Human Relations
A Job Oriented Approach
Fifth Edition

Andrew J. DuBrin

Professor of Management
College of Business
Rochester Institute of Technology

PRENTICE HALL CAREER & TECHNOLOGY
Englewood Cliffs, New Jersey 07632

Library of Congress Cataloging-in-Publication Data

DuBrin, Andrew J.
    Human relations : a job oriented approach / Andrew J. DuBrin. --
5th ed.
        p.   cm.
    Includes bibliographical references and index.
    ISBN 0-13-395526-5
    1. Industrial sociology.   2. Personnel management.
3. Organizational behavior.   I. Title.
HD6955.D82 1992
658.3--dc20   91-24201
                                                        CIP

Acquisition editor: *Maureen P. Hull*
Production editor and interior design: *Jacqueline A. Martin*
Copy editor: *Eleanor Walter*
Cover designer: *Karen Salzbach*
Prepress buyer: *Ilene Levy*
Manufacturing buyer: *Ed O'Dougberty*
Supplements editor: *Lisamarie Brassini*
Editorial Assistant: *Marianne J. Bernotsky*

© 1992 by Prentice Hall Career & Technology
Prentice-Hall, Inc.
A Simon & Schuster Company
Englewood Cliffs, New Jersey 07632

Printed in the United States of America
10 9 8 7 6 5 4 3

ISBN 0-13-395526-5

Prentice-Hall International (UK) Limited, *London*
Prentice-Hall of Australia Pty. Limited, *Sydney*
Prentice-Hall Canada Inc., *Toronto*
Prentice-Hall Hispanoamericana, S.A., *Mexico*
Prentice-Hall of India Private Limited, *New Delhi*
Prentice-Hall of Japan, Inc., *Tokyo*
Simon & Schuster Asia Pte. Ltd., *Singapore*
Editora Prentice-Hall do Brasil, Ltda., *Rio de Janeiro*

Once again,
to my daughter Melanie

CONTENTS

PREFACE

Does the world need another textbook about human behavior in organizations? One answer is, "yes, because few of the major problems have yet been solved. Perhaps this book will enable organizations to reach new heights of productivity, job satisfaction, internal harmony, and quality of work life." From a less grandiose standpoint, it is important to note seven features of the fifth edition of the book that I believe justify its writing.

First, the field of human relations and organizational behavior is a continuously expanding body of knowledge. Textbooks become dated quickly. This book is a concise yet comprehensive analysis of understanding and dealing effectively with human problems in organizations.

The target audiences for this book are students of human relations, organizational behavior, and industrial sociology in colleges, and participants in supervisory and management training courses. The text is also suited for applied psychology and organizational psychology courses that emphasize practice more than research and theory.

The text includes traditional topics plus a range of contemporary issues. Among the latter are organizational fun and humor, organizational culture, getting along in a bureaucracy, computer-generated stress, sexual harassment, intuition in decision making, and self-defeating behavior.

Second, the emphasis in this text is upon the reader and what he or she can do to handle situations. In contrast, most other human relations and organizational behavior texts emphasize how managers should handle employees.

Third, the approach to writing this book resembles that used in communicating with a general audience, without sacrificing scholarship. My intent is to avoid being patronizing, condescending, overly conversational, or excessively informal. I try to retain reader interest by writing in a style suited both to students without work experience and to experienced workers.

Fourth, classical topics that have suffered from overexposure, such as Maslow's need hierarchy, Theory X and Theory Y, and the Hawthorne studies, are not the major focus. Instead, this book emphasizes modern developments stemming from these keystone ideas, such as the expectancy theory of motivation and employee involvement groups.

Fifth, every major concept presented in the text is illustrated with an example—a feature that was enthusiastically received by readers of the four previous editions. However, I have avoided giving two examples to illustrate one concept.

Sixth, I try to explain how many of the concepts I present can be used to enhance individual and organizational effectiveness, including the improvement of productivity and satisfaction. Such application of knowledge is woven into the body of the text rather than placed in a separate, implications-for-management section.

Seventh, some attention is devoted to how knowledge in human relations and organizational behavior is gathered, including research methods. A separate learning module about research methods is presented as an appendix. Feedback from students suggests that the appendix has been helpful to them in preparing term papers. Students have also used it to help them conduct live research in the workplace.

The text is accompanied by a comprehensive instructor's manual with tests. The manual contains 900 test questions, chapter outlines and lecture notes, answers to discussion questions and case problems, and comments about the exercises. The 900 test questions are also available in a computerized version called Test Manager, and is available in 3½- and 5¼-inch discs. In addition, it includes step-by-step instructions for the use of computer-assisted scenario analysis (CASA).

CASA is a user-friendly way of using any word processing program to assist in analyzing cases. The student enters an existing case into the computer, and then analyzes it by answering the case questions in the text. Next, the student makes up a new scenario or twist to the case, and **enters this scenario in boldface into the case.** The case questions are reanalyzed in light of this new scenario. Any changes in the answers are **printed in bold.** CASA give the student experience in a creative application of word processing. Equally important, it helps the student develop a "what-if" or contingency point of view in solving human relations problems.

CHANGES IN THE FIFTH EDITION

Several important new features are included in this edition of *Human Relations: A Job Oriented Approach.* I have added a new chapter, "Foundations of Individual Differences." The chapter on stress and burnout has been replaced by a chapter on wellness and stress, reflecting the current emphasis in the field. The chapter on organizational culture and quality of work life has been deleted, but much of the information is now included in the chapter about organizational culture and change.

Many new topics have been added, many old ones have been deleted, and more than half of the cases, examples, and exercises from the fourth edition have been replaced. In more of the examples and cases, the organization is identified. Among the new or greatly expanded topics in this edition are customer service training, organizational fun and humor, wellness, the cognitive resource theory of leadership, cross-cultural factors in work relationships, practical intelligence, and rebounding from career adversity. Information about conducting a job campaign now appears in the appendix.

ACKNOWLEDGMENTS

A book of this nature requires the cooperation of many people to write and publish. My primary thanks go to my editorial team, Maureen P. Hull, Jackie Martin, Marianne J. Bernotsky and Eleanor Walter. I also thank the marketing and production staffs at Prentice Hall for their contribution to this project. The instructors who adopted the four previous editions of this book receive my enthusiastic appreciation. Many of them have contributed constructive suggestions that have been incorporated into this edition.

I thank the following people for their comments and suggestions that have helped to shape this edition of the text: Stephen C. Branz, Triton College; John M. Cozean, Central Piedmont Community College; Donna Hanley, Vincennes University; Ruth Kellar, Indiana Vocational Technical College; C. Russell Nickel, Washington State University; Burl Worley, Allan Hancock Community College; F. A. Zaccaro, Hofstra University; Dorothy E. Harrison, Temple Junior College; Jo Ann P. Reaves, Florence-Darlington Technical College; Gerald D. Slusser, Germanna Community College; N. B. Winstanley, the Rochester Institute of Technology. In addition, three published reviews of previous editions of this text provided excellent suggestions that have been incorporated into this edition. The reviewers were Kenneth J. Miller, Lockwood, Andrews & Newman, Inc.; M. Peter Scontrino, private practice; and Melissa Levi, Data General Corporation. A number of my students have also contributed suggestions for improvement from the standpoint of the learner.

Thanks also to Carol Bowman for the very positive impact she has had on my writing and the rest of my life. Thanks finally to Melanie DuBrin, Douglas DuBrin, and Drew DuBrin for their long-term interest in this book.

Andrew J. DuBrin
Rochester, New York

The Field of Human Relations

LEARNING OBJECTIVES

After reading and studying this chapter and doing the exercises, you should be able to

1. Define human relations and give an example of the practice of human relations.

2. Provide a brief historical sketch of the human relations movement.

3. Describe how scientific research contributes to knowledge of human relations.

4. Explain the contingency point of view in human relations.

5. Explain why human relations is not simply common sense.

A t the peak of the season for mailing out promotional letters for mail-order purchases of vinyl shoes, a word processing technician named Jennifer walked into the office of her boss, Shirley. With a disgruntled and distressed look on her face, she exclaimed:

> "Shirley, I'm leaving this job the end of the week. I can't take another day of sitting behind my word processor. As a word processing technician, I don't even feel like a human being. Nobody talks to me; they just fill my in-basket with bundles of letters to process. By midmorning every day I get a headache from staring at the display screen. That constant whirring of the disk drive stays in my ears hours after I leave the job at night. I didn't go to school to become an extension of a computer."
>
> "But Jennifer, you can't quit this week. Most of our profits for the year are dependent upon our completing our mailings within the next fifteen days. Quit us now, and nobody else will ever hire you as a word processing technician. Can't you take hard work?"
>
> "Insult me all you want, but my health is more important than my job as a word processing technician for sending out junk mail."

The supervisor involved in this exchange was encountering a human relations problem. So was her employee. Shirley was insensitive to the problems Jennifer faced; thus she was doing a poor job of managing job stress as experienced by an employee. If Shirley had been more adept at detecting signs of computer-generated stress, she might have dealt with Jennifer's problem before it caused Jennifer to leave.

Whenever anybody confronts a problem at work dealing with people, either individually or in groups, he or she is *potentially* making use of human relations. We emphasize the word *potentially* because not everything done to cope with the human element in work organizations can be considered human relations. If human relations were conceived in this manner, it would be a field of knowledge and practice without bounds.

What then is human relations? As defined here, **human relations** is the art and practice of using systematic knowledge about human behavior to achieve organizational and personal objectives. Since human relations borrows ideas from several fields, it is also a body of knowledge in addition to being a practice or an art. An effective executive is a practitioner of human relations. So is an effective member of a task force to improve the quality of service within a hospital. Human relations is also important in personal life. But here we are concerned about the workplace.

Both managers and nonmanagers practice human relations in their work. **Managers** are employees who accomplish work through others and have the authority to use resources, such as company money, to get things done. Nonmanagers are also called **specialists** or **individual contribu-**

tors, employees who accomplish work primarily by themselves rather than through others. Specialists and individual contributors have much less authority to use organizational resources.

HUMAN RELATIONS AND ITS RELATED FIELDS

Human relations is a field that gathers much of its systematic knowledge from the social and behavioral sciences, as well as from organizational behavior, which emerged as a field of study in the 1960s. Classification schemes differ, but the social sciences are now generally considered to be economics, political science, and history. The three primary behavioral sciences are usually considered to be psychology, sociology, and anthropology. Today, organizational behavior could rightfully be added as a behavioral science. If a diligent scholar were to trace the sources of most scientific studies undergirding human relations principles, he or she would discover that psychologists and sociologists are the largest contributors, with organizational behaviorists gaining ground. More specifically, the body of knowledge now called human relations stems from the findings and observations of organizational psychologists and organizational behaviorists.

The disciplines, fields, and professions dealing with human behavior in work settings overlap considerably, making rigid distinctions among them difficult to draw. These distinctions are not particularly vital when you deal with the application of knowledge. For instance, about twelve different disciplines are now concerned with job stress and burnout. It is much more important to help distressed employees than it is to assign credit to the right discipline for having developed a particular concept about stress management.

Organizational Behavior

Organizational behavior (OB) is the study of individuals and groups in organizations. As such, organizational behavior and human relations are quite similar in terms of the topics they study and the fields of knowledge upon which they are based. The big difference between them lies in the dimensions of technical depth, research sophistication, and amount of theory. Human relations today is essentially a less technical and more applied version of organizational behavior. Textbooks in human relations and organizational behavior contain many identical topics, but organizational behavior texts examine the topics more from a theoretical and research-oriented perspective. Note, however, that we are not reinforcing the overdrawn stereotype that because organizational behavior is more theoretical, it is impractical. Good theories, such as the law of gravity in physics and the law of effect in psychology, are very practical. (The *law of* *effect* states that behavior that is rewarded tends to be repeated.) If you believed in neither you would not fear jumping off buildings; nor would you bother to praise your new kitten for having properly used a litter pan.

Human Resource Management

This field, also referred to as *personnel,* is a hybrid, similar in scope to human relations. Human resource management (HRM) differs from human relations primarily because it is concerned with the application of a wide variety of personnel techniques and the administration of laws relating to employer-employee relationships. A personnel specialist must use human relations knowledge and techniques, but must also be conversant with personnel testing, employee training, compensation programs, and employee attitude surveys, among numerous other techniques. Not every human resource management practitioner, however, is expected to be knowledgeable about all aspects of the field. The field has its own subspecialties. A knowledge of current legislation, such as that dealing with worker disabilities and family leave, is also essential.

THE HUMAN RELATIONS MOVEMENT

The historical development of human relations knowledge applied to work warrants some attention. One reason is that some contributions of early human relations research are still relevant today. For example, an older finding still true today is that workers have social needs that they attempt to satisfy on the job.[1] The history of human relations is also important because it provides a framework for understanding modern developments.

The Hawthorne Studies

The human relations or behavioral school of management began in 1927 with a group of studies conducted at the Hawthorne plant in Cicero, Illinois of Western Electric, an AT&T subsidiary.[2] These studies were prompted by an experiment carried out by the company's engineers between 1924 and 1927. Following the scientific management tradition, these engineers were applying research methods to solve job-related problems.

Two groups were studied to determine the effects of different levels of illumination on worker performance. One group received increased illumination, while the other did not. A preliminary finding was that when illumination was increased, the level of performance also increased.

Surprisingly to the engineers, productivity also increased when the level of illumination was decreased almost to moonlight levels. One interpretation of these results was that the workers involved in the experiment enjoyed being the center of attention; they reacted positively because management cared about them.

The phenomenon is referred to as the **Hawthorne effect,** the tendency of people to behave differently when they receive attention because they respond to the expectations of the situation. In a research setting, this could mean that the people in the experimental group perform better simply because they are participating in an experiment. In a work setting, this could mean that employees perform better when they are part of any program—whether or not that program is really valuable.

As a result of these preliminary investigations, a team of researchers, headed by Elton Mayo and Fritz J. Roethlisberger from Harvard, conducted a lengthy series of experiments extending over a six-year period. The conclusions they reached served as the bedrock of later developments in the human relations approach to management. Among their key findings were the following:

- Economic incentives are less potent than generally believed in influencing workers to achieve high levels of output.
- Leadership practices and work group pressures profoundly influence employee satisfaction and performance.
- Any factor influencing employee behavior is embedded in a social system. For instance, to understand the impact of pay on performance, you also have to understand the climate in the work group and the leadership style of the superior.

A major implication of the studies conducted by Mayo and his associates was that the old concept of an economic person motivated mainly by money had to be replaced by a more valid concept. The replacement concept was a social person. He or she is motivated by social needs, desires rewarding on-the-job relationships, and is more responsive to work group pressures than to managerial control.[3]

Leadership Styles and Practices

As a consequence of the Hawthorne studies, worker attitudes, morale, and group influences became a concern of researchers. A notable development of this nature occurred shortly after World War II at the University of Michigan. A group of social scientists formed an organization, later to be called the Institute for Social Research, to study those principles of leadership associated with highest productivity.

Based upon research with office workers, an important conclusion was that supervisors of high-producing units behaved differently from those of low-producing units. Among the noted differences in style were that supervisors of productive groups, in comparison to their lower producing counterparts, were:

- More emotionally supportive of subordinates.
- More likely to play a *differentiated role*—plan, regulate, and coordinate the activities of subordinates, but not become directly involved in work tasks.
- More likely to exercise general rather than close or "tight" supervision.

Similar studies were conducted at Ohio State University. Among the key findings also was that people-oriented leadership was generally more effective than production-oriented leadership.[4] Today it is recognized that the requirements of the situation determine the most effective leadership style. (See the discussion following about the contingency viewpoint.) However, the historical significance of the studies cannot be dismissed. From this research stemmed leadership training programs designed to make supervisors more aware of the feelings, attitudes, and opinions of group members. Unfortunately, many of these early programs overemphasized people awareness and paid insufficient attention to the other aspects of a supervisor's job.

Organization Development

Another major development in the human relations movement is the proliferation of programs and techniques designed to move organizations toward more honest and authentic ways of dealing with work problems and each other. Today many private and public organizations participate in some form of **organization development (OD)** with the hope of improving organizational effectiveness.

Sensitivity training, the first widespread formal organizational development technique, owes its historical roots to the work of Kurt Lewin.[5] In the mid-1940s, Lewin formalized the technique of bringing a group of people together and helping them examine how their attitudes were received by other members of the group. Additionally, group members were given information about group dynamics. This activity was undertaken as part of a project to make local leaders from several communities understand and implement the new Fair Employment Practices Act.

The group discussion and feedback to members involved in this project became formalized as the T-group, a central aspect of sensitivity training. In 1947, the National Training Laboratory was established at Bethel, Maine, by a group of social scientists from the Massachusetts Institute of Technology and the National Education Association. Organization development today still emphasizes teamwork as illustrated in the accompanying box.

TEAMWORK IN THE OFFICE

Employees of Aid Association for Lutherans (AAL), an insurance company run by a fraternal society, speak in glowing terms of AAL's transformation. One day several years ago, the entire insurance staff of 500 clerks, technicians, and managers loaded their personal belongings onto office chairs and bid farewell to co-workers. All 500 employees then rolled down the halls to their new work areas.

Within two hours, AAL's home office employees had converted from the department structure typical of insurance companies into all-purpose teams that required little supervision. Changing to work teams has already been responsible for a 20 percent increase in productivity and a reduction in case processing time by as much as 75 percent.

AAL switched to teamwork primarily to process insurance cases more rapidly, and thus provide better service to its field agents and policyholders. Previously, all life insurance cases were handled by one unit, health insurance by another, and support services by a third. This division often resulted in some cases being bounced from one section to another, leading to embarrassing delays.

Under the new system, the insurance department is divided into five groups, each serving a geographic group of agents. Each group is composed of three or four teams of twenty to thirty employees who can carry out all of the 167 tasks formerly divided among the three sections. Team members are cross-trained to learn skills that connect the tasks that used to be the responsibility of only one section. Field agents in each district deal solely with one team and develop close working relationships with its members. In the eyes of the agents, working with the home office is now much more personal.

The abrupt switch from a traditional way of working to teams brought mixed feelings among employees. "There was uncertainty and a lot of broken friendships when we moved to the new system, and personally I feel more tension," one worker said. Yet most employees now like the team approach because it allows them to manage themselves. An exception is that some employees prefer not to have managerial responsibility.

Team members put up banners to signify their team's excellence and hold spontaneous parties when they achieve production and quality goals.

Source: As reported in "Work Teams Can Rev Up Paper-Pushers, Too," *Business Week,* Nov. 28, 1988, pp. 64–72.

Industrial Humanism and Concern for the Total Person

Partly as a by-product of the Hawthorne studies arose a new philosophy of human relations in the workplace. Elton Mayo was one of two key figures in developing this philosophy of **industrial humanism.** He cautioned managers that emotional factors (such as a desire for recognition and appreciation) were a more important contributor to productivity than were physical and logical factors. Mayo argued vigorously that work should lead to personal satisfaction for employees.

Mary Parker Follett was another key figure in advancing the cause of industrial humanism in the 1930s. Her experience as a management consultant led her to believe that the key to increased productivity was to motivate employees, rather than simply to order better job performance. The keys to both productivity and democracy, according to Follett, were cooperation, a spirit of unity, and coordination of effort.[6]

In the modern era the philosophy of industrial humanism shifted gradually to a concern for the welfare of the total person, and not just the welfare of the person as a worker. Among the manifestations of this trend are programs to help employees deal with personal problems, stay well, develop their careers, and provide for their children during working hours. A few words will be said about such programs here, and they will all be reintroduced at appropriate places in the text.

Almost all large and medium-sized firms today engage in some type of positive program to help employees deal with stress. Leading the list are **employee assistance programs (EAPs),** formal facilities to help employees whose performance has declined because of distracting personal problems. EAPs take the form of referral to an outside agency, an on-site counseling service, or a combination of the two. The most frequent problems experienced by visitors to an EAP are alcoholism, drug abuse, financial problems, and family problems.

A closely related but newer thrust of the human relations movement is a concern for employee **wellness,** a focus on good mental and physical health rather than simply the absence of disorders. Wellness programs include such activities as exercise facilities on company premises, lectures about stress management and diet, and financial bonuses for not filing medical claims.

Another way employers express concern for the total individual is through **career development programs,** planned approaches to helping employees enhance their careers while at the same time meshing individual and organizational goals. Career development programs help workers make career decisions that will move them closer to self-fulfillment.

An increasing number of employers today assist parents in providing for the welfare of their young children during working hours. A few have child-care facilities on company premises, while others make arrangements with child-care agencies located nearby. A more recent trend is to help employees arrange for care of elderly parents during working hours.[7]

Industrial humanism and concern for the total individual can benefit the organization as much as the worker. It has been argued that a major motive behind the human relations movement was to prevent unionization. When workers are highly satisfied with their conditions of employment, they are less likely to vote for a labor union. Another argument is that child-care programs increase productivity because parents using these facilities can concentrate better on their work. Also, working parents are less likely to quit when child care is available.

HOW SCIENTIFIC RESEARCH CONTRIBUTES TO HUMAN RELATIONS

Much of the knowledge of human relations and organizational behavior is based on research. An example of the contribution of scientific research to human relations is found in a study on the impact of flexible working hours on productivity.[8] Conducted by a team of researchers, this study is considered relevant to practitioners of human relations because so much attention is being paid these days to improving productivity. Reliable information about the effects of flexible working hours on productivity would help both managers and human relations specialists make sound policy.

It is generally accepted that giving employees a say in setting a portion of their working hours improves job satisfaction. The study reviewed here examines the topic of **productivity:** the ratio of output to input, taking quality of work into account.

Purpose of the Study

The purpose of the study was to examine the effect of **flextime** (flexible working hours) on productivity due to improved coordination of physical resources in the work unit. A previous study suggested that when workers have to share resources, such as equipment, they waste some time waiting to use the equipment. With flexible working hours, fewer people are at work simultaneously. This results in less waiting time, therefore increasing the potential for increased productivity.

One hypothesis (educated guess) is that the flextime group with limited physical resources will show a significantly higher level of productivity than its comparable control group. A **control group** is a comparison group that is similar to the group being studied except that it is not exposed to the variable being studied. The second hypothesis is that a flextime group without limited resources will not show a significantly higher level of productivity than its control group.

The researchers were also interested in investigating whether any changes observed would take place immediately, over a long period of time, or both. The time dimension is important because many changes brought about with human relations techniques prove to be short-lived.

Methods and Procedures

The study was conducted in two government agencies. The agency from which the experimental groups were selected had implemented an agencywide flextime program. The agency from which the control groups were selected did not have a flextime program. Both agencies place employees on an eight-hour day, forty-hour week. The range of working hours for the experimental agency is from 7:00 A.M. to 6:00 P.M. Employees have to work their full eight hours within this *bandwidth*. The core hours of required on-the-job presence are from 9:00 A.M. to 3:30 P.M. The lunch period can be from one-half hour to one hour in length. The control agency works from 8:30 A.M. to 5:00 P.M. with a thirty-minute scheduled lunch.

The experimental and control groups selected from the agencies were the programmers and data entry operators. One reason these groups were selected was because they had quantifiable, direct measures of productivity. The productivity measure for the programmers was the mean amount of central processing unit time used per month (how much time the programmers were actually using the computer). The productivity measure for the data entry clerks was the mean number of accurate entries per person per month.

These groups were also selected because the programming group shared a limited physical resource, the computer. Equally important, the data entry group did not share a resource; each operator had his or her own machine. Over the two-year period of the study, the number of experimental group programmers ranged from fifty-seven to sixty-three; the control group ranged in size from fifty-nine to sixty-nine. For the data entry operators, the experimental groups ranged from sixteen to twenty, and the control group from thirty-three to forty-two. Productivity measures were expressed as per person/per month averages.

Results of the Study

The major finding from this study was that the shared use of physical resources influenced the relationship between flextime and productivity. Programmers—who shared resources—were more productive when working a flexible rather than a fixed schedule. Data entry operators—who did not share resources—were about equally productive when working under flexible and fixed hours. Table 1–1 presents these findings.

Compare the improvement scores of the experimental groups with the control groups for both data entry operators and programmers in the table. Notice, for example, that the productivity for the experimental

TABLE 1-1 Productivity Measures for Programmer and Data Entry Groups for the Three Testing Periods

Group	Time		
	Pretest	Posttest	Long posttest*
Data entry operators†			
Flexible hours (experimental) mean	32,498	32,900	31,932
Fixed hours (control) mean	37,550	36,982	38,178
Programmers‡			
Flexible hours (experimental) mean	26.66	35.49	37.71
Fixed hours (control) mean	27.12	28.72	28.49

*The long posttest periods began after one year.

†The productivity measure for data entry operators is the mean number of cards accurately punched per month.

‡The productivity measure for programmers is the mean number of hours of central processing unit time used per person, per month.

Source: David A. Ralston, William P. Anthony, and David J. Gustafson, "Employees May Love Flextime, But What Does It Do to the Organization's Productivity?" *Journal of Applied Psychology,* May 1985, p. 277. Adapted with permission.

group of data entry operators did not improve after flexible working hours were introduced. In fact, the control groups seemed to show a slight improvement even though they remained on fixed working hours. None of the improvement scores for the data entry groups are significant. In contrast, the experimental group of programmers showed a big improvement in productivity scores after it was assigned flexible working hours.

The study also found no significant productivity difference between the flextime data entry operators and the control group. Although the differences between the experimental and control group may appear substantial (31,932 vs. 38,178 in the long posttest), they were not statistically significant. In contrast, the programmers had significantly higher levels of productivity during the posttest periods than did the fixed time comparison group. These differences held for the entire study.

Implications for Human Relations

If these findings hold in similar studies, management will be able to identify groups within its organization from whom productivity improvements may be expected with flextime. The researchers note that in addition to a high-demand, shared physical resource, one other group characteristic is important: The groups assigned to flextime should have a consistently high workload so that productivity increases are possible. Based on this study, the practitioner of human relations can now be optimistic about the contribution of flexible working hours to increased productivity—when the workers share equipment.

One criticism of this study is that the productivity measure for programmers reflected a very limited definition of productivity. The measure simply noted how much use was made of the computer, and not the quality of the work produced. What criticism can you make of the scientific value of this experiment?

THE CONTINGENCY (IT DEPENDS) VIEWPOINT

A major assumption of modern human relations and organizational behavior is that most human problems in organizations require a **contingency viewpoint.** According to the contingency viewpoint, the best solution to a given problem depends upon certain key factors in the situation. The opposite of the contingency viewpoint is the assumption that certain universal principles of human behavior can be applied effectively to virtually all situations. The contingency viewpoint does not deny that certain principles apply in most situations, but that to apply these principles, individual differences and situational factors have to be taken into consideration.

Assume that a manager wants to increase the amount of work produced by group members. One of the best-established facts about human behavior is that goals lead to increased performance. Goal setting is thus a universal principle that applies in virtually all situations. However, if the manager in question used a contingency viewpoint, he or she would search for the best way to apply goal setting considering the particular group members. For example, these people might perform best when the goals were fairly difficult, and set reasonably far into the future. A group of less capable and self-reliant workers might respond best to less difficult goals set in the very short range—even within an hour.

The contingency viewpoint in human relations will be particularly apparent in later discussions of individual differences (Chapter 2) and leadership (Chapter 9). For example, effective leaders vary their approach to group members according to such individual differences as their maturity and values. Effective leaders bear down more heavily on underachievers!

HUMAN RELATIONS AND COMMON SENSE

A systems analyst complained angrily, "Why did my company send me to this workshop on human relations? Anybody with half a mind knows that human relations is just common sense." Unfortunately, this analyst is only partially correct. Common sense is sometimes an adequate substitute for knowledge of human relations or organizational behavior. Yet many times it is not. Here we examine several reason why common sense is not a complete substitute for human relations knowledge.

Common sense is uncommon. A minority of people are highly effective in dealing with other people on the job or in personal life. Aside from those rare individuals who intuitively know how to cope with a variety of people in an effective manner, most people are plagued with interpersonal problems. Virtually all organizations have problems involving people. Thus, if common sense (meaning native good judgment, not requiring formal knowledge) were widely held, there would be fewer problems involving people. Because few people have substantial common sense in matters dealing with other people, the study of human relations becomes necessary.

Human relations sharpens and refines common sense. People with the most common sense often derive the most personal benefit from human relations training. They build upon strengths, which in general has a bigger payoff than does overcoming weaknesses. Through common sense, the interpersonally competent individual may be able to handle many situations involving people. With a few refinements, his or her handling of people may be even more effective.

Anne, a sales manager, prided herself on her sales conference techniques. She felt that more was accomplished in her meetings than in most others. Yet Anne was still not satisfied. As she told her human relations consultant, "I figure we can still get more out of our meetings. I detect that people are not really talking to each other about the problems facing them. I want communication to flow even better than it does now."

The human relations consultant asked about the physical arrangements in the conferences. Anne explained how people sat around a table with their notebooks, ashtrays, and water pitchers placed in front of them. "Now I see what you are doing wrong," said the consultant. "You are setting up a few structural barriers to communication. Get the people out in the middle of the room, seated in a circle. Let them put their notebooks aside. Get them physically closer to each other."

Anne tried this technique in her next conference, and it worked. Communication barriers broke down as people no longer psychologically hid behind tables, notebooks, ashtrays, and name placards. Anne was already effective with people, but by introducing the concept of *overcoming physical barriers to communication* to her repertoire, her effectiveness multiplied.

Human relations sometimes disproves common sense. A final major reason why having common sense does not make the study of human relations superfluous is that common sense can be wrong. Instances exist in which the commonsense explanation to a problem is inferior to the explanation provided by systematic knowledge about human behavior. Common sense, for example, tells us that persistence is usually the key to success. "If at first you don't succeed, try, try again," contends the old adage. A study conduced in several organizations with hundreds of managers and professionals suggests, however, that persistence on the job can backfire. Those people who pressed their demands too often wound up receiving smaller salary increases and lower performance ratings from their superiors.[9] How do you explain these findings?

HOW THIS BOOK WILL HELP YOU

A person who carefully studies the information in this book and incorporates many of its suggestions into his or her mode of doing things should derive the two benefits listed below. People vary so widely in learning ability, personality, and life circumstances that some will be able to attain some objectives and not others. For instance, you might be so shy at this stage of your development that you will not want to try some of the conflict resolution techniques. Or if you are locked into a family business, you may be uninterested in career planning.

Awareness of relevant information. Part of feeling comfortable and making a positive impression in any work organization is being familiar with relevant general knowledge about the world of work. By reading this book you will become conversant with many of the buzz words at work, such as *empowerment, quality circles,* and *VDT stress.*

Development of human relations skills. Anybody who aspires toward higher-level jobs needs to develop proficiency in such human relations skills as how to motivate people, how to communicate, and how to counsel subordinates with substandard performance. Studying information about such topics in this book, coupled with trying them out now or when your job situation permits, should help you develop such skills.

Summary of Key Points

- Human relations is the art and practice of using systematic knowledge about human behavior to achieve organizational and personal objectives. Any time you confront a work problem dealing with people, the potential exists for making use of human relations.
- Human relations (HR) receives most of its knowledge from the social and behavioral sciences, including organizational behavior (OB). Human relations and organizational behavior cover essentially the same topics, but OB places more emphasis on research and

theory, while HR is more applied in nature. The field of personnel or human resource management (HRM) is also related to human relations, although HRM is more concerned with applying personnel techniques and the administration of laws relating to employer-employee relationships.

- The human relations movement began with the Hawthorne studies. Among their major implications was that social as well as economic factors motivate workers. As a consequence of the Hawthorne studies, employee attitudes, morale, and group influences became a concern of social science researchers. Much of their research was conducted on leadership styles and practices.

- The philosophy of industrial humanism stems from the Hawthorne studies. It examines carefully how emotions and motivation contribute to productivity. In the modern era, industrial humanism has shifted to a concern for the welfare of the total person, not just the person as a worker. Employee assistance programs and company-sponsored child care are examples of industrial humanism.

- Much of the knowledge of both HR and OB is based on experimental, or scientific, research. Such research is characterized by using experimental groups, control groups, and statistical analysis. The experiment on the impact of flextime on productivity reported in this chapter illustrates the scientific method in HR and OB.

- A major assumption of modern human relations and organizational behavior is that most human problems require a contingency viewpoint. According to this viewpoint, the best solution to a given problem depends upon certain key factors in the situation.

- Common sense is not a complete substitute for human relations knowledge, for several reasons: Common sense is relatively uncommon; human relations sharpens and refines common sense; and human relations sometimes disproves common sense.

- A formal study of human relations will lead to both awareness of information relevant to work, and the development of a variety of skills in dealing with others.

Questions and Activities _____

1. Almost all organizations now make some direct use of human relations ideas or techniques, such as goal setting and participative management. Why do you think HR has "caught on"?

2. If human relations is so important, should all companies have a human relations department?

3. Describe how a former or present boss practiced *good* human relations.

4. Describe how a former or present boss practiced *poor* human relations.

5. Why should organizations be concerned about the whole person (rather than just the person as a worker)?

6. How does working in the type of team described at AAL (the insurance company) differ from being a member of a traditional department?

7. Do human relations and organizational behavior appear to be sciences? Explain your answer.

8. The study on flexible working hours was based on data processing personnel in a government agency. How confident would you be about generalizing to other settings its conclusion about the contribution of flextime to productivity?

9. An executive once said, "If the contingency viewpoint is true, it must mean that everything depends upon the situation. Human relations theories are therefore useless." What is the correct rebuttal to this statement?

10. A student scored 29 percent on the multiple-choice portion of a test based on the first six chapters of an earlier edition of this book. He was the same student who said in class, "This course is easy. The book is all common sense." How do you explain what probably happened?

A HUMAN RELATIONS CASE PROBLEM
"We Can't Afford Human Relations Around Here."

Tammy Phillips was happy to be hired by Bradbury Foods as a supervisor in the main processing plant. It was apparent to her that being a supervisor so soon after graduation would be a real boost to her career. After about a month on the job, Tammy began to make some critical observations about the company and its style of management.

To clarify things in her own mind, Tammy requested a meeting with Adam Green, plant superintendent. The meeting between Tammy and Adam included a conversation of this nature:

Adam: Have a seat, Tammy. It's nice to visit with one of our new supervisors. Particularly so when you didn't say you were facing an emergency that you and your boss couldn't handle.

Tammy: (*nervously*) Mr. Green, I want to express my appreciation for your willingness to meet with me. You're right, I'm not facing an emergency. But I do wonder about something. That's what I came here to talk to you about.

Adam: That's what I like to see—a young woman who takes the initiative to ask questions about things that are bothering her.

Tammy: To be truthful, I am happy here and I'm glad I joined Bradbury Foods. But I'm curious about one thing. As you may know, I'm a graduate of a business college. A few of the courses I took emphasized using human relations knowledge to manage people—you know, kind of psychology on the job. It seems like the way to go if you want to keep employees productive and happy.

Here at Bradbury it seems that nobody uses human relations knowledge. I know that we're a successful company. But some of the management practices seem out of keeping with the times. The managers make all the decisions. Everybody else listens and carries out orders. Even professionals on the payroll have to punch time clocks. I've been here for almost two months and I haven't even heard the term "human relations" used once.

Adam: Oh, I get your point. You're talking about using human relations around here. I know all about that. The point you're missing, Tammy, is that human relations is for the big, profitable companies. That stuff works great when business is good and profit margins are high. But around here business is so-so, and profit margins in the food business are thinner than a potato chip. Maybe someday when we get fat and profitable we can start using human relations. In the meantime, we've all got a job to do.

Tammy: I appreciate your candid answer, Mr. Green. But when I was in college, I certainly heard a different version of why companies use human relations.

1. What is your evaluation of Adam's contention that human relations knowledge is useful primarily when a firm is profitable?
2. To what extent should Tammy be discouraged?
3. What should Tammy do?
4. Based on your experiences, how representative of most managers is Adam's thinking?

A HUMAN RELATIONS EXERCISE
Developing a Contingency Point of View

The contingency point of view states that the most effective human relations strategy depends upon the situation. Few people disagree with this statement, but it is not easy to implement contingency behavior. To raise your level of awareness about the importance of contingency behavior, do the following exercise by yourself or within a group, as requested by your instructor.

Assume that three recent graduates want to demonstrate superior human relations skills on the job, and that each one takes a different job. Offer advice for demonstrating superior human relations skills in each of the following situations. Emphasize the unique type of behavior most appropriate for each situation.

Carlotta becomes a first lieutenant in the U.S. Army, and decides that she wants to work her way up the ranks.

Justin is hired as a software specialist for Sun Computer, a fast-growing company located in "Silicon Valley" in northern California. His primary concern is to be accepted by his peers.

Jose is hired as a supervisor of "cast members" (workers who interact directly with guests) at Disneyland. Jose wants to be known for his superior human relations skills, because the way to get ahead at Disneyland is to be effective with guests and co-workers.

Notes

1. Mel E. Schnake, *Human Relations* (Columbus, OH: Merrill, 1990), p. 20.
2. An original source of information about the Hawthorne studies is Elton Mayo, *The Human Problems of an Industrial Civilization* (New York: Viking, 1960). A summary and synthesis of these classic studies is found in Phillip L. Hunsaker and Curtis W. Cook, *Managing Organizational Behavior* (Reading, MA: Addison-Wesley, 1986), pp. 19–20, A19–A21.
3. Interpretation made by James A. F. Stoner and R. Edward Freeman, *Management,* 4th ed. (Englewood Cliffs, NJ: Prentice Hall, 1989), p. 49.
4. Arnold S. Tannenbaum, *Social Psychology of the Work Organization* (Belmont, CA: Wadsworth, 1966), p. 74.
5. Robert J. House, "T-group Education and Leadership Effectiveness: A Review of the Empiric Literature and a Critical Evaluation," *Personnel Psychology,* Spring 1967, p. 2.
6. Robert Kreitner, *Management,* 4th ed. (Boston: Houghton Mifflin, 1990).
7. Ruth Thaler-Carter, "Team Up to Meet Child-care Needs," *HRMagazine,* March 1990, pp. 44–48.
8. David A. Ralston, William P. Anthony, and David J. Gustafson, "Employees May Love Flextime, but What Does It Do to the Organization's Productivity?" *Journal of Applied Psychology,* May 1985, pp. 272–79.
9. Stuart M. Schmidt and David Kipnis, "The Perils of Persistence," *Psychology Today,* November 1987, pp. 32–34.

Suggested Reading

BOONE, LOUIS E., and BOWEN, DONALD D. *The Great Writings in Management and Organizational Behavior,* 2nd ed. New York: Random House, 1987.

GERSICK, CONNIE J. G. "Time and Transition in Work Teams: Toward a New Model of Group Development." *Academy of Management Review,* March 1988, pp. 9–41.

LEVERING, ROBERT. *What Makes Some Employers So Good (and Most So Bad).* New York: Random House, 1988.

LOCKE, EDWIN A., and associates, eds. *Generalizing from Laboratory to Field Settings.* Lexington, MA: Lexington Books, Heath, 1986.

MAJCHRZAK, ANN. *The Human Side of Factory Automation: Managerial and Human Resources Strategies for Making Automation Succeed.* San Francisco: Jossey-Bass, 1988.

MATTESON, MICHAEL T., and IVANCEVICH, JOHN M. *Management and Organizational Behavior Classics,* 4th ed. Homewood, IL: Irwin, 1989.

OTT, J. STEVEN, ed. *Classic Readings in Organizational Behavior.* Pacific Grove, CA: Brooks/Cole, 1989.

PIERCE, JON L., and associates. *Alternative Work Schedules.* Newton, MA: Allyn and Bacon, 1989.

PUGH, P. S., HICKSON, D. J., and HININGS, C. R. *Writers on Organizations,* 3rd ed. Newbury Park, CA: Sage, 1985.

WREN, DANIEL A. *The Evolution of Management Thought.* New York: Wiley, 1987.

2

Foundations
of Individual Differences

LEARNING OBJECTIVES

After reading and studying this chapter and doing the exercises, you should be able to

1. Identify the major implications of individual differences on the job.

2. Explain how individual differences in work behavior stem from mental ability, values and attitudes, physical abilities, and demographic factors.

3. Give examples of culturally based individual differences in work behavior.

4. Summarize the basics of the behavioral model of human beings.

T o use human relations knowledge effectively you must be aware of how people are similar and how they are different. General principles of human behavior, such as how people are motivated and how they react to pressure, provide general guidelines for dealing with people in the workplace. At the same time, it is important to appreciate the uniqueness of people. For example, a general principle is that people perform better when offered a reward. The fact of individual differences suggests, however, that it is necessary to understand which particular reward will work for the person you are trying to motivate.

In this chapter we explore several major contributors to individual differences in work behavior, and then tie the information together in a model of human beings. References to individual differences are also woven into many other topics in the text, such as motivation, creativity, and interpersonal skill training.

IMPLICATIONS OF INDIVIDUAL DIFFERENCES ON THE JOB

Individual differences moderate or influence how people respond to many things about their job. A company might install new lighting, considered to be badly needed by 80 percent of the workforce. Twenty percent of the employees would probably grumble that the work area is too brightly lit. Six

HOW LONG HAVE YOU BEEN IN OUR TRANSLYVANNIA REGIONAL OFFICE?

illustrative ways in which individual differences have important implications for human relations are noted here.

1. *People differ in productivity.* A recent analysis of individual differences in work behavior illustrates the magnitude of human variation in job performance. The researchers synthesized studies involving over 10,000 workers. They found that as jobs become more complex, individual differences have a bigger impact on work output.[1] An outstanding industrial sales representative might produce 100 times as much as a mediocre representative. In contrast, an outstanding data entry technician might produce only twice as much as a mediocre one. (An industrial sales job is more complex than the work of a data entry technician.)

2. *People differ in ability and talent.* Factors such as ambition, desire, self-confidence, a favorable appearance, and the ability to play office politics are not sufficient for getting the job done. People also need the right abilities and talents to perform any job well. Ability is thus a major source of individual differences that influence job performance. For example, a talented newscaster will outperform a newscaster with very little talent.

3. *People differ in the importance they attach to interesting work.* People with a passion for work are looking for stimulating, exciting, or enriching jobs. About one-third of the workforce is not looking for stimulating, exciting work. They prefer jobs that require a minimum of mental involvement and responsibility. Some people prefer to daydream on the job and find their self-fulfillment through recreational and family life. For such workers, a repetitive job is the most pleasing.

4. *People differ in the style of leadership they prefer and need.* Many workers like as much freedom as possible on the job and can function well under a looser leadership style. Other individuals want to be supervised closely by their manager. People also vary with respect to the amount of supervision they require. In general, less competent, less motivated, and less experienced workers need more supervision. One of the biggest headaches facing a manager is how to supervise people who need close supervision but who resent it when it is administered.

5. *People differ in their need for contact with other people.* As a by-product of their personality traits and occupational interests, people vary widely in how much people contact they need on the job to keep them satisfied. Some people can work alone all day and remain highly productive. Others become restless unless they are engaged in business or social conversation with another employee. Sometimes a business luncheon is scheduled more out of a manager's need for social contact than out of a need for discussing job problems.

6. *People differ in their degree of commitment and loyalty to the firm.* Many employees are so committed to their employers that they act as if they were part owners of the firm. As a consequence, committed and

loyal employees are very concerned about producing quality goods and services. They also maintain superior records of attendance and punctuality, which helps reduce the cost of doing business. At the other extreme, some employees feel very little commitment or loyalty toward their employer. They feel no pangs of guilt when they produce scrap or when they miss work for trivial reasons.

Be aware that not all differences in job performance and behavior stem from individual characteristics. Sometimes the way in which the employer treats people encourages these differences. For example, a company that treats people shabbily may not earn their commitment and loyalty.

MENTAL ABILITY

Mental ability, or intelligence, is one of the major personal differences that affects job performance and behavior. Highly abstract job problems can best be solved by intelligent workers. In a dramatically uncomplex job, such as stuffing envelops seven hours a day, being less bright would be an advantage.

The term **intelligence,** as it is used here, refers to problem-solving ability. Intelligence quotient, or IQ, is just one measure of intelligence. Because the particular test score called IQ is so widely known, many people regard IQ as synonymous with intelligence.

Here we describe two important aspects of mental ability: the components of intelligence, and practical intelligence.

Components of Intelligence

Intelligence consists of more than one component: It is not a pure characteristic. The preponderance of evidence suggests that it consists of a **g (general) factor** along with **s (special) factors** that contribute to problem-solving ability. Scores on tests of almost any type (such as math, mechanical ability, or reading skill) are somewhat influenced by the g factor.[2] The g factor helps explain why some people seem to perform so well in so many different mental tasks. Although the specific components of intelligence are debatable, at a minimum they include verbal and numerical abilities.

One widely used mental ability test, the Employee Aptitude Survey, is based on the idea that intelligence is composed of many components or factors. It is worth noting these components, because they are a source of individual differences related to job performance. Five illustrative dimensions follow:[3]

1. *Verbal comprehension:* the ability to use words in thinking and in both spoken and written communication. Good verbal skills are an

asset in a wide variety of occupations, including sales representative, executive, and telemarketing specialist.

2. *Numerical ability:* the ability to handle numbers, engage in mathematical analysis, and do arithmetic calculations. Among the occupations calling for good numerical comprehension are financial analysis, computer programming, tax advising, and engineering.

3. *Space visualization:* the ability to visualize forms in space and manipulate objects mentally, particularly in three dimensions. This ability is a critical requirement for drafting technicians, engineers, and other technical personnel. Space visualization is also an important component of mechanical aptitude.

4. *Word fluency:* the ability to use words quickly and easily, without an emphasis on verbal comprehension. This ability is called for in positions requiring extensive oral or written expression, such as technical writer or tour guide.

5. *Symbolic reasoning:* the ability to manipulate abstract symbols mentally and to make judgments and decisions which are logically sound. Symbolic reasoning also involves the ability to evaluate whether adequate information is available to make definite decisions. This ability is required in high-level positions, particularly in those classified as technical or scientific.

Practical Intelligence

Many people, including psychologists, are concerned that the traditional way of understanding intelligence inadequately describes mental ability. An unfortunate implication of intelligence testing is that intelligence as traditionally calculated is largely the ability to perform tasks related to scholastic work. Thus a person who scored very high on an intelligence test could follow a complicated instruction manual, but might not be "street smart."

To overcome the idea that intelligence mostly involves the ability to solve abstract problems, the concept of **practical intelligence** has been proposed. It means that intelligence is composed of several aspects, such as creativity, in addition to academic intelligence.

Several theories of practical intelligence have been proposed. A useful idea for human relations is that there are three different subtypes of intelligence. One subtype is *componential,* the traditional type of intelligence needed for solving difficult problems. The second subtype is *experiential,* the type of intelligence required for imagination and combining different things in different ways. The third subtype is *contextual,* the type of intelligence required for adaptation to your environment or changing your environment to suit your needs. Contextual intelligence is necessary to be street smart.[4]

The idea of practical intelligence helps explain why a person who has a difficult time getting through school can still be a successful business-person, politician, or athlete. Practical intelligence seems to incorporate the ideas of common sense and wisdom. One major reservation some have about practical intelligence is the implication that people who are highly intelligent in the traditional sense are not practical thinkers. In truth, most executives and other high-level workers score quite well on tests of mental ability. These tests usually measure componential intelligence.

PERSONALITY

"We're not going to promote you to department head," said the vice president to the analyst. "Although you are a great troubleshooter, you've alienated too many people in the company. You're too blunt and insensitive." As just implied, most successes and failures in people-contact jobs are attributed largely to interpersonal skills. And personality traits are an important contributor to interpersonal, or human relations, skills. The subject of individual differences in personality must therefore be given consideration in any serious study of human relations.

Personality refers to those persistent and enduring behavior patterns that tend to be expressed in a wide variety of situations. A person who is brash and insensitive in one situation is likely to behave similarly in many other situations. Your personality is what makes you unique. Your walk, your talk, your appearance, your speech, and your inner values and conflicts all contribute to your personality.

Although most people agree that personality is related to job performance, researchers have had difficulty measuring its contribution. Recent research has shown, however, that personality traits can be good predictors of job performance when the traits are properly matched with the occupation and the organization. The researchers found, for example, that accountants with a strong work orientation received high performance ratings. The explanation is that to be successful, it is necessary for an accountant in a firm to work long hours and to complete projects on time. Such behavior is especially crucial during peak months in the year.

The study also found that *ascendancy* (or pushiness) had a negative relationship to performance ratings. Accountants in the firm studied must be cooperative, able to work easily with others, and respectful of the authority of partners if they wanted to succeed.[5] (Only good office politicians need apply!)

The remainder of our discussion in this section further emphasizes how individual differences in personality influence job performance and behavior. Toward this end we will discuss personality traits and needs, and the Sixteen Personality Factor Questionnaire™.

Personality Traits and Needs

Among the many ways to study individual differences in personality is to observe how people differ on important traits. Many years ago, Henry Murray developed a list of human needs that lead to personality traits, and others have updated his work.[6] A **need** is an internal striving or urge to do something. Thus if you have strong need to dominate people, a noticeable personality trait of yours will be dominance.

Personality traits and needs influence people to act in certain ways. Each need results in a propensity to behave in a particular way. The dominant person will gravitate toward leadership positions or frequently get into arguments with others. Figure 2–1 describes eleven important person-

Need and accompanying personality trait	Example of type of job behavior of person who has strong need
Achievement: to accomplish something difficult.	Tries hard in all competitive activities; sets up own business.
Affiliation: to seek out personal relationships.	Tries to be "one of the gang."
Aggression: to attack or punish others; to overcome people.	Uses hard sell tactics as sales representative.
Autonomy: to act independently and to be free of constraints.	Takes job as branch manager; feels uncomfortable when closely supervised.
Deference: to admire and support a person in authority; to conform to custom.	Prefers to call superiors by title (Mr., Ms., Dr.); respectful as a subordinate.
Dominance: to influence others toward your way of thinking, often by forceful methods.	Often takes over in meetings; volunteers to be the leader; good at the hard sell.
Nurturance: to help, support, take care of weak and needy people.	Works well with disadvantaged people; develops team members but may be overprotective.
Order: to put things in order; to achieve balance, neatness, and precision.	Keeps work area neat; carefully prepares reports; keeps good files and databases.
Power: to control other people and resources; to seek recognition and fame.	Orients life around rising to the top; likes to be powerful in appearance, action, and speech.
Authoritarianism: to want power and status differences between self and others; to want to make major decisions.	Makes major decisions with little input from others; influenced mostly by people of high rank and status.
Thrill seeking: to seek out constant excitement and risk talking.	Seeks out assignments involving high risks and high payoffs; makes creative suggestions; becomes bored readily.

FIGURE 2–1 How Personality Traits Based on Needs Influence Behavior

ality traits determined by needs. To the right of each need is a sampling of the type of behavior that corresponds to that particular need. In this context, the terms *need* and *trait* are used almost interchangeably.

The Sixteen Personality Factor Questionnaire (16PF)™

The 16PF is widely used to measure dimensions, or components, of personality related to job behavior and performance.[7] Figure 2–2 presents the 16PF profile, and defines the two ends of each personality dimension. The 16PF includes scales for sixteen normal personality characteristics that are the building blocks of a theory of personality. Much like the atomic model in chemistry, the traits in the 16PF combine in varying degrees to become the structure of individual personality.

By dividing the sixteen scales into ten scores, more than 10 quadrillion (10^{16}) personality categories can be identified. For example, the person whose profile is depicted in Figure 2–2 scored 5 on warm, 10 on abstract thinking, 6 on emotional stability, 8 on dominance, and so forth. Virtually every person who takes the test receives a slightly different profile, which is consistent with the idea that everybody has a unique personality.

The 16PF is frequently used in business and industry for selection and promotion of employees by making predictions about such factors as sales effectiveness, work efficiency, tolerance for routine, and stability of employment. For example, hotel reservations sales agents (those who take reservations over 800 numbers) should score high on warmth, low on abstract thinking, and high on self-sufficiency.

VALUES

Another important source of individual differences on the job is **values,** strongly held beliefs that serve as guides to action. Employees who value hard work are obviously more likely to be better motivated than people who do not value hard work. Values also influence ethical choices.

> An insurance sales agent sold a disability policy to a 60-year-old customer. The policy did not provide the customer the coverage he requested. When the agent's manager reviewed the policy, he chastised her for selling the wrong policy. The agent shrugged her shoulders and said, "What's the difference? There is very little chance he will file a claim before he retires."

In terms of the agent's values, there is nothing wrong with deceiving a customer. Yet in terms of the manager's values, customers should not be deceived about coverage. (Laws governing disability insurance may also be shaping the manager's values.)

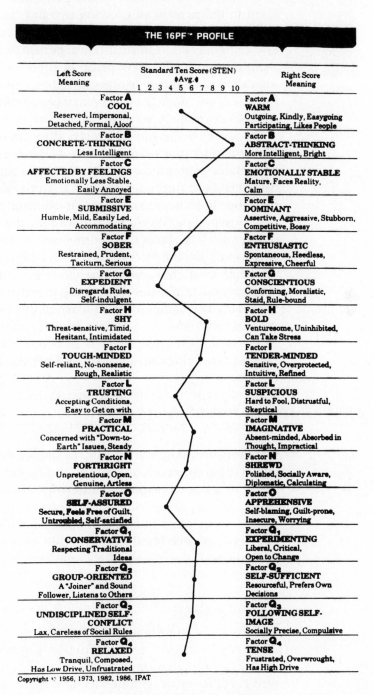

THE 16PF™ PROFILE

Left Score Meaning	Standard Ten Score (STEN) ♦Avg.♦ 1 2 3 4 5 6 7 8 9 10	Right Score Meaning
Factor **A** **COOL** Reserved, Impersonal, Detached, Formal, Aloof		Factor **A** **WARM** Outgoing, Kindly, Easygoing Participating, Likes People
Factor **B** **CONCRETE-THINKING** Less Intelligent		Factor **B** **ABSTRACT-THINKING** More Intelligent, Bright
Factor **C** **AFFECTED BY FEELINGS** Emotionally Less Stable, Easily Annoyed		Factor **C** **EMOTIONALLY STABLE** Mature, Faces Reality, Calm
Factor **E** **SUBMISSIVE** Humble, Mild, Easily Led, Accommodating		Factor **E** **DOMINANT** Assertive, Aggressive, Stubborn, Competitive, Bossy
Factor **F** **SOBER** Restrained, Prudent, Taciturn, Serious		Factor **F** **ENTHUSIASTIC** Spontaneous, Heedless, Expressive, Cheerful
Factor **G** **EXPEDIENT** Disregards Rules, Self-indulgent		Factor **G** **CONSCIENTIOUS** Conforming, Moralistic, Staid, Rule-bound
Factor **H** **SHY** Threat-sensitive, Timid, Hesitant, Intimidated		Factor **H** **BOLD** Venturesome, Uninhibited, Can Take Stress
Factor **I** **TOUGH-MINDED** Self-reliant, No-nonsense, Rough, Realistic		Factor **I** **TENDER-MINDED** Sensitive, Overprotected, Intuitive, Refined
Factor **L** **TRUSTING** Accepting Conditions, Easy to Get on with		Factor **L** **SUSPICIOUS** Hard to Fool, Distrustful, Skeptical
Factor **M** **PRACTICAL** Concerned with "Down-to-Earth" Issues, Steady		Factor **M** **IMAGINATIVE** Absent-minded, Absorbed in Thought, Impractical
Factor **N** **FORTHRIGHT** Unpretentious, Open, Genuine, Artless		Factor **N** **SHREWD** Polished, Socially Aware, Diplomatic, Calculating
Factor **O** **SELF-ASSURED** Secure, Feels Free of Guilt, Untroubled, Self-satisfied		Factor **O** **APPREHENSIVE** Self-blaming, Guilt-prone, Insecure, Worrying
Factor **Q₁** **CONSERVATIVE** Respecting Traditional Ideas		Factor **Q₁** **EXPERIMENTING** Liberal, Critical, Open to Change
Factor **Q₂** **GROUP-ORIENTED** A "Joiner" and Sound Follower, Listens to Others		Factor **Q₂** **SELF-SUFFICIENT** Resourceful, Prefers Own Decisions
Factor **Q₃** **UNDISCIPLINED SELF-CONFLICT** Lax, Careless of Social Rules		Factor **Q₃** **FOLLOWING SELF-IMAGE** Socially Precise, Compulsive
Factor **Q₄** **RELAXED** Tranquil, Composed, Has Low Drive, Unfrustrated		Factor **Q₄** **TENSE** Frustrated, Overwrought, Has High Drive

Copyright © 1956, 1973, 1982, 1986, IPAT

FIGURE 2–2 The 16PF™ Profile

Source: The Institute for Personality and Ability Testing, Inc., P.O. Box 188, Champaign, IL. 61820, 1988 catalog. Reproduced with permission.

A person is not born with a particular set of values. He or she learns them in the process of growing up, and many values are learned in early childhood. One important way we acquire values is through observing others, or modeling. Quite often a person who values quality was reared around people who took pride in their work. Models can be anyone we identify with, such as parents, teachers, friends, siblings, and even public figures. If we identify with a particular person, the probability is high that we will develop some of his or her major values.[8]

Another major way in which values are learned is through the communication of attitudes. The attitudes we hear expressed directly or indirectly help shape our values. Assume that your family and friends talked about using credit to purchase goods and services as an evil practice. You might therefore hold negative values about installment purchases.

Unstated but implied attitudes may also shape your values. If key people in your life showed no enthusiasm when you talked about becoming successful, you might not place such a high value on career success. If, on the other hand, the same key people encouraged conversation about career success, you might develop strong career values.

Many key values are also learned through religion, and thus become the basis for society's morals. A basic example is that all religions emphasize treating other people fairly and kindly. To "knife anybody in the back" is considered immoral both on and off the job.

PSYCHOMOTOR ABILITY AND PHYSICAL SKILLS

Various psychomotor and physical skills can be important sources of individual differences on the job, and can be job requirements. (*Psychomotor* refers to a motor response caused by the mind.) An example of a high-paying job requiring excellent vision is commercial airline pilot. Managerial work may not require many specific physical skills, but managers must have enough eye-hand coordination (a psychomotor skill) to operate computers.

Psychomotor Abilities

Eye-hand coordination, dexterity, manipulative ability, and the like are needed for many jobs, particularly at the first few job levels. People show extreme variation in this ability, even after extensive training. For example, some repair technicians have more mechanical aptitude and talent than others. Such mundane tasks as reloading paper into printers and changing ribbons do not come easily to every office worker.

Psychomotor skills can be subdivided into components. Three of these components are as follows:

Control precision: needed for tasks requiring finely controlled muscular adjustments such as moving a gauge to a precise setting, or programming a VCR.

Manual dexterity: needed for tasks involving skilled arm and hand movements in manipulating large objects under conditions of speed. Many assembly line jobs require good manual dexterity, and the same skill is required to change a car's tire.

Reaction time: the ability to respond to a signal. Fast reaction times are required for truck drivers and process control technicians, including those working in nuclear reactor plants. (Process control technicians watch computerized dials, which may indicate when something like a malfunctioning machine requires immediate attention.)

Physical Skills

People also show a wide range of physical abilities, and those differences can influence job performance. An ophthalmology medical technician, for example, may have to stand up most of the work day. He or she may not be able to sit down while administering visual tests to patients. Should that person be physically challenged (disabled), special accommodations will need to be made. Many jobs, including many involved with factories and mills, require good physical condition. Many postal carriers have had to resign because of bad backs or ailing feet (or the inability to run fast enough from angry dogs). A butcher may be required to manipulate cuts of meat weighing up to 200 pounds.

Many physical skills can be developed. In the past, women were excluded from certain occupations, such as telephone pole climber, because it was assumed that they lacked the appropriate physical skills. Now many telephone pole climbers are female. With practice, any able-bodied person can learn to scale a telephone pole.

DEMOGRAPHIC CHARACTERISTICS

Demographic, or statistical, characteristics of a person are *sometimes* related to job performance and behavior. For example, people in their 60s are more likely than those in their 20s to experience aching feet when required to stand for prolonged hours. Consequently, it might become more difficult for them to smile at unpleasant customers later in the day. However, the experience of an older employee is an advantage for such tasks as directing a major business corporation or flying a commercial passenger plane.

As the workforce becomes more culturally diverse, demographic factors could increase in importance. The Bureau of Labor Statistics estimates that women will occupy 64 percent of the new jobs by the year 2000. The number of blacks and Hispanics in the workforce is expected to increase nearly twice as fast as the number of whites. Furthermore, the number of workers ages 16 to 24 years old will drop by almost 2 million by the end of the century. As a result, the average age of employees will climb from 36 today to 39 by the year 2000, and to 41 in 2020.

Although demographic factors are responsible for some differences in job performance, individual differences within a particular demographic group are still more important. It might be true in general that working parents with preschool children are absent more frequently than are parents with grown children. Nevertheless, a worker with preschool children might have a retired parent who takes over in emergencies.

Age and Experience

The stereotype that older workers are more productive may not be as true as is generally thought. One study of 24,000 government workers found that age was barely related to performance. Experience, or seniority, did have a slight relationship to job performance. (Experience refers to how much time a person has been performing a particular job or type of job.) An enlightening aspect of the study indicated that both age and experience predicted performance better for jobs requiring higher levels of complexity or mastery than for other jobs.[9] The position of a mortgage officer is an example of a complex job.

A review of twenty-two years of articles studying the relationship between age and performance (involving almost 40,000 workers) found that age and job performance were generally unrelated. However, among workers in the 17- to 21-year-old category, older employees tended to be more productive.[10]

Even if being older and more experienced does not always contribute to job performance, older workers do have some other notable attributes. In contrast to younger workers they have lower absenteeism, turnover, illness, and accident rates; higher job satisfaction; and more positive work values.[11]

Sex Differences

A topic of intense debate and continuing interest is whether men and women differ in aspects of behavior related to job performance. The evidence suggests that there are few differences between males and females that will affect their job performance.[12] Despite this general finding, it is helpful to examine some of the specific job performance–related differences between men and women. Most of the differences that do exist can be attributed more to learning than to heredity (or nurture rather than nature).

Conformity. Women show a stronger tendency to conform to influence attempts. For example, women might be more influenced by persuasion from their boss. This tendency is much stronger in group than in individual situations. These differences are much less noticeable among the current generation of women.[13]

Influence tactics. Several findings that do not fit common sense have emerged in the study of differences in influence tactics between men and women. A study of 225 supervisors and 244 subordinates examined a variety of influence tactics, including assertiveness and making bargains with subordinates. Men and women chose about the same influence tactics. Also, the tactics chosen did not differ whether the person being influenced was male or female.[14]

A recent study investigated self-reports of influence tactics chosen by 176 men and 161 women in mostly higher-level jobs. As in the previous study, many similarities were found in the influence tactics used by men and women. Important differences were also noted. The findings contradicted some popular beliefs about how men and women go about gaining advantage. Men were significantly more likely than women to perceive themselves as relying on charm, manipulative tactics, and personal appearance to achieve results and gain advantage.[15] A follow-up study found that men make far more use of joking and kidding to influence others, according to the perceptions of both men and women. Women were more likely to use compliments.[16]

Cooperation vs. competition. Males tend to be more competitive and less cooperative than females. These differences were particularly pronounced before large numbers of women occupied higher-level positions. Recent observations suggest that career women tend to compete more than cooperate with other career women. In fact, they are sometimes prone to engage in devious tactics to block the success of women co-workers.[17] In this way, women might be treating women the same way many men treat other men (see Chapter 11).

Creativity. Few differences in creativity are found among boys and girls, and this pattern continues through adulthood.[18] In some situations women are more creative than men because women tend to be more emotionally expressive (a stimulant to creativity).

Leadership behavior. Some people argue that women have certain acquired traits and behaviors which suit them for people-oriented leadership positions. Among these are the abilities to resolve conflict among group members, listen to people and counsel them, and size up people. It is also argued that women's natural sensitivity to people gives them an edge over men in encouraging group members to participate in decision making.[19]

Absenteeism. Mothers of young children tend to be absent from work more frequently than are male workers with or without children. However, mothers of grown children probably do not have higher absenteeism rates than do male workers. Furthermore, when adequate child-care facilities are available, these differences in male-female absenteeism rates shrink. Absenteeism differences between men and women thus reflect differences in the roles of men and women rather than in their characters.[20]

Race

Because employers and society in general are committed to providing equal employment opportunity, information about the impact of race on job performance is important. A study of 8,500 enlisted personnel in the U.S. Army found that race (here, black, white, or Hispanic) had a very small effect on performance ratings. A similar small effect was found for sex. The jobs studied were entry-level positions, such as tank crewman, supply specialist, and medical specialist. Among the findings were that blacks were rated higher than whites on military bearing (pose, posture, and polish), but lower than whites on technical skill, job effort, and personal discipline.[21]

Recently a comparable number of white and black managers in three different companies were studied. The black and white managers were comparable in terms of age, length of time with the employer, job function, and rank in the organization. The study found that black managers received slightly lower performance ratings than did white managers. The differences were found for both technical and interpersonal aspects of performance. Black managers also reported having less job discretion and lower feelings of acceptance than did white managers. The researchers offered this explanation:

> The results of the present study, with its demographically comparable sample of blacks and whites, strengthen the conclusion that blacks may be excluded from opportunities for power and integration within organizations and that such exclusion may be detrimental to their job performance.[22]

Marital Status and Number of Dependents

Differences in job performance can also stem from marital status and number of dependents. Married employees are less likely to be absent from work or quit, and tend to have higher job satisfaction than do unmarried people.[23] It is also possible that divorced parents with child custody, and single people living with a partner, are also more reliable. Workers, especially females, with a larger number of dependents tend to be absent more frequently. As mentioned previously, when adequate child-care arrangements are available these differences may diminish.

CULTURALLY BASED INDIVIDUAL DIFFERENCES

The culture in which people are reared influences their work behavior. Although culture may be regarded as a group rather than an individual factor, it functions as a source of individual differences. People from different cultural backgrounds may respond quite differently to the same situation. For example, workers from rural areas tend to feel more kinship with co-workers than do workers from large urban areas. This is one reason why programs designed to foster teamwork tend to fare better in nonurban areas.

The internationalization of workplaces has made an awareness of culturally based individual differences more important than ever. For example, a substantial number of sales associate positions in New York City and Los Angeles are held by people from Asia and the Middle East. A New York retail store manager raised in the United States would therefore have to be sensitive to cultural differences. For example, a sales associate from India might regard the manager as abdicating responsibility if the manager asked the associate for her opinion on how to handle a customer problem.

Another major cultural difference in job behavior occurs between North Americans and Japanese. North Americans are predisposed by culture to welcome confrontation and conflict in the workplace, while Japanese tend to avoid confrontation and conflict. This cultural difference helps explain why Japanese often smile even when they strongly disagree with the other person's position on a work issue.[24]

The general principle for handling cultural differences is to be sensitive to their existence. Be aware that culturally based differences in work behavior exist, and be ready to make some adjustments to these differences. A specific example: An employee raised in Taiwan might be more predisposed to accept a manager's authority than an employee from Sweden might be. Figure 2–3 illustrates mistakes, or *cultural bloopers,* to avoid should you be on assignment in various countries. Some of the same ideas would apply if you were dealing with people from a foreign country in your native land.

A MODEL OF HUMAN BEHAVIOR BASED ON INDIVIDUAL DIFFERENCES

To help tie together much of the preceding information on individual differences, we present a model of human behavior that takes into account the uniqueness of people. The model could also prove helpful in another way. To deal effectively with individuals or small groups in a work environment, you need a basic framework for understanding human beings. Even if the framework you choose is not the most sophisticated available, it is better than no framework at all. A framework gives you a starting point for arriving

- Insisting on getting down to business quickly in most countries outside the United States. (In most countries, building a social relationship precedes closing a deal.)
- Pressuring an Asian job applicant or employee to brag about his or her accomplishments. (Boasting about professional achievements makes Asians feel self-conscious; they prefer to let the record speak for itself.)
- Inviting a Korean associate's wife to a dinner meeting. (Inviting a Korean's wife along is considered to be in poor taste.)
- Asking a Latin American supervisor to solicit group opinion before taking action. (Latin Americans generally expect the manager to be the voice of authority.)
- Telling Indians you prefer not to eat with your hands. (If Indians are not using cutlery when eating, they expect their guest to do likewise.)
- Misinterpreting "We'll consider it" as "Maybe" when spoken by a Japanese. (Japanese negotiators mean "No" when they say "We'll consider it.")
- Thinking that a businessperson from England is unenthusiastic when he or she says, "Not bad at all." (English people understate positive emotion.)
- Giving small gifts to Chinese people when conducting business. (Chinese are offended by these gifts.)
- Not giving small gifts to Japanese when conducting business. (Japanese are offended by *not* receiving these gifts.)
- Appearing in shirt sleeves at a business meeting in Germany. (Germans believe that a person is not exercising proper authority when he or she appears at a meeting without a jacket.)
- Being overly rank-conscious in Scandinavian countries. (Scandinavians pay relatively little attention to a person's organizational rank.)
- Appearing perturbed when somebody shows up late for a meeting in most countries outside the United States. (Time is much less valued outside the United States.)

FIGURE 2-3 Cultural Mistakes to Avoid in Selected Countries

Source: Several of the errors are based on Sandra Thierderman, "Overcoming Cultural and Language Barriers," *Personnel Journal,* December 1988, pp. 34–40; Jon Pepper, "U.S. Exec Often Doesn't Fit In at Japanese Firm," Gannett News Service story, Mar. 29, 1990; "International Business Tips," *The Pryor Report,* Aug. 1987, p. 11.

at conclusions about people, but it should not be an intellectual strait-jacket that prevents you from making spontaneous observations.

To use a sports analogy, in developing tennis strategy you might use the general assumption that the best way to beat (deal effectively with) an opponent is to keep him or her running. According to your basic framework about human behavior on the tennis court, a person kept on the move hits more erratically than does a person who has the opportunity to hit from one position. You might find this the best strategy to use against most people, but now and then you might have to reformulate your strategy. You might encounter a player who returns the ball best when he or she is kept running about the court. When forced to hit many balls from the same position, that particular opponent feels too constricted and therefore becomes more erratic.

Basic Nature of the Model

Figure 2–4 is a basic model of behavior that reflects current thinking about how people respond to external forces.[25] There are four key elements: (A) the stimulus or outside force, (B) the person, (C) internal or external behavior, and (D) results. We will describe and illustrate the model.

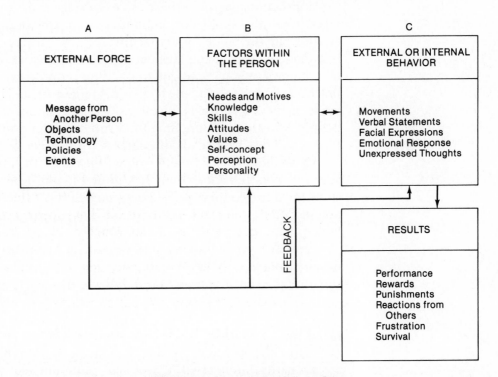

FIGURE 2–4 A Behavioral Model of Human Beings

Source: Adapted with permission from Henry L. Tosi, John R. Rizzo, and Stephen J. Carroll, *Managing Organizational Behavior* (Marshfield, MA: Pitman Publishing 1986), p. 114.

It incorporates two basic viewpoints about how people learn and are motivated: cognitive and noncognitive.

The **cognitive viewpoint** emphasizes the internal mental processes that take place whenever a person is subject to an external force. People behave according to how they react to the stimulus. If people are in control of their senses, they make rational choices—they seek to maximize gain and pleasure and minimize loss and pain. To make these rational choices, the person attempts to evaluate the merits of external stimuli (any force that produces an effect).

The **noncognitive viewpoint** emphasizes that behavior is determined by the rewards and punishments an individual receives from the environment. Instead of behavior being influenced by an evaluation of the environment, the consequences of one's past behavior influence future behavior. A noncognitive model of behavior is also called a **reinforcement model** because rewards and punishments reinforce or strengthen responses.

External Force

The behavioral model of human behavior begins when an external force acts upon a person. These forces can take many forms, including messages from others, objects, technology, company policies, or some event. To illustrate the model, visualize this scenario. You receive an unexpected telephone message from Jack, an old friend. After a few moments of small talk, he says to you: "I've got an exciting proposition to offer you. I am a branch manager for one of the world's largest financial services firm. Our latest marketing thrust is to sell individual retirement accounts (IRAs) to people who are just launching their careers. Since you are enrolled in college, you must have loads of contacts with career beginners."

"Just think what a bundle you will make for the rest of your life. Since very few people cancel their IRA policies, you'll be collecting commissions for thirty to forty years from practically all the people you sign up. And just think, you can work for us full-time or part-time. It all depends on how quickly you want to become rich."

Another way of looking at the factors in (A) is that they are the causes or antecedents of behavior. The message from Jack will cause you to do something, even if you just politely hang up.

Factors Within the Person

The external forces (A) act upon factors within the person (B), which are primarily intellectual, emotional, physiological, and physical attributes. Among them are needs and motives, knowledge, skills, attitudes, values, personality, self-concept, and perceptions. These attributes explain and regulate human behavior. All of the attributes are intangible, but they are nevertheless very important aspects of human behavior. They help explain and regulate human behavior.

A given external force will interact with the factors within the person that are most relevant at the time. These factors will influence how a person will respond to the external force. An important point about these factors is that they are all based partly upon past experience. For instance, your attitude toward selling a financial service would be influenced by past experience with life insurance sales representatives. Here is a brief rundown of how the factors listed in (B) could influence your response to Jack's proposition:

Needs and motives. If you have a strong need for accomplishment, you may respond positively to Jack's message. A strong motive for wanting to learn more about the deal would be a desire to increase your income. If you needed more money to continue your formal education, you might be very interested in Jack's proposition.

Knowledge. Your knowledge of IRAs, selling, and the spending preferences of career beginners will also influence your response to Jack's offer. Your knowledge could be valid, invalid, or some combination of the two. If you have limited knowledge of IRAs and selling, you might pay little attention to the message. If you believe that students would be eager to start retirement accounts, you would respond positively. If your knowledge tells you that students have no interest in opening retirement accounts, you might not think much of Jack's offer.

Skills. A person's perceived skills influence how he or she will respond to a stimulus. If you perceive yourself to have good sales, communications, or analytical skills, you may be positively inclined toward Jack's proposal. If you do not perceive yourself to have the relevant skills, you will be more hesitant to get involved.

Attitudes. Our **attitudes,** or predispositions to respond, directly influence our receptiveness to an external force. You would be more inclined to respond positively to selling IRAs if you had favorable attitudes toward sales work, retirement planning, and working while attending school. Negative attitudes toward these activities would lead you away from exploring the job further.

Values. People judge the merits of external stimuli in terms of their values. You would be more likely to explore the IRA venture if you valued money, challenge, and uncertainty. If your values lay in the opposite direction, you would be less inclined to pursue the venture.

Self-concept.   Your **self-concept** is simply what you think of yourself or who you think you are. If your self-concept includes the idea that you are a go-getter and a winner, you might be inclined toward exploring Jack's idea further. If your self-concept includes the idea that you succeed only in low-risk situations, you might not want to proceed.

Perception.   How people interpret things in the external world is referred to as **perception.** Your perception of Jack, IRAs, insurance companies, and sales work will profoundly influence your decision to explore the idea further. For instance, if you perceive Jack to be honest and sincere, you will be interested. If you perceive him to be devious and slick, you might respond, "Thanks anyway, but I'm very busy these days."

Personality.   Personality is a comprehensive concept that includes many of the other factors within the person listed in (B) of Figure 2–4. An example of a relevant personality factor influencing whether you decide to get involved with selling IRAs is your degree of extroversion. An extroverted person is more likely than an introverted person to engage in this type of difficult selling. Another relevant personality trait would be one's level of optimism. Only an optimist would try to sell retirement funds to newcomers to the full-time work force, and to part-time workers.

External or Internal Behavior

Characteristics of the person influence behavior. In response to the external force, the person behaves in some way (C). These behaviors include movements, verbal statements, facial expressions, emotional responses, and unexpressed thoughts. If Jack's proposition interested you, the consequent behaviors would include positive statements to him, a happy facial expression, and an increase in your heart rate.

Characteristics of the person and behavior are closely connected because behavior stems from these characteristics. Furthermore, some characteristics of a person cannot be separated from behavior. For example, skills exist only when they are manifested in behavior, and attitudes usually exist only as thoughts.

Results

Behavior (C) leads to some result or impact on the outside world. Some of the results are intended and some are not. For instance, the intended result of offering assistance to a co-worker is to help him or her and perhaps receive appreciation in return. If you are rebuffed, the result will be frustration. If you decide to follow up on Jack's offer, the results (D) you achieve could include performing as expected, receiving financial rewards, getting recognition from others, and financial survival.

The arrows in Figure 2–4 indicate that behavior and its results serve as feedback to a person. People learn from their behavior and from its effects. If you jumped at the opportunity to work with Jack and you succeeded, the feedback might include a strengthening of your self-concept, the development of your sales skills, and an increased readiness to respond to similar offers in the future.

Implications and Uses of the Behavioral Model

The model just presented has some important implications for understanding and dealing with others. We will mention a few of them now. Of course, many of the topics in this text provide more information for understanding and dealing with others. To repeat, the model is intended only as a starting point in explaining human behavior on the job.

The person and the environment contribute to behavior. The standard formula to represent how a person behaves is this:

$$B = f(P \times E)$$

The verbal expression is, "Behavior is a function of the person interacting with the environment." What we do in a given situation results from the combined influence of our internal characteristics and external forces. Thus a person with strong work values will express these values strongly when a company policy rewards initiative. A person's analytical skills may not be of much help if they are working with the wrong technology.

One direct application of the $B = f(P \times E)$ formula is that you have to understand both the person and the external forces faced by that person in order to understand his or her behavior. If you wanted to help the person perform well, you might need to change the external force (such as the choice of co-workers) to a more favorable one.

Behavior has multiple causes. Both on and off the job, a person's behavior is determined by a number of environmental stimuli and internal characteristics. These stimuli and characteristics may produce a number of different behaviors. An application of this idea is that you should not be personally hurt if your well-intended actions are rejected. Suppose you have good reason to believe that your weekly results are outstanding. You review these results with your boss, and she says, "Not good enough; why can't you work harder?" Your boss may not be responding simply to your results, but to a recent chastisement she received from her boss about producing more.

Self-explanations for behavior may be inaccurate. An important message from this model is that people may not be aware of the forces and motives that are causing their behavior. You therefore cannot always assume that their explanations for their actions are correct. Suppose that you are a supervisor and an employee says to you, "No thanks, I don't want to volunteer to be the first to use that new computer application. I'm so overloaded now that I don't want to fall behind schedule." Further conversation may reveal that the employee really wants to try the new computer application. His problem is he is not confident he has enough computer knowledge to perform well. You may need to encourage him or arrange for additional training.

Individual differences are important. In dealing with others it is essential to recognize that people differ in many significant ways. The sources of these differences are shown in the list of factors within the person (B) in Figure 2–4. An implication of these individual differences is that you may have to understand the uniqueness of a person in order to deal effectively with him or her. If a person is strongly motivated by money, talking about financial rewards will help you motivate that person. Another factor is that if you think somebody has a weak self-concept, avoid insulting that person. To do so will make that person very defensive and ineffective.

Does the concept of individual differences mean that human relations and organizational behavior can provide no firm guidelines for dealing with others? Decidedly not; there are many valid generalizations that give you guidelines for dealing with others. These generalizations can be used as starting points in dealing with others; they may then need to be modified to adapt to individual differences. Here are three general principles of human relations:

- People perform better when they set goals.
- Criticizing people in public makes them defensive.
- When faced with a crisis, employees prefer that the leader take forceful charge of the situation.

We will be discussing generalizations about job-oriented behavior throughout the text. We will also make frequent references to how individual differences influence behavior. Understanding and dealing effectively with others always involves finding the right balance between general principles of human behavior and individual differences.

Summary of Key Points

- The implications of individual differences on the job include the fact that people differ in these ways: (1) how well they produce on the job; (2) ability and talent; (3) the importance they attach to interesting work; (4) the style of leadership they prefer and need; (5) their need for contact with other people; (6) their degree of commitment and loyalty.
- Mental ability, or intelligence, is related to performance in a wide variety of medium- and higher-level occupations. Intelligence con-

sists of a general factor and specific factors such as verbal comprehension, numerical ability, and symbolic reasoning. The idea of practical intelligence means that intelligence is exhibited in mental activities of various kinds and that the study of intelligence must entail the study of these mental activities.

- Personality refers to those persistent and enduring behavior patterns of an individual that are expressed in a wide variety of situations. Individual differences in personality influence job performance and behavior. Certain needs of people, such as the need to be dominant over others, are often transformed into personality traits. Such traits then influence them to behave in certain ways, such as trying to control others. The Sixteen Personality Factor Questionnaire™ (16PF) measures dimensions of personality (such as group-oriented vs. self-sufficient) that relate to job behavior and performance.

- Values, another source of individual differences in job behavior, are often acquired through listening to and observing others.

- Various psychomotor and physical skills can be important sources of individual differences, and can be job requirements. Three important psychomotor skills are control precision, manual dexterity, and reaction time.

- Demographic characteristics of a person are sometimes related to job performance and behavior. Although these characteristics can be related to job performance, individual differences within a particular demographic group are still more important. Evidence was summarized about the following demographic characteristics: age and experience (can be important in more complex jobs); sex (few consistent differences related to job performance); race (most of the differences found can be trace to unequal opportunities in the workplace); marital status and number of dependents (people with partners may be more dependable but child-care responsibilities can increase absenteeism).

- The culture in which a person is reared influences work behavior. Although culture is a group rather than an individual factor, it functions as a source of individual differences. People from different cultures may respond quite differently to the same situations.

- A behavioral model of human beings presented here is based on both a cognitive and a noncognitive viewpoint. The model contains these key elements: (A) an external force acts upon (B) factors within the person to result in (C) external or internal behavior, which leads to (D) results such as performance and rewards. The behavior and its results serve as feedback to the person.

- Implications of this model include these points: The person and the environment contribute to behavior; behavior has multiple causes; self-explanations for behavior may be inaccurate; individual differences are important. The primary application of the model is to help you understand and deal effectively with other workers.

Questions and Activities

1. Give three examples of individual differences in job performance that you have observed among people on any job.
2. What are two important ways in which you are different from most other people?
3. Identify two occupations you think require a very high degree of problem-solving ability. Explain your answer.
4. Give an example of "contextual intelligence" as practiced by a professional-level worker such as a sales representative or a manager.
5. How might personality factors influence one's performance as a student?
6. How might the need for thrill seeking be satisfied on the job?
7. Identify the approximate standard ten score (STEN) on several traits that you think would be ideal for a top-level business executive (see Figure 2–2).
8. What do you think employers mean when they say they are looking to hire people with the "right values"?
9. Based on the discussion in the text, how does length of experience appear to be related to job performance?
10. Based on the discussion in the text, in what type of job situation might sex be related to job performance?
11. Why should business people be so concerned about committing a cultural blooper?

A HUMAN RELATIONS INCIDENT
The Rocky Mountain Accountant

Bart Belladonna had worked very hard to create a good life for himself. His lifestyle has been one of working hard and playing hard. He grew up in Utah, not far from a major ski area, where he also attended high school and college. Bart became a good enough skier to make his high school team. He majored in accounting and business administration at college. His first professional employment was as a junior accountant for an insurance firm located in a suburb of Denver, Colorado. Bart considered himself very fortunate to have landed a good job near some of the best ski areas in North America.

Bart approached his job with his characteristic high level of enthusiasm. His first three performance appraisals, given at six-month intervals, were outstanding. One day Bart's boss approached him with this offer:

"Bart, we love you around here. But the good of the firm as a whole comes before local considerations. Company headquarters in Chicago has offered you a position as an internal auditor. The job begins in thirty days. The position is a great stepping stone to bigger and better things with the firm. You'll receive an immediate $5,000 per year salary increase."

Bart was stunned. He asked his boss for one day to think about the offer. The next day he told his boss, "I'm very grateful for the promotion you have offered me. It would really be exciting to work as an auditor. And I agree it would be a big boost in my career. But I don't want to leave Colorado. This is God's country, especially when you're a skier. I'm not wiling to trade the beauty of the Rocky Mountains for life in the big city."

His boss retorted, "Bart, grab hold of yourself. With a $5,000 a year raise, you can fly out to Colorado for a ski trip at least twice a year. Are you a ski bum or an ambitious accountant? I just don't understand you."

"I'm sorry you put it that way," said Bart. "But my decision is final. I want to stay put here in Colorado."

1. Explain what happened here, using the behavioral model presented in Figure 2–4.
2. How does this case relate to values?
3. How would you evaluate the human relations effectiveness of Bart's boss?

A HUMAN RELATIONS CASE PROBLEM
Flipping Burgers in Yugoslavia

Belgrade, Yugoslavia, was the location of the first McDonald's to open in a Communist country. Management ran into an unexpected problem: Turnover is high, because employees find they have to work like Westerners (very hard) but get paid like East Europeans (very low). During the first few months of operation, forty employees—about one-third of the operation—have quit their jobs, despite a high unemployment rate.

Predrag Dostanic, managing director of the restaurant, blames misperceptions about the West gathered from American movies shown on Yugoslav television. Dostanic said, "That is all a result of drastically incorrect concepts about international business, implanted in people's minds by such American TV series as 'Dynasty.'"

"Those who have left us thought they would earn high wages only by virtue of working for an American enterprise," said an official from a state enterprise that entered into a joint venture agreement with McDonald's.

Dostanic added, "Those young people who quit probably also expected they could do their jobs the Yugoslav way—relax at work but still receive their wages."

The fast food outlet, located on a downtown square, has drawn large crowds since it opened, selling an average of 6,000 meals daily in its first month.

"The work has been so hard that I could not stand it any more," said a former employee. "If my salary was adequate to the work, I might have stayed."

The McDonald's employees, mostly young people trained to work at counters and in the kitchen, receive about $170 per month, which is slightly above the average Yugoslavian wage.

"Maybe there is something good in all these unexpected staff problems," said the state enterprise official. "Only the best workers will survive."

1. How does this case relate to individual differences?
2. How does this case relate to values?
3. What recommendations would you make to the managing director of McDonald's in Belgrade to decrease turnover and get the restaurant workers to be more productive?

Source: As reported in Dusan Stojanovic, "Belgrade McDonald's Hits Snag," Associated Press story, May 26, 1988.

Notes

1. John E. Hunter, Frank L. Schmidt, and Michael K. Judiesch, "Individual Differences in Output Variability as a Function of Job Complexity," *Journal of Applied Psychology,* February 1990, pp. 28–42.

2. John Hawk, "Real World Implications of g," *Journal of Vocational Behavior,* December 1986, p. 411.

3. "Employee Aptitude Survey (EAS)," © 1952–1983, *The Psychological Corporation Harcourt Brace Jovanovich, Inc.,* 1990 catalog.

4. Robert J. Sternberg and Richard K. Wagner (eds.), *Practical Intelligence: Nature and Origins of Competence in the Everyday World* (New York: Cambridge University Press, 1986).

5. David V. Day and Stanley B. Silverman, "Personality and Job Performance: Evidence of Incremental Validity," *Personnel Psychology,* Spring 1989, pp. 25–36.

6. Henry A. Murray, *Explorations in Personality* (New York: Oxford University

Press, 1938); Robert B. Ewen, *An Introduction to Theories of Personality,* 3rd ed. (Hillsdale, NJ: Erlbaum, 1988).

7. Published by the Institute for Personality and Ability Testing Inc., Champaign, IL.

8. Milton Rokeach, *The Nature of Human Values* (New York: The Free Press, 1973).

9. Bruce J. Avolio, David A. Waldman, and Michael A. McDaniel, "Age and Work Performance in Nonmanagerial Jobs: The Effects of Experience and Occupational Type," *Academy of Management Journal,* June 1990, pp. 407–22.

10. Glenn M. McEvoy and Wayne F. Cascio, "Cumulative Evidence of the Relationship Between Employee Age and Job Performance," *Journal of Applied Psychology,* February 1989, pp. 11–17.

11. Susan R. Rhodes, "Age-related Differences in Work Attitudes and Behavior: A Review and Conceptual Analysis," *Psychological Bulletin,* March 1983, pp. 328–67.

12. Stephen P. Robbins, *Organizational Behavior: Concepts, Controversies, and Applications,* 4th ed. (Englewood Cliffs, NJ: Prentice Hall, 1989), p. 44.

13. H. Joseph Reitz, *Behavior in Organizations,* 3rd ed. (Homewood, IL: Irwin, 1987), p. 443.

14. David Kipnis, Stuart M. Schmidt, and Ian Wilkinson, "Intraorganizational Influence Tactics: Explorations in Getting One's Way," *Journal of Applied Psychology,* August 1980, pp. 440–52.

15. Andrew J. DuBrin, "Sex Differences in Endorsement of Influence Tactics and Political Behavior Tendencies," *Journal of Business and Psychology,* Fall 1989, pp. 3–14.

16. Andrew J. DuBrin, "Sex and Gender Differences in Influence Tactics," *Psychological Reports,* 1991, pp. 635–46.

17. Judith Briles, *Women to Women: From Sabotage to Support* (New York: New Horizon Press, 1988).

18. Reitz, *Behavior in Organizations,* p. 176.

19. Judy Rosener, "Ways Women Lead," *Harvard Business Review,* November–December 1990, pp. 119–25.

20. Robbins, *Organizational Behavior,* p. 46.

21. Elaine D. Pulakos and associates, "Examination of Race and Sex Effects on Performance Ratings," *Journal of Applied Psychology,* October, 1989, pp. 770–80.

22. Jeffrey H. Greenhaus, Saroj Parasuraman, and Wayne M. Wormely, "Effects of Race on Organizational Experiences, Job Performance Evaluations, and Career Outcomes," *Academy of Management Journal,* March, 1990, p. 80.

23. Robbins, *Organizational Behavior,* p. 46.

24. Jon Pepper, "U.S. Exec Often Doesn't Fit In at Japanese Firm," Gannett News Service story, Mar. 29, 1990.

25. This section of the chapter is based on Henry L. Tosi, John R. Rizzo, and Stephen J. Carroll, *Managing Organizational Behavior* (Marshfield, MA: Pitman, 1986), pp. 113–16.

Suggested Reading _____

ALLPORT, GORDON W. *Personality: A Psychological Interpretation.* New York: Henry Holt, 1937.

ANASTASI, ANNE. *Psychological Testing,* 6th ed. New York: Macmillan, 1988.

CAMPION, MICHAEL A. "Ability Requirement Implications of Job Design: An Interdisciplinary Perspective." *Personnel Psychology,* Spring 1989, pp. 1–24.

DOBBINS, GREGORY H., CARDY, ROBERT L, and TRUXILLO, DONALD M. "The Effects of Purpose of Appraisal and Individual Differences in Stereotypes of Women on Sex Differences in Performance Ratings: A Laboratory and Field Study." *Journal of Applied Psychology,* August 1988, pp. 551–58.

DORTCH, C. THOMAS. "Job-Person-Match: A Case Example." *Personnel Journal,* June 1989, pp. 58–61.

DYCHTWALD, KEN, and FLOWER, JOE. *Age Wave: The Challenges and Opportunities of an Aging America.* Los Angeles: Tarcher, 1989.

GOLDSTEIN, ARNOLD P., and KRASNER, LEONARD. *Modern Applied Psychology,* New York: Pergamon, 1987.

MCAFEE, R. BRUCE, and CHAMPAGNE, PAUL J. "Employee Development: Discovering Who Needs What." *Personnel Administrator,* February 1988, pp. 92–98.

PETERS, ROGER. *Practical Intelligence: Working Smarter in Business and the Professions.* New York: Harper & Row, 1987.

VACCARO, ANTHONY J. "Personality Clash: How Do Individual Personalities Affect Job Performance and the Job Environment?" *Personnel Administrator,* September 1988, pp. 88–92.

3

Work Motivation and Productivity

LEARNING OBJECTIVES

After reading and studying this chapter and doing the exercises, you should be able to

1. Explain the meaning of work motivation and productivity.
2. Explain how goals contribute to motivation.
3. Pinpoint how human needs are tied in with work motivation.
4. Know how to apply expectancy theory to motivate people.
5. Sketch a program of using positive reinforcement in a work setting.
6. Understand the role of self-determination in motivation.
7. Develop a strategy for increasing your own motivation.

I n recent years, work motivation has surfaced as a topic of major concern for American society. One reason for this heightened interest is the need to make our organizations more competitive. Many firms are at a competitive disadvantage because so many entry-level workers have such a weak work ethic. The shortage of workers to fill many entry-level and skilled jobs has increased the importance of motivating present workers, rather than attempting to replace them.[1] Motivation is also important because: "consistently and correctly used motivational techniques can help turn a department or company with slumping morale and productivity into a galvanized unit of dragon-slayers."[2]

Before proceeding, we need to pinpoint two meanings of a frequently used term, **motivation.** One meaning is an internal state that leads to effort expended toward objectives. **Work motivation** is therefore effort expended toward organizational objectives. Another meaning of the term is an activity performed by managers or any other person to get others to accomplish work.

The term *productivity* also requires definition because it is used so frequently in conjunction with motivation. A major reason for motivating workers is to make them more productive. Generally speaking, productivity refers to how much a person accomplishes in a given period of time. A productive person accomplishes a lot (achieves output) without consuming too many resources (input). **Productivity** is thus the ratio of output to input, taking into account both quantity and quality. The productivity formula is shown in Figure 3–1.

Quality is an important part of productivity. If quality is not included in the productivity formula, a worker who generated a large amount of unacceptable work in a short period of time would be considered productive. The concept of quality also allows for the fact that a worker could produce a small amount of high-quality work in a long period of time and still be considered productive. If it took you all week to produce one successful five-word advertising slogan, you could consider yourself productive.

Productivity is tied in with motivation because motivation is an important contributor to productivity. However, the concept of productivity relates to every topic in this book. Productivity is built into the definition of human relations, since HR deals with improving effectiveness—a major component of productivity. It can be argued that no human relations technique is valuable if it does not enhance productivity or satisfaction.

$$\text{Productivity} = \frac{\text{Output (quantity and quality of goods and services produced)}}{\text{Input (amount of human, material, and financial resources consumed)}}$$

FIGURE 3–1 The Meaning of Productivity

COGNITIVE VERSUS NONCOGNITIVE EXPLANATIONS OF MOTIVATION

Explanations of human motivation can be divided into cognitive and noncognitive, or reinforcement, theories.[3] Cognitive models emphasize that people make conscious decisions about their behavior, such as, "Yes, I'll push for extra sales because my company is known to reward good performance." A cognitive explanation of motivation also emphasizes the fact that people are driven by internal forces that guide their behavior. Among such forces are the quest to satisfy needs for achievement, power, self-fulfillment, and affiliation with others. All but one of the explanations of motivation presented in this chapter are cognitive in nature.

Noncognitive explanations of motivation are based upon reinforcement theory. They are also referred to as behavior modification, or OB mod. A reinforcement model looks to external factors rather than the inner person for an explanation of why people behave as they do. The external factors emphasized are the rewards and punishments that condition behavior. Noncognitive explanations contend that workers engage in motivated behavior when their behavior leads to a reward or an escape from punishment. The noncognitive motivational approach described in this chapter is behavior modification.

Although the cognitive and noncognitive models differ, they overlap and can be used simultaneously to understand and control behavior. Inner strivings cause initial behavior, but external forces are major factors in future behavior. In other words, inner motives may trigger behavior, but satisfaction or other rewards derived from performance will cause it to be repeated and even improved. Dissatisfaction, of lack of appropriate reward, causes reduction or elimination of the behavior.[4]

A return to the behavioral model presented in Figure 2–4 will illustrate this important point further. The model contains both cognitive and reinforcement explanations of why people behave as they do. For instance, one aspect of the model contends that people's motives at the time determine whether they will spring into action (cognitive explanation). And whether they repeat that behavior depends upon the rewards or punishment they receive from the environment (noncognitive explanation).

Cognitive and reinforcement models of motivation are also used jointly in company programs designed to boost productivity. For example, need theory (cognitive explanation) is referred to to help determine which rewards would be useful in a program of positive reinforcement to control absenteeism (noncognitive explanation).

GOAL THEORY AND MOTIVATION

Almost every modern work organization has some form of goal-setting program to improve performance and productivity. Setting goals is basic to all motivational programs in organizations and to boosting your own level of motivation. Goal-setting theory helps explain both the importance of goal setting and the characteristics of goals that lead to improved performance.

Basic Facts

The best established facts of goal theory are shown in Figure 3–2. Underlying goal theory is the basic premise that behavior is regulated by values and conscious intentions or goals.[5] A **goal** is defined simply as what the person wants to accomplish. Our values create within us a desire to do things consistent with them. Goal-setting theory also contends that difficult goals lead to a higher level of performance than do easy goals. Although setting difficult goals is effective, goals should not be set so unrealistically high that they result in frustration due to failure.

It is also important to make goals specific, such as "sell ten cars this month," rather than general, such as "do your best." The goals people work toward tend to lead to improved performance regardless of whether these goals are set by them or the organization—providing that the individual accepts the goal.

Goals also are more effective when the person knows that they will be used to evaluate performance. Furthermore, the person should receive feedback on the goals and should be rewarded for reaching the goals.[6]

Research Evidence

A substantial amount of research has been carried out in organizations and laboratories to test the basic propositions of goal theory. Over twenty years of evidence indicate that setting goals (and implementing them) consistently improves performance.[7] Furthermore, when goals are set for both the work groups and individual workers, the results are even more

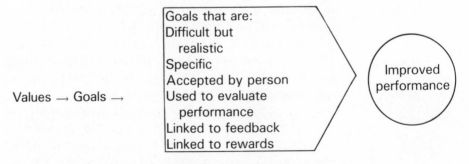

FIGURE 3–2 The Basics of Goal Theory

impressive.[8] The evidence is also quite consistent that difficult goals enhance performance more than easy goals do.

A basic example of the type of research used to test goal theory was carried out to investigate how well goal theory worked in another culture. Ninety-two women in a small eastern Caribbean island served as subjects. They made children's clothing at home and were paid on a piece-rate basis. Workers were free to complete any quantity: No quotas were set.

Subjects were randomly assigned to one of three groups. Goals were assigned to members of one experimental group based on previous production. The new goal was 20 percent above the individual's previous high production. Members of another experimental group were asked to "do their best." The control group received no change in instructions. The group with specific and difficult goals clearly outperformed the other two groups. Women who were assigned the goal of a 20 percent increase in performance earned twice as much as members of the control group and 47 percent more than the "do your best" group.[9]

Research evidence is inconsistent about the importance of people participating in their own goal setting. It would seem that when people participate in setting their own goals, they would tend to perform better. A recent study, however, concluded that when people are assigned a goal, they enjoy the task more than if *they* set the goal. The subjects were business students whose task was to join Tinkertoy® pieces to form a helicopter model.[10] (Maybe having to set goals interfered with the pure joy of earning extra credits to play with Tinkertoys!)

Other studies have shown that participation makes an indirect contribution to goal setting. Participation in goal setting can improve performance when

1. participation leads to the setting of a specific goal;
2. the specific goal is more difficult than the one set by the supervisor;
3. participation improves acceptance of the goal by the employee.[11]

MOTIVATION THROUGH NEED SATISFACTION

The most basic explanation of work motivation is that employees work to satisfy needs or motives. In review, a need is a craving or deficit of a physiological (such as hunger) or psychological (such as acceptance) nature. A **motive** is a force that requires satisfaction, such as the desire to gain power. In practice, the terms are used interchangeably. To motivate people, you give them an opportunity to satisfy important needs or motives.

You find out what these needs are by asking people what they want, or by observing what interests them. For instance, the way to motivate a recognition-hungry subordinate is to tell that person, "If you perform 10 percent above quota for six consecutive months, we will get you a plaque signifying your achievement to hang on your wall."

All need theories of motivation stem from this simple but true premise: People strive to satisfy needs. Here we describe two historically important need theories of motivation, Maslow's hierarchy and Herzberg's two-factor theory. Although both theories are now considered oversimplified, they have alerted managers to the importance of human needs. These theories have also set the stage for contemporary developments in motivation such as expectancy theory. We will outline other important human needs and motives for seeking satisfaction on the job.

MASLOW'S NEED HIERARCHY

Abraham **Maslow's need hierarchy** is sometimes referred to as a self-actualizing model of people. Maslow reasoned that human beings have an internal need pushing them on toward self-actualization (fulfillment) and personal superiority. However, before these higher-level needs are activated, certain lower-level needs must be satisfied.[12] A poor person thinks of finding a job as a way of obtaining the necessities of life. Once these are obtained, that person may think of achieving recognition and self-fulfillment on the job. When a person is generally satisfied at one level, he or she looks for satisfaction at a higher level.

Maslow arranged human needs into a five-level hierarchy. Each level refers to a group of needs—not to one need for each level. These need levels are described in ascending order, and shown in Figure 3–3.

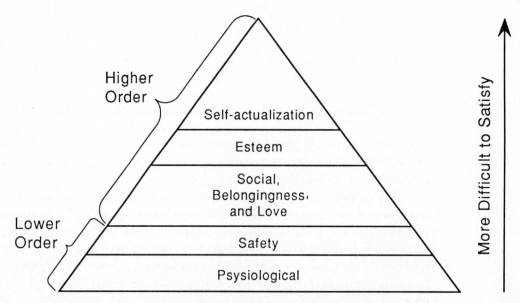

FIGURE 3–3 Maslow's Need Hierarchy

1. *Physiological needs* refer to bodily needs, such as the requirement for food, water, shelter, and sleep. In general, most jobs provide opportunity to satisfy physiological needs. Nevertheless, some people go to work hungry or in need of sleep. Until a person gets a satisfying meal or takes a nap, he or she will not be concerned about finding an outlet on the job for creative impulses.

2. *Safety needs* include a need to feel safe from physical and emotional injury. Many jobs, such as those of police officers or taxi drivers, frustrate a person's need for safety. Therefore, many people would be motivated by the prospect of a safe environment. People who do very unsafe things for a living, such as driving race cars, find thrills and recognition more important than safety. Many people are an exception to Maslow's need hierarchy.

3. *Social needs* are essentially love or belonging needs. Unlike the two previous levels of needs, they center around a person's interactions with others. Many people have a strong urge to be part of a group and to be accepted by that group. Peer acceptance is important in school and on the job. Many people are unhappy with their jobs unless they have the opportunity to work in close contact with others.

4. *Esteem needs* represent an individual's demands to be seen as a person of worth by others—and to himself or herself. Esteem needs are also called *ego* needs, pointing to the fact that people want to be seen as competent and capable. A job that is seen by yourself and others as being worthwhile provides a good opportunity to satisfy esteem needs.

5. *Self-actualizing needs* are the highest levels of needs, including the need for self-fulfillment and personal development. True self-actualization is an ideal to strive for, rather than something that automatically stems from occupying a challenging position. A self-actualized person is somebody who has become what he or she is capable of becoming. Few of us reach all our potential, even when we are so motivated.

The extent of need satisfaction.   Not everybody can have as much need satisfaction as he or she wishes. Maslow estimated that the typical adult satisfies about 85 percent of physiological needs; 70 percent of safety and security needs; 50 percent of belongingness, social, and love needs; 40 percent of esteem needs; and 10 percent of self-actualization needs.[13]

There are substantial individual differences in the amount of need satisfaction. Some construction jobs, for example, frustrate both physiological and safety needs. Ordinarily there is much more opportunity for approaching self-actualization when a person occupies a prominent position, such as a top executive or famous athlete. However, a person with lower goals and talents could approach self-actualization by occupying a lesser position.

The need hierarchy in perspective. Maslow's need hierarchy is a convenient way of classifying needs and has spurred millions of people to take the subject of human motivation seriously. Its primary value has been to highlight the importance of human needs in a work setting, and explain why people always crave something. Giving a person recognition one day, for example will not usually keep him or her satisfied for very long.

Three frequent misinterpretations of the need hierarchy should be avoided. One is that people behave as they do because of their quest to satisfy one particular need. In reality, many different needs are dominant at any one time. For example, a software developer may satisfy a number of needs (including recognition, esteem, and self-satisfaction) by developing a piece of software that solves a problem. A second misinterpretation is to view the ladder as a rigid one-step-at-a-time procedure. Each level of need does not have to be totally satisfied before a person can be motivated by a higher-level need. A third, and perhaps the most damaging, misinterpretation of the need hierarchy is that it represents all human needs. To repeat, the ladder represents need *categories*. As such, they reflect only a sampling of human needs. Other important needs include those mentioned in Chapter 2.

Herzberg's Two-Factor Theory

In 1966, Frederick Herzberg reported research suggesting that some elements of a job contribute to satisfaction and motivation.[14] Such job elements are called *satisfiers* or *motivators*. Although individuals and groups vary somewhat in the particular elements they find satisfying or motivating, they generally refer to the *content* (guts) of the job: achievement, recognition, challenging work, responsibility, and the opportunity for advancement. When satisfiers or motivators are not present on the job, the impact tends to be neutral rather than negative. Following this theory, one way to motivate most people is to provide them with the opportunity to do interesting work or to receive a promotion.

In contrast, some job elements appeal more to lower-level needs. Called *hygiene factors* or *dissatisfiers,* they tend to be noticed primarily by their absence. The purpose of dissatisfiers is to prevent dissatisfaction. For instance, you may grumble about having to work in a hot, cramped office with no windows. Because of it you may experience job dissatisfaction or even be demotivated. But a cool, uncrowded office with a view of the ocean will probably not increase your level of job satisfaction or motivation (at least according to Herzberg).

Evaluation. The two-factor theory has had a considerable impact on management thought. Job enrichment, discussed in Chapter 4, is an application of Herzberg's theory. Many studies and observations support key ideas of the two-factor theory. For example, many employees rank "recognition when I've done a good job" above such motivators as competitive salary.[15]

Other research and opinion suggest that the premises of the two-factor theory are not so accurate. For one, Herzberg and his associates erred by assuming that virtually all workers attach so much importance to their jobs. A complex, challenging, variable, and autonomous job is motivational to people who are searching for self-fulfillment in the workplace. This may be true for the majority of people occupying higher-level positions, but may not apply to every worker.

Salary is a prime example of a job element that acts as a motivator for some people and a dissatisfier (used to prevent dissatisfaction) for others. When you currently are worried about money you will work hard, given the chance to earn the amount of money you want. Another confounding factor is that money satisfies so many different needs. Given enough money, you can buy status, recognition, and even accomplishment. To illustrate, money can lead to accomplishment because it can buy education or a small business venture. Although the two-factor theory downplays the importance of money as a motivator, financial incentives are one of the most effective motivators available. In recognition of this fact, an increasing number of companies attempt to directly relate pay to how well the worker has performed.[16] Gainsharing programs, to be described later in this chapter, use financial incentives to enhance productivity.

Another major reservation about the two-factor theory is its contention that hygiene factors can prevent dissatisfaction, but cannot satisfy or motivate workers. The research evidence tends to refute this contention.[17] It seems logical to any experienced person that hygiene factors, such as working conditions or quality of supervision, could influence an employee's level of motivation or satisfaction. Would your level of satisfaction or motivation increase if you were assigned a beautiful office overlooking a bay, with a competent, warm, and friendly assistant seated outside?

Comparison of the Two Theories

The theories of Maslow and Herzberg support each other. As shown in Figure 3–4, satisfiers and motivators relate to the higher-level needs. Similarly, dissatisfiers and hygiene factors relate to lower-level needs. One major difference between the Maslow and Herzberg theories is that, according to the former, an appeal to any level of need can be a motivator. Herzberg contends that only appeals to higher-level needs can be motivational. Figure 3–4 also suggests how to apply these two theories to a job situation.

Achievement, Power, and Affiliation Needs

People seek to satisfy many higher-level needs on the job in addition to those mentioned in Maslow's hierarchy. Among these specific needs or motives are competence, control over one's environment, achievement, power, and affiliation. The last three have been studied extensively by psychologist David McClelland and many others.[18] Much human behavior on

Maslow's need hierarchy	Herzberg's two-factor theory	Managerial action
	Satisfiers or motivators	
Self-actualization Self-esteem	Achievement Recognition Work itself Responsibility Advancement Growth	Allow these factors to be present to increase satisfaction and motivation.
	Dissatisfiers or hygiene factors	
Social (love, belonging) Safety and security Physiological	Company policy and administration Supervision Working conditions Salary Relationship with co-workers Personal life Status Job security	Keep these factors at adequate level to prevent dissatisfaction and demotivation.

FIGURE 3–4 Comparison of the Need Hierarchy and Two-Factor Theory

the job can be explained by strong motives to achieve important things, acquire power, and affiliate with others.

Achievement need. Many managers and other ambitious people have a strong **achievement need,** the desire to set and accomplish goals for their own sake. People with strong motives for achievement are self-motivated; they persist in their efforts without prodding and prompting from others. Money, status, and power are secondary considerations to these individuals. People with a strong achievement need show three consistent behaviors and attitudes:

- personal responsibility for solving problems;
- a preference for establishing and reaching moderate or realistic goals, but not taking foolish risks;
- a preference for situations that provide frequent feedback on results.[19]

A strong achievement need is important for managerial work, particularly for **entrepreneurs**—people who establish and operate innovative business enterprises. The achievement need, as well as the needs for power and affiliation, was originally studied by the Thematic Apperception Test (TAT). Subjects were asked to write a story giving their interpretation of a drawing. For instance, the following interpretation of a picture of a man seated at a desk would indicate a need for achievement:

> The man sitting there is doing some short-range planning. He's trying to figure out how to take advantage of a downturn in business so he can make the best use of time. I'll bet he's thinking of a new service his company can offer that will really help people.

Like other needs and motives, the achievement need can be measured by a personality test. The person taking the test is asked to indicate the strength of his or her preference for a job with certain characteristics, such as

> the probability is very high that you will influence a large number of people; or
> the probability is very low that you will have a chance to start a new activity from scratch.[20]

Power need.   Another important motive of people in organizations is the **power need,** the desire to control other people and resources. People who climb to the top of organizations often have a strong drive for both achievement and power. The two needs complement each other: Achievement motivation directs people to accomplish worthwhile things; power motivation directs people to take control and draw attention to their own effect on the world.

The need for power can drive us to serve our self-interest or the welfare of others. David McClelland draws the distinction between *personalized* and *socialized* power.[21] An individual with a personalized power motive wants to control and manipulate others mostly for personal gain. A person with a socialized power motive desires power in order to serve the good of the organization or society. An executive who organizes a fundraising campaign for a new hospital probably has a socialized power need. Nevertheless, it is not always clear which power motive is dominant. The executive may look forward to having the hospital named in his or her honor, which may be an expression of a personalized power need.

Affiliation.   The **affiliation need** is a desire to seek close relationships with others and to be a loyal employee or friend. Affiliation is a social need, while achievement and power are self-actualizing needs. A person with a strong need for affiliation finds compatible working relationships more important than high-level accomplishment and exercising power. Successful executives therefore have stronger needs for achievement and power than for affiliation.

Thrill Seeking

Our discussion of needs so far still does not explain why some people crave constant excitement on the job, and are even willing to risk their lives to achieve thrills. The answer may lie in the **Type T personality,** an individual driven to a life of constant stimulation and risk taking.[22] A strong craving for thrill seeking can have some positive consequences for the organization, including a willingness to perform such dangerous feats as setting explosives, capping an oil well, fighting a fire, controlling a radiation leak, and introducing a product in a highly competitive environment.

The Type T personality also creates problems for employers. These individuals may be involved in a disproportionate number of accidents, drive while intoxicated just for the added excitement and risk, and take risks with company property. For example, Brett, an information systems specialist, was a known sensation seeker. Off the job he participated in hang gliding, ski jumping, and motorcycle racing. On the job he once wiped out an important file stored on a computer disk. Asked how the incident happened, Brett told his irate boss:

> I admit it, I'm guilty. I was looking to pull a stunt on the computer that no one had pulled before. I tried to make a copy of the file by taking the file out of the B drive and saving it on another disk I put back into the B drive. If I had taken the time to read the manual, this mistake wouldn't have happened. But I like the thrill of trying out my little tricks with the computer.

A person who uses thrill seeking for constructive purposes is a **T-plus.** His or her counterpart who gets into trouble with thrill seeking is a *T-minus.* T-plus people can be quite productive because they are often creative. The famous business promoter and sailing enthusiast Ted Turner appears to be a T-plus person. Can you think of another T-plus person?

MOTIVATION THROUGH EXPECTANCY THEORY

The **expectancy theory (ET)** of work motivation is based on the premise that how much effort people expend depends upon how much reward they expect to receive in return. Expectancy theory is really a group of theories based on a rational-economic view of human nature.[23] The theory assumes that people choose among alternatives by selecting the one that appears to have the biggest personal payoff at the time. Given a choice, most people will opt for a work assignment that will benefit them the most. The self-interest aspect of motivation underlying ET is also found in other theories of motivation—people try to satisfy their own needs and will strive for rewards they think are worthwhile.

Expectancy theory is currently receiving considerable attention in the human relations and organizational behavior field. Part of its popularity is due to its integration of much valid knowledge about work motivation. It is also useful in diagnosing whether motivation will occur in a given situation.

Basic Components

All versions of expectancy theory have four major components: expectancy, instrumentality, valence, and the calculation of motivation. A glimpse at ET is presented in Figure 3–5.

1. Expectancy is the probability assigned by the individual that effort will lead to performing the task correctly. An important question rational people ask themselves before putting forth effort to accomplish a task is this: "If I put in all this work, will I really get the job done properly?" Each behavior is associated in the individual's mind with a certain expectancy or subjective hunch of the probability of success. Expectancies range from 0 to 1.0. The expectancy would be zero if the person thought there were no chance of performing the task correctly. An expectancy of 1.0 would signify absolute faith in being able to perform the task properly. Expectancies thus influence whether you will even strive to earn a reward. Self-confident people have higher expectancies than do less self-confident people. Being well trained will also increase your subjective hunch that you can perform the task.

2. Instrumentality is the probability assigned by the individual that performance will lead to certain outcomes or rewards. When people engage in a particular behavior, they do so with the intention of achieving a desired outcome or reward. In the version of ET presented here, instrumentalities also range from 0 to 1.0.

If you believe there is no chance of receiving the desired reward, the assigned probability is zero. If you believe the reward is certain to follow from performing correctly, the assigned probability is 1.0. For example: "I know for sure that if I show up for work every day this month, I will receive my paycheck."

The performance mentioned in relation to expectancy is a first-level outcome, and is rooted in the job itself. If you work hard, you expect to do such things as produce goods, supply a service, or achieve quality. Instrumentalities deal with second-level outcomes—the rewards associated with

Person will be motivated under these conditions	A.	Expectancy is high: Person believes he or she can perform the task.
	B.	Instrumentality is high: Person believes that performance will lead to certain outcomes.
	C.	Valence is high: Person highly values the outcomes.

FIGURE 3–5 A basic version of expectancy theory

performing. An instrumentality can also be regarded as the hunch that a first-level outcome will lead to a second-level outcome. For instance, you might have a strong belief that if you produce high-quality work, you will receive recognition from the organization.

3.   Valence is the value, worth, or attractiveness of an outcome. In each work situation there are multiple outcomes, each with a valence of its own. For instance, if you make a substantial cost-saving suggestion for your employer, potential second-level outcomes include cash award, good performance evaluation, promotion, recognition, and status. Valences ranges from −100 to +100, in the version of ET presented here. (We believe the usual method of placing valences on a −1.00 to +1.00 scale does not do justice to the true differences in preferences.) A valence of +100 means that you strongly desire an outcome. A valence of −100 means that you are strongly motivated to avoid an outcome, such as being fired. A valence of zero means that you are indifferent toward an outcome, and is therefore of no use as a motivator.

The Calculation of Motivation

Motivation is calculated by multiplying expectancies, instrumentalities, and valences. This relationship is expressed by the formula:

$$\text{Motivation} = \text{Expectancy} \times \text{Instrumentality} \times \text{Valence}$$

An example from career planning will help explain how this process works. Margot believes strongly that she will be able to complete a program of study in engineering technology. She thus has a high expectancy, perhaps 0.90. She believes a little less strongly that an engineering technology program will lead to a high-paying, interesting job. Her instrumentality is 0.85. Yet Margot strongly values a potential career in engineering technology. Her valence is 95. When these three components are multiplied ($0.90 \times 0.85 \times 95 = 73$), it appears that Margot's motivation will be strong. To develop a valid analysis of her motivation, it would be necessary to calculate her motivation for several different outcomes, such as income, status, and career satisfaction. Motivation could also be calculated for several different expectancies. In addition to her expectancy about graduation, Margot would have expectancies for other hurdles, such as getting through a certain course.

One important implication of the formula is that a zero value for expectancy, instrumentality, or valence would result in zero motivation, because any number multiplied by zero is zero. Another implication of the formula is that it helps explain why some people engage in behaviors with low expectancies, such as trying to invent a successful new product, write a best-selling novel, or win a lottery. The compensating factor is the large valences attached to the second-level outcomes associated with these accomplishments.

How Ability and Motivation Are Linked to Performance

Figure 3–6 depicts how ability and motivation are linked to perform-ance. In order to achieve performance and productivity, both motivation and ability must be present.[24] Ability in this context includes organiza-tional support, because people need help to make good use of their abili-ties. Support includes the right equipment, tools, and help from co-workers. If either motivation or ability is absent, no performance will be possible. It is important to recognize the contribution of ability in bringing about performance, because our culture tends to overdramatize the contri-bution of motivation. Too many people uncritically accept the statement, "You can achieve anything you want if you try hard enough." In reality, a person also needs the proper education, ability, tools, and technology.

Evaluation and Implications of Expectancy Theory

Expectancy theory has been well researched, and many studies sup-port its basic ideas. Walter B. Newsom has summarized how supervisors of various groups have reacted to expectancy theory: "These people say the theory is a powerful diagnostic tool in determining why individuals they have supervised have or have not been motivated."[25]

One study calculated the motivational scores of 703 unionized con-struction workers, using measures of expectancy, instrumentality, and va-lence (as described earlier). The researchers found a strong positive relationship between the motivational scores and the levels of effort re-ported by the workers.[26] In other words, ET proved to be a useful indicator of job motivation.

Based on the type of opinion and research just described, expectancy theory has some important implications for enhancing motivation:

1. *Training and encouragement are important.* Managers should give employees the necessary training and encouragement to be confident they can perform the required task. Some employees who appear to be poorly motivated simply lack the right skills and self-confidence.
2. *The link between rewards and performance should be explicit.* Em-ployees should be reassured that if they perform the job up to stan-

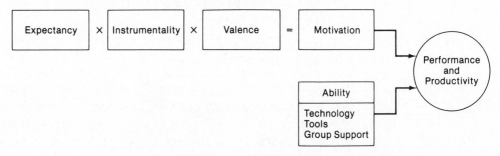

FIGURE 3–6 How Motivation and Ability Influence Performance and Productivity

dard, they will receive the promised reward. It is sometimes helpful for employees to speak to co-workers about whether they received promised rewards.

3. *The meaning and implications of second-level outcomes should be explained.* It is helpful for employees to understand the value of certain outcomes, such as receiving a favorable performance appraisal. (For example, it could lead to a salary increase and promotion.) People strive harder to achieve outcomes they know to be valuable.

4. *Individual differences in valences must be understood.* To motivate employees effectively, managers must discover individual differences in preferences for rewards. An attempt should be made to offer a worker rewards to which he or she attaches a high valence. For instance, one employee might value a high-adventure assignment; another might attach a high valence to a routine, tranquil assignment.

MOTIVATION THROUGH BEHAVIOR MODIFICATION

The most widely used formal method of motivating employees is **behavior modification,** an attempt to change behavior by manipulating rewards and punishments. Behavior modification is based upon two key concepts: the law of effect and environmental determinism. According to the **law of effect,** behavior that leads to a positive consequence for the individual tends to be repeated, while behavior that leads to a negative consequence tends not to be repeated.

The law of effect is a basic principle of psychology. Environmental determinism is a philosophy that stems from this principle. According to **environmental determinism,** our past history of reinforcement determines, or causes, our current behavior. The rewards and punishments we have received make up much of this history.

As mentioned earlier in the chapter, behavioral modification makes no reference to internal cognitions, such as needs or motives that influence behavior. Instead, reinforcers shape our lives. If smiling at people brought you the approval you wanted in the past, you will smile again when you want approval. The environmental event that determined your behavior was approval.

The balance of our discussion of behavior modification consists of a summary of behavior modification strategies, a list of rules for its application, and a description of gainsharing.

Behavior Modification Strategies

Behavior modification is an entire field of study itself. Nevertheless, the techniques of behavior modification can be divided into four strategies:

Positive reinforcement (PR) means increasing the probability that behavior will be repeated by rewarding people for making the desired response. The phrase *increase the probability* means that PR improves learning and motivation, but is not 100 percent effective. The phrase *making the desired response* is also noteworthy. To use PR properly, a reward is contingent upon the person doing something right. Simply paying somebody a compliment or giving them something of value is not positive reinforcement. Behavior modification always implies linking consequences to what the person has or has not accomplished.

PR is used much more frequently in behavior modification programs in organizations for two primary reasons: (1) It is more effective than punishment, and (2) it creates less negative publicity than a systematic use of employee punishments.

Negative reinforcement is rewarding people by taking away an uncomfortable consequence of their behavior. It is the withdrawal or avoidance of a disliked consequence. You are subject to negative reinforcement when you are told, "Your insurance rate will go down if you receive no traffic violations for twelve months." The uncomfortable consequence removed is a high insurance premium. Removing the undesirable consequence is contingent upon your making the right response—driving within the law.

Be careful not to confuse negative reinforcement with punishment. Negative reinforcement is the opposite of punishment. It involves rewarding someone by removing a punishment or uncomfortable situation.

Punishment is the presentation of an undesirable consequence, or the removal of a desirable consequence, because of unacceptable behavior. A supervisor can punish an employee by suspending the employee for violating an important safety rule. Or the employee can be punished by taking away his or her chance to earn overtime because of violating the rule.

Extinction is decreasing the frequency of undesirable behavior by removing the desirable consequence of such behavior. (It does *not* refer to getting rid of an employee forcibly.) A company might use extinction by ceasing to pay employees for making frivolous cost-saving suggestions. Extinction is sometimes used to extinguish annoying behavior. Assume that an employee persists in telling ethnic jokes. The joke telling can often be extinguished by the group agreeing not to laugh at the jokes.

Rules for the Use of Behavior Modification

To use behavior modification effectively on the job, certain rules and procedures must be followed. Although using rewards and punishments to motivate people seems straightforward, behavior modification requires a systematic approach. The following rules emphasize positive rewards, but they also incorporate the judicious use of punishment. The rules are specified from the standpoint of the person trying to motivate another individual.[27]

Rule 1: Choose an appropriate reward or punishment.   An appropriate reward or punishment is one that is (a) effective in motivating a given employee, and (b) feasible from the company standpoint. If one reward does not motivate the person, try another. When positive motivators do not work, it may be necessary to use negative motivators (punishment).

It is generally best to use the mildest form of punishment that will motivate the person. For example, if an employee writes personal letters during the day, the person might simply be told to put away the letters. Motivation enters the picture because the time not spent on letters can now be invested in company work. If the mildest form of punishment does not work, a more severe negative motivator is selected.

A list of potential rewards and forms of punishment to use on the job is presented in Tables 3–1 and 3–2. These can be kept in mind in the quest for appropriate rewards and punishments.

Rule 2: Supply ample feedback.   Behavior modification cannot work without frequent feedback to individuals. Feedback can take the form of simply telling people when they have done something right or wrong. Brief memos or messages sent via the person's computer are another form of

---

TABLE 3–1   Rewards of Potential Use in a Job Setting

Monetary
Money in form of salary increases, bonuses, profit sharing; company stock; discount coupons; movie, theater, or dinner passes

Durable gifts
Pen-and-pencil sets; watches and clocks; recognition pins and rings; trophies; small appliances such as toasters, hair dryers

Food and dining
Company picnics; department parties; coffee, tea, or soft drinks, and pastry; holiday turkeys and fruit baskets; cocktail party; banquet for top performers

Job- and career-related
Challenging new assignment; do more of preferred task; filling in for the boss; good performance appraisal; promotion; freedom to choose own work activity; tuition refund; assignment of new machine such as personal computer or video camera

Social and pride-related
Recognition and praise; expression of appreciation; privy to gossip and confidential information; asking employee for advice and suggestions; pat on the back; written note of appreciation

Status symbols
Office with window, private office, bigger office; bigger or fancier desk; plaque indicating accomplishment; freedom to personalize work area (such as painting mural on wall); exclusive use of machine or telephone

---

TABLE 3–2   Punishments of Potential use in Job Setting

Feedback on undesired behavior
Documentation of poor performance
Criticism
Withdrawal of privileges
Undesirable assignment, including being assigned the worst
   equipment owned by the company
Threat of sanctions
Fining
Threat of poor reference if fired
Withholding of any valued reward
Probation
Suspension
Firing

---

feedback. Be aware, however, that many employees resent seeing a message with negative feedback flashed across their video display terminal.

Rule 3: Do not give everyone the same size reward.   Average performance is encouraged when all forms of accomplishment receive the same reward. Assume one employee made substantial progress in reducing the production of defective parts. He or she should receive more recognition (or other reward) than an employee who made only a minor contribution to the problem.

Rule 4: Find some constructive behavior to reinforce.   This rule stems from the principle of behavior shaping. **Behavior shaping** is the rewarding of any response in the right direction, and then rewarding only the closest approximation. Using this approach, the desired behavior is finally attained. Behavior shaping is useful to the manager because the technique recognizes that you have to begin somewhere in teaching an employee a new skill, or motivating the employee to make a big change. It works in this manner:

> Assume that your desk is so messy that you lose important files. Using the principle of behavior shaping, your boss would reward you whenever you make progress in keeping your desk in order. For instance, if your boss notices that you no longer keep old coffee containers on your desk, he or she might comment, "I can see improvement in your work area. Keep up the progress."

Rule 5: Schedule rewards intermittently.   Rewards should not be given on every occasion for good performance. **Intermittent rewards** sustain desired behavior longer and also slow down the process of behavior fading away when it is not rewarded. If each correct performance results in a reward, the behavior will stop shortly after a situation in which no reward is received.

Another problem is that a reward which is given continuously may lose its impact. A practical value of intermittent reinforcement is that it saves time. Few managers have enough time to dispense rewards for every correct response forthcoming from subordinates.

Rule 6: Rewards and punishments should follow the observed behavior closely in time. For maximum effectiveness, people should be rewarded shortly after doing something right, and punished shortly after doing something wrong. A built-in feedback system, such as a computer program working or not working, capitalizes upon this principle. If as a supervisor you are dispensing the rewards and punishments, try to administer them the same day they are earned.

Rule 7: Ignoring certain types of behavior may extinguish them. When people are not rewarded for repeating a desired behavior, they will often discontinue that behavior. For example, if exceptionally good performance goes unnoticed, an employee may lose enthusiasm for being exceptional. As one disgruntled assistant said, "Nobody cares if I get out the department reports on time, so why should I?"

Rule 8: Tell people what they must do to be rewarded. The employee who has a standard against which to measure job performance will have a built-in feedback system. One of the many reasons a sport like basketball is so motivating is that the path to a reward is so clear-cut. A player can readily see that by putting the ball through the hoop, a reward will be forthcoming (one, two, or three points).

Rule 9: Do not punish in front of others. The form of punishment chosen should be enough to eliminate the undesired behavior. Being punished in front of co-workers is humiliating. In response, the person may become defensive and angry, and lose respect for the manager.

Rule 10: Make the reward or punishment fit the behavior. People inexperienced in applying PR often overdo the intensity of spoken rewards. When an employee does something of an ordinary nature correctly, a simple word of praise, such as "Good job," is preferable to something like "Fantastic performance!"

Rule 11: Change the reward periodically. Rewards do not retain their effectiveness indefinitely. Employees lose interest in striving for a reward they have received many times in the past. This is particularly true of a repetitive statement, such as "Nice job," or "Congratulations." It is helpful for the person dispensing rewards to study the list of potential rewards and try different ones from time to time.

Rule 12: Avoid "jelly bean" motivation.   Closely related to rule 10 is the admonition against **jelly bean motivation,** the heaping of undeserved rewards upon another person.[28] It is an acknowledgment of performance that has never materialized. A typical example is a manager saying "Keep up the good work" to an employee who has accomplished virtually nothing all day.

Gainsharing

Our discussion of behavior modification so far has emphasized workers receiving rewards or punishments based on their individual accomplishments. Behavior modification can also be applied on an organizationwide basis by offering rewards for group performance above a targeted level. A frequently used program of this type is **gainsharing,** a group incentive program that enables employees to share in the financial benefits of any improvements in productivity to which they contribute.

The two key elements of a gainsharing program.   Gainsharing involves two fundamental elements. The first is a committee of production employees and managers whose primary purpose is to evaluate workers' suggestions on ways of improving productivity. Another purpose of the committee is to develop a trusting relationship between managers and nonmanagers through two-way communication.

The second element of a gainsharing program is an incentive plan, in which employees are paid a bonus based on the amount of production increase over a base level for a prescribed time period. Behavior modification is involved because employees are rewarded only if they increase production over the base level. Although rarely carried out in practice, the employees could be punished by receiving a pay cut if production slipped below the base level.

The key to a successful gainsharing program, is to establish a trusting and open relationship between employees and management. Gainsharing is, in return, a potentially effective technique for developing this trusting relationship. Trust develops as employees realize they have an input into the company's success, and that they are rewarded if their ideas improve productivity.[29]

Gainsharing at Volvo.   The Volvo plant at Kalmar, Sweden, illustrates the type of contribution gainsharing can make. The program has been in operation since the mid-1980s. Kalmar workers receive their gainsharing bonus twice a year, even though the results portion is calculated every fourteen days. The seven bonus factors are (1) capital costs for total inventories; (2) person-hours per car, including direct and indirect production workers; (3) consumption of added materials; (4) consumption of materials and supplies; (5) spoilage and adjustments; (6) quality index, based on a point-scoring system; and (7) hours worked by office workers.

The gainsharing program was favorably received by most of the employees, and a few quantitative results were obtained that relate directly to productivity and quality. Since the inception of gainsharing, capital costs for total inventories have declined substantially. The index of person-hours per car has reflected a steady decline of about five points per year. Some of this decline can be attributed to an improved operating system developed by industrial engineers. A survey of employee opinion indicated that 82 percent of employees believed that gainsharing stimulated their interest in achieving high quality.[30]

SELF-DETERMINATION AND INTRINSIC MOTIVATION

Despite the success of behavior modification programs, such programs have been vehemently criticized for preoccupying people with external rewards, such as bonuses. Critics of behavior modification contend that workers should be motivated by the joy of work. (The two-factor theory of motivation supports this principle.) An alternative to behavior modification is **self-determination theory,** the idea that people are motivated when they experience a sense of choice in initiating and regulating their actions. Instead of looking to somebody else for rewards, a person is motivated by intrinsic aspects of his or her task.

The Rationale Behind Self-determination Theory

Intrinsic motivation theory (the idea that the work itself is rewarding) and self-determination go hand in hand. According to the theory of intrinsic motivation, individuals are active agents rather than passive recipients of environmental forces. Two factors can affect perceptions of intrinsic motivation. Certain characteristics of the task (such as challenge, autonomy, and feedback) can promote intrinsic motivation because they allow for satisfaction of needs for competence and self-determination. An individual's perceptions of why he or she performs a task can also affect intrinsic motivation. Specifically, intrinsic motivation may increase when people perceive that they perform tasks for themselves rather than for an external reward. This is true because such perceptions provide individuals with the opportunity to satisfy their self-determining needs.

In contrast, when an individual performs a task to achieve an external reward (such as money or recognition), the perceived cause of the behavior shifts from within the individual to the external reward. Money or recognition is literally controlling the person's actions. In this instance, the individual no longer perceives that he or she is self-determining, and as a result intrinsic motivation may decrease.[31]

The Problems Associated with Extrinsic Rewards

Self-determination theory relies heavily on the fact that rewards have some disadvantages. Robert Albanese notes that extrinsic (external) rewards can sometimes lower a person's job performance and be demotivating. This relationship is more likely to be true when people are performing a creative task. It has been further observed that the allure of extrinsic rewards can cause people to

focus narrowly on a task,

perform the task as quickly as possible,

lose interest in the intrinsic rewards (such as a sense of achievement),

see themselves as less free and less self-determining.[32]

Despite these legitimate problems associated with extrinsic rewards, it would be folly for a company to abandon financial bonuses and other forms of positive reinforcement. Even the most competent technical people (those who enjoy the nature of their work) expect recognition from management. Also, people who love the creativity of their work, such as professional athletes, musicians, and scriptwriters, demand huge financial incentives for performing their craft. The sensible solution for companies is to follow the practice of balancing extrinsic and intrinsic rewards. A commercial real estate broker said this:

I agree that these internal rewards are very good. I get a thrill out of putting together an important deal. It makes me feel good about myself, and I crave the excitement. But I also want to see a fat commission check when the deal is tied up in a neat bundle.

MOTIVATION THROUGH THE RIGHT ORGANIZATIONAL CULTURE

The motivational methods described so far are aimed at motivating people individually or in small groups. A macro (overall or strategic) way of enhancing motivation is to establish an environment or organizational culture that encourages hard work. **Organizational culture** is a system of shared values and beliefs that actively influence the behavior of organization members. Simply put, the organizational, or corporate, culture is its norms. Charles O'Reilly presents evidence that culture can be a mechanism for social control. As such, the right organizational culture can engender employee commitment, which translates into strong work motivation. The wrong organizational culture can conversely lead to low commitment and weak motivation.[33]

A new organizational culture cannot be implemented as readily as a behavior modification program can. It takes a long time to develop a culture that fosters strong motivation and productivity. It is difficult to reach firm conclusions about organizational culture because the concept is so abstract. Nevertheless, an organizational culture that fosters strong motivation would have several of these characteristics:[34]

1. *An atmosphere that rewards excellence by giving big rewards to top performers.* This characteristic is double-edged: Outstanding performers get big raises and promotions while poor performers do not get promoted, get few raises, and may even be terminated.

2. *An atmosphere that rewards creative thought by giving tangible rewards to innovators.* At the same time, few penalties are imposed on people whose creative ideas lead to failure. Penalties for failed ideas discourage innovation.

3. *A pervasive belief that the organization is a winner.* If employees perceive that they belong to a winning team, they will tend to be highly motivated. Proud organizations like IBM, Domino's Pizza, and Panasonic capitalize on this aspect of culture.

4. *A spirit of helpfulness that encourages employees to believe they can overcome setbacks.* Employees believe that when they face job hurdles, the company will provide assistance.

HOW DO YOU MOTIVATE YOURSELF?

People often interpret theories about work motivation as a way to motivate others to accomplish their jobs. Of equal importance, a study of motivation should help you energize yourself. In general, applying the theories discussed in this chapter to yourself should help you understand the conditions under which you are likely to work hard. Following are several specific suggestions and strategies for self-motivation.

Set goals for yourself. Goals are fundamental to human motivation. Set yearly, monthly, weekly, daily, and sometimes even morning or afternoon goals for yourself. For example, "By noontime I will have emptied my in-basket and made one suggestion to improve safety practices in our shop." Longer-range, or lifetime, goals can also be helpful in gathering momentum to spur yourself on toward higher levels of achievement. However, these have to be buttressed by a series of short-range goals. You might have the long-range goal of becoming a prominent architect, but first it would be helpful to earn an A in a drafting course.

Identify and seek out your motivators. Having read this chapter and done some serious introspection, you should be able to identify a few of your personal motivators. Next, find a job that offers them to you in ample supply. You might have good evidence from your past experience that the opportunity for close contact with people (comradeship or good interpersonal relationships) is a personal motivator. Find a job that involves working in a small, friendly department.

Owing to circumstances, you may have to take whatever job you can find, or you may not be in a position to change jobs. In that situation, try to arrange your work so that you have more opportunity to experience the reward(s) you are seeking. Assume that solving difficult problems excites you, but your job is 85 percent routine. Develop better work habits so that you can more quickly take care of the routine aspects of your job. This will give you more time to enjoy the creative aspects of your work.

Get feedback on performance. Few people can sustain a high level of drive without getting an objective or subjective opinion on how well they are doing. Even if you find your work exciting, you still need feedback. Photographers may be enamored of the intrinsic aspects of their work. Yet photographers, more than most people, want their work displayed. A display delivers the message, "Your work is good enough to show to other people."

If your boss or company does not recognize the importance of feedback or simply forgets to tell people how they are doing, don't be hesitant to ask an occasional question: "Is my work satisfactory so far?" "How well am I doing in meeting the expectations of my job?" "I haven't heard anything good or bad about my performance. Should I be worried?"

Apply behavior modification to yourself. The information presented earlier in this chapter about motivating others through behavior modification can also be applied to yourself. To boost your own motivation through behavior modification, you have to (1) decide whether you should be rewarded or punished for your acts, and (2) administer these rewards or punishments. If the idea of self-punishment is distasteful to you, try using a system which relies solely on positive reinforcers. In any event, you become both jury and judge!

One helpful way to use behavior modification by yourself is to determine which of the twelve rules described earlier would make the most sense in your particular situation. Much depends on which particular motivational problem you are facing.

Increase your expectancies. A practical way of using expectancy theory to increase your own motivational level is to increase your subjective probability that your effort will lead to good performance on a given task. One way to increase your expectancy is to increase your level of skill with respect to a task for which you want to be highly motivated. If a person has the necessary skills to perform a particular task, that person will usually raise his or her subjective hunch that he or she can get the task accomplished.

A strategy for increasing your expectancies in a wide variety of situations is to raise your general level of self-confidence. Self-confident people tend to have high subjective hunches that they can achieve performance in many situations. Raising your self-confidence is a long and gradual process. Its key ingredient is to begin with a small success and build up to bigger successes in an increasing number of situations.

*Raise your level of self-expectation.** In Greek mythology, Pygmalion was a sculptor who carved an ivory statue of a maiden and fell in love with it (her?). The statue was brought to life in response to his prayer. According to the Pygmalion effect in motivation, if your boss or teacher has high expectations of you, that will raise your level of performance—even if these high expectations are not communicated to you directly. Although less evidence exists about the possibility of turning the Pygmalion effect inward, it is conceivable that if you raise your self-expectations, you can raise your own performance. The net effect is the same as if you had increased your level of motivation. Raising your self-expectation means about the same thing as having a **positive mental attitude,** a conviction that you will succeed.

The combination of several of the above-mentioned self-motivational techniques will usually be more effective than using only one. A combination of goal setting and high self-expectations is particularly recommended for achieving high motivation.[35]

Summary of Key Points

- Work motivation refers to effort expended toward organizational objectives. It also refers to an activity performed by managers or

*Note carefully that we are referring here to expectations in a general sense, not in reference to ET. The confusion is unavoidable.

other people who try to get others to expend effort. Productivity refers to how much a person accomplishes in a given period of time. It is the ratio of output to input, taking into account both quality and quantity.

- Explanations of motivation can be divided broadly into cognitive and noncognitive, or reinforcement, theories. Cognitive theories emphasize that people make conscious decisions about their behavior and that they are driven by inner strivings. Reinforcement theories emphasize the role of the environment, especially rewards and punishments, in molding behavior. Cognitive and noncognitive explanations can be mutually supportive.

- According to goal theory, behavior is regulated by values and conscious intentions, or goals. Goals lead to improved performance if they are realistically difficult, specific, accepted by the person, used to evaluate performance, linked to feedback, and linked to rewards. Participation in goal setting improves performance indirectly because it may increase goal difficulty and acceptance.

- A popular cognitive conception of motivation is that people work to satisfy needs that are not currently being met. The famous need hierarchy of Maslow contends that people have an internal need pushing them on toward self-actualization. However, needs are arranged into a five-step hierarchy. Before higher-level needs are activated, certain lower-level needs must be satisfied. In ascending order, the groups of needs are physiological, safety, love (or belonging), esteem, and self-actualizing (such as self-fulfillment).

- Herzberg's two-factor theory states that some elements of a job, called *satisfiers* or *motivators,* give us a chance to satisfy higher-level needs. These elements or factors include achievement, recognition, and challenging work. In contrast, some job elements appeal more to lower-level needs and are called *dissatisfiers* or *hygiene* factors. They refer to the job setting and include company policy, supervision, physical working conditions, and status. Satisfiers are noted primarily by their presence, while dissatisfiers are noted primarily by their absence.

- Much human behavior on the job can be explained by people's strong motives to achieve important things, acquire power, and affiliate with others. The achievement need is the desire to set and accomplish goals for their own sake. Entrepreneurs have strong achievement needs. The need for power is the desire to control other people and resources. Power motives can be directed to personal gain or to social good. The need for affiliation is a desire to seek close relationships with others and to be a loyal employee or friend.

- Some job behavior can be explained by the need for thrill seeking, which is found in Type T personalities. Thrill seeking can be channeled into constructive or destructive purposes.

- Expectancy theory (ET) assumes that people are decision makers who choose among alternatives by selecting the one that appears to have the biggest personal payoff at the time. ET has three major components: expectancy about the ability to perform, instrumentality (the hunch that performance will lead to a reward), and valence (the value attached to the reward). Motivation is calculated by multiplying the numerical values for all three. ET has several important implications for managing people, including linking rewards to performance and understanding individual differences in preferences.

- Behavior modification is an attempt to change behavior by manipulating rewards and punishments. Its key principle is the law of effect—behavior that leads to a positive effect tends to be repeated, while the opposite is also true. The basic behavior modification strategies are positive reinforcement, negative reinforcement, punishment, and extinction.

- Rules for the effective use of behavior modification include: choose an appropriate reward or punishment; supply ample feedback; do not give everyone the same reward; schedule rewards intermittently; give rewards and punishments soon after the observed behavior; give equitable rewards and punishments; change rewards periodically; avoid "jelly bean" motivation (undeserved rewards).

- Gainsharing is a group incentive program that enables employees to share in the financial benefits of any improvements in productivity to which they have contributed. As such it is a form of behavior modification. The key elements of gainsharing are a committee to evaluate suggestions for productivity improvement, and the payout of bonuses.

- An opposite point of view to behavior modification is self-determination theory. It emphasizes that people prefer to control their own behavior and are therefore more motivated by intrinsic than by extrinsic rewards. A combination of intrinsic and extrinsic rewards is recommended here.

- An overall strategy of motivation is to establish an organizational culture that encourages hard work. This includes giving big rewards to top performers, encouraging innovation, and a pervasive belief that the organization is a winner.

- Suggestions and strategies for self-motivation include: set goals; identify and seek out your motivators; get feedback on performance; apply behavior modification to yourself; increase your expectancies that you can perform; and raise your level of self-expectation.

Questions and Activities _____

1. What evidence can you present that the United States has a work ethic problem?

2. Is motivation a characteristic of an individual that can be generalized from one situation to another? For example, do people who work hard seem to also play hard?

3. Which is a more optimistic interpretation of human behavior, a cognitive or noncognitive model?

4. When asked his goals for the season, a basketball coach replied, "To win every game, of course." How motivational might this goal be for the players?

5. How can you tell what psychological need a person is trying to satisfy?

6. Maslow's need hierarchy is still widely quoted and discussed thirty-five years after it was first published. What do you think accounts for its continued appeal?

7. What steps should a manager take to apply the two-factor theory of motivation to his or her work group?

8. How might an individual gather the necessary information to formulate an accurate instrumentality in a given situation?

9. Identify several rewards listed in Table 3–1 that you think would be particularly effective in motivating managers and professionals. Explain your reasoning.

10. Answer question 9 for entry-level service workers, such as hamburger preparers in a fast-food restaurant.

11. What are some squabbles you predict might take place as a result of a gainsharing program?

12. Do you think that the leading researcher in self-determination theory, Edward Deci, would appreciate a plaque recognizing his contribution?

A HUMAN RELATIONS INCIDENT
The Police Misspellers

Sergeant Maureen O'Brien grabbed a crime investigation report from her desk and placed it in front of her boss, Lieutenant José Lugo. Pointing to the report, she said to Lieutenant Lugo: "See all these circled words? They indicate spelling errors. Officer Gaudion made twenty-eight spelling errors in one investigation report. I wish I could say that Gaudion is an exception. The truth is that he is far from the worst speller in our platoon. I wish I could get the officers in my platoon to make fewer spelling errors on their daily reports."

With a concerned expression on his face, Lugo commented: "What steps have you taken so far to improve the spelling of your officers?"

"I've done about what I think is feasible. As you know, there is no money in the budget for purchasing word-processing equipment. The electronic spell checkers on those rigs would sure be a big help. I've made sure that our department has given each officer a pocket dictionary. I've also given them clear instructions to use the dictionary when needed. Another step I've taken is to schedule a training program in report writing for all platoon members. The sessions will be held this spring. I'm hoping that will cure the problem of so many misspellings."

"Maureen, I'm not so sure the report writing workshop will do the trick. Your officers are adults. If they haven't learned to be good spellers yet, I doubt a one-day workshop will cure their problems. Your real problem might be that your officers have no desire to be better spellers. Have you thought about that?"

"I have given some thought to the matter. In fact, I've told each officer with a spelling problem that I want very much for him or her to commit fewer spelling errors on police reports."

"Maureen, between now and the next time we talk, I want you to develop a better plan for motivating your officers to make fewer spelling mistakes," concluded José

1. To what extent do you think the frequent spelling errors made by the officers reflect a motivational problem?
2. What approach would you recommend Sergeant O'Brien take to motivate her platoon to become better spellers?

A HUMAN RELATIONS CASE PROBLEM
The Stale Rewards

Charlie Adamski is the postmaster of a large mail-processing facility. One factor in his annual performance review is the number of accidents occurring during the work year. Most accidents typically occur either on the workroom floor, where the mail is processed, or on the street, during mail delivery. On occasion, a postal employee in a more sedentary job will experience an accident.

Adamski keeps on the lookout for ways to reduce work-related accidents without incurring costs that will adversely affect other measures of his performance. Several years ago he instituted a program of providing coffee and doughnuts to any unit that did not have a chargeable accident within the previous quarter. Adamski would arrive in the conference room with the coffee and doughnuts, and a plaque commemorating that quarter's achievement. Usually, he would then give a brief speech congratulating the unit before he hurried off to his next appointment. This motivational program has been in place for about three years.

The employees in the accounting section had had only one accident in all the time Barbara Catrett was their manager. One winter day Connie Raven broke her wrist after slipping and falling in the parking lot when it had not been adequately cleared of snow. As a result of this low-accident record, the walls of the accounting section were cluttered with plaques.

Relevant facts about the department employees include the following:

> Barbara Catrett, manager. Mid-thirties, health and fitness conscious, a casual dieter.
>
> John Valvano, supervisor. Mid-thirties, has a mild diabetic condition, generally passes on sweets.
>
> Connie Raven, technician. Early forties, very overweight, not on a serious diet.
>
> Ed Small, technician. Late fifties, still relatively trim, will eat one of anything.
>
> Linda Yang, technician. Early twenties, just discovering that she can no longer eat everything, constantly dieting.
>
> Frieda Fromholtz, technician. Late forties, hates sweets.
>
> Cheryl Friedman, technician. Early forties, watches her weight, but will not refuse sweets.
>
> Bob Gambrelli, technician. Late forties, has a medical condition that prevents him from eating most sweets.

One day Charlie arrived with the usual fanfare in the accounting section to deliver his quarterly rewards. About halfway through his typical speech, he stopped and said: "I'm getting pretty tired of these things. Aren't you? Hasn't everybody had enough doughnuts? These aren't even that good. I wish someone would come up with another way to reward the areas that have done a good job of avoiding accidents."

Barbara looked around the room and observed everybody looking pensive. Each employee was jotting down ideas, waiting for Charlie to give the cue to speak. Charlie then said, "If you think of anything, let me know," and walked out of the conference room.

1. What concerns do you think the department members are likely to have about Adamski's program of behavior modification?

2. What rules for applying behavior modification did Adamski violate?

3. How can Adamski revitalize his motivational program?

Source: Case researched by Barbara P. Catrett, Rochester Institute of Technology.

Notes _____

1. Raymond A. Katzell and Donna E. Thompson, "Work Motivation: Theory and Practice," *American Psychologist,* February 1990, p. 144.

2. Kenneth M. Dawson and Sheryl N. Dawson, "How to Motivate Your Employees," *HRMagazine,* April 1990, p. 78.

3. Donald B. Fedor and Gerald R. Ferris, "Integrating OB Mod with Cognitive Approaches to Motivation," *Academy of Management Review,* January 1981, pp. 115–25.

4. Observation by Henry F. Houser, in book review, *Personnel Psychology,* Autumn 1985, p. 626.

5. Gary P. Latham and Edwin A. Locke, "Goal Setting—A Motivational Technique That Works," *Organizational Dynamics,* Autumn 1979, pp. 72–75.

6. F. Christopher Earley and associates, "Impact of Process and Outcome Feedback on the Relation of Goal Setting to Task Performance," *Academy of Management Journal,* March 1990, pp. 87–105.

7. Robert J. Vance and Adrienne Colella, "Effects of Two Types of Feedback on Goal Acceptance and Personal Goals," *Journal of Applied Psychology,* February 1990, p. 68.

8. Terence R. Mitchell and William S. Silver, "Individual and Group Goals When Workers Are Interdependent: Effects on Task Strategies and Performance," *Journal of Applied Psychology,* April 1990, p. 191.

9. Jane Punnett, "Goal Setting: An Extension of the Research," *Journal of Applied Psychology,* February 1986, pp. 171–72.

10. Christina E. Shalley, Greg R. Oldham, and Joseph F. Porac, "Effects of Goal Difficulty, Goal-Setting Method, and Expected External Evaluation on Intrinsic Motivation," *Academy of Management Journal,* September 1987, pp. 553–63.

11. Miriam Erez, P. Christopher Earley, and Charles L. Hulin, "The Impact of Participation on Goal Acceptance and Performance: A Two-Step Model," *Academy of Management Journal,* March 1985, pp. 63–64; Vance and Colella, "Effects of Two Types of Feedback on Goal Acceptance," p. 75.

12. An original source of the need hierarchy is Abraham Maslow, "A Theory of Human Motivation," *Psychological Review,* 50 (1943), pp. 370–96; a new synthesis of Maslow's ideas is Maslow, *Motivation and Personality,* 3rd ed. (New York: Harper & Row, 1987).

13. James L. Gibson, John M. Ivancevich, and James H. Donnelly, Jr., *Organizations: Behavior, Structure, Processes,* 6th ed. (Plano, TX: Business Publications, 1988), p. 142.

14. An original source of the two-factor theory is Frederick Herzberg, *Work and the Nature of Man* (Cleveland: World, 1966).

15. "Rewards Have Value," *Personnel Journal,* October 1989, p. 2.

16. Thomas Rollins, "Pay for Performance: Is It Worth the Trouble?" *Personnel Administrator,* May 1988, pp. 42–46.

17. David E. Terpstra, "Theories of Motivation—Borrowing the Best," *Personnel Journal,* June 1979, p. 377.

18. Michael J. Stahl, "Achievement, Power, and Managerial Motivation: Selecting Managerial Talent with the Job Choice Exercise," *Personnel Psychology,* Winter 1983, pp. 775–89; David C. McClelland, *Power: The Inner Experience* (New York: Irvington, 1975).

19. David C. McClelland, *The Achieving Society* (New York: Van Nostrand, 1961).

20. Stahl, "Achievement, Power, and Managerial Motivation," p. 776.

21. McClelland, *Power: The Inner Experience.*

22. Research cited in John Leo, "Looking for a Life of Thrills," *Time,* Apr. 15, 1985, pp. 92–93.

23. An original version of expectancy theory is Victor H. Vroom, *Work and Motivation* (New York: Wiley, 1964). A later synthesis similar to the version presented in this text is Henry L. Tosi, John R. Rizzo, and Stephen J. Carroll, *Managing Organizational Behavior* (Marshfield, MA: Pitman, 1986), pp. 240–46.

24. Tosi, Rizzo, and Carroll, *Managing Organizational Behavior,* p. 242.

25. Walter B. Newsom, "Motivate, Now!" *Personnel Journal,* February 1990, p. 52.

26. Research cited in Robert Albanese, *Management Update,* Fall 1988 (South-Western Publishing Co.).

27. An authoritative source on the use of behavior modification in organizations is Fred Luthans and Robert Kreitner, *Organizational Behavior Modification and Beyond: An Operant and Social Learning Approach* (Glenview, IL: Scott, Foresman, 1984).

28. Kenneth Blanchard, "Jelly Bean Motivation: Know When to Applaud Your Workers and When to Leave Them Alone," *Success!,* February 1986, p. 8.

29. A. B. Cecala, S. J. Liebowitz, and W. D. Presutti, "Gainsharing: A Technique to Improve Management-Employee Relations and Mine Productivity," *Mining Science and Technology,* vol. 8, 1989, p. 215.

30. William C. Hauck and Timothy L. Ross, "Sweden's Experiments in Productivity and Gainsharing," *Personnel,* January 1987, pp. 61–67.

31. Edward L. Deci, James P. Connell, and Richard M. Ryan, "Self-Determination in a Work Organization," *Journal of Applied Psychology,* August 1989, p. 580; Edward L. Deci and Richard M. Ryan, *Intrinsic Motivation and Self-Determination in Human Behavior* (New York: Plenum, 1985).

32. Alphie Kohn, "Incentives Can Be Bad for Business," *Inc.,* January 1988, cited in Albanese, *Management Update.*

33. Charles O'Reilly, "Corporations, Culture, and Commitment: Motivation and Social Control in Organizations," *California Management Review,* Summer 1989, pp. 9–25.

34. Michael E. Cavanagh, "In Search of Motivation," *Personnel Journal,* March 1984, p. 81.

35. Dov Eden, "Pygmalion, Goal Setting, and Expectancy: Compatible Ways to Boost Productivity," *Academy of Management Review,* October 1988, pp. 639–52.

Suggested Reading _____

HIRST, MARK K. "Intrinsic Motivation as Influenced by Task Interdependence and Goal Setting." *Journal of Applied Psychology,* February 1988, pp. 96–101.

KLEIN, HOWARD J. "An Integrated Control Theory Model of Work Motivation." *Academy of Management Review,* April 1989, pp. 150–72.

LOCKE, EDWIN A., and LATHAM, GARY P. *A Theory of Goal Setting and Task Performance.* Englewood Cliffs, NJ: Prentice Hall, 1990.

MERCHANT, JOHN E. "Motivating Entry-Level Service Workers." *Management Solutions,* March 1988, pp. 43–45.

MILLSAPS, JOHN. "Creating Motivation Programs from Within." *Personnel Administrator,* June 1988, pp. 113–14.

OST, EDWARD. "Gain Sharing's Potential." *Personnel Administrator,* July 1989, pp. 92–96.

PAULSEN, KEVIN M. "Gain Sharing: A Group Motivator." *Management World,* May/June 1989, pp. 24–25.

SUTTON, CHARLOTTE, D., and WOODMAN, RICHARD W. "Pygmalion Goes to Work: The Effects of Supervisor Expectations in a Retail Setting." *Journal of Applied Psychology,* December 1989, pp. 943–50.

WRIGHT, PATRICK M. "Operationalization of Goal Difficulty as a Moderator of the Goal-Difficulty Relationship." *Journal of Applied Psychology,* June 1990, pp. 227–36.

WRIGHT, PATRICK M. "Test of the Mediating Role of Goals in the Incentive-Performance Relationship." *Journal of Applied Psychology,* October 1989, pp. 699–705.

4

Job Satisfaction and Morale

LEARNING OBJECTIVES

After reading and studying this chapter and doing the exercises, you should be able to

1. Illustrate the difference between job satisfaction and motivation.
2. Pinpoint important consequences of job satisfaction and dissatisfaction.
3. Explain how job satisfaction is measured.
4. Identify major causes of or contributors to job satisfaction.
5. Describe general strategies for improving job satisfaction and morale.
6. Describe how modified work schedules and telecommuting contribute to job satisfaction and morale.

E very day is a new challenge. I never know what tough problem is going to hit my desk. If I didn't have a job like this to look forward to, my life would be empty." (A truck fleet supervisor at a soft-drink bottling company)

"My job is a constant hassle. I'm tired to doing other people's dirty work. If I won a lottery tomorrow, I would kiss this job goodbye." (An expediter in a tire-manufacturing company)

The sentiments just expressed illustrate the range of attitudes people have toward their jobs. Some people find their jobs a major contributor to the quality of their lives, while others are intensely dissatisfied. The statements are also an indicator of job satisfaction and morale. **Job satisfaction** is the amount of pleasure or contentment associated with a job. **Morale** is a mixture of feelings, attitudes, and sentiments that contribute to a general feeling of satisfaction. These two meanings are so close that the terms can be used interchangeably. Both morale and satisfaction refer to contentment with one's job and one's employer.

Repeated studies have demonstrated that about three-fourths of workers, all categories combined, are reasonably satisfied with their jobs.[1] As you might suspect, people in high-level, well-paying, and prestigious jobs have the highest satisfaction. Job satisfaction is of current interest because of both humanitarian and economic reasons. High job satisfaction can lead to positive ends, such as loyalty to the company and good mental health. Low job satisfaction can lead to negative ends, such as high turnover and poor mental health. Our discussion of job satisfaction will include causes, consequences, measurement, and improvement.

ARE YOU SATISFIED, MOTIVATED, OR BOTH?

Job satisfaction and motivation are related but not identical. Satisfaction refers to satisfaction of a need often resulting in a state of contentment. Motivation refers to expending effort toward a goal. One way to visualize the relationship between satisfaction and motivation is to use a four-way diagram indicating the extremes—highs and lows—with the middle conditions omitted. These four different possibilities are shown in Figure 4–1.

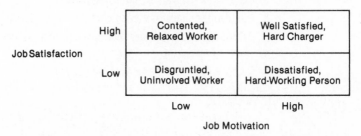

FIGURE 4–1 Four Relationships Between Job Satisfaction and Motivation

Contented, relaxed worker. Many people who have worked into a comfortable rut in a bureaucratic organization fall into this category. Some people derive job satisfaction from working in a relaxed, nonpressured atmosphere. If they had to work too hard, they would experience job dissatisfaction. Family businesses, too, have their share of contented individuals who expend very little effort toward achieving company goals.

Disgruntled, uninvolved worker. People who fit into this category are often experiencing stress. They dislike their jobs, yet work just hard enough to prevent being fired or receiving serious reprimands. Entry-level service workers often fall into this category. However, there are some people in managerial positions who dislike their jobs and are not particularly interested in working. Economic necessity (such as the need to pay bills) forces them to work.

Dissatisfied, hard-working person. Many people with a professional orientation work hard even if they are currently dissatisfied with their company, management, or working conditions. Often people with technical training find themselves in jobs that do not properly challenge their capacities. They nevertheless persevere, believing that conditions will improve or they can change jobs later. A professionally oriented person would not want to damage his or her reputation by performing poorly, even if a particular job were unsatisfying.

Well satisfied, hard charger. A person in this category is usually on the path toward self-fulfillment. A quarterback on a winning professional football team fits into this category. Many branch managers and successful small-business persons are also satisfied and hard-working. A young man with a small but busy and profitable landscaping business said of his work: "I happily work ten hours a day because landscaping is my contribution to a better planet."

CONSEQUENCES OF JOB SATISFACTION AND DISSATISFACTION

Extremes in satisfaction and morale are of major significance to individuals and the organization. Here we focus on the following consequences of job satisfaction and dissatisfaction: productivity, cooperative behavior and good citizenship, absenteeism and turnover, job stress and burnout, safety, quality of work life, and life satisfaction.

Productivity

A long-standing debate is whether high job satisfaction and morale improve productivity. The most accurate answer is that in the long run, there are many instances in which job satisfaction does increase productivity.

However, this is not always the case. For instance, "dissatisfied hard chargers" are productive because they hope that hard work will lead them to a better job. Another exception is that a satisfied employee might have faulty equipment that lowers his or her productivity.

High job satisfaction is particularly important for the productivity of employees whose work involves extensive contact with people. One study showed that managers with high job satisfaction were more likely to:

- listen to others,
- show awareness and concern for the feelings of others,
- be tactful,
- have good emotional control,
- accept criticism.[2]

These behaviors are more likely to improve the productivity of workers whose jobs involve extensive contact with people. For instance, it is important for human resource specialists and sales representatives to listen to others and be tactful. These workers cannot be effective without listening to others and being tactful.

Cooperative Behavior and Good Citizenship

Although high satisfaction may not always lead to high productivity, it often leads to good results in other aspects of job performance. These helpful aspects of performance center around cooperative behavior and good citizenship. Specifically, employees with high job satisfaction are likely to:

- help co-workers with a job-related problem,
- accept orders without a fuss,
- tolerate temporary impositions without a complaint,
- help to keep the work area clean and uncluttered,
- make timely and constructive statements about the department or its manager to outsiders,
- promote a work climate that is tolerable and minimizes the distractions caused by conflict between workers,
- protect and conserve company resources, such as parts, supplies, and money.[3]

Supervisors appreciate these behaviors because they make their job easier. If you exhibit the behaviors characteristic of a satisfied employee, it will strengthen your relationship with your boss.

Absenteeism and Turnover

Employees who dislike their jobs are absent more frequently and are also more likely to quit. This is one of the best-documented facts about the negative consequences of low job satisfaction. A recent synthesis of twenty-one studies has pinpointed which aspects of dissatisfaction contribute the most to absenteeism: (1) Absence frequency and duration (length of absence) is most closely associated with dissatisfaction with the work itself, and (2) absence frequently is related to dissatisfaction with co-workers and to overall satisfaction.[4]

Evidence also exists that if the cause of discontent is modified, job satisfaction will increase and turnover will decrease.[5] A supermarket manager describes an incident supporting this idea:

> Our turnover rate for checkout clerks was pushing 40 percent. That's too high, even for this business. Our interviews with checkout clerks who quit showed that most of them objected to getting approval on checks for customers who had checking privileges. Waiting for a supervisor to approve the checks created delays in handling other customers. The checkout clerks hated the growling and angry stares from the impatient customers. We removed the check-approval requirement and our turnover decreased to 25 percent.

Job Stress and Burnout

Chronic job dissatisfaction is a powerful source of stress and burnout. The employee may not see a satisfactory short-term solution to escaping this type of stress. An employee who feels trapped in a dissatisfying job may withdraw by such means as high absenteeism or tardiness; or the employee may quit.

Employees under prolonged job stress stemming from job dissatisfaction often consume too much alcohol, tobacco, prescription drugs, and illegal drugs. These employees are costly to the company in terms of time lost from the job and payments for medical expenses, including increased medical insurance premiums. Details about stress and burnout appear in Chapter 5.

Safety

Poor safety practices are another negative consequence of low satisfaction and morale. Some of the lost time just mentioned can be attributed to job accidents. When people are discouraged about their jobs, they are more likely to have accidents. An underlying reason behind such accidents is that discouragement may take attention away from the task at hand, and inattention leads directly to accidents. Many injuries from power tools can be attributed to the operator not paying careful attention to his or her work.

Quality of Work Life

Modern organizations devote considerable resources to helping employees achieve a high **quality of work life (QWL).** Programs aimed at improving the quality of work life grant employees increased decision-making authority about important matters. The increased responsibility leads to increased job satisfaction for those workers who value more responsibility.

A high quality of work life can also be a consequence of job satisfaction. Workers who perceive their work life to be of high quality will generally be more satisfied.

Life Satisfaction

Job and career satisfaction have a spillover effect on satisfaction with life in general. A four-year study of 1,100 workers investigated the link between job and life satisfaction. It was found that increases in satisfaction with supervision, pay, and promotion are likely to increase life satisfaction. Conversely, decreases in these factors tend to decrease life satisfaction.[6]

An analysis of studies involving almost 20,000 workers further confirms the fact that high job satisfaction can make life more pleasant. An interesting sidelight of the study is that prior to twenty years ago, the relationship was stronger for men than for women. Now that more women are committed to careers outside the home, job satisfaction also contributes substantially to their life satisfaction.[7]

THE MEASUREMENT OF JOB SATISFACTION AND MORALE

Organizations periodically measure job satisfaction for two reasons. First, they believe that job satisfaction is important in its own right. Second, they believe that measuring job satisfaction provides an index of organizational effectiveness (see Chapter 16). The three primary methods of measuring job satisfaction and morale are attitude surveys, observing actual behavior, and conducting meetings with employees.

Employee Attitude Surveys

Attitude surveys are the standard method of measuring job satisfaction and morale. These surveys always involve written questionnaires, but may also include interviews with employees. Interviews are helpful in explaining the meaning of survey findings. For instance, in one survey 75 percent of the employees said the company's salary system was unfair. Follow-up interviews helped uncover the reason for this perception: New employees were often hired at wages higher than those of current employees in comparable jobs.

Employee attitude surveys cover a wide range of topics related to job satisfaction and organizational effectiveness. Almost every survey asks questions about standard topics, such as attitudes toward the company and supervision, pay, and working conditions. The survey may also investigate attitudes toward topics of current concern, such as a takeover by another firm or subcontracting of work to another country. Figure 4–2 lists topics frequently measured in attitude surveys.

Written questionnaires. Questionnaires based on rating scales are the most frequently used formal method of measuring job satisfaction and morale. An example of a widely used scale to measure job satisfaction is the Job Descriptive Index. The JDI measures attitudes in five areas: work, supervision, people, pay, and promotions. Respondents are asked to mark each one as yes (Y), no (N), or cannot decide (?) as it relates to their job. A sampling of these questions is given in Figure 4–3.

Individual and group interviews. Interviews have three key purposes in an employee attitude survey. First, they can be used with a small sample of employees to identify topics worth exploring. Second, they can be used with small samples to learn directly about employee attitudes. Third, after the results are in, they can be used to explore some of the findings in depth.

Interviews offer the advantages of gaining in-depth information and exploring the causes of certain attitudes. Potential disadvantages of interviews are that they are time-consuming, cannot be conducted anonymously, and are subject to interview bias. Bias would occur, for example, if the interviewer had a preconceived idea of where employees stood on an issue. The interviewer might then look for statements to confirm his or her position.

Leadership, supervision, and management
Job itself
Co-workers
Physical working conditions
Pay, benefits, and other rewards
Career advancement and job security
Commitment to and identification with the organization
Job stress
Training and development
Physical environment
Disciplinary procedures
Management of the firm
Company climate (general working atmosphere)

FIGURE 4–2 Topics Addressed in Most Employee Attitude Surveys

	Work		*Supervision*
N	Routine	Y	Asks my advice
Y	Creative	Y	Praises good work
N	Tiresome	N	Doesn't supervise enough
Y	Gives a sense of accomplishment	Y	Tells me where I stand

	People		*Pay*
Y	Stimulating	Y	Income adequate for normal expenses
Y	Ambitious	N	Bad
N	Talk too much	N	Less than I deserve
N	Hard to meet	N	Highly paid

	Promotions
Y	Good opportunity for advancement
Y	Promotion on ability
N	Dead-end job
N	Unfair promotion policy

FIGURE 4–3 Sample Items from the 72-item Job Descriptive Index with "Satisfied" Responses Indicated

Source: The Job Descriptive Index is copyrighted by Bowling Green State University. The complete forms, scoring, key, instruction and norms can be obtained from Dr. Patricia Cain Smith, Department of Psychology, Bowling Green State University, Bowling Green OH 43404. Reprinted with permission.

Observing Actual Behavior

Employee attitudes can often be gauged by directly observing employees' behavior. Among the behaviors that suggest low satisfaction and morale are high absenteeism, turnover, tardiness, high scrap rates, low quality, time wasting, and reading the newspaper during working hours. In general, any form of psychological sabotage could be an indicator of job dissatisfaction.

Despite the obvious validity of linking satisfaction and behavior, the two may not be directly related in the short run. Some employees whose behavior is constructive may be harboring resentment. Their professional pride keeps their behavior on track, yet their dissatisfaction makes them turnover candidates.

Meetings with Employees

Another approach to measuring satisfaction and morale is for managers to meet with groups of employees and encourage them to express what is on their minds. These sessions are also referred to as gripe sessions. In a typical setup, a high-ranking manager would meet with a group of about fifty employees at their work site or in a company cafeteria. By encouraging employees to talk freely about their likes and dislikes, the executive hopes to measure the pulse of the organization.

Meetings with employees do provide many insights about areas of satisfaction and dissatisfaction within the firm. An important limitation of this method is that many employees believe it is unwise to be observed making negative statements about the company. A human resource professional made this comment about the meeting:

> It would take a naive employee to "let it all hang out" at one of these sessions. Top management does have a sincere interest in learning about how employees see things. But if you are too negative in your statements, you can be branded as a troublemaker. Besides, many problems in the firm can be traced to the mistakes of top management. You don't hear many employees directly confronting top management.

Up to this point in the chapter we have examined the nature of satisfaction, along with its consequences, and how it is measured. We now focus on the reasons why people experience job satisfaction and dissatisfaction.

CAUSES OF JOB SATISFACTION AND DISSATISFACTION

The two-factor theory of job motivation described in Chapter 3 is also an explanation of job satisfaction. The same elements that contribute to motivation also lead to satisfaction. For example, achieving recognition for one's ideas will both motivate and satisfy most people. Although the two-factor theory has merit in understanding the causes of job satisfaction, it is not the only plausible explanation. Here we present a list of external and internal causes of job satisfaction. External causes relate to the job and the company; internal causes relate to personality factors and personal attitudes.

Again, we caution that the general factors to be presented can be superseded by individual differences. For instance, "mentally challenging work" is a satisfier for most people. However, some people are dissatisfied with mentally challenging work because they prefer to daydream while on the job.

External Causes of Job Satisfaction

Certain factors that lead to an enriched job or a comfortable work atmosphere increase job satisfaction for employees with at least an average work ethic. An **enriched job** is one that allows the worker to perform more interesting and responsible tasks. As you study these factors,[8] evaluate whether they would enhance your job satisfaction.

Mentally challenging work. Most employees crave some intellectual challenge on the job. This need can be met by such means as getting a trouble-shooting assignment, training another employee, or making suggestions for productivity improvement. For instance, an assistant restaurant manager might be asked how the restaurant can decrease the amount of food wasted in the kitchen.

Reasonable physical demands. Work with reasonable physical demands is satisfying. In contrast, work that pushes an employee's physical limits usually becomes unsatisfying. Taxing physical work carried out for long periods of time becomes a source of physical and mental fatigue. A manager of an international company put it this way: "I've been flying back and forth between this country and far-flung locations for ten years. The wear and tear is getting to me. The flights themselves are bad enough. Being hung up in airports for hours and even days is worse. I want a different job where I can put most of my energy into doing the job rather than surviving travel."

Contact with end user.   The opportunity to interact with the person who ultimately uses your goods and services enhances job satisfaction. Most jobs call for employees to submit their work to their boss or a co-worker, such as an assistant preparing a letter for the department manager. Contact with an end user or client includes these examples: a systems analyst talking to an office supervisor about the backlog of paperwork in the supervisor's department; a production worker visiting a customer to help install a piece of equipment.

Personal accountability. A satisfying job makes workers accountable for their results. In this way they can accept congratulations for a job well done and blame for a job done poorly.

Scheduling of own work. Satisfying jobs grant employees the freedom to schedule some part of their own work, such as deciding when to tackle which assignment. Self-employed workers usually are in control of their own schedules. As described later, organization-employed persons are being granted more opportunities to schedule their own work.

Meaningful rewards. Job satisfaction increases directly when employees receive meaningful rewards for performance. A meaningful reward is fair, informative, and in line with a person's needs or goals. A *fair* reward is in line with the size of a worker's contribution. An example would be a note of congratulations from an executive for having performed well on a task force assignment.

An *informative* reward is one that tells you how well you have performed, such as a blinking computer message stating, "You are 20 percent ahead of quota right now." A reward *in line with one's needs or goals* is a reward that has a high valence for the person. An example would be an employee who is heavily in debt receiving a large salary increase or bonus.

Rewards are so closely linked with job satisfaction that another explanation of the link is worthy of attention. According to the *performance-*

reward-satisfaction model, if you perform well and receive an equitable reward, your satisfaction will increase.[9] Your perception is important: Job satisfaction occurs only when you think the reward is fair and you perceive it to be valuable. A key implication of this model is that workers are satisfied when they perform well. The commonsense version of this relationship is that we perform well on those tasks we find satisfying.

Helpful co-workers and superiors.   Helpful in this sense means giving the employee an opportunity to achieve important job values, such as interesting work, pay, and promotions. Job satisfaction is also enhanced when co-workers and superiors have basic values that mesh with others of the employees. For example, an employee with a strong work ethic will experience job satisfaction if he or she works with others who value hard work. Furthermore, the co-workers and superiors should minimize conflict and confusion.

More power and authority.   A consistent theme in human relations and organizational behavior is that many workers at all levels would enjoy having more power and authority.[10] When workers are "empowered" they often respond with higher levels of job satisfaction and productivity. Gainsharing, as described in the previous chapter, is one of the many methods described in this text of giving workers more power and authority.

Internal Causes of Job Satisfaction

The causes of job satisfaction described in this section stem primarily from personality characteristics and personal values. However, internal factors also influence whether external factors cause satisfaction. A good example would be the performance-reward-satisfaction model described above: Satisfaction occurs when the person perceives the reward to be fair and valuable.

Interest in the work itself.   Job satisfaction stems directly from being interested in what you are doing. Terms to describe this inherent interest in work include *craft instinct, pride in work,* and *self-rewarding work.* Whichever term is used, the message is the same: People who love their work experience high job satisfaction.

A feeling of self-esteem.   Work that satisfies a person's need for self-esteem contributes directly to job satisfaction. High-status occupations contribute more to self-esteem than do those of low status. The individual in search of self-esteem on the job is thus dependent upon society's perceptions of the status of specific occupations. Feelings of self-esteem also stem from doing work the individual sees as worthwhile. This perception is less influenced by external standards than is the status associated with a particular job or occupation.

Optimism and flexibility. An optimistic and flexible person is predisposed to be a satisfied employee. A pessimistic and rigid person will most likely be a dissatisfied employee. Every company has its share of "pills" who always find something to complain about. No matter what the company does to satisfy such a person, he or she finds another source of dissatisfaction.

Related to the optimism-pessimism explanation of job satisfaction is the possibility that satisfaction has an inherited basis. People appear to have a biologically based trait that predisposes them to see positive or negative content in their lives. This genetic trait can show up as a predisposition to job satisfaction or dissatisfaction.[11]

Thirty-four sets of identical (monozygotic) twins reared apart were studied to investigate the idea of a genetic basis to job satisfaction. It was found that the sets of twins had much more similar levels of job satisfaction than did a comparison group of people not reared together.[12] (The people in the comparison groups had jobs similar to those of the sets of twins.) Because the twins had identical heredity and similar job satisfaction, it could be concluded that heredity contributes to job satisfaction.

Positive self-image. As Robert A. Baron observes, people possessing a positive self-image are generally more satisfied with their jobs than are those possessing a negative self-image.[13] A possible explanation is that the people who view themselves negatively tend to view most things negatively. This is similar to the adage, "You have to like yourself first before you can like other people." In this case, you have to like yourself first before you can like your job.

Positive expectations about the job. People with positive expectations about their jobs are frequently more satisfied than are those with low expectations. These expectations illustrate a self-fulfilling prophecy. If you expect to like your job, you will behave in such a way that those expectations will be met. Similarly, if you expect your job not to satisfy your needs, you will do things to make your expectations come true. Assume that a person expects to earn low commissions in a sales job. The person's negativism may come through to customers and prospective customers, thus ensuring low commissions.

Good personal adjustment. People who report good personal adjustment away from work tend to have above-average job satisfaction. One reason is that an enjoyable personal life makes job frustrations more tolerable. A more fundamental reason offered by Baron is that the skills that help you do well in personal life are also helpful on the job. Among these skills are the abilities to get along with others and to face situations confidently.[14]

Research evidence for the relationship of personal adjustment to satisfaction comes from a study of **negative affectivity,** a tendency to experience aversive emotional states. People with high negative affectivity tend to be distressed, agitated, pessimistic, and dissatisfied. As a consequence they are poorly adjusted and may alienate themselves from co-workers. The subjects for the study were 315 members of the professional staff of a large international professional service firm. Not surprisingly, a significant relationship was found between having high negative affectivity and low job satisfaction.[15] People who suffer from negative emotional states tend to experience low job satisfaction.

GENERAL STRATEGIES FOR IMPROVING SATISFACTION AND MORALE

Since job satisfaction and morale have such important consequences, many managerial activities are directed toward improving satisfaction and morale. It can be argued that almost any constructive action taken by a manager will have some positive impact on satisfaction and morale. A discussion of strategies for improving satisfaction and morale therefore encompasses all of what is known about being an effective manager. Here we will sample several general strategies. In the next two sections of the chapter, we describe the use of modified work schedules to improve satisfaction.

Design Enriched Jobs

A standard approach to improving job satisfaction is to conduct a job enrichment program. Jobs are redesigned to give them many of the characteristics described in the section about external causes of job satisfaction. Job enrichment can be conducted with individuals or groups. Both approaches to enrichment are aimed at increasing satisfaction and productivity.

In the group approach to job enrichment, a team of workers is assigned responsibility for a total task instead of working in an assembly-line fashion.[16] (Refer back to Chapter 1). Each team member receives the personal satisfaction of being able to perform a variety of tasks. A team member in a claims processing unit of an insurance company expresses her attitude toward being a team member:

> Before we switched to teams, I would come to work each day and look at the hopeless stack of claims in front of me, waiting to be processed. I would do my little part, and pass the claim along the line. Now we are organized to perform all the necessary functions for a group of agents in one region. It's as if I'm running a little business of my own. I'm proud of what I do, and I would never want to let the team down.

Remedy Substandard Conditions

The commonsense solution to job satisfaction and morale problems is to remove substandard conditions. This strategy assumes that the true, underlying problem has been recognized. Employees may complain about something in the work environment, such as poor heating or cooling. If the underlying dissatisfaction is really with the quality of supervision—but employees are unwilling to say so—improving the heating and cooling system will not improve satisfaction.

An example of a management technique perceived by many workers to be a substandard condition is **computer-aided monitoring,** or using a computer to help keep track of employee output and activity. To its critics, monitoring is a repressive managerial control practice, conjuring up images of "Big Brother is watching." Proponents, however, perceive monitoring as necessary to conducting business and helpful in providing feedback to workers.

A typical example of computer-aided monitoring is telephone monitoring, which is used by the Tax Collection Division of the Internal Revenue Service. The supervisor listens in on employees' work-related calls, usually without the employee's awareness. The objective component is continuous computer tracking of performance measures, such as the employee's average length of phone conversation, number of calls completed, and number attempted.[17] Simultaneously, the supervisor views on a video display terminal the case being handled.

A study of computer-aided monitoring in the Tax Collection Division suggested that dissatisfaction with monitoring can be reduced if supervisors use the system in a constructive and helpful way.[18] For example, they should emphasize the system as a tool for providing helpful feedback. In effect, the supervisors would be remedying a substandard condition.

Display Concern for Employees

Managers who openly show concern for the feelings, attitudes, and opinions of employees contribute to high morale. People feel better and often work better when they receive reassurance and support from the boss. Concern for employees can also be expressed by such means as asking for suggestions, expressing sympathy about employee problems, and asking questions about an employee's family.

Displaying concern for employees is particularly important when the firm is going through a period of upheaval, such as after the company is taken over by another. Under these conditions, many employees feel that management is much more concerned about cutting costs than about employee welfare.[19]

Another important way of being considerate is to pay attention to employees. A standard managerial technique for paying attention to employees is to visit them at their work areas periodically. During the visit, the manager can chat with the employee about work-related topics and solicit ideas for improvement. These periodic incidents of *management by wandering around* should not be overdone; the purpose of management by wandering around is for the manager to keep in touch with people and problems, not to interrupt the flow of work.

Create Fun in the Workplace

Fun and humor on the job can help reduce tension, resolve conflict, and raise productivity and satisfaction.[20] These potential advantages of fun have prompted many companies to build fun into the job. Deliberate attempts to enhance workplace fun can be divided into three categories. The easiest approach is to conduct activities such as company picnics, fairs, and special days designed to make employees happy. A typical example is a "jeans day" on which all workers are encouraged to dress informally. Along the same lines, many companies sponsor cookie-and-milk breaks in the afternoon, styled after grade school.

Another company-organized fun activity is for customer contact personnel to conduct a "worst customer of the week" program. Its purpose is to help relieve the tension of dealing with unreasonable customers. A teller won her bank's weekly contest by describing the antics of an elderly customer. With a long line waiting behind him, the customer insisted that the teller wash the money he was withdrawing. The customer said he wanted to avoid any contagious diseases caused by germ-laden money. (Do you think the customer was being unreasonable?)

A second, more difficult to implement approach is to train managers in telling jokes and making witty, work-related comments. Humor consultants are sometimes hired to help managers develop such skills. Although humor is encouraged, managers are discouraged from making ethnic, sexist, or racist jokes.

A sales manager who had attended a humor workshop returned to the office to conduct a serious meeting about declining sales. He opened the meeting by saying, "Ladies and gentlemen, yesterday I completed a computerized analysis of our declining sales. According to the results of my spreadsheet analysis, if we continue our current trend, by the year 2001 we will have sales of negative $2,750,000. No organization can support those figures. We've got to reverse the trend."

A third form of organizational fun is to create assignments that are fun to accomplish. This category of fun is akin to job enrichment and self-determining work. In reporting on his research into organizational fun, David J. Abramis reported, "Some top executives we interviewed told us that challenge is one of the most fun parts of their work."[21]

Offer Satisfying Employee Benefits

Virtually all organizations offer full-time, permanent employees some type of benefits in addition to wages. One of the many purposes of these benefit programs is to increase job satisfaction and morale. Benefits include such wide-ranging plans and programs as medical insurance, dental insurance, retirement pay, parental leave, child care on company premises, tuition reimbursement, discount purchasing, tickets to athletic events, and expense-paid trips to professional meetings.

A type of employee benefit geared specifically toward increasing productivity and satisfaction is recognition programs. Because recognition is a basic human need (refer back to Chapter 3), the popularity of these programs is not surprising. A representative list of types of recognition programs and types of awards is presented in Figure 4–4.

BOOSTING SATISFACTION AND MORALE THROUGH MODIFIED WORK SCHEDULES

A widely used specific method of boosting job satisfaction and morale is to give employees more say about their hours of work. As noted in Chapter 1, flexible working hours can also increase productivity. For many employees in private and public firms, the standard eight-hour day with fixed starting and stopping times has ended. A variety of modified work schedules have replaced the standard week.

A **modified work schedule** is any formal departure from the traditional hours of work, excluding shift work and staggered work hours. Shift work refers to working evenings or nights instead of days. Staggered work

Types of Programs	Types of awards
Length of service	Plaques and certificates
Retirement	Accessories and jewelry
Safety	Merchandise
Attendance	Watches
Productivity	Sales incentives
Sales	Savings bonds
Superior performance	Cash bonus
Employee of the week/month/quarter/year	Trophies
	Travel incentives
Quality	Ribbons and pins
	Company stock

FIGURE 4-4 Typical Recognition Programs and Awards

Note: Items in both columns are listed in decreasing order of frequency. However, there is no particular relationship between the accomplishment or activity in the first column and the award in the second.

Source: Based on information gathered by Globe Research Corporation, in 1988 and published in Morton E. Grossman and Margaret Magnus, "The $2.1 Billion Rash of Awards," *Personnel Journal,* May 1989, pp. 73–74.

hours refer to employees in the same firm working different eight-hour blocks, such as 10 to 6 instead of 9 to 5. The two most widely used modified work schedules are flextime and the compressed work week. Work-at-home programs are steadily increasing, and job sharing has also gained some acceptance.

Flextime

More frequent use is made of flextime in offices than in factories, mills, foundries, construction sites, or stores. The major reason is that the system works best when employees do not depend on each other for accomplishing work. Office employees can often do their work by themselves. In contrast, in a lumber mill, certain work would have to stop if the crane operator were not on the job. Basic formats of flextime are shown in Figure 4–5 and Figure 4–6.

Flextime's Contribution to Satisfaction

Numerous reports and studies have shown that flextime enhances job satisfaction. It will be sufficient here to summarize the results of two reports involving large numbers of workers.

Flextime in three service industries. A study of company experience with clerical workers on flextime was conducted among 400 companies in the banking, insurance, and utility industries.[22] The results were based on the reports of company officials, not experimental results. In all three indus-

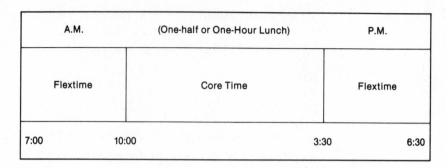

FIGURE 4–5 Typical Flextime Working Hours Schedule

A.M.	(One-half or One-Hour Lunch)	P.M.
Flextime	Core Time	Flextime

7:00   10:00   3:30   6:30

FIGURE 4–6 Flextime Schedule with Two Core Periods

tries, an overwhelming majority of company officials noted greater levels of job satisfaction with flextime. Flextime was noted as making a contribution to job satisfaction by 94 percent of banks, 93 percent of insurance companies, and 100 percent of gas and electric companies. Job satisfaction levels did not change for 5 percent of the banks studied, and for 7 percent of the insurance companies.

Flextime was also found to boost productivity (as measured by quantity and quality of work), decrease lateness and absenteeism, and reduce the amount of overtime used. The results of this survey could therefore be interpreted as indirect evidence that job satisfaction can lead to productivity improvement.

Modified work schedules in a Volvo plant. The Volvo plant in Koping, Sweden, used flextime to combat the problems of labor shortages, high employee turnover, and absenteeism. (Turnover and absenteeism are typically associated with low job satisfaction.) Volvo management developed seven possible shifts to utilize all 168 hours in a week. The multi-shift system makes it easier for employees to move back and forth between night and day, full-time and part-time shifts. Although shift work is usually not classified as flexible working hours, the Koping employees had many choices of hours and could switch to different shifts. Volvo officials thought that the flexible work schedules would make it easier to attract employees with preschoolers and school-age children.

Paul Bernstein observes that after twelve years with the multi-shifts, the experiment has been a success. Productivity is high, and absenteeism has held at 9 percent, a low rate for Sweden.[23]

Compressed Workweek

A **compressed work week** is a full-time work schedule that allows 40 hours to be accomplished in less than five days. The usual arrangement is 4-40 (working four ten-hour days). Many employees enjoy the 4-40 schedule because it enables them to have three consecutive days off from work. A 4-40 schedule usually allows most employees to take off Saturdays and Sundays. Important exceptions include police workers, hospital employees, and computer operators.

A relatively infrequent compressed work week, the 3-38 work schedule, was implemented for eighty-four information systems personnel.[24] Under a 3-38 schedule, the employee crams a full week's work into three work days of approximately 12½ hours each. One reason for trying the 3-38 schedule was that information systems workers were regularly assigned to overtime. The resulting six- and seven-day weeks became a source of frustration and fatigue for many workers. Management reasoned that 3-38 would enable six-day coverage, using two 12½ hour shifts per day. At the same time, there would be no overtime and no reduction in pay from that earned under the 5-40 schedule.

In addition to modifying the regular work schedule, the information systems workers also had their jobs upgraded. Prior to going on 3-38, there were three different jobs, each performed by different employees. The job titles were burster/decollator, input/output operator, and console operator. To implement the new schedule, all employees had to do all jobs. The effect was to enlarge the variety of tasks and increase responsibility.

The new work schedule deviated substantially from a traditional one. The day shift was from 6:00 A.M. to 6:30 P.M., Monday through Saturday; the night shift was 6:00 P.M. to 6:30 A.M., Sunday through Saturday. Overtime pay was granted for hours beyond 12½; on Saturdays and Sundays employees earned time-and-a-half, assuming they had already worked 37½ hours. (Before reading of the effect of this schedule on job satisfaction, imagine your attitude toward such a schedule.)

Job satisfaction was measured with several questionnaires, including the Job Descriptive Index. Eighteen months after implementation, employees assigned to a 3-38 schedule still preferred it over their previous work arrangement with the company. The employees most likely to favor the new schedule (1) participated in the decision to implement the new schedule; (2) received an upgraded job with the schedule; and (3) had strong higher-order needs (as measured by a separate questionnaire).

Several results of the study tied in with productivity. Fatigue did not appear to be a problem. Payoffs to the organization included reductions in sick time, overtime, and personal leave time.

Compressed work weeks also have their disadvantages. Many employees find it both fatiguing and inconvenient from a personal standpoint to work ten consecutive hours. Even in situations where employees are strongly in favor of the compressed work week, employers may discover significant problems. An engineering service group conducted a four-month experiment with a 4-40 schedule. The white-collar employees involved saw such advantages as being able to conduct personal business more efficiently, avoiding a difficult morning commute, and improved productivity due to work continuity. Management stopped the program, however, because it appeared that customer service had not really improved.[25] An executive from another company that discontinued the compressed work week explains his company's reasons:

The employees loved the program, but we stopped it for a very good reason. Under the usual eight-hour schedule, many of our best employees would stay a couple of hours to get their work done. In this way we would usually be getting about forty-six hours per week of productivity from these conscientious employees. Under the 4-40 program, nobody would stay past ten hours. In this way, we lost all our casual overtime. If you wanted somebody to come in for the fifth day, you would have to pay that person.[26]

Telecommuting

Another deviation from the traditional work schedule is **telecommuting,** an arrangement in which employees perform their regular work duties from home or at another location. Usually the employees use computers tied into the company's main office. Yet you can be a telecommuter, or teleworker, without a computer. For instance, you might work at home as an advertising copywriter, a garment maker, or a drafting technician. In addition to communicating by computer, telecommuters also attend meetings on company premises, and stay in telephone contact. Today, approximately 16 million corporate employees work at home full- or part-time, and the numbers are increasing.

Advantages of telecommuting. Telecommuting can work well with self-reliant, self-starting, and self-disciplined employees who also have relevant work experience. Work-at-home employees are usually people who request such an arrangement, and therefore are likely to experience high job satisfaction. Employees derive many benefits from working at home, including easier management of personal life, lowered commuting and clothing costs, and fewer distractions from co-workers. Telecommuting offers these potential advantages to the employer:[27]

Increased productivity. Where direct measurements are possible, productivity increases have averaged about 50 percent, with many reported increases of over 100 percent.

Lower overhead. Because the employees are providing some of their own office space, the company can operate with smaller offices. A marketing research executive noted that because of its work-at-home program, the company was able to greatly expand its client load without renting additional space.

Reduced absenteeism and turnover. It takes a serious illness for an employee not to be able to work at home. Turnover is decreased because telecommuting jobs are not yet in ample supply in a given community.

Access to a wider range of employee talent. Companies with work-at-home programs are almost always deluged with résumés from eager job applicants. The wider talent bank includes parents (mostly mothers) with young children, employees who find commuting uncomfortable, and others who live far away from the firm.

Disadvantages of telecommuting. Work-at-home programs must be used selectively because they also have many potential disadvantages to both employee and employer. The careers of telecommuters may suffer because they are not visible to management and cannot establish valuable contacts in the office. Many telecommuters complain of the isolation from co-workers. Also, they may be exploited because they may feel compelled to work on company problems late into the night and on weekends. Many telecommuters find it difficult to concentrate on work because of the many potential distractions at home.

A potential disadvantage of work-at-home programs to the employer is that it is difficult to build loyalty and teamwork when a large number of workers rarely come to the office and/or interact much with co-workers. Teleworkers are also difficult to supervise and therefore may have much more latitude in attending to personal matters when they should be thinking about company problems. (If work-at-home employees are assigned readily measured tasks such as data entry or report writing, this disadvantage is minimized.) Another problem is that the organization may miss out on some of the creativity that stems from the exchange of ideas in the traditional office.

Telecommuting at a computer consulting firm. One of the most extensive uses of telecommuting is at F International, a computer consulting firm founded by Steve Shirley. Her firm (Shirley is a woman) specializes in designing integrated office information systems, evaluating hardware and software, and helping managers use micro and personal computers. F International employs more than 1,000 freelancers in the United Kingdom, the Netherlands, and Denmark. All the freelancers, including Shirley, work from their homes. About 84 percent of the employees are women.

The consultants spend about 40 percent of their time working at home; the balance of their work is spent on client premises. Most of the communication among employees takes place by phone and at periodic company meetings. Asked how she organizes and oversees the work of over 1,000 employees working from home, Shirley replied:

> Quality control, which is what you're talking about, is no different in a service industry than on a production line. You take samples so that every now and again you actually have a look.[28]

Job Sharing

Job sharing is a modified work schedule in which two people share the same job, both usually working half-time. The two sharers divide up the job according to their needs, such as dividing up days of the work week. The people sharing the job might be two friends, a husband and wife, or two employees who did not know each other before sharing a job. An example of job sharing would be for one person to work mornings and the other to work afternoons. If the job were complex, the two sharers would have to spend some overlap time discussing the job.[29]

Job sharing has its greatest appeal to people whose family responsibilities are incompatible with a full-time job. A typical situation of job sharing comes about when two friends decide they both want a responsible job, but can only work part-time. Employers benefit from job sharing because employees are likely to be more productive in four hours than in eight hours of work. Also, if one employee is sick, the other will still be available to handle the job for the half day.

Job sharing has several disadvantages to the employees and the employer. You are unlikely to be recommended for promotion if you can only make a half-time commitment to the firm. The firm may have difficulty evaluating, supervising, and rewarding job sharers. For example, should both receive identical raises? How does the company know which should receive credit or blame when something goes right or wrong?

Why Modified Work Schedules Improve Job Satisfaction

Modified work schedules, particularly flextime, boost job satisfaction for two important reasons. One underlying reason is that employees appreciate exerting control over their work schedules.[30] Flextime is a form of participative decision making: Employees help decide which hours of the day they will work. Control and participation of this kind gives employees the feeling that they are being treated as responsible adults.

Another important reason is that modified work schedules make life easier for many employees. Since employees are not confined to the conventional work day, they can accomplish such personally important things as

- sleeping late on work days,
- avoiding rush-hour commuting,

- attending conferences with children's teachers,
- taking care of personal errands, such as visits to physicians, dentists, therapists, banks, car dealers, and realtors during normal working hours (this is an advantage because not all these matters can be handled at nights and on Saturdays),
- avoiding the routine of fixed working hours,
- scheduling vacations at times when recreation facilities are not overly crowded.

Summary of Key Points

- Job satisfaction is the amount of pleasure or contentment associated with a job. Morale is a mixture of feelings, attitudes, and sentiments that contribute to a general feeling of satisfaction. About three-fourths of workers, all categories combined, are reasonably satisfied with their jobs.

- Job satisfaction and motivation are not identical. People can experience different or similar levels of satisfaction and motivation at the same time. One example is the well-motivated person who works hard despite dissatisfaction with the present job.

- Job satisfaction and dissatisfaction have many important consequences to the individual and the organization. Job satisfaction sometimes leads to increased productivity, particularly for jobs dealing with people. Other consequences of satisfaction and dissatisfaction are related to (1) cooperative behavior and good citizenship, (2) absenteeism and turnover, (3) job stress and burnout, (3) safety, (4) quality of work life, and (5) life satisfaction.

- Job satisfaction and morale are frequently measured because they are important themselves and are related to organizational effectiveness. The three primary methods of measuring job satisfaction and morale are employee attitude surveys, observing actual behavior, and meeting with employees. Attitude surveys use both written questionnaires and interviews.

- Job satisfaction is caused by both external and internal factors; however, a person's perception influences whether an external factor leads to satisfaction. External causes of job satisfaction are tied in with an enriched job. They include mentally challenging work, reasonable physical demands, contact with end user, personal accountability, scheduling of own work, meaningful rewards, helpful co-workers and superiors, and more power and authority.

- Internal causes of job satisfaction include interest in the work itself, a feeling of self-esteem, optimism and flexibility, positive self-image, positive expectations about the job, and good personal adjustment.

- Many managerial activities are geared toward improving satisfaction and morale. Among them are to design enriched jobs, remedy substandard conditions, display concern for employees, create fun in the workplace, and offer satisfying employee benefits.

- Modified work schedules are formal departures from the traditional hours of work, excluding shift work and staggered work hours. Flextime is a method of organizing the hours of work so that employees have flexibility in choosing their own hours. Employees are required to work one or two core periods, but can vary their starting and stopping times. Flextime is known to have a positive impact on satisfaction, and may also improve productivity.

- A compressed work week is a full-time work schedule that allows 40 hours of work to be accomplished in less than five days, such as 40 hours of work in three days. Telecommuting is an arrangement by which employees perform regular work duties from home or another location. Most telecommuting jobs involve communication over a computer. Job sharing is a modified work schedule in which two people share the same job, both usually working half-time.

- Modified work schedules contribute to job satisfaction for two general reasons. First, employees enjoy exerting control over their own schedules. Second, these schedules make it easier for employees to manage both their careers and their personal life.

Questions and Activities _____

1. Why is understanding job satisfaction so important in an era of labor shortages in many types of jobs?
2. What kind of a job would make you a "well-satisfied hard charger"?
3. Identify two jobs for which you think satisfaction would be related to productivity.
4. Identify two jobs for which you think satisfaction would *not* be related to productivity.
5. How do cooperative behavior and good citizenship contribute to organizational productivity?
6. Identify several ways in which workers can be given more power and authority.
7. What relationships do you see between being satisfied on the job and being satisfied in the role of a student?
8. Why does computer-aided monitoring lower the job satisfaction of some workers?
9. Give the rest of the class an example of "fun on the job" that you have witnessed. Your answer can take any of the three forms of fun described in this chapter.

10. Assume that you are responsible for hiring three telecommuters. What information about a candidate would you need to convince yourself that he or she would work effectively at home?

A HUMAN RELATIONS CASE PROBLEM
The Disgruntled Cashiers

Rite-Buy is a chain of twenty-one supermarkets, spread out over a 200-mile radius. The company has been in business for thirty-five years and is generally profitable. Despite the presence of larger supermarket firms in their areas, Rite-Buy has been able to hold a satisfactory share of the market. The firm caters to the middle-class and lower-middle-class buyer who wants to avoid both high prices and poor quality food.

Rite-Buy's biggest business problem is high employee turnover, particularly among cashiers (checkout clerks). Melody Parker, vice president of personnel, was asked by the president to investigate the problem and make some recommendations. Three months later she was asked to present her preliminary findings. She told the president, "I see no strong pattern yet. The best I can come up with is that most of our cashiers dislike their jobs. I have conducted exit interviews with a dozen or so clerks who have resigned in the last few months. I have also interviewed employees who have stayed on the payroll more than four months.

"Maybe we need a more systematic study. But I don't notice anything in particular that Rite-Buy can do, other than double the wages of cashiers and decrease the number of customers they have to serve. If we carried out either action, Rite-Buy would go belly up. To reach the financial goals you have established for the firm, the store managers cannot offer higher wages."

The president said to Parker, "Let me see some of the interview reports. I'd like to review a handful myself, to see if I can find a trend."

"Okay," said Parker. "I'll be back in a few moments with some of my interview notes. I'll get the file for the cashiers. Our turnover rates for workers in other areas are about right for the industry."

Twenty minutes later, Parker brought her file to the president. He glanced through the file, and then began to read them in order. Excerpts of these interviews follow.

Bill Kingsley, 18-year-old part-time employee: "I'm leaving Rite-Buy because this job is the pits. You work harder than on an assembly line and the pay is much lower. I could take the job part-time when I was in high school. Now I need to make a better buck. I know I can do better than $5 per hour someplace else."

Nellie Baxter, 59-year-old full-time employee: "I'm sorry I'm leaving the job because the hours were good. I liked the way my schedule would change from week to week. But my feet, legs, and arms can't take it anymore. I'm so sore after a day's work that I usually have to soak in a tub of hot water for an hour when I come home. Then I hardly have energy for anything else but watching a little TV and going to sleep."

Sue Godwin, 33-year-old part-time employee: "I'm not leaving because of Rite-Buy management. You guys are great. It's the customers that are driving me away. You managers should work a checkout counter every once and awhile. The worst people are the coupon clippers. They have no mercy. The line can be twenty customers long and they drag out a month's supply of coupons for you to redeem. You can feel the pressure building up as the person in back of the coupon clipper gets impatient.

"The coupon clippers aren't nearly as bad as the weirdos who challenge you on every price. They have the nerve to say things like, 'I thought the diet soda was on special today. You gave me the regular price.' Even worse, they tell you when you have overcharged them one cent on a twenty-five-pound bag of dog food."

Manuel Garcia, 22-year-old full-time employee: "I'm leaving out of respect for my friends and personal life. How can a single guy develop a good social life when he has to work most nights and Sundays? I miss being out with my friends. You tell me that if I keep up the good work, I might become a store manager. The problem is that the store manager has an even worse schedule than a cashier. I hope to find an office job."

Sandra Yang, 28-year-old full-time employee: "I found the job too physically confining. I always felt boxed in by this little work area. The register is in front of me, and the shelf for bagging is right in back of me. You have about as much room to move around in as a bus driver. I'm the physical type who likes some space. Besides that, work like this can give you varicose veins. I'm looking for a job that's better for me physically."

With a sigh of exasperation, the president said to Parker, "I see what you mean, that there's no consistent pattern. The cashiers who have left have different opinions about what's wrong with the job. If you hear of any fully automated checkout counters, let me know. In the meantime, keep working on the problem. I'll also give it some thought."

1. What recommendations would you make for reducing the turnover of the cashiers?
2. Should Parker also be interviewing the cashiers who were so satisfied with their jobs that they did not quit?
3. Evaluate Parker's position that store managers cannot afford to pay higher wages for cashiers.

A HUMAN RELATIONS CASE PROBLEM
The Inflexible Flextime

Dave Pietro, division manager at Imaging Industries, called a meeting with his supervisors to make an important announcement. After taking care of some routine business he said, "Results of this year's opinion survey indicate that 90 percent of the employees in our division would prefer flexible working hours. Upper management is convinced that a flextime program is an inexpensive way of boosting morale and improving the quality of work life. You know as well as I do that a happy employee will generally be more productive.

"I'd like to get your opinion on how best to implement the system. Please turn in your recommendations to me by next week."

The supervisors discussed the new program among themselves and were ready to make recommendations to Dave the next week. They did not reach agreement on starting and quitting time ranges. The supervisors did agree, however, that the section secretary would ensure compliance with payroll regulations. Under the current system the hours of work are preprinted on the time cards, and employees only have to sign their names. The secretary collects the signed cards, obtains the supervisor's signature, and sends the cards to the payroll department. Under flextime, the secretary would have to verify the accuracy of each employee's time card, thus adding to her workload.

Two of the supervisors, John and Gary, advocated a two-hour flexible time range. Rich and Yolanda, the other two supervisors, recommended a one-hour flexible time range. Another much-discussed issue was how much flexibility to allow around the lunch break. It was finally decided that every employee must take a minimum time for lunch break. The supervisors reasoned that making lunchtime flexible would be an unhealthy choice because many people would skip lunch in order to leave earlier in the afternoon.

After the supervisors presented six drafts of a proposal to management over a period of three months, the flextime program was implemented. The key provisions of the flexible working hours program were as follows:

1. Starting times will fluctuate between 7 and 8 A.M. The minimum lunch break will be 42 minutes, but it can be extended to 90. Quitting time can fluctuate between 3:42 to 5:30 P.M. depending on starting time and lunch break.

2. All employees will work during the core hours of 8 to 11:30 A.M., and 1:00 to 3:42 P.M.

3. Employees interested in using flextime for a certain week are required to schedule and post a notice by their desk the preceding

Friday. Copies of the schedule must be available to the employee's supervisor and the unit secretary.

4. Meetings will be scheduled when possible during core hours. The employee is responsible for attending meetings called outside of core hours.

After the flextime program was in operation for six months, Dave called a meeting to discuss progress. He began the meeting by expressing his concerns: "It appears that something isn't right. The latest figures show that less than 5 percent of our employees are using flextime. I'm disappointed. I'd like for you folks to survey your workers and get some feedback."

Gary, one of the production supervisors, held a feedback session with his workers several days after learning that Dave wanted feedback. Lisa, a manufacturing technician, offered these observations: "This flextime program is a joke. Flexibility to me means the ability to make decisions day by day, depending on my personal situation. Having to schedule my work time isn't flexibility in my dictionary. Unfortunately, I cannot schedule either my children's illnesses or baby-sitting conflicts."

Tom, a production specialist, said, "I must be one of that 5 percent who consistently uses flextime. I live close to work and my kids are still very young. It is therefore a good opportunity for me to have lunch with them. A ninety-minute lunch break is great."

Stan, another production supervisor, learned from his group that the workers don't want to do so much paperwork just to get half an hour of flexibility.

When the supervisors met again with Dave, Stan served as the spokesperson. He informed Dave, "After meeting with all our employees, we've concluded that our current flextime program isn't going to boost production or raise morale. It looks like we've set up a system to serve our convenience. We were too conservative in our approach. The program has to be changed."

Dave thanked the supervisors for their input and proposed that they meet to discuss a plan modification in two weeks. The group accepted the challenge.

1. What did the company do wrong in planning its flextime program?
2. What changes should be made in the program?
3. Is it possible that supervisors would generally have difficulty with a flextime program? Explain.
4. What is your reaction to Dave's contention that job satisfaction generally boosts productivity?

Source: Case researched by Edna H. Soltero, Rochester Institute of Technology, 1990.

Notes ───

1. John M. Ivancevich and Michael T. Matteson, *Organizational Behavior and Management* (Plano, TX: Business Publications, 1987), p. 65.

2. Stephen J. Motowidlo, "Does Job Satisfaction Lead to Consideration and Personal Sensitivity?" *Academy of Management Journal,* December 1984, p. 914.

3. Thomas S. Bateman and Dennis W. Organ, "Job Satisfaction and the Good Soldier: The Relationship Between Affect and Employee 'Citizenship'," *Academy of Management Journal,* December 1983, p. 588.

4. K. Scott Dow and G. Stephen Taylor, "An Examination of Conflicting Findings on the Relationship Between Job Satisfaction and Absenteeism: A Meta Analysis," *Academy of Management Journal,* September 1985, p. 608.

5. Charles L. Hulin, "Effects of Changes in Job Satisfaction Levels on Employee Turnover," *Journal of Applied Psychology,* April 1968, pp. 122–26.

6. Thomas I. Chacko, "Job and Life Satisfactions: A Causal Analysis of Their Relationships," *Academy of Management Journal,* March 1983, p. 167.

7. Marianne Tait, Margaret Youtz Padgett, and Timothy T. Baldwin, "Job and Life Satisfaction: A Reevaluation of the Strength of the Relationship and Gender Effects as a Function of the Date of the Study," *Journal of Applied Psychology,* June 1989, pp. 502–7.

8. Edwin A. Locke, "The Nature and Causes of Job Satisfaction," in *Handbook of Industrial and Organizational Psychology,* ed. Marvin D. Dunnette (New York: Wiley, 1986), p. 1328; Frederick Herzberg, "The Wise Old Turk," *Harvard Business Review,* September–October 1974, pp. 70–80.

9. Edward E. Lawler III and Lyman W. Porter, "The Effects of Performance on Satisfaction," *Industrial Relations,* October 1987, pp. 20–28.

10. William C. Byham, *Zapp!—The Lightening of Empowerment—How to Improve Quality, Productivity, and Employee Satisfaction* (Pittsburgh: Development Dimensions Incorporated, 1988).

11. Barry M. Staw and Jerry Ross, "Stability in the Midst of Change: A Dispositional Approach to Job Attitudes," *Journal of Applied Psychology,* August 1985, p. 471.

12. Richard D. Arvey and associates, "Job Satisfaction: Environmental and Genetic Components," *Journal of Applied Psychology,* April 1989, pp. 187–92.

13. This and the next two factors are credited to Robert A. Baron, *Understanding Human Relations: A Practical Guide to People at Work* (Newton, MA: Allyn & Bacon, 1985), pp. 315–16.

14. Baron, *Understanding Human Relations,* pp. 315—-16.

15. Ira Levin and Joseph P. Stokes, "Dispositional Approach to Job Satisfaction: Role of Negative Affectivity," *Journal of Applied Psychology,* October 1989, pp. 752–58.

16. F. K. Plous, Jr., "Redesigning Work: A Chicago Bank Eliminates the 'Paperwork Assembly Line'," *Personnel Administrator,* March 1987, p. 99.

17. John Chalykoff and Thomas A. Kochan, "Computer-Aided Monitoring: Its Influence on Employee Job Satisfaction and Turnover," *Personnel Psychology,* Winter 1989, p. 809.

18. Chalykoff and Kochan, "Computer-Aided Monitoring," p. 821.

19. Dorri Jacobs, "Maintaining Morale During and After Downsizing," April 1988, pp. 5–13.

20. W. Jack Duncan and J. Philip Feisal, "No Laughing Matter: Patterns of Humor in the Workplace," *Organizational Dynamics,* Spring 1989, pp. 18–30.

21. David J. Abramis, "Fun at Work," *Personnel Administrator,* November 1989, p. 70.

22. J. Carroll Swart, "Clerical Workers on Flexitime: A Survey of Three Industries," *Personnel,* April 1985, pp. 40–44.

23. Paul Bernstein, "The Ultimate in Flexitime: From Sweden, by Way of Volvo," *Personnel,* June 1988, p. 74.

24. Janina C. Latack and Lawrence W. Foster, "Implementation of Compressed Work Schedules: Participation and Job Redesign as Critical Factors for Employee Acceptance," *Personnel Psychology,* Spring 1985, pp. 75–92.

25. Spyros Economides, D. N. Reck, and Allen J. Schuh, "Longer Days and Shorter Weeks Improve Productivity," *Personnel Administrator,* May 1989, pp. 112–14.

26. Case example contributed by Don Buffum, Rochester Institute of Technology, 1990.

27. The advantages and disadvantages of telecommuting are from Andrew J. DuBrin and Janet Barnard, "Job Satisfaction and Productivity Consequences of Work-at-Home Programs," research in progress, 1991; "Telecommuting: Is Your Operation Ready?" *Research Institute Personal Report for the Executive,* July 15, 1986, pp. 4–5; Lynne F. McGee, "Setting Up Work at Home," *Personnel Administrator,* December 1988, pp. 58–62.

28. Eliza G. C. Collins, "A Company Without Offices," *Harvard Business Review,* January–February 1986, p. 127.

29. Renee Magid, *The Work and Family Challenge,* management briefing (New York: American Management Association, 1990), pp. 43–44.

30. Lois E. Tetrick and James M. LaRocco, "Understanding, Prediction, and Control as Moderators of the Relationships Between Perceived Stress, Satisfaction, and Psychological Well-Being," November 1987, p. 543.

Suggested Reading

BAKER, CAROLYN A. "Flex Your Benefits." *Personnel Journal,* May 1988, pp. 54–61.

BUNNING, RICHARD L. "Rewarding a Job Well Done." *Personnel Administrator,* January 1989, pp. 60–64.

FRYXELL, GERALD E., and GORDON, MICHAEL E. "Workplace Justice and Job Satisfaction as Predictors of Satisfaction with Union and Management." *Academy of Management Journal,* December 1989, pp. 851–56.

Iseri, Betty A. "Flexible Benefits: A Growing Option." *Personnel,* March 1990, pp. 30–32.

Landon, Lucy. "Pump Up Your Employees." *HRMagazine,* May 1990, pp. 34–37.

Newman, Stuart. "Telecommuters Bring the Office Home." *Management Review,* December 1989, pp. 40–43.

Olmsted, Barney, and Smith, Suzanne. *Creating a Flexible Workplace: How to Select and Manage Work Options.* New York: AMACOM, 1989.

Pierce, Jon L., Dunham, Randall B., and Barber, Alison E. *Alternative Work Schedules.* Needham Heights, MA: Allyn & Bacon, 1989.

Shaffer, Garnett Stokes. "Patterns of Work, and Nonwork Satisfaction." *Journal of Applied Psychology,* February 1987, pp. 115–24.

Sweeney, Paul D., McFarlin, Dean B., and Inderrieden, Edward J. "Using Relative Deprivation Theory to Explain Satisfaction with Income and Pay Level: A Multistudy Examination." *Academy of Management Journal,* June 1990, pp. 423–36.

5

Wellness
and Stress

LEARNING OBJECTIVES

After reading and studying this chapter and doing the exercises, you should be able to

1. Explain the meaning of wellness and identify strategies for achieving wellness.

2. Summarize the physiological, psychological, and behavioral symptoms of job stress.

3. Describe the worksite consequences of job stress.

4. Identify the major sources of stress related to factors within the individual.

5. Identify the major sources of stress related to factors within the job and organization.

6. Develop a strategy for managing stress within yourself.

7. Describe a few organizational methods of managing stress.

Overcoming the ravages of job stress is important today; in addition, considerable emphasis is now being placed on preventing illness and staying well. Well employees are not simply those who are not sick; they are vibrant, relatively happy, and able to cope with life's problems. A **wellness program** is a formalized approach to preventive health care. This explains why company-sponsored fitness and wellness programs are often referred to as *workplace health promotion programs*. By promoting health, these programs help prevent employees from developing physical and mental problems caused or aggravated by excessive stress.

A major challenge in achieving wellness is to understand and manage stress. George Vaillant, the Harvard research psychiatrist, contends that effective adaptation to stress permits us to live.[1] As the term is used here, **stress** is the internal reaction to any force perceived as a threat to disturb a person's equilibrium. If you perceive something to be dangerous or threatening, you will experience the bodily response known as stress. Even a positive event, like marriage or the birth of a child, can cause stress. The force bringing about the stress is the **stressor.**

Stress is often associated with strain, yet the two terms differ in an important way. **Strain** is the adverse effects of stress on an individual's mind, body, and actions. To add just one more complexity, stress is also tied in with **burnout,** a state of exhaustion stemming from long-term stress. Burnout is a set of behaviors that result from strain. Later in this chapter we will give separate attention to burnout. Keep this relationship in mind to sort out the key terms mentioned so far:

Stressors → stress → strain → burnout
Preventing and controlling stress → wellness

STRATEGIES FOR ACHIEVING WELLNESS

Achieving wellness is desirable in order to enhance both work and personal life. Wellness helps a person develop a positive self-image and ward off harmful amounts of stress. A useful and interesting way of understanding wellness is the **PACT model,** developed by Marjorie Blanchard.[2] According to this model, a well person has perspective, autonomy, connectedness, and tone.

Perspective means understanding the big picture in life. People with good perspective have a purpose and goals. They know where they are headed in life, yet they are still interested in the present. By keeping a good perspective, they do not blow out of proportion daily stresses (such as dealing with an angry customer).

Autonomy refers to feeling in control. Autonomous people have the skills and knowledge necessary to make choices, and can manage their daily activities to let them achieve goals set at different time periods.

Connectedness means having positive relationships with people, such as friends, family, and co-workers. A connected person also feels some attachment to his or her physical environment. Such a person might not consciously pollute the environment.

Tone is the condition that results when people exercise regularly, pay attention to sound nutrition, and practice stress management techniques (to be described later). People who are toned have high energy levels and positive feelings about their physical appearance. The activities in most company wellness programs center around achieving tone through exercise, improved diet, and stress management.

Wellness and Physical Fitness Programs

Company wellness and fitness programs are implemented at three levels of intensity and depth. Level I consists of awareness programs that include newsletters, health fairs, screening sessions, posters, flyers, and classes. These activities may not necessarily improve health or bring about changes in behavior; however, they are useful in making workers aware of specific consequences of unhealthful habits.

Level II programs bring about lifestyle modification by providing specific programs, such as physical conditioning and proper methods of performing physically demanding tasks. The programs may last several months or may be available on an ongoing basis. Level II programs are aimed at helping the employee develop lifelong healthy habits, and may use behavior modification to achieve their goal. Workers are provided with the knowledge to help change negative health habits.

Level III programs attempt to create an environment that helps workers sustain their healthy lifestyles and behaviors. A Level III program fosters participation in a healthy lifestyle by providing a fitness center at the workplace, making healthy food available, and removing unhealthy temptations (such as candy or soft drink machines). Although a Level III program could be conducted independently, it is usually an outgrowth of ongoing Level I and II programs.[3]

An evaluation of a number of fitness and wellness programs concluded that participating in them can increase fitness and reduce risk factors for coronary heart disease. These programs also are effective in reducing absenteeism, injuries, and health care costs. Such gains have been achieved mostly in white-collar settings, with an average participation rate of only 15 to 30 percent of eligible employees.[4] The accompanying box describes a Level II program and the results it achieved.

THE FITNESS CENTER AT ENZON

ENZON Inc., a leader in drug-delivery technology, faced a formidable challenge. The company wanted to build teamwork while at the same time decrease operating expenses, particularly its rapidly escalating health insurance costs. To achieve this twin goal, all 100 employees were enlisted to form a partnership with management in building a healthy staff and reducing health care expenses.

A 2,000-square-foot employee fitness center, located on company premises, was the centerpiece of their plan. Open to all employees, it includes a sixteen-unit circuit weight-training station, two computerized treadmills, two computerized bicycles, one computerized rowing machine, and a stair-climbing machine. The weights and aerobic equipment are located in a room lined with mirrors and glass. The facility includes a spring water cooler and a refrigerator for natural soda and fruit juice. Locker rooms with full shower facilities are located on site. The fitness center is open and supervised from 6:30 to 8:30 A.M., 11:30 A.M. to 2:30 P.M., and 4:30 to 7:00 P.M., Monday through Friday.

Before employees began the program, a fitness coordinator tested them for their fitness levels. Among the specific tests are cardiovascular condition, flexibility, percentage of body fat, muscular strength, and abdominal strength. Based on the results, a fitness program was designed for each participant.

The wellness aspect of the program includes lectures on such subjects as crime awareness, stress management, and nutrition. ENZON also offers its employees "freedom from smoking" workshops. Cholesterol testing, blood pressure screening, and recreational events are also part of the fitness program.

ENZON management believes that its wellness center has both improved the quality of life at the company and reduced certain expenses. Specific benefits noted include:

a more productive workforce,

less absenteeism,

healthy families and an emotionally stable workforce,

improved recruiting capabilities,

better teamwork,

fewer hospital admissions,

fewer surgeries,

fewer insurance claims,

fewer accidents,

reduced turnover.

Source: As reported in Neil C. Torino, "An Ounce of Prevention," *Human Resources Forum,* April 1990, pp. 1–3.

THE SYMPTOMS AND CONSEQUENCES OF STRESS

If you experience stress, you display certain signs or symptoms indicating that you are trying to cope with a stressor. These symptoms can also be considered the consequence of stress. With few exceptions, you experience these symptoms only if you perceive the force to be threatening or challenging. An important exception is the stress associated with physical factors, such as disease. For example, an overdose of radiation will trigger a stress response in your body, even if you are not aware of the presence of radiation. The symptoms and consequences of job stress are organized here into five categories: physiological, psychological, behavioral, sex differ-ences, and job performance.

Physiological Symptoms and Consequences

The body's physiological and chemical battle against the stressor is the **fight-or-flight response.** The person tries to cope with the adversity in a head-on battle or tries to flee the scene. The physiological changes within the body are virtually identical for different stressors. All types of stressors produce a chemical response within the body, which in turn produces short-term physiological changes.

Among the most common reactions are increases in heart rate, blood pressure, blood glucose, and blood clotting. The best-documented fact about physiological stress symptoms is that stressful life events, such as divorce or incurring a large debt, are associated with elevated cholesterol and blood pressure levels.[5] To help recognize some of these stress symptoms, recall your internal bodily sensations the last time you were in an automobile accident or heard some wonderful news.

If stress is continuous and accompanied by these short-term physiological changes, certain annoying or even life-threatening conditions can occur. Among them are heart attacks, strokes, hypertension (high blood pressure), increased cholesterol level, migraine headaches, skin rashes, ulcers, allergies, and colitis.

Unfortunately, prolonged stress also leads to a weakening of the body's immune system, which makes recuperation from illness difficult.[6] People experiencing emotional stress may have difficulty shaking a common cold or recovering from pneumonia. Accumulating evidence is also beginning to show that some forms of cancer, including leukemia and lymphomas, are related to prolonged stress reactions.[7] In general, any disorder classified as *psychosomatic* is precipitated by emotional stress.

Although most of the physiological consequences of stress described here are negative, the right amount of stress prepares us for meeting difficult challenges and spurs us toward peak performance. This issue is explored in the section on stress and job performance.

Psychological Symptoms and Consequences

The psychological or emotional symptoms of stress cover a wide range and show substantial individual differences. Much depends upon the person's cognitive evaluation of the situation. Assume that two people are faced with the same stressor: The company decides to fire both in order to reduce costs. Person A may be triggered into a depressed mood, mixed with feelings of anger and self-blame. Person B may be triggered into a surge of enthusiasm, mixed with feelings of independence and relief. He or she races home and announces, "Hooray, I've finally found the right excuse to start my own business."

Among the more frequent psychological consequences of stress are tension, anxiety, discouragement, boredom, complaints about bodily problems, prolonged fatigue, feelings of hopelessness, and various kinds of defensive thinking and behavior. People may also experience disturbed inner states as a result of intense or prolonged stress. Here we will describe three of the major psychological consequences of stress, recognizing that psychological and behavioral responses to stress overlap.

Emotion. When faced with stress, people typically react with some form of emotional response. Among the most significant emotional patterns for job-related behavior are anger, fear, and anxiety. The expression of these emotions can be both direct and indirect. A manager who has been demoted may express his anger directly by telling other people in the company how thoughtless the company has become. He may express his anger indirectly by taking an inordinately long time to learn his new job and making frequent errors in the process.

Fear is displayed in response to several job-related stresses. In times of recession many people fear losing their jobs. Their fear reaction typically is to become more and more hesitant to take risks that involve innovative solutions to problems. People fear making mistakes because they fear the resulting penalty. When threats of job loss are high, people fear being fired as a consequence of having made a mistake.

Anxiety is known as a feeling of apprehension and fearfulness in the absence of specific danger. People experience anxiety when the source of stress is felt, but its implications are not exactly known. A middle manager in a bank talked about his anxiety this way:

> I'm not sure what all these changes mean to me personally, but they have made me so tense that my stomach is churning. I know the bank is trying to promote more women into officer positions. That must mean that fewer men will be promoted, but nobody has said that for sure. Also, a good number of New York City banks have moved into our area. That could have some bad implications for us, but I have seen no problems yet.

Emotional disorder. The vast majority of people have the resilience to handle work pressures without becoming so distressed or disturbed that they succumb to emotional illness. A minority of people, perhaps one in ten, react to severe job pressures by experiencing an emotional disorder. Many of these people were in fragile emotional shape before they experienced the severe job stress. Unfortunately, the job pressure became the "last straw" that brought about emotional disorder. On balance, it should be kept in mind that some jobs—such as air traffic controller or emergency medic—are bad for your mental health.

Behavioral Symptoms and Consequences

Psychological or emotional symptoms of job stress indicate how people think and feel when placed under job pressures. These symptoms often lead to actual behavior that is of particular concern to the student of human relations in organizations. Among the more frequently observed behavioral consequences of job stress are the following:

- Agitation, restlessness, and other overt signs of tension, including moving your legs back and forth toward each other while seated at a meeting.
- Forgetting to carry out routine activities such as answering mail or returning telephone calls.
- Accident proneness exhibited by an employee who has a good safety record in the past, or an increased accident frequency experienced by an employee who is already known to be accident prone.
- Drastic changes in eating habits, including decreased or increased food consumption. Under heavy stress, some people become junk food addicts.
- Increased cigarette smoking, coffee drinking, alcohol consumption, and use of illegal drugs.
- Increased use of prescription (legal) drugs, such as tranquilizers and amphetamines, including diet pills.
- Panic-type behavior, such as making impulsive decisions.
- Errors in concentration and judgment.

This list is a sampling of the behavioral consequences of job stress. Hundreds of symptoms are possible. When workers are placed under too much stress, it tends to exaggerate their weakest tendencies. For instance, a person with a strong temper who usually keeps cool under pressure may throw a tantrum when faced with a crisis.

Sex Differences in Stress Symptoms

About a dozen scientific studies have investigated whether men and women tend to have different stress symptoms. The most pronounced difference is that women tend to exhibit symptoms of low emotional well-being to a greater extent than men do. For instance, women are more likely to get depressed and also report higher rates of emotional discomfort.

In response to stress, men are more likely to suffer from coronary heart disease, cirrhosis of the liver, suicide, and alcoholism. Yet minor physical ailments, such as headaches, dizziness, and stomach upsets, are reported to be more prevalent in women than men. The overall evidence suggests that men are more prone to serious and incapacitating illness in response to stress. Women more often tend to suffer from less severe psychological problems, yet they have a greater incidence of acute symptoms.[8]

Job Performance Consequences

Few people can escape work stress. This is fortunate, because escaping all forms of stress would be undesirable. An optimum amount of stress exists for most people and most tasks. It is referred to as **eustress,** or positive stress. The inverted J-shaped relationship shown in Figure 5–1 depicts this relationship. In most situations, job performance tends to be best under low to moderate amounts of ordinary stress.

Too much stress makes people temporarily ineffective because they may become distracted or choke. This negative type of stress is called **distress.** Mental health workers estimate that as many as 15 percent of executives and managers suffer from critical levels of job stress that will eventually affect their job performance.[9] Similarly, stress-related disorders now account for 15 percent of all occupational disease claims.[10] Too little stress, on the other hand, tends to make people lethargic and inattentive.

Previously it was believed that performance improves steadily as stress is increased, until the stress becomes too intense. It is now believed that performance decreases more rapidly as stress increases. The wrong type of stressor can also produce stress that rarely improves job performance, even in small doses. Support for this point was obtained from research conducted with 200 employees in four firms. The study indicated that negative stress was generally associated with lowered productivity. Also, an optimal level of negative stress was not found.[11] Another study also found that negative stress, such as time urgency, interfered with solving complex problems.[12]

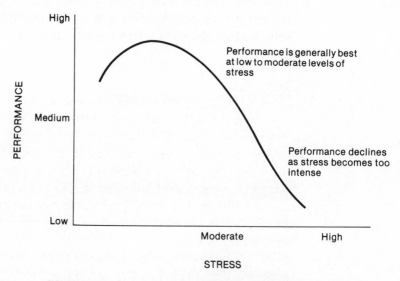

FIGURE 5–1 The Short-term Relationship Between Stress and Job Performance

A conclusion to consider is that for most people, challenge and excitement improve job performance. Irritation and threatening events, such as an intimidating boss, generally lower performance.

INDIVIDUAL SOURCES OF STRESS

People often experience job stress based primarily upon their personalities, or their perceptions of situations, values, and goals. Here we will describe a sampling of individual sources of negative job stress: discrepancy between reality and expectations, Type A behavior, belief in external locus of control, heavy family and personal demands, dislike for rules and regulations, limited tolerance for ambiguity, and negative lifestyle factors.

Discrepancy Between Reality and Expectations

Stress can develop when a person's expectations (what is wanted) and reality (what the person has) are too far apart.[13] This stressor often arises with respect to career aspirations. Approximately 1 percent of jobs in any firm are truly executive (policymaking) positions. Thus only a small minority of people who aspire to become executives can be satisfied. The result is a large number of frustrated, dissatisfied people who suffer from the stress of disappointed expectations. Another problem is that many organizations today are reducing the number of managerial positions, making it even more difficult to be promoted.

The stress created by not becoming wealthy and powerful is virtually a pure case of culturally induced stress. With the current trend of people seeking self-fulfillment through work and a high quality of life in general, it is possible that this type of job stress may be on the decline. The leveling off of boom times throughout the world has also had a dampening effect on the career expectations of many young people. Frustrated ambitions are less likely to happen when career expectations are modest.

Type A Behavior

A person who exhibits **Type A behavior** is demanding, impatient, and overstriving, and therefore prone to distress. Type A behavior has two main components. One is a tendency to try to accomplish too many things in too little time. This leads the Type A individual to be impatient and demanding. The other component is free-floating hostility. Because of their sense of urgency and hostility, these people are irritated by trivial things. On the job, people with Type A behavior are aggressive and hard-working. Off the job, they keep themselves preoccupied with all kinds of errands to run and things to do.

Type A personalities frequently have cardiac diseases (such as heart attacks and strokes) at an early age. But not every hard-working and impatient individual is prone to severe stress disorder. Hard chargers who like what they are doing—including many top executives—are remarkably healthy and often outlive less competitive people. A key factor is that these people are not particularly hostile. Being hostile is a bigger contributor to heart disease than being impatient is. One approach to lowering the risk for heart disease is to learn to become less hostile and more trusting.[14]

Belief in External Locus of Control

If you believe that your fate is controlled more by external than internal forces, you are probably more susceptible to stress. People with an **external locus of control** believe that external forces control their fate. Conversely, people with an **internal locus of control** believe that fate is pretty much under their control.

The link between locus of control and stress works in this manner: If people believe they can control adverse forces, they are less prone to the stressor of worrying about them. For example, if you believe that you can always find a job, you will worry less about unemployment. At the same time, the person who believes in an internal locus of control usually experiences a higher level of job satisfaction.[15] Work is less stressful and more satisfying when you perceive it to be under your control.

What about your locus of control? Do you believe it to be internal? Or is it external?

Heavy Family and Personal Demands

People who place a high premium on leading a full family and personal life often find themselves in conflict between work and home life. The conflict typically leads to negative job stress.[16] In order to prosper in one's career, some sacrifices are often necessary in terms of personal life. Only the truly well-organized individual can juggle things sufficiently well to perform well both at work and at home. The constant tugging between the two creates stress for many people. The stronger the value the person places on both areas of life, the greater the potential conflict and stress.

Dislike for Rules and Regulations

Another way of creating stress for yourself in a large organization is to develop an intense dislike for rules and regulations. The pattern of rebelling against rules and regulations within a bureaucracy has been labeled bureautic (not bureaucratic) behavior. Such people come to be seen as malcontents by others in the firm.[17] The reason bureautic personalities face so much stress is that they are continually fighting rules and regulations.

Limited Tolerance for Ambiguity

A **limited tolerance for ambiguity** is a tendency to be readily frustrated when situations and tasks are poorly defined. People with a limited tolerance for ambiguity are prone to frustration and stress because job responsibilities are often ambiguous. For instance, a staff specialist might be told by the boss: "Take care of things while I'm out of town." A command of this type can be interpreted in many ways. (More will be said about ambiguous instructions in our discussion of role ambiguity later in the chapter.)

The combination of a Type A personality and limited tolerance for ambiguity increases the chances of distress. A recent study demonstrated that for Type A individuals, an increase in ambiguity is related to an increase in systolic blood pressure, diastolic blood pressure, and triglyceride levels.[18] (Triglyceride is tied in with fatty acids in the arteries that can contribute to heart disease.)

Negative Lifestyle Factors

A **negative lifestyle factor** is any behavior that predisposes one to stress, such as poor eating and exercise habits and heavy consumption of caffeine, alcohol, and other drugs. People who accumulate these negative lifestyle factors are predisposed to work stress.[19] The reason is that they are in a weakened physical and mental condition. An employee who said he was "freaking out from his job" was referred to the company physician. The physician made these observations about the employee:

> Little wonder that Mr. Watkins displays stress symptoms. He is forty pounds overweight, smokes one pack of cigarettes per day, ingests five diet soft drinks during the day, and backs that up with a six-pack of beer each night. His favorite foods all contain a high percentage of animal fat. If he doesn't change his lifestyle, any unusual job pressures may lead him to a heart attack.

ORGANIZATIONAL SOURCES OF STRESS

In many instances, the employer must take the primary blame for creating job stress. We use the word *primary* because neither the individual nor the organizational is fully to blame when the person experiences stress. A worker under stress usually has the option to speak up and deal with the problem in a constructive manner. Here we describe ten frequently observed organizational sources of stress, as noted in Figure 5–2.

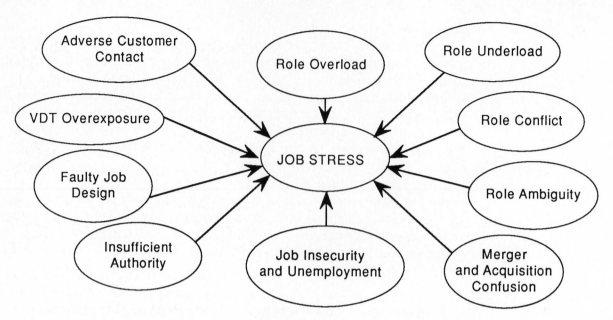

FIGURE 5-2 Frequently Observed Organizational Stressors

Role Overload

Role overload is a burdensome workload. It can create stress for an individual in two ways. First, the person may accumulate fatigue and thus be less able to tolerate annoyances and irritations. Think of how much easier it is to become provoked over a minor incident when you lack proper rest. Second, a person subject to exorbitant work demands may feel perpetually behind schedule, which in itself creates an uncomfortable, stressful feeling.

Heavy work demands are considered part of an executive's life. However, many people of lower rank and income are also asked to give up much of their personal freedom and work under continuous pressure during working hours.

Role Underload

A major stressor facing people early in their careers is **role underload,** having too little work to perform. The most general form of underutilization takes place when an employee is given tasks to perform that he or she thinks could be performed by somebody of less education and training. Many employees in professional and technical jobs lament, "Why did they hire a business graduate to do this job? Any clerk could do it equally well."

Role underload creates stress because it frustrates one's desire to make a contribution to the organization. Also, role underload is a stressor because it creates ambiguity. The underutilized person may wonder, "What am I doing here? Why was I hired? Doesn't the company think I can make a contribution?"

Role Conflict

A major organizational stressor is **role conflict,** having to choose between competing demands or expectations. If you comply with one aspect of a role, compliance with the other is more difficult. A basic example would be receiving contradictory orders from two people above you in the organization. Four types of role conflict have been identified:[20]

Intrasender conflict occurs when one person asks you to accomplish two objectives that are in apparent conflict. If your boss asked you to hurry up and finish your work but also decrease your mistakes, you would experience this type of conflict (plus perhaps a headache!).

Intersender conflict occurs when two or more senders give you incompatible directions. Your immediate superior may want you to complete a crash project on time, but company policy temporarily prohibits authorizing overtime payments to clerical help.

Interrole conflict results when two different roles that you play are in conflict. Your company may expect you to travel 50 percent of the time, while your spouse threatens a divorce if you travel over 25 percent of the time.

Person-role conflict occurs when the role(s) your organization expects you to occupy are in conflict with your basic values. Your company may ask you to fire substandard performers, but this could be in conflict with your humanistic values.

Role Ambiguity

Role ambiguity is a condition in which the job holder receives confusing or poorly defined expectations. Workers in all kinds and sizes of organizations are often placed in a situation where job responsibilities are sloppily defined. As we mentioned in the discussion about individual sources of stress, many people become anxious when faced with role ambiguity. One reason is that being out of control is a stressor. If you lack a clear picture of what you should be doing, it is difficult to get your job under control. Here is a representative example of role ambiguity:

> A man was hired into a management-training program and given the elegant title of "assistant to the general manager." After three days of reading company manuals and taking plant tours, he pressed for an explanation of what he was supposed to be doing in the assignment. His boss told him, "Just try to make yourself useful. I'll be going out of town for two weeks. If you have any questions, ask my secretary for help."

Merger and Acquisition Confusion

A special case of role ambiguity is the confusion that often occurs surrounding corporate mergers and acquisitions. (Worry about job loss, as described following, is also present.) After a corporate merger, employees are often confused about reporting relationships, which policies to follow, handling customer service problems, and so forth. Confusion also occurs because it becomes difficult to get some types of work accomplished after the merger is completed. Many people spend considerable amounts of time looking for new jobs and playing politics in order to cope with the organizational changes. As a result, they have less time to coordinate with and help other workers.[21]

Job Insecurity and Unemployment

People have traditionally worried about losing their jobs because of budget cuts and automation. Two current sources of job insecurity are layoffs caused by mergers and acquisitions, and the quest for "lean" organizations. Layoffs often occur after one firm acquires or merges with another for two primary reasons: (1) The merged organization will have duplicate positions, such as two vice presidents of finance, and (2) the organization may have to trim the payroll in order to save money. Major expenses involved in purchasing another firm include stock purchases and legal fees.

A **lean organization** is one in which there is a minimum of nonessential functions and employees. Figuratively, the "fat" has been trimmed from the firm. In order to achieve leanness, many large firms have laid off as much as 30 percent of their workforce. Worrying about whether they will become one of the next to be laid off or asked to retire early becomes a stressor for many workers.

Unemployment itself generates more stress than does the threat of job insecurity. Unemployed people, in comparison to employed people, have much higher rates of depression, suicide, homicide, child abuse, and spouse abuse. One study of joblessness showed that people unable to find jobs express low self-esteem, personal powerlessness, and many forms of psychosomatic distress.[22] Part of the problem is that the identity of many people is related to their occupation. Being unemployed is thus a blow to their self-perception.

The stressful nature of unemployment is further illustrated by **early executive mortality,** a tendency for recently retired executives to die much sooner than expected. A psychiatrist who has studied post-retirement executive deaths contends that "executives are dying not with their boots on, but with their retirement plans clutched in their hands."[23]

Insufficient Authority

An axiom of management is that people need the right kind and amount of authority to accomplish their jobs. If people do not have enough authority to carry out their assigned tasks, the situation can be stressful. Imagine yourself as a supervisor given a job to accomplish in a short period of time. You will be held responsible if you fail, but you are not given sufficient authority to work your subordinates overtime or hire additional help.

If you are conscientious, or worried about your job, the situation will act as a stressor.

Faulty Job Design

Another important source of job stress centers around flaws within the design of jobs. The job of air traffic controller, for example, is widely recognized as a stress inducer. To illustrate, each air traffic controller at O'Hare airport in Chicago is responsible for landing a plane every two minutes. Simultaneously, the controller must monitor a half dozen others on the screen. Since the pressures are so great, controllers are allowed to work only ninety consecutive minutes during peak hours. Despite these precautions, turnover is high, tenure is short, and psychosomatic disorders, such as ulcers and high blood pressure, are epidemic.[24]

VDT Overexposure

A type of faulty job design deserving separate mention is an unintended consequence of computerization. Working with computers can lead to **VDT stress,** an adverse physical and psychological reaction to prolonged work at video display terminals. Because of continuous work flow and terminal design, some VDT operators may perform as many as 10,000 keyboard strokes per hour. Such a rate places severe strain on hand and wrist muscles, often leading to repetitive motion disorders. Additional symptoms often reported by VDT workers after long hours of operation include headaches; neck/aches; fatigue; hot, tired, and watery eyes; and blurred vision; and backaches.[25]

Adding to the impact of VDT stress is the controversy about whether prolonged exposure to computer monitors can contribute to miscarriages and birth defects. The National Institute of Safety and Health contends that VDTs *do not* emit unsafe levels of electromagnetic radiation (a possible contributor to miscarriages).[26]

Much of VDT stress can be prevented by VDT operators taking frequent rest breaks and using a well-designed combination of work table, chair, and video display terminal. Being comfortable while working prevents much physical strain. Along these lines, San Francisco enacted a bill in 1991 regulating the use of VDTs. Employers with more than fifteen employees must supply antiglare shields, wrist rests, and adjustable chairs. Employees required to work four or more hours will be authorized to take a fifteen-minute rest break every two hours.

Adverse Customer Interaction

Interactions with unpleasant customers can be a major stressor, as revealed by a study of ninety-three employees. Stressful events frequently cited were customers losing control, using profanity, badgering and harassing employees, and lying. The employees interviewed said that these adverse customer interactions affected the quality of their work environment.[27] Part of the problem is that the sales associate often feels helpless when placed in conflict with a customer. Management declares that "the customer is always right." Furthermore, the store manager usually sides with the customer in a dispute with the sales associate.

JOB BURNOUT: ONE CONSEQUENCE OF LONG-TERM STRESS

Job burnout is a condition of emotional, mental, and physical exhaustion, along with cynicism toward work, in response to long-term stressors. It is the final stage of an adverse reaction to stress. Burnout sufferers experience physical symptoms such as lingering colds, headaches, backaches, sleep problems, complexion problems, and stomach distress. Mental and emotional symptoms of burnout include cynicism, irritation, frustration, procrastination, and difficulties in concentration.

Burnout was originally observed primarily among people helpers, such as nurses, social workers, and police workers. It then became apparent that people in almost any occupation could develop burnout. Conscientiousness and perfectionism contribute to burnout. If you strive for perfection, you stand a good chance of being disappointed about not achieving everything. Organizations also play a role in contributing to burnout. If your efforts go unappreciated and you are given very little emotional support, your chances for burnout increase.

Before reading about burnout, answer the burnout checklist shown in Figure 5–3. The remainder of our discussion about burnout concerns the behavior of burnout victims and tactics for managing burnout.

Behaviors Associated with Burnout

Several burnout symptoms have already been mentioned. Three major behavioral patterns indicate that burnout is present.[28]

1. *Emotional, mental, and physical exhaustion.* Burnout victims are exhausted. When asked how they feel, these people typically answer that they feel drained or used up, at the end of their rope, physically fatigued. Often the burnout victim dreads going to work even though he or she was once idealistic about what could be accomplished.

2. *Withdrawing from people.* Burnout victims try to cope with emotional exhaustion by becoming less personally involved with co-workers. The burned-out employee develops a detached air, becomes

Directions: Check each of the following statements that generally or usually applies to you.

1. I feel tired much more frequently than I used to. ____
2. I get very irritated at people lately. ____
3. I suffer from a number of annoying physical problems, such as neckaches and backaches. ✓ ____
4. I often feel that I am losing control of my life. ____
5. I'm feeling pretty depressed these days. ____
6. I get down on myself too often. ____
7. My life seems to be at a dead end. ____
8. My enthusiasm for life has gone way down. ____
9. I'm tired of dealing with the same old problems. ____
10. I've pretty much withdrawn from friends and family. ____
11. Not much seems humorous to me anymore. ____
12. There's really nothing for me to look forward to at work or at school. ____
13. It's difficult for me to care about what's going on in the world outside. ____
14. My spark is gone. ____
15. I know that I have a problem, but I just don't have the energy to do anything about it. ____
16. I usually dread going to work or school. ____
17. My friends say that my temper is getting pretty short. ____
18. I don't get nearly enough appreciation from my boss. ____
19. I've begun to feel sorry for myself. ____
20. I find it difficult to get out of bed in the morning. ____

Interpretation: The more of these statements that apply to you, the more likely it is that you are experiencing burnout. If you checked fifteen or more of these statements, it would be helpful to discuss your feelings with a mental health professional.

FIGURE 5–3 The Burnout Checklist

cynical of relationships with others, and feels callous toward others and the organization.

3. *Low personal accomplishment.* The final aspect of burnout is a feeling of low personal accomplishment. The once idealistic employee begins to realize that there are too many barriers to accomplishing what needs to be done. Often he or she lacks the energy to perform satisfactorily. Managers suffering from burnout hurt the organization because they create a ripple effect, spreading burnout to subordinates.

INDIVIDUAL METHODS OF STRESS MANAGEMENT

Because stress is such a widespread problem, many techniques have been used to help reduce or prevent stress. The distinction between methods of reducing and preventing stress is not clear-cut. For example, proponents of physical exercise as a way of managing stress and its concomitant tension say that physical conditioning not only reduces stress, but gives you a way of life that helps you prevent stress. Methods of stress management in the control of the individual vary from highly specific techniques (such as the relaxation response) to more global methods that reflect a lifestyle. Among the latter would be maintaining a diet that is free of caffeine, alcohol, excessive sugar, and non-nutritious ("junk") food.

In this section we describe methods of stress management that are basically in control of the individual. Two of these methods, exercise and diet, have already been mentioned in relation to wellness and need not be repeated. In the following section our attention turns to the organization's role in stress management.

Identify Your Own Stress Signals

An effective program of stress management begins with self-awareness. Midge Wilson, a clinical psychologist, urges that you learn to identify your own particular reactions to stress. Take note of their intensity as well as the time of the day when the symptoms occur. Often the mere act of keeping a record of stress symptoms lessens their incidence and severity. It is likely that this phenomenon is related to the realization that you are starting to take charge of your health.

Once you have learned to pick up warning signs, the next step is to identify *what* and *how* you were thinking and feeling prior to the onset of the symptoms. For example, if your boss tells you that your report is needed in a hurry you may begin to fret. What usually triggers stress reactions is your own stream of negative thoughts, such as, "I will be criticized if this report isn't finished on time," or, "If this report isn't perfect, I'll be fired."

It is crucial to learn how to terminate unproductive, worrisome thoughts. A recommended technique is that of thought-stopping, or canceling. It works this way: Choose either the term "stop" or "cancel" and quietly but emphatically repeat it whenever you catch yourself engaging in anxiety-provoking thought. At first, this may be as many as fifty to 100 times per day.[29]

Although being aware of stress signals is important, too much self-focused attention can be a problem. You may become oversensitive to potential stress symptoms, to the point of becoming a hypochondriac.[30]

Eliminate or Modify the Stressor

Underlying any approach to reducing stress is this key principle. Until you take constructive action about reducing stress itself or removing the causes of stress, you will continue to suffer. One value of tranquilizing mediation is that it calms down a person enough so that he or she can deal constructively with the source of stress.

At times, the first step taken to overcome a source of stress or to reduce the discomfort of stress may seem modest. However, the fact that you are now working toward a solution to your problem may make you feel better about the problem. To illustrate, if you find that working Saturday mornings is creating problems between you and your spouse, it behooves you to deal constructively with that problem. Discuss the problem with your boss and/or your spouse. One man facing this problem spoke to his supervisor and was pleased to learn that he could substitute working late on Thursday nights for his Saturday assignment.

Improve Your Work Habits

People typically experience job stress when they feel they are losing, or have lost, control of their work assignments. Perhaps you are familiar with the distress associated with the feeling that you are hopelessly behind schedule on several important tasks. Conscientious people, in particular, experience distress when they cannot get their work under control. Improving your work habits and time management will help you relieve this source of stress. Chapter 18 is devoted entirely to work habit improvement and time management.

Everyday Methods of Relaxation

The simple expedient of learning to relax is an important method of reducing the tensions brought about by both positive and negative stress. A sample of everyday suggestions for relaxing is presented in Table 5–1. If you can accomplish these, you may not need formal methods of tension reduction, such as tranquilizing medication or biofeedback training.

The Relaxation Response

The **relaxation response (RR)** is a bodily reaction in which you experience a slower respiration rate and heart rate, lowered blood pressure, and lowered metabolism. The response can be brought about in several ways, including meditation, exercise, or prayer. By practicing the RR, you can counteract the fight-or-flight response associated with stress.[31]

TABLE 5–1   Everyday suggestions for relaxation

1. Have at least one brief idle period every day.
2. Talk over problems with a friend.
3. Take a nap when facing heavy pressures.
4. Have a good laugh (laughter is an excellent tension reducer).
5. Smile at least five minutes every day.
6. Concentrate intensely on your work or reading, or on a sport or hobby (concentration is a natural tension reducer).
7. Avoid becoming stressed about things over which you have no control.
8. Breathe deeply, and between inhaling and exhaling, tell yourself you can cope with the situation.
9. When feeling tight, focus on a specific muscle and attempt to loosen it by gently moving that part of the body.
10. Have a quiet place or retreat at home.
11. When feeling stressed, visualize yourself in an unusually pleasant situation.
12. Take a leisurely vacation during which virtually every moment is not programmed.
13. Finish something you have started, however small. Accomplishing almost anything reduces some stress.
14. Stop drinking so many caffeinated or alcoholic beverages. Try fruit juice or water instead.
15. Stop to smell the flowers, make friends with a preschool child, or play with a kitten or puppy.
16. Strive to do a good job, but not a perfect job.
17. Become well organized and get your work under control.
18. Hug somebody you like today.

According to cardiologist Herbert Benson, four things are necessary to practice the RR: a quiet environment, an object to focus on, a passive attitude, and a comfortable position. The RR is to be practiced ten to twenty minutes, twice a day. To evoke the relaxation response, Benson advises: "Close your eyes. Relax. Concentrate on one word or prayer. If other thoughts come to mind, be passive, and return to the repetition."[32]

Transcendental Meditation

An old but still widely practiced relaxation technique is **transcendental meditation (TM),** a process of establishing a physiological state of deep rest. The TM technique is relatively simple, once learned. It consists of getting into a comfortable upright position, closing the eyes, and relaxing for twenty minutes in the morning and evening. The mind is allowed to drift, with no effort or control required. During TM the mind focuses on what is known as a mantra, a sound assigned to the meditator by the teacher. The mantra takes the form of a relaxing sound such as "om."

At its best, TM produces deep rest and relaxation. The meditator shows distinct physiological changes, including a decrease in heart and respiratory rate and lower bodily metabolism. Meditators frequently note that they feel more relaxed or less hurried than before they began to meditate.

TM reached fad proportions in the 1960s and 1970s. It has now stabilized as an accepted technique for reducing employee health problems. A dramatic example of the contribution of TM is the experience of a Detroit chemical company. Impressed with his personal experiences with TM, the president encouraged his employees to meditate. During a three-year period, absenteeism among those practicing TM fell by 85 percent, and sick days among those workers dropped by 30 percent.[33]

Rehearsal of the Stressful Situation

Imagine yourself having the unpleasant task of having to resign from one job in order to take a better one. You are tense, and your tension level increases as the day progresses. (You have already tried the relaxation response, but you still have butterflies!) One approach to relaxing enough to handle this situation is to rehearse this scenario mentally. Most important, rehearse your opening line, which might be something like, "Scott, I've asked to see you to discuss something very important," or "Scott, the company has been very nice to me, but I've decided to make an important change in my life."

It is also helpful to anticipate other aspects of the scenario, such as what you would do if Scott told you that he would not accept your resignation. Or worse, what you would say if Scott turned on you and began to call you ungrateful and unappreciative?

Choosing the Best Stress Management Technique

A logical question at this point is whether different stress management techniques are particularly helpful for different people or different stressors. A general answer to this question is not yet available. Nevertheless, we do know that not all techniques work equally well for everybody. For instance, many impatient individuals would find it tension-provoking to disrupt their work by practicing transcendental meditation or the relaxation response. Of perhaps greater significance, relaxation techniques in general may be harmful for some people. Several reports indicate that some people become more anxious or tense when they try to relax. Among their symptoms are restlessness, profuse perspiration, trembling, and rapid breathing.[34]

The best general rule is to try different stress management techniques until you find one that is effective. For instance, you might find attacking the stressor much more useful than the relaxation response. If one technique decreases your symptoms to your satisfaction, use it again. Since most stress techniques take time to learn, give each one a fair trial. If it does not work for you, move on to another.

ORGANIZATIONAL METHODS OF STRESS MANAGEMENT

Employers have an important responsibility for reducing and preventing job stress and burnout. It is also part of management's responsibility to create enough stress in the job environment to keep employees challenged and stimulated. Bored employees are often both unhappy and unproductive. In keeping with the major emphasis of this chapter, we will describe several general and specific strategies for reducing and preventing stress in addition to wellness and fitness programs.

Practice Good Human Resource Management

It has been noted that effective stress management essentially boils down to good human resource management.[35] What constitutes good human resource (or personnel) management is a book-length subject in itself. Human resource programs include those for employee selection, training, compensation, motivation, and assistance with personal problems (described following). Any one of these programs, properly administered, will help prevent and sometimes reduce stress. For instance, if the right employee is selected for a job, he or she will perform well. Good performance, in turn, helps prevent the stress stemming from job dissatisfaction and feelings of self-doubt.

Managers outside the human resource department can also help reduce and prevent stress by practicing good management. One approach would be to clarify responsibilities. Many forms of job stress are created by ambiguity about what employees are supposed to be doing. A study of burnout provides another example of how good management can reduce the consequences of stress. It was shown that employees treated with consideration by supervisors were less likely to develop burnout.[36] (Consideration in this context refers to such behaviors as listening to employees and giving them positive feedback.)

Good communication helps reduce stress in such ways as clarifying job responsibilities and encouraging employees to talk over their problems. Also, misunderstandings are reduced, which leads to less stress caused by conflict.

Modifying the Organization Structure

Rearranging or modifying the organizational structure can sometimes reduce and prevent stress. The object is to redesign the structure so that the stressful elements in a job are reduced to a healthy level. One basic example would be to reduce the span of control (number of direct subordinates) of a manager who was overwhelmed with dealing with so many subordinates. The establishment of a complaint department also helps reduce stress for employees who previously had to deal directly with irate customers. Now all complaints are channeled through one thick-skinned employee.

Participative Decision Making

Some employees find it stressful to be left out of important decisions that directly affect their welfare. Therefore another managerial action capable of reducing stress reactions in some employees is the use of participative decision making (PDM). A caution is that participation in routine and trivial decisions is transparent to employees and might tend to increase, not decrease, job stress.[37] The underlying psychology to PDM as a stress reducer is perhaps that many people feel better when they believe that they are in control of their jobs. Participating in decision making is one way of gaining more control.

Establish a Supportive Organizational Climate

Organizational climate is the general atmosphere or personality of an organization. Climate can influence employee stress levels in several ways. A firm that has genuine concern for the welfare of people will trigger less stress than a firm that disregards the feelings of people. A supportive climate tends to increase job satisfaction and productivity. Simultaneously, such a climate decreases job stress.

An extensive study conducted in Japanese industry gives credence to the idea that a supportive climate can decrease employee stress. After administering a 596-item questionnaire to 130,000 employees, psychologist Hiroto Kobuta noted that the organization climate influences employee stress. Employees with the most stress worked for *tight companies,* those with rigid and inflexible policies. In contrast, employees who experienced less stress worked for *loose companies,* those with flexible policies.

The tie-in with a supportive climate is that the loose companies were more supportive of employees. The corporation's policy on loans to employees illustrates the difference. A rigid company would set a maximum loan and hold to it, regardless of the reason for the loan. A loose company would allow the personnel department to take into account unusual circumstances, and bend the rule if warranted.[38]

Employee Assistance Programs (EAPs)

Some employees have personal problems that create so much stress that their job performance suffers. In response to this situation, a substantial number of employers of all sizes offer employee assistance programs. In a recent survey, 80 percent of the companies responding said they had an EAP.[39] Some of the personal problems handled by an employee assistance program, however, are closely related to the job. For instance, an employee might increase his or her use of alcohol because of work stress. Most large- and medium-size organizations have EAPs of their own, or belong to an EAP that s erves many firms. EAPs are found in both private and public organizations.

General Format of an EAP Employee assistance programs take a variety of forms, from simple referral services to fully staffed in-house programs. Having a referral service means that employees who visit the EAP coordinator are in turn referred to an outside agency for help. Employees come to the attention of the EAP in three primary ways: urging by supervisors, self-referral, and co-workers calling someone's attention to the problem. In other instances, family and friends urge an employee to visit the company

EAP. The accompanying box provides a representative summary of the operations of an employee assistance program. This particular program is used by a number of companies.

Professional specialists employed by the EAP include physicians, clinical psychologists, social workers, nurses, alcohol counselors, drug counselors, career counselors, financial counselors, and lawyers. These specialists hint at the most frequent type of problems referred to an EAP. Among them are alcohol dependency, drug dependency, financial problems, marital problems, personality clashes on the job and legal problems. The abuse of legal drugs has become as big a problem as that of illegal drugs. For example, many employees overuse sedatives to the point of suffering impaired job performance.[40]

Although supervisors may recommend that employees seek help, the EAP program is designed to be voluntary. Employees therefore make the ultimate decision to seek help themselves. In many organizations, however, supervisors place subtle pressure on problem employees to obtain help from the EAP.

Confidentiality An essential feature of EAPs is that they are confidential. Publicity about the program emphasizes its confidentiality. Brochures, notices, and articles in company newspapers all state that the program is confidential and that records remain in EAP files only. Neither the personnel department nor an employee's manager has access to EAP records. However, if the EAP specialist thinks that the employee is homicidal, suicidal, or a potential saboteur, these confidences will be broken. Despite the confidentiality of EAPs, the company is aware of which people they refer to the EAP. Yet most EAPs do not reveal the names of self-referrals.

On balance, EAPS have proved to be cost-effective. The cost of these programs is returned many times in terms of the improved job performance of employees who are treated successfully. For example, approximately 75 percent of alcoholics referred to EAPs later return to satisfactory job performance. Twenty-five percent of human resources professionals in one survey said the company EAP contributed to increased productivity.[41] Some people question the glowing reports of EAPs, because they are usually based on figures from people who operate these programs.

AN EMPLOYEE ASSISTANCE PROGRAM BROCHURE

We know that the people who walk in our doors each day are more than just employees. They're one of a kind individuals with complex lives and complex problems. And when a personal problem is making life difficult, it's also making work difficult. The care and attention an EAP provides will help an employee accurately assess the problem and find a way to resolve it.

We're offering this service because we're concerned about each employee's personal well-being and also because it makes good financial sense.

WHAT IS IT? It's a service that provides confidential counseling to help resolve personal problems of an employee.

WHAT TYPES OF PROBLEMS CAN THE EAP HELP SOLVE? The program is set up to help people with all types of personal problems— marital conflict, alcoholism, financial jams, emotional problems, family conflict, etc.

Sometimes people can solve these problems on their own but often outside help makes the difference between stopping a problem cold or going through a long period of struggle and coping, a period when people are unable to be themselves at home or at work.

HOW LONG DO COUNSELING SESSIONS LAST AND HOW MANY ARE NECESSARY? Individual sessions usually last an hour. Sessions for couples and families may last 30 to 45 minutes longer.

Most problems can be handled in three to four sessions—with hard work by both the counselor and you. At the end of these sessions you will have either resolved the problem or developed a detailed plan of action to resolve it, a plan that makes sense to you because you create it along with the counselor. Sometimes this plan may involve referral to a resource other than PPC. This only occurs when long-term assistance, specialized care or hospitalization is needed.

IS COUNSELING REALLY CONFIDENTIAL? YES. EVERYTHING DISCUSSED IN COUNSELING SESSIONS IS COMPLETELY CONFIDENTIAL. Most employees make their own appointments and can rest assured that their employer won't even know their names. PPC simply does not reveal names of self-referred employees. In some instances, employees are referred to the EAP by their supervisor because of a performance problem. When this is the case the supervisor is given only the following details:

Whether or not the employee kept the appointment.

Whether or not the employee has decided on and is following a plan to solve the personal problem.

All discussion between the counselor and the employee is strictly confidential.

IF MY SUPERVISOR REFERS ME TO THE EAP AND I USE IT, WILL MY FUTURE WITH MY EMPLOYER BE JEOPARDIZED? *ABSOLUTELY NOT.* As always, your job performance determines your future. The decision to use the program is yours and whatever you decide will be respected. On-the-job performance is what counts, not your participation in the EAP.

HOW DO I MAKE AN APPOINTMENT WITH A COUNSELOR? You can arrange an appointment by calling PPC directly between 8:30 A.M. and 5:15 P.M., Monday through Friday. An assistant will answer the phone (if you would rather speak directly with a counselor, just ask). The assistant will ask the name of your employer, your name, and when you would like an appointment.

WHAT HAPPENS WHEN I GO TO THE PPC OFFICE? You'll be met by an assistant who will either take you immediately into a counselor's office or show you to a private waiting room where you can sit, have some coffee, and relax until your counselor is free to see you.

The counselor will begin by reviewing a "Statement of Understanding" describing PPC services and pointing out the confidentiality of the service. The counselor will answer any general questions you have and then ask why you are seeking assistance. This begins the session.

The counselor will not tell you what to do about your problem, but will discuss your situation and help you make up your own mind about what you think, feel and want. If the counselor asks questions, it will be to help you get a better perspective on your situation.

WHERE DOES COUNSELING TAKE PLACE? PPC provides offices at various locations for your convenience. When you call, ask the assistant for locations in your area.

Source. Reprinted with permission of Personal Performance Consultants, St. Louis, MO

Summary of Key Points _____

- Wellness and fitness is the new thrust in stress management. By promoting health, wellness and fitness programs prevent employees from developing physical and mental problems caused or aggravated by excessive stress. Stress is the internal reaction to any force, positive or negative, perceived as a threat to a person's equilibrium. The force bringing about the stress is the stressor, and burnout is exhaustion stemming from long-term stress.

- The PACT model offers a way of understanding wellness. A well person has perspective (the big picture), autonomy (feels in control), connectedness (with people), and tone (physical and mental conditioning).

- Wellness and physical fitness programs are designed to help employees achieve wellness. Level I programs create awareness of wellness and fitness; Level II programs bring about lifestyle modification through such programs as physical conditioning; Level III programs create a healthy environment, such as offering an on-site fitness center.

- Stress has a variety of physiological, psychological, and behavioral symptoms and consequences. The physiological symptoms are tied in with the fight-or-flight response when faced with a stressor. Psychological symptoms include fear, anxiety, and in extreme cases, emotional disorder. A major job-related symptom of stress is errors in concentration and judgment. Men tend to have more severe stress symptoms than women, but women have a greater incidence of minor symptoms.

- An optimum amount of stress exists for most people and most tasks. Too much stress makes people temporarily ineffective; too little stress tends to make people lethargic and inattentive. Some types of negative stress, whatever the amount, do not help job performance.

- People often experience job stress based on their personality, or their perception of the situation, values, and goals. Among these major individual sources of stress are discrepancy between reality and expectations, Type A behavior, belief in external locus of control, heavy family and personal demands, dislike for rules and regulations, limited tolerance for ambiguity, and negative lifestyle factors.

- Job burnout is the final stage of an adverse reaction to stress that includes physical, mental, and emotional symptoms. In burnout, cynicism is pronounced. The major behaviors associated with burnout are as follows: emotional, mental, and physical exhaustion; withdrawing from people; and low sense of personal accomplishment. Relief from burnout requires treatment of the stress aspects.

- Organizational sources of stress include the following: role over-load, role underload, role conflict, role ambiguity, confusion relating to mergers and acquisitions, job insecurity and unemployment, insufficient authority, faulty job design, VDT overexposure, and adverse customer interaction.

- Methods the individual can use to reduce and prevent job stress include the following: Identify your own stress signals, eliminate or modify the stressor, improve your work habits, use everyday methods of relaxation, try the relaxation response, practice transcendental meditation, and rehearse the stressful situation. It is important to select a technique that suits your style and circumstance.

- Organizational methods of reducing and preventing stress include the following: Practice good human resource management, modify the organization structure, engage in participative decision making, establish a supportive organizational climate; and use employee assistance programs. Employee assistance programs help employees deal with personal or work problems that are stressful enough to lower job performance. The supervisor may refer the stressed employee to the EAP, where the employee is then assigned to the right treatment facility.

Questions and Activities

1. How might people use the PACT model to improve their life?
2. Experience has shown that relatively few blue-collar workers take advantage of company wellness and fitness programs. How would you explain this finding?
3. How do you personally know when you are stressed out?
4. How might a manager introduce the right amount of stress into the work environment?
5. Which personal characteristics of yours do you think currently, or will in the future, create stress for you?
6. Identify two jobs which you think creative negative stress for most incumbents, and pinpoint the stressors.
7. It has been said that people who are psychologically hardy (able to roll with the punches) are likely to avoid most forms of job stress. What is your opinion?
8. What form of "adverse customer interaction" have you personally observed?
9. Why do so many people brag about being burned out?
10. Suppose you had financial problems serious enough to impair your job concentration. Would you volunteer to seek help through your firm's EAP? Why or why not?

11. Interview a person in any high-pressure job. Find out if that person experiences stress, and how he or she copes with the stress.

A HUMAN RELATIONS CASE PROBLEM
The Stress Epidemic

Wendy Fernandez, human resources manager at Great Western Insurance Company, sifted through her mail and telephone messages on Tuesday morning. She found about thirty-five requests from supervisors to speak to her about employee health problems. Perplexed about this accumulation of problems, Fernandez conferred with Pete Martin, her assistant.

"What's happening around here that could conceivably be creating so many health problems?" asked Wendy. "Are toxins floating through the air conditioner? Is the L.A. smog seeping through the building? Are our supervisors putting too much pressure on the workforce?"

"Most likely none of the above," responded Pete. "I think we have a classic case of job stress induced by an outside agent. Let me show you this ad that appeared in the Sunday newspapers. I think the ad is putting ideas into the heads of our employees."

JOB PROBLEMS?
If you suffer from
nervousness,
low energy, irritability, insomnia, depression,
headaches, or other disabling psychological symptoms
that are a result of
EMOTIONAL STRESS, HARASSMENT, PHYSICAL INJURY
OVERWORK
while on the job,
telephone
(213)655-9999
or
(818)999-8888.
No cost to you.
You may be entitled to substantial benefits.
COMPENSATION PAYMENTS
EVALUATION
TREATMENTS

CALL ANY TIME FOR FREE APPOINTMENT
Se Habla Español
PSYCH SERVICES CENTER
MDs and PhDs

Wendy looked intently at the ad, and then said: "What a weekend for me to be out of town on vacation. I didn't catch the paper this weekend. We certainly can't stop this clinic from advertising. Yet we should alert our managers that this ad could be influencing how employees feel about their health. I suspect it could lead employees to exaggerate their symptoms."

Pete reflected, "That's the business these clinics are in. They prey upon the suggestible and the greedy. For instance, who doesn't feel under emotional stress and overworked these days?"

"I agree with your opinion," said Wendy. "Yet we cannot interfere with any employee's right to complain about health problems or contact this clinic.

"What I intend to do is discuss this problem with top management as soon as possible. My tentative plan is to send out a bulletin to all managers giving them tips on how to handle complaints about stress and health," said Wendy.

"Have you thought of the possibility that all these complaints will subside once the novelty of the ad has worn off?" asked Pete. "Besides that, a few employees will go to the clinic and find out that a few symptoms of discomfort will not lead to a settlement in their favor. Word will then get back that unless you have a real problem, going through one of these clinics will get you nowhere."

"That could be," said Wendy. "But I still think this problem needs careful consideration by top management."

1. What action, if any, do you think top management should take about the increase in employee complaints?
2. Should this problem even be brought to the attention of top management?
3. Which of the problems mentioned in the ad might be attributed to work stress?
4. Do you think that placing this ad is an ethical business practice? Explain your reasoning.
5. Do you think that these ads "prey upon the suggestible and the greedy"?

A HUMAN RELATIONS EXERCISE
Are You Dealing with Stress Properly?

How well do you cope with stress in your life? Gauge your ability with the following quiz developed by George S. Everly, Jr., for the U.S. Department of Health and Human Services.

1. Do you believe that you have a supportive family? If so, score 10 points.

2. Give yourself 10 points if you actively pursue a hobby.

3. Do you belong to some social activity group that meets at least once a month (other than your family)? If so, score 10 points.

4. Are you within five pounds of your "ideal" body weight, considering your health, age, and bone structure? If so, give yourself 15 points.

5. Do you practice some form of "deep relaxation" at least three times a week? These include meditation, imagery, yoga, etc. If so, score 15 points.

6. Give yourself 5 points for each time you exercise 30 minutes or longer during the course of an average week.

7. Give yourself 5 points for each nutritionally balanced and wholesome meal you consume during an average day.

8. If during the week you do something that you really enjoy and is "just for you," give yourself 5 points.

9. Do you have some place in your home where you can go to relax or be by yourself? If so, score 10 points.

10. Give yourself 10 points if you practice time management techniques in your daily life.

11. Subtract 10 points for each pack of cigarettes you smoke in an average day.

12. Do you use any drugs or alcohol to help you sleep? If so, subtract 5 points for each evening during an average week that you do this.

13. During the day, do you take any drugs or alcohol to reduce anxiety or calm you down? If so, subtract 10 points for each time you do this during the course of an average week.

14. Do you ever bring home work in the evening? Subtract 5 points for each evening during an average week that you do this.

Scoring and Interpretation

Calculate your total score. A "perfect" score would be 115 points. The higher your score, the greater your ability to cope with stress. A score of 50 to 60 points indicates an adequate ability to cope with most common stressors. Experts advise against using drugs or alcohol to deal with stress, and instead advocate exercising, eating a balanced diet, and using relaxation techniques to minimize the effects of stress.

Source: U.S. Department of Health and Human Services, 1986.

Notes _____

1. Quoted in book review appearing in *The Academy of Management Review,* October 1989, p. 602.

2. Majorie Blanchard, "Wellness Programs Produce Positive Results," *Personnel Journal,* May 1989, p. 30.

3. Deborah L. Gebhardt and Carolyn E. Crump, "Employee Fitness and Wellness Programs in the Workplace," *American Psychologist,* February 1990, pp. 263–64.

4. Gebhardt and Crump, "Employee Fitness and Wellness Programs," p. 270.

5. Brian D. Steffy, "Workplace Stress and Indicators of Coronary-Disease Risk," *Academy of Management Journal,* September 1988, p. 687.

6. Steven F. Maier and Mark Laundenslager, "Stress and Health: Exploring the Links," *Psychology Today,* August 1986, p. 44.

7. Maier and Laundenslager, "Stress and Health," p. 44.

8. Todd D. Jick and Linda F. Mitz, "Sex Differences in Work Stress," *Academy of Management Review,* July 1985, pp. 410–12.

9. "Stress: The Test Americans Are Failing," *Business Week,* April 1988, p. 74.

10. Helen LaVan, Marsha Katz, and Wayne Hockwarter, "Employee Stress Swamps Workers' Comp," *Personnel,* May 1990, p. 61.

11. R. Douglas Allen, Michael A. Hitt, and Charles R. Greer, "Occupational Stress and Perceived Organizational Effectiveness: An Examination of Stress Level and Stress Type," *Personnel Psychology,* Summer 1982, pp. 359–70.

12. Kenneth E. Friend, "Stress and Performance Effects of Subjective Work Load and Time Urgency," *Personnel Psychology,* Autumn 1982, pp. 623–33.

13. *Staying on Top of Stress* (booklet) (Daly City, CA: Krames Communications, 1990), p. 4.

14. Redford Williams, *The Trusting Heart: Good News About Type A Behavior* (New York: Times Books, 1989).

15. Carl R. Anderson, Don Hellreigel, and John W. Slocum, Jr., "Managerial Response to Environmentally Induced Stress," *Academy of Management Journal,* June 1977, p. 260.

16. Sheldon Zedeck and Kathleen L. Mosier, "Work in the Family and Employing Organization," *American Psychologist,* February 1990, p. 240.

17. Victor Thompson, "Bureaucracy and Innovation," *Administrative Science Quarterly,* June 1975, pp. 1–20.

18. John D. Howard, David Cunningham, and Peter A. Rechnitzer, "Role Ambiguity, Type A Behavior, and Job Satisfaction: Moderating Effects on Cardiovascular and Biochemical Responses Associated with Coronary Risk," *Journal of Applied Psychology,* February 1986, p. 99.

19. William H. Hendrix, Nestor K. Ovalle II, and R. George Toxler, "Behavioral and Physiological Consequences of Stress and Its Antecedent Factors," *Journal of Applied Psychology,* February 1985, p. 188.

20. Daniel Katz and Robert L. Kahn, *The Social Psychology of Organizations* (New York: Wiley, 1966), p. 184; Richard G. Netemeyer, Mark W. Johnston,

and Scot Burton, "Analysis of Role Conflict and Role Ambiguity in a Structural Equations Framework," *Journal of Applied Psychology,* April 1990, pp. 148–57.

21. John M. Ivancevich and associates, "Worksite Stress Management Interventions," *American Psychologist,* February 1990, p. 260.

22. Joan Wolinsky, "Black Jobless Suffer Despair, Self-Blame," *Monitor,* October 1982, p. 21.

23. Quoted in Steven K. Paulson, "Studying Executive Deaths," The Associated Press, June 19, 1990.

24. This problem still exists today, although originally reported in the 1978 edition of Katz and Kahn, *Social Psychology,* p. 599.

25. Larry Reynolds, "New Illnesses in the Age of Computers," *Management Review,* August 1989, p. 56.

26. Norma R. Fritz, "VDTs: Reducing the Risk," *Personnel,* September 1988, pp. 4–5.

27. James D. Brodzinski, Robert P. Scherer, and Karen A. Goyer, "Workplace Stress: A Study of the Internal and External Pressures Placed on Employees," *Personnel Administrator,* July 1989, pp. 77–78.

28. Susan E. Jackson and Randall S. Schuler, "Preventing Employee Burnout," *Personnel,* March–April 1983, p. 59; Hugh F. Stallworth, "Realistic Goals Help Avoid Burnout," *HRMagazine,* June 1990, p. 169.

29. Midge Wilson, "First Aid for Stress," *Success!,* September 1982, p. 13.

30. Michael R. Frone and Dean B. McFarlin, "Chronic Occupational Stressors, Self-Focused Attention, and Well-Being: Testing a Cybernetic Model of Stress," *Journal of Applied Psychology,* December 1989, p. 882.

31. Herbert Benson, *The Relaxation Response* (New York: Morrow, 1975).

32. Herbert Benson (with William Proctor), *Beyond the Relaxation Response* (New York: Berkley Books, 1985), pp. 96–97.

33. Norma R. Fritz, "In Focus," *Personnel,* January 1989, p. 5.

34. Frederick J. Heide, "Relaxation: The Storm Before the Calm," *Psychology Today,* April 1985, p. 18.

35. Michael T. Matteson and John M. Ivancevich, *Controlling Work Stress: Effective Human Resource and Management Strategies* (San Francisco: Jossey-Bass, 1987).

36. Joseph Seltzer and Rita E. Numerof, "Supervisory Leadership and Subordinate Burnout," *Academy of Management Journal,* June 1988, pp. 439–46.

37. John M. Ivancevich and Michael T. Matteson, "Organizations and Coronary Heart Disease: The Stress Connection," *Management Review,* October 1978, p. 122.

38. David Cohen, "Japanese Face Up to Stress on the Job," *Monitor,* December 1985, p. 8.

39. "79 percent of Companies Have EAPs; Most Use Community Services," *American Society for Personnel Administration/Resource,* April 1989, p. 2.

40. Michael E. Cavanagh, "The Dilemma of Legal Drug Abuse," *Personnel Journal,* March 1990, p. 124.

41. "79 percent of Companies Have EAPs," p. 2.

Suggested Reading

APPELBAUM, STEVEN H., and SHAPIRO, BARBARA T. "The ABCs of EAPs." *Personnel,* July 1989, pp. 39–46.

CAVANAGH, MICHAEL E. "What You Don't Know About Stress." *Personnel Journal,* July 1988, pp. 52–59.

FALKENBERG, LOREN E. "Employee Fitness Programs: Their Impact on the Employee and the Organization." *Academy of Management Review,* July 1987, pp. 511– 22.

HATFIELD, MARK O. "Stress and the American Worker." *American Psychologist,* October 1990, pp. 1162–64.

KLEIMAN, MARCIA. "Ease the Stress of Change." *Personnel Journal,* September 1989, pp. 106–12.

MCGEE, GAIL W., FERGUSON, CARL E. JR., and SEERS, ANSON. "Role Conflict and Role Ambiguity: Do the Scales Measure These Two Constructs?" *Journal of Applied Psychology,* October 1989, pp. 815–18.

PRITCHARD, ROBERT E., and POTTER, GREGORY C. *Fitness, Inc.: A Guide to Corporate Health and Wellness Programs.* Homewood, IL: Dow-Jones Irwin Books, 1990.

SHAFER, WALT. *Stress Management for Wellness.* New York: Holt, Rinehart, and Winston, 1987.

SLOAN, RICHARD P., and GRUMMAN, JESSIE C. "Does Wellness in the Workplace Work?" *Personnel Administrator,* July 1988, pp. 42–48.

SPECTOR, PAUL E., DWYER, DANIEL J., and JEX, STEVE M. "Relation of Job Stressors to Affective, Health, and Performance Outcomes: A Comparison of Multiple Data Sources." *Journal of Applied Psychology,* February 1988, pp. 11–19.

STURGES, JOHN S. "A Method for Merger Madness." *Personnel Journal,* March 1989, pp. 60– 69.

THOMPSON, DENNIS. "Wellness Programs Work for Small Employers, Too." *Personnel,* March 1990, pp. 26–28.

6

Job Conflict

LEARNING OBJECTIVES

After reading and studying this chapter and doing the exercises, you should be able to

1. Specify the major reasons why so much job conflict exists.
2. Explain how job discrimination, including sexual harassment, creates job conflict.
3. Understand why line vs. staff conflicts occur so frequently.
4. Be aware of both the constructive and destructive sides of conflict.
5. Acquire new methods of handling conflict on your own.
6. Know specific techniques for dealing with difficult people.
7. Summarize several methods that organizations use to reduce and prevent conflict.

THE MEANING OF JOB CONFLICT

As Chuck, a transportation specialist, walked into his office, he noticed that another desk had been moved in. Upset, Chuck grabbed the phone and called the maintenance department. The maintenance worker who answered informed Chuck that he had been told to move the desk in because the office was now to be shared by two employees. Chuck slammed down the receiver, picked up the other desk, and hurled it into the hallway. Hearing the commotion, Chuck's boss came running to the spot where the desk landed. Chuck's boss suspended him for three days without pay.

The unfortunate incident with Chuck and his boss illustrates two related meanings of conflict. A conflict is a situation in which two or more goals, values, or events are incompatible or mutually exclusive. The major incompatibility here is that Chuck wants a private office, while the organization wants his office to be shared. A conflict is also a strife, quarrel, or battle. Chuck and his boss quarreled, since Chuck's behavior was incompatible with organizational rules—no throwing company property around!

How Conflict Is Related to Stress, Frustration, and Anger

Conflict is a stressor, as described in the discussion of role conflict in Chapter 5. One reason why Chuck acted so irrationally is that he experienced stress when his private office was taken away without warning. Conflict is also tied in with frustration and anger.

Conflict typically leads to **frustration,** a blocking of need or motive satisfaction. Chuck was frustrated because the new desk blocked his motive to maintain the status of having a private office. Frustration, in turn, leads to **anger,** a feeling of extreme hostility, indignation, or exasperation. Throwing a desk into the hall is obviously an act of anger. Anger alters the body's physiology and chemistry. These changes are part of the body's fight-or-flight response when faced with a stressor.

Levels of Conflict

Conflict encompasses many kinds of behavior in the workplace. A major reason is that conflict occurs at four levels. *Conflict within the individual* occurs when two or more motives clash, such as wanting more pay and less responsibility. *Interpersonal conflict* occurs when two people clash, such as two office workers both wanting to gain control of the department's personal computer. *Intergroup conflict* takes place when two groups have incompatible desires, goals, or motives. For example, two departments might both want a bigger share of the budget. *Interorganizational conflict* takes place when two firms have incompatible goals, such as one company attempting a hostile takeover of another. Here we emphasize interpersonal conflict, although other levels of conflict will also be mentioned.

The underlying theme of this chapter is that every organization has some conflict between individuals and groups, and in some organizations, conflict is rampant. One implication is that if you cannot tolerate conflict and are unwilling to learn methods of resolving it, you should avoid jobs that involve interaction with people.

SOURCES OF CONFLICT

Job conflict has many causes. Here and in the following section we discuss leading sources, or causes, of job conflict. A list such as this needs continuous updating. New sources of conflict emerge from time to time, such as the conflict being created currently by hostile takeovers of one company by another. Although specific sources of conflict can be identified, all conflict arises from the underlying theme of incompatibility among goals, values, or events.

Competition for Limited Resources

An underlying source of job conflict is that few people can get all the resources they want. These resources include money, material, and personnel. Conflicts arise when individuals and organizational units squabble over the available resources. Even in a prosperous organization, resources have to be divided in such a manner that not everybody gets what he or she wants, as the following example shows:

A special staff meeting was called to discuss an emergency situation as perceived by Pete, the corporate treasurer of a prefabricated housing company. He made this plea to the rest of the staff: "I don't think you realize the gravity of the situation. We are in danger of not meeting our next payroll. We owe the banks $17 million and our receivables aren't coming in fast enough to pay off our notes. I told you people several months back that we need to begin cutting back on a few of the luxuries. We may be a glamour company to the world outside, but we need some restraint internally."

The marketing vice president interrupted with her notes: "But, Pete, we *have* cut back in many areas at your suggestion. We decided to postpone the construction of our southern plant for the time being. We've cut down on overtime except for emergency situations. We've even discontinued the practice of paying for spouses on company trips."

Replied Pete, "What irritates me, Jane, is the gluttony of marketing. You're as aware of our need for restraint as anybody on the management team. I've been denied the right to hire an additional cost accountant who would have probably paid for himself or herself anyway. I learned yesterday that the president has authorized the purchase of another corporate jet without even consulting me. Why can't the marketing department impress our potential customers with the two jets we already have?"

"There you go again, Pete, taking an accountant's view of the world," retorted Jane.

Differences in Objectives

When two groups have major differences in objectives or goals, the potential for conflict is high. Everybody working for the same organization should have the same ultimate objective (the success of the organization). Yet this does not always happen in practice. Sales groups, for example, are often in conflict with other units. The conflict occurs because the sales force emphasizes closing deals rather than such considerations as the profitability of the new business. A running conflict exists between the sales and underwriting (rate setting and acceptance of the policy) groups in many insurance companies.

For instance, sales people at one for-profit medical insurance company refer to the underwriting group as the "policy-prevention" department. As the sales people see it, the underwriters go out of their way to find reasons to reject applicants for insurance.

Conflict-Prone Job Responsibilities

A **role** is a set of behaviors or attitudes appropriate to a particular position, regardless of who occupies that position. Roles thus determine what people ought to do as a function of their position. Certain jobs are conflict-prone because of the role occupied by the job holder. Auditors, quality-control specialists, safety specialists, and industrial engineers are examples of workers in conflict-prone occupations. When your job involves criticizing or improving upon the work of others, a high potential for conflict exists. One student expressed the very nature of conflict-prone job responsibilities in her comments about campus security officers:

> It's nothing personal. Those people are paid to be mean. Most students can't afford the types of car that you can count on to start when you want them to. The result is that during a cold spell we often have to abandon our cars for a couple of days. Often you get a ten-dollar ticket that you can't afford. Worse is when you get the car towed away.

Differences in Personal Characteristics

A variety of personality and cultural differences among people contribute to job conflict. One contributor to conflict is the differences in values that stem from differences in age. The *generation gap* can lead to conflict because members of different generations may not accept the other group's values. Cooperation is sometimes difficult to achieve between older and younger members of a department because older workers question the seriousness of purpose of the younger workers. Simultaneously, the younger workers believe that the older workers are resistant to change and blindly loyal to the company.

Personality Clashes

Many workplace disagreements arise because people simply dislike each other. A **personality clash** is thus an antagonistic relationship between two people based on differences in personal attributes, preferences, interests, values, and styles. A personality clash reflects negative chemistry between two people, while personal differences are based more specifically on a value clash.

People involved in a personality clash often have difficulty specifying why they dislike each other. The end result, however, is that they cannot maintain an amiable work relationship. A peculiarity about personality clashes is that people who get along well may begin to clash after working together for a number of years. Many business partnerships fold because the two partners eventually clash.

Abrasive and Aggressive Personalities

Some people are predisposed toward job conflict because they are abrasive. An **abrasive personality** is one who is self-centered, isolated from others, perfectionistic, contemptuous, and prone to attack.[1] The abrasive personality literally rubs other people the wrong way.

Closely related to abrasive personalities are **aggressive personalities,** people who frequently physically or verbally attack others. Accurate figures about the incidence of violence on the job are difficult to obtain. Nevertheless, assault (both verbal and physical) is the second most important issue addressed by arbitrators.[2] (An *arbitrator* is an outside party who acts in the role of a judge in settling disputes.) Physical assault is often preceded by verbal assault, because an argument triggers a physical attack. Both verbal and physical attacks are classified as job conflict.

Hostile Takeovers of Corporations

A trend in modern business is for firms to expand by purchasing other firms, usually through buying stocks. In many instances, the second firm does not want to be acquired by the first, resulting in a **hostile takeover.** Interorganizational conflict occurs in a hostile takeover because the owners of the firms in question are at odds. Since many of the managers in the acquired firm think they will be dismissed, they enter into frequent conflict with managers of the acquiring firm. The chairman of an energy company makes this comment about hostile takeovers:

> We see companies which took decades to build, companies which have enhanced the welfare of communities, states, and the nation, raided and dismembered for the benefit of a select few.[3]

Although some people defend hostile takeovers as an appropriate expression of free enterprise,[4] takeovers undeniably are a source of job conflict. Even when the takeover is friendly, some conflict is likely to be generated among the members of the two firms.

Whistle Blowing

Whistle blowing is the disclosure of organizational wrongdoing to parties who can take action. Wrongful deeds brought to outsiders' attention include safety defects in automobiles, toxic substances in the work environment, overcharging the government, and cost overruns by the government. A person who blows the whistle on an employer typically enters into conflict with the employer. Although many forms of retaliation by the employer are illegal, the whistle blower usually fares poorly in the firm. For instance, a whistle blower may be passed over for promotion, receive below-average salary increases, and be given undesirable assignments.[5]

Job Discrimination

Job discrimination is an unfavorable action brought against a person because of a characteristic of that person unrelated to job performance. All forms of job (or employment) discrimination are likely to be declared illegal if brought to court. According to the Equal Employment Opportunity Commission (EEOC), there are six major areas where discrimination may occur: age, handicaps (disabilities), national origin, race or color, religion, and sex.[6] Discrimination on the basis of marital status or sexual orientation is usually included under sex discrimination.

Less publicized forms of job discrimination include unfavorable employment decisions against people who are overweight, bald, below average in height, or physically unattractive. Discrimination can also take the form of language. (More will be said about discrimination in language in Chapter 9.)

An important aspect of job discrimination is **disparate treatment,** whereby members of a protected group receive unequal treatment or are evaluated under different standards. A protected group is composed of people who have been discriminated against in the past. Two examples of disparate treatment that have been judged in violation of the law are as follows:[7]

- A Hispanic woman was discharged for poor attendance by an electronics firm. However, three workers of other national origins with equivalent records were retained.
- A 61-year-old supervisory chemist performed badly as a supervisor, but well as a chemist. Learning that he was to be discharged, he sought a chemist's position with the same employer. He was unquestionably better qualified than the 26-year-old who received the job. The older chemist was rejected because the vacancy was an entry-level position, reserved for recent college graduates.

Job discrimination becomes a source of conflict to the extent that the individual feels blocked because of a characteristic not under his or her control. The person who wishes to remedy the discrimination is forced into conflict. The person must now confront his or her supervisor or lodge a formal complaint. And the conflict does not end there. A person who wins a job discrimination ruling may become perceived as a troublemaker and therefore lose stature in the firm. One woman who won a discrimination claim against her employer said in retrospect: "I should have just found another job and quit. It's no fun being treated like an ingrate."

Sexual Harassment

A substantial number of employees find themselves in conflict because they are sexually harassed by a superior or a co-worker. Estimates of the number of women sexually harassed range from 40 percent to 90 percent. In recent years, one-third of harassment complaints have been filed by males.[8] **Sexual harassment** can be generally defined as any unwanted attention of a sexual nature from someone in the workplace, resulting in discomfort and/or interference with the job. It can include something as violent as rape or as subtle as a sexually oriented comment about someone's body or appearance.

Two types of sexual harassment are recognized by the courts. In *quid pro quo* sexual harassment, the individual suffers job loss, or threatened loss of a job benefit, as a result of his or her responses to a request for sexual favors. The demands of a harasser can be explicit or implied. A manager promising an employee a promotion in exchange for sexual favors, and then not promoting the employee because the employee refused, is *quid pro quo* harassment.

The other form of sexual harassment is hostile environment harassment. It occurs when someone in the workplace creates an intimidating, hostile, or offensive working environment. No tangible loss has to be suffered in this form of sexual harassment. An employee who is subjected to sexually suggestive comments, lewd jokes, or advances is a victim of hostile environment harassment.

Sexual harassment creates conflict because the harassed person has to make a choice between incompatible motives. One set of motives is to get ahead or at least keep the job. But to satisfy this motive, the person is forced to sacrifice the motive of holding on to his or her moral values or preferences. The values and preferences include not submitting to sexual advances or being placed in an uncomfortable environment.

Sexual harassment is considered a form of employment discrimination because the harasser treats people unequally based upon their sex. The subordinate who does submit receives preferential treatment, while the employee who does not submit receives negative treatment. Title VII of the Civil Rights Act of 1964 is still the key piece of legislation in the United States that makes sexual harassment illegal. Canadian law is also quite explicit about the illegality of forcing people to trade sex for job favors, or harassing them sexually in other ways. The accompanying box provides suggestions for dealing with sexual harassers, recognizing that most companies having strict anti-harassment policies.

HOW TO HANDLE OR PREVENT SEXUAL HARASSMENT

The potential or actual victim of sexual harassment is advised to use the methods and tactics described below to deal with the problem.

FORMAL COMPLAINT PROCEDURE

Whenever an employee believes that he or she has encountered sexual harassment, or if an employee is suspected to be the perpetrator of sexual harassment, the complainant should report the incident to his or her immediate superior (if that person is not the harasser) or to the next higher level of management if the supervisor *is* the harasser. The supervisor contacted is responsible for contacting the equal employment opportunity officer immediately regarding each complaint. The officer will explain the investigative procedures to the complainant and any supervisor involved. All matters will be kept strictly confidential, including private conversations with all parties.

DEALING WITH THE PROBLEM ON YOUR OWN

The easiest way to deal with sexual harassment is to nip it in the bud. The first time it happens, respond with a statement such as: "I won't tolerate this kind of talk." "I dislike sexually oriented jokes." "Keep your hands off me."

Write the harasser a stern letter shortly after the first incident. Being confronted in writing dramatizes your seriousness of purpose in not wanting to be sexually harassed.

Tell the actual or potential harasser: "You're practicing sexual harassment. If you don't stop, I'm going to exercise my right to report you to management." Or: "I think I heard you right. Would you like to accompany me to the boss's office and repeat what you said to me?"

LINE VS. STAFF CONFLICT

A comprehensive form of conflict in most large organizations is that between line and staff authority. **Line authority** deals with the primary purposes of the firm, such as the authority of a sales manager in a business. Line managers therefore have direct authority to make decisions about using company resources. **Staff authority** deals with the secondary purposes of the firm, such as the authority of a safety and health specialist in a manufacturing firm. Staff managers therefore have indirect authority because they advise line personnel and provide support services, such as the photocopying center in a bank. Support workers, such as data entry technicians and office assistants, can also be classified as staff personnel.

Line and staff workers experience conflict for most of the reasons described earlier in this chapter. Line vs. staff conflict is considered to be the major form of conflict between groups in organizations.[9] Four more specific reasons help explain the prevalence of conflict between line and staff.

Territorial Encroachment

In general, the staff person advises the line person. The latter may accept or reject this advice as he or she sees fit in getting things accomplished. In some instances a staff person has considerable power. For example, if the company lawyer says a particular sales contract is absolutely illegal, management will probably draw up a more acceptable contract. At other times a staff person may be ignored. A personnel research specialist might inform management that its methods of selecting employees are unscientific and unsound. Management may ignore the advice.

Staff specialists and line generalists often enter into conflict when the line worker perceives the staff worker to be encroaching on his or her territory. In the personnel research example just cited, the plant manager and the personnel manager may say to each other: "Who does this character from the home office think he is, telling us how to select people? Our plant is running well. Why is he bothering us?"

Line people see staff people as encroaching on their territory in another important way. Whenever a staff specialist makes a suggestion for improvement to a manager, it automatically implies that present conditions need improvement. If the industrial engineer says, "My methods will improve your efficiency," the implication is that the manager is not efficient in his or her current mode of operation.

Conflicting Loyalties

Many staff specialists come into conflict with line personnel over the issue of loyalty to their discipline vs. their organization. The staff person feels this role conflict because he or she may want to adhere to a professional code that conflicts with tasks assigned by the firm. An accountant in an electronics firm faced this dilemma when he disapproved of the company's earnings statement. He felt that the company was using almost fraudulent accounting practices, yet his company pressured him to approve the statement. He finally approved the financial manipulations asked for by the president, but simultaneously wrote a letter of protest. His guilt about violating accounting ethics finally led him to resign from the company. Four months after he resigned, the company declared bankruptcy.

Separation of Knowledge and Authority

In large organizations few executives have sufficient knowledge to carry out their responsibilities. They are dependent upon lower-ranking staff advisers to furnish the appropriate information. For instance, an executive may have to choose a course of action based upon technical advice that he or she does not fully understand. Dependence on the staff specialist may become a source of conflict.

Another source of conflict arises when the specialist resents being evaluated by a generalist whom he or she feels lacks the appropriate background to evaluate the work fairly. A performance appraisal of an engineering technician by a construction superintendent led to a confrontation. The superintendent told the technician he was performing "barely adequately" in his job. In response, the technician replied: "What makes you think you are qualified to evaluate my technical work? You have no specialized background in engineering."

Formal vs. Informal Authority

When a line manager wants something accomplished, he or she often has the formal authority to influence the behavior of others. When the department manager requests that the maintenance department repair a venetian blind, the maintenance department usually recognizes this as a legitimate request. Should the same request be made by an engineer in the department, the maintenance department might feel that the request is unauthorized. Staff specialists, and sometimes staff managers, must often go beyond their formal authority in getting things accomplished. Staff and line may thus come into conflict over one or more basic aspects of organizational life.

To compensate for their limited formal authority, staff personnel frequently resort to informal authority to get things accomplished. When a staff person is perceived as misusing informal authority, the result can be intensified conflict. One personnel manager attempted to enhance his informal authority by intimating to line managers that he worked closely with the president, and therefore indirectly held much power. One of his frequently used phrases was "Today when I was talking to Mr. Walker (the president). . . . " One day the head of manufacturing asked Mr. Walker if he had seen the personnel manager recently. Walker replied, "I hardly ever see him. He reports two levels below me." From that point on few people listened to the requests of that personnel manager.

THE CONSTRUCTIVE AND DESTRUCTIVE SIDES OF CONFLICT

Job conflict, like other stressors, has both constructive and destructive consequences. The right amount of conflict may enhance productivity, while too much conflict decreases productivity. Figure 6–1 depicts this general relationship between conflict and productivity, which is almost identical to the stress/performance relationship. Here we describe what happens when conflict is moderate and when it is too high.

Constructive Consequences of Conflict

You can probably recall an incident in your life when conflict proved to be beneficial in the long run. Perhaps you and your boss hammered out a compromise to a problem troubling you only after you complained about working conditions. Properly managed, moderate doses of conflict can produce such benefits as these:

> *Talents and abilities may emerge in response to conflict.* When faced with conflict, people often become more innovative than they would be in a tranquil situation. For instance, when an organizational unit is fighting with management to justify its existence, it will usually provide a creative explanation of how it contributes to organizational effectiveness.
>
> *Conflict can lead to innovation and change.* Concerns about the welfare of preschool children with working parents have led to mild

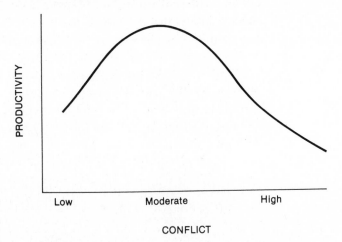

FIGURE 6–1 The Relationship Between Job Conflict and Productivity

conflict between children's advocacy groups and company executives. Many companies originally complained that child-care facilities were not the responsibility of management. Recently, however, many companies have voluntarily provided child-care facilities for their employees.

In the aftermath of conflict, organizations often learn useful methods of resolving and preventing conflict. A case in point is employee meetings with top management, as described in Chapter 4. These sessions originated because employees wanted more of a voice in company matters. Now employee meetings have become institutionalized in many places. Consequently top management learns of problems before they become major crises.

Conflict can provide diagnostic information about problem areas in the organization. If the quality assurance and production departments are in constant conflict, it might indicate that production is using inferior methods or quality assurance is being unrealistic. Either condition requires an adjustment.

As a result of conflict, unity may be reestablished. For instance, two warring departments may become more cooperative with each other in the aftermath of confrontation.

Destructive Consequences of Conflict

As you would suspect, conflict can have destructive consequences to both individuals and the organization. Among the more frequently observed are these:

Conflict consumes considerable managerial time. Managers report that they spend as much as 20 percent of their time at work dealing with conflict and its consequences.[10] The net result may be lowered managerial productivity, since less time is spent on problems that can increase profits or save money.

Conflict often results in extreme demonstrations of self-interest at the expense of the larger organization. Units of an organization or individual people will place their personal welfare over that of the rest of the firm. For instance, a labor union may call a strike, or a company may engage in a lockout, primarily to demonstrate power.

Prolonged conflict between individuals can harm emotional and physical well-being. Stress disorders are a frequent consequence of organizational conflict, because conflict can be a potent stressor.

Time and energy can be diverted from reaching organizational goals when workers are in conflict. In addition, money and material can be wasted. One such example is a meeting called more for the purpose of settling interdepartmental disputes than for discussing how to improve productivity.

The aftermath of conflict may have high financial and emotional costs. Both physical and psychological sabotage lead to adverse financial consequences. At the same time, management may develop a permanent distrust of its workforce, even if only a few people were in fact saboteurs. One of the costliest consequences is disgruntled former employees returning to the company in a violent rage and opening fire on innocent people.[11] Fortunately, this is a rare occurrence.

Conflict may result in a "me vs. them" attitude. Divisiveness of this type can ruin team spirit and the desire to work toward common goals. Each side in the dispute becomes concerned with gaining personal advantage and devalues the ideas of the other. Stalemates may result as team members refuse to modify their positions.[12]

Conflict may result in the falsification of information and the distortion of reality. When in conflict, some individuals may be led to lie in order to defend a position. A common manifestation of this problem is falsely accusing the other side when mistakes happen. In one government agency, a budget officer falsely accused a planning group of giving her inaccurate forecasts that resulted in a budget overrun.

So far our discussion of conflict has focused on meaning, sources, and consequences. This information helps us understand conflict and therefore can contribute to managing or resolving conflict. It is also important to be familiar with some specific strategies and tactics for resolving conflict.

CONFLICT HANDLING MODES

Before describing specific methods of resolving conflict, an overview of conflict handling modes is useful. The quiz presented in Figure 6–2 leads to a four-way categorization of conflict-management styles. Although a fresh approach, it is similar to an established framework for understanding how people handle conflict.[13]

INDIVIDUAL METHODS OF CONFLICT RESOLUTION

Because of the inevitability of job conflict, a career-minded person must learn effective ways of resolving conflict. In this section we concentrate on methods of conflict resolution that you can use on your own. All are based somewhat on the underlying philosophy of **win-win,** the belief that after conflict has been resolved both sides should gain something of value. Similarly, the organizational methods of resolving conflict described in the next section are based on a win-win philosophy. A situation in which no-

A QUIZ TO SEE WHETHER YOU FIGHT OR FLEE

Do you handle conflict calmly? Take the following quiz and find out. Check the box that most closely fits your typical reaction to the situation described.

Part I: The Quiz

1. When someone is overly hostile toward me, I usually:
    a. _____ respond in kind
    b. _____ persuade him or her to cool down
    c. _____ hear the person out
    d. _____ walk away.

2. When I walk in on a heated argument, I'm likely to:
    a. _____ jump in and take sides
    b. _____ mediate
    c. _____ keep quiet and observe
    d. _____ leave the scene.

3. When I suspect that another person is taking advantage of me, I:
    a. _____ try to get the person to stop
    b. _____ rely on persuasion and facts
    c. _____ change how I relate to the person
    d. _____ accept the situation.

4. When I don't see eye to eye with someone, I typically:
    a. _____ try to get him or her to see things my way
    b. _____ consider the problem logically
    c. _____ search for a workable compromise
    d. _____ let the problem work itself out.

5. After a run-in with someone I care about a great deal, I:
    a. _____ try to make him or her see it my way
    b. _____ try to work out our differences
    c. _____ wait before renewing contact
    d. _____ let it lie.

6. When I see conflict developing between two people I care about, I usually:
    a. _____ express disappointment
    b. _____ try to mediate
    c. _____ watch to see what develops
    d. _____ leave the scene.

7. When I see conflict developing between two people who are relatively unimportant to me, I usually: (score same responses as in question 6).

8. The feedback people give me indicates that I:
    a. _____ push hard to get what I want
    b. _____ try to work out differences

    c. ____ take a conciliatory stance

    d. ____ sidestep conflict.

9. When having serious disagreements, I:

    a. ____ talk until I've made my point

    b. ____ talk a little more than I listen

    c. ____ listen and make sure I understand

    d. ____ listen passively.

10. When someone does something that angers me, I generally:

    a. ____ use strong, direct language

    b. ____ try to persuade him or her to stop

    c. ____ go easy, explaining how I feel

    d. ____ say and do nothing.

Part II: Score Analysis

When you've completed the questions, add all the As, Bs, Cs and Ds to find where you collected the most responses. Then consider these profiles:

A. Aggressive/Confrontive. If you picked mostly *A* responses, you feel best when you're able to direct and control others. Taken to extremes, you can be intimidating and judgmental. You are generally contemptuous of people who don't stand up for themselves, and you feel frustrated when you can't get through to someone.

B. Assertive/Persuasive. If you scored high in this category, you may be from the "use your head to win" school of conflict management—strong-willed and ambitious, but not overbearing. You'll use persuasion, not intimidation, and are willing to compromise to end long-running conflicts.

C. Observant/Introspective. People who score high here don't get fired up. They listen to the opponent's point of view, analyze situations and make a factual pitch for their case. But in the end, they will defer to opponents in the interest of harmony.

D. Avoiding/Reactive. A high score suggests that you avoid conflict and confrontation at all costs, suppress your feelings— strong as they may be—to keep peace.

Observation: No one style of conflict management is better than another. Most people use all four, depending on the situation. But if you rely too much on one, start shifting your approach.

FIGURE 6–2 Are You Conflict-tolerant?

Source: Reprinted with permission from *Executive Strategies,* National Institute of Business Management, Feb. 20, 1990, p. 6.

body wins is referred to as **lose-lose.** The individual methods of conflict resolution discussed here are these:

1. confrontation and problem solving,
2. negotiation and bargaining,
3. disarming the opposition,
4. image exchanging.

Confrontation and Problem Solving

The ideal approach to resolving any conflict is to confront the real issue, and then solve the problem. Blake and Mouton note that confrontation means taking a problem-solving approach to differences and identifying the underlying facts, logic, or emotions that account for them. When conflicts are resolved through confronting and understanding their causes, people feel responsible for finding the soundest answer.[14]

Confrontation can proceed gently in a way that preserves a good working relationship, as shown by this example. Assume that Mary, the person working at the desk next to you, loudly cracks chewing gum while she works. You find the gum chewing both distracting and nauseating. If you don't bring the problem to Mary's attention, it will probably grow in proportion with time. Yet you are hesitant to enter into an argument about something that a person might regard as a civil liberty (the right to chew gum in public places).

A psychologically sound alternative is for you to approach her directly in this manner:

You: Mary, there is something bothering me that I would like to discuss with you.

She: Go ahead, I don't mind listening to other people's problems.

You: My problem concerns something you are doing that makes it difficult for me to concentrate on my work. When you chew gum you make loud cracking noises that grate on my nerves. It may be my hangup, but the noise does bother me.

She: I guess I could stop chewing gum when you're working next to me. It's probably just a nervous habit.

Negotiating and Bargaining

Conflicts can be considered situations calling for **negotiating or bargaining,** conferring with another person in order to resolve a problem. When you are trying to negotiate a fair salary for yourself, you are trying to resolve a conflict. At first the demands of the two parties may seem incompatible, but through negotiation a salary figure may emerge that satisfies both. Managers and staff people must negotiate both internally (for example, with subordinates and bosses) and externally (for example, with suppliers and government agencies).[15] Five negotiating and bargaining tactics will be sufficient to illustrate the nature of the process.[16]

Focus on interests, not positions.   Rather than clinging to specific negotiating points, keep your overall interests in mind and try to satisfy them. Remember that the true object of negotiation is to satisfy the underlying interests on both sides. Here is how this strategy works:

> Your manager asks you to submit a proposal for increasing productivity, and you see it as an opportunity to acquire an additional staff member. When you submit your ideas, you learn that management is really thinking about additional computerization, not additional staff. Instead of insisting on their hiring a new worker, be flexible. Ask to be included in the decision making for acquiring an additional computer. You will reduce your workload (your true interest), and you may enjoy such secondary benefits as having helped the company increase productivity.[17]

Compromise.   The most widely used negotiating tactic is **compromise,** settlement of differences by mutual concessions. One party agrees to do something if the other party agrees to do something else. Compromise is a realistic approach to resolving conflict. Most labor-management disputes are settled by compromise. For instance, labor may agree to accept a smaller salary increase if management will subcontract less work to other countries.

Some people argue that compromise is not a win-win tactic. The problem is that the two parties may wind up with a solution that pacifies both but does not solve the problem. One example would be purchasing for two department heads half the new equipment each one needs. As a result, neither department really shows a productivity gain. Nevertheless, compromise is both inevitable and useful.

Begin with a plausible demand or offer.   The commonsense approach to negotiation suggests that you begin with an extreme, almost fanciful demand or offer. The final compromise will therefore be closer to your true demand or offer than if you opened the negotiations more realistically. A plausible demand is useful because it shows you are bargaining in good faith. Also, if a third party has to resolve a conflict, a plausible demand or offer will receive more sympathy than an implausible one will.

> A judge listened to the cases of two people who claimed they were the victims of age discrimination by the same employer. The lawyer for the first alleged victim asked for $10,000,000 in damages; the lawyer for the second victim asked for $200,000. The first person was awarded $50,000 in damages, and the second person $150,000. An inside

source reported that the judge was so incensed by the first lawyer's demands that she decided to teach him a lesson.

Allow room for negotiation.   Although it is advisable to begin with a plausible demand, one must allow room for negotiation. A basic strategy of negotiation is to begin with a demand that allows room for compromise and concession. If you think you need $5,000 in new software for your department, you might begin negotiations by asking for a $7,000 package. Your boss offers you $4,000 as a starting point. After negotiation, you may wind up with the $5,000 you need.

Make small concessions gradually.   Making steady concessions leads to more mutually satisfactory agreements in most situations.[18] Gradually you concede little things to the other side. The hard-line approach to bargaining is to make your concession early in the negotiation and then grant no further concession. The tactic of making small concessions is well suited to purchasing a new car. In order to reach a price you consider acceptable, you might grant concessions, such as agreeing to finance the car through the dealer or purchasing a service contract.

Additional suggestions for effective negotiation are presented in the accompanying box. Effective negotiation, as with any other form of conflict resolution, requires extensive practice and knowledge of basic principles and techniques.

SUGGESTIONS FOR EFFECTIVE NEGOTIATION

1. *Find out how much authority the other side has before negotiating.* For instance, why waste time trying to sell something to someone who lacks the authority to close the deal?

2. *Determine a best alternative to a negotiated agreement (BATNA) before you begin negotiating.* If you know what you can obtain for yourself without negotiating, you are less likely to accept a bad deal.

3. *Legitimize your demand.* A printed demand or offer helps convince the other side of the legitimacy of your demand or offer. An example would be a letter from your company stating the maximum that can be paid for an electronic typewriter.

4. *Ask for something in return for any concession you make.* By asking for mutual concessions, you will not feel you have been taken advantage of.

5. *Negotiate on your own turf.* Negotiators tend to do better when the other side comes to their office. This tactic is also referred to as the "home court advantage."

6. *Nibble.* Ask for a small concession after the other side thinks the deal is closed, such as asking for a can of spot remover after purchasing a couch. ("Nibble," however, is more manipulative in nature than win-win.)

Disarming the Opposition

In many instances of interpersonal conflict the other individual has a legitimate complaint about specific aspects of your behavior. If you deny the reality of that person's complaint, he or she will continue to harp on that point and the issue will remain unresolved. By agreeing with that criticism of you, you may set the stage for true resolution of the problem.

Agreeing with criticism made of you by a superior is effective, because by doing so you are then in a position to ask for his or her help in improving the situation. Rational managers realize that it is their responsibility to help subordinates overcome problems, not merely to criticize them. Imagine that you have been chronically late with reports during the last six months. It is time for a performance review and you know that you will be reprimanded for your tardiness. You also hope that your boss will not downgrade all other aspects of your performance because of your tardy reports. Here is how disarming the opposition would work in this situation:

Your boss: Have a seat. It's time for your performance review, and we have a lot to talk about. I'm concerned about some things.

You: So am I. It appears that I'm having a difficult time getting my reports in on time. I wonder if I'm being a perfectionist. Do you have any suggestions?

Your boss: Well, I like your attitude. Maybe you *are* trying to make your reports too perfect before you turn them in. I think you can

Table 6–1   An image-exchanging list between you and your boss, based on a conflict about punctuality

You: My side of the story	**What I think is your side of the story**
a. I'm usually on time for work.	a. I'm not very dependable.
b. I live on the other side of town.	b. I live too far from the office.
c. Public transportation is unreliable in this city.	c. I take the last possible bus.

Your boss: My side of the story	**What I think is your side of the story**
a. You are late too often.	a. I'm as punctual as most people in the office.
b. If you cared more about your job, you would consider moving closer to the office.	b. I think you don't take my transportation problems seriously.
c. If you got out of bed earlier, you could take an earlier bus.	c. I try hard to get here on time. It's not my fault that I'm late sometimes.

improve in getting your reports in on time. Try not to figure everything out to five decimal places. We need thoroughness around here, but we can't overdo it.

Image Exchanging

The essential point of **image exchanging** is that you and your antagonist make it clear that you understand the other person's point of view. Empathy of this kind may then lead to a useful and productive compromise. A convenient application of this method is for you to list on a sheet of paper (1) your side of the argument, and (2) what you think is the other person's side of the argument. Next, he or she does the same for you. Table 6–1 is an example of how images might be exchanged. Each person makes up an image sheet without consulting the other person. After the images are exchanged, discussion (and sometimes fireworks) begins.

ORGANIZATIONAL METHODS OF RESOLVING CONFLICT

Organizations have developed many formal approaches for resolving conflict because of the recurring nature of conflict in the workplace. Since employees are demanding more rights than in the past,[19] these organizational methods are more important than ever. Some organizational methods of conflict resolution focus on problem solving, while others involve making physical changes in the organization. The techniques to be described here are these:

1. appeals procedures,
2. superordinate goals,
3. the ombudsman,
4. exchange of members,
5. changing the organization structure.

Appeals Procedures

Appeals procedures are the most conventional method of resolving job conflict. When you cannot resolve your conflict or gripe at one level, you appeal to a higher authority. The higher authority is ordinarily the common boss of the people in dispute or a member of the human resources department. However, top management in some organizations maintains an **open-door policy,** in which any employee can bring a gripe to its attention without checking with his or her immediate manager. The open-door policy is popular as a grievance procedure, because it allows problems to be settled quickly. The manager may not necessarily take sides with the employee, but he or she has the opportunity to talk about the problem shortly after it occurs. In this way the problem is less likely to fester.

> Rick, a purchasing agent, asked his boss in passing if he would be eligible for parental leave. Rick and his wife were expecting a baby in a few months, and he wanted to stay home with the baby for thirty days. The boss was in a hurry at the time of the request and did not pay much attention to Rick's proposal. Upset over the incident, Rick dropped in to see the vice president of materials management, who listened carefully to Rick's problem, and then suggested that Rick speak to his boss again. The vice president called Rick's boss shortly after the meeting, and asked him to pay more attention to Rick's request. Rick did speak to his boss again, and was informed that his leave (without pay) would certainly be granted.

Sample appeals procedures. Appeals procedures exist in both union and nonunion firms. An appeals procedure used in virtually every union firm is the **grievance procedure,** a formal mechanism for filing employee complaints. The grievance procedure is outlined in a written agreement between the union and the company. The procedure generally follows this format: If a union member thinks that he or she has been treated unfairly by the supervisor, that employee can ask the union steward to get involved in the dispute. If the dispute is not resolved at that level, it is moved to the next higher level. Both company and union management are represented at each higher level. If all else fails, an outside arbitrator acts as a judge to solve the dispute.

An example of a grievance procedure in a nonunion firm is an appeal to a hearing officer. A **hearing officer** is a staff specialist who is employed by the firm to arbitrate disputes between employees and management. Even though hearing officers are organization members, they are supposed to be impartial. Before a grievance gets to a hearing officer, it has been heard at lower levels. Hearing officers are more likely to be found in government agencies than in business firms.

The hearing officer grievance procedure produces winners and losers. Compromise settlements take place at lower levels. A hearing officer's decision cannot be appealed within the firm. Nevertheless, any citizen can hire legal counsel to attempt to overrule an employee's decision.

A key advantage of the hearing officer system is that the officer is an expert in labor relations. A disadvantage is that some employees believe that a hearing officer cannot be neutral, since he or she is paid by the employer.[20]

Problems associated with appeals procedures.   One valid criticism of the appeals procedures is that when the higher-ranked third party settles the dispute, the person or group that has lost may not be psychologically committed to the decision. However, since so many people are culturally conditioned to accept third-party rulings, this approach often works.

Appeals procedures in organizations also have a hidden danger for the individual. You may win your appeal, but you may fall into disfavor with the person with whom you had the conflict. It is therefore best to try to work out your problem through confrontation and problem solving. A man who brought a dispute with his boss to higher management, and won, tells what ultimately happened to him:

> I can't prove that my boss tried to get even. But he sure didn't make life easy for me after higher management ruled in my favor. I never seemed to get a choice assignment, nor did I ever receive a compliment. My performance ratings also went down, even though I was working harder than ever. My solution was to keep bugging the personnel department until I got a transfer.

Superordinate Goals

Organizational conflict can sometimes be resolved by helping the people in dispute to recognize that they are striving for common goals requiring cooperative effort. These **superordinate goals** are common ends that might be pursued by two or more groups, yet cannot be achieved through the independent efforts of each group separately.[21] Superordinate goals do not replace or eliminate the goals of each group. Instead, they represent a higher purpose toward which everybody can strive. An illustration of the establishment of superordinate goals to resolve conflict took place in a health maintenance organization (HMO).

The pediatric and administrative services departments were in frequent conflict over such issues as scheduling of workloads, referrals to outside psychiatric services, and working conditions. Several meetings were called in an attempt to resolve conflicts between the two departments. Despite these efforts, the squabbles continued. Annoyed and outraged by what he perceived as immature behavior, the health director told the two departments: "Forget about your petty differences. I'll help you work them out. If you both can't get your acts together, our HMO will be losing more patients than we can afford and still stay in business. You're cutting your own throats, and I want you to stop."

Shortly thereafter, the pediatric and administrative services departments began to work more cooperatively together. Being confronted with the importance of pursuing superordinate goals helped them gain insight into their counterproductive behavior.

The Ombudsman

A number of organizations have created a new position to help resolve employee conflicts. The **ombudsman** is a neutral person designated by the firm to help employees process complaints.[22] *Ombudsman* is the Scandinavian term for a person who helps citizens process complaints against government and cut through red tape. The ombudsman must be skilled in resolving conflict and knowledgeable about organizational procedures.

An ombudsman is granted the right to speak to anybody at any level in the company. He or she is sometimes seen as a lay therapist or a priest. Unlike an arbitrator, the ombudsman does not have the power to make a decision, but he or she can bring a problem to the attention of higher management.

What kind of conflict can an ombudsman help resolve? In one company an employee and his supervisor had a heated discussion about whether the supervisor was discriminating against the employee because he was black. Claimed the supervisor, "It's your attitude, not your race, that is holding you back from good assignments in my department." The employee brought the problem to the attention of the ombudsman (himself a black man). After the ombudsman brought the problem to higher management, the plant superintendent, ombudsman, and supervisor conferred about the problem. The employee was given a trial favorable assignment (night supervisor on a rotating basis). His attitude improved because of his favorable treatment, and the problem of perceived discrimination seemed to disappear.

Exchange of Members

Empathy helps reduce conflict. One way to acquire empathy for the other side is to work in their department. Exchanging members between groups in conflict (or groups having the potential for conflict) is thus another helpful approach to conflict resolution. Reassigning people in this way can achieve the benefit of introducing different viewpoints in the affected groups. As the group members get to know each other better, they tend to reduce some of their distorted perceptions of each other. For the exchange method to work, the group members exchanged must be willing and able to tackle the new assignments.

Changing the Organization Structure

A widely used approach to conflict resolution is to change the structure or shape of an organization in such a way that the sources of conflict are minimized. The underlying assumption in reducing or preventing conflict by modifying the structure is that personality clashes are not at the root of certain conflicts.

Modifying the organizational structure is a useful way of reducing or eliminating many forms of role-based conflict. Manufacturing and marketing are so frequently in conflict that resources are wasted in settling their disputes. Manufacturing accuses marketing of being willing to sell anything to a customer, even if the product cannot be manufactured at a profit. Furthermore, manufacturing contends that marketing wants everything accomplished on an unrealistically short schedule. Marketing, in turn, accuses manufacturing of being inflexible and unresponsive to the demands of customers.

A common solution to this problem has been the creation of a buffer position between manufacturing and marketing. Called something like "marketing liaison specialist" or "demand specialist," this individual becomes the communications bridge between the two groups. He or she interprets the demands of both groups to each other. The plan works except when the interface person feels that he or she has a superfluous job.

Summary of Key Points _____

- A conflict is a situation in which two or more goals, values, or events are incompatible or mutually exclusive. A conflict is also a strife, quarrel, or battle. Conflict is a stressor, and typically leads to frustration and anger. Conflict can occur within the person, or among people, groups, and organizations. Conflicts are inevitable within organizations.
- Job conflicts exist for many reasons, including the following: competition for limited resources, differences in objectives, conflict-prone job responsibilities, differences in personal characteristics, personality clashes, abrasive and aggressive personalities, hostile takeovers of corporations, whistle blowing, job discrimination, and sexual harassment.

- An almost inevitable form of conflict in modern organizations is that between line and staff personnel (and groups). Contributing reasons to this conflict include concerns over territorial encroachment, staff's partial loyalty to its discipline, line personnel's dependence on the expertise of staff people, and staff's quest for more authority.

- Job conflict has both constructive and destructive consequences. Positive consequences of conflict include the emergence of talents and abilities, innovation and change, and learning new methods of resolving conflict. Destructive consequences include wasted time, extreme self-interest, emotional and physical harm, and high financial and emotional costs.

- A good starting point in understanding conflict resolution is to recognize that people have different conflict-handling modes. Under the framework presented here, the four modes are aggressive/confrontive, assertive/persuasive, observant/introspective, and avoiding/reactive. It is best not to rely too much on one approach.

- Confrontation and problem solving is the ideal method of resolving conflict. Negotiating and bargaining is a major approach to resolving conflict. It includes focusing on interests rather than positions, compromise, beginning plausibly, allowing room for negotiation, and making small concessions gradually. Disarming the opposition and image exchanging are also useful methods of resolving conflict.

- Organizational methods of resolving conflicts include appeals procedures, establishing superordinate goals, using an ombudsman, exchanging members among organizational units, and changing the organizational structure.

Questions and Activities

1. Is a basketball game a conflict? Why or why not? Answer the same question for a mountain climb.

2. How might conflict among students be seen as "competition for limited resources"?

3. Identify a public figure whom you think can be accurately classified as an abrasive or aggressive personality. On what basis did you reach your conclusion?

4. Almost no top executive in a major corporation is under age 35. To what extent does this fact indicate the presence of age discrimination?

5. Several analyses have concluded that sexual harassment is very costly. What do you imagine are the costs associated with sexual harassment?

6. A production supervisor complained to the company fitness and wellness coordinator that the exercise program she had developed

was eating into productive work time. She, in turn, said the supervisor had a "dinosaur mentality." How does this incident illustrate line vs. staff conflict?

7. What is the difference between focusing on interests vs. focusing on positions?

8. Identify three occupations in which resolving conflict is a major part of the job.

9. Give your own example of changing the organization structure in order to resolve conflict.

10. Based on the opinion of students, the study of job conflict is one of the most useful topics in human relations and organizational behavior. How do you account for its applied value?

A BUSINESS PSYCHOLOGY CASE PROBLEM
Smokers' Rights

Child-Decor, a manufacturer of children's furniture, recently placed a total smoking ban on employees. The official policy stated that company employees were not allowed to smoke on company premises, but they were allowed to smoke outside the building. If caught smoking inside the factory or office they would be subject to discipline, such as written documentation in their personnel files, suspension, or demotion. Repeated violators would be subject to dismissal.

Company president Bill Garrison, himself a former two-pack-a-day smoker, was proud of Child-Decor's new policy. In a speech to employees, he stated: "Our company has taken a giant step forward in creating a safe work environment. We are helping hundreds of our employees avoid the biggest job hazard they will ever face—passive smoking. It is much more dangerous than anything else you will inhale in a furniture factory. Every Child-Decor employee has a right to breathe air unpolluted with carcinogens. I am certain that the few remaining smokers among you will agree that the health and safety of the majority must take precedence over the addictions of the minority.

"My door is always open to discuss our new policy. And please keep your supervisors informed of any difficulties encountered in creating a smoke-free environment."

Thirty days after the new policy began, Garrison asked his administrative assistant, Kathy Chang, to investigate how well the policy was working. While wandering around the office and the factory, Chang spoke to a number of Child-Decor employees to obtain a clear perspective on how well the smoking ban was being received.

"To be truthful," commented Bruce Garcia, a production scheduler, "this new policy is making me physically sick. And I intend to fight back.

These smokers are revolting. They gather outside every doorway to smoke throughout the day. When you walk in on a still day you hit this wall of putrid smoke. It's as bad as the restrooms used to be, when smoking was only allowed there. Smokers should not be allowed to smoke within fifty feet of a building entrance."

Inge Goldfarb, an office assistant, offered these observations with anger in her voice: "Never in my fifteen years of working for this company have I been treated so shabbily. Forcing me to go outside my building to engage in a perfectly legal activity smacks of totalitarianism. What right do nonsmokers have to make smoking a crime? Show me the scientific evidence that smoking in a ventilated area is harming people who do not smoke. If you ask me, Mr. Garrison has gone overboard."

Terry McWorth, an industrial engineer, said to Chang: "It's too early to provide hard data, but I think the smoking ban is lowering productivity. I've heard a lot of complaints that the smokers are spending too much time outside the building smoking. They are missing time from work, and people have to be shifted around to cover for them. It's a tough sell to convince a nonsmoking worker to cover for a smoker who is outside the building puffing away.

"Another problem the smoking ban has created is that I see evidence of hard feelings between some smokers and nonsmokers. The smoking ban has been divisive. It shows up in little ways, like a smoker not cooperating with a nonsmoker. The reason seems to be that the smoker now feels like a second-class citizen."

Melody Lewis, a purchasing assistant, informed Chang: "I and a few other smokers are willing to put up with this policy for now. So far the weather has been cooperating. But can you imagine being forced to smoke outside the building when it's snowing, raining, sleeting, or freezing cold? Smoking outside in 100-degree weather wouldn't be too comfortable either. It's ludicrous. Give us back our smoking lounge, and treat us like human beings. This is a furniture factory, not a prison. I'm getting ticked off at these smug nonsmokers who have made life so uncomfortable for us."

Gil McAlister, a customer service representative, told Chang: "I like the policy. I was smoking a pack a day on the job. I'm now down to ten cigarettes, and I enjoy the breaks outside. Since it's company policy to smoke outside, I don't have to feel guilty. I wish those other smokers would stop complaining. They may be killing off a good thing."

Chang reported back to Garrison that the ban on smoking inside the building was creating problems, and she wondered if something should be done about the situation. "There are more animosities created than is good for the company," said Chang.

1. What actions, if any, should the company take to resolve conflict between smokers and nonsmokers?

2. If Garrison does take steps to resolve conflict between smokers and nonsmokers, which methods of conflict resolution would you recommend?

3. What is your opinion about whether the rights of smokers are being violated?

A HUMAN RELATIONS CASE PROBLEM
Who Has the Right to Tell Whom What to Do?

Midge Baxter, the quality control manager at her company, was sorting through her morning mail. She came across a bulletin from the human resources department announcing a new training film, "How to Spot the Employee Drug Abuser." Under the announcement was a form to be filled out by managers indicating when they would be available for a screening of the film.

As Baxter threw the announcement into a wastepaper basket, she thought to herself, "If I did everything the personnel department wanted me to, I would have very little time to supervise the department."

One week later, Baxter received another bulletin from the human resources department. It was labeled "second notice." This time Baxter wrote across the bulletin, "Sorry, no time to attend your film."

Two days later Baxter was visited by her boss, Vince Gomez. He explained to Baxter, "We've been getting some complaints from the human resources department about you. They say that you won't cooperate with them, and they want me to do something about it."

"I resent those comments from the human resources department," said Midge. "They are complaining because I won't buy into some of their programs. I'm not saying their programs are not worthwhile. It's just that I have the right to choose how to budget my time.

"I don't like the heavy-handed tactics they are using to force me to cooperate. Are the line departments here to please staff departments? Who has the right to tell whom what to do?"

1. How does this case incident illustrate line vs. staff conflict?

2. How much authority should the human resources department have in influencing Baxter to view their film?

3. How else might have the human resources department have attempted to resolve the conflict with Baxter?

4. How should Gomez handle the conflict between Baxter and the human resources department?

A HUMAN RELATIONS ROLE PLAY
Image Exchanging

Assume that Vince Gomez attempts to resolve this conflict by getting Midge Baxter and a representative from the human resources department to exchange images. One person plays the role of Baxter, and another the role of the human resources manager who reported her lack of cooperation to Gomez. Play out an image exchange, going through the steps outlined in Table 6–1. The four key elements are as follows: (1) Baxter's side of the story, (2) Baxter's perception of the human resources official's side of the story, (3) the human resources official's side of the story, and (4) the human resources official's perception of Baxter's side of the story.

After the two sides have exchanged images, both engage in additional dialogue about their conflict.

Notes

1. Harry Levinson, "The Abrasive Personality at the Office," *Psychology Today,* May 1978, p. 78.

2. Charles Gold, "Assault on the Job," *Management Solutions,* June 1986, p. 5.

3. Michel T. Halbouty, quoted in Robert Metz, "Hostile Takeovers Will Damage Corporate Health Over the Long Term," *Rochester Democrat and Chronicle,* June 26, 1985, p. 10D.

4. T. Boone Pickens, Jr., "Professions of a Short-Termer," *Harvard Business Review,* May–June 1986, pp. 75– 79.

5. Janet P. Near and Marcia P. Miceli, "Retaliation Against Whistle Blowers: Predictors and Effects," *Journal of Applied Psychology,* February 1986, p. 137.

6. *1984 Guidebook to Fair Employment Practices* (Chicago: Commerce Clearing House Inc., 1983).

7. Donna E. Ledgerwood, "Workplace Relationships in the Federal Sector," a presentation for employees of Dallas region, United States Office of Personnel Management, May 1989.

8. Maureen P. Woods and Walter J. Flynn, "Heading Off Sexual Harassment," *Personnel,* November 1989, p. 45; Diane Feldman, "Harassment Touches All in Workplace," *Management Review,* April 1989, p. 8.

9. James L. Gibson, John M. Ivancevich, and James H. Donnelly, Jr., *Organizations: Behavior, Structure, Processes,* 6th ed. (Plano, TX: Business Publications, 1988), p. 313.

10. Robert A. Baron, "Reducing Organizational Conflict: The Role of Attributions," *Journal of Applied Psychology,* August 1985, p. 434; Rekha Karambayya and Jeanne M. Brett, "Managers Handling Disputes: Third-Party

Roles and Perceptions of Fairness," *Academy of Management Journal,* December 1989, p. 687.

11. Martha T. Moore, "When Terror Stalks the Workplace," *USA Today,* Sept. 25, 1989.

12. H. Kent Baker and Philip I. Morgan, "Building a Professional Image: Handling Conflict," *Supervisory Management,* February 1986, p. 25.

13. The standard approach is explained in Evert Van De Vliert and Boris Kabanoff, "Toward Theory-Based Measures of Conflict Management," *Academy of Management Journal,* March 1990, pp. 199–209.

14. Robert R. Blake and Jane S. Mouton, *The Managerial Grid III* (Houston: Gulf Publishing, 1985), p. 101.

15. George S. Odiorne and Earl Brooks, *Managing by Negotiations* (New York: Van Nostrand Reinhold, 1984), p. 1.

16. Andrew J. DuBrin, *Contemporary Applied Management,* 3rd ed. (Homewood, IL: Irwin, 1989), pp. 73– 95.

17. "Negotiating Without Giving In," *Executive Strategies,* Sept. 19, 1989, p. 6.

18. Mark S. Plovnick and Gary N. Chaison, "Relationships Between Concession Bargaining and Labor-Management Cooperation," *Academy of Management Journal,* September 1985, pp. 697–704.

19. "Beyond Unions: A Revolution in Employee Rights Is in the Making," *Business Week,* July 8, 1985, p. 72.

20. Alan Balfour, "Five Types of Non-Union Grievance Systems," *Personnel,* March–April 1984, pp. 67–76.

21. Don Hellriegel, John W. Slocum, and Richard W. Woodman, *Organizational Behavior,* 4th ed. (St. Paul, MN: West Publishing, 1986), p. 286.

22. Thomas J. Condon, "Use Union Methods in Handling Grievances," *Personnel Journal,* January 1985, p. 72.

Suggested Reading

AFZALUR, RAHIM M. (ed.). *Managing Conflict: An Interdisciplinary Approach.* Westport, CT: Praeger, 1989.

BENNETT-ALEXANDER, DAWN. "Sexual Harassment in the Office." *Personnel Administrator,* June 1988, pp. 174–88.

CHAMPAGNE, PAUL J., and McAFEE, BRUCE R. "Auditing Sexual Harassment." *Personnel Journal,* June 1989, pp. 124–39.

DANA, DANIEL. *Talk It Out! Four Steps to Managing People Problems in Your Organization.* Amherst, MA: Human Resource Development Press, 1990.

EDWARDS, P. K. *Conflict at Work: A Materialist Analysis of Workplace Relations.* Oxford: Basil Blackwell, 1986.

HABIB, GHAZI M. "Measures of Manifest Conflict in International Joint Ventures." *Academy of Management Journal,* December 1987, pp. 808–16.

JANDT, FRED E. *Win-Win Negotiation: Turning Conflict into Agreement.* New York: Wiley, 1987.

MANNIX, ELIZABETH A., THOMPSON, LEIGH L., and BAZERMAN, MAX H. "Negotiation in Small Groups." *Journal of Applied Psychology,* June 1989, pp. 508–17.

NOLLEN, STANLEY D. "The Work-Family Dilemmas: How HR Managers Can Help." *Personnel,* May 1989, pp. 24–30.

TJOSVOLD, DEAN. *Managing Conflict: The Key to Making Your Organization Work.* Minneapolis: Team Media, 1989.

WALL, JAMES A., JR., and RUDE, DALE E. "Judges' Mediation of Settlement Negotiations." *Journal of Applied Psychology,* May 1987, pp. 234–39.

7

Creativity
and Problem Solving

LEARNING OBJECTIVES

After reading and studying this chapter and doing the exercises, you should be able to

1. Identify the stages of creative thought.
2. Explain several key misperceptions about creativity.
3. Show how creativity fits into problem solving and decision making.
4. Obtain preliminary insight into your creative potential.
5. Explain how organizations can contribute to the creativity of workers.
6. Acquire several tactics and strategies for becoming a more creative problem solver.

A| major strategy for making an important contribution to your employer is to solve problems uniquely and imaginatively. An observation expressed by two human resource specialists, and echoed by many others, is this:

> Creative decision making and problem solving are two of the most important talents that employees can possess, talents that are necessary for the financial health and prosperity of any firm. Unless a firm can respond with unique products and services, innovative marketing strategies, and creative responses to complex problems, it may find itself losing sales, shares of the market, and profits.[1]

As implied from the above, **creativity** is the ability to develop good ideas that can be put into action. To qualify as creative, an idea must be original, adaptive (or useful), and meaningful to others.[2] Imaginative but useless ideas are thus not considered creative in this context. **Creative problem solving** stems from creativity. It is the ability to overcome obstacles by approaching them in novel ways.[3]

THE STAGES OF CREATIVE THOUGHT

Since the importance of creativity has long been recognized, much effort has been devoted to understanding the process by which creative ideas surface. Here we are concerned with the five stages in a person's thinking and behavior that produce a creative result.[4]

1. *Problem finding.* The individual discovers that something is worth working on or becomes aware that a problem or disturbance exists. A housing developer might say, "People are getting more and more concerned about the cost of heating and cooling their homes. We've come a long way in offering more efficient cooling and heating systems. What else can we do?"

2. *Immersion.* The individual concentrates on the problem and becomes immersed in it. He or she will recall and collect information that seems relevant, dreaming up alternatives without refining or evaluating them. The housing developer might say, "It seems to me that other industries have been faced with the problem of consumer resistance to the energy costs of using their products."

3. *Incubation.* After assembling the information, the individual keeps it in the back of his or her mind for a while. It has been hypothesized that the subconscious mind begins to take over. Although the individual is not actively working on the problem, it is simmering in the mind. It is therefore justifiable to go for a walk during working hours to engage in creative problem solving. While the problem is simmer-

ing, the subconscious may be trying to arrange the facts into a meaningful pattern.

4. *Insight.* If you have ever experienced a sudden insight about a vexing problem, you will understand this step in the creative process. The problem-conquering solution flashes into the mind at an unexpected time, such as while about to go to sleep, showering, or jogging. Creative people often carry notebooks to record these flashes of insight. The housing developer achieved her flash of insight while in a shopping mall: "Why not build compact homes to save energy, just like compact cars?"

5. *Verification and application.* The individual sets out to prove that the creative solution has merit. Verification procedures include gathering supporting evidence, logical persuasion, and experimenting with the new idea. The builder might conduct some market research about the market's acceptance of compact houses sold in other locations. Or the builder might take the plunge and build a few houses for speculation.

Tenacity is usually required at the application stage of creative thought, since most novel ideas are rejected as being impractical. Most experienced idea generators recognize that rejection is part of the game. For example, many inventions and developments that later proved to be huge successes were at first rejected by several companies. Xerography and the personal computer are two historically significant cases in point.

MISPERCEPTIONS ABOUT CREATIVITY

Before proceeding, it is important to dispel four misperceptions or myths about creativity. One is that people can be classified accurately as creative or noncreative. In reality, creativity is like height, intelligence, or strength. People vary considerably in these dimensions, but everyone has *some* height, *some* intelligence, and *some* strength. Creativity is therefore not like some intangible psychic organ, present in some and absent in others.[5]

A second misperception about creativity is that it can be exercised only in a limited number of fields, such as physical science, the arts, and advertising. These types of creativity could be labeled scientific or artistic creativity. Yet creative problem solving can be exercised in almost any field. You can engage in creative problem solving in such diverse settings as manufacturing, office work, administrative work, and home repairs.

A third misperception is that all creative ideas are complex and technical. In reality, most useful ideas are magnificently simple. A classic example is the whole new industry that was formed when two young men decided that computers could be used in homes and small businesses as well as in large organizations. The two creative problem solvers were Steve Jobs and Steve Wozniak, founders of Apple Computer.

A final myth is that creativity cannot be controlled, managed, or rushed. In reality, in some situations a deadline can be imposed for reaching a creative solution to a problem. A specialist at the Center for Creative Leadership has found that managers can aim at specific, controlled results. One such approach to forcing creativity is the *excursion technique*. This technique was used when NASA was trying to design some sort of buttonlike, zipperlike material that astronauts could manipulate while wearing bulky gloves in space.

After working unsuccessfully on the project for a while, the excursion technique was utilized. The group was asked to construct fantasies based on the words "rain forest." One group member described an image he had in his mind of running through the forest and having the thorns and stickers tear at his clothes. This image led to the development of velcro.[6]

CREATIVITY, PROBLEM SOLVING, AND DECISION MAKING

Creativity is not an end in itself, but an important part of any responsible job—solving problems and making decisions. Difficult problems usually require a creative solution. Although problem solving and decision making are part of the same general process, an important distinction can be drawn between them. **Problem solving** is a method of closing the gap between the actual situation and the desired situation. **Decision making** is the process of choosing among the alternatives that exist to solve the problem.

The type of decision faced by a person determines how much creativity will be required. A **programmed,** or routine, **decision** is one whose alternative solutions are determined by rules, procedures, or policies. For instance, deciding what to do when a printer ribbon is used up is a programmed decision. A **nonprogrammed,** or unique, **decision** requires a new solution because alternatives have not been prescribed in advance. For instance, deciding what kind of insurance business can be offered to the world is a nonprogrammed decision.

Creativity is required to make effective programmed decisions. In many situations, creativity is discouraged when you are faced with a programmed decision. What would happen if a bank teller deviated from standard procedure in cashing a check from a stranger without proper identification?

Here we are concerned primarily with the creative aspects of solving problems and making decisions. However, we must note that creativity is exercised within the context of decision making.

Decision-Making Styles

A good starting point in understanding problem solving and decision making is to recognize that there are two basic styles of decision making, analytical and intuitive. Analytical, or rational, decision making is purposely systematic. When using the analytical style, the person solves problems in an orderly, step-by-step fashion, as in the decision-making steps outlined in Figure 7–1.

The analytical style uses logical thinking, and follows the scientific method. When contemplating an investment, the person using an analytical decision-making style would carefully evaluate the available evidence. The prospective investment would be carefully evaluated against other investment vehicles before the person reaches a decision.

The intuitive style relies more on quick judgments, "gut reactions," and "feel." Intuitive decision making is an important part of being creative. Russ Holloman notes that intuitive decisions call for imagination and courage, whereas the analytical decision is best made by a methodical, deliberate person.[7]

Making use of both styles. Although there are two basic decision-making styles, many effective thinkers shift back and forth between the two styles as the situation requires. Both approaches can and should be used as complementary components when faced with a problem. Returning to the investment example, your intuition might point you toward an exciting investment opportunity. Before plunking down your money, it would be helpful for you to engage in analytical decision making.

Limitations to rational decision making.   Current thinking is that the rational model has been overemphasized. Several researchers have noted that decision making is seldom highly logical and systematic. Instead, it is a mixture of the analytical and the intuitive.[8]

Decision making is often confused because there are so many problems needing attention, and so many emotional factors that enter in. The explosion of the Challenger spacecraft is a tragic example. Decision makers at Morton Thiokol Inc., manufacturers of the booster rocket, knew that their engineers were concerned about the safety of their seals. It had long been known that problems with the seals could be aggravated by low temperatures. However, when the Morton Thiokol officials knew that NASA was impatient to launch on time, officials suppressed the negative evidence.

Observe carefully that both Morton Thiokol and NASA officials were swayed by subtle political forces to neglect information about safety. A *political force* in this context is a pressure to take a course of action in order to please somebody. Morton Thiokol officials wanted to please NASA officials, and NASA officials wanted to please Congress and the public by launching on time.

Another problem with carrying rational decision making too far is that it leads to *analysis paralysis.* The decision maker deals with so many facts that he or she becomes confused, overwhelmed, and unable to make a decision.

The alternative to the rational model of decision making is not to discard facts and figures in making a decision. Instead, the decision maker should attempt to accumulate an ample amount of reliable facts, and then trust his or her intuition. Trusting hunches may mean making some decisions on the basis of incomplete data, but it does allow you to become a creative problem solver. An important part of obtaining reliable facts is to trust the source of those facts.

Decision-Making Steps

According to the rational view of decision making, the process consists of seven steps: Recognize the problem, diagnose the problem, generate creative alternatives, weigh alternatives, choose an alternative, implement the chosen alternative, and evaluate the decision. Figure 7–1 outlines the decision-making steps. In some situations the steps overlap, and the decision maker may skip a step or jump back and forth between steps. Working your way through all these steps may be arduous, but good decision making is hard work.[9]

Recognize the problem.   Problem solving and decision making involve either having a problem assigned to you or finding one. Creative people are usually good problem finders—they recognize a problem when others are unaware of it. For instance, several companies today are involved in *remanufacturing*— rebuilding worn-out equipment and selling it to the public. The rebuilt product, such as a car or bus, can be sold much less ex-

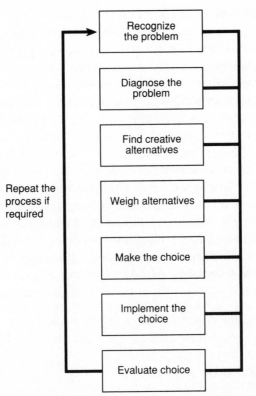

FIGURE 7–1 The Steps in Problem Solving and Decision Making

pensively than a new product. The man who found the problem of people wanting new cars at used car prices thought of the idea while working his way through college as a junkyard attendant.[10]

Diagnose the problem.   Assume that instead of looking for a problem, you are faced with the problem of needing money for furthering your education, purchasing a home, or getting married. The second step in problem solving and decision making is to diagnose, or clarify, the problem and its causes. It is essential to have some idea of both the actual and the desired situation.

In the example, you may decide you need an additional $7,000 to make the intended purchase. Conceivably, it is true that you need to find a satisfactory way to earn an additional $7,000. Or the real problem could be that you must discover a way to pare down your expenses by $7,000 within the next year.

According to George P. Huber, problem exploration often suffers because of the tendency to define the problem in terms of a proposed solution.[11] For example, you may think that you need $7,000 to have a proper wedding. Yet many people get married for under $200! And many managers find that instead of needing a bigger budget next year, they can achieve the same result by introducing more efficient work methods.

Generate creative alternatives.   The essence of creativity is found in this step: Generate a number of sensible alternatives to the problem at hand. A sound decision is more likely when the decision maker chooses among a number of alternatives. Conversely, many people make poor decisions simply because they did not search long enough for a good alternative. The effectiveness-reducing behavior frequently exhibited at this point is to evaluate each alternative that presents itself, rather than to concentrate on generating many alternatives. If you need an additional $7,000, it's worth your time to dig for many alternatives.

One precaution to take in generating alternative solutions is not to rely exclusively upon your own ideas. People who love their own ideas simply because they have produced them are said to suffer from *ideonarcissism*.[12] Instead of relying on your own thinking exclusively, solicit suggestions from superiors, co-workers, and friends.

A major hurdle in finding an outstanding creative alternative is that it is difficult to know all the relevant facts. When large amounts of seemingly relevant information are available, the decision maker is advised to engage in **humble decision making**.[13] Humble means that the person must admit that all the relevant facts cannot be gathered and processed.

Weigh the alternatives.   In order to make an intelligent choice, the advantages and disadvantages of each alternative should be specified. To illustrate, one approach to raising $7,000 after taxes would be to work twenty hours per week, at $8 per hour, for fifty weeks. This alternative might have the advantage of raising the proper amount of money. Yet it might have the disadvantage of playing havoc with your regular job, schooling, or personal life. A recommended method of weighing alternatives is to list the advantages and disadvantages of each on a separate sheet of paper.

Choose an alternative.   It is important to weigh each alternative; yet the process cannot go on too long. At some point you have to take a stand in order to solve an individual or organizational problem. You have to trust your intuition and take a chance with a plausible alternative. Intuition and hunches are now considered key aspects of managerial decision making. Most breakthrough decisions are made by business leaders who trust their hunches and seize an alternative without endless analysis.

Implement the chosen alternative.   This step centers around planning and following through on the activities that must take place for the chosen alternative to solve the problem. It can also be regarded as converting the decision. So often people make a decision but fail to implement it. Under these circumstances, no decision has been made at all. Let us assume that the money-making alternative you choose is to become a distributor for a milk substitute. Your earnings will come from sales you make yourself and from commissions paid you based on your lining up other distributors. (This alternative does run the risk of your losing some friends.)

Evaluate the decision.   The final stage of the problem-solving and decision-making process involves evaluating the quality of the decision made. Answering the deceptively simple question, "How effective is the decision I made?" is a complex activity. If the decision maker has a clear perception of what the decision was supposed to accomplish, evaluating the decision is somewhat easier. In the situation here, the decision maker has focused upon earning $7,000 within a year without badly disturbing other facets of life. If selling the milk substitute meets these criteria, the decision has been a good one. If this course of action proves to be unprofitable and overly time-consuming, the decision can be considered a poor one. In this case the problem has not been solved, and the decision maker returns to step 1.

Evaluating the outcome of a decision is important for another basic reason. Feedback of this type can improve decision-making skills. One might say, for example, "This time around I chose an alternative without giving careful thought to how difficult it would be to implement." Similarly, evaluation helps the problem solver know if the true problem has been solved. For example, some people find a creative way to make more money because they think that the lack of money is the root of their problems. If the person obtains more money, but is still unhappy, the true problem has not been solved. Maybe the person is really lacking in self-esteem.

To evaluate decisions accurately, the decision maker needs to develop and use a strong feedback system. Many managers have difficulty finding the consequences of their actions because they lack reliable information. Subordinates are often reluctant to bring bad news to the attention of superiors. According to a research report on managerial decision making, the higher a manager's position, the more limited are the feedback channels from below.[14]

Computer-Assisted Decision Making

Acceptance of the role of intuition in decision making has led to computer programs that help one make better use of hunches and intuition when attempting to solve problems. Two forms of computer-assisted decision making are decision-making software and artificial intelligence.

Decision-making software is any computer program that helps the decision maker work through the problem-solving and decision-making steps. These programs guide you through the actual steps outlined in Figure 7–1. In addition, they ask questions about such things as your values, priorities, and the importance you attach to such factors as price and durability.

Three representative decision-making programs are Trigger, Lightyear, and Expert Choice. Each is designed for use with personal computers. The decision-making process used in these programs is referred to as intuitive because the programs rely more on human judgment than heavy quantitative analysis. The purpose of these programs is to improve the quality of decisions, rather than make computations or generate data. A decision-making program could help a manager decide whether to market a new product through sales representatives, by telephone, or by direct mail.

Artificial intelligence (AI) is the capability of the computer to perform functions usually considered part of human intelligence, such as learning, reasoning, and listening. *Expert systems* are a subset of artificial intelligence programs that attempt to achieve the skill of experts in solving difficult problems like making decisions about mortgage applications.[15] Through the use of artificial intelligence, or an expert system, the computer can be made to think much like a person.

One approach to artificial intelligence is to program a computer to ask a series of "if-then" questions, simulating human logic. A second approach is to build enormous databases to incorporate as many facts as possible to fit a particular situation. Another approach is to build a system that links facts the way they might be linked in the human brain. As you might suspect, the technology for artificial intelligence is complex and esoteric.

Artificial intelligence programs are now available for personal computers. The more advanced use natural language commands rather than traditional computer commands. One of these programs, called Sales Activity Manager, helps track information such as how fast products are selling or how well particular sales representatives are performing. Using a voice command, the sales manager might ask: "How's business in Indianapolis?"

Artificial intelligence programs are promising because they approximate the way people really think. A really effective artificial intelligence program would function much like a knowledgeable personal assistant who would listen to questions and respond with accurate answers. As an expert in the field explains, "Using AI helps you catch more information than just numbers. It tells you to 'watch out for this' or 'take a look at that,' thereby helping you to do a better job."[16]

WHAT IS YOUR CREATIVE POTENTIAL?

A logical starting point in studying creativity is to gain a tentative awareness of your creative potential. Here we confine our measurement of creative potential to two illustrative exercises. Do not be overly encouraged or dejected by any results you achieve on these tests. They are designed to give only preliminary insights into whether your thought processes are similar to those of creative individuals.

RHYME AND REASON TEST

Creativity expert Eugene Raudsepp observes that exercises in rhyming release creative energy; they stir imagination into action. While doing the following exercises remember that rhyme is frequently a matter of sound and does not have to involve similar or identical spelling. This exercise deals with light and frivolous emotions.

After each "definition," write two rhyming words to which it refers.

EXAMPLES

1. Large hog
2. Television
3. Cooperative female

Big ____	pig ____
Boob ____	tube ____
Game ____	dame ____

NOW TRY THESE:

1. Happy father
2. False pain
3. Formed like a simian
4. Highest-ranking police worker
5. Voyage by a large boat
6. Corpulent feline
7. Melancholy fellow
8. Clever beginning
9. Heavy and unbroken slumber
10. Crazy custom
11. Lengthy melody
12. Weak man
13. Instruction at the seashore
14. Criticism lacking in effectiveness
15. A person who murders for pleasurable excitement
16. Musical stringed instrument with full, rich sounds
17. Courageous person who is owned as property by another
18. Mature complaint
19. Strange hair growing on the lower part of a man's face
20. Drooping marine crustacean
21. A man, short in height, accompanying a woman

See the end of chapter for answers and interpretation.

Source: Eugene Raudsepp with George P. Hough, Jr., *Creative Growth Games* (New York: Harcourt Brace Jovanovich, 1977). Reprinted with permission.

CREATIVE PERSONALITY TEST

The following test will help you determine if certain aspects of your personality are similar to those of a creative individual. Since our test is for illustrative and research purposes, proceed with caution. Again, this is not a standardized psychological instrument. Such tests are not reprinted in general books.

Directions: Answer each of the following statements as "mostly true" or "mostly false." We are looking for general trends; therefore, do not be concerned if you answer true if they are mostly true and false if they are mostly false.

	Mostly True	Mostly False
1. Novels are a waste of time. If you want to read, read nonfiction books.	_____	_____
2. You have to admit, some crooks are very clever.	_____	_____
3. People consider me to be a fastidious dresser. I despise looking shaggy.	_____	_____
4. I am a person of very strong convictions. What's right is right; what's wrong is wrong.	_____	_____
5. It doesn't bother me when my boss hands me vague instructions.	_____	_____
6. Business before pleasure is a hard and fast rule in my life.	_____	_____
7. Taking a different route to work is fun, even if it takes longer.	_____	_____
8. Rules and regulations should not be taken too seriously. Most rules can be broken under unusual circumstances.	_____	_____
9. Playing with a new idea is fun even if it doesn't benefit me in the end.	_____	_____
10. So long as people are nice to me, I don't care why they are being nice.	_____	_____
11. Writing should try to avoid the use of unusual words and word combinations.	_____	_____
12. Detective work would have some appeal to me.	_____	_____
13. Crazy people have no good ideas.	_____	_____
14. Why write letters to friends when there are so many clever greeting cards available in the stores today?	_____	_____
15. Pleasing myself means more to me than pleasing others.	_____	_____
16. If you dig long enough, you will find the true answer to most questions.	_____	_____

See end of chapter for answers and interpretation.

CHARACTERISTICS OF THE CREATIVE WORKER

Before attempting to improve your own creativity, it is helpful to know the characteristics of creative workers. A **creative worker** is someone who approaches problems in a new or unique way.[17] Studies point toward one distinguishing overall characteristic: Creative people are more emotionally loose and open than less creative people.

The emotional looseness of creative people is often manifested in practical jokes and other forms of playfulness. For example, a packaging design engineer roomed with another woman who collected stuffed animals. While the stuffed-animal collector was away for the weekend, the design engineer dressed all the animals in her own clothing. She even put high heels on a stuffed giraffe. The joke worked. The animal collector was distressed about a delayed flight home. However, she laughed so hysterically upon seeing her dressed-up animals that her distress was relieved.

Robert R. Godfrey has grouped the characteristics of creative workers into three broad areas: knowledge, intellectual abilities, and personality. The following list incorporates his thinking with that of other writers and researchers.[18]

Knowledge. Creative thinking requires a broad background of information including facts and observations. Knowledge is the storehouse of building blocks for generating and combining ideas. Many years of immersion in a field may be required to make an outstanding creative contribution.[19]

Intellectual abilities. Included here are cognitive abilities, such as intelligence and abstract reasoning.

- Creative people, by definition, are *intuitive,* as described throughout this chapter. They often experience a sudden illuminating flash of judgment when faced with a problem, known as the "aha experience."
- Creative people tend to be *bright rather than brilliant.* Extraordinarily high intelligence is not required to be creative, but creative people are good at generating alternative solutions to problems in a short period of time.
- Creative people have a *youthful curiosity* throughout their lives. Their curiosity is not centered just on their own field of expertise. Instead, their range of interests encompasses many areas of knowledge, and they generate enthusiasm toward almost any puzzling problems.
- Creative people are *open and responsive* to feelings and emotions and the world around them.

Personality. Included here are the emotional and nonintellectual aspects of an individual that facilitate being creative.

- Creative people tend to have a *positive self-image.* They feel good about themselves but are not blindly self-confident. Because they are reasonably self-confident, creative people are able to cope with criticism of their ideas.
- Creative people have the *ability to tolerate isolation.* Isolation is useful because it helps put a person into a receptive mood for ideas. Working alone also helps creative people avoid the distractions of talking to others. (Creativity, however, is sometimes facilitated by interaction with others.)

- Creative people are frequently *nonconformists*. They value their independence and do not have strong needs to gain approval from the group.
- Creative people often have a *Type T personality*. Their thrill-seeking tendencies often lead to outstanding creativity because finding imaginative solutions to problems is thrilling.[20]
- Creative people are *persistent*. Persistence is important, because finding creative solutions to problems is hard work and requires intense concentration.

Synthesizing these lists leads to a general picture of the creative person. He or she is more loose than tight, open than closed, flexible than rigid, playful than always serious, adventuresome than safety-seeking. Several of these characteristics support the popular stereotype of the creative person as somewhat of a maverick, both intellectually and socially.

ORGANIZATIONAL CONTRIBUTIONS TO CREATIVITY

To achieve creative solutions to problems and to think of new opportunities, an organization needs more than creative people. Creativity is the combined influence of people with creative potential working in an environment that encourages creativity. Here we examine three related ways in which organizations contribute to creativity: having a favorable climate for creativity, conducting creativity-training programs, and fostering intrapreneurship.

A Favorable Climate for Creativity

Organizations that are able to capitalize upon much of the creative potential of their members have certain characteristics in common. One underlying characteristic is that organizational members are given encouragement and emotional support for attempts at creativity. As you read the following list of more specific characteristics, notice that many of the characteristics of creative organizations are similar to those of creative people.[21]

- Group norms, or an organizational culture, that encourages and expects creativity from group members. This is perhaps the single most important characteristic of a creative organization.
- Rewards, including recognition and money, are given to employees whose innovative ideas have tangible payoffs. (At Eastman Kodak, for example, three workers in one year received $50,000 each for their money-saving ideas.)

- Managers at the top of the organization who support innovation and imagination.
- An organizational structure flexible enough to bend with whatever pressures innovation may bring.
- A process already established for developing new ideas into products or services.
- A trustful management that does not overcontrol people.
- Open channels of communication among members of the organization; a minimum of secrecy.
- Considerable contact and communication with outsiders to the organization.
- Large variety of personality types.
- Willing to accept change, but not enamored with change for its own sake.
- Enjoyment in experimenting with new ideas.
- Encourages people of various education levels and generalists (not only specialists) to contribute new ideas.
- Attempts to retain creative people even during times of financial difficulty.
- Little fear of the consequences of making a mistake.
- Selects people and promotes them primarily on the basis of merit.
- Uses techniques for encouraging ideas, such as suggestion systems, special recognition for patent awards, and brainstorming.
- Sufficient financial, managerial, human, and time resources to accomplish its goals.

Creativity-Training Programs

In recognition of the importance of creativity, a quarter of all companies with more than one hundred workers offer creativity training. The goal of many of these programs is to help develop quality products and services. Most creativity-training programs center around two major themes. One is helping the trainee develop more flexible thinking and other characteristics of a creative person. The other theme is using the problem-solving and decision-making steps described earlier.[22]

A representative example of a creativity-enhancing exercise used in these programs is the random-word technique. Here is how the approach works:

> You're a product manager at Reynolds Metals. Your boss has just read how Arm & Hammer strategists increased sales of baking soda by 70 percent: They suggested that homemakers put a box in the refrigerator to absorb food odors. The boss would like you to make a similar breakthrough for your company—come up with new uses for Reynolds Wrap.

You select a concrete word at random to use as an idea hook in your brainstorming session. Cracking your trusty *American Heritage* dictionary at page 159, word number six, you get "costume." Hmmmm. How about putting directions on the back of the Reynolds Wrap package, showing parents how to make Halloween costumes for kids from aluminum foil? "Mr. Mirror"; "The Silver-Horned Wonder Woman." You get the idea.

Aside from being used as part of training programs, the random-word technique has been applied successfully to business problems. A highly successful line of Campbell's soups was conceptualized in a random-word brainstorming session. The dictionary word was "handle." This led the group to "utensil," and finally "fork." "The soup you can eat with a fork!" a team member joked. Nobody can eat soup with a fork. However, the unconscious mind seizing the idea hook, supplies another answer instantly: " . . . unless it's incredibly full of meat and vegetables and other good stuff." The payoff from this exercise was Campbell's "Chunky" soups.[23]

Fostering Intrapreneurship

The focus of creativity in many organizations is on individuals who develop and implement new ideas for products and services. Ordinarily one associates new products and services with business organizations. However, many nonprofit firms, such as government agencies, educational institutions, and hospitals, are also concerned about offering innovative services to the public. Here we describe the nature of entrepreneurship and intrapreneurship, and what organizations are doing to foster this type of creativity.

The nature of entrepreneurship and intrapreneurship. An entrepreneur establishes and manages a business in an innovative manner. Note the distinction between anybody who operates a small business and a true entrepreneur—an entrepreneur offers an innovative product or service. If you establish a company that manufactures and sells laser guns for home repairs, you are an entrepreneur (and a small business owner). If you open a newsstand in a hotel lobby, you are a small business owner but not an entrepreneur. Approximately 650,000 people open small businesses each year in the United States and Canada. Very few of these people are true entrepreneurs.

An **intrapreneur** is a company employee who engages in entrepreneurial thinking and behavior for the good of the firm. Intrapreneurs work somewhat independently inside the firm, with the mission of developing a new product or service.[24] The intrapreneur benefits from the company's backing, and the company benefits from the intrapreneur's productivity. Like an entrepreneur, the intrapreneur begins small. If the new product becomes successful, the intrapreneur commands more resources.

Intrapreneurship has burgeoned in recent years because it is generally recognized that most innovation comes from small organizations. Ideally, the intrapreneur pursues his or her product idea with the intensity of an entrepreneur. Don Estridge, the IBM executive whose business unit developed the IBM PC, made this comment about the importance of smallness: "If you're competing against people who started in a garage, you have to start in a garage."[25]

Organizations are taking many steps to foster entrepreneurial thinking within a bureaucracy. The general thrust of these actions is to exempt intrapreneurs from many of the restrictions and controls usually imposed in a large firm. At the same time, intrapreneurs are given extra resources and special privileges.[26]

The establishment of skunk works. Several large firms, including Hewlett-Packard and 3M, allow selected employees to operate out of **skunk works,** a secret place to conceive new products. The term derives from the fact that something secret and unpleasant is thought to be going on in these off-site locations. Skunk works employees are given latitude in pursuing new products. Major products conceived in skunk works include jet fighter technology and a giant-screen video monitor.

Identification and recognition of intrapreneurs. Intrapreneurs are risk takers—they will pursue ideas and get volunteer help before they receive permission from the firm. Companies are now making an effort officially to recognize employees with ideas for breakthrough products. Once the potential intrapreneur is identified, he or she is officially encouraged by a top executive.

Allocation of more resources. Many intrapreneurs who have become corporate superstars have used unauthorized resources from their companies to develop their product. Much of the work they have done on new products was originally on their own time. Although not every new idea can be funded, many high-tech companies are now providing money, material, and human resources for intrapreneurs. Another way of giving the intrapreneur resources is to form special project teams to help develop a promising new product.

IMPROVING YOUR CREATIVITY THROUGH SELF-HELP

Creativity can sometimes be improved through formal training programs. At other times, do-it-yourself techniques can be equally beneficial. Here we describe seven strategies and techniques many people have used outside of formal training programs to improve their own creative behavior.

Overcome Traditional Mental Sets

Most techniques of creativity improvement are based on the same principle: To think creatively, you must overcome a traditional mental set. A **traditional mental set** is a conventional way of looking at things and placing them in familiar categories. Overcoming traditional mental sets is necessary to loosen up emotionally and intellectually. As long as you remain a "tight" person, your creativity will be inhibited.

Alcohol and other drugs sometimes provide the user with a temporary state of emotional and intellectual looseness that can stimulate the creative process. However, the loss of intellectual alertness from extensive use of these substances usually more than offsets the advantage of temporary looseness.

Overcoming traditional ways of looking at things is a mechanism by which a person can become emotionally and intellectually looser. A traditional, or rigid, way of looking at something is referred to as a **perceptual block.** People frequently cannot solve problems in a creative manner because they are bound by preconceived ideas. Until person can look beyond the normal ways of doing things, he or she will probably not find a solution. A case in point is the development of the automatic teller machine (ATM). The mental set needed to be overcome was that human contact was required for bank customers to withdraw funds. (Customers had been able to deposit funds in overnight depositories for many years.)

Use Brainwriting

Brainstorming, in its usual format, is a technique that involves group members thinking of multiple solutions to a problem. **Brainwriting** is arriving at multiple solutions to a problem by jotting down ideas while working by yourself. Learning to overcome traditional mental sets will help you develop the mental flexibility necessary for individual and group brainstorming.

An important requirement of brainwriting is that you set aside a regular time (and perhaps place) for generating ideas. The ideas discovered in the process of routine activities can be counted as bonus time. Even five minutes a day is much more time than most people are accustomed to use in thinking creatively about job problems. Give yourself a quota with a time deadline.

IdeaFisher, a computer program, has been developed to facilitate brainwriting. The software contains a list of over 3,000 very specific questions designed to help the user think of solutions to business problems, such as developing a marketing strategy or inventing a new product or service. As part of the program, over 60,000 words, expressions, people, places, and things are cross-referenced in over 700,000 ways. Associations to your key word are broken down into subcategories.[27] Assume that you were trying to develop a new marketing campaign for cheese. *IdeaFisher* would help you develop a giant list of things and ideas associated with cheese.

Develop a Synergy Between Both Sides of the Brain

Neurological and psychological studies of the brain have shed light on creativity. Researchers have been able to demonstrate that the left side of the brain is the source of most analytical, logical, and rational thought. It performs the tasks necessary for well-reasoned arguments. The right side of the brain grasps the work in a more intuitive, overall manner. It is the source of impressionistic, creative thought. People with dominant right brains thrive on disorder and ambiguity—both characteristics of a creative person. (These differences in brain dominance relate directly to decision-making styles.)

The argument that the left side of the brain controls logic and the right side of the brain controls intuition has been disputed by biopsychologist Jerre Levy, among others. Her studies show that any mental activity is carried out by both sides of the brain simultaneously. Joined by the corpus callosum, the two hemispheres work together in harmony.[28]

Whether you believe that both sides of the brain work independently or interdependently, the message for creativity improvement is the same. Both logical and intuitive thinking are required. The creative person needs a fund of accessible facts in order to combine them to solve problems. He or she also needs to rely on hunches and intuition to achieve flashes of insight.

The highly creative person achieves a synergy between the two sides of the brain. **Synergy** is a combination of things with an output greater than the sum of the parts. The unique capabilities of both sides of the brain are required. Robert Gundlach, a physicist who has amassed 133 patents in over thirty years of work, explains it this way:

> Being creative means developing a synergy between the left half of the brain—the analytical half—and the right half of the brain—the creative half. I learned that at home during my childhood. My mother was an artist, a painter of landscapes. My father was a chemist, and inventor of Wildroot hair oil. Both my parents influenced me equally well.[29]

Use Nonlinear Thinking

The usual, logical approach to obtaining creative ideas is *linear thinking,* moving from one idea to another in step-by-step fashion. One moves from thought A to thought B to thought C and so forth. According to Edward Glassman, another approach is nonlinear creativity (or thinking). Ideas leap from A to L to Z to R to E, and so forth. Something useful may eventually merge out of bizarre intermediaries and remote associations. Glassman furnishes this example:

During a discussion about how to prevent ice from breaking power lines, somebody suggested, "Let's train bears to climb the telephone poles in winter and shake loose the ice that accumulates and breaks the transmission wires." A second person, again in jest, suggested putting pots of honey on top of the poles so that the bear would make the climb in the first place. A third person humorously suggested using helicopters to place the pots of honey on the poles, another bizarre idea.

All this humorous and bizarre thinking led to a practical solution, used for many years: The downdraft from the helicopters flying over the wires knocks off the ice before the wires break.[30]

Maintain and Use an Idea Notebook

Good ideas are hard to come by, yet they are readily forgotten in the press of normal activities. A standard creativity improvement device of people who are dependent upon novel ideas for their livelihood is to keep an idea notebook with them at all times—including one at bedside. When an idea of any possible merit flashes across your mind, it should be entered in a notebook reserved for that purpose. It is also essential that the idea notebook be referred to frequently to see which ideas are now ready for refinement and implementation.

Borrow Creative Ideas

Copying the successful ideas of others is a legitimate form of creativity. Knowing when and which ideas to borrow can help you behave as if you were an imaginative person yourself. One source of good ideas is conversations with people from other departments and specialties. If you maintain contact with managers and specialists from your own firm or other firms, you will have a pipeline to potentially useful ideas. Reading also serves as a useful source of creative ideas. Newspapers, general magazines, trade magazines, and nonfiction books frequently contain novel ideas about improving your job effectiveness.

A delicate issue is whether you should tell others the source of your novel suggestions. Do you think it is proper to take full credit for ideas you have borrowed from people or printed sources?

Don't Be Afraid to Try and Fail

If you try a large number of ideas, projects, or things, a large number of them will probably fail. Relatively few ideas ever become accepted and implemented. Yet your number of "hits" will be much higher than if you tried only a few creative ideas and all of them were successful. It is the absolute number of successes that counts the most, not the percentage of successes.

Summary of Key Points _____

- Creativity is the ability to develop good ideas that can be put into action. Creative problem solving stems from creativity, and is the ability to overcome obstacles by approaching them in novel ways. The five stages of creative thought are: problem finding, immersion, incubation, insight, and verification and application.

- Misperceptions about creativity include these: People can be accurately classified as creative or noncreative; creativity can be exercised only in artistic and scientific fields; all creative ideas are complex and technical; and creativity cannot be controlled, managed, or rushed.

- There are two basic styles of decision making: analytical and intuitive. Analytical decision making is purposely systematic, following an orderly, step-by-step fashion. The intuitive decision-making style relies more on quick judgments, and is tied in closely with creativity. Many effective thinkers shift back and forth between the two styles as required by the situation.

- Current thinking is that the rational model of decision making has been overemphasized. In reality, decision making is often confused because there are so many problems requiring attention, and so many emotional factors involved. Another limitation to rational decision making is that it may lead to "analysis paralysis." Big decisions should be based on both facts and hunches.

- Creativity takes place within the context of solving problems and making nonprogrammed (unique) decisions. Decision making can be divided into seven steps: Recognize the problem; diagnose the problem; generate creative alternatives; weigh the alternatives; choose an alternative; implement the chosen alternative; evaluate the decision.

- Computer-assisted decision making can be helpful in improving intuition. Decision-making software helps one work through the steps in problem solving and decision making, yet emphasizes the qualitative factors. Another form of computer-assisted decision making is artificial intelligence, a computer program that simulates human thinking.

- Creative potential can be measured with some degree of accuracy by taking tests designed for that purpose. The tests sampled here include those requiring you to behave creatively and to compare certain aspects of your personality with those of creative people.

- Characteristics of the creative worker can be subdivided into knowledge, intellectual abilities, and personality. A synthesis of this information is that the creative personality is more loose than tight, open than closed, flexible than rigid, playful than always serious, and adventuresome than safety-seeking.

- Organizations contribute to creativity in several ways. One is by having a climate favorable for creativity. The general approach is to give emotional support and encouragement to members and have group norms favoring creativity. The creative climate also possesses characteristics similar to those of creative people, including an enjoyment in experimenting with new ideas.

- Creativity-training programs in organizations also contribute to creativity. The programs tend to emphasize the development of flexible thinking, and guide people toward using the decision-making steps. The illustrative training program described here is the random-word technique. Fostering intrapreneurship also enhances creativity. It is accomplished by (1) the establishment of skunk works, (2) identification and recognition of intrapreneurs, and (3) allocation of more resources for intrapreneurs.

- Often creativity can be improved by self-help techniques. Among them are (1) overcome traditional mental sets, (2) use brainwriting, (3) develop a synergy between both sides of the brain, (4) use nonlinear thinking, (5) maintain and use an idea notebook, (6) borrow creative ideas, and (7) don't be afraid to try and fail.

Questions and Activities

1. How might a person use knowledge about the stages of creative thought to find a creative solution to a problem?
2. How might information about the misperceptions of creativity be used to inspire workers to become more creative?
3. What is the predominant decision-making style of the leader of your country? Provide supporting evidence.
4. How can a manager benefit from the concept of "humble decision making"?
5. At what point do you think artificial intelligence will replace the need for professionals, such as physicians and financial consultants (stockbrokers)?
6. Do you know anybody who is highly creative yet unsuccessful by conventional standards? What accounts for the person's lack of success?
7. To what extent would a very strict boss be effective in encouraging creativity from team members? Explain your reasoning.
8. Identify a work or personal problem that you think would be well suited to the random-word technique.
9. Some people believe that being creative did them more harm than good on the job. How do you explain this comment?
10. Ask a creative problem solver you know how he or she became creative. Be prepared to discuss your findings in class.

A HUMAN RELATIONS CASE PROBLEM
The Food Company Skunk Works

Melrose Foods is a large food manufacturer and processor consisting of twenty-one divisions. Many of these divisions are smaller companies purchased in recent years. The executive office, headed by Gardner Appleby, recently decided to establish a research and development group whose responsibility it would be to develop new food products. Appleby explained it in these words to the corporate staff and division heads:

"The time has arrived for Melrose to copy the high-tech approach to R&D [research and development]. Effective July 1 of this year, we are building our own skunk works. The executive office has chosen Manuel Seda for this key assignment. As you recall, Manuel was a dynamically successful entrepreneur who established Tangy Tacos. Starting in his mother's kitchen, he built up a national distribution for his product in three years. We bought Tangy Tacos for its growth and profitability. But even more important, we bought the talent of Manuel Seda.

"Tangy Tacos will be headed by Wanda Morales while Manuel is on indefinite assignment as manager of our skunk works. Manuel will begin with six competent employees. He and his group can have all the budget they need, so long as it looks like they are on the path to developing successful products."

At this point in Appleby's presentation, Garth Laidlaw, division head of Tiger Pet Foods, waves his hand. "We need clarification, Gardner. You mention that the skunk works will be funded as long as it looks like they are about to develop successful products. Developing a successful new food product is a risky business. About 90 percent of new product ideas never make it to the marketplace. And about half of the 10 percent that do arrive on the market fail within one year."

"I'm aware of those dismal statistics," said Appleby. "But without a push on new product development, Melrose Foods is doomed to stagnation and mediocrity.

"Members of the management team, let us all move forward toward a successful skunk works. And let us all wish Manuel the best of luck."

Three months after the skunk works was established, Seda received a visit from Appleby. After a brief tour of the facility, Appleby said to Seda: "Manuel, I do get the impression that there is a lot of activity going on here, but it does not seem to be focused activity. Could you give me an update?"

"Gardner, it's premature to expect results. We have been set aside so that we can think at our own pace. This is not a crash program. Don't forget, I had been working in the food business for three years before I thought of the idea for Tangy Tacos."

"It's true, we are not expecting immediate results from the skunk works, but you are a pretty well funded group. Could you please give me a hint of any new product idea you have developed so far?"

Seda answered: "Actually we are pretty excited about one new idea. It's a form of instant fish called 'Sudden Seafood.' Today's busy and health-conscious professional will love it. You add boiling water to pulverized seafood, and you get a mashed-potato-like substance that is actually tasty seafood. We would certainly be the first on the market."

"Revolting," responded Appleby. "I would definitely turn thumbs down on Melrose investing money to market instant fish. Maybe you should interest our Tiger Pet Foods division in that idea. It could be used when traveling with cats."

Three months later, Appleby revisited Seda at the skunk works. The president said, "I'm just doing an informal check again. What new product idea is the skunk works toying with these days?"

"I think we have a real winner on the drawing board," said Manuel. "The country is sick of wimpy soft drinks that have no real flavor, no gusto, and give no boost to the psyche. We have been experimenting with a raspberry-flavored soft drink that has four times the caffeine and three times the sugar of anything on the market. Its tentative name is 'Razzle Razzberry.' It's destined to be a winner."

"Hold on, Manuel. You're running counter culture. The country is moving away from heavy soft drinks and you're suggesting a product that's practically a narcotic. It sounds like our skunk works might be getting carried away."

"Gardner, it's too bad you don't like this promising idea. Maybe I could meet with you and other members of the executive office to discuss the mission of the company skunk works. I don't feel things are going right."

"It sounds to me like you're getting a little touchy," said Appleby.

1. How would you evaluate Appleby's approach to evaluating the output of the skunk works?

2. Do you think Seda is getting a little touchy?

3. Are Gardner's review sessions justified?

4. What do you think of Seda's request to review the mission of the skunk works with the executive office?

5. What is your hunch about the potential success of Sudden Seafood and Razzle Razzberry?

A HUMAN RELATIONS CASE PROBLEM
The Traditional Thinkers

Laura Madison, president of Elgin's Department Store, met with her team of managers at a Sunday brunch. After the meal was served, Madison began her formal presentation with these words:

"I've called this special meeting only because I have to deal with a topic that is better handled in person than by memo. Elgin's has reached a crossroads, and its fate is in your hands. Our share of the market in all five locations has shown a steady decline over the past five years. We have got to do something about this problem, or we will be closing our doors within several years.

"As you know, we've conducted consumer surveys to find out what our customers like about us and what they don't like. The message I get from this survey is that Elgin's lacks imagination. Some customers think we are a bland store that has become blander. If we are to survive, we have to freshen our thinking. We have become too set in our ways."

After Madison continued on for ten minutes about the importance of Elgin's becoming a more imaginative store, she asked the group for questions. Don Battles, the advertising director, was the first to raise his hand:

"Laura, we have heard your charges about Elgin's being bland and lacking imagination. Could you please give us a few specifics?"

"I don't want to offend anybody in particular, but I guess I will have to be more specific," said Madison. "Above all, we don't do anything unusual as a store. Take this Christmas season as a good example. The motif our store chose was to decorate the store with Santa Claus, reindeer, and elves. How traditional can you be?

"Another example is that our special sales are just like everybody else's. We run ads announcing that everything in the store is marked down by a certain percent. That's so mundane. Furthermore, our stores are not distinctive. They remind me of an average Main Street or mall department store.

"I'm afraid we have become dull, dull, dull! If I don't get some fresh ideas from you people soon, I'm going to have to hire some creative talent from outside. Next question please," said Laura Madison, as her management group looked stunned.

After two minutes of silence, Mary Jo Fenton, a merchandising coordinator, asked: "Laura, you set the tone for new ideas in this store. We expect you to take the lead in pointing us in new directions."

"Maybe you have a point, Mary Jo. You now know that I want Elgin's to move forward with more innovation."

1. What do you think of Madison's conclusion that her managers are traditional thinkers?

2. If her diagnosis of the problem is correct, what steps could be taken to help the managers become less traditional in their thinking?

3. What do you think of Madison's approach to solving the problem of limited imagination?

4. What do you think of Madison's idea of threatening to hire some creative talent from the outside?

5. Is Mary Jo Fenton justified in assuming that the president should be setting the tone for the store?

Notes

1. Although this quote is old, it is just as relevant today. David R. Wheeler, "Creative Decision Making and the Organization," *Personnel Journal,* June 1979, p. 394.

2. Edward H. Meyer, "Creativity in Business," *Business Week's Guide to Careers,* September 1985, p. 27; Lesley Dormen and Peter Edidin, "Original Spin," *Psychology Today,* July/August 1989, p. 49.

3. "Creativity: A Special Report," *Success!,* March 1985, p. 54.

4. James A. F. Stoner and R. Edward Freeman, *Management,* 4th ed. (Englewood Cliffs, NJ: Prentice Hall, 1989), p. 409.

5. Dormen and Edidin, "Original Spin," p. 48.

6. S. S. Gryskiewciz and J. T. Shields, "Targeted Innovation," *Issues and Observations,* November 1983, p. 4.

7. Russ Holloman, "The Light and Dark Sides of Decision Making," *Supervisory Management,* December 1989, p. 34.

8. John L. Brown, "Executive Judgment: The Intuitive/Rational Ratio," *Personnel,* December 1985, p. 48; Daniel Araoz, "Thinking for Success," *Human Resources Forum,* August 1989, p. 4.

9. Ted Levitt, "Decisions," *Harvard Business Review,* January–February 1989, p. 6.

10. "A Growing Love Affair with the Scrap Heap," *Business Week,* April 29, 1985, p. 69.

11. George P. Huber, *Managerial Decision Making* (Glenview, IL: Scott, Foresman, 1980), p. 13.

12. Darrell W. Ray and Barbara L. Wiley, "How to Generate New Ideas," *Supervisory Management,* November 1985, p. 9.

13. Amitai Etzioni, "Humble Decision Making," *Harvard Business Review,* July–August 1989, p. 132.

14. Morgan W. McCall, Jr., and Robert E. Kaplan, *Whatever It Takes: Decision Makers at Work* (Englewood Cliffs, NJ: Prentice Hall, 1985).

15. Dorothy Leonard-Barton and John J. Sviokla, "Putting Expert Systems to Work," *Harvard Business Review,* March–April 1988, p. 93.

16. Nancy Madlin, "Artificial Intelligence: No Longer Science Fiction," *Management Review,* June 1988, p. 60.

17. "Finding Creative Workers," *Research Institute Personal Report for the Executive,* Oct. 1, 1985, p. 4.

18. Robert R. Godfrey, "Tapping Employees' Creativity," *Supervisory Management,* February 1986, pp. 17–18.

19. Dormen and Edidin, "Original Spin," p. 49.

20. Frank Farley, "The Big T in Personality," *Psychology Today,* May 1986, p. 48.

21. Robert R. Blake and Jane Srygley Mouton, "Don't Let Group Norms Stifle Creativity," *Personnel,* August 1985, pp. 28–33; Maurice I. Zeldman, "How Management Can Develop and Sustain a Creative Environment," *Advanced Management Journal,* Winter 1980, pp. 23–27.

22. Charlene Marmer Solomon, "Creativity Training," *Personnel Journal,* May 1990, pp. 65–71.

23. Bryan W. Mattimore, "Breakthroughs," *Success!,* November 1988, p. 46.

24. Gifford Pinchot III, *Intrapreneuring* (New York: Harper & Row, 1985).

25. Quoted in Keith Atkinson, "Intrapreneurs: Fostering Innovation Inside the Corporation," *Personnel Administrator,* January 1986, p. 43.

26. Franck A. deChambeau and Fredericka Mackenzie, "Intrapreneurship," *Personnel Journal,* July 1986, pp. 40–45.

27. Bryan M. Mattimore, "Mind Blasters," *Success!,* June 1990, pp. 46–47.

28. Jerre Levy, "Right Brain, Left Brain: Fact and Fiction," *Psychology Today,* May 1985, p. 44; Terence Hines, "Left Brain/Right Brain Mythology and Implications for Management and Training," *Academy of Management Review,* October 1987, pp. 600–606.

29. John J. Byczkowski, "Invention's a Necessity at Xerox," *Rochester Democrat and Chronicle,* January 1983, p. 1F; David Dorsey, "The Curious Cowboy," *Upstate,* April 20, 1986, p. 6.

30. Adapted from Edward Glassman, "Creative Problem Solving," *Supervisory Management,* January 1989, pp. 21–26.

Suggested Reading _____

ACKOFF, RUSSELL L. *The Art of Problem Solving.* New York: Wiley, 1987.

BOTTGER, PRESTON C., and YETTON, PHILIP W. "Improving Group Performance by Training in Individual Problem Solving." *Journal of Applied Psychology,* November 1987, pp. 651–57.

DRUCKER, PETER F. *Innovation and Entrepreneurship.* New York: Harper & Row, 1985.

GLASSMAN, EDWARD. "Creative Problem Solving: Your Role as Leader." *Supervisory Management,* April 1989, pp. 37–42.

HUGHES, THOMAS P. *American Genesis: A Century of Invention and Technological Enthusiasm.* New York, Viking, 1989.

KIRRANE, DIANNE, and KIRRANE, PETER R. "Managing by Expert Systems." *HRMagazine,* March 1990, pp. 37–39.

MITROFF, IAN I. *Break-Away Thinking: How to Challenge Your Business Assumptions (and Why You Should)*. New York: Wiley, 1988.

RUSSO, J. EDWARD, and SCHOEMAKER, PAUL J. H. *The 10 Barriers to Brilliant Decision Making and How to Overcome Them*. New York: Doubleday/Currency, 1989.

SINNOTT, JAN D. (ed.). *Everyday Problem Solving: Theory and Application*. Westport, CT: Praeger, 1989.

VANGUNDY, ARTHUR B. *Creative Problem Solving: A Guide for Trainers and Managers*. Westport, CT: Quorum, 1987.

Chapter 7 Appendix

ANSWERS AND INTERPRETATION TO CREATIVITY TESTS

RHYME AND REASON TEST

Obviously, the more of these rhymes you were able to come up with, the higher your creative potential. You would also need an advanced vocabulary to score very high (for instance, what is a "simian" or a "crustacean"?). Ten or more correct rhymes would tend to show outstanding creative potential, at least in the verbal area. Here are the answers:

1. Glad dad	12. Frail male
2. Fake ache	13. Beach teach
3. Ape shape	14. Weak critique
4. Top cop	15. Thriller killer
5. Ship trip	16. Mellow cello
6. Fat cat	17. Brave slave
7. Sad lad	18. Ripe gripe
8. Smart start	19. Weird beard
9. Deep sleep	20. Limp shrimp
10. Mad fad	21. Short escort
11. Long song	

If you can think of a sensible substitute for any of these answers, give yourself a bonus point. For example, for number 9, how about a booze snooze?

CREATIVE PERSONALITY TEST

The answer in the *creative direction* for each question is as follows:

1. Mostly false	9. Mostly true
2. Mostly true	10. Mostly true
3. Mostly false	11. Mostly false
4. Mostly false	12. Mostly true
5. Mostly true	13. Mostly false
6. Mostly false	14. Mostly false
7. Mostly true	15. Mostly true
8. Mostly true	16. Mostly false

Give yourself a plus one for each answer you gave in agreement with the keyed answers.

How Do You Interpret Your Score?

As cautioned earlier, this is an exploratory test. Extremely high or low scores are probably the most meaningful. A score of 12 or more suggests that your personality and attitudes are similar to those of a creative person. A score of 5 or less suggests that your personality is dissimilar to that of a creative person. You are probably more of a conformist (and somewhat categorical) in your thinking, at least at this point in your life. Don't be discouraged. Most people can develop in the direction of becoming a more creative individual.

8

Working Effectively within a Group

LEARNING OBJECTIVES

After reading and studying this chapter and doing the exercises, you should be able to

1. Appreciate why it is important to understand group behavior.
2. Develop a tentative strategy for improving your team play.
3. Describe the mechanics of brainstorming and the nominal group technique.
4. Explain how quality circles operate.
5. Summarize the major potential contributions of group effort.
6. Summarize the potential hazards of group effort, including groupthink.

G roups are vital to the understanding of human relations because they are the basic building blocks of the larger organization. The department you are assigned to, the division your department belongs to, the people you share a work break with, and the special committee you are assigned to are among the many groups found within an organization. A group has an identity of its own that transcends that of its members. For instance, a group of people may laugh at a comment that its members individually would not find humorous. And a group can accomplish a task that could not be accomplished by combining the contributions of its individual members. In recent years much attention has been paid to the ability of groups to achieve such ends as improving the quality of products and services and increasing productivity.

A **group** is two or more people who interact with each other, are aware of each other, are working toward some common purpose, and perceive themselves to be a group. Two police officers making their rounds in a squad car would constitute a group. So would the executive committee of an energy corporation. In contrast, ten people waiting for a bus would not be a real group. Although they might converse, their interaction would not be on a planned or recurring basis. Nor would they be engaged in collective effort—a fundamental justification for forming a group.

The study of groups is justified only if people behave differently in groups than they do individually. A grisly example can be used to illustrate the point that group and individual behavior are not the same. Twelve times during the last thirty years, riots among fans at soccer games have resulted in multiple deaths. Most of these deaths resulted from trampling. Yet almost none of the tramplers would individually stomp to death another soccer fan. Only a group can incite such violence.

Groups are also responsible for positive accomplishments, such as increased creativity and problem solving. The thrust of this chapter deals with the positive side of group effort, such as group decision making, quality circles, and effective meetings.

FORMAL VS. INFORMAL GROUPS

Since groups are such an important part of the workplace, they have been classified and described in many ways. The two major types of groups of most importance to the study of human behavior in organizations are formal and informal groups. Much of this book is concerned with the behavior of people in formal and informal groups.

Formal Groups

A **formal group** is one deliberately formed by the organization to accomplish specific tasks and achieve objectives. Formal groups are designated by the organization chart, with each group having its own box. At times formal groups are indicated on the bulletin board or through office memos (for example, "The undernamed people are hereby assigned to the safety committee."). Formal groups of a relatively permanent nature are called command groups, while those of a more temporary nature are called committees and task forces.

Command groups are the most prevalent clustering of people in almost any work organization. They consist of a manager and the group members. The formal organization is composed of a group of interconnected command groups. According to the linking-pin concept, managers are the linking pins between the many formal groups in the organization. As such each manager is a member of at least two command groups (see Figure 8–1).[1]

Command groups are easy to identify. Usually they have names that bring attention to their identity, such as information systems department, marketing division, public safety department, and department of radiology. Typically a person is assigned to only one command group at a time. Yet that same person may be assigned simultaneously to one or more special purpose temporary groups.

A **committee** is a group of people brought together to help solve a problem, usually by studying the problem and then offering advice to some higher authority. Standing committees are permanent, as illustrated by a planning committee that helps the firm cope with the future. The majority of committees are temporary. The committee is assigned a problem to study, such as establishing better relations with citizens groups. Once the committee has finished its work, its recommendations are given to a high-ranking official. It is not unusual for the same committee to be reinstated next year, but this time new members are chosen. Governments and educational institutions rely heavily on the committee system to bring about important changes.

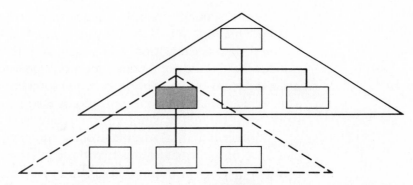

FIGURE 8–1 The Linking-pin Concept Whereby the Manager Represents the Group in the Next Level of Management

A **task force** is composed of a group of employees assigned to carry out a specialized activity, often with a time deadline. The task force usually has more formal authority to implement its recommendations than does a committee. In getting the task accomplished, it is necessary for group members to coordinate their efforts. Often members of the task force are from different departments. In some instances, members of a command group have a minimum of interaction. For instance, two accountants working in the same payroll department might be handling different projects and therefore work independently of each other. By definition, then, members of a task group must work cooperatively.

Another type of formal group is the **interorganizational group,** composed of members of organizations with common concerns who meet regularly. Group members are typically from nonprofit organizations. An example is community agency representatives who meet to develop services for pregnant teens.[2] Interorganizational groups can also be composed of business people, such as a group of company presidents who meet regularly to discuss common concerns about educating the workforce.

Informal Groups

An organization cannot be understood by studying its formal groups alone. Informal groups are also important. An **informal group** is one that arises out of individual needs and the attraction of workers to one another. These groups evolve naturally to take care of people's desire for friendship and companionship. Informal groups appear at all levels in the organization. Two examples of informal groups are as follows:

- Four computer operators form a jogging club that meets three days per week at lunch to run two miles.
- Three managers from different parts of the company commute to work together every business day when they are all in town. Often they discuss current events and the stock market, but they also discuss company business while commuting to work.

As the second example suggests, informal groups are often work-related. One function of the informal organization is to fill in the gaps left by the formal organization. Few organizations have a written job description for the "coffee pot tender," yet such a position arises on a rotating basis in a good many offices. Similarly, when somebody in your department is absent for legitimate reasons, you might take care of his or her emergency work, even though it is not a formal part of your job.

Another potential advantage of the informal group is that the members may develop a mutual friendship off the job that carries over to the job. The result is that ties to the formal group become stronger, as exemplified by people becoming more loyal to the company as a consequence of bowling together.

HOW TO BE A TEAM PLAYER

Teamwork is heavily emphasized today, as evidenced by the grouping of workers into self-managing teams.[3] Being a team player is thus more important than ever (see the accompanying box). The same principle applies to both managers and individual contributors. As the linking pin concept indicates, each manager is a member of two groups: his or her own work group, and a group of managers.

Five suggestions are offered here which get at the essence of being a team player: Be cooperative, promote the team concept, share information and opinions, be candid with other team members, and provide emotional support to co-workers.

WINNING IN BUSINESS REQUIRES TEAMWORK

James A. Perkins, former football player and now senior vice president of personnel for Federal Express, brings a strong sense of team spirit to his position. Perkins sees a direct correlation between the way Federal Express treats its employees and the way the overnight courier is treated by its customers.

Perkins has stayed with Federal Express for over fifteen years primarily because the company's loyalty to employees is as strong as its commitment to profits. Perkins said he learned the value of teamwork from his parents and coaches. "You can't win on your own. It's necessary to work with other people effectively."

His current team is the human resources people at Federal Express. He is known in his company for his integrity, fairness, and straightforward, candid way of dealing with confusing situations. If another person presents his or her ideas in a garbled manner, Perkins will say, "I don't have the slightest idea of what you're talking about."

In reflecting on his company, Perkins says, "Working at Federal Express is far beyond anything I have ever envisioned. I feel like I have been a key player on one of the best management teams in corporate America. I feel a tremendous amount of pride in having been a member of the team. From my perspective, I've been playing on a Super Bowl team, and I feel just great about it."

Source: As reported in Martha I. Finney, "Talents of a Team Player," *Personnel Administrator,* November 1988, pp. 44–47.

Be cooperative. If you display a willingness to help others and work cooperatively with them, you will be regarded as a good team player. Organizations cannot function without cooperative effort. If people do not cooperate with each other, the system breaks down. Not all employees are concerned about the smooth functioning of the total organization, but they do value cooperation from their co-workers. An excellent way of being cooperative is to handle the customer or client problems of a co-worker when he or she is not available: "_____ is out sick today, but perhaps I can help you."[4]

Promote the team concept.   A critical part of promoting the team concept is to emphasize "we" rather than "I" when talking about work accomplishments. The rationale here is that almost all accomplishments in an organization are really group accomplishments. A convenient way of emphasizing the "we" concept is to share credit with co-workers for your good ideas and accomplishments: "Here is the report I synthesized based on important input from Sally, Tom, and Rick."

Share information and opinions.   Sharing of this nature helps foster a spirit of teamwork because sharing leads to closeness both on and off the job. Tamara, a public relations specialist, illustrates how information and opinions may be shared in a work setting:

> At a typical staff meeting Tamara makes comments such as: "Let me share with you some important information I've picked up on that topic"; "I have some scuttlebutt that might be worth something"; or "Let me give you my candid, very personal reaction to your proposal."

Be candid with other team members.   Similar to the suggestion just made, be open with co-workers in order to encourage mutual trust. Trust, in turn, leads to teamwork and group effectiveness. Jack Welch, the chairman and chief executive officer of General Electric, has attempted to foster teamwork by promoting traits such as candor and trust.[5] A good starting point in gaining the trust of other team members is to be as open and honest as the situation will allow.

A sales representative made a candid comment that helped win him the trust of team members. He said, "I wish I could take full credit for having beat out the competition on that humongous order you all heard about. But it sure helped having my mother's best friend as the president of the company that placed the order."

Another important way of being candid is to inform co-workers about your plans, in order to minimize the feeling that you tried to surprise them on purpose. An example would be to inform others in advance that you will be making a suggestion for reorganizing the department at the next staff meeting. A variation of this tactic is to gather suggestions from co-workers before finalizing your plan.

Provide emotional support to co-workers.   An effective team player as well as an effective leader provides emotional support to members. Support of this nature can take the form of verbal encouragement for ideas expressed, listening to a co-worker's problems, or even providing help with a knotty technical problem. A direct approach would be to say to a co-worker who looked to be in a sullen mood, "It looks as if this isn't the best day in your life. Is there anything I can do to help?"

Our attention turns next to another important part of being a group member: leading or participating in meetings.

CONDUCTING OR PARTICIPATING IN AN EFFECTIVE MEETING

A substantial portion of working within groups takes place in the context of a meeting, including staff meetings and committee meetings. A new development is to conduct work unit meetings, composed of supervisors and workers at the first one or two job levels.[6] A consistent estimate is that managers, professionals, and technical employees spend about 30 percent of their time in meetings. Senior executives spend about half their work days in meetings.[7]

It is fashionable to decry meetings with statements such as "Ugh, not another meeting." Negative jokes about committee meetings circulate freely, such as, "A committee is a place where minutes are taken and hours are lost," or "The primary purpose of a committee is to avoid action." Despite these criticisms, collective effort would be very difficult without formal meetings.

A constructive viewpoint about meetings is not to eliminate them, but to follow guidelines for improving their effectiveness. Both leaders and participants share responsibility for attaining effectiveness. In this context, *effectiveness* refers to goal attainment and member satisfaction.

Suggestions for the Meeting Leader

Select qualified members and rely upon their expertise. Members of effective meetings are qualified for their assignments from the standpoint of knowledge and interest. For instance, if a person is planning to quit a company in six months, he or she would have little interest in serving on a profit-sharing committee and therefore would make a meager contribution. During the meetings, it is important for the leader to rely on the expertise of members. An obvious but often overlooked point is that a meeting cannot achieve its full purpose unless members help solve the problems.

Have a specific agenda. Efficient and effective meetings typically have a planned agenda that is given to participants in advance of the meeting. Simultaneously, it is important that the head of the meeting steer the group toward staying with the agenda. When members ask, "What are we supposed to talk about today?" or take off on tangents during the meeting, time wasting is the most probable result.

Strive for balanced contributions by members. A skillful leader often has to curtail the contribution of verbose and domineering members. Equally important, the chairperson has to coax more reticent members to contribute their ideas. Without a balanced contribution, a committee fails to achieve its fundamental purpose of being a democratic process.

The leader should seriously consider the ideas and suggestions of the participants. In order to encourage employee involvement and participation, ideas from the group should be seriously considered. Dave Day suggests that when appropriate, these views should be incorporated into decisions that affect the work group.[8] When a participant's total suggestion cannot be accepted, it is often possible to use part of the idea submitted.

> During a work unit meeting, a bank teller suggested that bank employees wear team clothing to dramatize the team banking concept. Sensing that most of the group disliked the idea, the leader said, "I like the idea of using a team symbol. How about metal buttons with a message something to the effect that we're part of the First National team?"

Effort should be directed toward surmountable problems.   Many problem-solving groups make the mistake of spending time discussing "who is to blame for the problem," or "what should have been done to avoid the problem."[9] Rather than try to change the past—an impossible task—it is better to focus on how things can be improved in the future.

The meeting should start and stop on time.   Meetings that start on time create a stronger sense of urgency and purpose than do meetings that begin late. If the leader guarantees that the meeting will end on time, much fidgeting and looking at watches is eliminated. Also, members will work harder at covering the planned agenda if a time limit is imposed. An agenda should be planned to fit comfortably into the allotted time.

Strive for consensus, not total acceptance.   Few groups composed of assertive individuals will reach total agreement on most agenda items. It is more realistic to strive for **consensus**—a state of harmony, general agreement, or majority opinion with a reasonable amount of disagreement still present. When consensus is achieved, each member should be willing to accept the plan because it is logical and feasible. The following suggestions are designed to help the leader achieve consensus:

1. Encourage participants to clarify and build on one another's ideas. Be sure that everyone's ideas are heard.
2. Avoid vigorous or heated arguments in favor of one person's position, especially your own. Encourage the team not to let itself be railroaded by one or two people.
3. Strive for win-win solutions (or plans), instead of such methods as majority vote, averaging and coin flipping. Win-win means that everyone feels reasonably comfortable with what is going to happen. This is where you should be when you believe that you have a consensus.[10]

Be enthusiastic.   To help increase productivity and satisfaction, display enthusiasm. Show respect for the importance of the meeting to the group, to the task at hand, and to the organization. Conducting a meeting is an act of leadership, and enthusiasm is an important leadership requirement.

Suggestions for the Meeting Participant

Most of the suggestions mentioned above for the meeting leader can also be transposed to the participant's perspective. For instance, while leaders should rely on member expertise, members should contribute their expertise. The following suggestions will help you avoid frequent errors committed by meeting participants.

Make the right amount of contribution. The person who dominates a meeting is perceived just as negatively as the noncontributor. Give other people a chance to contribute, but do not be so unassuming that you become passive.

Be punctual and stay for the entire meeting. If you will be late or have to leave early, let the leader know in advance.

Keep your comments brief and pointed. One of the major problems facing the meeting leader is to keep conversations on track. Help the leader by setting a good example for the other participants.

Be supportive toward other members. If another participant says something of value, give that person your approval by such means as nodding your head or smiling. Support of this type encourages the free flow of ideas. Being supportive includes being tolerant of viewpoints considerably different from yours.

Listen carefully to the leader and other participants. Show by your nonverbal behavior that you are concerned about what they are saying. For example, look attentive and enthusiastic.

Take your turn at being the leader during the meeting. To accomplish this you might volunteer to make a report during the meeting or head a subcommittee that will report back to the group later.

Avoid disruptive behavior, such as belittling another participant, frequent laughter, nail clipping, wallet cleaning, newspaper reading, napping, or yawning. Many a career has been set back because of poor etiquette displayed in a meeting.

GROUP DECISION MAKING AND PROBLEM SOLVING

Decision making and problem solving are major activities carried out in meetings. In organizations most complex problems are solved, and therefore most decisions are made, by groups. The information presented in Chapter 7 about individual decision making and creativity also applies to groups because groups still rely on individuals for ideas. However, a substantial amount of information about decision making in groups deserves separate treatment. Here we examine four group approaches: general problem-solving groups, group brainstorming, the nominal group technique, and quality circles.

General Problem-Solving Groups

When a group of workers at any level gather to solve a problem, they typically hold a discussion rather than rely on a formal group decision-making technique. These general meetings are likely to produce the best results when they follow (1) the suggestions for conducting a meeting, and (2) the decision-making steps. Table 8–1 describes recommended steps for conducting group decision making. You will observe that these steps follow quite closely the decision-making steps presented in Figure 7–1.

TABLE 8–1   Steps for effective group decision making

1. *Identify the problem.* Describe specifically what the problem is and how it manifests itself.

2. *Clarify the problem.* If group members do not perceive the problem the same way, they will offer divergent solutions to their own individual perceptions of the problem.

3. *Analyze the cause.* To convert "what is" into "what we want," the group must understand the causes of the specific problems and find ways to overcome those causes.

4. *Search for alternative solutions.* Remember that multiple alternative solutions can be found to most problems.

5. *Select alternatives.* Identify the criteria that solutions must meet, then discuss the pros and cons of the proposed alternatives. No solution should be laughed at or scorned.

6. *Plan for implementation.* Decide what actions are necessary to carry out the chosen solution to the problem.

7. *Clarify the contract.* The contract is a restatement of what group members have agreed to do, and deadlines for accomplishment.

8. *Develop an action plan.* Specify who does what and when to carry out the contract.

9. *Provide for evaluation and accountability.* After the plan is implemented, reconvene to discuss progress, and to hold people accountable for results that have not been achieved.

Source: Derived from Andrew E. Schwartz and Joy Levin, "Better Group Decision Making," *Supervisory Management,* June 1990, p. 4.

Group Brainstorming

Brainstorming is a conference technique of solving specific problems, amassing information, and stimulating creative thinking. The basic technique is to encourage unrestrained and spontaneous participation by group members. The term *brainstorm* has become so widely known that it is often used as a synonym for a clever idea. Developed by advertising executive Alex Osburn over forty-five years ago, brainstorming really means to use the *brain* to *storm* a problem.[11]

Today brainstorming is used both as a method of finding alternatives to real-life problems and as a creativity training program. In the usual form of brainstorming, group members spontaneously call out alternative solutions to a problem facing them. Any member is free to enhance or "hitchhike" upon the contribution of another person. At the end of the session, somebody sorts out the ideas and edits the more unrefined ones.

Brainstorming is widely used to develop new ideas for products, find names for products, develop advertising slogans, and solve customer problems. For instance, the idea for pet seatbelts emerged from a brainstorming session. Brainstorming has also been used to develop a new organization structure in a government agency, and is now widely used in developing software.

Rules for brainstorming. Adhering to a few simple rules or guidelines helps ensure that creative alternative solutions to problems will be forthcoming from the procedure. The brainstorming process usually falls into place without frequent reminders about guidelines. Nevertheless, here are eight rules to improve the chances of having a good session:

1. *Group size should be about five to seven people.* Too few people and not enough suggestions are generated; too many people and the session becomes uncontrolled. However, brainstorming can be conducted with as few as three people.
2. *Everybody is given the chance to suggest alternative solutions.* Members spontaneously call out alternatives to the problem facing the group. (Another approach is for people to speak in sequence.)
3. *No criticism is allowed.* All suggestions should be welcome; it is particularly important not to use derisive laughter.
4. *Freewheeling is encouraged.* Outlandish ideas often prove quite useful. It's easier to tame a wild idea than to originate one.[12]
5. *Quantity and variety are very important.* The greater the number of ideas put forth, the greater the likelihood of a breakthrough idea.
6. *Combinations and improvements are encouraged.* Building upon the ideas of others, including combining them, is very productive. "Hitchhiking" or "piggybacking" is an essential part of brainstorming.

7. *Notes must be taken during the session by a person who serves as the recording secretary.* The session can also be taped, but this requires substantial time to retrieve ideas.

8. *Do not overstructure by following any of the seven ideas too rigidly.* Brainstorming is a spontaneous group process.

Brainstorming at an airline. A representative example of the output from brainstorming is the "no ifs, ands, or butts" advertising campaign developed at Northwest Airlines that banned smoking on all its flights. (Northwest pioneered the smoking ban.) The majority of Northwest passengers are business travelers, and the airline's previous advertising campaign had emphasized its frequent-flier program. However, the airline had become more aggressive about attracting leisure travelers with programs such as clubs that offer travel packages. The no-smoking campaign was aimed at both markets.

Northwest executives developed the idea for the campaign during a brainstorming session. The output from the session was supported later by market research. Although one-third of airline passengers are smokers, Northwest said its research showed that the vast majority of consumers favored smoke-free flights.[13]

The Nominal Group Technique

At times a leader is faced with a major problem that would benefit from the input of group members. Because of the magnitude of the problem, it would be helpful to know what each member thought of the others' positions on the problem. Brainstorming is not advisable because the problem is still in the exploration phase, and requires more than a list of alternative solutions. A problem-solving technique has been developed to fit this situation. The **nominal group technique (NGT)** is a group problem-solving technique that calls people together in a structured meeting with limited interaction. The group is called "nominal" because people first present their ideas without interacting with each other, as they would in a "real" group. However, group discussion does take place at a later stage in the process.

George P. Huber provides a general description of the NGT that will help you gain insight into the process.

> Imagine a meeting room in which seven to ten individuals are sitting around a table in full view of each other. At the beginning of the meeting they are not speaking to one another. Instead, each individual is writing ideas on their pads of paper. At the end of five to ten minutes, a structured sharing of ideas takes place. Each individual, in round-robin fashion, presents one idea from his or her private list. A recorder or leader writes that idea on a flip chart in full view of other members. There is still no discussion at this point of the meeting—only the recording. Round-robin listing continues until all members indicate they have no further ideas to share.[14]

The output from this phase is a list of ideas, such as, "Why not sell three small schools and replace them with one large, central building?" or "I wonder if we should be talking about consolidation until we first obtain more information about population trends in this district." Next, discussion of a very structured nature takes place; this is called the interactive phase of the meeting. Questions and comments are solicited for each idea posted on the flip chart. ("What do you folks think about this idea of selling the smaller school buildings and constructing one new, large building?")

When this process of asking for reactions to the ideas is complete, independent evaluation of the ideas takes place. Each group member, acting alone, indicates his or her preferences by ranking the various ideas proposed. Again, these ideas may be alternative solutions to the problem or factors the group should take into consideration in trying to solve the problem. At this stage, we know the average rank the group has attached to each idea.

Since its development over two decades ago, the nominal group technique has gained considerable acceptance and recognition. It has been widely applied in business, industry, health, education, social service, and government. The process does the job of generating alternatives, keeping "bloopers" to a minimum, and satisfying group members. Much of the success of the NGT can be attributed to the fact that it follows the logic of the problem-solving method and allows for group participation. It is also somewhat more disciplined than conventional brainstorming.

Quality Circles

A **quality circle** is a small group of employees from the same department who voluntarily and regularly meet in order to identify, analyze, and solve problems related to the work group. During the last two decades this group problem-solving technique has seen rapid growth, and is considered a major form of participative management. The wide-scale adoption of QCs stems from the perception that they were a major contributor to Japan's high annual rate of productivity growth.

Usually about six to twelve volunteers from the same department constitute the circle. Group members receive training in problem solving, statistical quality control, and the functioning of work groups. QCs typically recommend solutions for productivity and quality problems which are then passed along to management for approval and implementation. A facilitator who is a consultant or a staff specialist helps train circle members and keeps the group running smoothly.

Goals and objectives of QC programs include (1) quality improvement, (2) productivity improvement, and (3) improved quality of work life through employee involvement. The group usually meets four hours a month on company time. Members get recognition, and in rare instances, financial rewards for their suggestions.[15]

The balance of our discussion of quality circles centers around the details of the process, and the factors associated with its success.

The QC process: group problem solving in action. All quality circles are designed to gather employee suggestions about work-related topics. Quality circle meetings are well-structured group problem-solving sessions. As such, they are far removed from employee gripe sessions or "free-for-alls." Meetings take place in a conference room or other suitable space furnished with the necessary supplies and equipment needed to discuss topics and perform analyses. Organizations fine-tune the QC approach to fit their needs. Nevertheless, six major steps in the process can be identified, as shown in Figure 8–2.[16]

Step 1: Problem identification. The circle members develop a list of problems tied directly to their jobs. The quality circles are not established with the intention of solving all the company's ills. Because circle members are regarded as experts in their own jobs, it is important that the problems be associated directly with the work.

Step 2: Problem selection. The QC members select from the total group of problems those they choose to tackle. A QC expert suggests: "It is advisable to address simple problems initially so that the circle develops confidence in the techniques that its members have been trained to use, in themselves operating as a group, and in management's endorsement of the program."

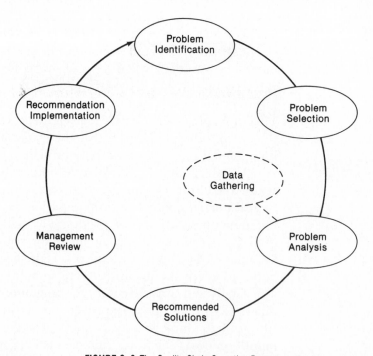

FIGURE 8–2 The Quality Circle Operating Process

Step 3: Problem analysis.   In this step of the process, QC members apply analytical techniques to identify the cause of the problem, to gather information, and to sort out possible remedies. The QC may need to use company data that bears directly on the problem. It may also be necessary to call on experts from different departments to avoid duplication of effort.

One of the analytical techniques often used in the problem analysis stage is the **80–20 principle.** It states that 80 percent of the results or problems are usually caused by 20 percent of the activities. For instance, 80 percent of the sales volume is often contributed by 20 percent of the customers. In a QC, an 80–20 analysis might reveal that 80 percent of customer complaints can be attributed to 20 percent of the features of a product. By identifying the 20 percent problem area, QC members can then make suggestions for improvement.

Step 4: Recommended solutions.   In most instances the QC will arrive at a firm recommendation or a few alternative solutions. QCs have developed a good reputation for arriving at cost-effective solutions to tangible work problems.

Step 5: Management review.   The output of the circle is a formal presentation to the QC's department manager regarding the statement of the problem, the analysis, and recommendations. For many QC members, this represents the first time they have ever made a presentation to management. Management retains the prerogative of implementing or not implementing the QC recommendations.

Step 6: Implementing the recommendation.   Once a recommendation has been approved by management, its implementation usually does not meet with much resistance. Employees outside the QC generally accept its value and appreciate the fact that the opinions of operating personnel have been incorporated into the suggestions.

Evaluation of quality circle effectiveness.   Quality circles are widely used by both private and public organizations. The Internal Revenue Service provides an illustration of a governmental application of quality circles. QCs were incorporated into the IRS after a troublesome filing season for 1985 taxes. Thousands of people filed complaints because tax refunds were mailed late.

The widespread use of quality circles has prompted extensive evaluation of their effectiveness. One of the most comprehensive evaluations of QCs synthesized the results of thirty-two studies. Fifteen of these studies showed uniformly positive results. The positive results were reported in terms of consequences both to individuals and to organizations, and included higher job satisfaction, improved product quality, and increased productivity.

Eight of the thirty-two studies identified negative consequences (decreases in job satisfaction and productivity) to the individual and the organization. One of these results was found at a division of Honeywell Inc., one at a computer firm, one among government employees, and five at the Department of Defense. The researchers who prepared the report suspected that the organizational climate in the Department of Defense may not be appropriate for the conduct of QCs. Also, the QCs may not have been conducted long enough to obtain good results.[17]

A study of seventy-three employees organized into eight QCs over a three-year period indicates that positive results with QCs may not be long-lasting. The purpose of the study was to assess the individual and organizational consequences of quality circles. Scores for individual consequences of job satisfaction, commitment to the organization, performance, and intentions to quit improved gradually over two years. After this time period, all the scores decreased back to their initial levels. During the same period, management's perception of the effectiveness of the QC program followed the same pattern.[18] An optimistic interpretation of these results is that QCs are excellent short-range morale and productivity boosters.

Key elements of successful QC programs.   Whether a QC succeeds or fails depends heavily on the conditions under which it is implemented and on certain characteristics of the circle.[19] As with most human relations techniques, it is important to explicitly state the goals of the program, such as improving product quality or increasing productivity. When good employee-management relations already exist, the quality circle is predisposed to success. One reason is that the employees are less likely to believe that management is using the QC merely to squeeze extra productivity from them.

It is important for circle leaders to solicit opinions from the group, because the QC is a technique of participative management. Employees who volunteer for membership in the QC should be competent and interested in making an extra contribution, and they should receive ample training. QC members should receive some external rewards for outstanding suggestions. These external rewards can include recognition and money. Payment for suggestions, however, is controversial because it may create resentment among nonmembers of the quality circle.

POTENTIAL CONTRIBUTIONS OF GROUP EFFORT

Working within a group has many advantages, including synergy—the total output of the group is greater than the sum of the individual contributions. Another major advantage of group effort is that it frequently enhances the job satisfaction of members because of the opportunity to satisfy needs, such as affiliation, recognition, and self-esteem.

A lengthy experiment was conducted to determine the contribution of groups to problem solving and decision making. The subjects in the study were twenty-two learning groups that formed the basis for instruction in twenty-five organizational behavior courses taught over a five-year period. In the team learning format the vast majority of class time is spent actually working on group problem solving. Data for individual vs. group decision making comparisons were collected from a series of individual and group tests about the subject matter. Some of the tests were quite advanced, requiring students to synthesize and analyze concepts.

The results showed that the mean group score was 89.9; the best individual score was 82.6; and the average individual score was 74.2. In comparing group scores with individual best scores, it was found that 215 of the 222 groups (97 percent) outperformed their best member. Based on these results, the researchers concluded:

> The greatest contribution of this study is an unequivocal demonstration that, in a setting similar in many ways to a typical work environment, a vast majority of groups can outperform their most knowledgeable member on decision-making tasks.[20]

POTENTIAL HAZARDS OF GROUP EFFORT

Despite the many contributions of group effort, including decision making, work groups have some major potential disadvantages for the organization and group members. Four notable ones are shirking of individual responsibility, conformity to mediocre performance, stifling of creativity, and groupthink.

Shirking of Individual Responsibility

For those people not strongly work oriented, group assignments are sometimes an invitation to shirk responsibility. Unless assignments are carefully drawn and both group and individual objectives exist, an undermotivated member can often squeeze by without contributing his or her fair share. The shirker risks being ostracized by the group, but may be willing to pay this price rather than work hard. Shirking of individual responsibility is commonly found in groups such as committees, task forces, and project teams.

Shirkers run the risk of exposure. The heads of temporary groups are often required to write a report estimating the contribution of individual members. If the same person is perceived to have been a noncontributor in several groups, he or she may not be invited back for special assignments. (In regular work units, the work of individuals is readily measured, because people work against goals and quotas.)

Conformity to Mediocre Performance

Group membership exerts pressures on individuals to conform to group standards in such ways as thinking like the average member and producing at approximately the same level as co-workers. These standards are referred to as **group norms,** the unwritten expectations for members that tell them what they ought to do. Norms become a standard of what each person should or should not do within the group. The norms often influence the level of goal difficulty set by the individual.[21]

Conformity in thinking can sometimes be detrimental. For instance, one design engineer in a group of five may believe that a car-braking mechanism is unsafe. After learning that the co-workers think the braking mechanism is safe, the engineer may reflect, "If the other members of the group disagree with me, I'm probably wrong. Why be an oddball? I'll call the braking mechanism safe." Such an act of conformity has two negative consequences. First, the engineer may be right. A pronouncement about the unsafe features of the braking mechanism could save lives (or at least a later recall) if brought to the attention of management. Second, by not casting an opinion and going along with the group, the engineer's contribution is almost zero. As one manager said about his subordinates, "If they all agree with me, why do I need all of them?"

Conformity in actions can lead to lowered performance and career retardation. A potential hazard of being accepted by your work group and identifying with its members is that you will go along with mediocre performance standards. To the extent that you try to remain "one of the gang," you will not be able to distinguish yourself from others. Your allegiance to the group may make it difficult for you to advance into management or to perform your job in a superior manner. Groups sometimes foster mediocre performance.

> Nancy took the best job she could find for the summer, a housekeeper position at a resort hotel. As she perceived the situation, the pay was good, the hours delightful, and the beach superb. However, Nancy was subject to some uncomfortable group pressures. She explains what happened: "I felt some kind of obligation to do my best for the hotel owners. They were treating me fine, and I wanted to reciprocate. I charged into my jobs, literally singing as I went about my chores. Within a week I found that the other housekeepers were almost forcing me to take a coffee or soft drink break with them. They told me I was cleaning too many rooms an hour. They wanted me to slow down so they wouldn't look bad. My decision was to tell them to do what they wanted, and I would do what I wanted. My decision was the right one. I was invited back the next year as a supervising housekeeper."

Stifling of Creativity

Closely related to the problem of conformity to mediocre performance is the fact that group norms can stifle creativity. The group may foster the attitude that innovative thinking disturbs the status quo and is therefore undesirable. One manifestation of norms stifling creativity is when the person who initiates an original idea is given no recognition by the group. Unless the person is a strong individualist, he or she will probably not pursue the idea. Blake and Mouton furnish an example of how one company coped with the problem of creativity-stifling norms.

> A large utilities company was able to solve problems arising from the norms that were hampering a project team's progress in making key decisions. Pressures were mounting after unexpected fuel cost increases and new technological developments triggered huge first-quarter losses.
>
> The engineering division manager faced a number of tough decisions concerning the newest plant. His project team began to flounder, even though he had handpicked the members who seemed to be best available. After he and another manager discussed the problem, and examined the norms and culture of their company, they realized that operations were conducted primarily on a "compromise" basis. Few people wished to "rock the boat" by suggesting plans or programs that departed from past precedents. To solve the problem, they developed a norm-shifting action plan that zeroed in on the major problems. For in-

stance, they openly discussed their drift toward mediocrity and then wrote a short description of the problems as they perceived them.[22]

Groupthink

A potential disadvantage of group decision making is **groupthink,** a deterioration of mental efficiency, reality testing, and moral judgment in the interest of group solidarity. Groupthink is an extreme form of consensus that results in a decision fiasco. The group thinks as a unit, believes it is impervious to outside criticism, and begins to have illusions about its own invincibility.

Examples of groupthink.   Groupthink was first observed by Irving L. Janis in his research on governmental policy groups faced with difficult problems in a complex and changing environment. A widely cited example of groupthink relates to the United States invasion of Cuba in 1961. President John F. Kennedy and his staff decided to invade Cuba at the Bay of Pigs, despite information that the invasion would fail and damage our relations with other countries. Arthur Schlesinger, Jr., one of Kennedy's closest advisers, stated that he had strong reservations about the invasion proposal, yet he failed to present his opposing views. He felt his dissenting opinions were unlikely to sway the group away from the invasion plan and would probably have made him appear to be a "nuisance."[23]

More recent government examples of what appears to be groupthink are the approval of the Challenger launch despite strong warnings, and the Iran-Contra affair (illegally using arms sales to Iran to fund the Contras in Nicaragua). A business example is the decision of Chrysler Corporation executives to sell as new cars that they had personally sampled. The illusion of newness was created by dolling up the cars and turning back the odometers. The following case history, also from business, helps explain the process of groupthink.

> The field of management information systems (MIS) provides a current example of the hazards of groupthink. The project involved was a complex decision support system for corporate planners. Far into the project, the systems vice president admitted: "We had gotten sucked into something that was doomed to fail from the start." The excitement about the project camouflaged obstacles that should have forced a serious rethinking of the decision.
>
> Unfortunately, the obstacles to the project's success were the same as its reputed benefits. The system would be powerful and flexible enough to help planners anticipate future corporate needs more accurately than in the past. However, the system was so sophisticated that it was too complicated for the planners to use. The systems vice president analyzed why this possibility was not foreseen.

"It sounded so good," said the vice president. "Planning is such a tedious process, and with this system we were going to make users a lot more powerful. We felt we were really accomplishing something." Eventually the system was phased out in favor of a simple system that programmers can change as conditions dictate. "I guess," said the vice president, "that when you sense something is too good to be true, it probably is."[24]

Groupthink was responsible for the construction of an unusable system because no group member was willing to challenge the value of the system. The intelligent and well-trained people assigned to the project insulated themselves from the real world in which the system would be used.

Glen Whyte believes that many instances of groupthink can be explained by decision makers seeing themselves as choosing between losses that are inevitable. The group believes that a sure loss will occur unless action is taken. Caught up in the turmoil of trying to make the best of a bad situation, the group takes a bigger risk than would any individual member. The arms-for-hostages deal (Iran-Contra) was perceived by those who made it as a choice between losses. The status quo of American citizens held hostage by terrorist groups was a certain loss. Making an arms deal with Iran created some hope of averting that loss, although the deal would most likely fail and create more humiliation.[25]

How to prevent groupthink. If you are a group leader, consider taking the following steps to guard against the potential dangers of groupthink:

- Encourage all members of the group to express doubts and criticisms of proposed solutions to problems.
- Show by example that you are willing to accept criticism.
- Divide the group into subgroups to develop ideas. Then have the subgroups confront one another to examine why they differ.
- Periodically invite qualified outsiders to meet with the group and provide suggestions.
- If groupthink seems to be emerging, bring it to the attention of the group. For instance, you might say, "I get the impression that we are too eager to think as one. What is your reaction to the problem?"[26]

Summary of Key Points

- Groups are the building blocks of the larger organization. A group is defined as a collection of people who interact with each other, are aware of each other, are working toward some common purpose, and perceive themselves to be a group.

- Many different types of groups exist in an organization. A major classification of groups is formal vs. informal. A formal group is one deliberately formed by the organization to accomplish specific tasks. Command groups, committees, and task forces are the main types of formal groups. Another formal group is the interorganizational group. An informal group is one that evolves naturally to take care of people's desire for companionship; however, it may also serve organizational purposes.

- Being a team player is an important part of working within a group. Strategies for achieving this end include being cooperative, promoting the team concept, sharing information and opinions, being open and honest, informing others of your plans, and providing emotional support to co-workers.

- Both the meeting leader and members contribute to an effective meeting. Points for the leader to keep in mind include these: Rely on the expertise of qualified members, have a specific agenda, strive for consensus, and be enthusiastic. Points for participants include these: Make the right amount of contribution; make brief, pointed comments; support other members; listen to others; take your turn at leading the meeting; and avoid disruptive behavior.

- Group decision making and problem solving are frequently practiced in organizations. The four group approaches described here are general problem-solving groups, group brainstorming, the nominal group technique, and quality circles. General problem-solving groups follow the suggestions for conducting a meeting and the decision-making steps.

- In brainstorming, a group of people spontaneously call out alternatives to a problem facing them. Any group member is free to enhance or piggyback upon the idea of another member. Notes are taken during the sessions.

- The nominal group technique (NGT) is a method of exploring the nature of a problem and generating alternative solutions. It involves a group of seven to ten individuals contributing their written thoughts about the problem, and then all other members responding to their ideas. Members rank or rate the ideas, and the final group decision is the pooled outcome of the individual votes.

- A quality circle is a small group of employees from the same department who voluntarily and regularly meet in order to identify, analyze, and solve problems related to the work group. Organizations usually adapt the QC format to their particular circumstances. However, the typical steps are as follows: problem identification, problem selection, problem analysis (including data gathering), recommended solutions, management review, and implementing the recommendation.

- Whether a quality circle succeeds or fails depends heavily on conditions under which it is implemented, and on certain characteristics of the circle. Positive results, for example, are more likely to occur when top management is committed to the program, and QC members receive external rewards for their contribution.

- Group effort can lead to higher levels of productivity than individual effort will, and is often more satisfying than individual work is. A long-term experiment reported in the chapter demonstrated that for learning groups, 97 percent of groups outperformed their best member.

- Group effort has some potential hazards, including shirking individual responsibility, conformity to mediocre performance, stifling of creativity, and groupthink (an extreme form of consensus in which the group loses its powers of critical analysis).

Questions and Activities

1. Explain whether the class for which you are reading this book is a formal group.

2. Explain whether a professional baseball team is a formal or an informal group.

3. Give two examples of professional-level jobs for which being a team player is especially important.

4. What behaviors can you recommend for letting co-workers know that you are really more interested in "we" than "I"?

5. How might the suggestions for conducting oneself in a meeting be applied to the classroom?

6. What similarity do you see between brainwriting (see Chapter 7) and the nominal group technique?

7. How might quality circles be used to improve customer service in a department store?

8. Some companies have found that quality circles generate a higher number of useful ideas when there is frequent rotation among members. Why might this be true?

9. In what way do quality circles differ from brainstorming?

10. Obtain one valid example of groupthink by speaking to people with experience working in groups. Be prepared to discuss your findings in class.

A HUMAN RELATIONS CASE PROBLEM
The Uneasy Metric Conversion

Diane Turtino, director of County Social Services, looked forward to her Monday afternoon staff meeting. Eager to receive acceptance for her new program, she opened the meeting with these words:

"I'm not one for lengthy introductions to important topics. I have a major program for your approval. It could make us pacesetters in the social services field. By following my basic program, we will demonstrate that the county government means business about moving into the 21st century.

"I'm proposing that effective July 1 of this year, our agency make the switch from the decimal to the metric system," said Turtino. "No more hesitation; no more blocking the inevitable. From July 1 forward, we think metric around here. When I read client files, I want to see their height and weight expressed in centimeters and kilograms. When you tell me they need heating fuel, I want to know how many liters, not how many gallons.

"As most of you know," she continued, "the federal government is required by a 1988 act to use the metric system in its procurements, grants, and other business activities. Congress has officially designated metric as our preferred measurement system for trade and commerce."

Carlos Alvarez, director of housing, was the first to react: "Diane, I hear what you're saying, but I'm not in total agreement. I think you would need ten levels of approval to make the switch. We still receive a big chunk of our funding from state and federal sources. The federal government has gone metric, but the state hasn't. If we fall out of line with the state's official procedures, we could get penalized; maybe even lose some of our funding."

Jean LaMont, director of administrative services, spoke next: "Diane, I wish you and I had discussed this before you made up your mind. Are you aware of the administrative nightmare you would be creating by converting to metric? We'd have to calculate metric equivalent for all the data in our files. Whenever we sent files to out-of-county agencies, we'd get a barrage of complaints."

Turtino replied: "I hear some resistance from the group surfacing. But any worthwhile change will have its critics. So I won't be dissuaded by a few negative comments."

Gilbert Chen, director of income maintenance, commented: "Diane, you're dealing with more than a few negative comments. So far the metric conversion program has had its biggest impact on the federal government, and diary and calendar makers. Now engagement calendars and the like all contain metric conversion tables. So why bother with a program that hasn't really caught hold? In Canada, it's a different story. But we are in the United States."

Helen Moore, director of child services, summed up: "I make a motion that we postpone the idea of converting to metric. Perhaps we should set up a task force to study the issue more carefully."

Reluctantly, Turtino said: "Okay, who seconds the motion to postpone further discussion on the metric conversion program? After we vote on this motion, we will introduce the motion of setting up the necessary task force."

As the group considered the motion, Turtino thought: "What did I do wrong? Maybe I should have just issued an edict to convert to the metric system."

1. Explain why Diane Turtino should or should have not used group decision making on the metric conversion project.
2. What does this case illustrate about the advantages and disadvantages of group decision making?
3. What is your evaluation of Turtino's group decision-making technique?

A HUMAN RELATIONS CASE PROBLEM
The QC Complainers [27]

Kerry Industries formed a quality circle in its automatic bagging manufacturing operations. The QC was formed because the level of machine bag failures was unacceptably high. Rebags and equipment failures were running at 20 percent and 10 percent, respectively. The goal set for the QC improvements were rebags at a 5 percent level in six months, and equipment failures at 2 percent in three months.

Plant management moved quickly to give the QC the support it needed, including ample budgeting and hiring an outside consultant. The QC met ten hours the first month, and five hours per month thereafter. After six months, the goal of 5 percent rebags was met. Equipment failures were reduced to 3 percent. Circle members believed they could achieve the goal of 2 percent improvement within another month.

As the circle completed its first six months of operation, Denise Gonzalez, the circle leader, asked to speak with Chris Kantor, the plant manager. Four minutes into their meeting, Gonzalez said to Kantor: "Let me be candid. Our group has met with excellent success. We've made tremendous strides in overcoming the two key problems in the bagging operations. But I don't think the members are going to bring forth any more money-saving suggestions."

"Why not?" asked Kantor, "You've been doing so beautifully so far."

"Because we're tired of being ripped off by management," said Gonzalez. "If one of us had submitted those great ideas to a suggestion system, he or she would have received about $4,000 in suggestion money. Since the suggestions have come out of the circle, all we will get is a recognition plaque to hang on the wall. None of us thinks that's very fair."

"Denise I don't think you are taking this in the right spirit," said Kantor. "I will discuss your concerns with my staff and then get back to you soon."

1. What should Kantor do about the demands of the QC members for financial rewards for their efforts?
2. What should the company policy be about paying for suggestions made through the suggestion system but not the QC?
3. What is your opinion of the ethics of how circle members are behaving?

A HUMAN RELATIONS EXERCISE
A Quality Circle Simulation

The purpose of this exercise is to simulate the workings of a QC. The class is divided into QCs of five to seven members, with each group appointing one person as supervisor. Next, each group has the task of improving upon the quality of a product or service familiar to most people. Potential products and services to choose from include a ten-speed bicycle, the student chair found in most classrooms, a backpack, the ballpoint pen, and student recreational facilities on campus.

Before proceeding with the exercise, it is important to review the workings of a QC described in this chapter and/or the suggested readings. The output of the group should be some tangible, potentially cost-effective, and feasible suggestions. It may be necessary to consult some people outside the circle to obtain some technical ideas. Excluding outside consultation, about twenty-five minutes is required to conduct this simulation.

Notes

1. Rensis Likert, *New Patterns of Management* (New York: McGraw Hill, 1961), p. 113.
2. Janice H. Schopler, "Interorganizational Groups: Origins, Structure, and Outcomes," *Academy of Management Review,* October 1987, p. 703.
3. A representative example is found in James E. Ellis, "Monsanto Is Teaching Old Workers New Tricks," *Business Week,* Aug. 21, 1989, p. 67.

4. George Prince, "Recognizing Genuine Teamwork," *Supervisory Management,* April 1989, p. 25.

5. Russell Mitchell, "Jack Welch: How Good a Manager," *Business Week,* Dec. 14, 1987, p. 92.

6. Jack J. Phillips, "We've Got to Keep Meeting Like This," *Personnel,* January 1988, p. 42.

7. Harry J. Lifton, "The Meeting Society, Part I," *Human Resources Forum,* December 1989, p. 4.

8. Dave Day, "Make the Most of Meetings," *Personnel Journal,* March 1990, p. 34.

9. Gary Dessler, *Human Behavior: Improving Performance at Work* (Reston, VA: Reston Publishing, 1980), p. 277.

10. Francis X. Mahoney, "Team Development, Part 4: Work Meetings," *Personnel,* March–April 1982, pp. 52–53.

11. Jack Halloran and Douglas Benton, *Applied Human Relations: An Organizational Approach,* 3rd ed. (Englewood Cliffs, NJ: Prentice Hall, 1987), p. 360.

12. Jack Halloran, *Applied Human Relations: An Organizational Approach* (Englewood Cliffs, NJ: Prentice Hall, 1978), p. 214.

13. Carol Cain, "Northwest Takes Lead on Smoking Ban," Gannett News Service, April 20, 1988.

14. George P. Huber, *Managerial Decision Making* (Glenview, IL: Scott, Foresman, 1980), p. 199.

15. Edward E. Lawler III and Susan A. Mohrman, "Quality Circles After the Fad," *Harvard Business Review,* January–February 1985, p. 66.

16. Robert J. Shaw, "Tapping the Riches of Creativity Among Working People," *Management Focus* (Peat, Marwick, Mitchell & Co.), September–October 1981, pp. 27–29.

17. Murray R. Barrick and Ralph A. Alexander, "A Review of Quality Circle Efficacy and the Existence of Positive-Finding Bias," *Personnel Psychology,* Autumn 1987, pp. 579–92.

18. Ricky W. Griffin, "Consequences of Quality Circles in an Industrial Setting: A Longitudinal Assessment," *Academy of Management Journal,* June 1988, pp. 338–58.

19. Sandy J. Wayne, Ricky W. Griffin, and Thomas S. Bateman, "Improving the Effectiveness of Quality Circles," *Personnel Administrator,* March 1986, pp. 79–88; Barrick and Alexander, "A Review of Quality Circle Efficacy," p. 587.

20. Larry K. Michaelsen, Warren E. Watson, and Robert H. Black, "A Realistic Test of Individual Versus Group Consensus Decision Making," *Journal of Applied Psychology,* October 1989, pp. 834–39; the quote appears on p. 836.

21. Edwin A. Locke and Gary P. Latham, *A Theory of Goal Setting and Task Performance* (Englewood Cliffs, NJ: Prentice Hall, 1990), p. 117.

22. Robert R. Blake and Jane Srygley Mouton, "Don't Let Group Norms Stifle Creativity," *Personnel,* August 1985, pp. 31–32.

23. Irving L. Janis, *Victims of Groupthink: A Psychological Study of Foreign Policy Decisions and Fiascos* (Boston: Houghton Mifflin, 1972), pp. 39–40.

24. Martin Lasden, "Facing Down Groupthink," *Computer Decisions,* June 1986, pp. 52–53.

25. Glen Whyte, "Groupthink Reconsidered," *Academy of Management Review,* January 1989, p. 47.

26. David R. Hamptom, *Contemporary Management* (New York: McGraw-Hill, 1977), pp. 184–85.

27. The statistics in this case were researched by Roger H. Hinds.

Suggested Reading ───

ALLCORN, SETH. "Understanding Groups at Work." *Personnel,* August 1989, pp. 28–36.

HARDAKER, MAURICE, and WARD, BRYAN K. "How to Make a Team Work." *Harvard Business Review,* November–December 1987, pp. 112–20.

KIEFFER, GEORGE DAVID. *The Strategy of Meetings.* New York: Simon & Schuster, 1988.

LEFTON, ROBERT E. "The Eight Barriers to Teamwork." *Personnel Journal,* January 1988, pp. 18–24.

LYNCH, ROBERT. "The Shoot Out Among Nonteam Players." *Management Solutions,* May 1987, pp. 4–12.

REICH, ROBERT B. "Entrepreneurship Reconsidered: The Team as Hero." *Harvard Business Review,* May–June 1987, pp. 77–83.

ROSEN, NED. *Teamwork and the Bottom Line: Groups Make a Difference.* Hillsdale, NJ: Lawrence Erlbaum, 1989.

SMITH, KENWYN K., and BERG, DAVID N. *Paradoxes of Group Life.* San Francisco: Jossey-Bass, 1987.

TANG, THOMAS LI-PING, TOLLISON, PEGGY SMITH, and WHITESIDE, HAROLD D. "The Effect of Quality Circle Initiation on Motivation to Attend Quality Circle Meetings and on Task Performance," *Personnel Psychology,* Winter 1987, pp. 799–814.

TYSON, TREVOR. *Working with Groups.* Melbourne, Australia: Macmillan, 1989.

9

Leadership
and Influence

LEARNING OBJECTIVES

After reading and studying this chapter and doing the exercises, you should
be able to

1. Identify several tactics leaders use to influence group members.
2. Summarize the traits and behaviors that are related to effective
managerial leadership.
3. Describe three approaches to classifying leadership styles.
4. Describe the two major contingency theories of leadership.
5. Explain the entrepreneurial style of leadership.
6. Identify techniques for developing teamwork.
7. Understand how to develop your leadership potential.

L eadership is a central topic of interest to professionals, managers, and leaders alike, because it is "the glue which holds organizations together."[1] Leadership is no longer just the domain of a company president or a few top managers. In today's world, take-charge ability is important at all levels of management.[2] People who perform the day-to-day work of an organization, and who are in direct contact with customers and clients, often require stronger leadership than do top-level workers. Furthermore, the current emphasis on team structures means that the supervisors have to provide leadership to help foster teamwork.

Leadership is the process of influencing employees to attain organizations' goals, excluding illegal and immoral methods of persuasion. For instance, influencing employees to kick back part of their pay by threatening them with loss of their jobs is not considered to be leadership. If influence is not necessary, leadership has not been exerted. Employees will often perform their jobs adequately without the benefit of coaching, prompting, cajoling, or being inspired by the boss. In these situations, leadership is not necessary to achieve good job performance. However, if a manager helps employees achieve performance they would not have achieved without his or her influence, leadership has been exercised.

The concepts of leadership, management, and supervision are not identical. Management and supervision involve a wide variety of activities, such as planning, controlling, organizing, scheduling, negotiating, and leading (or directing). Many people are effective in the administrative aspects of a managerial or supervisory job, but few people are effective leaders. Effective leadership involves bringing about important changes, such as turning around a troubled work unit. To get you started thinking about what leadership involves, take the quiz presented in Figure 9–1.

INFLUENCE TACTICS USED BY LEADERS

Because leadership is an influence process, it is important to be aware of the tactics leaders use to influence others. Much of the discussion about power and politics in Chapter 11 is relevant to understanding how leaders influence people. Here we summarize research findings, and some opinion, about influence tactics used by leaders. Most of these tactics can be used by managers and individual contributors.

1. *Charisma.* The ability to lead others, based on personal charm, magnetism, and emotion, is referred to as **charisma**.[3] This type of influence is also referred to as transformational leadership. A **transformational leader** is one who helps organizations and people make positive changes in the way they do things. He or she moves a stagnant or troubled organization to higher ground. Bernard Bass described a particular transformational leader in these words:

TEST YOUR LEADERSHIP SKILLS

Rate yourself on basic leadership characteristics:

	Always	Sometimes	Rarely
1. I'm a good listener.	☐	☐	☐
2. I'm accessible.	☐	☐	☐
3. I'm decisive	☐	☐	☐
4. I'm gracious.	☐	☐	☐
5. I "keep it simple."	☐	☐	☐
6. I'm optimistic.	☐	☐	☐
7. I give credit where due.	☐	☐	☐
8. I confront problems.	☐	☐	☐
9. I speak directly.	☐	☐	☐
10. I acknowledge mistakes.	☐	☐	☐
11. I have a "can do" attitude.	☐	☐	☐
12. I'm enthusiastic.	☐	☐	☐
13. I seek strong subordinates.	☐	☐	☐
14. I have a positive attitude.	☐	☐	☐

TO SCORE:

Number of responses in **Always** column $\times$ 5 = _____

Number of responses in **Sometimes** column $\times$ 3 = _____

Number of responses in **Rarely** column $\times$ 1 = _____

Total score (add the three totals): _____

ANALYZE YOUR SCORE

More than 50: You have a great deal of natural leadership ability!

30 to 50: You have a good base of leadership characteristics.

Less than 30: Underdeveloped leadership skills may be hampering your ability to manage and supervise successfully. It will be helpful for you to study leadership and attend a leadership development course.

FIGURE 9–1 Some Basic Thoughts About Leadership

Source: Pryor Resources Inc., P.O. Box 2951, Shawnee Mission, KS 66201. Reprinted with permission.

When facing a crisis, Cynthia inspires her team's involvement and participation in a "mission." She solidifies with simple words and images and keeps reminding her staff about it. She has frequent one-to-one chats with each of her employees at his or her work station. She is a consultant, coach, teacher, and mother figure.[4]

2.   *Leading by example.* A simple but effective way of influencing group members is **leading by example,** or leading by acting as a positive model. The ideal approach to leading by example is to be a "do as I say and do" manager. He or she shows consistency between actions and words. Also, actions and words confirm, support, and often clarify each other. For example, if the firm has a dress code and the supervisor explains the code and dresses accordingly, he or she provides a role model that is consistent in words and actions. The action of following the dress code provides an example that supports and clarifies the words used in the dress code.[5]

3.   *Assertiveness.* You are **assertive** when you are forthright with your demands and express both the specifics of what you want done and the feelings surrounding your demands. An assertive leader might say, "I'm very upset about the number of errors in your report. I want it cleaned up by tomorrow at 4:30." A leader might also be assertive by checking frequently on a subordinate.

4.   *Rationality.* Appealing to reason and logic is used frequently by strong leaders. Pointing out the facts of a situation to a group member in order to get the person to act is an example of rationality.

5.   *Team play.* Influencing others by being a good team player has been identified as a key tactic for getting work accomplished. The suggestions presented about team play in Chapter 8 are all part of this influence tactic.

6.   *Ingratiation.* Getting somebody else to like you is another influence tactic. Two specific ingratiating behaviors noted in a study were "acted in a friendly manner prior to asking for what I wanted" and "praised the subordinate just before asking for what I wanted." (Strong leaders tend not to rely heavily on ingratiating tactics.)

7.   *Sanctions.* A **sanction** is the use of threats of punishment or actual punishment to get somebody to act in a particular way. Influence tactics of this nature include (a) giving the person no salary increase or preventing that person from getting a pay raise, and (b) threatening the subordinate with loss of promotion.

8.   *Exchange.* A widely used tactic is to influence others through the use of reciprocal favors. An example of exchange would be promising to endorse an employee's request for transfer providing he or she takes on an unpleasant short-term assignment.

9.   *Upward appeal.* In upward appeal, the leader exerts influence by getting a more powerful person to carry out the influence act. A specific example is: "I sent the guy to my superior when he wouldn't listen to me.

That fixed him." More than occasional use of upward appeal weakens the manager's stature in the eyes of group members and superiors, thus eroding effectiveness as a leader.

10. *Joking and kidding.* Recent research has documented that joking and kidding are widely used to influence others in the workplace. Good-natured ribbing is especially effective when a straightforward statement might be interpreted as harsh criticism. In an effort to get an employee to clean up his work area, one manager said: "I don't object to the appearance of your cubicle. But the Environmental Protection Agency is coming through next week. I don't want us to be cited for sight pollution." The worker smiled, and then proceeded to clean up his work area.

11. *Charm and appearance.* A leader can sometimes influence others by being "charming" and creating a positive appearance. A survey showed that both men and women rely on charm to accomplish work tasks.[6]

The next major issue about leaders we address is what traits and behaviors are often associated with success as a leader.

LEADERSHIP TRAITS AND BEHAVIORS

Leadership is best understood when the leader, the group members, and the situation in which they are placed are analyzed. Nevertheless, the leader remains an important consideration in understanding leadership. One justification for studying leadership traits is that the most widely read books on the topic emphasize leadership qualities, such as integrity and a sense of vision.[7] Another justification is that the traits of leaders are related closely to the degree to which they are perceived to be leaders. For example, managers who are perceived to be good problem solvers are more likely to be accepted as leaders.[8]

A realistic view is that certain traits and behaviors contribute to effective leadership in a wide variety of situations. Correspondingly, similar situations require similar leadership traits and behaviors. To illustrate, a person who was effective in running a production operation in a newspaper could probably run a production operation in a book bindery. There would be enough similarity among the type of subordinates and machinery to make the situations comparable. In contrast, a high school football coach might fail dismally as the managing editor of a fashion magazine. The two situations would call for dramatically different kinds of leadership.

Contemporary writers usually draw a sharp distinction between the traits of people (including their motives, characteristics, and attitudes) and their behavior (what they actually do). Leadership theorists are the most adamant about this point, contending that it is much more profitable to study what leaders actually do than to focus on their traits. It is important to recognize, however, that behavior is attributable to both traits and the situation. Assume that an emotionally warm person occupies a leadership position. The trait of warmth will lead the person to the desirable leadership behavior of being supportive of group members.

Extensive research continues to be conducted on which traits, motives, characteristics, behaviors, and skills contribute to effective managerial leadership. The discussion in the following two sections is based on research and opinion about leadership effectiveness.[9] The distinction between traits, motives, and personal characteristics vs. behaviors and skills is not always clear-cut. For example, enthusiasm can be regarded as both a trait and a behavior.

Traits, Motives, and Personal Characteristics

The traits, motives, and characteristics that follow are a sampling of traditional and current thinking about contributors to leadership effectiveness. Our choice of these nine traits does not imply that traits not on the list are unimportant.

Power motive. Effective executives have a strong need to control resources. Leaders with high power drives have three dominant characteristics: (1) They act with vigor and determination to exert their power; (2) they invest much time in thinking about ways to alter the behavior and thinking of others; and (3) they care about their personal standing with those around them.[10] The high need for power is important because it means that the leader is interested in influencing others.

Achievement motive.   Managerial leaders find joy in accomplishment for its own sake. They enjoy the thrill associated with initiating a project and seeing it through to completion. Achievement motivation contributes to leadership effectiveness of both entrepreneurs and managers who work for an employer.

Problem-solving ability.   A current theory of leadership supports what has been known for many years: Effective leaders have good problem-solving ability. According to **cognitive resource theory,** intelligent and competent leaders make more effective plans, decisions, and strategies than do leaders with less intelligence or competence.[11] Despite the importance of problem-solving ability for leadership, an advanced capacity for solving abstract problems can be disadvantageous. The president of a barge company makes this comment about intelligence and leadership success.

> Sometime, a less than top IQ is an advantage because that person doesn't see all the problems. He or she sees the big problem and gets on and gets it solved. But the extremely bright person can see so many problems that he or she never gets around to solving any of them.[12]

Self-confidence.   In virtually every leadership setting it is important for the leader to be realistically self-confident. A leader who is self-assured without being bombastic or overbearing instills confidence in subordinates. Aside from being a psychological trait, self-confidence or self-assurance refers to the behavior exhibited by a person in a number of situations. It is akin to being cool under pressure. We can conclude that a given person is a confident supervisor if he or she displays such behavior as retaining composure when an employee threatens to file a grievance or calmly helping an employee fix a jammed machine when the department is behind schedule.

Initiative.   Exercising initiative, or being a self-starter, refers to taking action without support and stimulation from others. A person aspiring to leadership assignments should recognize that initiative is a characteristic looked for in potential leaders. Initiative is also related to problem-finding ability—you need to exercise initiative to search for worthwhile problems.

Vision.   Top-level managers need a visual image of where they see the organization headed and how it can get there. Organizational progress is dependent upon the top executive having this sense of vision. A major finding of a survey of what managers look for in their leaders is that a leader should inspire a shared vision, including an uplifting and ennobling future.[13] Vision also contributes to leadership effectiveness at lower levels in the organization. Many workers would like to know where their unit is headed, and what they can do to contributes to that future.

Enthusiasm. In almost all leadership situations it is desirable for the leader to be enthusiastic. The same model applies: A trait (enthusiastic) leads to behavior (enthusiasm). Subordinates tend to respond positively to enthusiasm, partially because enthusiasm may be perceived as a reward for constructive behavior. Enthusiasm is also a desirable leadership trait because it helps build good relationships with subordinates. The trait can be expressed both verbally ("Fabulous job" or "I love it") and nonverbally (through gestures, touching, and so forth).

Internal locus of control. As described in Chapter 5, people with an internal locus of control believe that they are the primary cause of events happening to them. Supervisory leaders with an internal locus of control are favored by group members.[14] Part of the reason is that an "internal" person is perceived as more powerful than an "external," because he or she takes responsibility for things happening.

Insight into people and situations. **Insight** is a depth of understanding that requires considerable intuition and common sense. Insight into people and situations involving people is an essential characteristic of managerial leaders. A manager with good insight is able to make better work assignments and do a better job of training and developing subordinates. The reason is that such a manager makes a careful assessment of the strengths and weaknesses of subordinates. Another major advantage of being insightful is that the leader can size up the situation and adapt his or her leadership approach accordingly. For instance, in a crisis situation, group members would welcome a directive and decisive style of leadership.

Behavior and Skills

Following are key behaviors and skills associated with effective managerial leadership. Which behavior and skill is most important depends heavily on the particular situation. Supportiveness, for example, is most important when group members are not self-sufficient.

Credibility and integrity. Data from 7,500 managers indicate that honesty is the most sought after leadership trait. Group members measure honesty by the deeds (behavior) of leaders. Leaders are considered honest by their constituents when they follow through on promises. In a related study, it was found that of all behaviors describing leadership, the most essential was the leader's display of trust of others.[15]

Technical competence. An effective leader has to be technically or professionally competent in some discipline, particularly when leading a group of specialists. It is difficult to establish rapport with group members when you do not understand what they are doing and they do not respect your technical skills. At a minimum, the manager of specialists has to be *snow proof* (not readily bluffed about technical matters by subordinates). Thomas R. Horton, president of the American Management Association, made these comments about technical competence and leadership:

> It is a fantasy that a really good manager can manage anything. The best managers have always been those who really know their business, and know it inside out. Bill Marriott, Jr., of the Marriott Corporation, has built that organization into the fastest growing hotel chain in the world. Marriott attributes his success to the fact that he thoroughly knows the hotel and restaurant business. He spends about half his time outside the office visiting Marriott properties.[16]

Sensitivity to people.   It has long been recognized that being sensitive to the needs of people is an important leadership behavior. Recent research documents the fact that insensitivity prevents many up-and-coming managers from reaching the top. In a study of top executives, psychologists compared "derailed" executives with those who had progressed to senior management positions. The leading category of fatal flaws was insensitivity to others, characterized by an abrasive, intimidating, bullying style.[17] Abrasive and intimidating behavior is most likely to show up when the manager is placed under stress.

Effective work habits.   In today's information-based world of work, it is important for organizational leaders to possess effective work habits. (Chapter 18 deals exclusively with this topic.) Even if directing the activities of artistic, free-spirited individuals, the leader contributes to organizational effectiveness if he or she is well-organized. For example, in an advertising agency somebody needs to keep track of contracts, budgets, and expense accounts.

Supportiveness   Supportive behavior toward subordinates is frequently associated with leadership effectiveness. A supportive leader (one who gives encouragement and praise to subordinates) usually increases morale and often increases productivity. Supportive behavior stems from personal characteristics such as empathy, warmth, and flexibility.

Maintaining high expectations.   Effective leaders consistently hold group members to high standards of performance, which raises productivity. Setting high expectations for others becomes a self-fulfilling prophecy. Workers tend to live up to the expectations set for them by their superiors. Setting high expectations might take the form of encouraging subordinates to establish difficult goals.

Providing feedback. Letting subordinates know where they stand is another vital leadership behavior. Feedback of this nature has two aspects. First, employees must know where they stand with respect to performance goals. In this way, if they are falling short, they can take corrective action. Second, employees must be informed when a job is being done well. Such information is a crucial ingredient of positive reinforcement.

Stability under pressure. Effective leaders are steady performers, even under heavy workloads and uncertain conditions. Remaining steady under conditions of uncertainty contributes to effectiveness because it helps subordinates cope with the situation. When the leader remains calm, group members are reassured that things will work out satisfactorily. Stability is helpful for another reason: It helps the managerial leader appear professional and cool under pressure.

Recover quickly from setbacks. Effective managerial leaders are resilient—they bounce back quickly from setbacks such as budget cuts, demotions, and being fired. An intensive study of executives revealed that they don't even think about failure, and don't even use the word. Instead, they rely on synonyms, such as "mistake," "glitch," "bungle," and "setback."[18] In practice, this means that the leader sets an example to subordinates by not crumbling when something big goes wrong. Instead, the leader tries to conduct business as usual.

LEADERSHIP STYLES

The study of leadership behaviors progressed naturally to the study of **leadership styles,** the typical pattern of behaviors engaged in by the leader when dealing with employees. Styles can also be considered stereotypes of how leaders behave in most situations. It is well recognized that effective leaders try to match their style to the situation at hand—they use insight. Here we describe three of the most enduring methods of categorizing leadership styles:

1. The leadership continuum, based on the amount of authority retained by the leader.
2. Theory X and Theory Y, based on the assumptions the leader makes about group members.
3. The Leadership Grid®, based on the leader's relative concern for people and task accomplishment.

The Leadership Continuum

The leadership continuum, or classical approach, classifies leaders according to how much authority they retain for themselves vs. how much is turned over to the group. Three key points on the continuum are autocratic, participative, and free-rein leaders (see Figure 9–2).

Autocratic style. **An autocratic leader** attempts to retain most of the authority granted the group. Autocratic leaders make all the major decisions and assume that subordinates will comply without question. Leaders who use this style give minimum consideration to what group members are likely to think about an order or decision. An autocrat is sometimes seen as rigid and demanding by subordinates.

Although the authoritarian (a synonym for autocratic) leadership style is not in vogue, many successful leaders are autocrats. One example is Larry Rawl, the chairman and CEO of Exxon Corp. He moves quickly in making major decisions and is not overly concerned with group opinion. A business reporter notes that Rawl's tough, inward-looking style seems to fit a more competitive world with no room for the gentle and polite managers who once headed blue chip companies.[19]

The autocratic style generally works best in situations in which decisions have to be made rapidly, or group opinion is not needed. One situation calling for autocratic leadership would be extinguishing a forest fire. Another would be a company undergoing liquidation.

Participative style. **A participative leader** is one who shares decision-making authority with the group. The participative style encompasses so much of the leadership continuum that it is useful to divide it into three subtypes: consultative, consensus, and democratic.

Consultative leaders solicit opinions from the group before making a decision, yet they do not feel obliged to accept the group's thinking. Leaders of this type make it clear that they alone have authority to make the

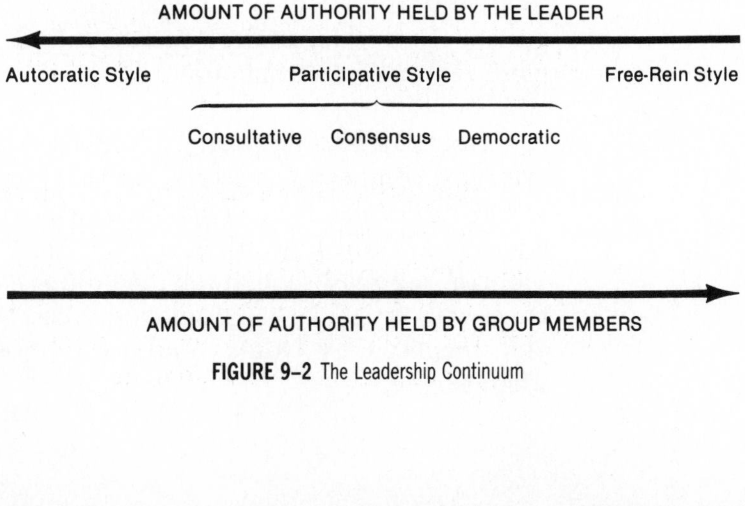

AMOUNT OF AUTHORITY HELD BY THE LEADER

Autocratic Style   Participative Style   Free-Rein Style

Consultative   Consensus   Democratic

AMOUNT OF AUTHORITY HELD BY GROUP MEMBERS

FIGURE 9–2 The Leadership Continuum

final decisions. A standard way to practice consultative leadership would be to call a group meeting and discuss an issue before making a decision. One technique for practicing consultative leadership is **management by wandering around.** The process involves visiting worksites and informally chatting with people about their work as a means of collecting input and boosting morale. (See the accompanying box.)

K-MART CEO WALKS THE AISLES

Joseph E. Antonini, CEO of K-Mart, visits company stores by darting here and there and touching everything in sight. His wanderings around have helped to rejuvenate the giant discounter. Antonini's mission is to look for holes that need filling, to see that the stores are well kept, and to converse with customers and workers.

As he visits a clothing department, he comments, "Well displayed, that's good." Then it's on to another department, accompanied by local and district managers. As he proceeds with his wanderings around, Antonini both gives advice and listens for valuable input.

Source: Facts as reported in *Business Week: The Corporate Elite,* Oct. 21, 1988, pp. 56–57.

Consensus leaders encourage group discussion about an issue and then make a decision that reflects the consensus (general agreement) of group members. Japanese managers typically use a consensus style of decision making. Consensus-style leaders thus turn over more authority to the group than do consultative leaders. The consensus leadership style results in long delays in decision making because every party involved has to agree.

Democratic leaders confer final authority on the group. They function as collectors of opinion and take a vote before making a decision. Democratic leaders turn over so much authority to the group that they are sometimes classified as free-rein leaders. The group usually achieves its goals when working under a democratic leader. Democratic leadership has more relevance for community activities than for most work settings.

Evaluation of the participative style. The three participative styles are suited to managing competent and well-motivated people who want to get involved in making decisions and giving feedback to the leader. A participative style is also useful when the manager wants employees to commit to a course of action. A supervisor might ask the group, "What should we do with group members who smoke in nonsmoking areas?" If the group agreed on a fitting punishment, they would tend to accept the punishment if it were administered.

Leonard R. Sayles observes that the participative style is necessary to meet the requirements of rapidly changing organizations. As organizations become more change-oriented, the relationship between superiors and subordinates will continue to depart from the traditional hierarchical view of "us" and "them." In the past, participative leadership styles were often perceived as motivational aids. Now, they are seen as a necessity to implement change.[20]

If procedures or alternative solutions to a problem have already been agreed upon, participative management is superfluous. For instance, in highly repetitive, machine-paced operations, little room is left for employee problem solving. Another example is that the vast majority of bank employees are not asked to participate in making decisions about setting interest rates on loans. Such decisions are made in the executive suite.

Another problem is that participative decision making is often resisted by first-level managers and middle managers because they worry about losing power and having to do extra work. Since participative management is on the upswing, supervisors and middle managers must learn to adapt to the system. The participative style works best when there is regular communication between managers and employees. Regular communication makes it easier to obtain employee suggestions.[21]

Free-rein style. A **free-rein leader** is one who turns over virtually all the authority to the group. This person issues general goals and guidelines to the group and then does not get involved again unless requested. The only limits imposed on the group are those specified by the leader's boss. Such an extreme degree of freedom is rarely encountered in a work setting. One exception would be a pure research laboratory where scientists and engineers are granted freedom to tackle whatever problems they find interesting.

Styles Based on Assumptions Made About People (Theory X and Theory Y)

A widely quoted and historically important method of classifying leadership styles is based on differences in assumptions made about people. Douglas McGregor, a social psychologist, developed this explanation of leadership because he wanted managers to challenge their own assumptions.[22] McGregor believed that these traditional assumptions were often false, leading to the demotivation of subordinates. He divided assumptions into two extremes, Theory X and Theory Y.

Theory X managers take the traditional, distrustful view of people, and therefore behave autocratically. Consequently, Theory X managers supervise quite closely. The Theory X style is based upon these assumptions:

1. People dislike work, and therefore try to avoid it.
2. People dislike work, so managers are forced to control, direct, coerce, and threaten subordinates to get them to work toward organizational goals.
3. People prefer to be directed, to avoid responsibility, and to seek security. In general, they are unambitious.

Theory Y managers are trustful of subordinates, and therefore allow them to participate in decision making. The Theory Y style is based on these assumptions:

1. Physical and mental work is a natural part of life, and thus not disliked by people.
2. People are self-motivated to reach goals to which they feel committed.
3. People are committed to goals, providing they attain rewards when the goals are reached.
4. Under favorable conditions, people will seek and accept responsibility.
5. People have the capacity to be innovative in solving job-related problems.
6. People are basically bright, but in most job settings their potential is underutilized.

The Leadership Grid® Styles

The **Managerial Grid®**, developed by Blake and Mouton, is a widely used method of classifying leadership styles. It was republished as the Leadership Grid in 1991. The grid is also a comprehensive system of leadership training and organization development. Grid leadership styles are based on the extent of a person's concern for production and people (see Figure 9–3).[23] Concern for production includes such matters as results, the bottom line, performance, profits, and mission. It is rated on a 1 to 9 scale on the horizontal axis. Concern for people is reflected in such matters as showing support for subordinates, getting results based on trust and respect, and worrying about employees' job security. Concern for people is rated on a 1 to 9 scale on the vertical axis.

Key grid positions. The benchmark styles on the Leadership Grid® are described here, and are also explained in Figure 9–3.

9,1 In the lower right corner is a maximum concern for production combined with a minimum concern for people. A leader with this orientation concentrates on maximizing production by exercising power and authority, and dictating what people should do.

1,9 In the top left corner is the manager with a minimum concern for production and a maximum concern for people. Primary attention is placed on good feelings among subordinates and co-workers, even at the expense of achieving results.

1,1 In the lower left corner is the manager with a minimum concern for both production and people. The 1,1-oriented manager does only the minimum required to remain a member of the firm.

5,5 In the center is the 5,5 orientation. Managers with this style are "middle-of-the-roaders" who do their job but avoid making waves, and conform to the status quo.

9,9 In the upper right corner is the 9,9 orientation, which integrates concerns for production and people. It is a goal-directed team approach

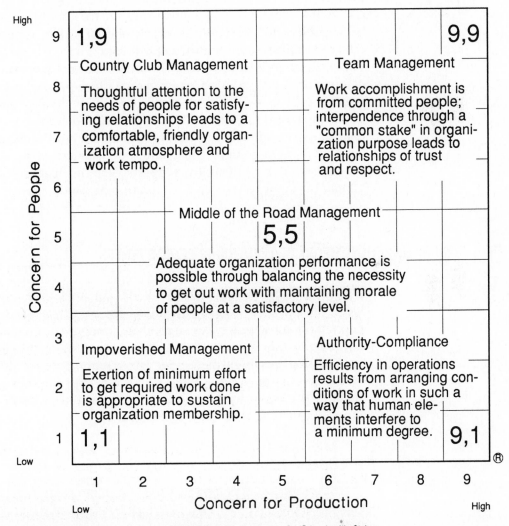

FIGURE 9-3 The Leadership Grid® Leadership Styles

Source: The Leadership Grid® Figure from *Leadership Dilemmas–Grid Solutions*, by Robert R. Blake and Anne Adams McCanse, Houston; Gulf Publishing Co., p.29. Copyright © 1991, by Scientific Methods, Inc. Reproduced by permission of the owners.

that seeks to gain optimum results through participation, involvement, and commitment.

Managers generally have one dominant style, such as 9,1. In addition, they have a backup style. The latter tends to be used when the dominant style does not achieve the desired results. For instance, you might attempt a 9,9 approach, only to find that most of the members are not so enthusiastic about their work. It might then be necessary to shift to a 9,1 approach.

Which style is best?   Blake and Mouton argue strongly for the value of team management (9,9). The team management approach usually results in improved performance, low absenteeism and turnover, and high employee satisfaction. "9,9" management relies on trust and respect, which helps bring good results. A synthesis of a number of studies supports the idea that effective leaders score highly on both concern for people and production. The researchers who analyzed the studies caution, however, that each leadership situation should be investigated before prescribing the best leadership style.[24]

Similarly, the Leadership Grid® does not dictate that the manager mechanically use one style in trying to lead such different groups as entry-level workers in a yogurt shop and a department of information systems specialists. The philosophy suggests that the leader use principles of human behavior to size up the situation at hand.

FIEDLER'S CONTINGENCY THEORY OF LEADERSHIP EFFECTIVENESS

A **contingency theory of leadership** specifies the conditions under which a particular style of leadership will be effective. Fred E. Fiedler developed the most widely researched and quoted contingency model.[25] His contingency theory states that the best style of leadership is determined by the situation in which the leader is working. Here we describe how the style and situation are evaluated, and the overall findings of Fiedler's contingency theory. Although Fiedler's theory is difficult to understand, it is important for understanding leadership.

Measuring Leadership Style (The Least-Preferred Co-worker Scale (LPC)

A manager's leadership style is classified as relationship-motivated or task-motivated, similar to the concern for production vs. concern for people. The intermediate style is labeled socioindependent (although not much attention has been paid to this style). Fiedler says that leadership style is a relatively permanent aspect of behavior, thus difficult to modify. He reasons that once you understand your leadership style, you should work in situations that match your style. Similarly, the organization should help managers match leadership styles and situations.

The least-preferred co-worker (LPC) scale measures the degree to which a leader describes favorably or unfavorably his or her least-preferred co-worker. The latter is an employee with whom you could work the least well. A leader who describes the least-preferred co-worker in relatively favorable terms tends to be relationship-motivated. In contrast, a person who describes his or her least-preferred co-worker in an unfavorable manner tends to be task-motivated, or less concerned with human relations. In short, if you can tolerate your enemies, you are relationship-motivated. The LPC asks the leader to describe the person with whom he or she can work least well by making ratings such as:

Friendly ___ ___ ___ ___ ___ ___ ___ ___ Unfriendly
           8 7 6 5 4 3 2 1

Tense ___ ___ ___ ___ ___ ___ ___ ___ Relaxed
           1 2 3 4 5 6 7 8

A major problem with the LPC scale is that many people who take it, and researchers who study it, question its validity. The exercise at the end of the chapter presents a much simpler approach to measuring your leadership style.

Measuring the Leadership Situation

The contingency theory diagnoses situations into three basic classifications: high control, moderate control, and low control. (Earlier versions of the model used the term *favorability* instead of control.) A high-control situation is considered favorable for the leader, while a low-control situation is considered unfavorable. The control classifications are determined by rating the leadership on its three dimensions, based on straightforward questionnaires:

1. Leader-member relations measure how well the group and the leader get along.
2. Task structure measures how clearly the procedures, goals, and evaluation of the job are defined.
3. Position power measures how much authority the leader possesses to hire, fire, discipline, and grant salary increases to group members.

The three dimensions are listed in decreasing order of importance. Leader-member relations contribute as much to situation favorability as do task structure and position power combined. The leader therefore has the most control in situations where relationships with members are the best.

The Leader-Match Concept and Overall Findings

The major proposition in the contingency theory is the **leader-match concept**—leadership effectiveness depends on matching leaders to situations where they can exercise most control. It states specifically:

1. Task-motivated leaders perform the best in situations of high control and low control.
2. Relationship-motivated leaders perform the best in situations of moderate control.
3. Socioindependent leaders tend to perform the best in situations of high control.

Rationale for the leader-match concept. Various explanations have been offered for the leader-match concept. Fiedler's most recent thinking on the topic is presented here. His analysis is that task-motivated leaders perform better in highly favorable situations because they do not have to be concerned with the task. Instead, they can work on relationships. In moderately favorable situations, the relationship-motivated leader works well because he or she can in fact work on relationships and not get involved in overmanaging.

Also, in very low-control or unfavorable situations, the task-motivated leader is able to structure and make sense out of confusion. The relationship-motivated leader wants to give emotional support to group members or call a committee meeting.[26]

Summary of research findings. A summary of the findings on which the leader-match concept is based is presented in Figure 9–4.

To interpret the model, look first at the situational factors at the bottom of the figure. There are eight possible combinations of leader-member relations, task structure, and leader position power. This is true because all three variables are divided into two categories. Leader-member relations can be good or poor; task structure can be high or low; and position power may be strong or weak. The result is eight possible situations, shown as cells I through VIII. Cells I, II, and III are very favorable for exercising control, while cell VIII is very unfavorable for the leader to exercise control.

Leadership style is also represented in Figure 9–4. The two categories for which the most research has been conducted are the relationship-motivated and the task-motivated (or high LPC and low LPC). Findings for the socioindependent (mixed style) are more tentative. Below each situation is shown the leadership style found to be most strongly associated with effective group performance in that situation. Task-motivated leaders perform the best in situations of high control and low control. These extreme situations are represented by cells I, II, III, and VIII. Note that cell III is classified as favorable despite the leader having to deal with an unstructured task. The other major conclusion is that relationship-motivated leaders are most effective when the situation is moderately favorable.

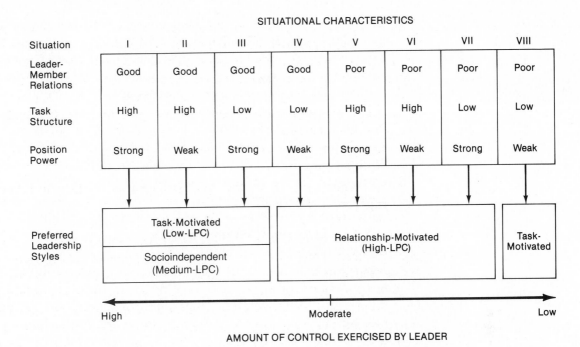

FIGURE 9–4 Fiedler's Findings on Leadership Performance and Favorability of the Situation

A major contribution of Fiedler's work is that it has prompted others to conduct studies about the contingency nature of leadership. It has also alerted leaders to the importance of sizing up the situation in order to gain more control. For instance, if a situation were unfavorable, it could be made more favorable by granting the leader more position power, or by increasing task structure.

A major problem with Fiedler's model centers around matching the situation to the leader. In most situations, the amount of control the leader exercises varies from time to time. For instance, a relationship-motivated leader might ask for a transfer if the situation became too favorable for exercising control.

ENTREPRENEURS AND INTRAPRENEURS AS LEADERS

Many entrepreneurs and intrapreneurs use a similar leadership style that stems from their key personality characteristics and circumstances. A general picture emerges of task-oriented and charismatic leaders. Entrepreneurs drive themselves and others relentlessly, yet their personalities inspire others. Entrepreneurs and intrapreneurs often possess the characteristics and behaviors described following.[27] Recognize, however, that authorities disagree about whether an entrepreneurial personality exists.

1. *A strong achievement need.* Entrepreneurs have stronger achievement needs than do most managers. Building a business is an excellent vehicle for accomplishment. The high achiever shows five consistent behaviors and attitudes: a desire to (a) achieve through one's own efforts and take responsibility for success or failure, (b) take moderate risks that can be handled through one's own efforts, (c) receive feedback on level of performance, (d) introduce novel, innovative, or creative solutions, and (e) plan and set goals.[28]

2. *High enthusiasm and creativity.* Related to the achievement need, entrepreneurs and intrapreneurs are typically enthusiastic and creative. Their enthusiasm, in turn, makes them persuasive. As a result, entrepreneurs are often perceived as charismatic by their employees and customers. Some entrepreneurs are frequently so emotional that they are regarded as eccentric.

3. *Always in a hurry.* Entrepreneurs and intrapreneurs are always in a hurry. When engaged in one meeting, their minds typically begin to focus on the next meeting. Their flurry of activity rubs off on group members and others around them. Entrepreneurs often adopt a simple dress style in order to save time. "He wears slip-on shoes so he doesn't have to bother with laces in the morning; he grows a beard; she cuts her hair short. Everything is hurry, hurry."[29]

4. *Visionary perspective.* Entrepreneurs and intrapreneurs, at their best, are visionaries. They see opportunities others fail to observe. Specifi-

cally, they have the ability to identify a problem and come up with a solution.

5. *Uncomfortable with hierarchy and bureaucracy.* Entrepreneurs are not ideally suited by temperament to working within the mainstream of a bureaucracy. Many successful entrepreneurs are people who were frustrated by the constraints of a bureaucratic system. A typical example is the entrepreneur who sells his or her business to a larger firm, thus becoming a division president. Within two years, the entrepreneur leaves the firm because of frustration with rules and regulations imposed from above. Intrapreneurs, by definition, fit reasonably well into a bureaucracy, yet they do not like to be restrained by tight regulations.

6. *A much stronger interest in dealing with customers than with employees.* One of the reasons why entrepreneurs and intrapreneurs have difficulty with bureaucracy is that they focus their energies on products, services, and customers. Some entrepreneurs are gracious to customers and money lenders but brusque with company insiders.

To further your insight into the entrepreneurial personality and leadership style, here is a description of an entrepreneur provided by one of her employees:

> Sarah is an absolute madwoman. She is always on the go, always thinking, and always wanting to get something done. She often handles two phone calls at once. We all love Sarah, and we worry about her having a heart attack. A normal workweek for Sarah is seventy-five hours. If it weren't for her cellular phone, she would never take a vacation. Sarah has made her million dollars, but rumor has it she's planning another new business.
>
> A problem we have with Sarah is that it's hard to get her to sit still and listen to problems about employees or review reports.

THE LEADER'S ROLE IN ENCOURAGING TEAMWORK

As emphasized throughout this text, teamwork is an important requirement in the modern organization. A key role for the leader is therefore to encourage teamwork. To meet this expectation, there are many actions a leader can take.[30] The most effective way to encourage the emergence of teamwork is by example. If the leader is a good team player, team members will follow. An overall strategy the team leader should use is to cultivate the attitude among members that working together effectively is an expected standard of conduct.

An obvious but often overlooked method of team-building is to encourage cooperation, rather than intense competition, within the group. One such method would be for the leader to praise employees for having collaborated on joint projects. Perhaps the best-known way to encourage teamwork is to rally the support of the group against a real or imagined threat from the outside. Beating the competition makes more sense when the competition is outside your own organization.

Many minor problems between the manager and group members fester into major problems. The major problems, is turn, adversely affect team spirit and productivity. In order to resolve little problems, the group leader should keep open the channels of communication within the group. Keep in mind that good teamwork includes emotional support to members. Such support can take the form of verbal encouragement for ideas expressed, listening to a group member's problems, or even providing help with a knotty technical problem.

Laughter is a natural team-builder that enhances understanding and empathy, which are essential to group cohesiveness. Simple techniques that work well are daily calendars with humorous stories, and in-group jokes at work unit meetings.[31] Teamwork on the athletic field is enhanced by team symbols, such as uniforms and nicknames (Boilermakers, Orangemen, Lady Longhorns, and so forth). Symbols are also a potentially effective team-builder in the worksite. Company jackets, caps, T-shirts, mugs, and business cards can be modified to symbolize an organizational subunit.[32]

It is important to avoid the common mistake of creating in-groups and out-groups within your unit. The team members who are "in" may cooperate with each other, but the "outs" probably will not cooperate with the "ins." Furthermore, this type of favoritism tends to breed dissension instead of teamwork.[33]

Finally, a key strategy in encouraging teamwork is to reward the group as a whole when such rewards are deserved. A popular form of group incentive is to reward good group performance with an organization-paid banquet. Scheduling the banquet on a weekend, and inviting spouses and guests, is even a bigger morale booster. This is important because teamwork depends on high morale.

DEVELOPING YOUR LEADERSHIP POTENTIAL

Much of this book deals directly and indirectly with information that could improve your leadership effectiveness. The following chapter on communications is a case in point. Improving your communications effectiveness would be one way to enhance your ability to lead people. And Chapter 13, "Interpersonal Skill Training," describes programs often used to improve managerial skills. Formal education and leadership development programs also contribute to enhancing leadership potential. The accompanying box describes a popular leadership and teamwork development program. Here we describe three strategies for developing your leadership potential, in addition to studying and participating in formal programs.

WILDERNESS CAMP BUILDS LEADERSHIP

In the cold predawn light of the Rockies, a dozen executives of the Champion Spark Plug Company shiver into jogging gear. They wheeze through a twenty-minute run on a winding pine forest trail, reluctantly plunge half-naked into a rushing mountain stream, and then head off to climb some rocks.

It's all in a day's work at the Colorado Outward Bound School, where the hard-charging managers learn teamwork in the wild. Over the next five days, the spark plug executives would discover fears they never knew they had. Among their daily feats, they clawed up a seventy-foot cliff blindfolded and scaled a 13,000-foot peak, posing for photographs at the summit like an Everest assault team.

"In a couple of days I'll be back in the office saying, 'Wow, did I do all that stuff?' " said the manager of Champion's international manufacturing operations.

The executives were sent to Outward Bound as an experiment by Champion, one of a growing number of companies introducing an adventure into management training to build camaraderie and cultivate leadership. Part of the idea of these programs is to confound, surprise, shock, and scare managers into breaching preconceived limits and thinking about new ways of doing things.

The programs are often a mixture of seminars, scout camp, serious reflection and good-natured jokes about sore muscles. The training party reflects a shift in what companies are seeking in a leader. They still want scrappy soldiers who are not afraid to brawl with rivals to achieve success. But they also want people with compassion, humility, vision, and willingness to manage by consensus, not edict. Many of the exercises, such as scaling a twelve-foot wall, require exceptional teamwork.

Source: As reported in Rick Gladstone, "Executives Take Their Insecurities Outdoors," Associated Press, Sept. 25, 1988.

---

1. Acquire broad experience. Because leadership is situational, a sound approach to improving leadership effectiveness is to attempt to gain supervisory experience in different settings. A person who wants to become an executive is well-advised to gain supervisory experience in at least two different organizational functions, such as marketing and operations.

First-level supervisory jobs are an invaluable starting point for developing your leadership potential. It takes considerable skill to manage a fast-food restaurant or direct a public playground during the summer. A first-level supervisor frequently faces a situation where subordinates are poorly trained, poorly paid, and not well motivated to achieve company objectives.

2. Modeling effective leaders. Another strategy for leadership development is to observe capable leaders in action and then model some of their approaches. You may not want to copy a particular leader entirely, but you can incorporate a few of the behavior patterns into your own leadership style. For instance, most inexperienced leaders have difficulty confronting others. Observe a skilled confronter handle the situation, and try that person's approach the next time you have unfavorable news to communicate to another person.

3. Self-development of leadership traits and behaviors. Our final recommendation for enhancing your leadership potential is to study the leadership traits, characteristics, and behaviors described earlier in this chapter. As a starting point, identify several attributes you think that you could strengthen within yourself, given some determination and perhaps combined with the right training program. For example, you might decide that with effort you could improve your initiative and enthusiasm. You might also believe that you could remember to be more supportive of co-workers and subordinates. It is also helpful to obtain feedback from valid sources about which traits and behaviors you particularly need to develop.

Summary of Key Points

- Leadership is the process of influencing employees to achieve organizational goals, excluding illegal and immoral methods of persuasion. Leading, or directing, is one function of management or supervision. Among the influence tactics used by leaders are charisma, leading by example, assertiveness, rationality, team play, ingratiation, exchange of favors, upward appeal, joking and kidding, and charm and appearance.

- Leadership is situational, yet some traits, motives, and personal characteristics contribute to effectiveness in many situations. Among them are the power and achievement motives, problem-solving ability, self-confidence, initiative, vision, enthusiasm, internal locus of control, and insight.

- Behaviors and skills related to leadership effectiveness include credibility and integrity, technical competence, sensitivity to people, effective work habits, supportiveness, maintaining high expectations, providing feedback, stability under pressure, and resiliency.

- A leadership style is the typical pattern of behavior engaged in by the leader when dealing with employees. The leadership continuum classifies leaders according to how much authority they retain for themselves. Styles are autocratic, participative (including consultative, consensus, and democratic), and free-rein. The participative style works best with people who are competent and well-motivated.

- The Leadership Grid® styles classify leaders according to how much concern they have for both production (task accomplishment) and people. Team management, with its high emphasis on production and people, is considered the ideal. The Theory X and Theory Y styles are based on the assumptions a manager makes about people. Theory X assumptions lead to an autocratic style, while Theory Y assumptions lead to a participative style.

- Fiedler's contingency theory states that the best style of leadership is determined by the situation in which the leader is working. Style, in Fiedler's theory, is measured by the least-preferred co-worker scale (LPC). You are relationship-motivated if you have a reasonably positive attitude toward your least-preferred co-worker. You are task-motivated if your attitude is negative, and you are socioindependent if your attitude is neutral. Situational control, or favorability, is measured by a combination of the quality of leader-member relations, the degree of task structure, and the leader's position power.

- The key proposition of Fiedler's theory is the leader-match concept: In situations of high control or low control, leaders with a task-motivated style are the most effective. In a situation of moderate control, a relationship-motivated style works best. In a high-control situation, a socioindependent style is best.

- An important style of leader is the entrepreneur or intrapreneur. The entrepreneurial style stems from the leader's personal characteristics and the circumstances of self-employment. The entrepreneurial and intrapreneurial styles include these elements: a strong achievement need, high enthusiasm and creativity, hurriedness, visionary perspective, discomfort with bureaucracy, and preference for dealing with customers rather than employees.

- A key role for the leader is to encourage teamwork. Many actions taken by the leader foster this result. They include setting the right example, encouraging cooperation, maintaining open communication channels, giving emotional support, sharing laughter, using team symbols, minimizing the creation of in-groups and out-groups, and using group incentives.

- A recommended approach to developing your leadership potential is to acquire supervisory experience in several different situations. Also, it is helpful to model effective leaders and to develop those traits and characteristics associated with effective leadership.

Questions and Activities

1. How does knowledge about the basic organization functions, such as accounting, production, and marketing, contribute to a person's ability to be an effective leader?

2. How do you explain the observation that joking and kidding can be effective influence tactics?

3. What can a leader do to be more "charming"?

4. Now that you have studied this chapter, what do you think of the once-popular statement, "Leaders are born, not made"?

5. Give an example of insightful behavior on the part of any leader you have observed personally or through the media.

6. Which leadership style do you think would be the most effective in supervising a group of teenage recruits in a busy new fast-food restaurant? Explain your reasoning.

7. What might be the negative side effects of "management by wandering around"?

8. Place the leader of your country on the Leadership Grid®, and justify your placement.

9. Based on Fiedler's contingency theory, explain how a leader can modify a situation in order to exert more control.

10. What would be a useful strategy in dealing with a manager who fit perfectly the entrepreneurial leadership style?

11. What similarities do you see between the suggestions for being a team player offered in Chapter 8 and those offered here for fostering teamwork?

A HUMAN RELATIONS CASE PROBLEM
What Kind of a Leader is Sue Wong?

Sue Wong, an office manager at Great Western Mutual, recently took a leadership development course sponsored by her company. The major thrust of the course was to teach supervisors how to implement participative management. In the words of the course leader, "Today, almost all employees want to get involved. They want a say in all important decisions affecting them. The era of the industrial dictator is over."

Wong was mildly skeptical about the course leader's universal endorsement of participative management. Yet she decided that if this is what the company wanted, she would adopt a more participative style. Wong took extensive notes on how to implement participative decision making.

Six months after the leadership development program was completed, the human resources department attempted to evaluate its impact. One part of the evaluation consisted of interviews with managers who had attended the program. Managers were asked how they liked the program and how it had helped them. Another part of the program evaluation was to speak to employees about how the course had influenced their boss's approach to supervision.

Rick Alluto, the company training director, conducted several of the interviews with employees. He spoke first with Amy Green, a claims processor who reported to Sue Wong. Alutto told Green that her answers would be kept confidential. He said that the purpose of these interviews was to evaluate the leadership effectiveness training program, not to evaluate the manager.

Green responded, "It would be okay with me if Sue did hear my comments. I have nothing very critical to say. I think that the leadership training program was very useful. Sue is a much better manager now than she was before. She's much more aware that the people in her group have something useful to contribute. Sue asks our opinion on everything.

"I'll give you an example," Green continued. "Sue was going to order a new office copier. In the past she might have just ordered a new copier and told us when it was going to be delivered. Instead, we held three meetings to decide which copier to purchase. Three of us formed a committee to study the problem. We finally chose a copier that everybody in the office agreed would be okay. We even obtained approval from the new office assistant. It sure made him feel good."

Green concluded, "I think that every manager at Great Western should learn how to be a participative manager."

Alutto then spoke to Kent Nelson, another claims analyst reporting to Sue Wong. Nelson said that he appreciated the fact that the interviews would be confidential. However, he hoped that the drift of his comments would get back to Wong, as long as he was not identified. Nelson offered this evaluation:

"Sue has gone downhill as a manager ever since she took your training program. She has become lazier than ever. Sue always did have a tendency to pass off too much work to employees. Now she's gone overboard. The recent purchase of a photocopying machine is a good example. Too many people spent too much time deciding which machine to purchase. To make matters worse, a committee of three people was formed to research the matter. It seems to me that we can make better use of working time.

"If Sue keeps up this approach to supervision much longer, she won't have a job. We will be doing all of her work. How can you justify a supervisor's salary if other people are doing her work?"

Alutto thought, "I wonder if Amy and Kent are talking about the same supervisor. Their comments make it difficult for me to know whether the development program is getting the job done."

1. What does this case tell us about contingency management?
2. How do you explain the different perceptions that Green and Nelson have?
3. What might be wrong with the leadership development program?
4. Can you offer Sue Wong any suggestions for making better use of consensus decision making?
5. What is the counterargument to Nelson's point about Wong not justifying her pay?

A HUMAN RELATIONS CASE PROBLEM
The Overwhelming Leader

Sam Giovanni founded his chain of hardware stores about forty years ago by opening a small retail outlet in a residential neighborhood. Giovanni's prices were competitive with other retail outlets, and his physical layout was modest. Nevertheless, Giovanni Hardware was an immediate success. The competitive edge his store offered was a personalized approach to customer service.

Giovanni's approach to personalized service had a distinct meaning. Each associate was given four months of intensive training about the store's merchandise and how to advise customers on do-it-yourself projects. If an associate did not know the answer to a customer problem, he or she was instructed to ask Giovanni or his brother or sister, who also worked at the store.

Two years after founding the company, Giovanni opened another store. Over a period of twenty years, he opened ten more stores. Twelve Giovanni Hardware stores are now in operation. Several of these stores evolved into huge warehouse-style home centers that sell lumber and plumbing supplies as well as a full range of hardware items. After the twelfth store was opened, Giovanni was working seventy-five hours a week, taking care of such major business problems as merchandising, employee selection, and bank negotiations. Also, he regularly walked through the aisles of his stores greeting customers and sometimes helping them make purchase decisions.

To ease the workload on himself and his siblings, Giovanni hired an operations manager, Joe Danville, and a merchandise manager, Peggy Seacrest. Danville's main job was to oversee the store operations. All twelve store managers reported to him. Seacrest's job was to help the Giovannis with purchasing, and to make decisions about new types of merchandise for the stores. Both Danville and Seacrest were required to clear any major decision with Giovanni or his siblings.

Three months after being hired, Danville faced a major operating decision. A hurricane had hit the area and knocked out power lines, hampered telephone service, and created floods leading to stalled traffic. After studying the situation for an hour, Danville went into the office of Katrina Giovanni, Sam's sister. "Katrina," he said, "my decision is to close all the stores for the day. Conditions are getting out of hand, and I don't want any storm-related accidents to happen to our employees or customers."

Katrina responded, "Joe, you and I don't have the authority to make such a big decision. Sam is off the coast of Florida this week on a fishing trip. He can't be reached. We'll have to stay open through our normal operating hours. Sam is still the boss."

"Then why did you hire me as an operations manager if I don't have the authority to close the stores in a hurricane? Giovanni Hardware can no longer afford to operate as a one-person band."

"I sympathize with you," said Katrina, "but Sam is still the boss."

Discouraged by his conversation with Katrina, Danville decided to drop the issue. He thought, "I'll speak to Sam about this problem a few days after he gets back from Florida. I just can't get through to Katrina."

The next day was a hectic one for Danville, the store managers, and other employees. The hurricane had done considerable damage to several storefronts. Debris had to be cleaned up, broken windows had to be replaced with plywood, and insurance claims had to be filed. To ease some of the tension, Joe asked Peggy Seacrest if she could meet with him for breakfast the following day. She obliged.

"Peggy," said Joe, "I'm wondering if you're experiencing the same kind of problem that I am. I was hired here as a professional manager, but I'm not being treated like a professional. This place is still clearly Sam Giovanni's operation. He's still the big decision maker."

Seacrest laughed and said, "Joe, I know what you're saying. I was hired to help the chain adopt some innovative merchandising policies. I agreed to touch base with Sam or his brother or sister on major decisions. Checking with them is a waste of time. They always tell me that they will have to speak to Sam before giving me approval.

"Sam's a great guy and a smart businessperson. Yet he really doesn't listen to my merchandising ideas. He only approves of those ideas that he would have thought of without my input. He sees himself as the only person capable of making major merchandising decisions for Giovanni Hardware. Sam just won't let go. He may be an inspired leader to the old-time employees, but he has a small-business mentality. I think his attitude is going to stifle our growth."

"I agree," said Joe Danville, "yet I don't know how to change things for the better."

1. How would you describe Sam Giovanni's leadership style?
2. What do you think of Seacrest's assessment that Giovanni has a small-business mentality?
3. What changes in Giovanni's leadership style would you recommend?
4. Assuming that Danville and Seacrest want to stay with Giovanni Hardware, what should they do about their working relationship with Sam Giovanni?

A HUMAN RELATIONS EXERCISE
What Is Your Leadership Style?

The following quiz will help you assess your leadership style, whether you are currently a boss or might be in the future. Answer "agree" or "disagree" to the left of each statement.

_____ Ambition is essential in leadership.

_____ Outdated methods in industry must be eliminated, in spite of people's feelings.

_____ Know-how and initiative are two of the most important qualities a person can have.

_____ What gets done is more important than how pleasant it is to perform the task.

_____ A supervisor's job is more important than that of a social worker.

_____ Newspapers don't give enough space to people who complete worthwhile projects.

_____ My primary goal in life is to reach the top of the heap.

_____ The greatest satisfaction for me is the feeling of a job well done.

_____ Friends are more important than career ambition.

_____ Schools should put less emphasis on competition and more on getting along with others.

Scoring and interpretation. Task-motivated bosses would answer "agree" to items 1 through 8, and "disagree" to items 9 and 10. Relationship-motivated bosses would answer "disagree" to items 1 through 8, and "agree" to items 9 and 10. Give yourself one point for each answer that follows these patterns, and consider a score of 3 to 5 in either category as average. Any score above 6 is high and indicates that you would be (or are) either strongly task-motivated or relationship-motivated as a boss.

Source: Excerpted and adapted with permission from Salvatore Didato, "Do Your Employees Like You or Respect You? It's Hard to Have Both," *Rochester Democrat and Chronicle,* Jan. 19, 1985, p. 14B.

Notes

1. Adapted from book review in *Personnel Psychology,* Summer 1979, p. 454.

2. John P. Kotter, *The Leadership Factor* (New York: Free Press, 1988).

3. Jay A. Conger, A. Kanungo, and N. Rabindra, and associates, *Charismatic Leadership: The Elusive Factor in Organizational Effectiveness* (San Francisco: Jossey-Bass, 1988).

4. Bernard M. Bass, *Leadership and Performance Beyond Expectations* (New York: Free Press, 1985).

5. R. Bruce McAfee and Betty J. Ricks, "Leadership by Example: 'Do as I Do!' " *Management Solutions,* August 1986, p. 10.

6. The influence tactics listed above are from: David Kipnis, Stuart M. Schmidt, and Ian Wilkinson, "Intraorganizational Influence Tactics: Explorations in Getting One's Way," *Journal of Applied Psychology,* August 1980, pp. 440–52; Chester A. Schriesheim, and Timothy R. Hinkin, "Influence Tactics Used by Subordinates: A Theoretical and Empirical Analysis and Refinement of the Kipnis, Schmidt, and Wilkinson Subscales," *Journal of Applied Psychology,* June 1990, pp. 246–57; Andrew J. DuBrin, "Sex and Gender Differences in Tactics of Influence," *Psychological Reports,* 1991, 68, pp. 635–46.

7. One of many examples is Warren G. Bennis, "Bennis on Leadership," *Human Resources Forum,* July 1990, p. 4.

8. Robert G. Lord and associates, "A Meta-Analysis of the Relationship Between Personality Traits and Leadership Perceptions: An Application of Validity Generalization Procedures," *Journal of Applied Psychology,* August 1986, pp. 402–10.

9. General references here are Bass, *Leadership Beyond Expectations,* and Burt K. Scanlon, "Managerial Leadership in Perspective: Getting Back to Basics," *Personnel Journal,* March 1979, pp. 168–71.

10. David C. McLelland and Richard Boyatzis, "Leadership Motive Pattern and Long-Term Success in Management," *Journal of Applied Psychology,* December 1982, p. 737.

11. Fred E. Fiedler and Joseph E. Garcia, *New Approaches to Effective Leadership: Cognitive Resources and Organizational Performance* (New York: John Wiley, 1987).

12. Quoted in Priscilla Petty, "If You've Been in Your Job Long, You Need to Freshen Up on Ambition," Gannett News Service, Sept. 30, 1986.

13. James M. Kouzes and Barry Z. Posner, *The Leadership Challenge: How to Get Extraordinary Things Done in Organizations* (San Francisco: Jossey-Bass, 1987).

14. Avis L. Johnson, Fred Luthans, and Harry W. Hennessey, "The Role of Locus of Control in Leader Influence Behavior," *Personnel Psychology,* Spring 1984, p. 70.

15. James M. Kouzes and Barry Z. Posner, "The Credibility Factor: What Followers Expect from Their Leaders," *Management Review,* January 1990, p. 30.

16. Thomas R. Horton, "American Management: Myths and Realities," paper presented at Rochester Institute of Technology, April 17, 1986.

17. Morgan W. McCall, Jr., and Michael M. Lombardo, "What Makes a Top Executive?" *Psychology Today,* February 1983, p. 28.

18. Warren Bennis and Burt Nanus, "The Leadership Tightrope," *Success!,* March 1985, p. 62.

19. John A. Byrne, "The Rebel Shaking Up Exxon," *Business Week,* July 18, 1988, pp. 104–5.

20. Leonard R. Sayles, "Leadership for the Nineties," *Issues & Observations,* Spring 1990, p. 9.

21. Leonard M. Apcar, "Middle Managers and Supervisors Resist Moves to More Participatory Management," *The Wall Street Journal,* Sept. 16, 1985, p. 1.

22. Douglas McGregor, *The Human Side of Enterprise* (New York: McGraw-Hill, 1960), pp. 33–57.

23. Robert R. Blake and Anne Adams McCarse, *Leadership Dilemmas and Solutions* (Houston: Gulf Publishing, 1991).

24. Bruce M. Fisher and Jack E. Edwards, "Consideration and Initiating Structure and Their Relationships with Leader Effectiveness: A Meta-Analysis," *Academy of Management Best Papers Proceedings 1988,* p. 204.

25. Fred E. Fiedler, Martin M. Chemers, and Linda Mahar, *Improving Leadership Effectiveness: The Leader Match Concept,* 2nd ed. (New York: Wiley, 1984); E. Leroy Plumlee, "A Visit with Fred Fiedler," *Management Newsletter* (published by Houghton Mifflin), December 1989, pp. 2–7.

26. Plumlee, "A Visit with Fred Fiedler," p. 4.

27. Based in part on Daniel Goleman, "The Psyche of the Entrepreneur," *The New York Times Magazine,* Feb. 2, 1986, pp. 30–32, 59, 68; Franck A. deChambeau and Fredericka Mackenzie, "Intrapreneurship," *Personnel Journal,* July 1986, p. 40.

28. John B. Miner, Norman R. Smith, and Jeffrey S. Bracker, "Role of Entrepreneurial Task Motivation in the Growth of Technologically Innovative Firms," *Journal of Applied Psychology,* August 1989, p. 554.

29. Priscilla Petty, "The Budding Entrepreneur Is Dissatisfied, Energetic, and a Visionary," *Rochester Democrat and Chronicle,* April 24, 1984.

30. Andrew J. DuBrin, *Contemporary Applied Management,* 3rd ed. (Homewood, IL: Irwin, 1989), pp. 164–79; Paul S. George, "Teamwork Without Tears," *Personnel Journal,* November 1987, pp. 122–29.

31. George, "Teamwork Without Tears," p. 124.

32. George, "Teamwork Without Tears," p. 126.

33. Dave Day, "Beating the In-Group–Out-Group Problem," *Supervisory Management,* August 1989, pp. 17–21.

Suggested Reading

BENNIS, WARREN. *Why Leaders Can't Lead: The Unconscious Conspiracy Continues.* San Francisco: Jossey-Bass, 1989.

DePree, Max. *Leadership Is an Art*. Garden City, New York: Doubleday/Currency, 1989.

Gardner, John W. *On Leadership*. New York: Free Press, 1990.

Goktepe, Janet R., and Schneier, Craig Eric. "Role of Sex, Gender Roles, and Attraction in Predicting Emergent Leaders." *Journal of Applied Psychology,* February 1989, pp. 165–67.

Marsick, Victoria J., Turner, Ernie, and Cederholm, Lars. "International Managers as Team Leaders." *Management Review,* March 1989, pp. 46–49.

Vroom, Victor H., and Jago, Arthur G. *The New Leadership: Managing Participation in Organizations*. Englewood Cliffs, NJ: Prentice Hall, 1988.

Zaleznik, Abraham. *The Managerial Mystique: Restoring Leadership in Business*. New York: Harper & Row, 1989.

————. "Real Work." *Harvard Business Review,* January–February 1989, pp. 57–64.

10

Communicating with People

LEARNING OBJECTIVES

After reading and studying this chapter and doing the exercises, you should be able to

1. Explain the basic steps in the communication process.

2. Describe the major communication pathways in organizations.

3. Understand the importance of nonverbal communication in organizations.

4. Be sensitive to cross-cultural differences in nonverbal communication.

5. Pinpoint techniques and strategies for overcoming communications problems in organizations.

6. Develop a plan for improving your communication effectiveness.

W hy isn't this project ready for shipment today?" barked the manager. "I told you to get it done as soon as you could get to it."

"That's why it isn't done," replied the group member. "I was too busy to get to it."

The communication problem just described took place because the phrase "as soon as you can get to it" was interpreted differently by the two people involved. The mixup that took place illustrates that communication breakdowns are responsible for many problems that take place on the job.

Communication is the sending, receiving, and understanding of messages. It is also the basic process by which managers and staff specialists accomplish their work. A manager can coordinate the work of others only if he or she receives information from some people and transmits it to others. And staff specialists can have their recommendations implemented only if they are communicated to management in a useful manner. Even those whose work does not primarily involve people must communicate with others to ask questions or explain their work. Communication is also important because effective communication skills have always been considered a success factor for managerial workers.

The information in this chapter is aimed at reducing communication problems among people. We approach this end in two ways: First, we explain the nature of many facets of interpersonal communication. Second, we describe methods of overcoming communication problems in organizations and methods of improving your communication skills.

STEPS IN THE COMMUNICATION PROCESS

One way to understand how people communicate is to examine the steps involved in transmitting and receiving a message (see Figure 10–1). The process involves the following sequence of events: ideation, encoding, transmission over a medium, receiving, decoding, understanding, and taking action. The clouds in the diagram in Figure 10–1 symbolize barriers that can arise at any step in communication.

The process is cyclical. Upon decoding a message, understanding it, and then taking action, the receiver sends out his or her own message. The cycle is therefore repeated at least once. Assume Conrad wishes to communicate to his boss, Barbara, that he wants a salary increase.

Step 1 is *ideation* by Conrad. He organizes his thoughts about this sensitive problem. This stage is both the origin and the framing of the idea or message in the sender's mind. Conrad says to himself, "I think I'll ask for a raise."

Step 2 is *encoding*. Here the ideas are organized into a series of symbols (words, hand gestures, body movements, drawings) designed to com-

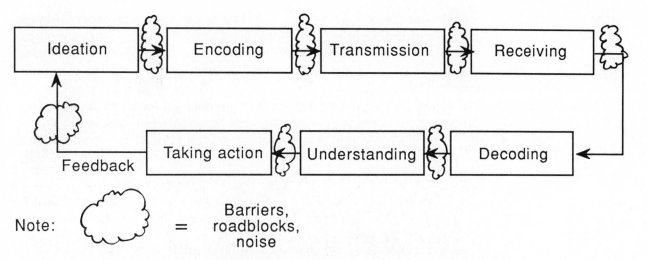

FIGURE 10-1 A Basic Model of Communication Process

municate to the intended receiver. Conrad says, "Barbara, there is something I would like to talk to you about when you have the time."

Step 3 is *transmission* of the message orally or in writing. In this situation, the sender chose the oral mode.

Step 4 is *receiving* of the message by the other party. Barbara can only receive the message if she is attentive to Conrad. Not being attentive is a barrier to communication.

Step 5 is *decoding* the symbols sent by the sender to the receiver. In this case decoding is not complete until Barbara hears the whole message. The opening comment, "Barbara, there is something I would like to talk about. . . . ," is the type of statement often used by employees to broach a sensitive topic, such as discussing a resignation or salary increase. Barbara therefore listens attentively for more information.

Step 6, *understanding,* follows upon the decoding process. Barbara has no trouble understanding that Conrad wants a salary increase. When communication barriers exist (as described in the next section of this chapter), understanding may be limited.

Step 7 is *taking action*. Barbara understands Conrad's request, but does not agree. She acts by telling Conrad that he will have to wait three more months until his salary will be reviewed. Action is also a form of feedback, because it results in a message being sent back to the original sender from the receiver.

COMMUNICATION DIRECTIONS

Messages between and among people in organizations flow in three primary directions—downward, sideways, and upward. It is also possible, but not easy, to communicate in a diagonal or circular direction. People who are adept at sending messages in one direction are not necessarily skilled at communicating in other directions. For example, some people are politically motivated to become good upward communicators, but they fail to communicate in a meaningful way to their peers or to lower-ranking employees.

The problems encountered in communicating messages in these three directions include the general communication problems discussed later in the section "Overcoming Communication Problems and Barriers." Here we will mention one or two unique problems of downward, sideways, and upward communication.

Downward Communication

The purpose of downward communication is to send information from higher levels of the organization to lower levels. Through downward communication management is able to carry out its basic functions of planning, organizing, controlling, and directing. When you receive an evaluation of your performance, you are the recipient of downward communication.

A problem with downward communication is that too many managers overemphasize it at the expense of inviting upward communication. Messages are sent to employees, but not enough effort and time is devoted to learning if the message has been properly received. (Think back to the chapter opener.)

Another problem with some forms of downward communication is that subordinates tend to regard communications from above as indicators of dissatisfaction. The underlying sentiment is, "If management wrote a memo about the topic, it must be that we're doing something wrong."

Sideways Communication

Communication among employees at the same level is crucial for the accomplishment of work. Good coordination is the product of good communication. For instance, an employee who hears a customer complaint directly should communicate that information to a co-worker who can correct the problem. A study of problems encountered in different communication directions found that horizontal communication is the most effective process. One specific finding was that horizontal messages arrive on time about 75 percent of the time. The researcher noted that some of this communication efficiency can be attributed to formal structures, such as quality circles and project teams.[1]

Horizontal communication is less efficient when workers are isolated from each other by being grouped into different departments. The isolation leads to limited understanding, which in turn leads to rivalry and friction. One way of overcoming this type of conflict is to give people the opportunity to talk to one another in interdepartmental meetings. Other methods of improving horizontal communication are job rotation, after-hours gatherings, and conferences.

Upward Communication

Upward communication is the flow of information from lower levels to higher levels, or from employees to management. Without upward communication, management works in a vacuum, not knowing if messages have been received properly, or if other problems exist in the organization.

> Faced with decreasing profits, a large retailer decided to cut costs by reducing substantially the number of store employees. Customer service became so poor that many customers left the store in a huff or complained to store managers. Fearful of informing top management that the cost-cutting plan was driving away customers, information about customer complaints was not relayed to top management. By the time top management became aware of the customer service problems, sales had declined to a dangerously low level.

Despite the importance of upward communication, it is usually limited. Table 10–1 summarizes findings from Allan D. Frank's study of organizational communication in over 100 firms.[2] The people answering the questionnaire were human resource professionals. One interpretation of the data is that upward communication is not responded to enthusiastically, nor is it very welcome.

One barrier to upward communication is that many employees see management as being both inaccessible and unresponsive. Workers often

TABLE 10–1 How effective is upward communication?

Question	Percent	Response categories
"When messages are sent	0.7%	Almost never/very little
upward through formal	20.7	Sometimes/little
channels, how frequently	30.0	Often
does the receiver respond	32.0	Very often/great
to the message?"	16.7	Almost always/very great
"To what extent are	10.0	Almost never/very little
employees encouraged by	32.7	Sometimes/little
management to send	—	Often
messages upward in the	39.3	Very often/great
organization?"	18.0	Almost always/very great

Source: Adapted from Allan D. Frank, "Trends in Communication: Who Talks to Whom," *Personnel*, December 1985, p. 42. Reprinted with permission from the American Management Association.

feel that their bosses are too busy to be disturbed, or they simply cannot find them when they want to. Also, workers may not trust the upward channels and may be fearful of using them.[3]

FORMAL AND INFORMAL COMMUNICATION PATHWAYS

In addition to traveling in more than one direction, messages are sent over more than one pathway. Organizational communication takes place over both formal and informal channels or pathways.

Formal Communication Pathways

Formal communication pathways are the official, sanctioned paths over which messages are supposed to travel. As such, they are easy for most employees to understand and accept. Two key determinants of formal communication pathways are the organization structure and the flow of work.

Organization structure. The organization structure, as revealed by the organization chart, describes who reports to whom. It simultaneously dictates communication pathways. In large organizations, these pathways can be complex. As many as twelve levels of management are often found in large corporations and government agencies. Assume that a chairman of the board decides that helping to find jobs for the spouses of transferred employees is a corporate responsibility. A policy statement is then made that managers should make an effort to help the spouse of a transferred employee find a job in the new location.

Figure 10–2 shows the formal communication pathway for this message. The formal pathway indicates the least complicated route over which the message will be transmitted. In practice, the route may be much more circuitous. One side route would be managers talking to other managers at the same level about this new corporate responsibility.

Work flow. Formal communication pathways are also heavily influenced by the **work flow,** the routing of work from one person or department to another. If you are a quality specialist, you might be expected to communicate your observations directly to a supervisor. A sales representative might initiate work for a credit analyst. The "rep" makes a tentative sale on a big piece of equipment. Before the customer is approved for receiving the equipment prior to paying for it in full, the credit analyst must approve the customer's credit rating.

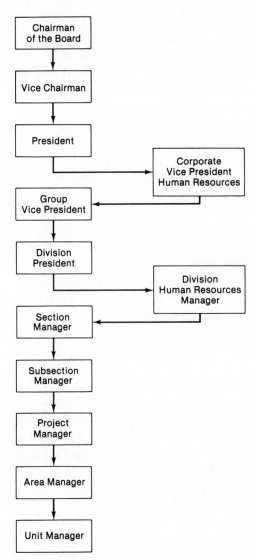

FIGURE 10–2 Formal Communication Pathway for Message from Top to Bottom of a Large Business Organization

Informal Communication Pathways

Organizations cannot get their work accomplished by means of formal communication channels alone. A supplementary system of communication, called informal communication pathways, is also needed. An **informal communication pathway** is an unofficial network of communications used to supplement a formal pathway or channel. Many of these pathways arise out of necessity. For example, employees may consult with someone outside their department to solve a technical problem. Three key aspects of informal communication pathways are the grapevine, the rumors it carries, and gossip.

The grapevine. The **grapevine** is the major informal communication channel in an organization. The term refers to tangled wires or branches that can distort information. Yet there are times when information transmitted along the grapevine is undistorted and accurate. For example, valid news about a pending company merger often passes along the grapevine before it is officially announced.

The grapevine is sometimes used deliberately by management to transmit information it may not want to transmit formally. One example would be to feed the grapevine with news that salary increases will be below average this year.[4] When the salary increases turn out to be average, most employees will be relieved and therefore satisfied.

A related use of the grapevine is to measure the reaction of employees to an announcement before it is transmitted through formal channels.[5] If the reaction is bad, management can sometimes modify its plans. One company wanted to test employee reaction to a productivity improvement plan to shorten lunch breaks by ten minutes. An administrative assistant made casual mention of the plan in the cafeteria, and news about the plan spread rapidly. Reaction to the shortened lunch break was so negative that the company abandoned the plan.

Rumors. A **rumor** is a message transmitted through the organization, although not based on any official word. Usually rumors travel along the grapevine, sometimes with the assistance of a communication hub (a person who transmits information regularly).[6] The biggest problem with rumors is that they are capable of disrupting work and lowering morale. If you are ruminating over a rumor, you are likely to divert effort away from your job. As the rumor travels along the grapevine, it will cause some people to do foolish things—like begin to look for a new job when it is not necessary.

Communication specialists have formulated suggestions for dealing with rumors that plague organizations both internally and externally.[7] The same principles can sometimes be used to combat rumors circulated about an individual.

- First, try to wait it out. The rumor may run its course before doing too much damage.
- If the rumor persists, make it news. If you talk about the rumor and deny it, then nobody has an exclusive. Everybody has heard about it.
- Act promptly to determine how far a rumor has spread by contacting customers, vendors, and the public.
- To cut the rumor short, communicate the information that people want. Do so promptly, clearly, accurately, and factually. At the same time, keep open formal communication channels and shorten them whenever possible to encourage more direct interaction. An open-door policy is helpful here.

- Ridicule a rumor that is absolutely untrue. Call it preposterous, stupid, crazy. People may then ridicule those who repeat it.
- As a countermeasure, feed the grapevine with actual information to get the facts through informal communication channels. If the rumor is of grave enough consequences, have members of top management meet with small groups of employees to place matters in proper persepctive.

Walter St. John suggests that preventive measures are perhaps the most effective strategy for managing rumors. He advises management to be alert to situations that promote rumors. Among them are employees being confused about what is happening and information is unclear, incomplete or lacking; people feeling powerless to attain their desires on the job; and excessive anxiety and conflict present in the workplace.[8]

Gossip. A special form of rumor is **gossip**—the idle talk or tidbits of information about people that are passed along informal communication channels. We all know that gossip can hurt reputations and waste time. Yet gossip also serves a number of useful organizational purposes. It can be a morale booster, a socializing force, and a guidebook to group norms.

Gossip can improve morale by adding spice and variety to the job. It may even make some highly repetitive jobs bearable. Robert Wieder notes that in an increasingly technological and depersonalized workplace, gos-

sip may be an important humanizing factor. At the same time, it is a source of employee team spirit.[9]

Gossip serves as a socializing force because it is a mode of intimate relationship for many employees. People get close to each other through gossip. It also serves as the lifeblood of personal relationships on the job. Gossip acts as a guidebook because it informs employees of the real customs, values, and ethics of the work environment. For instance, a company might state formally that no employee can accept a gift of over $10 from a supplier. Gossip may reveal, however, that some employees are receiving expensive gifts from suppliers. Furthermore, the company makes no serious attempt to stop the practice.

NONVERBAL COMMUNICATION IN ORGANIZATIONS

Most of our discussion so far has emphasized the use of words, or verbal communication. However, a substantial amount of communication between people takes place at the nonverbal level. **Nonverbal communication (NVC)** refers to the transmission of messages through means other than words. A nonverbal communication can be regarded as a *silent message*. These messages accompany verbal messages and sometimes stand alone. The general purpose of NVC is to communicate the feeling behind a message. For instance, you can say "no" either with a clenched fist or with a smile to communicate the intensity of your negative feelings.

A widely quoted study by Albert Mehrabian dramatizes the relevance of nonverbal communication. He calculated the relative weights of three elements of overall communication. The words we choose account for only about 7 percent of our impact on others; our voice tone accounts for 38 percent; our facial expressions for 55 percent. Nonverbal behavior therefore accounts for 93 percent of the impact of a message.[10] This famous study should not be interpreted to mean that 93 percent of communication is nonverbal. It deals with the impact of your message, and does not mean that the content of your message is unimportant.

Nonverbal communication is a broad topic. The three aspects covered here are modes of transmission, problems revealed by body language, and cross-cultural differences.

Modes of Transmission of Nonverbal Communication

Nonverbal messages can be transmitted in many modes, as described following. Later, we also describe mirroring, because it is an interesting application of nonverbal messages.

Environment. The setting or environment in which you send a message can influence the receiving of that message. Assume that your manager invites you out to lunch to discuss a problem. You will think it is a more important topic under these circumstances than if the manager had lunch with you in the company cafeteria.

Other important environmental silent messages include room color, temperature, lighting, and furniture arrangement. A person who sits behind a large, uncluttered desk, for example, appears more powerful than a person who sits behind a small, messy desk.

Interpersonal distance. The placement of one's body in relation to someone else (proxemics) is widely used to transmit messages. In general, getting physically close to another person conveys a positive attitude toward him or her. Putting your arm around someone is generally interpreted as a friendly act. (Some people, however, recoil when touched by someone other than a close friend.) Kenneth Blanchard observes that if an employee feels at ease with a manager's style, the employee will face the manager in a casual, relaxed manner. If the employee turns away, he or she is literally giving the manager the cold shoulder.[11]

Practical guidelines for judging how close to stand to another person in the United States and Canada, or in a similar culture, are shown in Figure 10–3.

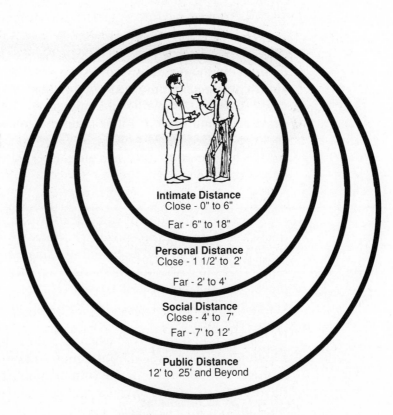

Intimate Distance
Close - 0" to 6"

Far - 6" to 18"

Personal Distance
Close - 1 1/2' to 2'

Far - 2' to 4'

Social Distance
Close - 4' to 7'

Far - 7' to 12'

Public Distance
12' to 25' and Beyond

FIGURE 10–3 Four Circles of Intimacy

Posture.   Your posture communicates a variety of meanings. Standing erect usually conveys the message that the person is self-confident and experiencing positive emotion. Slumping makes a person appear to be lacking in self-confidence or down in the dumps. Another interpersonal meaning of posture involves the direction of leaning. Leaning toward the sender suggests that you are favorably disposed toward his or her message; leaning backward communicates the opposite message. Openness of the arms or legs serves as an indicator of liking or caring. In general, people establish closed postures (arms folded and legs crossed) when speaking to people they dislike.

Gestures.   Positive attitudes toward another person are shown by frequent hand movements. In contrast, dislike or disinterest usually produces few gestures. An important exception is that some people wave their hands furiously while arguing. Gestures are also said to provide clues to a person's levels of dominance and submission. Research by two anthropologists indicated that the gestures of dominant people are typically directed outward toward the other person. Examples include a steady, unwavering gaze and touching one's partner. Submissive gestures are usually protective, such as touching oneself or shrugging one's shoulders.[12]

Facial expressions.   Using your head, face, and eyes in combination provides the clearest indications of interpersonal attitudes. Looking at the ceiling—without tilting your head—combined with a serious expression almost always communicates the message, "I doubt what you're saying is true." As is well known, maintaining eye contact with another person improves communication. To maintain eye contact, it is usually necessary to move your face and eyes with the other person. Moving your face and eyes *away* from the other person is often interpreted as defensiveness or a lack of self-confidence.

Voice tone.   The tone of voice deals with aspects such as pitch, volume, quality, and rate of the spoken word. As with most nonverbal messages, there is a danger in overinterpreting a single voice quality. A team member might speak to you about the status of a project in a high-pitched voice, not out of fear but because of laryngitis. Three emotions frequently experienced on the job—anger, boredom, and joy—often can be interpreted from voice quality.

Anger is best perceived when the source speaks loudly, at a fast rate, in a high pitch, with irregular inflection and clipped enunciation. Boredom is often indicated by moderate volume, pitch, and rate, and a monotone inflection. Joy is often indicated by loud volume, high pitch, fast rate, upward inflection, and regular rhythm.[13]

Problems Revealed by Body Language

Nonverbal messages sometimes signal the existence of problems. For example, if a vendor promises you a delivery date while looking away from you and blushing, you might suspect that the date is unrealistic. Table 10–2 describes body language cues that could be indicative of significant problems.

TABLE 10–2   Body language signals of job problems

---

1. *Stress.* Signs of stress include:

A blank expression or phony smile,

Tight posture, with arms held stiffly at the person's side,

Abrupt motions, such as suddenly shifting the eyes, a quick turn of the head, nervous tapping of a leg,

Sudden mood shifts in speech, from toneless and soft answers to animinated and loud ones.

2. *Lack of comprehension.* When you give instructions and encounter silence or a lack of questions, look for signs of doubt or uncertainty. Examples include:

Knitted brows,

A deadpan expression,

Tentative, weak nodding or smiling,

One slightly raised eyebrow,

"Yes" or "I see," in a strained voice,

"I understand," accompanied by looking away.

3. *Hesitation.* Spot employee reluctance to speak out on sensitive topics by tracking these signals:

A slight raising of the head and eyebrows,

Unconsciously lifting one finger,

Licking the lips,

Deep breathing with eye contact.

4. *Disagreement.* You can spot hostile submission, as opposed to genuine agreement, by watching for these indicators:

A downward movement of the body or eyes, or both, resembling bowing to authority,

Closed eyes and a hand put over the nose, as if the person is saying, "Oh no!"

5. *Fraud and deception.* Fabrication and fraudulence is best detected through body movement. Inability to maintain eye contact is less reliable. Be on guard for these signs:

Inappropriate finger or foot tapping,

Body shifting or some other movement that suddenly appears.

Source: "Body Language," *Executive Strategies,* June 5, 1990, p. 8; Pauline E. Henderson, "Communication Without Words," *Personnel Journal,* January 1989, p. 27.

Cross-Cultural Differences in Nonverbal Communication

People from different cultures obviously speak and write different languages. Cultural differences in language can also be found within the same country, such as some groups using "go" to mean "say." A variety of cross-cultural differences can also be found with respect to nonverbal communication. Being aware of the existence of these differences in body language will alert you to look for them when dealing with people from another culture. A sampling of these differences follows:

- A Japanese person smiling and nodding connotes understanding, not necessarily agreement.
- In many Asian cultures it is considered improper to look a superior in the eye too often. A bowed head is therefore a sign of deference, not an indicator of low self-confidence.
- Asians may smile to avoid conflict, rather than to show approval.
- British, Scandinavians, and other Northern Europeans prefer plenty of space between themselves and another person. They seldom touch when talking. In contrast, French, Italians, Latin Americans, and Eastern Europeans tend to stand close together, and they often touch one another, indicating closeness or agreement.[14]
- A German manager appearing in shirt sleeves at a business meeting would be displaying substantial indifference, while an American or Canadian would just be behaving informally.

OVERCOMING COMMUNICATION PROBLEMS AND BARRIERS

Communication problems in organizations are ever-present. Some interference usually takes place between ideation and action, as suggested by the "clouds" in Figure 10–1. The type of message influences the amount of interference. Routine or neutral messages are the easiest to communicate. Interference is most likely to occur when a message is complex, emotionally arousing, or clashes with a receiver's mental set.

An emotionally arousing message deals with topics such as a relationship between two people or money. A message that clashes with a receiver's mental set requires the person to change his or her typical pattern of receiving messages. Try this experiment: The next time you visit a restaurant, order dessert first and the entree second. The server will probably not receive your dessert order because it deviates from the normal sequence.

Here we will describe strategies and tactics for overcoming some of the more frequently observed communication problems in organizations, as outlined in Table 10–3. The following section deals with another major

---

TABLE 10–3   Overcoming barriers to communication

---

1. Understand the receiver.
2. Minimize defensive communication.
3. Use multiple channels.
4. Use verbal and nonverbal feedback.
5. Use bias-free language.
6. Avoid information overload.
7. Establish a culture of open communication.
8. Use mirroring to establish rapport.

---

strategy for overcoming communication barriers—improving your communication skills.

Understand the Receiver

Understanding the person you are trying to reach is a fundamental principle of overcoming communication barriers. The more you know about your receiver, the better able you are to effectively deliver your message. Three important aspects of understanding the receiver are (1) developing empathy, (2) recognizing his or her motivational state, and (3) understanding the other person's frame of reference.

Developing **empathy** requires placing yourself in the receiver's shoes. To accomplish this you have to imagine yourself in the other person's role and assume the viewpoints and emotions of that individual.[15] For example, if a supervisor were trying to communicate the importance of customer service to sales associates, the supervisor might ask himself or herself, "If I were a part-time employee being paid close to the minimum wage, how receptive would I be to messages about high-quality customer service?" To empathize you have to understand another person. *Sympathy* means that you understand and agree.

The receiver's **motivational state** could include any active needs and interests operating at the time. People tend to listen attentively to messages that show promise of satisfying an active need. Management usually listens attentively to a suggestion framed in terms of cost savings or increased profits.

People perceive words and concepts differently because their vantage points and perspectives differ. Such differences in **frame of reference** create barriers to communication. To reduce this barrier, you have to understand where the receiver is "coming from." A manager attempted to chastise a team member by saying, "If you keep up your present level of performance, you'll be a repair technician all your life." The technician replied, "That's good news," because he was proud of being the first person in his family to hold a skilled job. Understanding another person's frame of reference requires empathy.

Minimize Defensive Communication

An important general communication barrier is **defensive communication**—the tendency to receive messages in such a way that our self-esteem is protected. Defensive communication is also responsible for people sending messages to make themselves look good.[16] For example, when being criticized for low production, an investment banker might blame the advertising agency used by her firm.

Overcoming the barrier of defensive communication requires two steps. First, people have to recognize the existence of defensive communication. Second, they have to try not to be defensive when questioned or criticized. Such behavior is not easy because of the unconscious or semiconscious process of **denial**—the suppression of information we find uncomfortable. For example, the investment banker just cited would find it uncomfortable to think of herself as being responsible for below-average performance.

Use Multiple Channels

Repetition enhances communication, particularly when different channels are used to convey the same message. Effective communicators at many job levels follow up spoken agreements with written documentation. Since most communication is subject to at least some distortion, the chances of a message being received as intended increase when two or more channels are used. It has become standard practice in many firms for managers to use a multiple-channel approach to communicate the results of a performance appraisal. The subordinate receives an oral explanation from the superior of the results of the review. The subordinate is also required to read the form and indicate by signature that he or she has read and understands the meaning of the review.

Use Verbal and Nonverbal Feedback

Ask for feedback to determine if your message has been received as intended. A frequent managerial practice is to conclude a meeting with a question such as, "Okay, what have we agreed upon?" Unless feedback of this nature is obtained, you will not know if your message has been received until the receiver later carries out your request. If the request is carried out improperly, or if no action is taken, you will know that the message was received poorly.

Feedback is also important because it provides reinforcement to the sender, and few people will continue to communicate without any reinforcement.[17] The sender is reinforced when the receiver indicates understanding of the message. When the original receiver indicates that he or she understands the message, that person becomes the sender. A nod of approval would be an appropriate type of nonverbal reinforcement for the sender to receive.

Other forms of nonverbal feedback are also important. Following are two examples of nonverbal behavior that could help you interpret whether your message is being received as intended.

- You are making a sales pitch about encyclopedias to a family. Both the husband and the wife move forward in their chairs toward you, while the two adolescent children lean back on their chairs. You probably have the parents just about sold on the proposition, but need to work more with the children.
- You ask your boss when you will be eligible for a promotion. He looks out the window, cups his mouth to cover a yawn, and says, "Probably not too far away. I would say your chances aren't too bad." Keep trying. He is not yet sold on the idea of promoting you in the near future.

Receiving feedback enables you to engage in two-way communication, which is usually superior to one-way communication. One reason why written messages fail to achieve their purpose is that the sender of the message cannot be sure what meanings are attached to its content. Electronic mail creates a similar barrier. Instead of interacting directly with another person in the office, a message is sent to the other person's VDT. In the process the human touch (specifically, the feeling behind the message) is often lost. The antidote is to communicate in person those messages that are likely to have an emotional meaning.

Use Bias-Free Language

An important implication of semantics is that certain words are interpreted by some people as a sign of bias. When people perceive a statement to be biased, or discriminatory, an emotional barrier may be erected against the message being sent. The use of bias-free language therefore avoids one type of discrimination and helps to overcome one more communication barrier. An example of a biased statement would be for a supervisor to say, "I need a real man for this job." The bias-free expression would be, "I need a courageous person for this job."

Table 10–4 presents a list of biased words and terms, along with their bias-free equivalent. Recognize, however, that your choice of words can never please everybody. For instance, many women prefer to be addressed as "Miss" or "Mrs." rather than "Ms."

Avoid Information Overload

A major communication barrier facing today's manager or professional is **information overload,** the state of receiving more information than one can handle. So much information comes across one's desk that it is often difficult to figure out which information should receive one's atten-

TABLE 10–4   Biased terms and their bias-free substitutes

	Biased	Bias-free
Sex-related	Girl (for adult)	Woman
	Boy (for adult)	Man
	Salesman, saleswoman	Sales representative
	Lady engineer	Engineer
	Cleaning woman, maid	Housekeeper, cleaner
	Cleaning man	Custodian, cleaner
Disabilities	Handicapped	Physically challenged
	Blind†	Visually impaired
	Confined to a wheelchair	Uses a wheelchair
Race	Nonwhite, nigger	Black, African-American; Asian; person of color
	Indian	Native American; Native Canadian
	Eskimo	Native American; Native Canadian
	Newfie	Newfoundlander
	Whitey, honkey	White, white person, Caucasian
	"Scottish in me"	"My frugality"
	Ethnic jokes	Jokes with nationality unspecified

Note: Many people who cannot hear prefer the term "deaf" as a matter of deaf pride. "Hearing-impaired" may soon be considered biased.

†From a technical standpoint, visually impaired refers to some seeing ability rather than total blindness.

tion and which should be discarded. If all office communications were attended to, the actual work of the firm would go unattended.[18] Photocopying machines and computer printers have been a major contributor to information overload.

A flood of information reaching a person is a communication barrier because people have a tendency to stop receiving when their capacity to process information becomes taxed. Literally, their "circuits become overloaded" and they no longer respond to messages.

Steps are already being taken to deal with the problem of information (or communication) overload. It is becoming common practice for managers to be sent only summaries of general information, while critical information is sent in fuller form. You can decrease the chances of succumbing to information overload by organizing and sorting through information before plunging ahead with reading. Do you think students suffer from information overload?

Establish a Culture of Open Communication

An organizationwide strategy for improving interpersonal communication is to establish a culture that encourages a free and open exchange of ideas and information. Len Sandler observes that the less information given to employees, the more active the company grapevine. Rumors, gossip, half-truth, innuendo, exaggeration, and facts become blended together to fill the communication void.[19]

One way of promoting a climate of open communication is for organization members to strive to share useful information. Another way is for managers to be receptive to employee suggestions for improvement. Along these lines several companies have begun "Operation Speakeasy," a type of employee meeting (as described in Chapter 4). This new form of meeting brings together a different group of employees each month with two or three executives. The employees represent their department in presenting suggestions, concerns, and questions. The climate is positive and productive, and a one-month limit is set on responding to the issues raised.[20]

Use mirroring to establish rapport.

Communication can often be improved through **mirroring.** To mirror someone is to subtly imitate that individual. The most successful mirroring technique is to imitate another's breathing pattern. If you adjust your own breathing rate to match someone else's, you will soon establish rapport with that individual. Eric H. Marcus describes an example of how mirroring can be used to solve a management problem:

> A manager is confronted by an angry union shop steward concerning disciplinary action taken against a union member. In the normal course of events, the breathing rate of both people will fluctuate in keeping with the process of the discussion. In this case, rapid, shallow breathing, a subconscious signal of anger, will only elicit anger in response. But if the manager deliberately paces his or her own breathing rate to match that of the antagonist, and gradually decreases his or her breathing rate, tension will be reduced and rapport established.[21]

Mirroring sometimes takes the form of imitating a boss in order to win favor. Many subordinates show a relentless tendency to copy the boss's mannerisms, gestures, way of speaking, and dress.[22]

IMPROVING YOUR COMMUNICATION SKILLS

Aside from helping you to overcome communication barriers, effective communication skills are a success factor in organizational life. Unless you own a business or receive a political appointment, it is difficult to obtain a managerial or professional position without having adequate communication skills. A person intent upon improving his or her communication effectiveness should take a course, attend a workshop, or read books and articles geared toward that purpose.[23] Here we suggest a few methods to serve as a reminder for improving your communication effectiveness in four modes: face-to-face speaking, listening, writing, and nonverbal communication.

Face-to-Face Speaking

Most people could use improvement in public speaking, but only high-level executive positions require that the incumbent give speeches. What most people do need is improved ability to express their ideas in face-to-face encounters, such as conferences and two-way discussions. Implementing these experience-based suggestions should help you improve your face-to-face speaking skills.

1. Take the opportunity to speak in a meeting whenever it arises. Volunteer comments in class and committee meetings, and capitalize on any chance to be a spokesman for a group.

2. Obtain feedback by listening to tape recordings or dictating equipment renditions of your voice. Attempt to eliminate vocalized pauses and repetitious phrases (such as "okay" or "you know") that detract from your communication effectiveness. Ask a knowledgeable friend for his or her opinion on your voice and speech.

3. Use appropriate models to help you to develop your speech. A television talk show host or commerical announcer may have the type of voice and speech behavior that fits your personality. The goal is not to imitate that person, but to use him or her as a guide to generally acceptable speech and grammar.

4. Practice interviewing and being interviewed. Take turns with a friend conducting a simulated job interview. Interview each other about a controversial current topic or each other's hobby.

5. Practice expressing the feelings behind your factual statements. For example, you might rehearse an imaginary situation in which your boss has bypassed you for a special assignment several times. A factual question might be, "How does one get chosen for a special assignment?" A statement that combines facts with feelings is, "So far I have not been chosen for a special assignment. I'm worried that I'm doing something wrong, and I would like to discuss the situation with you."

Listening

Listening is a basic part of the communication process. Unless you receive messages as they were intended, you cannot perform your job properly or be a good companion. John W. Richter describes listening as our primary communication activity. Studies demonstrate that we spend about 80 percent of our waking hours communicating; 45 percent of that time is spent in listening.[24] Listening is a particularly important skill for managers because so much of their work involves eliciting information from others.

For example, in order for a manager to resolve conflict between two subordinates, the manager must listen to each side carefully. Despite the importance of listening, it has been estimated that the average listening efficiency is 25 percent.

Another key reason for improving the listening ability of employees is that insufficient listening is extraordinarily costly. Listening mistakes lead to retyping of letters, rescheduling of appointments, and reshipping of orders. Also of note, ideas get distorted by up to 80 percent as they travel up the chain of command of a large organization.[25]

Specific suggestions for improving listening skills are summarized in Figure 10–4. As with any other suggestions for developing a new skill, considerable practice (with some supervision) is needed to bring about actual changes in behavior. One of the problems a poor listener would encounter is the difficulty of breaking old habits in order to acquire these new habits.

Writing

Every reader of this book has probably already taken one or two courses designed to improve writing skills. Nevertheless, six suggestions are in order to serve as a refresher.

1. *Read a book or article about effective business report writing, or letter writing, and attempt to implement the suggestions it offers.* You are advised, however, that you may not want to follow the advice of one expert. What constitutes good writing is based to some extent on subjective opinion.

2. *Read material regularly that is written in the style and format that would be useful to you in your career.* The Wall Street Journal and *Business Week* are useful models for most forms of job-related writing. Managerial and staff jobs require you to be able to write brief, readily understandable memos and reports. If your goal is to become a good technical report writer, read technical reports in your field or specialty.

3. *Practice writing at every opportunity.* As a starting point, you might want to write letters to friends and relatives or memos to be placed in the file. Successful writers constantly practice writing. Stephen King, the popular mystery writer, says that writing is a matter of exercise: "If you work out with weights for fifteen minutes a day over a course of ten years, you will get muscles. If you write for an hour and a half a day for ten years, you will turn into a good writer.[26]

4. *Get feedback on your writing.* Ask a co-worker to critique a rough draft of your reports and memos. Offer to reciprocate; editing other people's writing is a valuable way of improving your own. Feedback from a person with more writing experience and knowledge than you is particularly valuable. For instance, comments made by an instructor about a paper would be highly valued.

These keys are a positive guideline to better listening. In fact, they're at the heart of developing better listening habits that could last a lifetime.

Eleven keys to effective listening	The bad listener	The good listener
1. Find areas of interest	Tunes out dry subjects	Seeks opportunities; asks "What's in it for me?"
2. Judge content, not delivery	Tunes out if delivery is poor	Judges content, skips over delivery errors
3. Hold your fire	Tends to enter into argument	Doesn't judge until comprehension is complete
4. Listen for ideas	Listens for facts	Listens for central themes
5. Be flexible	Takes intensive notes using only one system	Takes fewer notes; uses four or five different systems, depending on speaker
6. Work at listening	Shows no energy output; fakes attention	Works hard, exhibits active body state
7. Resist distractions	Is distracted easily	Fights or avoids distractions, tolerates bad habits, knows how to concentrate
8. Exercise your mind	Resists difficult expository material; seeks light, recreational material	Uses heavier material as exercise for the mind
9. Keep your mind open	Reacts to emotional words	Interprets color words; does not get hung up on them
10. Capitalize on the fact that *thought is* faster than speech	Tends to daydream with slow speakers	Challenges, anticipates, mentally summarizes, weighs the evidence, listens between the lines to tone of voice
11. Restate what you hear	Reacts to what he or she hears	Clarifies what he or she hears until other person says "Yes, this is what I'm saying."

FIGURE 10–4 Eleven Keys to Effective Listening

Source: John W. Richter, "Listening: An Art Essential to Success," *Success*, (September 1980), p. 26.

5. *Learn to use a word processor.* Writing will always be tedious unless you mechanize the process. Typing in place of writing by hand is a moderate step forward; learning to use a word processor is a giant step forward. My observation is that the true payoff from word processing is in writing quality, although the gains in speed may also be impressive. Writing quality improves because it is so easy to correct mistakes and edit as you go along. You can also rearrange your paragraphs. And when it comes time to do a second draft of your paper, you simply recall the original document from the computer memory and re-edit. Word processing programs usually include a spell checker and a thesaurus, both of which can improve writing quality.

6. Try out one of the many software packages for improving writing. These programs are designed to help improve spelling, grammar, sentence structure, sentence length and variety, and overuse of the passive voice. Some professional writers doubt the effectiveness of these programs, yet many students attest to their usefulness.

Nonverbal Communication

Nonverbal communication can also be improved, and printed information is becoming available for that purpose.[27] Here are five suggestions to consider:

1. *Obtain feedback on your body language by asking others to comment upon the gestures and facial expressions that you use in conversations.* Be videotaped conferring with another individual. After studying your body language, attempt to eliminate those mannerisms and gestures that you think detract from your effectiveness. Common examples include nervous gestures, such as moving knees from side to side, cracking knuckles, rubbing the eyes or nose, head scratching, and jingling coins.

2. *Learn to relax when communicating with others.* Take a deep breath and consciously allow your body muscles to loosen. The tension-reducing techniques discussed in Chapter 5 should be helpful here. A relaxed person makes it easier for other people to relax. You are likely to elicit more useful information from other people when you are relaxed.

3. *Use facial, hand, and body gestures to supplement your speech, but don't overdo it.* A good starting point is to use hand gestures to express enthusiasm. You can increase the potency of enthusiastic comments by shaking the other person's hand, nodding approval, smiling, or patting him or her on the shoulder.

4. *Avoid using the same nonverbal gesture indiscriminately.* To illustrate, if you want to use nodding to convey approval, do not nod with approval even when you dislike what somebody else is saying. Also, do not pat everybody on the back. Nonverbal gestures used indiscriminately lose their communication effectiveness.

5. *Use role playing to practice various forms of nonverbal communication.* A good starting point would be to practice selling your ideas about an important project or concept to another person. During your interchange, supplement your spoken messages with appropriate nonverbal cues, such as posture, voice intonation, gestures, and so forth. Later, obtain the other person's perception of the effectiveness of your nonverbal behavior.

Summary of Key Points _____

- Communication is the basic process by which managers and staff specialists accomplish their work, yet many communication problems exist in organizations. Communication among people is a complex process that can be divided into seven stages: ideation, encoding, transmission, receiving, decoding, understanding, and taking action.

- Communication in organizations flows in three primary directions: downward, sideways, and upward. Downward communication is used to send information from higher to lower levels; sideways communication is used to send messages to co-workers; and upward communication is used for sending messages up the organization.

- Formal communication pathways are determined to a large extent by the organization structure and the technological requirements of the situation. Three major manifestations of informal communication pathways in organizations are the grapevine, rumors, and gossip. False rumors can be disruptive to morale and productivity, and therefore should be dealt with quickly and openly.

- Nonverbal communication also plays an important part in sending and receiving messages. It includes such modes as the environment in which the message is sent, interpersonal distance, posture, gestures, facial expressions, and voice tone. Nonverbal messages can be observed to detect such job problems as stress, lack of comprehension, hesitation, disagreement, and fraud and deception. Cultural differences in nonverbal communication are worth observing.

- Methods of overcoming communication barriers include (1) understand the receiver, (2) minimize defensive communication, (3) use multiple channels, (4) use verbal and nonverbal feedback, (5) use bias-free language, (6) avoid information overload, (7) establish a culture of open communication, and (8) use mirroring to establish rapport.

- Effective communication skills are needed in order to succeed in managerial, staff, technical, and customer-contact positions. Four different modes of communication require attention: face-to-face speaking, listening, writing, and nonverbal communication. Suggestions for improvement in each of these four modes are presented in the chapter.

Questions and Activities _____

1. If communication skills are so important for managerial success, would acting experience help prepare a person for a managerial position?

2. Which steps or steps in the communication process are people the most likely to skip? Explain your reasoning.

3. Give two examples of sideways communication that take place on the job.

4. Give two examples of upward communication that take place on the job.

5. Which type of communication problem was illustrated by the Iran-Contra controversy of the Reagan administration?

6. In what way do deaf interpreters use both verbal and nonverbal communication?

7. The executive vice president of a telephone company had a videotape prepared of himself giving a speech about the importance of cost cutting. All employees were required to watch the videotape. What type of reception do you think it got?

8. What do you think of the ethics of mirroring to establish rapport?

9. What objections do you have to any of the "bias-free" terms listed in Table 10–4? To what extent do you think that some biased and bias-free terms change over time?

10. Identify a high-paying job for which communication skills are relatively unimportant. Explain why this is true.

A HUMAN RELATIONS INCIDENT
Memo Warfare

OFFICE MEMO

To: Office staff of Pleasure Time Travel Agency
From: Jerry Prince, owner and president
Subject: Budget overrun on photocopying

It has been brought to my attention that we are now 24 percent over budget on photocopying expenses, with a full one-third of the year remaining. Somehow this abuse of photocopy privileges must stop. This is certainly no way to run a travel agency. I see three alternatives facing us. Number one, we can close down the agency for the year, thus avoiding any more copying expenses (an alternative *most* of you would not desire). Number two, we can stop making photocopies for the rest of the year. Number three, we can all develop a responsible and mature approach to budget management by making more prudent use of the photocopier.

OFFICE MEMO

To: Jerry Prince

From: Sheila LaVal

Re: Your memo about photocopying

I read your recent memo with dismay, since it is my department that makes extensive use of the photocopying machine. We use copies mostly for very important purposes, such as getting trip information to clients in a hurry. Are we in the business of taking care of the travel needs of clients or in the business of pinching pennies on photocopying costs?

OFFICE MEMO

To: Sheila LaVal

From: Jerry Prince, president

Subject: Your response to my memo about photocopying

It is obvious to me, Sheila, that you are resisting the philosophy of budgeting. In today's business world, both the IBMs and the Pleasure Time Travel Agencies must learn to respect the limits imposed by budgets. Perhaps it is time that you and I had a serious discussion about this matter. Please make an appointment to see me at your earliest convenience.

1. What communication problems are illustrated by this incident?
2. Rewrite Prince's first memo in such a way that it will be less likely to make LaVal defensive.
3. Rewrite LaVal's memo in such a way that it will be less likely to make Prince counter-defensive.

A HUMAN RELATIONS CASE PROBLEM
Professionalism at Abilene Health Center

Joan McKenzie, the health care administrator at Abilene Health Center (AHC), had become concerned about the casual behavior of nurses at the center. McKenzie observed that some of the RNs (registered nurses) and LPNs (licensed practical nurses) were dressing and acting in a manner that detracted from the professional image of the health center. McKenzie set up a meeting to deal with what she perceived to be a problem of professionalism. At the outset of the meeting, McKenzie distributed an agenda that described the goals and objectives for the nursing staff. She instructed the people present to read the memo, and then said, "After you have digested the information, we will have a full group discussion of the issues raised." A copy of her memo follows:

To: All members of the AHC nursing staff
From: Joan McKenzie, health care administrator
Re: Professionalism

We are *professional* adults and must behave accordingly. Professionalism can be achieved by keeping the following goals and objectives in mind.

1. Provide comprehensive health care of high quality in a cost-effective manner which provides satisfaction to those who receive and those who deliver services.

2. Assist, guide, and direct each nurse to her or his highest potential. Help each nurse be the best she or he can be.

3. Maintain and improve respect, pride, and dignity for co-workers.

In order to resolve existing problems, please observe the following rules:

1. Cursing will not be tolerated.

2. Screaming, yelling or raising your voice is not acceptable.

3. Calling others names is not acceptable.

4. Everybody is to be at work from 8 A.M. to noon, and 1 to 5 P.M. If you have a problem with leaving at noon or 5 P.M., please call your supervisor one hour before that time.

5. If you are sick, you should call AHC before 8 A.M. at 442-0483. Lori Fanuco will answer the telephone and take your message. If there is no answer, please keep trying.

6. When you are asked to float to an area, please stay in that area and work appropriately.

7. There will be no nail-polishing in nurses' stations. Reading should be confined to nursing journals. Breaks must be taken in the break room.

8. As of May 1, the nursing staff is to wear white dresses or white pants or skirts with white or colored uniform-type tops. White nurses' shoes and sheer hose are also required. Name tags are to be worn by all employees at all times while at AHC.

9. A policies and procedures manual will be available in each nurses' station in the future.

As the nursing staff finished reading the memo, Joan McKenzie looked around the room to see if she could gauge their reaction.

Questions

1. How effective is the above memo from a communication standpoint?

2. What communication barriers might McKenzie be erecting?

3. What improvement in nonverbal communication is McKenzie seeking, as revealed by her memo?

4. How effective are the goals set forth in the memo (review Chapter 3)?

A HUMAN RELATIONS ROLE PLAY
Discussing a Controversial Memo

The role play is a follow-up to McKenzie's memo and meeting. One of the nurses at the meeting initiates a discussion of his or her reaction to the memo and its implications. The nurse feels that McKenzie is putting the nursing staff on the defensive by using accusatory and hostile language. McKenzie believes that her memo is a useful communication vehicle, and that the nurse is being too sensitive. One person plays the role of McKenzie, another person plays the role of the dissenting nurse. Several other people can play the roles of other meeting participants who want to express how they feel about McKenzie's written message.

Notes

1. Allan D. Frank, "Trends in Communication: Who Talks to Whom?" *Personnel,* December 1985, p. 42.

2. Frank, "Trends in Communication," p. 44.

3. Alan Zaremba, "The Upward Network," *Personnel Journal,* March 1989, p. 43.

4. Walter St. John, "In-House Communication Guidelines," *Personnel Journal,* November 1981, p. 877.

5. St. John, "In-House Communication Guidelines," p. 877.

6. Stephen P. Robbins, *Organizational Behavior: Concepts, Controversies, and Applications,* 2nd ed. (Englewood Cliffs, NJ: Prentice Hall, 1983), pp. 274–75.

7. Donald D. Simmons, "The Nature of the Organizational Grapevine," *Supervisory Management,* November 1985, p. 42.

8. St. John, "In-House Communication Guidelines," p. 877.

9. Robert S. Wieder, "Psst! Here's the Latest on Office Gossip," *Success!,* January 1984, pp. 22–25.

10. Cited in *Body Language for Business Success* (New York: National Institute of Business Management, 1989), p. 1.

11. Kenneth Blanchard, "Translating Body Talk," *Success!,* April 1986, p. 10.

12. Cited in Salvatore Didato, "Our Body Movements Reveal Whether We're Dominant or Submissive," Gannett News Service, Dec. 20, 1983.

13. John Baird, Jr., and Gretchen Wieting, "Nonverbal Communication Can Be a Motivational Tool," *Personnel Journal,* September 1979, pp. 607–10.

14. *Body Language for Business Success,* p. 21.

15. James L. Gibson, John M. Ivancevich, and James H. Donnelly, Jr., *Organizations: Behavior, Structure, Processes,* 6th ed. (Plano, TX: Business Publications Inc., 1988), p. 562.

16. Robert A. Giacalone and Stephen B. Knouse, "Reducing the Need for Defensive Communication," *Management Solutions,* September 1987, pp. 20–25.

17. Owen Hargie, ed. *A Handbook of Communication Skills* (New York: New York University Press, 1986), chapter 5.

18. Charles A. O'Reilly III, "Individuals and Information Overload in Organizations: Is More Necessarily Better?" *Academy of Management Journal,* December 1980, pp. 684–96.

19. Len Sandler, "Rules for Management Communication," *Personnel Journal,* September 1988, p. 42.

20. Joyce S. Anderson, "Blueprint for Real Open-Door Communication," *Personnel Journal,* May 1989, p. 32.

21. Eric H. Marcus, "Neurolinguistic Programming," *Personnel Journal,* December 1983, p. 972.

22. Larry Reibstein, "Mimic Your Way to the Top," *Newsweek,* Aug. 8, 1988, p. 50.

23. See the "Suggested Reading" section of this chapter. The business or communication skills section of libraries and bookstores have ample information on this topic.

24. John W. Richter, "Listening Is an Art Essential to Success," *Success!,* September 1980, p. 26.

25. C. Glenn Pearce, "Doing Something about Your Listening Ability," *Supervisory Management,* March 1989, p. 29.

26. "The Novelist Sounds Off," *Time,* Oct. 6, 1986, p. 80.

27. "Use Your Body Language," *Executive Strategies,* April 17, 1990, p. 4.

Suggested Reading

Barbee, George E. L. "Communicating with a Personal Touch." *Personnel Journal,* October 1989, pp. 38–45.

Barnum, C., and Wolniansky, N. "Taking Cues from Body Language." *Management Review,* June 1989, pp. 59–60.

Carnegie, Dale. *How to Win Friends and Influence People.* New York: Pocket Books (reprinted regularly) 1936.

Fiedlen, John S. "Meaning Is Shaped by Audience and Situation." *Personnel Journal,* May 1988, pp. 107–10.

Francis, Dave. *Unblocking Organizational Communication.* Brookfield, VT: Gower, 1987.

Goldhaber, Gerald M., and Barnett, George A. *Handbook of Organizational Communication.* Norwood, NJ: Ablex, 1988.

Hunt, Gary T. *Communication Skills in the Organization,* 2nd ed. Englewood Cliffs, NJ: Prentice Hall, 1989.

Mumby, Dennis K. *Communication and Power in Organizations: Discourse, Ideology, and Domination.* Norwood, NJ: Ablex, 1988.

Piotrowski, Maryann. *Effective Business Writing: Strategies and Suggestions.* New York: HarperCollins, 1990.

Van Tell, Terry. "Communicating with Your Employees and Boss." *Supervisory Management,* October 1989, pp. 5–10.

Walton, Donald. *Are You Communicating? You Can't Manage Without It.* New York: McGraw-Hill, 1989.

11

Power
and Politics

LEARNING OBJECTIVES

After reading and studying this chapter and doing the exercises, you should be able to

1. Differentiate between power and politics.
2. Identify the major sources and types of power in organizations.
3. Explain the empowerment process in organizations.
4. Describe a variety of political tactics and strategies.
5. Identify devious and unethical political tactics.
6. Understand how to control excessive amounts of political behavior.

Being competent in your job is still the most effective method of achieving career success.[1] After skill come hard work and luck as important success factors. A fourth ingredient is also important for success—political awareness and skill. Few people can achieve success for themselves or their group without having some awareness of the political forces around them and how to use them to advantage. It may be necessary for the career-minded person to take the offensive in using ethical political tactics. It may also be necessary to defend yourself against the maneuvers of people trying to discredit you or weaken your position.

As used here, **organizational politics** refers to gaining advantage through any means other than merit or luck. (Luck, of course, is what happens when preparation meets opportunity.) Politics are played to achieve power, either directly or indirectly. The power achieved may take such diverse forms as being promoted, being transferred, receiving a salary increase, or avoiding hard work. Office politics, job politics, and politically oriented behavior are all synonymous with organizational politics.

Our definition of organizational politics is nonevaluative, except that we draw a distinction between ethical and unethical politics. Many other writers on the topic regard organizational politics as emphasizing self-interest at the expense of others, or engaging in mysterious activities. Two such examples follow:

- Organizational politics consists of intentional acts of influence undertaken by individuals or groups to enhance or protect their self-interest when conflicting courses of action are possible.[2]

- Politics is the observable, but often covert, actions by which executives enhance their power to influence a decision.[3]

Power and politics are closely interrelated. In general, **power** refers to the ability to control anything of value, while **politics** refers to methods of acquiring power. The primary reason for behaving politically is to acquire power. More specifically, power has been defined as "the ability to mobilize resources, energy, and information on behalf of a preferred goal or strategy."[4] The concept of power is readily understood by anybody who has worked in a large organization or dreamed of becoming an influential person.

The career-advancement tactics described in Chapter 17 can also be considered part of organizational politics. In this chapter, we concentrate on political behavior geared toward gaining types of advantage other than promotion.

FACTORS CONTRIBUTING TO ORGANIZATIONAL POLITICS

Organizational politics is all around us. In most places, people jockey for position and try a variety of subtle maneuvers to impress the boss. To understand organizational politics, it is important to understand why such actions are omnipresent. These reasons include, but extend beyond, the use of politics to acquire power. The factors underlying organizational politics are summarized in Table 11–1

Pyramid-Shaped Organizations

The very shape of large organizations is the most fundamental reason why organizational members are motivated toward political action. Only so much power is available to distribute among the many people who would like more of it. As you move down the organization chart, each successive layer has less power than does the layer above. At the very bottom of the organization, people have virtually no power. Furthermore, organizations have been described as political structures that operate by distributing authority and setting the stage for the exercise of power.[5]

Every member of the top management team in eight microcomputer firms was interviewed on decision making and politics. The findings suggested that a pyramid-shaped structure fosters politics. According to the study, politics arises from power centralization (the consequence of a pyramid). Furthermore, autocratic executives (those who prefer to centralize power) engage in politics and generate political behavior among their team members.[6]

Competitiveness Within the Firm

A pyramid-shaped organization creates competition among employees seeking advancement. Other factors that breed competitiveness also foster politicking. For instance, when a firm hires a large number of ambi-

---

TABLE 11–1   Factors contributing to organizational politics

1. Pyramid-shaped organizations
2. Competitiveness within the firm
3. Subjective standards of performance
4. Environmental uncertainty
5. Emotional insecurity
6. Need for acceptance
7. A desire to avoid work
8. Machiavellian tendencies of people

---

tious people, competitiveness increases. When a firm is being trimmed down in size, employees compete for the remaining positions. Whatever the reason that compels people to compete with one another, they often resort to office politics to improve their competitive edge.

Subjective Standards of Performance

People often resort to job politics because they do not believe that the organization has an objective (fair) way of judging their suitability for promotion. Similarly, when management has no objective way of differentiating effective people from the less effective, they will resort to favoritism. The adage "It's not what you know but who you know" does apply to organizations that lack clear-cut standards of performance.

Environmental Uncertainty

Environmental uncertainty contributes to organizational politics in a way similar to subjective performance standards. When people, or the organizational subunits they represent, operate in an unstable and unpredictable environment, they tend to behave politically.[7] The reason could be that organizational politics is used to create a favorable impression because it is difficult to specify what a person really should be accomplishing in an uncertain situation. Since top management may not understand themselves how you should respond to the unstable environment, you resort to political approaches to win favorable evaluation from them.

Emotional Insecurity

Some people resort to political maneuvers to ingratiate themselves with superiors because they lack confidence in their talents and skills. As an extreme example, a Nobel prize–winning scientist does not have to curry favor with the administration of his or her university. The distinguished scientist's work speaks for itself. Winning a Nobel prize has given this scientist additional self-confidence; he or she is therefore emotionally secure. A person's choice of political strategy may indicate that he or she is emotionally insecure. For instance, an insecure person might laugh loudly at every humorous comment made by his or her boss.

Need for Acceptance

Many employees who practice politics in the office are not particularly intent upon climbing the organizational ladder. They simply want to be accepted and liked by others. To accomplish this end they do favors for others and carry out other relatively harmless ploys. Tom, a first-level supervisor, earned the nickname "Candy Man" based on one of his strategies for gaining acceptance from others. He kept a full candy dish on his desk, which helped maintain a steady stream of visitors.

Research evidence supports the idea that the need for acceptance leads to office politics. Interviews with sixty executives revealed that the executives often gave team members undeservedly high performance ratings in order to gain their acceptance. As one manager said, "You don't want to be the bad guy, the bearer of gloom."[8]

A Desire to Avoid Work

Some employees use various forms of office politics to avoid hard work. By performing favors for the boss, or showing the boss approval in a variety of ways, the poorly motivated employee escapes undesirable assignments. For example, a warehouse employee told a researcher that he was allowed to take naps in the storeroom because he ran personal errands for the boss.

Machiavellian Tendencies of People

A fundamental reason why people engage in political behavior is because they possess **Machiavellian tendencies,** a desire to manipulate other people. It also relates to an ability to shape the attitudes and desires of others so that it turns out for personal advantage. Research conducted by Gerald Biberman provided the evidence for the relationship between Machiavellianism and political behavior. He found a high correlation between scores on a test of Machiavellian attitudes and DuBrin's organizational politics scale.[9] An updated version of this scale is presented in Figure 11–1.

SOURCES AND TYPES OF POWER

Organizational power can be derived from many sources. How you obtain power depends to a large extent upon the type of power you are seeking. Therefore, to understand the mechanics of acquiring power you also have to understand what types of power exist and the sources and origins of these types of power. Here we examine four sources, or types, of power:

1. Power granted by the organization,
2. Power stemming from characteristics of the person,
3. Power of subordinates,
4. Power derived from capitalizing upon opportunity.

THE ORGANIZATIONAL POLITICS QUESTIONNAIRE

Directions: Answer each question "mostly agree" or "mostly disagree," even if it is difficult for you to decide which alternative best describes your opinion.

	MOSTLY AGREE	MOSTLY DISAGREE
1. The boss is always right.	_____	_____
2. It is wise to flatter important people.	_____	_____
3. If you do somebody a favor, remember to cash in on it.	_____	_____
4. Given the opportunity, I would cultivate friendships with powerful people.	_____	_____
5. I would be willing to say nice things about a rival in order to get that person transferred from my department.	_____	_____
6. If it would help me get ahead, I would take credit for someone else's work.	_____	_____
7. Given the chance, I would offer to help my boss build some shelves for his or her den.	_____	_____
8. I laugh heartily at my boss's jokes, even if I do not think they are funny.	_____	_____
9. Dressing for success is silly. At work, wear clothing that you find to be the most comfortable.	_____	_____
10. Never waste lunch time by eating with somebody who can't help you solve a problem or gain advantage.	_____	_____
11. I think using memos to zap somebody for his or her mistakes is a good idea (especially if you want to show that person up).	_____	_____
12. If somebody higher up in the organization offends you, let that person know about it.	_____	_____
13. Honesty is the best policy in practically all cases.	_____	_____
14. Power for its own sake is one of life's most precious commodities.	_____	_____
15. If I had a legitimate gripe against my employer, I would air my views publicly (such as writing a letter to the editor of a local newspaper).	_____	_____
16. I would invite my boss to a party at my home, even if I didn't like him or her.	_____	_____
17. An effective way to impress people is to tell them what they want to hear.	_____	_____
18. Having a high school or skyscraper named after me would be an incredible thrill.	_____	_____
19. Hard work and good performance are usually sufficient for career success.	_____	_____

	MOSTLY AGREE	MOSTLY DISAGREE
20. Even if I made only a minor contribution to a project, I would get my name listed as being associated with it.	_____	_____
21. I would never publicly correct mistakes made by my boss.	_____	_____
22. I would never use my personal contacts in order to gain a promotion.	_____	_____
23. If you happen to dislike a person who receives a big promotion in your firm, don't bother sending that person a congratulatory note.	_____	_____
24. I would never openly criticize a powerful executive in my organization.	_____	_____
25. I would stay late in the office just to impress my boss.	_____	_____

Scoring and interpretation: Give yourself a +1 for each answer you gave in agreement with the keyed answer. Note that we did not use the term *correct* answer. Whether an answer is correct is a question of personal values and ethics. Each question that receives a score of +1 shows a tendency toward playing organizational politics. The scoring key is as follows:

1. Mostly agree
2. Mostly agree
3. Mostly agree
4. Mostly agree
5. Mostly agree
6. Mostly agree
7. Mostly agree
8. Mostly agree
9. Mostly disagree
10. Mostly agree
11. Mostly agree
12. Mostly disagree
13. Mostly disagree
14. Mostly agree
15. Mostly disagree
16. Mostly agree
17. Mostly agree
18. Mostly agree
19. Mostly disagree
20. Mostly agree
21. Mostly agree
22. Mostly disagree
23. Mostly disagree
24. Mostly agree
25. Mostly agree

Based on a sample of 750 men and women managers, professionals, administrators, sales representatives, and business owners,* the mean score is 10. Scores of 1 through 7 suggest a below-average tendency to play politics. Scores between 8 and 12 suggest an average tendency to play office politics. Scores of 13 and above suggest an above-average tendency to play office politics, and a strong need for power.

FIGURE 11-1 How Political Are You?

*Andrew J. DuBrin, "Career Maturity, Organizational Rank, and Political Behavior Tendencies: A Correlational Analysis of Organizational Politics and Career Experience," Psychological Reports, 1988, vol. 63, pp. 531–37; DuBrin, "Sex Differences in Endorsement of Influence Tactics and Political Behavior Tendencies," Journal of Business and Psychology, Fall 1989, pp. 3–14.

Power Granted by the Organization

A standard method of classifying power is based upon whether the power stems from the organization or the individual. Three of these bases of power stem from the organization.[10]

Legitimate power.   Power granted by the organization is referred to as **legitimate power.** People at higher levels in the organization have more power than do people below them. However, the culture of an organization helps establish the limits to anybody's power. A company president who suggests donating most of the company profits to a political party may find his or her decision overruled by the board of directors. A supervisor who tells employees what hairstyle to wear may find such orders ignored. Employees disregard orders they perceive as being illegitimate.

Reward power.   The authority to give employees rewards for compliance is referred to as **reward power.** If a sales manager can directly reward sales representatives with cash bonuses for good performance, this manager will exert considerable power. Leaders can use reward power effectively only when they have meaningful rewards at their disposal.

Coercive power.   The power to punish for noncompliance is referred to as **coercive power.** It is based upon fear. As noted in Chapter 3, punishment and fear achieve mixed results as motivators. The leader who relies heavily upon coercive power runs the constant threat of being ousted from power.

Power Stemming from Characteristics of the Person

Two sources of power stem from characteristics or behaviors of the power actor: expert power and referent power. Both are classified as **personal power,** because they are derived from the person rather than the organization.

Expert power.   The ability to control others through knowledge relevant to the job, as perceived by subordinates, is **expert power.** You can also exercise expert power outside of a formal leadership position. An example is the engineering technician who is talented in getting industrial robots to work properly. The company becomes dependent on that individual, giving him or her some power in the form of special privileges.

To accumulate expert power, a leader should cultivate an image of experience and competence. A leader who appears confused, vacillates, or is obviously panicked will quickly lose expert power.[11]

Referent power.   The ability to control others based on loyalty to the leader, and the group members' desire to please that person, is **referent**

power. Charisma is the basis of referent power. Some of the loyalty to the leader is based on an identification with the leader's personality traits and characteristics. Financial executive Sanford I. Weill is an example of a charismatic leader. He is equally comfortable doing deals on Wall Street or conversing with people on Main Street. As Weill was on the verge of completing a major deal, a competitor described him in these terms.

> He's a man with broad vision, he has great inspirational leadership qualities, he's forceful, and what he's building is going to be a formidable competitor in the financial services business.[12]

Referent power can be increased by being considerate to group members, treating them fairly, and defending their interests to higher management. On the other hand, a leader can quickly lose referent power if he or she expresses hostility, distrust, and suspicion; rejects employees; or is indifferent to them.

Although both position power and personal power are important, effective leaders tend to rely more heavily on personal power to influence others.[13]

Power of Subordinates

Subordinate power is any type of power that organization members can exert upward in the organization. When subordinates perceive orders as nonlegitimate, they will rebel. Legitimate orders lie within a range of behaviors that the employee regards as acceptable—they fall within the zone of indifference. The **zone of indifference** encompasses those behaviors toward which the employee feels indifferent (does not mind). If the manager pushes beyond that zone, the leader loses power. For example, an administrative assistant will sometimes refuse to run personal errands for the boss, and a computer specialist may refuse to debug nonworking software on New Year's Eve. Do you think these people are being fair to their employers?

Legal rights also contribute to subordinate power. Federal, state, and provincial laws protect employees from discrimination and being forced to work with hazardous substances. For example, an employee has the right to refuse sexual advances from the boss because sexual harassment is illegal, as described in Chapter 6.

Power Derived from Capitalizing upon Opportunity

Power can be derived from being at the right place at the right time and taking the appropriate action. You also need to have the right resources to capitalize upon the opportunity.[14] It pays to be "where the action is" if you want to gain power through capitalizing upon opportunity. For example, if you work in a diversified company, the best opportunities lie in one of its growth divisions.

Working on an organizational problem will bring you power if you work on it at the right time. For instance, working on energy conservation during an energy crisis is power-enhancing. It is also important to take the right action at a time of crisis, such as introducing low-cost windmills to generate electricity. If a person lacks the necessary resources, such as the budget to invest in windmills, the power-enhancing opportunity will escape.

EMPOWERING OTHERS IN THE ORGANIZATION

An important new thrust in the use of power is for managers to systematically share power and control with group members.[15] Employees experience a greater sense of self-efficacy (effectiveness) and ownership of their jobs when they share power. **Empowerment** is defined as the process by which a manager shares power with subordinates, thereby enhancing their feelings of self-efficacy.[16] Sharing power with subordinates enables them to feel better about themselves and perform at a higher level. Two general

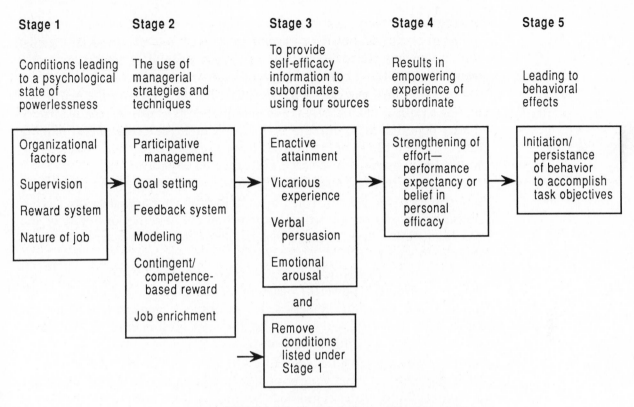

Stage 1	Stage 2	Stage 3	Stage 4	Stage 5
Conditions leading to a psychological state of powerlessness	The use of managerial strategies and techniques	To provide self-efficacy information to subordinates using four sources	Results in empowering experience of subordinate	Leading to behavioral effects

FIGURE 11-2 Five Stages in the Process of Empowerment

Source: *Jay A. Conger and Rabindra N. Kanungo, "The Empowerment Process: Integrating Theory and Practice,"* Academy of Management Review, *July 1988, p. 475.*

purposes are accomplished through empowerment: power sharing and increased employee motivation. The techniques to accomplish empowerment include participative management, goal setting, quality circles, giving feedback, and use of empathy.

Two scholars have developed a model of the empowerment process, as shown in Figure 11–2. According to the model, in order to empower employees managers have to remove conditions that keep employees powerless, such as authoritarian supervision or a low-control job. Employees must also receive information that increases their feelings of self-efficacy. When employees are empowered, they will take the initiative to solve problems and persist in the pursuit of task objectives.

DEVELOPING A PLAN FOR INCREASING YOUR POWER

Workers intent on increasing their power are advised to develop a plan, not dissimilar to developing a plan to obtain political office. The plan should include these components:[17]

1. *Establish goals that you want your political behavior to achieve.* Political behavior should be geared toward important goals, such as getting promoted, receiving a raise, or being transferred from a boss who is holding back your career.

2. *Evaluate the cost-effectiveness of your campaign.* Before selecting a political tactic, assess any potential costs of using it against its potential benefits. Many instances exist in which the costs of influencing others exceed the benefits derived from exerting influence. An example would be an attempt to discredit a respected executive.[18]

3. *Identify the true power.* To properly plan a political campaign, it is necessary to identify the true power holders in your organization. (A true power holder is a person who is very influential, whether or not he or she has high rank.) Subtle questioning of experienced workers can often achieve this end.

4. *Conduct a power analysis of the powerful people.* After you have identified the powerful players in the organization, figure out how much power each one possesses. For example, a powerful manager can make many decisions without having to confer with a superior. Having received a series of rapid promotions is also a sign of power.

5. *Size up your boss.* Because office politics begins with creating a favorable impression on your boss, it is important to understand his or her preferences and values. Find answers to questions such as, "What is my manager's most vexing problem?" or "What does my boss regard as good performance?"

6. *Analyze what type of politics is played by senior management.* Top-level political behavior often serves as an appropriate model for political tactics played below. For example, top management might underplay its power by means such as dressing casually or having the minimum number of assistants. If you emphasize looking and acting powerful by dressing formally, and requesting two personal assistants, you could fall into immediate disfavor.

ETHICAL POLITICAL TACTICS AND STRATEGIES

So far we have mentioned organizational politics without pinpointing specific tactics and strategies. In this section we describe a sampling of ethical political behaviors divided into four related categories: strategies and tactics aimed directly at gaining power, building relationships with superiors, building relationships with co-workers and lower-ranking employees, and avoiding political blunders.

Keep in mind that a given behavior is political only if it is intended to be political. If you dress stylishly because you want to be stylish, you are not behaving politically. If you dress stylishly just to please your superiors, you are acting politically.

Strategies and Tactics Aimed Directly at Gaining Power

All political tactics are aimed at acquiring and maintaining power (even the power to avoid hard work!). Described here are seven techniques aimed directly at acquiring power (see Table 11–2). The techniques for building relationships and avoiding political blunders described later are more indirect.

Develop power contacts. After powerful people have been identified, alliances with them must be established and maintained. Cultivating friendly, cooperative relationships with powerful organizational members can make your cause much easier to advance. These contacts can benefit you by supporting your ideas in meetings and other public forums.[19] One method of developing these contacts is to extend yourself socially, such as throwing a party and inviting powerful people and their partners or guests. A frequent practice is for the power-seeker to periodically invite power-holders to lunch or breakfast.

Form coalitions. An individual's power can often be increased by joining forces with others. As the adage states, "There is strength in numbers." A **coalition** is a specific arrangement of parties working together to combine their power. An important purpose of networking is to help build a coalition. Coalitions in business are a numbers game—the more people you can get on your side, the better. In one company, part-time and temporary workers from several different areas made a combined plea to management for better working conditions. They achieved demands such as some vacation pay and hourly increases for longevity. No one group of part-time or temporary workers had ever achieved any concessions from management.

Control vital information. Power accrues to those who control vital information, as indicated in the discussion of expert power. Many former government or military officials have found convenient power niches for themselves in industry after leaving the public payroll. Frequently such in-

---

TABLE 11–2 Strategies and tactics aimed directly at gaining power

1. Develop power contacts,
2. Form coalitions,
3. Control vital information,
4. Keep informed,
5. Acquire seniority,
6. Play "camel's head in the tent,"
7. Make a quick showing.

dividuals are hired as the Washington representative of a firm that does business with the government. The vital information they control is knowledge of whom to contact to shorten some of the complicated procedures in getting government contracts approved. The esoteric knowledge of how to write a proposal to suit the government's requirements also gives that individual power.

Controlling vital information becomes a devious and unethical strategy when the person controls information that is stolen or should be shared with others. An example would be when an executive switches firms and takes information about customers to a competing firm.

Keep informed.   In addition to controlling vital information, it is politically important to be kept informed. Management consultant Eugene Schmuckler aptly describes the situation in these terms:

> We are all aware of the significance of having one's name removed from the distribution list of internal memos. Although the information is not always accurate, we recognize the value of being able to tap into the corporate grapevine. Successful managers attempt to develop a "pipeline" or information source so that they can stay abreast and, in some cases, ahead, of what is happening in their organization. For the same reason, it is a wise individual who befriends the president's secretary. No other source offers the potential of information as does the executive secretary.[20]

Acquire seniority.   Longevity in an organization still garners some respect and privilege. Although seniority alone will not prevent you from being ousted from the organization or guarantee you more power, it helps. The compulsive job hopper is forever working against the implicit threat of the last in, first out personnel policy, even at the managerial level:

> One manager in the food business accepted a position with a Boston company as the manager of new product development. Three months after he arrived he was informed that the company had no funds left to invest in new product development. He was given one month's severance pay and faced with the embarrassment and awkwardness of finding a comparable level position. Eight months later, he found a job as a food-processing engineer at a substantially lower level of pay than his previous two positions.

Play "camel's head in the tent."   A gradual approach is sometimes the most effective means of acquiring power. Just as the camel works his way into the tent inch by inch, you might acquire power in a step-by-step manner until you emerge victorious. An administrative assistant in a furniture company took care, one by one, of all the details relating to a line of office furniture. Finally her boss said, "Rosalin, why don't we make you the product manager for office furniture? At this stage you know more about the product line than I do." Rosalin achieved just the position she wanted. If she had suggested at the outset that she be made product manager, her proposal might have been refused.

Make a quick showing. A display of dramatic results can be useful in gaining acceptance for your efforts or those of your group.[21] Once you have impressed management with your ability to work on that first problem, you can look forward to working on the problems that will bring you greater power. An information systems specialist provides this example of making a quick showing:

> Our group agreed to set up a database of credit ratings on customers. This was a bread-and-butter item, but we were willing to take on any assignment to show our skills. The database was a winner. We then suggested a program for tutoring executives on the use of personal computers. Based on our past success, our ideas were accepted. Our acceptance in the firm has gone way up now that we are working closely with key executives throughout the firm.

Building Relationships with Superiors

The political purpose of building good relationships with superiors is to gain power through means such as being recommended for promotion and key assignments. Good relationships can also be established with superiors for the nonpolitical purpose of trying to get the job accomplished. The tactics and strategies described next are outlined in Table 11–3.

Help your boss succeed. The primary reason why you are hired is to help your superior achieve the results necessary to succeed. Avoid an adversarial relationship with your boss. Also figure out both obvious and subtle ways of ensuring the boss's chances for success. One subtle way of increasing your boss's chances for success is to help that person out when he or she is

---

TABLE 11–3   Strategies and tactics for building relationships with superiors

1. Help your boss succeed,
2. Display loyalty,
3. Volunteer for assignments,
4. Appear cool under pressure,
5. Manage your impression,
6. Laugh at your boss's humor,
7. Use discretion in socializing with your boss.

---

under attack. One example would be to supply data to support your boss's position on a controversial issue.

Display loyalty. A loyal worker is a valued worker because organizations prosper more with loyal than disloyal employees. Blind loyalty, in which you believe your organization cannot make a mistake, is not called for. You may recall that such loyalty contributes to groupthink. An obvious form of loyalty to the organization is longevity. A study by an executive recruiting firm supports the value of this type of loyalty. The average chief executive of 1,300 of the nation's largest firms has spent 22.5 years with the firm. In some companies, 90 percent of the senior staff is promoted from within.[22]

Loyalty can also take other forms, such as defending your company when it is under attack, avoiding making negative statements about superiors, and using company products and services. For instance, if you work for an automobile manufacturer, owning a car made by a competitor is strongly frowned upon by management.

Volunteer for assignments. An easily implemented method of winning the approval of your superiors is to become a "handraiser." By volunteering to take on assignments that do not fit neatly into your job description, you display the kind of initiative valued by employers. Among the many possible activities to volunteer for are fundraising campaigns assigned to your company, committee membership, and working overtime when most people prefer not to (for example, on a Saturday in July). Committee assignments are also useful for being noticed by key people in the organization.

Appear cool under pressure. Although modern managers are supposed to express honest feelings, showing signs of panic generally hurts your reputation with influential people. Appearing to be in emotional control when things around you are falling apart helps convey the impression that you are worthy of additional responsibility. An example of coolness under pressure follows:

> The manager of a bank's data processing center was confronted by three employees who said they would resign by the end of the week unless the bank offered them a 10 percent salary increase. The manager replied, "Do what you think is best. If you resign now, I will recommend that you are never rehired by the bank. All three of you can readily be replaced in the short run by a quick call to one of our temporary help agencies." The employees decided not to quit, and to discuss their demands at a later date.

Manage your impression. This strategy includes behaviors directed at enhancing your image by drawing attention to yourself. Often the attention of others is directed toward superficial aspects of the self, such as clothing and appearance. Other variations of this strategy include telling people about your successes or implying that you are on the inside of activities. Displaying good manners has received renewed attention as a key part of impression management. Here is a sampling of the many suggestions for proper business etiquette offered by Letitia Baldrige:

- When you meet strangers at a business function, include the name of your firm with your name.
- In making introductions, remember that a young person should be introduced to an older one, that the person of lower rank should be introduced to a person of higher rank.
- Do not argue over who is going to pay when you are in a restaurant. Decide beforehand who is going to be the host.
- As the host at a restaurant, remember to have the server take your guest's order before your own.
- Wait until your boss or other superior invites you to lunch. Do not be pushy and invite them first.
- Remember, the secret of good manners is to make other people feel comfortable.[23]

Laugh at your boss's humor. When you indicate by your laughter that you appreciate your boss's sense of humor, it helps establish rapport between the two of you. An indicator of good two-way communication between people is that the two parties comprehend each other's subtle points. Most humor in the workplace deals with subtle meanings about work-related topics. To implement the tactic of laughing at your boss's jokes, you do not have to worry excessively about having heard the joke before.

Use discretion in socializing with your boss. A constant dilemma facing employees is how much and what type of socializing with the boss is appropriate. Advocates of socializing contend that off-the-job friendships with the boss lead to harmonious work relationships. Opponents say that socializing leads to **role confusion,** being uncertain what role you are occupying. One guideline is to have cordial social relationships with the boss of the same kind shared by most employees, such as group luncheons. Another guideline is to strive to be regarded as an employee rather than a member of the boss's family. By so doing, you will not fall into the trap of getting emotionally involved in the boss's personal problems.[24]

Building Relationships with Co-Workers and Lower-Ranking Employees

Another general strategy for increasing your power base is to form alliances with co-workers and employees of lesser rank. You need the support of these people to get your work accomplished. Also, when you are being considered for promotion, co-workers and lower-ranking employees may be asked their opinion of you. Here we describe seven representative techniques for cultivating employees at or below your level (see Table 11–4).

TABLE 11–4 Strategies and tactics for developing relationships with co-workers and lower-ranking employees

1. Develop allies,
2. Be a team player,
3. Express an interest in their work,
4. Be diplomatic,
5. Exchange favors,
6. Ask advice,
7. Follow group standards of conduct.

Develop allies. A general strategy for cultivating co-workers and lower-ranking employees is to create allies rather than enemies. Your allies can support you when you need help. It has been noted, for example, that the elevator starter in the lobby may alert you to the arrival of a VIP whom you might have missed. Equally important, a network of allies establishes you as a leader, which increases your chances for promotion.[25] Most of the other tactics in this section are specific ways of developing allies.

Be a team player. As described in Chapter 8, being a team player helps you work effectively as a group member. The same tactic is essential for developing allies among team workers. The group member who is not perceived as a team player will be hard pressed to gain the cooperation of co-workers and employees at lower levels.

Express an interest in their work. A simple yet valuable technique for cultivating lateral and downward relationships is to express genuine interest in the work of others. A basic way to accomplish this end is to ask other employees questions such as:

How is your work going?
How does the firm use the output from your department?
How did you master the software you use on the job?

Be diplomatic. Despite all that has been said about the importance of openness and honesty in building relationships, most people fail to be convinced. Their egos are too tender to accept the raw truth when faced with disapproval of their thoughts or actions. Diplomacy is still an essential part of governmental and office politics. Translated into action, diplomacy often means finding the right phrase to convey disapproval, disagreement, or discontent. Here is an example of a delicate situation and the diplomatic phrase used to handle it.

During a staff meeting, a co-worker suggests that the entire group schedule a weekend retreat to formulate a five-year plan for the department. The boss looks around the room to gauge the reactions of others to the proposal. You want to say: "What a stupid idea. Who needs to ruin an entire weekend to do something we could easily accomplish on a workday afternoon?" The *diplomatic response:* "I've heard that retreats sometimes work. But would spending that much time on the five-year plan be cost-effective? Maybe we could work on the plan during one long meeting. If we don't get the planning accomplished in that time frame, we could then consider the retreat."[26]

Exchange favors. Many of the informal agreements that take place on the job are based on exchanging favors with other employees. The tactic of exchanging favors is also referred to as *collecting and using IOUs*. The adept political player performs a favor for another employee without asking a favor in return. The IOU is then cashed in when a favor is especially needed.

Phil, a junior faculty member, agreed to cover a Saturday morning class for a senior faculty member, Alice, because she wanted to take a getaway weekend. Later that year Phil needed a letter of recommendation from two other faculty members in order to apply for tenure. He turned first to a close friend, and then turned to Alice, who was willing to help out such a cooperative colleague.

Ask advice. Asking advice on technical and professional topics is a good way of building relationships with other employees. Asking another person for advice—someone whose job does not require giving it—will usually be perceived as a compliment. Asking advice transmits the message, "I trust your judgment enough to ask your opinion on something important to me." You are also saying, "I trust you enough to think that the advice you give me will be in my best interest."

To avoid hard feelings, inform the person whose advice you are seeking that his or her opinion will not necessarily be binding. A request for advice might be prefaced with a comment such as, "I would like your opinion on a problem facing me. But I can't guarantee that I'll be in a position to act on it."

Follow group standards of conduct. A summary principle to follow in getting along with other employees is to heed **group norms,** the unwritten set of expectations for group members. If you do not deviate too far from these norms, much of your behavior will be accepted by the group. If you deviate too far, you will be subject to much rejection and therefore lose some of your power base. Yet if you conform too closely to group norms, higher management may perceive you as unable to identify with management. Employees are sometimes blocked from moving up the ladder because they are regarded as "one of the gang."

Avoiding Political Blunders

A strategy for retaining power is to refrain from making power-eroding blunders. Committing these politically insensitive acts can also prevent you from attaining power. A sampling of such political blunders is listed in Table 11–5, and described following.

Upstaging your boss. To upstage your boss (make him or her look bad) privately or in a group meeting is a quick way to ruin a relationship. Marilyn Moats Kennedy cautions against upstaging your boss even if that person is barely older than you, and, in your opinion, no more competent. In most organizations it is more important to respect rank than the person holding the position.[27] Upstaging can take many forms, including the following:

- Your boss is telling a good joke in a meeting, and you call out the punchline before he or she finishes.
- Your boss presents some technical facts, and you publicly correct these facts.
- Your boss says, "We're task-orientated around here." You respond, "You really mean task-*oriented*. But don't feel bad, most people make the same error."

Bypassing your boss. Protocol is highly valued in multilayered organizations. Going over your boss's head (or around the boss) to resolve a problem is therefore hazardous. You might be able to accomplish the bypass, but your career can be damaged and your recourses limited. In a court case, an oil company's dismissal of a manager was upheld because the manager had repeatedly ignored the chain of command. The manager would go over his superior's head, directly to the president.[28]

A general principle is that going over your boss's head is a blunder. Yet a boss-bypass may be necessary when you get no satisfaction from speaking directly to your immediate superior about an important problem. Asking your boss for permission to speak to a higher-ranking manager is a possible alternative. A sneak play will usually backfire.

TABLE 11–5   Political blunders to avoid

1. Upstaging your boss,
2. Bypassing your boss,
3. Being abrasive,
4. Being a naysayer,
5. Betraying confidences,
6. Challenging fond beliefs.

Being abrasive. An abrasive person is someone who "rubs people the wrong way." Being abrasive toward superiors will quickly hurt one's chances for promotion. Being abrasive toward co-workers and lower-ranking employees erodes one's power base more gradually. Abrasiveness may create enemies who will seize the opportunity to retaliate. One method of retaliation would be to mention to higher management that the abrasive individual "cannot get along with people." Such a reputation usually disqualifies a person for promotion.

Being a naysayer. If you become branded as a person who usually says that a new plan or proposal will not work, it could hurt your future. Pessimism of this type works as a demotivator and hampers interpersonal relationships on the job. A politically wise person therefore knows when to stop saying no to other people's dreams. Al Neuharth, the founder of *USA Today,* gives us insight into the potential self-destructiveness of being a naysayer. Neuharth was struggling to overcome the newspaper's problems in advertising and circulation. At the same time he was fighting internal battles with skeptics. Neuharth said:

> There was a category of people who were enemies from within. They took a lot of my time keeping my backside covered; time that I could have used more productively. There were people in finance who would

ask, "Why do you need 135,000 vending machines? Couldn't it be 99,000?" That was disruptive. The enemy from within didn't keep the job from getting done, but made it a lot more difficult. (One of the major financial critics was later passed over for the presidency of *USA Today*. Instead, the promotion went to an enthusiastic supporter of the *USA Today* venture.)[29]

Betraying confidences.   Unfortunately, there are no secrets in organizations. Nevertheless, if you want to preserve your reputation as a trusted individual, do not let it be known that *you* are a betrayer of confidences. One negative consequence of passing along confidential information is that you may lose the trust of people who count in your career, although many people in organizations cannot be trusted to keep secrets.

Challenging fond beliefs.   Most private and public organizations have certain fond beliefs that are implicit rather than stated: They are part of the organization culture. If you make public statements challenging the folklore of the organization, you may be branded as disloyal or unappreciative.

One such fond belief is that the company is the best in its field. Many a mediocre organization finds some rationalization to delude itself into believing that it is the industry leader in quality. A marketing manager might state that although the company product is highly priced, the quality-conscious buyer will always choose it. Another fond belief not to challenge is that the organization has virtually no waste and excess. When the topic of reducing the organization's size surfaces, it is a blunder for a lower-ranking insider to suggest that the company suffers from a surplus of managers.

Instead of challenging fond beliefs, make constructive suggestions for improvement that do not explicitly point out or poke fun at company weaknesses.

UNETHICAL AND DEVIOUS POLITICAL BEHAVIOR

Any technique of gaining power or favor can be devious if practiced in the extreme. A person who supports a boss by helping him or her carry company property out the door for personal use is being devious. Some approaches are unequivocally unethical, such as those described next. Each one of them is *precisely what we recommend you do not do*.

Discredit your rival.   Many devious political tactics are aimed at discrediting a rival or any person one wants to get in trouble. Specific techniques for discrediting rivals can be overt or covert. One technique is to make a direct accusation about a rival's job performance. A milder form of discrediting a rival is to simply raise questions about his or her capabilities. Raising questions is effective because it allows the other person to reach his or her own conclusions. For example, one might say to a superior, "Is Jennifer [the rival] losing enthusiasm for the job lately?"

Receive undue credit. A devious approach widely practiced by managers is to take credit for work performed by subordinates and not allow them to share in the recognition. A typical example would be this: You submit a useful idea to your boss. Your boss then proposes the idea to his or her boss without mentioning that it was your idea. One suggestion for dealing with this problem is to *discreetly* confront your boss about not receiving recognition for your ideas. Another approach is to present a valid reason for seeking recognition. For instance, you might point out that you want to earn recognition so you can advance in the organization.[30]

Embrace or demolish. This ancient strategy suggests that you remove from the premises rivals who suffered past hurts through your efforts. Those wounded rivals might retaliate when you are vulnerable. The origin of this strategy is found in Machiavelli's advice regarding the conquest of smaller nations:

Upon this, one has to remark that men ought either to be well-treated or crushed, because they can avenge themselves of lighter injuries, of more serious ones they cannot; therefore the injury that is done to a man ought to be of such a kind that one does not stand in fear of revenge.[31]

Divide and rule. An ancient military and governmental strategy, this tactic is sometimes used in business. The object is to have subordinates fight among themselves, therefore giving you the balance of power. If subordinates are not aligned with each other, there is an improved chance that they will align with a common superior. One company general manager used this technique to short-range advantage by dropping innuendoes during staff meetings.

Once in a meeting called to discuss the production schedule on a new product, Vic, the general manager, said to Don, the head of manufacturing, "They tell me engineering isn't holding up its end of getting things ready for production." Two weeks later Vic dropped another conflict-arousing comment, this time to the head of engineering: "It's too bad you're having so many problems with manufacturing trying to figure out how to build the product you've designed." Vic's techniques did create rivalry and hard feelings between engineering and manufacturing. Ultimately, his top staff saw through his divide and conquer tactics and his effectiveness as a leader was diminished. Realizing he was no longer effective as a leader, higher executives in the company asked him to resign.

Set up a person for failure.   The object of a setup is to place a person in a position where he or she will look ineffective. A newcomer considered by the company to have high potential was assigned to a manager's department. Suspecting that this new arrival might be intended as his replacement, the manager set up the newcomer to fail. He placed him in charge of an operation he knew nothing about. In a short period of time the acclaimed individual was in trouble on the job. Believing that they perhaps had overrated this man's potential, management transferred him to another department. He was also relegated to lesser tasks.

Blackmail.   Extortion is a longstanding criminal activity. It has also been used by company politicians to gain power and/or favor. A curious aspect of company blackmail is that one deviant person threatens to make public the deviant behavior of another, unless the former makes certain concessions to the latter. Blackmailers, however, lead a hazardous existence—they are liable to exposure at any time by the blackmailee.

CONTROLLING ORGANIZATIONAL POLITICS

Carried to excess, job politics can hurt an organization and its members. Too much politicking can result in wasted time and effort, thereby lowering productivity. Human consequences can also be substantial, including lowered morale and the turnover of people who intensely dislike playing office politics. Five particularly helpful approaches to combating job politics will be mentioned here.

Provide objective measurements of performance.   A primary reason we have so much politicking in some organizations is that those organizations do not provide objective methods of measuring performance. When a person knows exactly what it is he or she has to do in order to qualify for promotion, there is less need for political maneuvering. Even more fundamental, you tend to curry favor with a superior when there seems to be no other way to determine if you are competent in your job.

Provide an atmosphere of trust.   Several management observers have noted that this is the best overall antidote to excessive playing of politics. If people in a company trust each other, they are less likely to use devious tactics against each other. People often resort to cover-up behavior because they fear the consequences of telling the truth about themselves.

Set good examples at the top.   When people in key positions are highly political, they set the tone for job politicking at lower levels. When people at the top of the organization are nonpolitical in their actions, they demonstrate in a subtle way that political behavior is not desired. A new vice president squelched job politicking in a hurry through an unusual confrontation:

> Brad called his first official staff meeting as vice president of finance. After a few brief comments about his pleasure at joining the company, he said bluntly: "I've been here only two weeks, yet I've noticed some strange actions that I want stopped right now. I know it's part of our culture to please the boss, but don't be so naive about it. I'm not pointing the finger at any one person in particular, but you people have been milling around my office like birds waiting for crumbs. If you have some official business and you want to make an appointment with my assistant, Betty, fine. But if you don't have a legitimate business purpose in seeing me, don't drop by my office. We've got too many things to accomplish to spend time in coffee klatches."

Threaten to discuss questionable information in a public forum. People who practice devious politics usually want to operate secretly and privately. They are willing to drop hints and innuendoes and even make direct derogatory comments about someone else, provided they will not be identified as the source. An effective way of stopping the discrediting of others is to offer to discuss the topic in a public forum.[32] The person attempting to pass on the questionable information will usually back down and make a statement closer to the truth. Recognizing that all complaints are subject to open discussion usually discourages people who hope to engage a manager in political games.

Be impervious to an exposé. A person out to discredit you and your job has the best chance of succeeding when you have something to hide. A simple antidote for this is for you to establish an unquestionable record of professionalism and integrity. People can expose you only when you have engaged in some deviant or questionable act.

ORGANIZATIONAL POLITICS AND CAREER SETBACKS

People who do not achieve their career goals frequently attribute their lack of success to office politics. They believe that favoritism has worked against them—that a less deserving person has been promoted instead. At other times, people contend that office politics cost them their job. One way that this can happen is to form alliances with those whom the boss perceives to be enemies. Nevertheless, organizational politics should not be blamed for long-term career problems. Marilyn Moats Kennedy makes this analysis:

> It is the commonest thing in the world to say that you were a political victim. But maybe you victimized yourself. The number of people who are actually the victims of any concerted office plot or plan is pretty small.

> For instance, the most common way to victimize yourself is to say: "I
> don't want to do it that way. I want to do it my way." O.K., you've made a
> choice, and it's the wrong one. To me, politics is a process of choices.
> You get to choose the work environment. You even get to choose the
> boss you'll work for if you do your homework.[33]

We believe that Kennedy is essentially correct. However, contentions
about having been cast aside by political forces are not necessarily the
product of paranoid thinking. If you are politically naive, you probably
will not achieve the success you desire. The antidote is to practice ethical
and sensible organizational politics. One strategy would be for you to become recognized by upper management for your willingness to volunteer
for assignments and your participation in company and social functions.
Under such circumstances, politics might work in your favor. Another antidote is to leave an organization when you are convinced that you are no
longer aligned with powerful people. In this way you cannot permanently
blame organizational politics for retarding your career.

Summary of Key Points

- Organizational politics refers to gaining advantage through any
  means others than merit or luck. Power is the ability to mobilize resources, energy, and information on behalf of a preferred goal or
  strategy. Politics is thus used to attain power. Some political strategies are generally ethical, while others are clearly unethical.
- Contributing factors to organizational politics include (1) pyramid-
  shaped organizations, (2) competitiveness within the firm, (3) subjective standards of performance, (4) environmental uncertainty,
  (5) emotional insecurity, (6) need for acceptance, (7) a desire to
  avoid work, and (8) Machiavellian tendencies of people.
- Organizational power stems from four general sources: power
  granted by the organization, power stemming from characteristics
  of the person, the power of subordinates, and power derived from
  capitalizing upon opportunity. The last source of power stems from
  being in the right place at the right time, taking the right action, and
  having the right resources.
- An important current trend is empowerment, a process of sharing
  power with subordinates to enhance their feelings of self-efficacy.
  Empowerment leads to shared power and increased employee motivation. In order to empower employees, conditions leading to
  powerlessness must be removed. Employees must also receive information that increases feelings of self-efficacy.
- Planning is helpful for purposes of increasing one's power. Such
  planning includes establishing goals, determining the cost-
  effectiveness of using a given political tactic, identifying the true

power, and conducting a power analysis of the powerful people, sizing up your boss, and analyzing what type of politics is played by senior management.

- Strategies and tactics aimed directly at gaining power include develop power contacts, form coalitions, control vital information, keep informed, acquire seniority, play "camel's head in the tent," and make a quick showing.

- Strategies and tactics for building relationships with superiors include help your boss succeed, display loyalty, volunteer for assignments, appear cool under pressure, manage your impression, laugh at your boss's humor, and use discretion in socializing with your boss.

- Strategies and tactics for developing relationships with co-workers and those of lower rank include develop allies, be a team player, express an interest in their work, be diplomatic, exchange favors, ask advice, and follow group standards of conduct.

- Political blunders to avoid described here are upstaging your boss, bypassing your boss, being abrasive, being a naysayer, betraying confidences, and challenging fond beliefs.

- Unethical and devious political tactics sometimes practiced on the job include discrediting your rival, receiving undue credit, embrace or demolish, divide and rule, set up a person for failure, and blackmail.

- Five ways of controlling excessive politics are provide objective measurements of performance, provide an atmosphere of trust, set good examples at the top, threaten to discuss questionable information publicly, and be impervious to an exposé.

- Office politics can block career success. However, if political forces have worked against you, it may be necessary to start fresh in a new job. In this way, organizational politics cannot be held responsible for a permanent career setback.

Questions and Activities

1. Many people use the phrase "it's a political jungle" when describing their place of work. What do you think they mean?

2. Estimate the approximate score of the following people on the organizational politics questionnaire in Figure 11–1: the head of your country, Donald Trump, and your instructor in this course. Explain your logic.

3. Which tactic of organizational politics have you observed used most frequently in real life or in fiction? For what purpose was it used?

4. Is there such a thing as "classroom politics"? If classroom politics does exist, give two examples of it in practice.

5. What is your reaction to this statement? "Office politics is mostly for incompetents."

6. What are several specific steps top management could take to empower employees?

7. At what point in your career do you think you would be able to control vital information?

8. Interview a few experienced workers to obtain some examples of political blunders to avoid. Be prepared to discuss your findings in class.

9. Our research has shown a statistically significant tendency for people to receive a lower score on the organizational politics questionnaire later in their careers. How do you explain this finding?

10. October 16 is Boss's Day in the United States. What should an astute office politician do to observe boss's day?

A HUMAN RELATIONS CASE PROBLEM
Derek, The Ambitious Marketing Vice President

Derek is a 45-year-old marketing vice president for a tire manufacturer. Most managers in his company conduct their work in shirt sleeves. Derek wears a jacket even during the summer. His shirts are French-cuffed; his boots have three-inch heels. Derek's office is uniformly furnished in leather, chrome, and glass.

Derek's guests have no choice but to sit in chairs set at a level six inches lower than Derek's chair. Several photos and plaques adorn his office's walls. One photo shows him wearing a captain's cap, seated at the helm of a large speedboat; in another he is shaking hands with the mayor; a third depicts him standing while his wife and two children are seated. A plaque attests to the extraordinary number of miles he has traveled on a particular commercial airline. Another plaque gives Derek the accolade, "Outstanding Alumnus Award," based on both his community activities and his contribution to his college alumni fund.

In the three years that Derek has been the marketing vice president, his total number of subordinates has grown from fewer than fifty to over 100. Gloria, the personnel manager, commented on the growth:

> Derek might be accused of empire building, but you cannot justifiably say that he has created jobs that don't need doing. The marketing division is very efficient. It seems that everybody has a worthwhile function to perform. We get no complaints that employees in Derek's area are being underutilized. It's just that Derek keeps on picking up activities and functions that perhaps should be reporting somewhere else.

A case in point is the advertising department. We used to make extensive use of advertising agencies and their facilities. Now we do a good part of our advertising with in-house people. We use agencies more for special promotions and innovative campaigns. Before Derek took over, we had three people in the advertising department. We now have ten. Yet our total expenditure for advertising is less than before we revamped our approach to advertising.

Several months ago Derek made a presentation to the company president and the board of directors. Accompanied by his assistant and a neatly organized set of flip charts, Derek addressed the group:

Good afternoon. I wouldn't have requested a meeting unless I thought I had a plan for reorganization that would pay enormous dividends to Superior Tire. The reason I have not asked the other vice presidents to attend this meeting is that some will be personally affected by the proposed changes. Therefore, they would lack the objectivity necessary to judge my proposal. Self-interest and subjectivity can destroy any business proposal.

Everybody in this room realizes what a problem it is to be held accountable for something over which you have too little control. How can you hold a vice president of marketing responsible for the whims of the distribution department? My sales team might outsell another brand of tires in a given month. But if we can't get them delivered where they are needed, when they are needed, our good efforts are nullified. Cancellations because of late delivery are disastrous to our business.

One logical way to prevent this lack of coordination between sales and distribution is for my division to control distribution. People in that department should report to marketing, not manufacturing. When the distribution people boggle a shipment, I want to personally lay them out on the carpet. Distribution should be working for us. As things stand now, they sometimes try to tell us how much to sell and when to sell it. Ladies and gentlemen, let's put some realism back into the tire business.

1. How are the president and the board likely to react to Derek's proposal? How *should* they react?
2. What methods of power acquisition is Derek attempting?
3. What would you estimate Derek's score to be on the organizational politics questionnaire?
4. What are Derek's sources of power?
5. What does Derek's nonverbal behavior indicate about his need for power?

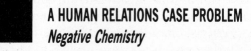

A HUMAN RELATIONS CASE PROBLEM
Negative Chemistry

Gunther Wortman looked forward to a career as a quality specialist. He began working for Micro Tech as a quality control inspector. As a result of hard work and additional study, he was promoted to quality control technician, and then to quality control supervisor. As a supervisor he now reported to Alan Tombak, manager of quality assurance. Four other supervisors also reported to Tombak.

Wortman approached his new job with his usual enthusiasm. He was proud to be a supervisor, and believed that his big career break had finally arrived. Gradually Wortman began to sense that things were not going so well for him in his new position. One day he felt particularly despondent. Ten days previously he had sent Tombak a detailed proposal for the use of a new inspection machine. So far Tombak had not even acknowledged his proposal.

Concerned about his feeling that things were not going so well between himself and his boss, Wortman decided to call Diane Garcia, a personnel specialist. He asked Garcia if she would join him for lunch to discuss a career problem he was facing. Wortman and Garcia agreed to meet for lunch the following Friday at a nearby sushi restaurant.

As the two dug into their fish, Wortman began to talk about his concern. "Diane, maybe you can help me," he said. "I just don't seem to be hitting it off with my boss, Alan Tombak. He hardly acknowledges my presence. He usually ignores my suggestions. He doesn't even laugh at my jokes. When I'm at a staff meeting with the other supervisors, he acts as if I don't even exist. Do you have any suggestions for handling this situation?"

Garcia said, "Gunther, it sounds like you do have a problem. Either you're paranoid, or you have failed to impress Tombak. I know you well enough to be sure that you're not paranoid. So there must be a real problem between you and Tombak. What have you done about the problem so far?"

"I've put my nose to the grindstone, as I have in every other assignment with Micro Tech. Nothing about me seems to impress Tombak. That's why I've asked for your help."

After thinking for a moment, Garcia responded, "I have a plan. This month I'm supposed to help the managers in your area with their human resources planning. This usually involves a discussion of key employees. I'll see what Tombak has to say about you. I'll then get back to you with my findings."

Ten days later, Garcia did help Tombak with human resources planning. The conversation led naturally to a discussion of the strengths and weaknesses of the supervisors reporting to Tombak. "What is your evaluation of Gunther Wortman, your newest supervisor?" asked Garcia. "Good question," said Tombak. "I don't really know what to make out of him. He does seem to try hard. But there's negative chemistry between us. The guy just doesn't turn me on as an employee. I think he's overrated. Maybe I'm missing something, but he's just a neutral entity to me. Yet I'm certainly not trying to get rid of him. That's all I can say."

Garcia thought, "Tombak has been brutally honest. Gunther and he just don't hit it off. I guess it's my duty as a friend to tell Gunther about this problem. But I wouldn't want him to leave Micro Tech over it."

1. Should Garcia give Wortman a full report of her feelings?
2. What should Wortman do about his problem of negative chemistry between himself and his boss?
3. Is Garcia acting ethically in her method of helping Wortman?
4. Should Wortman confront Tombak directly about his problem?

A HUMAN RELATIONS ROLE PLAY
The Negative Chemistry Confrontation

Assume that after hearing from Garcia, Wortman decides to confront his boss about the problem of negative chemistry. Wortman makes an appointment to discuss the problem with Tombak. He wants to improve—not worsen—his relationship with his boss. Tombak is upset by this confrontation, yet he wants to keep things on a level footing and not prompt Wortman to quit. Tombak sees no grounds for dismissing Wortman, yet he does not see him as a star on his team. The roles to be played, of course, are Gunther Wortman and Alan Tombak.

Notes _____

1. "Office Politics: How to Play Hardball, and When," *Executive Strategies,* March 6, 1990, p. 3.
2. Barbara Gray and Sonny R. Ariss, "Politics and Strategic Change Across Organizational Life Cycles," *Academy of Management Review,* October 1985, p. 707.
3. Kathleen M. Eisenhardt and L. J. Bourgeois III, "Politics of Strategic Decision Making in High-Velocity Environments: Toward a Midrange Theory," *Academy of Management Journal,* December 1988, p. 737.

4. Gerald P. Cavanagh, Dennis J. Moberg, and Manuel Velasquez, "The Ethics of Organizational Politics," *Academy of Management Review,* July 1981, p. 363.

5. Abraham Zaleznik, "Power and Politics in Organizational Life," *Harvard Business Review,* May–June 1970, p. 47.

6. Eisenhardt and Bourgeois, "Politics of Strategic Decision Making," pp. 737–70.

7. Dan L. Madison and associates, "Organizational Politics: An Exploration of Managers' Perceptions," *Human Relations,* February 1990, p. 95.

8. Clinton O. Longenecker, Henry P. Sims, Jr., and Dennis A. Gioia, "Behind the Mask: The Politics of Employee Appraisal," *The Academy of Management Executive,* August 1987, p. 187.

9. Gerald Biberman, "Personality and Characteristic Work Attitudes of Persons with High, Moderate, and Low Political Tendencies," *Psychological Reports,* 1985, vol. 57, p. 1309.

10. John R. P. French and Bertram Raven, "The Basis of Social Power," in *Studies in Social Power,* ed. Dorwin Cartwright (Ann Arbor, MI: Institute for Social Research, 1959); Timothy R. Hinkin and Chester A. Schriesheim, "Power and Influence: The View from Below," *Personnel,* May 1988, pp. 47–50.

11. Gary Yukl and Tom Taber, "The Effective Use of Managerial Power," *Personnel,* March–April 1983, p. 42.

12. Bill Sing, "He'll Head Wall Street Powerhouse," *Los Angeles Times,* Aug. 31, 1988.

13. Yukl and Taber, "The Effective Use of Managerial Power," p. 42.

14. Morgan McCall, Jr., *Power, Influence, and Authority: The Hazards of Carrying a Sword* (Greensboro, NC: Center for Creative Leadership, 1978), p. 5.

15. William C. Byham with Jeff Cox, *Zapp! The Lightening of Empowerment* (Pittsburgh: Developmental Dimensions International Press, 1989).

16. Jay A. Conger and Rabindra N. Kanungo, "The Empowerment Process: Integrating Theory and Practice," *Academy of Management Review,* July 1988, pp. 473–74.

17. Andrew J. DuBrin, *Winning Office Politics: DuBrin's Guide for the '90s* (Englewood Cliffs, NJ: Prentice Hall, 1990), pp. 33–52.

18. Stephen P. Robbins, *Training in Interpersonal Skills* (Englewood Cliffs, NJ: Prentice Hall, 1989), p. 176.

19. "On the Offensive," *Executive Strategies,* Aug. 21, 1990, p. 1.

20. Eugene Schmuckler, book review in *Personnel Psychology,* Summer 1982, p. 497.

21. William H. Newman, *Administrative Action: The Techniques of Organization and Management* (Englewood Cliffs, NJ: Prentice Hall, 1963), p. 90.

22. David Greising, "Company Loyalty Lifts Aggressive Executives Up the Corporate Ladder," *Chicago Sun Times,* Nov. 29, 1983.

23. Letitia Baldrige, "A Guide to Executive Etiquette," *Business Week Guide to Careers,* October 1986, pp. 60–63.

24. "Beware Your Boss's Tender Trap," *Research Institute Personal Report for the Executive,* May 28, 1985, p. 6.

25. "Power Comes to Those Who Plan for It," *Research Institute Personal Report for the Executive,* July 9, 1985, p. 5.

26. *The Super Achievers,* report published by the National Institute of Business Management Inc., 1988, pp. 11–12.

27. Marilyn Moats Kennedy, "How to Manage Your New Boss," *Business Week Careers,* March/April 1987, p. 94.

28. "How to Win at Organizational Politics—Without Being Unethical or Sacrificing Your Self-Respect," report published by *Research Institute Personal Report,* 1985, p. 4.

29. Peter Prichard, "Project Hindered by Non-Supporters in Financial Area," Gannett News Service, Sept. 19, 1987.

30. "How to Win at Organizational Politics," p. 15.

31. Niccolo Machiavelli, *The Prince* (New York: Modern Library, 1940), p. 73.

32. Robert P. Vecchio, *Organizational Behavior* (Hinsdale, IL: Dryden, 1988), p. 272.

33. "Playing 'Office Politics'—How Necessary?" (interview with Marilyn Moats Kennedy). *U. S. News & World Report,* January 12, 1981, p. 36.

Suggested Reading

BLOCK, PETER. *The Empowered Manager: Positive Political Skills at Work.* San Francisco: Jossey-Bass, 1987.

CAMERON, RANDOLPH W. *The Minority Executive's Handbook: Your Essential Map and Guide to Success Up the Corporate Ladder.* New York: Warner, 1989.

DILENSCHNEIDER, ROBERT. *Power and Influence.* Englewood Cliffs, NJ: Prentice Hall, 1990.

FLAMHOLTZ, ERIC, and RANDLE, YVONNE. *The Inner Game of Management.* New York: AMACOM, 1987.

GROVE, ANDREW S. *One-on-One with Andy Grove: How to Manage Your Boss, Yourself and Your Co-workers.* New York: Putnam, 1987.

HALL, JAY. "Putting Power to Work." *Management World,* November/December 1988, pp. 23–25.

MARK, J. PAUL. *The Empire Builders: Power, Money and Ethics Inside the Harvard Business School.* New York: Morrow, 1987.

POWELL, GARY N. *Women & Men in Management.* Newbury Park, CA: Sage, 1988.

WYSE, LOIS. *Company Manners: An Insider Tells How to Succeed in the Real World of Corporate Protocol & Power Politics.* New York: McGraw-Hill, 1987.

12

Employee Coaching and Counseling

LEARNING OBJECTIVES

After reading and studying this chapter and doing the exercises, you should be able to

1. Use the control model to improve employee performance.
2. Be familiar with the guidelines for employee coaching and counseling.
3. Pinpoint how a manager should handle the problem of alcohol and drug addiction on the job.
4. Develop insights into dealing with difficult people.
5. Describe outplacement counseling.

$\boxed{D}$ ebbie, the way you handle your job is really getting to be a problem," said her boss Charlie. "If I tell you to do some routine
thing, it does get done. But you never anticipate anything important.
And what I need is someone who can anticipate."

"Charlie, I wish you would be more specific," said Debbie. "Tell me
what you mean about my never anticipating anything important."

"I'm getting at things like this: You knew that I had a big meeting with
my boss Wednesday about the budget. Why did I have to ask you to
gather up the budget information? You should have had that information on my desk at least by the previous Friday."

This exchange between Charlie and Debbie represents a brief sample
of a vital part of managerial leadership. Effective managers spend considerable time coaching and counseling employees toward improved performance. Few managers face a situation in which all of their employees are so
competent that no assistance is required.

Coaching and counseling are similar but not identical processes.
Coaching is a method of helping employees grow and improve their job
competence by providing suggestions and encouragement.[1] **Counseling** is a formal discussion method for helping another individual overcome a problem or improve his or her potential. A counselor listens
more than a coach does and is more concerned with feelings than with
action. A coach might give you a tip on how to prepare tax depreciation
schedules properly. A counselor might listen to you complain about
how preparing depreciation schedules does not exactly fit your career
objectives.

Counseling, in general, involves the long-term development of an employee, whereas coaching deals with present job performance. In practice,
the terms counseling and coaching are often used synonymously, and no
great confusion is caused in doing so. Both techniques are primary methods for improving employee performance.

Coaching has several purposes. One is to reverse poor performance.
Often this involves helping the employee overcome maladaptive behavior
that results in substandard performance.[2] Another purpose is to assist effective employees reach even higher levels of performance. A sales manager,
for example, might help a competent sales representative achieve a higher
number of sales. Yet another purpose of coaching is to prepare the employee for promotion. It is common practice, for example, for a manager to
groom a subordinate to take over his or her job.

Dennis C. Kinlaw helps us appreciate the importance of coaching.
He asserts that the best managers achieve long-term superior performance by coaching, not by exerting heavy-handed control over team
members.[3]

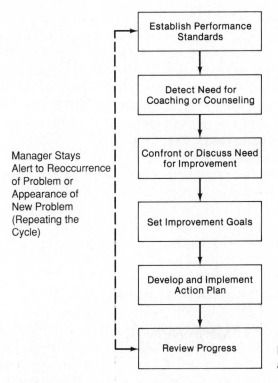

Establish Performance
Standards

Detect Need for
Coaching or Counseling

Confront or Discuss Need
for Improvement

Set Improvement Goals

Develop and Implement
Action Plan

Manager Stays
Alert to Reoccurrence
of Problem or
Appearance of
New Problem
(Repeating the
Cycle)

Review Progress

FIGURE 12–1 The Control Model for Coaching
and Counseling Employees

A CONTROL MODEL FOR COACHING AND COUNSELING

A recommended approach for coaching, counseling, and disciplining employees is the control model shown in Figure 12–1. It provides a systematic approach to improving performance. The model is most often used with substandard performers, but can also be used to assist good performers to do even better. The control model is divided into seven steps that should be followed in sequence.

Establish Performance Standards

As with any other control technique, performance standards must be defined before an employee can be informed that improvement is necessary. It is equally important to communicate these standards clearly to all employees. Defining acceptable performance also helps the manager spur on employees toward higher levels of performance. For instance, a manager might say to a packaging design specialist: "Your package designs are acceptable because our clients aren't complaining. Yet I think you can lend more creativity to your designs and get our clients excited about your work."

Detect Need for Coaching or Counseling

Detection is the process of noting when an employee's performance could stand improvement. To make such detections, the manager has to stay in contact with the activities of the department. Another approach to detection is for the manager to have frequent discussions with group members about their job performance. Straightforward questioning may uncover areas for improvement. One such question is, "How close are you to meeting the deadline on Project 37?"

When a worker displays a consistent pattern, rather than a one-time deviation from standard performance, coaching is usually required. Note one important exception to the "consistent pattern" principle: Some departures from acceptable performance or behavior are so significant they must be brought to the immediate attention of the employee. These departures relate to violations of company policy or the law.

Confront or Discuss Need for Improvement

After detecting the problem, the manager must bring it to the attention of the employee. Supervisors have a general tendency to dislike confronting subordinates because of the defensive or hostile reaction confrontation may elicit. A general principle here is for the manager to focus on the substandard behavior itself, and not upon the individual. People usually become defensive and uncooperative when they believe that their traits or personal characteristics are under attack. According to this principle, a teller who borrowed money informally from the bank teller might be approached in this manner:

> We have something serious to talk about. A routine audit showed that you borrowed $100 from your cash drawer before leaving for lunch. Apparently it was returned by the end of the day. Borrowing money from the bank without making formal application for the loan is absolutely forbidden. It could lead to a person's immediate dismissal.

A less effective approach would be to confront the teller about his or her "loan," and simultaneously insult the teller's character. To illustrate:

> I caught your little act of petty thievery. You were very sneaky about it. Don't use any lies to cover up for your dishonesty. You've been caught.

Direct confrontation of ineffective employees is difficult. A basic reason is that many managers feel uncomfortable about and have limited skills in criticizing employees. Supervisors generally mention three scenarios that concern them about confronting employees: employees who become hostile or angry, those who deny having a problem, and those who withdraw when criticized.[4] The suggestions for coaching and counseling present later in this chapter should help you develop confrontation skills. In addition, Figure 12–2 offers a few basic suggestions for providing corrective feedback.

Set Improvement Goals

To bring about change, it is helpful to set specific improvement goals that detail what kind of behaviors are required. Improvement goals that are vague, such as, "Become a more productive employee," do not give the person a specific improvement target. More helpful would be an improvement goal such as, "Do not leave a customer inquiry unprocessed for more than twenty-four hours." It is also helpful to set short-range rather than long-range goals in most disciplinary situations. By setting short-range goals, the subordinate can readily see if he or she is making progress. Assume that a manager is reviewing the work performance of a budget analyst whose reports are invariably late. The improvement goal for the next month might be for her to turn in three out of five reports on time. If this target is reached, she and her boss might make the goal four out of five on-time reports for the following month. For the third month, the goal might be five out of five timely reports.

Jointly set goals.   By collaborating with the boss in setting improvement goals, the employee feels emotionally involved in the counseling process.

You can make corrective feedback less traumatic for yourself and the employee by following these suggestions.

Be positive. The supervisor needs to display a positive attitude. Show a "can do" spirit that conveys a belief on your part that the employee will overcome the problem.

Be prepared. Know exactly what behaviors you find unacceptable, be able to give examples, and describe the undesirable consequences of the unacceptable behavior.

Be realistic. Make sure that the behavior you find unacceptable is something that the employee can control. Are the late reports something the employee can change, or must the company's information system be updated first?

Don't be completely negative. Be prepared to give the employee some positive feedback during the session. Exclusively negative feedback only is overwhelming.

Make feedback a two-way process. During the feedback session, give the employee the opportunity to comment. Listen carefully to the employee's side of the story.

FIGURE 12–2 How to Give Corrective Feedback to Employees

Source: Robert A. Luke, Jr., "How to Give Corrective Feedback to Employees," *Supervisory Management,* March 1990, p. 7.

It is also another way for the superior and the subordinate to share in the discipline situation. Nevertheless, at times the principle of mutual goal setting must be preempted by organizational realities. Assume that in the above instance, management needs all five reports on time before the third month. The manager would then be forced to impose goals upon the subordinate with an explanation of why these goals are necessary.

Sample goals.   Following are five improvement goals which specify the type of behavior that constitutes improved performance. As such, they can serve as a guide to action. Although these goals may appear to be set from the perspective of the organization, we can assume that achieving them is also in the best interest of the employee. Therefore, they may have been set jointly.

1. *Retail sales associate:* Decrease the number of bogus checks you accept by insisting upon proper identification before accepting a check.
2. *Human resources specialist:* Volunteer only for those projects that you have the time to take care of properly.
3. *Computer programmer:* Consider no programming assignment complete until you have run the program twice without error.
4. *Newspaper reporter:* Include no "facts" in your stories that cannot be authenticated by a second party.
5. *Truck driver:* No hitchhikers allowed unless the person given the ride is an accident victim.

Develop and Implement an Action Plan

An **action plan** is a description of what steps will be taken to improve performance. In some instances the action plan might be as simple as this: "Make a mental and written note to engage the security system when you leave the store at closing." At other times the action plan might be more complex, because new skills are required in order to improve performance. A group member might be preparing disorganized, clumsily written reports. Part of the action plan in this situation would be for the person to take a course in report writing.

The specific nature of the action plan is tied to the cause of the problem that is creating substandard performance, or blocking top-level performance. Marcia Ann Pulich has outlined some of the possible action plans for improving substandard performance:

1. *Change the work environment.* Redesigning a job would be one way of implementing this action plan. In one firm a sales order specialist would regularly express irritation toward customers when he had to handle more than one phone call simultaneously. The company solved the problem by installing a phone answering system that auto-

matically placed customers on hold when the specialist was handling another call.

2. *Improve the selection process.* Poor performance can sometimes be attributed to selecting the wrong person for the job. Future problems can be minimized by improving selection procedures.

3. *Improve training.* Performance can often be improved with adequate training, including the manager coaching the employee on a new work method or technique. For example, a manager might give an assistant more training in preparing a travel expense report.

4. *Improve communication.* Substandard performance, or less than peak performance, sometimes stems from poor communication between the manager and the employee. A frequent problem here is that the employee has not clearly understood instructions.

5. *Transfer.* If a mismatch exists between the employee and the job, a transfer to a job better fitting the employee's capabilities would be warranted. One difficulty in implementing this action plan is that other managers are often reluctant to accept an employee who is being transferred because of performance problems.

6. *Demote.* If an employee is demoted to a less demanding job, he or she may perform better. A successful demotion makes it possible for the employee to remain with the firm. Pulich notes, "Some employees actually welcome demotion because it places them in a position where they can again be successful and feel in control of their job performance." Nevertheless, the majority of employees will resent a demotion.

7. *Terminate.* When all other attempts at improving performance fail, including appropriate discipline, termination may be necessary. Current employment practice dictates that employees be given ample opportunity to improve before being terminated.[5]

Implementation stems logically from establishing the action plan. There are times, however, when action plans are drawn up but never implemented. As inferred from the above action plans, they must be implemented with sensitivity and tact.

Review Progress

After a subordinate is coached or counseled about improvement, some form of systematic follow-up is required. At an elementary level, the follow-up could consist of the supervisor checking to see that the desired actions have been taken. If the employee were coached not to wear jeans to staff meetings, his or her compliance with the request could readily be detected.

When the new behavior is more complex, formal review sessions are in order. For example, Phil, an engineering technician, might be coached about his relationships with engineers. An improvement goal is set: "Decrease incidences of conflict with engineers over technical matters." After three months, the technician and his manager might discuss progress toward this goal. The manager might have inquired in the engineering department about incidences of conflict, while Phil might have reached his own conclusions about his relationship with the engineers. When both agree that substantial progress has been made, the manager might conclude: "It looks as if we have this problem licked. We can touch base six months from now. In the interim, proceed as you have been doing. It's working."

Use of positive reinforcement. The comments made by the engineering manager above illustrate the use of positive reinforcement. Giving employees encouragement, or other forms of positive reinforcement, is one of the most effective tools for coaching and counseling at the disposal of the manager. Making rewards contingent upon good performance increases the probability that the improvements will be lasting. A major purpose, then, of the review sessions is for the manager to dispense rewards for tangible progress toward the improvement goals.

Use of discipline. Positive reinforcement usually works more effectively than punishment and other negative motivators in bringing about performance improvements. It is better to reward people for the improvement they have made than to punish them for the improvement they have not made. However, some employees respond better to punishment or the threat of punishment than to rewards. If progress has not been made, the control model suggests that it may be necessary to administer discipline. More will be said about discipline later in this chapter.

Repeating the Cycle

The coaching and counseling process is rarely completed. After progress is made in overcoming one aspect of deficient performance, channels of communication must remain open. One reason is that improvements are rarely permanent. A person whose performance improves may slip back to his or her previous level of performance, particularly under heavy job pressure.

> An automobile service manager was criticized by his boss for telling customers who brought their cars for servicing near quitting time to return the next day. He agreed to mellow in his approach. However, when the season for changeover to snow tires came back, so did the service manager's abruptness. Three customers complained to the dealership owner that they were treated rudely by the service manager. Additional counseling was necessary to correct an old problem.

COACHING AND COUNSELING LINKED TO PERFORMANCE APPRAISAL

A performance appraisal is a formal system of evaluating employee performance and conveying this evaluation to the employee. Performance appraisals meet two general purposes. First, they serve administrative purposes because they provide a basic for determining salary increases, promotions, terminations, and other personnel decisions. Second, performance appraisals serve developmental purposes to the extent that employees are provided with specific job feedback, assistance, and coaching and counseling to improve future job performance.[6] It should be noted that not every manager capitalizes upon the opportunity to coach and counsel that the performance appraisal session provides.

Dozens of methods have been developed for appraising employee performance. Many of these appraisal systems include some method of rating performance along such dimensions as quality of work, quantity of work, problem-solving ability, and creativity. In addition to or in place of measuring such traits and behaviors, many organizations measure employee performance against goals. One such system of goal setting and performance review is **management by objectives.** The employee's evaluation is linked to how well he or she attained goals (or objectives) that were jointly set with the superior. The type of goals set are similar to those described above in relation to improvement goals.

Coaching and counseling take place when the manager assists the group member do a better job of attaining goals that were not achieved in the most recent review period. Assume that an income tax preparer failed to achieve this goal: "Less than 2 percent of tax returns will contain a legitimate error later caught by the government or the client." A coaching dialogue might take this form:

SUPERVISOR:	"Your error rate was 10 percent last period. That's too high, and you failed to reach your goal. What's the problem?"
TAX PREPARER:	"I know it's too high. But I can't help it. The workload around here is gruesome."
SUPERVISOR:	"In what way is the workload gruesome?"
TAX PREPARER:	"It's rush, rush. Panic, panic. Get them in. Get them out."
SUPERVISOR:	"I don't hear the same complaint from many other preparers. Why is your situation different?"
TAX PREPARER:	"I'm not so good under pressure, I guess."
SUPERVISOR:	"Let's talk about why you aren't so good under pressure. Maybe we can help you learn how to manage pressure better."

TAX PREPARER: "I'm willing to listen. I need any help I can get."

SUPERVISOR: "I like your attitude. The company is sponsoring a priority-setting workshop that might help you a lot."

SUGGESTIONS FOR COACHING AND COUNSELING

Coaching and counseling employees requires skill. One way of acquiring this skill is to study basic principles, and then practice them on the job. Another way is to attend a training program for coaching and counseling that involves modeling (learning by imitation) and role playing. Here we describe thirteen suggestions for effective coaching and counseling, as outlined in Figure 12–3. These suggestions supplement the information about constructive criticism presented in Figure 12–2. If implemented with skill, the suggestions from both sources will improve the chances that coaching and counseling will lead to improved performance.

1. *Establish a comfortable atmosphere.*   The worker being counseled should be made to feel as much at ease as possible. Spare him or her the mental anguish of guessing the purpose of the meeting. Although a counseling or coaching session will often contain some elements of discipline, the employee should recognize that the atmosphere is friendly and constructive.[7]

2. *Provide specific feedback.*   Instead of making generalities about the employee's substandard performance or unacceptable behavior, pinpoint areas of concern. A generality might be, "You just don't seem as if

1. Establish a comfortable atmosphere.
2. Provide specific feedback,
3. Listen actively,
4. Encourage the employee to talk,
5. Give emotional support,
6. Help solve barriers to good performance,
7. Help establish realistic goals,
8. Reflect feelings,
9. Reflect content or meaning,
10. Interpret what is happening,
11. Give some constructive advice,
12. Gain a commitment to change,
13. Allow for modeling of desired performance and behavior.

FIGURE 12–3 Suggestions for Employee Coaching and Counseling

you're into this job." A specific on the same problem might be, "You neglect to call in on days that you are going to be out ill." Sometimes, it can be effective to make a generalization (such as not being "into the job") after you first provide several concrete examples.

3. *Listen actively.*   Listening is an essential ingredient in any counseling, coaching, or disciplinary session. An active listener tries to grasp both the facts and feelings of what is being said. Observing the employee's nonverbal communication is another part of active listening. The manager must also be patient and not poised for a rebuttal to any difference of opinion between him or her and the group member.

4. *Encourage the employee to talk.*   As implied in the previous example, part of being a good listener is encouraging the person being counseled, coached, or disciplined to talk. Counseling, in particular, is more effective when the person being counseled does most of the talking. A standard tactic of encouraging conversation is to ask *open-ended questions*. Closed questions do not provide the same opportunity for self-expression, and they often elicit short, uninformative answers.

An example of a closed question is, "Was it your fault that our personal computer was stolen?" An open-ended question, such as, "What were the circumstances surrounding the loss of the computer?" will encourage the employee to talk more expansively.

5. *Give emotional support.*   By being helpful and constructive, the superior provides much-needed emotional support to the subordinate whose performance requires improvement. A counseling or coaching session should not be an interrogation. An effective way of providing emotional support is to use positive rather than negative motivators.

6. *Help solve barriers to good performance.*   Many problems of poor work performance are caused by factors beyond the employee's control. By showing a willingness to intervene in such problems, the boss displays a helpful and constructive attitude and gives emotional support. One boss helped her advertising and sales promotion manager improve performance through a simple remedy:

Marketing manager:	The main job objective that you missed in this review period was having the fliers sent out on time to introduce our new line of personal computers. What happened?
Advertising and sales promotion manager:	As I've hinted several times in the past, our budget for support help is too tight. It was virtually impossible to have those fliers out on time without more help.
Marketing manager:	Then I'll get you more help, even if I have to lend you my own assistant one day a week.

7. *Help establish realistic goals.*   An improvement goal that a person cannot reach because of insufficient education, training, or native ability is unrealistic and usually leads to frustration stemming from failure. A sales manager leaned heavily upon one of his best sales reps to produce almost flawless reports that would be sent to the market research department. After failing to make the improvement desired by the manager for two consecutive review periods, the sales representative commented:

> Sorry, there is just nothing I can do to make my reports any better. One of the reasons I went into sales twenty years ago is that I hate paperwork. I want to cooperate with the market researchers. Let them interview me instead of my doing their work for them. I'm at my best dealing with customers, not doing staff work.

8. *Reflect feelings.*   The counseling professional is adept at reflecting feelings. Some reflection of feelings is recommended in a job situation (but too much is inappropriate). Reflection-of-feeling responses typically begin with, "You feel. . . ." Suppose you ask the shipping supervisor why a shipment was late. She answers, "Those jerks in manufacturing held me up again." You respond, "You are angry with manufacturing?" The head of shipping, now feeling encouraged, might vent her anger about manufacturing. Your reflection of feelings communicates the fact that you understand the real problem. Because the employee feels understood, she *might* be better motivated to improve.

9. *Reflect content or meaning.*   Reflecting feelings deals with the emotional aspects of a person. Reflecting content or meaning deals with the intellectual or cognitive aspects of a person. A good way of reflecting meaning is to rephrase and summarize concisely what the employee is saying. A substandard performer might say, "The reason I've fallen so far behind is that our department has turned into a snakepit. We're being hit right and left with impossible demands. My in-basket is stuffed a foot high." You might respond, "You are falling behind because the workload is so heavy." The employee might then respond something like, "That's exactly what I mean. I'm glad you understand my problem."

10. *Interpret what is happening.* An interpretation given by a manager in a counseling, coaching, or disciplinary session is an explanation of why the employee is acting in a particular manner. It is designed to give the employee insight into the true nature of the problem. For instance, a food service manager might be listening to the problems of a cafeteria manager with regard to cafeteria cleanliness. After a while the food service manager might say, "You're angry and upset with your employees because they don't keep a careful eye on cleanliness. So you avoid dealing with them, and it only makes problems worse." If the manager's diagnosis is correct, an interpretation can be very helpful.

11. *Give some constructive advice.* Too much advice-giving interferes with two-way communication, yet some advice can lead to improved performance. The manager should assist the subordinate in answering the question, "What can I do about this problem?"[8] Advice in the form of a question or suppositional statement is often effective. One example is, "Could the root of your problem be insufficient planning?"

12. *Gain a commitment to change.* Unless the manager receives a commitment from the subordinate to carry through with the proposed solution to the problem, the employee may tend to continue aimlessly as before. An experienced counselor-manager develops an intuitive feel for when employees are serious about turning around ineffective performance. Two clues that commitment to change is lacking are (a) overagreeing about the need for change, and (b) agreeing to change without display of emotion.

13. *Allow for modeling of desired performance and behavior.* An effective coaching technique is to show the employee by example what constitutes the desired behavior. The service manager alluded to earlier was harsh with customers when under heavy pressure. One way the boss coached the service manager was for the boss to take over the manager's desk during a busy period. The service manager then watched the boss deal tactfully with demanding customers.

DISCIPLINE AND PERFORMANCE IMPROVEMENT

The underlying assumption in counseling and coaching is that the organization is willing to provide assistance to an employee who wants to remain a member of the firm. Counseling and coaching are thus adjuncts to **corrective discipline**, any type of discipline that emphasizes improving employee behavior. In corrective discipline, employees are informed that their behavior is unacceptable and that corrections must be made if they want to stay with the firm. Offenses such as below-standard job perform-

ance, excessive absenteeism, tardiness, and gambling on company premises usually call for this type of discipline. We describe two types of
corrective discipline, progressive discipline and positive discipline. We
then describe **summary discipline**, an approach used for major violations
of company policy or the law.

Progressive Discipline (The Traditional Approach)

Progressive discipline is the administering of punishments in increasing order of severity until the person being disciplined improves or is
terminated. Many labor-management agreements call for progressive discipline, and most other organizations also practice this commonsense approach to improving substandard performance. Progressive discipline
proceeds in five steps:

Step 1: Counsel the employee about the problem.

Step 2: Oral warning—the employee is told that if the problem continues, more severe penalties will be in order.

Step 3: Written warning—if a second violation occurs, the manager again
counsels the employee but notes that a written violation will be
entered in his or her file. Written notice may also be given of future sanctions (organizational punishments).

Step 4: Suspension or disciplinary layoff—if another violation occurs, or
substandard performance persists, the employee is suspended
without pay or given a disciplinary layoff.

Step 5: Discharge—since the employee has been fairly warned, but still
does not improve, his or her employment is terminated.

Documentation is an important part of progressive discipline, as well
as with other types of discipline. The manager administering the discipline
must furnish a written or electronic record of the occurrence. It must also
be verified that the employee has been made aware of his or her disciplinary status.[9]

Although progressive discipline seems fair, its effectiveness in improving performance has been seriously questioned. A representative in-
dictment of progressive discipline appeared in *Harvard Business Review*.
The report concluded that few organizational systems are more accepted
yet less productive than the traditional progressive discipline. A major
problem is that progressive discipline prevents self-discipline.[10]

Positive Discipline (Motivating Employees to Improve Performance)

Positive discipline is an approach to improving substandard performance and behavior that emphasizes coaching, individual responsibility, and a mature problem-solving method.[11] Progressive discipline, in

contrast, places more emphasis on punishment. The control model for coaching, counseling, and disciplining incorporates positive discipline.

Positive discipline focuses on motivating employees to improve performance, rather than punishing them for poor performance. Written and verbal warnings are replaced with:

> Discussions and written reminders of employee responsibility. The term *reminder* is used in preference to *warning*.
>
> The employee's agreement to maintain certain standards of performance and behavior.
>
> A paid day off as the final step in the disciplinary process.[12]

The cornerstone of positive discipline is the **decision-making leave**, a paid one-day suspension to help the employee think through the disciplinary problem. If preliminary measures fail, the employee is given one day off with full pay. During the time off the employee is supposed to decide to remain on the job and meet performance standards, or resign. If the employee decides to remain with the firm, the supervisor helps that person develop improvement goals and action plans. The supervisor encourages the employee, but makes it clear that failure to reach goals will result in termination.

Many managers are naturally skeptical about the merits of a paid suspension for ineffective performance, yet the system appears to be working. A study conducted in the Tampa Electric Company found that decision-making leaves reduce the need for employees to get even with the organization. Also, employees did not abuse the system in an attempt to gain a "free day off." (One explanation here is that a one-day suspension, even with pay, would still be perceived as a punishment by most employees.) Tangible results of the positive discipline program included fewer terminations, less absenteeism, and virtually no formal employee complaints.[13]

Summary Discipline

Summary discipline is not as humanitarian as either progressive or positive discipline. It involves the immediate discharge of an employee for having committed a major offense. A labor relations official at Detroit Edison observes, "Offenses such as theft, physically assaulting a supervisor, and gross insubordination usually warrant immediate discharge regardless of the employee's previous work record."[14] In many companies, receiving kickbacks from suppliers is grounds for summary discipline.

Summary discipline can be used only when the violation is clear-cut, and ample evidence exists that the violation took place. If this is not the case, the employee can sue for **wrongful discharge**, the firing of an employee for arbitrary or unfair reasons. In recent years, many employers have been sued for wrongfully discharging employees. Many employees—acting alone, or assisted by their unions—have been awarded damages in these cases.[15]

Effective Discipline Through the Hot-Stove Rule

A useful guideline for applying discipline correctly is the **hot-stove rule**. According to this rule, a parallel can be drawn between discipline and touching a hot stove. A hot stove with its radiating heat gives *warning* that danger will be forthcoming if the stove is touched. Similarly, workers should be warned in advance of the consequences of rule violation. The punishment (in the form of a burn) is *immediate* and directly linked with the rule for not touching a hot stove.

Similar to the hot stove that immediately burns anybody who touches it, a rule should be applied *consistently*. The punishment administered by the stove is also *impersonal* and unbiased. It does not matter who touches the stove (the president or the custodial worker)—he or she will get burned. Finally, the punishment administered by the hot stove is *appropriate*. The offender usually receives a burn that will be remembered but will not do permanent damage.

COACHING AND COUNSELING SUBSTANCE ABUSERS

Alcoholism and drug abuse among employees and managers constitute a significant management problem. At least 10 percent of the workforce at any given time experiences lowered job performance because of **substance abuse**, the overuse of any substance that enters the bloodstream.[16] Substance abuse is usually associated with alcohol, prescription drugs, and illegal drugs. Yet it can also include the abuse of tobacco, coffee, soft drinks, nonnutritional food substances, and vaporous fluids. A recent analysis dramatizes the importance of dealing constructively with the two major types of substance abuse in the workplace.[17]

> Alcohol and drug abuse in the workplace is a problem that strikes all levels of workers in all types of jobs. The effects of substance abuse can be staggering. Substance abusers are three times more likely to cause a workplace accident, five times more likely to file a workers' compensation claim, and twice as likely to use sick leave as are "clean" employees. Substance abuse raises insurance costs $50 billion each year and costs employers an additional $436 billion in lost productivity, medical expenses, theft, and damage.[17]

Using the Control Model with Substance Abusers

Our recommended procedure for turning around the employee substance abuser stems directly from the guidelines contained in the control model in Figure 12–1. To use the control model, it is necessary for the manager to recognize common symptoms of substance abuse. These symptoms are summarized in Figure 12–4.

Alcohol abuse	Drug abuse
Sudden decrease in performance	Sudden decrease in performance
Decreased mental alertness	Decreased mental alertness
Long lunch hours, tardiness	Employee hiding out on premises
Unexplained absences from work	Unexplained absences from work
Altered gait	Dilated pupils
Slurred speech	Unusual bursts of energy and excitement
Frequent use of breath freshener	Prolonged and serious lethargy
Depressed mood	Unexplained states of apathy or elation
Trembling of hands and body	Errors in judgment and concentration
Errors in judgment and concentration	Urgent financial problems
Financial problems	Sleepy appearance to eyes
Sleepy appearance to eyes	Frequent sniffing
Denial of drinking problem	Appearance of being detached from reality
Lost time due to physical illness	Elaborate alibis for work deficiencies
Elaborate alibis for work deficiencies	Denial of drug problem

FIGURE 12–4 Symptoms of Alcohol and Drug Abuse

Assume that Ralph, an advertising account executive, uses cocaine off the job, and sometimes during working hours. Janet, his immediate superior, observes that Ralph's performance is suffering. He is often late with work for clients, and he sometimes appears to be in a frenzied hyperactive state. Janet thus *detects* the need for counseling. Janet *confronts* Ralph about the problem: "The way you've been acting lately, I can't trust you with important work for clients. When you are in a frenzied state, you make serious errors, such as calling a client product by the wrong name. Go get help from the employee assistance program, or I will have to recommend severe disciplinary procedures."

Janet and Ralph then jointly *set the goal* of Ralph improving his concentration on work within fifteen days. The two then develop an *action plan* whereby Ralph gets help with his drug abuse problem through an EAP the agency uses. (The agency is not big enough to have its own EAP, so it uses one shared by many firms in the area.) The action plan is *implemented* by Ralph working closely with a drug counselor.

A *review of progress* is made weekly. Ralph has controlled his cocaine habit to the point that he does not display drug-related symptoms on the job, and his performance improves. Janet therefore gives Ralph encouragement and support for his progress. If at any point Ralph again shows signs of drug abuse on the job, Janet will *repeat the cycle.*

Drug and Alcohol Testing of Present Employees

Assume that the advertising agency described previously had a policy of terminating any employee known to use illegal drugs. Janet would then have been justified in referring Ralph for drug testing. His job performance was suffering, and she suspected cocaine use. However, referring an employee for drug testing is fraught with difficulty. Some people regard the testing of employees as a legitimate employment practice. Others regard such testing as a violation of civil liberties and an indignity. Another part of the controversy is that drug testing is not 100 percent reliable. Also, the amount of drugs in the bloodstream required to impair job performance is not known precisely.

The legally soundest policy about alcohol and drug abuse is to focus on job performance, not the use of alcohol or drugs themselves. A labor-relations attorney notes that the precise legal status of drug and alcohol testing remains undefined. An employer's use of testing has many potential liabilities. Random drug or alcohol testing invades personal privacy too far to be condoned. Yet drug testing of employees in occupations with high potential for serious accidents, such as pilots, bus drivers, and window washers, is defensible. Also, few legal objections have been voiced against the drug testing of job applicants. For example, the National Labor Relations Board (NLRB) has upheld an employer's right to require applicants to pass a drug test without approval from their labor union.[18]

DEALING WITH DIFFICULT PEOPLE

Another application of coaching and counseling is dealing with difficult, or problem, people. The control model applies here also, and includes confrontation, constructive criticism, and developing action plans. The information presented next can be applied to dealing with difficult subordinates and co-workers. Our discussion of the topic is organized around four tactics and methods: sympathize with personality quirks, use nonhostile humor, clamp down on needless dissension, and give recognition and affection.

Sympathize with Personality Quirks

A **personality quirk** is a persistent peculiarity of behavior that annoys or irritates other people. To defend against personality quirks, show sympathy for employees with these quirks, without submitting to all of their demands. Here are two frequently observed personality quirks, along with a counterthrust for each one.

1. *The person who has a strong need to be correct.* Employees with this quirk set up situations so that people who disagree with them are made to look foolish or naive. For example, "All well-educated and in-

telligent people believe as I do that this is the way we should go on this project. If anybody disagrees, please speak up now." (You can sympathize in this manner: "I recognize that you research everything before reaching an opinion, and that you are usually right. Nevertheless, I want to point out another perspective.")

2. *The person who resents control, direction, or advice from others.* Employees with this quirk are so oversensitive to being controlled that they misinterpret hints as suggestions, and orders as direct challenges to their intelligence and self-worth. (You might express sympathy—yet still get through to a person with this quirk—by a statement such as: "I know you like to be your own person. I admire you for it, but I have a small suggestion that could strengthen the graphics you put together.")[19]

Use Nonhostile Humor

Nonhostile humor can often be used to help a difficult person understand how his or her behavior is blocking others.[20] Also, the humor will help defuse conflict between you and that person. The humor should point to the person's unacceptable behavior, yet not belittle him or her. Assume that Kevin (whom you regard as difficult) says that he will not sign off on your report because you used the decimal instead of the metric system. You need Kevin's approval, because your boss wants unanimity from the group. You ask Kevin again the next day, and he still refuses to sign. To gain Kevin's cooperation, you might say:

> I swear on a stack of Bibles, one meter high, that all future reports will use the metric system. Will you please affix your signature, one centimeter below mine? By the way, did you see that 45.45-meter field goal the Green Bay kicker made in yesterday's game? With a grin on his face, Kevin replies, "Okay, give me the report to sign." (The humor here indicates that you respect Kevin's desire to convert to the metric system, but you also acknowledge that it can sometimes be impractical.)

Clamp Down on Needless Dissension

Constructive criticism is welcome in any healthy organization. A dissenter who has the good of the organization in mind can be handled with an appeal to reason. Explain to the person that sometimes he or she appears too harsh and disgruntled, and that it would be better to express criticism privately rather than in a staff meeting.

In contrast, a worker who repeatedly creates animosity by deceiving, lying, and accusing probably wants to achieve personal gain rather than be helpful. The most effective way to deal with this type of person is to warn him or her that such behavior will not be tolerated. Back up the oral warning with a stern letter.[21]

Give Recognition and Affection

Difficult people, similar to misbehaving children, are sometimes crying out for attention. By giving them recognition and affection, you *may* cause their counterproductive behavior to cease. If their negative behavior is a product of a more deeply-rooted problem, recognition and affection alone will not work. Other actions must be taken such as professional counseling. The most direct strategy is to give the misbehaving individual attention and affection. If the negative behavior stops, you have found the proper antidote. Recognition and attention could take the form of excessive compliments, or giving the person a special assignment. Include also a temporary title, such as "project director" or "program coordinator."

OUTPLACEMENT: COUNSELING AND COACHING SURPLUS EMPLOYEES

Another important form of job counseling and coaching is used when employees are considered surplus and must be dismissed for any reason other than summary discipline. About two-thirds of large firms offer some form of **outplacement**, company-sponsored programs to minimize the personal and organizational trauma associated with job loss.[22] Professional counseling is also part of outplacement because job loss pushes many people into a period of emotional instability.[23] The outplaced individual often becomes confused, angry, anxious, and depressed. The large number of mergers and acquisitions in recent years has spurred a rapid growth in outplacement services. These programs are administered by in-company specialists and by outside consultants.

Key Elements in an Outplacement Program

Programs vary from one firm to another, but they usually have four components. First is personal evaluation, whereby outplaced employees obtain a clear evaluation of themselves. Using tests, interviews, and other diagnostic procedures, outplacement counselors identify the counselee's strengths and weaknesses. Former employees are also taught to identify their transferable skills and professional goals, so that they can seek positions that will further their careers.

The second component is counseling and coaching about such topics as résumé writing, job search techniques, using contacts to advantage, and interview techniques (see Chapter 17). When the job search lingers on, counselees are provided with additional help, including gentle prodding to persist in the job search. Outplacement counseling typically emphasizes helping the job seeker find a job by using his or her self-generated contacts. As such, outplacement does not find a job for people. The third component is institutional support, in the form of a base of operations for conducting the job search. Included here are office space, telephones, clerical support, and photocopying privileges. Another aspect of outplacement is emotional support, in the form of job seekers working together to help each other find a job. These employees form their own support groups, discuss the job market, share tips, and bolster each others' egos.

Evaluation of Outplacement

On balance, outplacement services are well received by employees and regarded as worthwhile by employers. Outplacement services can be cost-effective because they often cut the time required for a successful job search in half. As a result, less money is required for unemployment compensation and separation payments. Outplacement also improves morale and is better for the company image than laying off large numbers of people without offering them help.

One criticism of outplacement services is that they are of unequal quality. The effectiveness of the service is highly dependent upon the skills of the counselor to help the job seeker deal with the trauma of being fired and finding new employment.[24] Another criticism is that outplacement services overmarket job seekers. Using highly polished techniques, employees are marketed into positions for which they are underqualified.[25] Often this process leads to putting the employees in a situation where they will once again be forced to look for new employment. And who wants to be outplaced more than once in a career?

Summary of Key Points

- Coaching and counseling are used to improve the performance of both good performers and substandard performers. Coaching helps employees grow and improve by providing suggestions and encouragement. Counseling serves a similar purpose but is more concerned with feelings than action, and focuses more on the long range.

- A recommended approach for coaching, counseling, and disciplining employees is a control model, consisting of seven steps: (1) establish performance standards, (2) detect need for coaching or counseling, (3) confront or discuss need for improvement, (4) set improvement goals, (5) develop and implement an action plan, (6) review progress, and (7) repeat the cycle if necessary.

- A substantial portion of counseling and coaching takes place in the context of performance appraisal—a formal system of both evaluating employee performance and conveying the evaluation to the employee. A natural opportunity for coaching is when the employee has not met an objective in a management-by-objectives system.

- Counseling and coaching can be improved by following these suggestions:

1. Establish a comfortable atmosphere.
2. Provide specific feedback.
3. Listen actively.
4. Encourage the employee to talk.

5. Give emotional support.
6. Help solve barriers to good performance.
7. Help establish realistic goals.
8. Reflect feelings.
9. Reflect content or meaning.
10. Interpret what is happening.
11. Give some constructive advice.
12. Gain a commitment to change.
13. Allow for modeling of desired performance and behavior.

- Counseling and coaching are also used in corrective discipline. One form of corrective discipline is progressive discipline, administering punishments in increasing order of severity until the person being disciplined improves or is terminated. Positive discipline emphasizes coaching and individual responsibility. It features a decision-making leave—a paid one-day suspension to help the employee decide about his or her future performance. Summary discipline is the immediate discharge of an employee for a major offense, and does not involve coaching and counseling. A general guideline for administering any form of discipline is the hot-stove rule, which recommends that discipline include a warning and be immediate, consistent, impersonal, and appropriate.

- Another application of counseling and coaching is dealing with difficult, or problem, people. The four tactics and methods recommended here are (1) sympathize with the personality quirks of others, (2) use nonhostile humor, (3) clamp down on needless dissension, and (4) give recognition and affection to the difficult person.

- Coaching and counseling substance abusers is also part of a manager's job. A recommended approach is to follow the control model, with an emphasis on using an employee assistance program as an action plan. Current legal opinion is to regard substance abuse as a management concern primarily when the abuse lowers job performance. Drug testing of current employees must therefore be limited to exceptional situations, such as those employees whose jobs can potentially endanger the lives of others.

- Outplacement services are company-sponsored programs intended to minimize the personal and organizational trauma associated with job loss. "Outplaced" employees can be substandard performers or those who are declared surplus for other reasons. Outplacement programs usually involve four types of activities: personal evaluation, counseling and coaching about job finding, institutional support such as office space, and emotional support.

Questions and Activities _____

1. In what way does the perspective of this chapter differ from the perspective of all previous chapters?
2. Why are job standards so important for coaching and counseling employees?
3. Which leadership style described in Chapter 9 do you think would include ample coaching and counseling? Explain your answer.
4. It has been said that an effective supervisor is a "coach" more than a "player." What does this statement mean to you?
5. How might individual differences influence how well an employee accepts corrective feedback?
6. Assume that you are a store manager. Explain how you would take through the control model a sales associate who is rude to customers.
7. Why is it important to include coaching and counseling in a performance appraisal?
8. How does effective coaching and counseling help decrease the chances of wrongful discharge suits?
9. To what extent do you think that "difficult people" represent a real problem for supervisors and co-workers?
10. Ask any experienced manager about the importance of coaching and counseling in a manager's job. Be prepared to discuss your findings in class.

A HUMAN RELATIONS CASE PROBLEM
The Hostile Loss-Prevention Manager

Mark Gulden, the zone loss-prevention manager (LPM) at Keystone Stores, prided himself on his managerial skill. As he explained to the case researcher, "I'm in complete control all the time. And control is the name of the game in the loss-prevention field. Inventory shrinkage is a big problem with us. We therefore have to keep an accurate account of our inventory. If a piece of merchandise has not been sold, and it is not on the shelf or in the storeroom, we can assume that it's been stolen.

"If I find an audit coming back from one of my stores, I demand an answer right away. And I don't pussyfoot. I let the local LPM know right away that a miss has been made that must be corrected. My LPMs respect me for my toughness as a manager."

Later, the case researcher spoke to several of the loss-prevention managers to learn of their perspective on the working relationship between the LPMs and their zone manager. Bud, a 24-year-old in charge of security at the highest volume store in his zone, offered these observations:

"I'm afraid for Mark Gulden. No doubt in my mind he's a Type A personality who is headed for an early heart attack. He takes his job too seriously. If Gulden finds one little error, he goes bananas. Sometimes he swears at me as if I have stolen some missing merchandise. I don't take it personally. I guess it's just his way. But overall I think Gulden gets the job done. No big complaint on my part."

Melissa, an LPM at another store in the zone, had this view of Gulden:

"So long as this is confidential, I can tell you with a straight face that the man is a lunatic. When things are going fine, he's fine. But when he sees a problem, he flies off the handle. He's a fire-spitting dragon who spits too much fire at the wrong people. Some days he swears at me over the phone. It ruins my whole day. In fact, I've got to do something about the problem soon. But I wouldn't want to lose my job over complaining to my boss."

1. How should Melissa deal with this problem?
2. Should Bud speak to Gulden about his method of criticism?
3. What type of coaching should Gulden be receiving from his boss?
4. Which principles of constructive criticism is Gulden violating?

A HUMAN RELATIONS CASE PROBLEM
Retail Rudeness

"Can you direct me toward the fireplace tool sets? You know, the tongs, brushes, and pick," asked the customer.

"Sorry, I can't help you," answered the store sales associate. "I just started working here last week. I don't know where nothing is. Just look around yourself."

"Good heavens, you are not familiar with the merchandise, or even with proper grammar. You do not belong on the floor," said the customer in a loud, angry tone. Before leaving the store, the customer demanded to see the manager, Tara Reeves. During the fifteen-minute interview with Reeves, the customer recounted her brief conversation with the sales associate. Reeves pleaded with the customer to forgive the matter this once, and she assured the customer of courteous treatment in the future.

The next day Reeves telephoned the corporate training director, Jesse Banks, to schedule a meeting about the issue of customer courtesy. Reeves and Banks met the next day.

"I hope that what I'm going to tell you will not make me appear weak as a store manager," Reeves began. "I suspect that the other branches are having the same problem. Some of our sales associates are so rude that they are driving our customers to use telephone and mail-order shopping services."

"Tell me more about the problem," said Banks. "I need some specifics."

"As the store manager, I receive a lot of complaints. To verify these customer complaints, I asked my husband and children to shop in my store, and then tell me what kind of treatment they received from the sales associates. They didn't bring back horror stories. Yet some of their observations were along the lines of those made by our other customers."

Reeves continued, "Many customers contend that our sales associates just ignore them. They carry on conversations with co-workers while the customer is trying to check out or ask for help. I've also received a few complaints about gum chewing. Another problem I've noticed is that some of our employees never look customers in the eye or smile at them."

"What have you done so far about the problem?" asked Banks.

"Sometimes I talk to our employees about the problem. I've even brought a few of the ruder ones into my office for a little discussion about customer courtesy."

"What do your employees say about the problem?" asked Banks.

"Most of them claim that it's the customer's fault. The customers show them very little respect. My sales associates say that some of the customers treat them like servants. There's also the problem of customers taking out their hostility on our sales associates."

"What would you like me to do about this entire problem?" asked Banks.

"Fix it," replied Reeves. "You're the corporate training director."

1. Whose responsibility is it to fix this problem?
2. How widespread are the various problems identified in this case?
3. Develop a realistic plan to deal with these problems.

A HUMAN RELATIONS EXERCISE
The Counseling and Coaching Acceptability Checklist

Employees vary considerably in what they consider to be acceptable areas for counseling and coaching on the job. Complete the following brief questionnaire, indicating whether you consider each statement
to be a warranted topic for counseling and coaching by a boss. Later, results for the entire class can be tabulated. Conclusions can then be
drawn about definite trends revealed by the data.

BEHAVIOR	OKAY FOR BOSS TO COUNSEL OR COACH EMPLOYEE ABOUT THIS MATTER	NOT OKAY FOR BOSS TO COUNSEL OR COACH EMPLOYEE ABOUT THIS MATTER
1. Employee consistently arrives at work two minutes late.	_____	_____
2. Employee chews garlic on the job.	_____	_____
3. Male employee wears dress to work.	_____	_____
4. Female employee wears man's suit to work.	_____	_____
5. Employee takes home about two ballpoint pens per week.	_____	_____
6. Accountant works on own income tax return during slow period at work.	_____	_____
7. Stockbroker reads *The Wall Street Journal* during office hours.	_____	_____
8. High-performing employee stays home from work on birthday and offers no other excuse for absence.	_____	_____
9. Employee falls asleep once during staff meeting.	_____	_____
10. Employee joins Communist Party.	_____	_____
11. While in the office, employee brags about the use of competitive product.	_____	_____
12. Employee has strong body odor.	_____	_____

Notes

1. Lynn McFarlane Shore and Arvid J. Bloom, "Developing Employees Through Coaching and Career Management," *Personnel,* August 1986, p. 34.

2. Derri Jacobs, "Coaching to Reverse Poor Performance," *Supervisory Management,* July 1989, pp. 21–28.

3. Dennis C. Kinlaw, *Coaching for Commitment: Managerial Strategies for Obtaining Superior Performance* (San Diego: University Associates, 1989).

4. Ellen K. Harvey and Colleen E. O'Malley, "Delivering Bad News: What to Do When Employees Get Emotional," *Supervisory Management,* July 1990, p. 4.

5. Marcia Ann Pulich, "What to Do with Incompetent Employees," *Supervisory Management,* March 1986, pp. 14–16.

6. Peter W. Dorfman, Walter G. Stephan, and John Loveland, "Performance Appraisal Behaviors: Supervisor Perceptions and Subordinate Reactions," *Personnel Psychology,* Autumn 1986, pp. 579–80.

7. Andrew E. Schwartz, "Counseling the Marginal Performer," *Management Solutions,* March 1988, p. 31.

8. Richard J. Walsh, "Ten Basic Counseling Skills," *Supervisory Management,* July 1977, p. 9.

9. Daniel M. Shidler, "Documenting Disciplinary Situations," July 1989, p. 15.

10. David N. Campbell, R. L. Fleming, and Richard C. Grote, "Discipline Without Punishment—At Last," *Harvard Business Review,* July–August 1985, p. 163.

11. Alan W. Bryant Jr., "Replacing Punitive Discipline with a Positive Approach," *Personnel Administrator,* February 1984, p. 79.

12. "Positive Discipline: Motivating Employees to Improve Performance," *Business Update,* vol. 1, no. 9, 1985, p. 15.

13. Campbell, Fleming, and Grote, "Discipline Without Punishment," pp. 163, 170.

14. Martin, "Five Principles of Corrective Disciplinary Action," *Supervisory Management,* January 1978, p. 24.

15. David A. Bradshaw and Linda Van Winkle Deacon, "Wrongful Discharge: The Tip of the Iceberg?" *Personnel Administrator,* November 1985, pp. 74–76; Steven A. Jesseph, "Employee Termination, 2: Some Do's and Don'ts," *Personnel,* February 1989, p. 37.

16. Roger K. Good, "A Critique of Three Corporate Drug Abuse Policies," *Personnel Journal,* February 1986, p. 96.

17. Book review, *HRMagazine,* February 1990, p. 10.

18. Michael R. Carrell and Christina Heavrin, "Before You Drug Test," *HRMagazine,* June 1990, p. 65.

19. Michael E. Cavanagh, "Personalities at Work," *Personnel Journal,* March 1985, pp. 55–64.

20. Kaye Loraine, "Dealing with the Difficult Personality," *Supervision,* April 1989, pp. 6–8.

21. *Mastering Office Politics: How to Finesse Your Way to Success* (New York: National Institute of Business Management, 1988), p. 46.

22. Hermine Zagat Levine, "Outplacement and Severance Pay Practices," *Personnel,* September 1985, p. 13.

23. Lisa L. Lancaster and Thomas Li-Ping Tang, "Outplacement Offers Safety Net for Displaced Workers," *Personnel Administrator,* April 1989, pp. 60–63.

24. Lewis Newman, "Outplacement the Right Way," *Personnel Administrator,* February 1989, pp. 83–86.

25. Joel A. Berak, "Termination Made Easier: Is Outplacement Really the Answer?" *Personnel Administrator,* April 1982, p. 71.

Suggested Reading

ADMINISTRATIVE MANAGEMENT SOCIETY. "Drug Testing: Employment Practices Are Changing." *Supervision,* July 1990, pp. 6–7.

BERNSTEIN, ALBERT J., and CRAFT, SYDNEY ROSEN. *Dinosaur Brains: Dealing with All Those Impossible People at Work.* New York: Wiley, 1989.

COOK, GERALD D. "Employee Counseling Session." *Supervision,* August 1989, pp. 3–5.

DANA, DANIEL. *Talk It Out! Four Steps to Managing People Problems in Your Organization.* Amherst, MA: Human Resource Development Press, 1990.

DAVIDSON, JEFFREY, and ALESSANDRA, ANTHONY. "Why Employees Should Be Told the Bad News." *Supervisory Management,* March 1989, pp. 12–13.

GRASSELL, MILT. "How to Supervise Difficult Employees." *Supervision,* July 1989, pp. 3–5.

HALSON, BILL. "Teaching Supervisors to Coach." *Personnel Management,* March 1990, pp. 36–39.

KLAAS, BRIAN S., and WHEELER, HOYT N. "Managerial Decision Making About Employee Discipline: A Policy-Capturing Approach." *Personnel Psychology,* Spring 1990, pp. 117–34.

REDECKER, JAMES R. *Employee Discipline: Policies and Practices.* Washington, DC: The Bureau of National Affairs, 1989.

WEISS, RICHARD M. "Writing Under the Influence: Science Versus Fiction in the Analysis of Corporate Alcoholism Programs." *Personnel Psychology,* Summer 1987, pp. 341–56.

13

Interpersonal Skill Training

LEARNING OBJECTIVES

After reading and studying this chapter and doing the exercises, you should be able to

1. Pinpoint the conditions under which interpersonal skill training will be effective in organizations.

2. Understand how interactive video is used for interpersonal skill training.

3. Explain how assertiveness training (AT) can improve your interpersonal effectiveness.

4. Identify and explain the key concepts in transactional analysis (TA).

5. Outline the basics of a customer service training program.

6. Describe the essential ingredient of a cultural awareness training program.

Sean, a credit analyst, was being considered for promotion to supervisor. So far, Sean had not been informed of this development. Roger, Sean's manager, was discussing his pending promotion with his boss and the human resources director. Roger spoke first: "I'm in Sean's corner. But the guy is just not ready for supervisory responsibility. He's a fine credit analyst. Sean has warded off many bad credit risks. But he gets under people's skin. Time and time again, he rubs people the wrong way.

"I wonder if there's a training program we can send Sean to that would help smooth out his rough edges?"

Scenarios similar to the one above take place so often that many human relations training programs have been developed to help workers improve their effectiveness in dealing with people. Our concern in this chapter is with training programs designed specifically to improve effectiveness in dealing with co-workers and customers. We therefore refer to them as **interpersonal skill training,** the teaching of skills in dealing with others so that they can be put into practice.

Interpersonal skill training is also referred to as *soft-skills* training to differentiate it from technical training. Soft-skills training builds interpersonal skills, including communication, listening, problem solving, negotiation, decision making, and customer service. Soft-skills training is more important than ever as organizations realize that a combination of individuals and technology is needed to produce results.[1]

Other chapters in this book describe activities that can develop soft skills, such as resolving conflict and listening. Here we describe training programs to enhance skills in assertiveness, conducting transactions with people, serving customers, and dealing with people from another culture.

FRAMEWORK FOR INTERPERSONAL SKILL TRAINING

Interpersonal skill training should proceed in a systematic manner that allows for correction and renewal. A model to achieve these ends is presented in Figure 13–1. The model states that you first identify what conditions need improvement, select an appropriate training program, allow for practice, and then apply the skill.

Identification of Individual and Organizational Needs

Before embarking upon any training program, it is important to identify what kinds of training are needed. Training of individuals should be based upon their **developmental needs,** the specific areas in which a person needs improvement. For instance, some people may be too shy, some too abrasive, and some may not give others the encouragement they need.

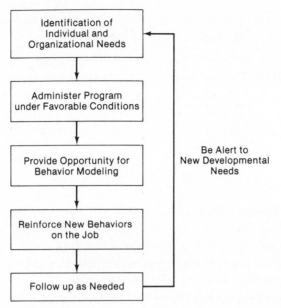

FIGURE 13–1 Framework for Interpersonal Skill Training

Ideally, a person's developmental needs should influence what particular interpersonal skill training program he or she attends.

Organizational requirements also weigh heavily in choosing a program to improve soft skills. In one company, managers might need improvement in effectively managing a multicultural workforce. To help remedy this situation, a program designed to improve sensitivity to people of different cultures might be selected.

Ideally, the interpersonal skill training programs chosen should match the needs of both the individual and the organization. The individual should acquire a valuable professional skill, and the organization should become more productive.[2] In the example just cited, the managers and the organization would benefit when the managers feel more comfortable leading a culturally diverse workforce. A questionnaire has been developed to help managers and training specialists identify individual and organizational developmental needs more precisely. Among the developmental needs assessed are motivating people, coaching and counseling, and team building.[3]

Administer Program under Favorable Conditions

Under the appropriate conditions, most human relations training programs can contribute to individual and organizational effectiveness. Under the wrong conditions, the program might even be harmful. In general, the program must be technically sound, the participants must have the capacity and willingness to change, and the organization must welcome the changes.

To determine whether a given program of interpersonal skills will be effective, answers should be sought to questions such as these:

1. Does the participant have the motivation and problem-solving ability to benefit from the program?
2. Is the participant involved sufficiently in the job to benefit from training?[4]
3. Is the program tied to the development needs of the participant?
4. Is the program tied to the objectives of the organization?
5. Will the organization provide the participant the opportunity to practice the new skills learned in the program?

Allow for Behavior Modeling

A standard way of learning interpersonal skills is to first observe somebody practicing them correctly and then to imitate or *model* that person. The process is similar to learning an athletic move or dance step by observing a competent performer. Modeling has been used effectively to train sales representatives in how to handle customer complaints. First, they observe an effective model handle such a problem situation in a film. Next, they role-play the constructive behavior shown by the model. For instance, one person would role-play the irate customer, while the other assumes the role of the sales rep handling the complaint.

Although behavior modeling usually leads to learning, it less frequently leads to improvement in actual job performance.[5] A challenge to the trainer and the manager, therefore, is to identify skills that are truly associated with good performance. For instance, teaching a sales rep to smile will not improve job performance unless smiling at customers actually leads to more sales.

Reinforce New Behaviors

If new learning is not practiced and reinforced, it will be forgotten. A case in point would be the situation of Derek, a chemist who attends an assertiveness training workshop. By the end of the workshop, Derek says to himself, "I agree with everything I've heard. I should learn to express my feelings in a positive, forthright manner. That way people won't take such advantage of me."

Back on the job, he receives no encouragement for attempting to be more assertive. He says to his boss, "My opinion as a chemist is that we cannot properly perform these experiments unless we purchase the equipment I recommended." His boss replies, "Accept the working conditions as they are or we will find somebody else to do your job. There are loads of good chemists out looking for work these days." After one or two more episodes like this, Derek decides to discontinue his attempts at being more assertive on the job.

Follow Up as Needed

A common failing of most interpersonal skill training programs is that they are "one-shot affairs." A person attends the program, perhaps tries out the new skills, and after a while returns to his or her former ways of doing things. A convenient way of circumventing this problem is for the organization to sponsor periodic "refresher" or "reminder" courses.

Be Alert to New Developmental Needs

As new skills are developed, they often create the need for the development of additional skills. Karen, a first-level supervisor, might attend a human relations workshop. She becomes more proficient at complimenting others and making them feel good. Because of this skill her subordinates now feel more comfortable in coming to her for help with work problems. Karen decides that she could benefit from a developmental program that would enhance her skills in coaching and counseling subordinates. As people improve their interpersonal skills, they often begin to identify areas for growth.

INTERACTIVE VIDEO FOR INTERPERSONAL SKILL TRAINING

A new technique for interpersonal skill training is the **interactive video,** a computer-assisted video system in which the trainee interacts with the training material. Interactive video is an extension of computer-based training that has been widely used to teach factual material. Interactive video appears to have promise for teaching interpersonal skills because the behavior of the actors on the screen is contingent upon the trainee's responses. To appreciate the possibilities of interactive video, it is necessary to visualize its hardware and software.

Interactive Video Hardware

The hardware for interactive video includes five elements, as illustrated in Figure 13–2: (1) TV monitor; (2) laser videodisc player, similar to the ones available for home stereos; (3) laser disc interface—the central component in an interactive video system (The interface fits into a slot of the microcomputer. It provides total user control of the videodisc player through a computer program executed on the computer.); (4) a computer—mainframe, mini, or micro; (5) an input-output device, such as a touch screen, mouse, or keyboard (voice commands may be forthcoming).[6]

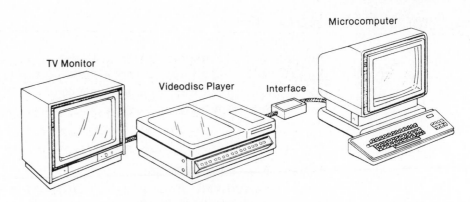

FIGURE 13-2 Hardware Required for Interactive Video

Source: Mary Jane Ruhl and Keith Atkinson, "Interactive Video Training: One Step Beyond," *Personnel Administrator,* October 1986, p. 70. Used with permission.

Interactive Video Software

The software for interactive video includes filming the training scenarios, and is thus complex and imaginative. Assume that an interactive video system were developed to help people deal effectively with threats of sexual harassment. The trainee observes the screen. One person says to another across the desk, "I think you are dressed very sexily today. You also look very sexy."

The following question flashes on the screen: Which of the two following statements should the woman make?

"Well, thank you, that is a nice compliment."

"That's strange. I don't feel sexy today, and I have no intention of dressing sexily. I'm here to conduct business."

If the trainee selects the first response, the man in the film responds, "I'm glad you took it as a compliment. Why don't we have dinner together after work?" If the trainee selects the second alternative, the man responds, "Okay, here are the figures I want you to review for me."

The effectiveness of an interactive video system depends upon creating plausible scenarios to illustrate what happens when the trainee makes a particular response. The different scenarios that surface on the screen when different responses are made are the *branches,* as illustrated above. The cycle for creating an interactive video begins with organizing a *storyboard.* Then the developer films the video and constructs the videodisc. Finally, the software is developed for graphics overlay and program control.[7]

The software or "courseware" often has to be tailor-made for a particular organization, and may take six months to develop. An interactive video training program is costly. Yet, the developers of these systems contend that the cost is less than that required for hiring classroom trainers. Do you think interacting with a videodisc is as effective as interacting with a live instructor?

ASSERTIVENESS TRAINING

A widely used method of improving interpersonal skills is **assertiveness training (AT).** AT is a self-improvement training program that teaches people to express their feelings and act with an appropriate degree of openness and candor. The method is derived from a technique of psychotherapy. The goals of assertiveness training include (1) know how you feel, (2) say what you want, (3) get what you want, and (4) overcome anxiety about confronting others.

Passive, Aggressive, and Assertive Behaviors

The true goal of assertiveness is to help an individual make a clear statement of what he or she wants, or how he or she feels in a given situation, without being abusive or obnoxious. It is also implied that the individual will learn to avoid the passive mode of suppressing feelings and actions. From another perspective, the nonassertive (passive) individual is stepped on and the aggressive person steps on others, whereas the assertive person deals with a problem in a mature and explicit manner. A frequent situation in organizational life—that of being appointed to a committee—can be used to illustrate these differences.

Opening his morning mail, project manager Lloyd notices a letter from another project manager, which says in part: "Congratulations, you have been appointed area captain to collect money for the Kidney Foundation. You will find it both an honor and a privilege to serve in this manner."

Lloyd is already heavily committed to community activities, including serving as a precinct worker in upcoming elections. He can respond in three different ways:

Passive behavior:
Lloyd does nothing and awaits further instructions. He is simmering with anger, but grits his teeth and hopes that the assignment will not be as time-consuming as he now estimates.

Aggressive behavior:
Lloyd grabs the phone, calls the other project manager, and says, "Who do you think you are, assigning me to your cockamamie committee? When I want to be on a committee, I'll volunteer."

Assertive behavior:
Lloyd calls the other project manager and says, "I appreciate your thinking of me in connection with your committee. But I choose not to serve. Good luck in finding another captain."

GUILT-FREE ASSERTIVENESS

HOW TO SAY WHAT YOU FEEL...AND FEEL GOOD ABOUT IT

Do you recognize yourself in any of these non-assertive personalities?

The Doormat
You get pushed around and stepped on more often than not

The Ostrich
It's hard for you to make eye contact, small talk or strike up a conversation

The Zipper
It's easier to keep your mouth shut than let people know how you really feel

The Nice Guy
You're so polite, easy-going and accommodating that you often get taken advantage of

Superman
You take on the problems of the world because you just can't seem to say no

SEMINARS INTERNATIONAL
A DIVISION OF KEYSTONE MANAGEMENT SYSTEMS, INC.
8780 Mastin
Overland Park, KS 66212

General Methods of Assertiveness Training

Although the specific content and format of assertiveness training programs differ, they concentrate on the development of the following kinds of skills.[8]

● The ability to cope with manipulation and criticism without responding in a like manner or withdrawing in fright with hurt feelings, guilt or shame, or the intention of later counterattack.

- The ability to make requests and state points of view in a confident, straightforward manner, without becoming pushy, annoyed, or angry.
- The ability to cooperate with others in solving problems in an adult manner, so that both parties are satisfied.
- How to manage others without being aggressive or manipulative.
- Resolving conflict through assertive behavior.

In order to acquire these skills, AT makes extensive use of role plays, role reversal, and modeling—much like many other interpersonal skill training programs. *Role plays* are used to create a situation in which the participants act out an assertive behavior they think would make them effective in a similar real-life situation. One example would be role playing a job interview. You want the job, but you don't want to appear either too desperate or too laid back. Role playing is helpful because it gives participants new experiences to be added to their repertoire and drawn upon later.

Role reversal is a process whereby one person pretends he or she is the adversary of the person who is acting assertively. (This is therefore a special type of role playing.) In this way the first person experiences what it is like to have to deal with an assertive person. Later, the two people reverse roles: The adversary becomes the assertive person and the assertive person becomes the adversary.

Modeling is an essential part of AT. Participants in the training program are given the opportunity to observe a person who displays assertive behavior. The model may be physically present or observed on a videotape.

Three Exercises for Developing Assertion Skills

So far we have described the general concepts underlying AT and the general exercises used in most AT programs. Here we look at three specific exercises designed to improve your assertion skills. You are encouraged to try them to develop a better understanding of how AT can lead to constructive change.

Exercise A: Learning the steps to assertion.   Some AT workshops begin by asking participants to engage in self-examination about their current level of assertiveness. The self-examination raises your level of awareness about your specific developmental needs. Here is one such AT self-examination exercise:

Steps to Assertion: A Checklist

1. Clarify the situation and focus on the issue. What is my goal? What exactly do I want to accomplish?
2. How will assertive behavior on my part help me accomplish my goal?

3. What would I usually do to avoid asserting myself in this situation?
4. Why would I want to give that up and assert myself instead?
5. What might be stopping me from asserting myself?
   a. Am I holding on to irrational beliefs? If so, what are they?
   b. How can I replace these irrational beliefs with rational ones?
   c. (For women only) Have I, as a woman, been taught to behave in ways that make it difficult for me to act assertively in the present situation? What ways? How can I overcome this?
   d. What are my rights in this situation? (State them clearly.) Do these rights justify turning my back on my conditioning?
6. Am I anxious about asserting myself? What techniques can I use to reduce my anxiety?
7. Have I done my homework? Do I have the information I need to go ahead and act?
8. Can I
   a. Let the other person know I hear and understand him/her?
   b. Let the other person know how I feel?
   c. Tell the other person what I want?[9]

Exercise B: Fogging. This subtle technique provides insight into the nature of assertiveness training. In **fogging,** you respond to manipulative criticism as if you were a fog bank. The criticism just passes through like a punch into a fog. You are thus virtually unaffected by the criticism, and you will be able to get across your point. The learner is instructed to offer no resistance to the criticism. Fogging is usually learned through the standard techniques of role playing, role reversal, and modeling. Here are three samples of fogging dialogue used in an AT program:

Critic: I see that you are as sloppy-looking as usual.
Learner: That's right. I look the same today as I usually do.
Critic: How atrocious! You made five errors in preparing that corporate tax return.
Learner: That's true. I counted the errors you red-circled. There were exactly five.
Critic: Have you ever thought of giving up your career and dropping out of college to become a beachcomber?
Learner: I could see some merit in dropping out of college and becoming a beachcomber.

Exercise C: Rehearsal. Another popular training exercise to improve your assertion skills is to rehearse an assertive response to an anxiety-provoking situation. By imagining how you would handle them, you should increase your skill in handling similar situations in real life. This time, imagine you are in the AT program, and rehearse your response to these two scenarios:

1. You are waiting in line at a bank to cash a check, and you are getting close to being late for an important appointment. A large, angry-looking man steps in ahead of you.

2. You diligently prepare a term paper. With considerable pride, you submit your report. It is returned one week later with a grade of "D," and the comments, "Incoherent piece of trash, shows almost no effort."

On balance, AT has proved to be a sensible and effective way of improving an important aspect of interpersonal relations—getting what you want without being too pushy, or not failing to get what you want because you are too passive. Part of AT's popularity can be attributed to its simplicity. Criticisms of AT center around two points. First, many graduates of AT programs become "pains in the neck" who push for demands deemed inappropriate by the organization. A study survey showed that persistence on the job can be self-defeating. Employees who placed too many demands on management tended to receive lower salary increases and performance appraisal ratings.[10] Second, many graduates wind up being assertive about trivial things while remaining unchanged in more important areas.

TRANSACTIONAL ANALYSIS TRAINING

Another notable interpersonal skill training program is **transactional analysis (TA),** a technique for improving interpersonal relationships that focuses on the transactions between people. A general goal of transactional analysis is to help people relate to each other in a mature, adult manner, thus easing tension and getting important things accomplished. An overview of key TA concepts is necessary to understand how TA can be applied to making you more effective on the job.[11]

Ego States

According to transactional analysis, the human personality is composed of three parts, called **ego states.** The three ego states are parent, adult, and child. A healthy person moves from one ego state to another depending upon the demands of the situation. Most work situations demand that the person behave in an adult manner.

The parent. The *parent* ego state dictates that we act as our parents once did. It is a body of recordings in the brain that reflect the unquestioned events perceived by a person during his or her childhood. According to TA, the parent is highly judgmental and moralistic. A person acting in the parent state will display such characteristics as being overprotective, distant, dogmatic, indispensable, and self-righteous. Clues that someone is acting in the parent state include wagging the finger to show displeasure, reference to laws and rules, and reliance on ways and values that were successful in the past.[12] ("I told you never to take an auto trip without first checking your oil and tires.")

The adult. When people are acting and thinking rationally, when they are gathering facts and making judgments based upon these facts, they are in the *adult* ego state. The adult is an information seeker and processor who basically follows the decision-making model described in Chapter 7.

You can tell that a person is in the adult ego state when he or she concentrates and engages in factual discussion.

The child. When people act and feel as they did in childhood, or when they behave immaturely, they are in their *child* ego state. It is the data recorded in the brain as a result of experiences taking place during ages one to five. Characteristics of the child include temper tantrums, creativity, conformity, depression, anxiety, dependence, fear, and hate. Because childhood experiences are so varied, people show varied behavior when in

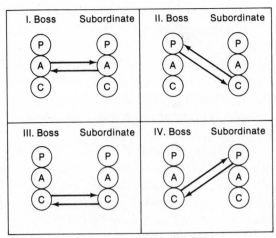

P is Parent; A is Adult; C is Child

FIGURE 13-3 Complementary Transactions

their child state. Despite this variation, a clue that a person is being a child is when he or she is nonlogical and demands immediate gratification of impulses. ("I want what I want when I want it.") Other clues are temper tantrums, giggling, coyness, attention seeking, and stony-faced silence.

The key to successful performance on and off the job is for the adult ego state to act as an executor and determine the appropriate expression of all three ego states during a specific situation. At a farewell party for a retiring executive, it would be helpful for middle managers to display a good deal of their child state. However, the adult should rescue the child before the middle managers exhibit such childlike behavior as rowdyism or drunkenness.

Analysis of Transactions

To apply TA, it is necessary to identify the transactions taking place between the ego states of people who are dealing with each other. In TA training, much time is devoted to analyzing transactions. Recognizing the ego states of the two people involved in the transaction can help the people communicate more effectively. Transactions are classified as *complementary* and *noncomplementary* (or crossed). Complementary transactions lead to effective interaction and *positive strokes* or ego-building compliments. Noncomplementary transactions lead to ineffective interaction and *negative strokes,* or ego-tearing insults.

Complementary transactions are shown in Figure 13–3. All are effective transactions because both people receive the positive stroking they want. In cell I, a boss acting in an adult ego state might say to an employee, "When will I get my report?" The employee replies, "It will be ready tomorrow at three o'clock."

In cell II, the boss, in a parent state, says, "Be here early tomorrow; it's an important day." To which the subordinate replies, "Don't worry, I'll be here."

In cell III, the child-acting boss says, "Let's have a few drinks at lunch." The subordinate replies, "Maybe we can even drink right up to quitting time."

In cell IV, the child-acting boss says, "We're so overwhelmed with work in this department, I don't think we'll ever catch up." In a parentlike fashion, the subordinate responds, "I'll get things under control."

Noncomplementary transactions, shown in Figure 13–4, result in negative strokes and ineffective transactions between people.

In cell I, the boss, in a child state, says, "I desperately need your cooperation," hoping for a parent response. Instead, the response is, "I'm doing all I can right now. What more do you expect?"

In cell II, the parent boss, hoping for a child response from his subordinates, says, "Your work is sloppy and needs immediate correction." Instead, a parentlike subordinate says, "I'll be the judge of the neatness of my work."

In cell III, an adult boss, hoping for an adult response, says: "Have you ever thought of getting help from the EAP?" Acting as a parent, the subordinate says, "That sir, constitutes an invasion of privacy."

In cell IV, a parent-acting boss says: "You are totally without self-discipline." Instead of acting as a whipped or obedient child, the subordinate responds in an adult manner, "In what way am I lacking in self-discipline?"

Ulterior transactions occur when communications break down because the real meaning of the message is disguised. The sender of the message says one thing but means another. In an ulterior transaction, the receiver of the message is usually unsure whether to respond to the surface message or its hidden meaning. When a person initiates an ulterior transaction, the person's body language is usually inconsistent with the spoken message. For example, a boss may say to an employee, "I'm happy that

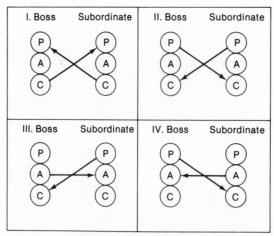

P is Parent; A is Adult; C is Child

FIGURE 13–4 Noncomplementary Transactions

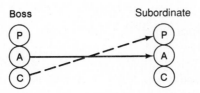

P is Parent; A is Adult; C is Child   **FIGURE 13–5** An Ulterior Transaction

you're not working so hard that you experience job stress." However, the boss speaks in a sarcastic tone, and shows a frown of disappointment. An ulterior transaction often leaves the receiver of the message confused about its true meaning.

As illustrated in Figure 13–5, the words of the boss appear to be coming from the boss's adult ego state. In reality, the message is coming from his child to the employee's parent. The boss wants the employee to see the need for working harder. The boss would have a better chance of achieving his or her goal by saying, "I would like you to work harder. Your current level of effort does not bring you up to company standard."

Life Scripts

Another key concept in TA is that the individual develops a life script—a plan or drama acted out during a person's life. It is as if people have a compulsion to live a preprogrammed life. Some people are forever manipulating others; some are losers; some are winners; some are chronic procrastinators. If a manager understands the script being followed by a subordinate, co-worker, or superior, it might make it easier to deal with that person. For example, if Michelle is a "winner," all things being equal her boss will send her out on a difficult mission.

In early childhood, the person develops a life script by being submerged in a culture, interacting with the family unit, viewing television, and being exposed to printed information. Part of developing a life script is finding answers to questions such as: Who am I? What am I doing here? Who are these people around me? What are these people doing here?

A damaging life script is **self-defeating behavior,** a pattern of doing something to oneself that interferes with goal attainment and happiness.[13] All of us know somebody for whom things appear to be going fairly well. Then suddenly the person does something senseless that brings on defeat. Among such self-defeating behaviors are vehemently criticizing your boss in a group meeting, and not handing in a term paper. These acts of self-sabotage become life scripts when the behavior occurs repeatedly.

An important goal of transactional analysis training is to help the individual substitute negative life scripts for positive ones. Trainees are sometimes confronted with their negative scripts. They are then made aware that they have the power to substitute positive scripts.

How to Use TA in Your Own Life

Transactional analysis is supposed to be of major benefit to its followers. Yet there is a big gap between reading about TA or attending TA training, and applying it to your own life. The comments made about TA in this chapter point you toward an understanding of several of its major concepts. Three examples will help you understand how TA might improve your communications—and therefore your relationships—with people.

Removing communication blocks. A direct application of TA is to overcome communication blocks between you and another person. The key here is to decide which ego state the other person is using: parent, adult, or child. You strive for a complementary transaction. If someone is acting as an adult, the best way to "get through" to that person is to act as an adult yourself. Child-to-child, parent-to-child, and child-to-parent transactions all help you communicate better with another individual. The interchanges between people presented earlier to explain Figure 13–3 are all examples of using TA to remove communication blocks.

Another important way of using TA to enhance communication is to follow its communication rules. Abe Wagner, the developer of these rules, believes that changing your words can change your personality. It also invites others to change their personalities. His rules relate directly to the idea of owning your own feelings, thoughts, and behavior, and no one else's. Six of his suggestions are as follows:

1. *Use the word "I."* Speak in the first person when you want to express your own point of view and feelings, instead of using "one," "people," or "they." The word "I" personalizes your comments and indicates that you take responsibility for your own ideas.

2. *Say "I won't" instead of "I can't."* To say "I can't" implies that you have no control over your action, and this is rarely the case. To say "I won't" implies that this is your decision not to do something.

3. *Avoid saying "I don't know" when you do know.* Save "I don't know" for occasions when you are asked for information you really do not have. If you do know something but are not willing to share your answer, "I'd rather not say" is an acceptable response.

4. *Avoid hedging.* When you have a definite point of view, avoid words like "perhaps," "probably," "maybe," and "I'm not sure." Definite points of view encourage others to be open with you in return.

5. *Don't try, do.* You communicate much stronger conviction to another person when you say you *will* do something, rather than you will *try* to do something. Which sounds more effective, "I will try to get back to you next week," or "I will get back to you next week"?

6. *Use eye contact.* Eye contact is an important part of nonverbal communication, and it is a good indicator of which ego state is operating. The child breaks eye contact; the parent looks down from above; the adult uses a comfortable, level gaze.[14]

Improving your leadership style. TA has much to say about leadership styles. If you want to be an autocratic boss, it is usually necessary to maintain parent-to-child transactions with people. In some situations, this helps you to overcome communication barriers. However, in the long run it is more beneficial to the organization to have more people relating to one another in an adult-to-adult manner. Such transactions require a participative style of management. Using this approach, the leader is able to achieve a climate of mutual trust and respect for each other's competence. A follower of TA will thus strive to be a participative leader in most situations.

The free-rein style is sometimes a child-to-child relationship. A leader of this type leaves subordinates to their own devices and provides no leadership. In the long range, the organization suffers and the individuals are left with a feeling of frustration because they have not accomplished much.[15]

Giving positive strokes to folks. An important message of TA is similar to that derived from reinforcement theory: You can enhance your relationships with others by dispensing positive reinforcement. Transactional analysis has a set of catchy terms of its own for the same approach to handling people. Perhaps you have met a person who attended a weekend workshop in TA or read a book on the subject. Often he or she will make statements such as, "Wow, that was a warm fuzzy," or "I guess you need some stroking." If TA makes you more sensitive to the importance of positive reinforcement in daily relationships, that alone is an important contribution.

How Good Is TA?

Transactional analysis training for improving interpersonal skills on the job has declined in popularity in recent years. The idea of scripts, however, has endured. TA does seem to lead to gains in human relations skills, but it does so in a cumbersome manner. Many of the standard TA ideas can be explained in much less complex, more practical terms. As one critic notes, the distinction between "I'm O.K." thought patterns and "I'm not O.K." thought patterns may be just a matter of self-confidence or self-esteem. Another criticism of TA is that its results are much more difficult to evaluate than those of other human relations training programs. For example, how do you measure whether a supervisor has begun to engage in a greater number of complementary transactions with subordinates?

CUSTOMER SERVICE TRAINING

A major thrust of interpersonal skill training is to help employees deal more effectively and courteously with customers. Private and public firms alike expect employees to respond to customer needs. In a public organization, such as a government agency, the customer is the public the agency serves. The general purpose of customer service training is to help organizations achieve a **customer orientation.** Such an orientation occurs when the delivery of goods and services is focused on customer needs and concerns.[16]

Customer service workers are responsible for one or more of three functions: sales, service (such as booking a hotel reservation), or problem-solving (such as exchanging defective merchandise). Customer service training programs often include lectures, role plays, questionnaires, films, and videos. The specific program outlined here is Quality Customer Service, as developed by William B. Martin. It consists of four major steps:

Send a positive attitude→ identify the needs of your customers→ provide for the needs of your customers→ work to ensure your customers' return.[17]

Step One: Send a Positive Attitude

Training participants are taught that customers want more than just the product or service offered. They also want to be treated well. Trainees rate themselves on such dimensions of customer service as:

I enjoy being of service to others.	10 9 8 7 6 5 4 3 2 1	People should help themselves.

Participants learn that quality customer service is strong on two dimensions. The *procedural side* of service consists of the established systems and procedures to deliver products and/or services. The *personal side* of service is how service workers, using their attitudes, behaviors, and communication skills, interact with customers. Outstanding service is important because repeat business is the lifeblood of any company, and will also help the worker advance.

Trainees are shown that a positive attitude is sent by (a) appearance, (b) body language, (c) the sound of one's voice, and (d) good telephone communication skills. To increase telephone skill, trainees are given such guidelines as the following:

- Answer the phone in a maximum of three rings.
- Actually smile when you answer the telephone.
- Identify yourself by name when answering a business-related telephone call.
- Communicate a sincere interest in the caller and in the information that is being requested or provided.
- Do not retaliate when a customer is rude or snippy.
- Never eat or drink while you are talking. If your mouth is full when the telephone rings, wait a few seconds before answering.
- End the conversation in an upbeat manner, with a summary of any action taken.

Step Two: Identify the Needs of Your Customers, Clients, or Guests

The key principle here is that the customer is the boss. To satisfy the boss, trainees are taught essential aspects of identifying customers' needs. Among these aspects are the following:

1. Assess how quickly the customer request must be handled.
2. Figure out what the customer might want, and offer to provide that service without requiring the customer to ask for it.
3. "Read" the customer by being attentive to both verbal and nonverbal signals. For example, a customer wearing out-of-fashion clothing may need assistance in choosing clothing.
4. Recognize that customers have the needs to be understood, feel welcome, feel important, and be comfortable.
5. Listen carefully to find out what the customer wants.
6. Obtain customer feedback by methods such as listening carefully to what customers, clients, and guests have to say. Feedback cards are also helpful.

Step Three: Provide for the Needs of Your Customers, Clients, or Guests

Customer needs are met through basic activities such as performing back-up duties (e.g., stocking, filing, recording information, and assisting with clean-up). Sending clear messages to customers and other employees is also important. Saying the right thing, including avoiding tactlessness, is vital to good customer service. The four basic customer needs described earlier can usually be met by (a) showing understanding, (b) making customers feel welcome, (c) helping customers feel important, and (d) providing a comfortable environment.

The Quality Customer Service Program also contains a segment on meeting the service needs of a customer through a computer. For example, trainees are instructed to never concentrate on a computer problem at the expense of a customer. Instead, get some assistance right away.

Step Four: Work to Ensure the Return of Your Customers, Clients, or Guests

A critical factor in obtaining repeat business is to satisfy customer complaints. Satisfaction would include listening carefully to the complaint, acknowledging the feelings, apologizing, and thanking the customer for bringing the problem to your attention. Going beyond what customers expect is good for repeat business. For example, the bank teller says, "Take this new checkbook cover. Yours looks as if it has served you well." Or the dining room server says, "May I bring you an extra plate so that you can share our special dessert?"

CULTURAL AWARENESS TRAINING

The internationalization of business has created a demand for training employees to deal effectively with people from other cultures. Developing interpersonal skills suited to another culture requires understanding the values and customs of people from that culture. The type of information presented in Chapter 2 about cultural mistakes to avoid in selected countries (review Figure 2–3) is usually included in cultural awareness training. **Cultural awareness training** is a formal method of helping people develop a sensitivity to local and national customs, and their importance in effective interpersonal relations. Among the training methods are readings on relevant information, lectures, films and videos, and experiential exercises, such as role playing and games.

Major Objective of Cultural Awareness Training

A major objective of cultural awareness training is to help workers cope with unanticipated events in a foreign culture. (Cultural differences within the United States and Canada are also extreme enough to warrant such training. For example, the values, speech, and customs of automotive workers in Tennessee are very different from those of their counterparts in Michigan.) A worker overwhelmed by a new culture will be unable to perform work effectively. Also, the ill-prepared individual may inadvertently offend a foreign host and jeopardize an important business relationship.

> An American manager attended a party while working in a Middle Eastern country. During the party, the manager inquired as to a native colleague's family. Because the constraints of that particular culture permit such an inquiry only among people who know one another quite well, the American alienated the colleague.[18]

Values Critical to International Effectiveness

Certain values held by many Americans are likely to precipitate conflict with workers from other countries. Because these values may be at odds with people of other cultures, they are often discussed in cultural awareness training.[19]

Individualism. In the American culture, individualism may motivate personal accomplishment, often resulting in competitiveness with group members. Individualism is considered much less important in other cultures. Among Chinese, Koreans, and Japanese, the group is preeminent on the job and in social life. Conformity and cooperation are therefore characteristic of Asian workers.

Informality. The informality of Americans can create conflict in other business cultures. Workers in other cultures are much less likely to address managers by their first name. Latin Americans value tradition, ceremony, and social rules more than do Americans.

Directness in negotiating. A striking difference between American negotiators and those in many foreign cultures concerns time. Saudi Arabian and Japanese negotiators alike are willing to spend many days negotiating a deal. Much of their negotiating activity is aimed at relationship building, and is unrelated to the task at hand.[20] This often frustrates the "strictly business" American.

Materialism. Americans and other Westerners tend to attach status to physical objects, such as designer-label clothes and watches. In some Eastern and Middle Eastern cultures, people (excluding royalty and wealthy people) are less materialistic. Instead, they emphasize finding and enjoying aesthetic and spiritual values.

Time orientation. A distinguishing cultural characteristic of American businesspeople is that they treat time as a precious resource that is continuously being depleted. Americans are therefore more likely than others to emphasize deadlines, punctuality, and showing up for appointments. (Again, cultural differences within the United States can also shape attitudes toward time.) In the Middle East, for example, a businessperson may keep a visitor waiting for a long time. The Middle Easterner will also prefer to allow a meeting to run as long as needed to accomplish a task.

The accompanying box provides additional insight into the type of training program used to prepare Americans to work in a specific foreign culture. Firms in other countries have similar programs to help their citizens deal with Americans.

JAPANESE CULTURE TAUGHT TO ASSIST U.S. BUSINESS

American businesspeople who don't know the Japanese language or culture are at a disadvantage with their Japanese counterparts, who expect respect from business associates. To help take care of this problem, Masahiro Iwashita is teaching a course at Purdue University for agricultural engineers who conduct business with Japanese companies. Students in this course learn elementary Japanese language, business practices, and information about Japanese companies.

Iwashita is an engineer in Osaka, Japan, with Kubota Ltd., a manufacturer of agricultural equipment. His students learn several differences in American and Japanese business practices, including the way to address business contacts. American businesspeople typically call each other by first names, while Japanese are rarely so informal. Working through the correct channels in business is important to the Japanese. Americans are sometimes prone to take shortcuts.

Iwashita said Americans erroneously believe that it is difficult for U.S. companies to conduct business in Japan. Several American companies have been successful, including Texas Instruments Inc. and International Business Machines Corp.

"Only the unsuccessful companies complain that the Japanese society is very difficult," Iwashita said. It's a matter of learning the subtle aspects of culture and business practices.

Source: As reported in Kay Shipman, "Japanese Culture Taught to Assist U.S. Business," Gannett News Service, May 18, 1987.

Summary of Key Points

- An interpersonal skill training program should first determine what kind of improvement is necessary, taking into account individual and organizational needs. The program should be administered under favorable conditions, it should provide for modeling or other active practice, and new learning should be reinforced by the organization. A follow-up refresher experience may be needed.

- A new technique for interpersonal skill training is interactive video, a computer-assisted video system in which the trainee interacts with the training material. A key feature of interactive video is that a different branch of the story develops contingent upon the trainee's response to a situation.

- Assertiveness training (AT) helps you to learn how to recognize and constructively state your true feelings in both work and social situations. An assertive person is forthright, rather than abusively aggressive or passive. Three important methods of AT are role playing, role reversal, and modeling. Specific training exercises include learning the steps to assertion, fogging, and rehearsal.

- Transactional analysis (TA) training has been widely applied to improving communication among people in work settings. Applying TA to the job requires that you learn its jargon and be able to analyze the transactions that take place between yourself and others. Most work situations demand that you behave in an adult manner to be truly effective. TA helps you recognize your "script" (roughly, a programmed pattern of behaving) and change it to your advantage. An example of a damaging life script is self-defeating behavior.

- TA can be applied to your own life in ways such as removing communication blocks with others, improving your leadership style (relate to subordinates in an adult-to-adult manner), and giving positive strokes to people.

- The general purpose of customer service training is to help organizations achieve a focus on customer needs and concerns. The customer service training program described here, Quality Customer Service, consists of four major steps: (1) send a positive attitude, (2) identify the needs of your customers, (3) provide for the needs of your customers, and (4) work to ensure your customers' return.

- Cultural awareness training is designed to help people develop a sensitivity to local and national customs and their importance in interpersonal relations. The major objective of such training is to help workers cope with unanticipated events in a foreign culture. Certain values can exert an influence on effectiveness in dealing with people from other cultures. These key values are individualism, informality, directness in negotiating, materialism, and time orientation.

Questions and Activities _____

1. How could one diagnose accurately what kind of interpersonal skill training is needed by an individual?

2. How could one diagnose accurately what kind of interpersonal skill training is needed by an organization?

3. For what types of work might assertiveness be particularly important?

4. How does one know when it is time to back off and not be so assertive?

5. Some highly successful people in all fields are abrasive, rude, and pushy. How would you therefore defend the importance of being assertive rather than aggressive?

6. Why is it important for a professional person on the job to usually behave in the adult ego state?

7. Identify two occupations in which being able to act in the child ego state is important from time to time.

8. Identify one of your dominant life scripts. Should it be changed?

9. Based on your experiences with customer service personnel, what would you identify as the major needs for customer service training?

10. In most European and Asian countries, businesspeople speak some English. Why would it therefore be important for an American businessperson to learn a European or Asian language?

A HUMAN RELATIONS CASE PROBLEM
It's Too Soon to Say Goodbye to Québec City

Ashley Parsons had been interested in the medical field since her adolescent years, but she did not wish to work directly with patients. While in high school, Ashley decided that a practical career choice would be to enter a health care–related business. She discussed with her parents and guidance counselor her interest in someday working for a medical products company. Ashley's plan was to first obtain a degree in business administration, and then find a position in a medical products company. Ashley's parents and guidance counselor agreed that her plan was well conceived, and encouraged her to proceed.

During her last year of business school in Vermont, Ashley conducted a thorough job search. The most exciting offer she received was from a medical products company based in Massachusetts. Ashley's position would entail selling a blood analyzer to hospitals, clinics, and wholesalers of medical equipment in Vermont, New Hampshire, Maine, northern New York State, and the province of Québec. However, she would be required to concentrate on Québec, because the company had barely explored that market. With careful planning, the job would involve approximately 60 percent travel.

Ashley quickly decided to accept the offer as a medical products representative. The base pay was satisfactory, the commission structure was excellent, and she valued the freedom she would have with so much travel. Ashley had studied four terms of French in high school. To further prepare herself for working in Québec, she would take an intensive two-month course in conversational French.

Ashley's job proceeded generally well during the first six months. Much of her work involved speaking to existing accounts about additional business. Existing accounts readily accepted her as the new representative in the territory. Ashley also had moderate success in creating new business with some medical clinics and hospitals.

Ashley worked the hardest to generate new business in Québec. During her first swing through the territory, the potential buyers Ashley called on reacted coolly to her presentation. Ashley decided to modify her person-to-person approach on her next trip to Québec. She would begin her conversation in French, hoping to establish rapport between herself and her prospects.

Ashley's new opening line was, "Bonjour. Je m'appelle Ashley Parsons. Comment allez-vous? Enchanté de faire votre connaissance. Je voudrais discuter les produits medical." [Good day. My name is Ashley Parsons. How are you? It's a pleasure to meet you. I would like to discuss medical products.] Two people who Ashley approached with this greeting immediately began to speak English. Two others smiled halfheartedly, and then spoke English. The fifth person replied "Excusez-moi, je suis trés occupé," [Excuse me, I am very busy] and terminated the meeting.

Discouraged by her rejection in both Montréal and Québec City, Ashley reviewed her experiences with her manager. His analysis was, "It sounds as if you're making the right moves to establish rapport in Québec. But maybe we should find a Québecois distributor to represent us up there. Maybe someone who isn't a native of Québec is a poor fit in the job. On the other hand, hiring a distributor would be a big problem. Our profit margins would be awfully thin.

"Your performance in the rest of your territory is fine. Maybe we could drop you from Québec, but assign you more of New York State."

"I'm not willing to say au revoir to Québec quite yet. Give me more time to prove myself," Ashley said.

1. What does this case tell us about international business?
2. How should Ashley overcome the problems she is facing?
3. What type of specific training would you recommend for Ashley?

4. What do you think the company should do about the Québec territory?

A HUMAN RELATIONS CASE PROBLEM
The Paternalistic Boss

Arthur Bennington, a department store manager, was receiving his annual performance appraisal from his boss, Shelly Wolf, the regional manager. Wolf began her evaluation with these comments:

"No doubt about it, Art, you have turned in another six months of sterling performance. Your sales volume is up 27 percent and your profits have increased 12 percent. I'm happy with your performance, but I do notice that your personnel costs are running high. Your profits might have increased more if your turnover were lower."

"Thank you for the compliment about a good year," Bennington replied. "I do think, though, that the high personnel costs are beyond my control. My sales help keep leaving because they dislike being supervised conscientiously."

"Art, I think your definition of conscientious might differ from the usual meaning of the word," Wolf said. "In your attempts to be conscientious you may be trying to exert too much control over the lives of your store personnel."

"Shelly, what do you mean, that I exert too much control?" asked Bennington.

"Here is the nature of the complaints we've been receiving through the personnel department and in unsolicited letters: A number of your employees think that you confuse your role as a store manager with that of an overpowering parent or relative. You told one of the women who quit that she would never amount to anything unless she finished business school. You told one of the men who quit that his punk hairstyle makes him unfit to associate with people from decent backgrounds. It could be that your preaching to your employees is driving them out the door."

"Shelly," replied Bennington, "You may be overreacting. What the younger generation needs from management is guidance that will help them in life, not just the job."

1. Do you think Wolf is justified in criticizing Bennington for his approach to supervision?
2. What type of interpersonal skill training do you think would be the most helpful to Bennington?

A HUMAN RELATIONS EXERCISE
What Are Your Developmental Needs?

The following exercise is designed to heighten your self-awareness of areas in which you could profit from personal improvement. It is not a test, and there is no scoring, yet your answers to the checklist may prove helpful to you in mapping out a program of interpersonal skills training.

THE INTERPERSONAL SKILLS CHECKLIST

Directions: Below are a number of specific aspects of behavior that suggest a person needs improvement in his or her interpersonal skills. Check each statement that is generally true for you. You can add to the validity of this exercise by having one or two other people who know you well answer this form as they think it describes you. Then compare your self-analysis with their analysis of you.

**PLACE
CHECK
IN THIS
COLUMN**

1. I'm too shy. _____
2. I'm too mean. _____
3. I'm too much of a bully. _____
4. I have trouble expressing my feelings. _____
5. I make negative comments about people too readily. _____
6. Very few people listen to me. _____
7. My personality isn't colorful enough. _____
8. People say that I'm a clown. _____
9. I don't handle myself in a very mature way. _____
10. People find me boring. _____
11. It is very difficult for me to criticize others. _____
12. I'm too serious most of the time. _____
13. I avoid controversy in dealing with others. _____
14. It is difficult for me to find things to talk about with others. _____
15. I don't get my point across very well. _____
16. _____ (fill in your own statement) _____

Now that you (and perhaps another person) have identified specific behaviors that may require change, action plans should be drawn. Describe briefly a plan of attack for bringing about the change you hope to achieve for each statement that is checked. Ideas for your action plan might come from information presented in this chapter or elsewhere in the text. Also investigate the suggested readings at the end of this and the previous chapter. A basic example would be to participate in an AT workshop if you checked "I'm too shy."

Notes

1. James C. Georges, "The Hard Reality of Soft-skills Training," *Personnel Journal,* April 1989, p. 41.

2. R. Bruce Dodge, "Learning-Centered Development," *Personnel Journal,* September 1989, p. 100.

3. Instrument available from Talico Inc., Jacksonville Beach, Florida.

4. Raymond A. Noe and Neal Schmitt, "The Influence of Trainee Attitudes on Training Effectiveness: The Test of a Model," *Personnel Psychology,* Autumn 1986, pp. 497–523.

5. James S. Russell, Kenneth H. Wexley, and John E. Hunter, "Questioning the Effectiveness of Behavior Modeling in an Industrial Setting," *Personnel Psychology,* Autumn 1984, p. 479.

6. Mary Jane Ruhl and Keith Atkinson, "Interactive Video Training: One Step Beyond," *Personnel Administrator,* October 1986, p. 70.

7. Ruhl and Atkinson, "Interactive Video Training," p. 70.

8. *American Management Association Course Catalogue,* August 1990–April 1991, p. 33.

9. Lynn Z. Bloom, Karen Coburn, and John Pearlman, *The New Assertive Woman* (New York: Dell, 1976), pp. 175–76.

10. Stuart M. Schmidt and David Kipnis, "The Perils of Persistence," *Psychology Today,* September 1987, pp. 32–34.

11. Two job-related explanations of TA are Muriel James and John James, *The OK Boss* (Reading, MA: Addison-Wesley, 1975), and Dorothy Jongeward and Philip Seyer, *Choosing Success—Transactional Analysis on the Job* (New York: Wiley, 1978).

12. James and James, *The OK Boss,* p. 32.

13. Rebecca C. Curtis, ed., *Self-Defeating Behaviors: Experimental Research, Clinical Impressions, and Practical Applications* (New York: Plenum, 1989).

14. Abe Wagner, *The Transactional Manager: How to Solve People Problems with Transactional Analysis* (Englewood Cliffs, NJ: Prentice Hall, 1981), p. 7.

15. Donald D. Bowen and Raghu Nath, "Transactions in Management," *California Management Review,* Winter 1975, pp. 82–83.

16. Ted Cocheu, "Refocus Performance Objectives Toward Greater Customer Service," *Personnel Journal,* April 1988, p. 116.

17. William B. Martin, *Quality Customer Service: The Art of Treating Customers as Guests* (Los Altos, CA: Crisp, 1987).

18. P. Christopher Earley, "Intercultural Training for Managers: A Comparison of Documentary and Interpersonal Methods," *Academy of Management Journal,* December 1987, p. 686.

19. Phitak Arvind V., *International Dimensions of Management* (Boston: Kent, 1983), pp. 22–26; see also 2nd ed., 1989.

20. Lennie Copeland, "China Opportunity: Amateurs Need Not Apply," *Personnel Administrator,* July 1985, p. 98.

Suggested Reading

BELL, CHIP, and ZEMKE, RON. "Coaching for Distinctive Service." *Management Review,* May 1989, pp. 27–30.

BOWEN, DAVID E., and associates. *Service Management Effectiveness.* San Francisco: Jossey-Bass, 1990.

CAMPION, MICHAEL A., and CAMPION, JAMES E. "Evaluation of an Interviewee Skills Training Program in a Natural Field Experiment." *Personnel Psychology,* Winter 1987, pp. 675–91.

GORDON, JACK, ZEMKE, RON, and JONES, PHILLIP, eds. *Designing and Delivering Cost-Effective Training,* 2nd ed. Minneapolis: Lakewood, 1988.

HARRIS, PHILIP R., and MORAN, ROBERT T. *Managing Cultural Differences,* 2nd ed. Houston: Gulf, 1990.

HICKS, WILLIAM D., and KLIMOSKI, RICHARD J. "Entry into Training Programs and Its Effects on Training Outcomes: A Field Experiment." *Academy of Management Journal,* September 1987, pp. 542–52.

MELNIC, JERRY. "Resilience Training: Reaping Success from Failures." *Personnel,* March 1989, pp. 74–77.

MORGOLIS, FREDRIC H., and BELL, CHIP. *Understanding Training Perspectives & Practices.* San Diego: University Associates, 1989.

ROBINSON, DANA GAINES, and ROBINSON, JAMES C. *Training for Impact: How to Link Training to Business Needs and Measure the Results.* San Francisco: Jossey-Bass, 1989.

WARSHAUER, SUSAN. *Inside Training and Development: Creating Effective Programs.* San Diego: University Associates, 1988.

14

The Effective Organization

LEARNING OBJECTIVES

After reading and studying this chapter and doing the exercises, you should be able to

1. Describe several external measures of an effective organization.
2. Describe several internal measures of an effective organization.
3. Summarize the systems view of organizational effectiveness.
4. Explain how productivity and quality are linked to organizational effectiveness.
5. Pinpoint the principles of organizational excellence as defined by Peters and Waterman.
6. Describe a few characteristics of well-managed companies as perceived by employees.

Y our reaction to many places of work you know about has probably been, "I wonder how they continue to operate." About other places you may have commented, "What a smooth-running outfit. No wonder they are tops in their field." This chapter examines the issue of what and who determines organizational effectiveness. A major justification for including this chapter is that so many organizations today are striving for effectiveness, if not excellence.

There are many different opinions of what constitutes an effective organization. Organizational effectiveness is therefore measured in different ways. Despite this diversity of opinion, we need a central definition of organizational effectiveness. As defined here, **organizational effectiveness** is the extent to which an organization is productive and satisfies the demands of its interested parties. Among the interested parties that need to be satisfied are employees, customers, clients, the general public, labor unions, and the governments.

Another complexity in evaluating organizational effectiveness is the time dimension. Some measures of organizational effectiveness deal with the long range, while others deal with the intermediate or short range. For instance, a company that loses money in one year may be temporarily ineffective. If the same company earns a profit after the first five years, it might be considered effective in the intermediate and long range.

A SYSTEMS VIEW OF ORGANIZATIONAL EFFECTIVENESS

Systems theory has contributed to the understanding of organizational effectiveness. As diagrammed in Figure 14–1, an organization is part of a larger system—society itself. An effective organization makes prudent use of natural resources (inputs), by processing them (process or throughput) into something useful for society (outputs). The effective organization is thus productive. As these outputs are placed in the environment, the effective organization changes in response to new demands from the environment. Often this means using different inputs.

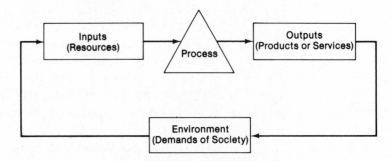

FIGURE 14–1 A Systems View of Organization

Another important aspect of systems theory is that organizations are open systems. They interact with the outside world, as noted by two elements of Figure 14–1: Outputs are fed into the environment, and the environment furnishes the inputs necessary to keep the organization functioning.

A business analogy will help explain these relationships further. An automobile dealership uses the *inputs* of (1) new and used cars, and (2) people, in the form of sales, shop, and office personnel, in order to provide a service to the public. The cars taken into the dealership are *processed* to the extent that they are prepared for sale and displayed on a lot or in a showroom. Offering financing and insurance programs to the public is part of the process that takes place in the dealership.

The *output* is private transportation for the public. As tastes and requirements change (for example, a demand for more luxurious automobiles), the dealership receives *feedback*. Such feedback helps inform the dealer and manufacturer what types of inputs (new cars) the dealer should be offering next. As long as the dealership responds to the tastes of the public, while at least breaking even, it will be able to meet its objective of delivering cars to the public. If these objectives are met, the organization is considered to be effective. The environment is thus the final evaluator of organizational effectiveness.[1]

PRODUCTIVITY, QUALITY, AND ORGANIZATIONAL EFFECTIVENESS

Private and public organizations alike strive to be productive and offer high-quality goods and services to the public. Quality should be considered part of productivity. Nevertheless, since productivity and quality are related but not synonyms, each topic requires separate attention. After describing productivity and quality, we will examine how employee factors can affect them adversely.

Productivity

Later in this chapter we present numerous criteria of organizational effectiveness. None of these criteria, or determinants of effectiveness, are so important that they override the importance of productivity. A modern definition of **productivity** is the use of resources. Low productivity has serious negative consequences. Among them are a business failing to make a profit, a health maintenance organization showing an operating loss, and a government agency losing its funding. High productivity has serious positive consequences of the opposite kind—profits, staying within budget, and retaining funding.

Productivity also has behavioral consequences. Morale tends to be high when people perceive themselves to be productive but not subject to exorbitant work demands. And morale tends to erode when an organization achieves low productivity. As described in Chapter 4, job satisfaction and morale can also influence productivity.

Quality

According to a leader in the quality movement, Philip B. Crosby, **quality is conformance to requirements.**[2] If the public and company officials require a watch battery to last 500 days, and it does, the battery has acceptable quality. Have you ever dialed 800-424-1040 to receive answers to a question about your federal income tax? If the service conformed to your requirements, you would conclude that the IRS is offering a high-quality service. If you spent four hours trying to get through and then were put on hold for five minutes, you would conclude that the service was of low quality. Customer service is thus an important aspect of a quality firm.

Providing high-quality goods and services has become a widely accepted measure of organizational effectiveness. An advertising strategy for some firms is to mention the quality of both their products and services, and the people making or providing them. Observe the mention of product and people quality in the accompanying box.

Employee Factors Contributing to Productivity and Quality Problems

Poor management practices, poor equipment, and inadequate technology are important contributors to productivity and quality problems. Employees also contribute to low productivity and quality. One major factor is poor motivation. Some employees are much more interested in leisure and personal life than in work. They regard productivity and quality improvement as somebody else's responsibility. When threatened with being fired, some of these employees may show a temporary spurt in productivity. After the threat wears off, they once again decrease their work effort.

Another important employee factor leading to work errors is poor attention. Even well-motivated workers sometimes have problems concentrating on their work because they are preoccupied with personal problems. A data entry specialist in a bank made a large number of errors in transferring information from canceled checks to monthly statement sheets. Customer complaints about mistakes not in their favor, along with an audit, brought the problems to management's attention. The data entry specialist blamed her errors on her concerns about personal finances.

Poor ability can also contribute to low productivity and quality. The employee may simply not be able to perform at the required level. Similarly, insufficient training and education can lower productivity and quality. A planning specialist in a government agency persisted in making forecasts that were out of line with past experience and common sense. When confronted about these unusual forecasts, the specialist said: "I apologize. I really don't understand how to use the right forecasting statistics. So I was probably way off in my calculations."

SELECTED MEASURES OF ORGANIZATIONAL EFFECTIVENESS

No single measure determines whether an organization is effective. For example, the criterion of profitability does not tell the whole story of an organization's effectiveness. A profitable firm may be creating undue stress for employees, leading to an exodus of people from the firm once they can find new jobs. Ultimately, what constitutes an effective organization depends upon a person's values—what he or she thinks is important.

A realistic view is that organizational effectiveness is usually measured by multiple criteria. To illustrate, an effective hospital would have to accomplish such ends as taking care of sick and injured people, staying within budget, providing employment to the disabled, contributing to an aesthetic environment, and conducting research. A substantial number of measures of organizational effectiveness are described next to help you appreciate the complexity of specifying what constitutes organizational effectiveness.[3]

To help clarify these many measures of effectiveness, they are sorted into two different types of measures. *External measures* refer to output variables, such as the production of goods and services. *Internal measures* refer to processes such as maintaining good morale and a high quality of work life.

As you read through these various measures of organizational effectiveness, it will become obvious that they are not all different from one another. For example, there is a high correlation between "profit making" and the "efficient use of resources." If resources are squandered, it will be difficult to make a profit.

External Measures of Organizational Effectiveness

External measures of organizational effectiveness center around the interaction of the organization with the outside world. As such, they are logical and fit into a systems view of organizations. Two major external measures, productivity and quality, have already been described.

Goal attainment is a general measure of how well the organization accomplishes what it set out to accomplish. Assuming that an organization's goals are not destructive or harmful to others, there is much to be said for this criterion. A subset of this criterion is *achieving new goals.* A successful organization emphasizes the attainment of new and important goals. An important new goal for a business firm, for example, might be to ward off a hostile takeover from a group of investment bankers.

Profit making, or a favorable "bottom line," is often considered the most important measure of effectiveness for a business. Unless a firm makes

If You Don't See This Symbol

You Won't Get This Guarantee.

We know that every call you make is important. That you rely on your cellular phone and your Rochester Tel Mobile service. Rochester Tel Mobile is so confident of its service, that we offer a Cellular Clear Call Guarantee.

To start with, we use state-of-the-art AT&T switching equipment to ensure quality. But if you're ever dissatisfied with the cellular transmission on any call, you don't have to pay for that call. It's free! And we'll repair your cellular equipment right the first time, or any additional labor charges are on us. And when you call us with a question, you'll talk to a courteous, professional customer service representative who is eager to help. If that's the kind of service you want, come to us or one of our authorized dealers. Because if you go somewhere else, you're going to end up with service from someone else.

And speaking of things that are free, we offer free local directory assistance. And services such as Call Waiting, Call Forwarding and Conference Calling are yours for the asking, with no monthly service charge. No one else gives you so much at no charge.

For a free brochure on why it pays to choose Rochester Tel Mobile, visit our service center or one of our authorized dealers. Or give us a call and we'll send the brochure to you. But remember to look for the Rochester Tel logo wherever you go. If you don't see it, you won't get our guarantee, and you won't get our special brand of service.

716-274-7000
2060 Brighton Henrietta Town Line Road
Rochester, New York 14623

RochesterTel
Mobile Communications

The Difference Is Clear

a profit, it cannot afford to accomplish other objectives, such as making charitable contributions or providing job training to culturally disadvantaged people. Yet an overemphasis on profit can result in such practices as firing people indiscriminately or imposing exorbitant work demands on employees.

Staying within budget is a nonprofit firm's equivalent of making a profit. Unless an organization stays within budget, it risks losing much of its public support. Managers of nonprofit organizations are as budget-conscious as those employed by for-profit businesses. Nonprofit firms that overspend risk extinction.

Social responsibility means that organizations have an obligation to groups in society—other than owners or stockholders—beyond that prescribed by law or union contract. One example of a socially responsible act would be for a company to help solve social problems that it causes or contributes to. A case in point would be a brewery that chooses to conduct an advertising campaign against driving while intoxicated. Many organizations today are behaving in a socially responsible way by providing child-care facilities for their employees.[4]

Practicing good ecology is the satisfaction of a number of groups in the organization's environment. Practicing good ecology is thus a more general case of being socially responsible. When certain key groups in society are satisfied, we can say that the organization is effective or successful.[5]

In a study of ninety-seven small businesses, the researchers identified seven different groups (constituencies) who have a vested interest in the welfare of the company. To the extent that these parties are satisfied, the organization can be classified as effective or successful. The seven groups are customers, creditors, suppliers, employees, owners, the community, and government. Many of the expectations these groups have of a small business are similar. For example, all groups want the company to stay in operation. Other concerns are more meaningful to one group than to another. The government is strongly interested in a given company obeying safety regulations, whereas a creditor would be more concerned about prompt payment of bills.[6]

The different criteria of organizational effectiveness used by the seven groups are shown in Figure 14–2. The same figure also illustrates an important theme of this chapter—that organizational effectiveness is multidimensional.

Growth is an increase in such factors as total workforce, plant capacity, assets, sales, profit, market share, and number of new products or services. To many observers, the absence of growth is the equivalent of organizational ineffectiveness. In the current era, however, the relevance of growth as a measure of effectiveness is diminishing. The reason is that many organizations are trimming down in size, including business corporations selling large units to other companies.

Voluntarism is the extent to which people want to continue as members of the organization. An organization that many people are eager to

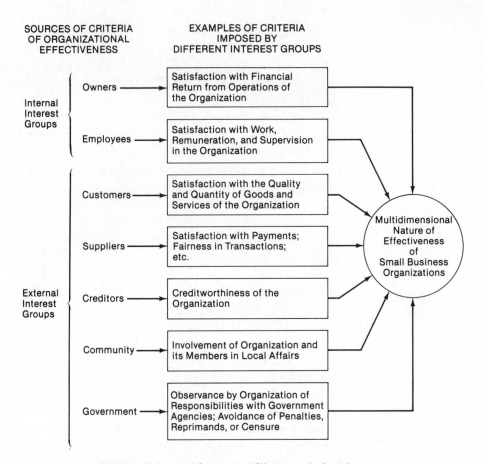

FIGURE 14–2 Criteria of Organizational Effectiveness for Small Businesses

join, and few want to leave, might be considered effective. Hewlett-Packard Corp. exemplifies an organization that scores high on voluntarism. When most of the members want to leave at the earliest opportunity, it could mean that the organization is ineffective. Among the exceptions are hospitals and prisons, where most of the employees want to remain, but the patients and prisoners, respectively, want an early exit.

Readiness to perform means carrying out the organization's purpose as required by its constituents. An organization that can successfully perform on short notice can be considered effective. A fire department that gets its firefighters out on time to minimize physical and human loss is an effective department. On the other hand, an orthopedic medical practice that requires people with backaches to wait three months for an appointment is not totally effective.

Survival means staying in existence over time by being able to cope with a changing environment. An organization that survives in the long range is probably meeting the demands of some section of society. A 100-year-old college is undoubtedly performing a legitimate service. A construction company that has been in business in the same community for forty years has obviously earned the right to survive.

A major contributor to survival is the organization's capacity to adapt to change. An adaptable organization has good problem-solving ability, combined with the capacity to react with flexibility toward changing environmental demands. Organizations with the ability to adapt to necessary changes have been labeled **organic.** In order to be adaptive or organic, the firm would have to receive valid information and then communicate it internally. Specialists, such as strategic planners and market researchers, play an important role in gathering and interpreting valid information from the environment.

Tom Peters exhorts managers to welcome change, in part because it leads to useful innovations. He states, "We must become improvement fanatics. We must constantly jigger and rejigger every procedure in our firms if we are to regain our competitiveness."[7]

Internal Measures of Organizational Effectiveness

An internal measure of organizational effectiveness relates to processes and techniques similar to those described throughout this text. For example, a successful organization would use effective methods of motivating and communicating with people, and would resolve disputes and grievances promptly and fairly. In our opinion, internal measures are less meaningful than external measures in determining organizational effectiveness. For instance, good motivational systems are relevant only if the people are motivated to engage in work that society thinks is valuable (an external measure of effectiveness). Following is a sampling of internal criteria of organizational effectiveness.[8]

A *sense of identity* is present when an organization is aware of what it is and what it is trying to accomplish. Strategic planning by executives contributes to an organization's sense of identity. In addition, when organization's members perceive it as it is perceived by others, a sense of identity is fostered. Ford Motor Co. and the United Way represent organizations with a strong sense of identity—both have a purpose that is seen by insiders and outsiders.

Good internal service occurs when organization members treat each others as customers, and are good corporate citizens. Another important symptom of good internal service is when various departments try hard to assist other departments. In an ineffective organization many workers say something to the effect of, "We could get our job done if only the field office would . . . ." or "If only sales would. . . ."[9]

Managerial skills is the ability of managers to accomplish tasks by working with and through people. Few people would argue that an organization can become or remain effective without managers who possess both task and interpersonal skills. Task skills are those related directly to work accomplishment. Interpersonal skills include the extent to which managers give support, facilitate constructive interaction, and generate enthusiasm for meeting goals and achieving superior performance.

Integration is achieved when the subparts of the organization fit together and therefore are not in severe conflict or working at cross purposes. When employees believe that they can prosper in an organization only by lying and stealing, the opposite of integration has occurred. When the various departments of a company realize that only through teamwork will they all succeed, integration occurs.

Planning and goal setting means figuring out what needs to be done and how to accomplish it. Successful organizations are typically committed to goal setting and action planning at all levels. For goals to be effective, they must be agreed upon and accepted. An organization increases its chances for success when the vast majority of members perceive the same goals for the organization. Such a scenario would take place only when top management clearly articulates the goals, or when the goal is obvious. Xerox Corporation experienced a high degree of goal agreement several years ago when the company was striving to win the Malcolm Baldrige Award for quality. A unified effort by employees at all levels contributed to their success.

Control is how well management measures performance and corrects deviations from desired performance. The control model described in Chapter 12 explains the nature of control of human performance. Controls are also important in areas such as finance, operations, inventory shrinkage, and safety and health.

Participative decision making is the extent to which people throughout the organization contribute to important decisions and make suggestions. An organization is likely to increase its effectiveness when it solicits expertise from a wide range of members. The higher the quality of the workforce, the higher the yield from participative decision making.

Morale is a predisposition in organization members to put forth extra effort in achieving organizational goals and objectives. As implied in Chapter 4, it includes feelings of commitment and extra effort on the part of the group. High morale contributes to effectiveness in such ways as retention of organization members, lower accident rates, less waste, and "good-mouthing" the organization in the community.

Turnover and absenteeism is an index of the rate of attraction of the organization to its members. The extent of avoidable turnover and absenteeism serves as a rough index of organizational effectiveness. Involuntary turnover and voluntary turnover detract from organizational effectiveness. A firm that is forced to terminate or lay off employees may have made errors in selection or in satisfying consumer demands. Turnover and absenteeism are significant indexes of organizational effectiveness because they are often caused by low morale.

Accident frequency and severity is the rate and intensity of job-related physical injuries to employees. Accident control is important for both humanitarian and economic reasons. An effective organization does not waste human life or incur needless fines. Nor does it pay excessive insurance premiums because of poor safety practices.

Placing a high value on human resources is yet another internal measure of organizational effectiveness. An effective organization has talented and motivated people whose value is recognized by the firm. Most organizations claim that human resources are their most valuable asset; successful firms believe it. An organization with talented people is usually in a better position to recover from adversity than a firm with less valuable human resources. Human resources of high value therefore contribute directly to organizational survival. Placing a value on human resources is so important that it has led to an activity called *human resource accounting.* One of its applications is to assess the true cost of losing a valuable employee.[10]

Courage in the face of adversity means coping effectively with hard times. Most managers become cautious and embrace the status quo just when new ideas are the most needed. This holding back can be attributed to a concern that one will be criticized or fired if the risky idea fails. A more effective organization is more willing to take a risk when it is most needed. One such legendary act of organizational courage was Chrysler's introduction of the mini-van at a time when the firm was close to defaulting on loans. The gamble paid off handsomely.

The importance of overcoming adversity has created a demand for executives with expertise in bringing troubled organizations back to health. Labeled *turnaround managers*, these executives take such drastic steps as laying off large parts of the workforce and selling off company assets.[11] When turnaround managers are successful, the organization regains its equilibrium and may return to health.

Trust between management and employees is a belief that the other side is acting in your best interest, combined with a mutual concern for each other. Trust contributes to organizational effectiveness because it builds employee loyalty and sometimes enhances motivation. Also, employees who trust management are willing to identify organizational problems because they do not fear being blamed for causing the problems. Consultant Gordon Shea observes that the actions of supervisors communicate how much they trust employees: "Tight control and heaviness of management—looking down people's throats—reveals low trust."[12]

PRINCIPLES OF ORGANIZATIONAL EXCELLENCE

Another way of understanding organizational effectiveness is to study the principles that guide successful organizations. Such an approach was undertaken by two best-selling books about management, *In Search of Excellence* and *Passion for Excellence.*[13] Peters and Waterman, the authors of the first book, selected their sample on the basis of opinions and facts about organizational performance. First, they interviewed executives who were known for their skill, experience, and wisdom. Next, they talked to a number of faculty members from a dozen business schools in the United States and Europe. Based on these discussions, and their own experience as management consultants, Peters and Waterman identified a number of excellent companies. They also discovered the principles underlying their excellence.

Two more steps were involved in choosing the final sample. The authors used six measures of long-term productivity (such as average return on capital). To qualify for the sample, a company had to be in the top half of its industry on at least four of the six measures for twenty-five years. Finally, industry experts were selected to rate the companies' history of innovativeness. Sixty-two companies were included in the final sample.[14]

Eight Principles for Excellence

The findings are described in the eight principles listed and defined in Table 14–1. A few of these principles are updated with the current thinking of their originators. Several of these principles emphasize the or-

---

TABLE 14-1   Eight principles for excellence

1. *Bias for action:* A preference for doing something—anything—rather than sending a question through many cycles of analyses and committee reports.

2. *Staying close to the customer:* Learning the customer's preferences and catering to them.

3. *Autonomy and entrepreneurship:* Breaking the corporation into small companies and encouraging them to think independently and creatively.

4. *Productivity through people:* Creating in *all* employees the awareness that their best efforts are essential and that they will share in the rewards of the company's success.

5. *Hands-on, value driven:* Insisting that executives keep in touch with the firm's essential business.

6. *Stick to the knitting:* Remaining with the business the company knows best. Many successful companies of the 1990s are focusing on *core competence,* such as General Electric operating only in markets where it can be number 1 or number 2.

7. *Simple form, lean staff:* Few administrative layers, few people at upper administrative levels.

8. *Simultaneous loose-tight properties:* Fostering a climate where there is dedication to the central values of the company, combined with a tolerance for all employees who accept these values.

Source: Compiled from Thomas J. Peters and Robert J. Waterman, Jr., *In Search of Excellence: Lessons from America's Best-Run Companies* (New York: Harper & Row, 1982); Anne Skagen, "Tom Peters as Performance Art," *Executive Management Forum,* June 1990, pp. 1–2; "Four Fs on Your Report Card? Yes!" *Executive Management Forum,* June 1990, p. 3.

ganization structure, such as principle 3—breaking the organization into small companies. Several principles emphasize behavioral tactics. An example is principle 1—a bias for action instead of overanalyzing problems. The remaining principles deal with organizational values and climate, such as fostering dedication to the values of the company.

Criticism of the Principles for Excellence

The approach under study to identify guiding principles of organizational success has met with considerable criticism from researchers. A current critical analysis of the principles of excellence builds upon past criticism and offers new quantitative data. Two researchers compared fourteen of the excellent firms to a larger sample from *Fortune's* 1,000 industrial firms on indicators of stock market performance. They also evaluated how well these firms fared on the four principles of excellence included in *Passion for Excellence* (leadership; closeness to the customer; innovation, autonomy and entrepreneurship; and productivity through people).

The study concluded that several of the firms included in the original list may not have been excellent, and other firms may have been erroneously excluded. Additionally, the results showed that three of the four excellence principles described in *Passion for Excellence* were unrelated to performance. However, the principle of innovation, autonomy, and entrepreneurship was significantly related to performance. It was therefore concluded that managers should be cautious about uncritically accepting these principles of excellence.[15]

Despite these well-founded criticisms, Peters and his associates have made a notable contribution to organizational effectiveness. They have reinforced a growing awareness that small units within larger bureaucratic structures tend to foster innovation.

Characteristics of the 100 Best-Run Companies

The two books just mentioned emphasized business success as the key measure of organizational effectiveness. Another book about organizational effectiveness, *The 100 Best Companies to Work For in America,* focused on job satisfaction instead of business success.[16] The authors of *100 Best Companies* interviewed hundreds of people about what they thought were the best places to work. Among the people interviewed were consultants, recruiters, friends, relatives, business school professors, reporters, media personnel, advertising people, and physicians. The top ten of the 100 were Bell Labs, Trammell Crow, Delta Airlines, Goldman Sachs, Hallmark Cards, Hewlett-Packard, IBM, Pitney Bowes, Northwestern Mutual Life, and Time Inc. Twenty-one of companies on this list of 100 were also included in the list of excellent firms cited by Peters and associates.

Once 100 fine employers were identified, the authors interviewed from six to thirty people in each company. The interviews were analyzed to arrive at a list of characteristics typical of a good employer, as shown in Table 14–2. A comparison of Tables 14–1 and 14–2 suggests that managers and employees do not agree strongly on what makes for an excellent company. The principles in Table 14–1 are derived mostly from managers' perceptions, while those in Table 14–2 are derived mostly from employee perceptions. However, both groups do mention such factors as autonomy, quality, values, and decentralization.[17]

A follow-up analysis investigated why the 100 "best" companies were such good places to work. The author of the study, Robert Levering, found employees with enthusiasm, dedication, and a sense of belonging. These best companies were perceived as partnerships between employers and employees.[18]

Yet another perspective on organizational effectiveness and job satisfaction is how well the company provides for the needs of working parents. *Working Mother* magazine observes that the best companies for women offer child-care assistance and "family-friendly" leave policies. In the magazine's 1990 annual survey, ten employers were cited for exceptionally progressive policies. Among them were Apple Computer, Beth Israel teaching hospital of Boston, HBO, IBM, and Merck, the drug manufacturer. All seventy-five companies cited in the 1990 list offered some form of child-care program or assistance, and long-term unpaid leaves with benefits. Some of these leaves stretched up to three years.[19]

TABLE 14–2   Characteristics of 100 best companies

---

1. Employees are made to feel that they are part of a team, or in some cases, a family.

2. Open communication is encouraged; people are informed of new developments, and are encouraged to offer suggestions and complaints.

3. Promotions are from within; employees are allowed to bid on jobs before outsiders are hired.

4. Quality is emphasized, enabling people to feel pride in the products or services they are providing.

5. Employees are allowed to share in profits through profit sharing or stock ownership or both.

6. Distinctions in rank between top management and employees in entry-level jobs are reduced. Everyone is addressed by his or her first name; executive dining rooms and exclusive perks for executives are barred.

7. Attention and resources are devoted to creating as pleasant a work environment as possible, and good architects are hired.

8. Employee activity in community service is encouraged by giving money to organizations in which employees participate.

9. Employee savings are assisted by matching the funds they save.

10. Employees are not laid off without management first making an effort to place them in other jobs within the company or elsewhere.

11. Physical fitness centers and regular exercise and medical programs are provided, indicating concern about employee health.

12. Employee skills are expanded through training programs and reimbursement of tuition for outside courses.

Source: From Robert Levering, Milton Moskowitz, and Michael Katz, *The 100 Best Companies to Work for in America* (Reading, MA: Addison–Wesley, 1984).

Summary of Key Points

- There are many different opinions of what constitutes an effective organization, and effectiveness can be measured for different time periods. A working definition used here is that organizational effectiveness is the extent to which an organization is productive and satisfies the demands of its interested parties.

- Systems theory helps us understand the nature of organizational effectiveness. An effective organization makes use of natural resources (inputs) by processing them into something useful for society (outputs). As these outputs are placed in the environment, the effective organization changes in response to the new demands from the environment.

- Productivity and quality are important aspects of organizational effectiveness. Quality is conformance to customer requirements. Organizations today are particularly concerned about offering high-quality goods and services, including customer service. Many productivity and quality problems are created by employees. Among the contributing factors are poor motivation, attention, and ability.

- Organizational effectiveness is usually measured by multiple criteria. External criteria of effectiveness include goal attainment, profit making, staying within budget, social responsibility, practicing good ecology, growth, voluntarism, readiness to perform, and survival.

- Internal measures of organizational effectiveness include a sense of identity, good internal service, managerial skills, integration of the subparts, morale, placing a high value on human resources, and trust between management and employees.

- Another approach to understanding organizational effectiveness is to identify the principles and characteristics that make organizations successful. The principles of organizational excellence identified by Tom Peters and his associates are (1) bias for action, (2) staying close to customers, (3) autonomy and entrepreneurship, (4) productivity through people, (5) hands-on, value driven, (6) stick to the knitting, (7) simple form, lean staff, and (8) simultaneous loose-tight properties. The accuracy of these principles has been questioned by researchers.

- Characteristics typical of a good employer, as perceived by employees, include such factors as making employees feel they are part of a team, open communications, promotion from within, a pleasant work environment, and minimizing layoffs. A factor contributing to these positive characteristics is a partnership between employers and employees. Another job satisfaction–related characteristic of effectiveness is how well an organization provides for the needs of working parents.

Questions and Activities

1. Provide an example of an organization you classify as being effective, and explain the reason for your choice.
2. Provide an example of an organization you classify as being ineffective, and explain the reason for your choice.
3. How does the systems view of organizational effectiveness coincide with the philosophy of "survival of the fittest"?
4. What is your reaction to the argument that high-quality goods often cost so much to make that they would have to be priced noncompetitively?
5. Which attributes of a product or service lead you to conclude that it is of high quality?

6. Since few organizations are ineffective by choice, why don't ineffective organizations become effective?

7. Identify several forces in the outside world that would make it difficult for an organization to become and remain effective.

8. Identify the interest groups that an educational institution must satisfy in order to be effective.

9. Which of the eight principles for excellence could a person apply to achieve individual (rather than organizational) excellence?

10. Some employees argue that providing special benefits to working parents discriminates against workers who do not need child-care assistance. What is your stance on this issue?

A HUMAN RELATIONS CASE PROBLEM
The Striving-for-Excellence Hospital

The management at AMI Palmetto General Hospital in Hialeah, Florida, is concerned about forces making it difficult for the hospital to be excellent. Among the forces straining the industry and Palmetto General include government regulations (payments based on diagnosis instead of incurred expense), physician and patient needs, ownership changes, and the general public's perception about the cost of care.

A "Visions of Excellence" program was established to meet some of the challenges just cited. The hospital addresses these issues by combining elements of traditional employee relations, programs with a customer service orientation, and an organizationwide commitment to excellence. Implemented several years ago, the program is designed to convey a collective vision of the hospital's direction. Furthermore, the program aims to show what can be done internally to make the visions of the future the realities of today.

The Visions of Excellence Program has seven themes and activities, as described next:

Physician appreciation month. Hospital employees hand out business cards with slogans to physicians practicing at the hospital. The cards bear such slogans as "Our Doctors Make the Difference," and "Thanks for Being There When We Needed You." After a physician has collected a card with each of the imprinted slogans, the physician exchanges the cards for a gift at the administration office. The Physician Appreciation Month is designed to show customers (the physicians) how much they are appreciated.

Commitment Pledge Month. During this month a seven-foot outline of the hospital is placed in the main hallway. Employees submit signed commitment cards to be used as "bricks" in building the hospital's future. Contributing employees are given a "Committed to Excellence" badge, and can later participate in a raffle for a prize.

Shake-Hands Week. To promote family pride and teamwork, a Shake-Hands Week is organized. Employees are assigned another employee to meet and shake hands with. The partners then estimate the number of forms returned as part of a hospital contest.

Employee Exchange Day. One employee from each department spends two hours working in another department to learn about a co-worker's job.

Patient Satisfaction Means Success (PSMS). To draw attention to a program of monitoring patient satisfaction, periodically one of the four words in PSMS is printed on each employee's payroll stuffer. All foursomes who together can present the correct phrase are eligible for a prize.

Employee Honor Roll. An honor roll is composed of the names of employees mentioned in letters of appreciation sent by patients to the hospital administration. Honor roll employees are listed on a poster in the lobby, and a gold star is posted for each time the employee is mentioned in a letter. Employees included on the honor roll are invited to a midafternoon cake and champagne party with members of the administrative staff.

Patient Census. A contest is held in which the employee correctly guessing the average daily patient census at noon on the last day of the fiscal year receives $1.00 for each hospital patient. The purpose of Patient Census is to develop involvement and understanding of the health care industry.

Typical prizes awarded in the above seven events are weekend ocean liner cruises, days off with pay, restaurant dinners, and gift certificates for local department stores.

1. What contribution do you think the Vision for Excellence program might actually be making to organizational effectiveness?
2. Why should a hospital be concerned about being so nice to physicians and patients?
3. What would the two-factor theory (see Chapter 3) predict about the contribution of the Vision for Excellence program to job motivation?

Source: As reported in Juan L. Pujol and Edward Tudanger, "A Vision for Excellence," HRMagazine, June 1990, pp. 112–16.

A HUMAN RELATIONS CASE PROBLEM
Big Blue's Quest For Excellence

Several years ago, the world's largest maker of office equipment and computers, International Business Machines Corp., decided to strengthen itself internally and in the marketplace. A major reason IBM decided to embark upon far-reaching changes was that earnings had dipped, and competitors were gaining ground.

Top management candidly admitted that some of its own practices, as well as a business downturn, were responsible for the company's slump. Task forces were assigned to answer such questions as: "Has IBM become so bureaucratic that some decisions are made too slowly?" "Has the company not paid enough attention to the needs of its customers?" The strategies enacted by IBM to improve its situation are summarized in the next several paragraphs.

IBM's top priority is cost-cutting. The company planned to reduce its costs 7 percent in a twelve-month period. Reduced costs include: $1 billion in capital spending; $500 million through attrition of employees (voluntary quits and retirements) and other personnel programs; and $500 million in discretionary spending for travel, consultants, expense accounts, and other miscellaneous costs.

A major thrust toward reducing costs and decreasing delays in decision making will be to reduce the force of 40,000 managers worldwide. At some IBM manufacturing facilities there are five or six layers of management. As each layer of management passes judgment on the merits of a decision, it can take a long time to make a needed change. A top IBM official noted that in many areas of the company, planning is so complex that making an important change takes a year. The company, however, is not talking about laying off managers. Instead, many managers who leave voluntarily will not be replaced, and many other managers will be reassigned to sales, professional, and technical positions.

IBM will strengthen its marketing force, which is already the biggest in the industry. The company decided to create 5,000 new sales and marketing jobs by transferring headquarters and manufacturing employees into customer-contact assignments. These moves were planned to increase the sales staff by 22 percent to 28,000 people. Another change planned was for marketing personnel to listen even more carefully to customers, so it can match their requirements. IBM also planned to install systems that incorporated equipment from competitors, a maneuver prohibited in the past.

Another improvement planned by IBM is to accelerate its strategy to diversify its product line. The company plans to offer more software and services (such as equipment maintenance) because this business is more profitable than selling hardware.

Another area of potential change was to examine IBM's strategy of relying so heavily on company insiders for innovative ideas. Many competitive companies hire people from other companies in order to bring new perspectives into the firm.

1. Relate the above changes proposed by IBM to the criteria of organizational effectiveness presented in this chapter.
2. Relate the above changes to the principles of excellence expounded by Peters and Waterman.
3. Relate the above changes to the characteristics of the 100 best companies.
4. What is your evaluation of the soundness of IBM's plan for strengthening itself? Offer at least one constructive criticism or caution.

A HUMAN RELATIONS EXERCISE
Organizational Survival

One criterion of organizational effectiveness is survival. Its rationale is that since so many organizations of all types do not survive, being able to survive deserves some credit. The purpose of this exercise is for you to estimate the "organizational survival rate" in your area. Proceed as follows:

1. Each member of the class telephone twelve organizations of any kind listed in the Yellow Pages of your local telephone directory. Make the sample somewhat random by such methods as calling every ninth (or any number you choose) firm listed.
2. If the phone is disconnected, assume the firm has not survived, or at least the local branch of the firm has not survived.
3. If somebody answers, politely state: "Thank you for answering. We are doing a brief survey of organizational survival rates. You have answered our question. We appreciate your cooperation, and thank you for your time."
4. Combine data to arrive at the rate of organizational survival from one year to the next in your area. (Telephone directories are reprinted each year.)

Before implementing your part of the assignment, write down your prediction of what percentage of organizations listed in the telephone directory are still in business.

Notes _____

1. William A. Pasmore, *Designing Effective Organizations: The Sociotechnical Systems Perspective* (New York: Wiley, 1988).

2. Philip B. Crosby, *Quality Without Tears: The Art of Hassle-Free Management* (New York: McGraw-Hill, 1984), p. 59.

3. Based on a synthesis of the literature in Robert B. Miles, *Macro Organizational Behavior* (Santa Monica, CA: Goodyear, 1980), pp. 356–59.

4. "Child Care Hits the Bottom Line," *Human Resources Forum,* July 1989, pp. 1–2.

5. Miles, *Macro Organizational Behavior,* p. 377.

6. Hal Pickle and Frank Friedlander, "Seven Societal Criteria of Organizational Success," *Personnel Psychology,* Summer 1967, pp. 165–78.

7. Tom Peters, "Learn to Love Change, but Not Without Training," syndicated column, Jan. 31, 1988.

8. Patrick E. Connor, *Organizations: Theory and Design* (Chicago: Science Research Associates, 1980), p. 440.

9. Jerry Plymire, "Internal Service: Solving Problems," *Supervisory Management,* May 1990, p. 5.

10. Eric G. Flamholtz, *Human Resources Accounting: Advances in Concepts, Methods, and Applications,* 2nd ed. (San Francisco: Jossey-Bass, 1985).

11. John O. Whitney, "Turnaround Management Every Day," *Harvard Business Review,* September–October 1987, pp. 49–55.

12. Quoted in Priscilla Petty, "Companies Must Cultivate an Atmosphere of Trust Among Employees," Gannett News Service syndicated column, Aug. 27, 1985.

13. Thomas J. Peters and Robert H. Waterman, Jr., *In Search of Excellence: Lessons from America's Best-Run Companies* (New York: Harper & Row, 1982); Thomas J. Peters and Nancy Austin, *A Passion for Excellence* (New York: Harper & Row, 1985).

14. Summary of research procedures based on book review by Terence R. Mitchell in *Academy of Management Review,* April 1985, pp. 350–55.

15. Michael A. Hitt and R. Duane Ireland, "The Quest for Excellence," *The Academy of Management Executive,* May 1987, pp. 91–98.

16. Robert Levering, Milton Moskowitz, and Michael Katz, *The 100 Best Companies to Work For in America* (Reading, MA: Addison-Wesley, 1984).

17. Mitchell book review, p. 352.

18. Robert Levering, *A Great Place to Work: What Makes Some Employers So Good (And Most So Bad)* (New York: Random House, 1988).

19. "75 Best Companies for Working Mothers," *Working Mother,* October 1990.

Suggested Reading _____

DuBrin, Andrew J. *Contemporary Applied Management: Behavioral Science Techniques for Managers and Professionals,* 3rd ed. Homewood, IL: Irwin, 1989, pp. 215–26.

ELLIG, BRUCE R. "Improving Effectiveness Through an HR Review." *Personnel,* June 1989, pp. 56–64.

FENNELL, MARY L., and ALEXANDER, JEFFREY A. "Organizational Boundary Spanning in Institutionalized Environments." *Academy of Management Journal,* September 1987, pp. 456–76.

GARVIN, DAVID A. *Managing Quality.* New York: Free Press, 1988.

HARRISON, MICHAEL I. *Diagnosing Organizations: Methods, Models, and Processes.* Newbury Park, CA: Sage, 1987.

MARX, GARY T. "The Case of the Omniscient Organization." *Harvard Business Review,* March–April 1990, pp. 12–16, 20–24, 28–30.

PASCARELLA, PERRY, and FROHMAN, MARK A. *The Purpose-Driven Organization: Unleashing the Power of Direction and Commitment.* San Francisco: Jossey-Bass, 1989.

PRICHARD, ROBERT D., and associates. "Effects of Group Feedback, Goal Setting, and Incentives on Organizational Productivity." *Journal of Applied Psychology Monograph,* May 1988, pp. 337–58.

SCHERRER, P. SCOTT. "From Warning to Crisis: A Turnaround Primer." *Management Review,* September 1988, pp. 30–36.

WATERMAN, ROBERT H., JR. *The Renewal Factor: How the Best Get and Keep the Competitive Edge.* New York: Bantam, 1987.

15

Getting Along in a Bureaucracy

LEARNING OBJECTIVES

After reading and studying this chapter and doing the exercises, you should be able to

1. Describe the difference between the popular and technical meanings of the term *bureaucracy*.

2. Specify key advantages and disadvantages of a bureaucracy.

3. Give your own example of an "inversion of means and ends."

4. Pinpoint several methods organizations can use to prevent or overcome problems sometimes created by a bureaucracy.

5. Pinpoint several methods individuals can use to cope with the problems sometimes created by a bureaucracy.

n its popular meaning, the term *bureaucracy* is associated with a number of negative attributes. Most people think a bureaucracy is an organization rampant with the rigid application of rules and procedures, slowness of operation, buck-passing, repetition of effort, empire building, exaggerated secrecy, and frustrated employees. Yet technically **bureaucracy** refers to a form of organization in which division of effort, rank, rules, and regulations are carefully defined. It is a rational, systematic, precise form of organization.

The bureaucratic design is still the dominant form of organization, although it rarely exists in pure form. Most large organizations supplement a bureaucracy with smaller nonbureaucratic units, such as projects and production work teams.

Most readers of this book have dealt or will deal with a bureaucracy as an employee, customer, client, or citizen. It is thus worthwhile to examine the nature of bureaucracies and suggest strategies and tactics for overcoming their potential problems.

CHARACTERISTICS OF A BUREAUCRACY

Max Weber, a German sociologist, believed that bureaucracy was the pure form of organization, designed to achieve efficiency and effectiveness. He also reasoned that a state bureaucracy was the most expedient method of dominating and controlling people.[1] A bureaucracy has certain identifying characteristics.

- *A division of labor based on functional specialization.* Thus companies have departments such as engineering, manufacturing, marketing, data processing, accounting, and personnel. People in these departments possess specialized information that contributes to the overall welfare of the firm.

- *A well-defined hierarchy of authority.* The person granted the most power sits at the top of the hierarchy (chairman of the board or president). As you move down the organization chart, people at each level have less power than do those people at the levels above them, as shown in Figure 15–1.

- *A system of rules covering the rights and duties of employees.* In a truly bureaucratic organization each person has a precise job description and knows what he or she can expect from the company. In a few large corporations, for example, you are entitled to an extra day's vacation should you get sick one day during your vacation.

- *Systems and procedures for dealing with work situations.* In a bank, for example, each teller knows exactly what to do when a customer wishes to deposit money in his or her account. No deviation from bank policy is encouraged or allowed.

- *Impersonality of interpersonal relations.* Even when you smile sweetly at the civil servant in the motor vehicle department, he or she will not renew your registration until you meet specified requirements.
- *Promotion and selection based on technical competence.* To make this characteristic of a bureaucracy true to life, technical competence must also include managerial or administrative competence. Thus in a bureaucracy laughing at your boss's jokes can never be an official reason for your receiving a promotion.

ADVANTAGES OF BUREAUCRACY

The world probably could not function without bureaucracy. Imagine the chaos if every supervisor at Proctor and Gamble established his or her own pay scale and retirement policies for workers. What would happen if every employee at Fuji discussed problems with the company president, rather than conferring with his or her immediate superior? Before describing the specific advantages of bureaucracy, observe the recent comments of organization theorist Elliot Jaques:

> Thirty-five years of research have convinced me that the managerial hierarchy is the most efficient, hardiest, and most natural structure ever devised for large organizations. Properly structured, hierarchy can release energy and creativity, rationalize productivity, and actually improve morale.
>
> The hierarchical kind of organization we call bureaucracy did not emerge accidentally. It is the only form of organization that can enable

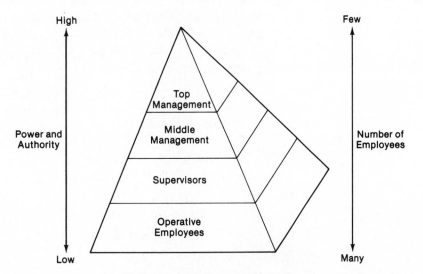

FIGURE 15-1 The Bureaucratic Form of Organization

a company to employ large numbers of people and yet preserve unambiguous accountability for the work they do. And that is why, despite its problems, it has so doggedly persisted.[2]

The advantages of bureaucracy described following, and outlined in Table 15–1, are forthcoming when the bureaucratic form of organization is properly applied.

Machinelike efficiency. At its best, a bureaucracy is a highly efficient form of organization. Weber believed that the fully developed bureaucratic mechanism compares with other organizations as does the machine with nonmechanical production methods. Under bureaucratic administration, precision, speed, and unambiguity are raised to an optimum point.[3]

IBM represents a modern example of what Weber envisioned when he spoke of a methodically efficient organization. A purchasing agent in one company had this comment to make about IBM's penchant for thoroughness: "When we don't know where something is in our company, we call our IBM account representatives. The people from IBM seem to know more about our company than we do."

Personally given orders become unnecessary. A bureaucratic manager can smugly point to the rulebook and say, "Any employee who is late five consecutive days will be docked one day's pay." He or she thus cannot be accused of discriminating against you personally, nor can you legitimately feel that you were unjustly treated. At its best, a bureaucracy prevents people from being treated arbitrarily or unfairly.

Repetition of orders is unnecessary. A bureaucratic manager can tell you that each day at closing time the money in your cash register must be balanced. In the future, this order does not have to be repeated. Somewhere in the back of the store a rulebook exists that tells you this must be done every day. Theoretically, given a carefully designed rulebook, employees would need a minimum of supervision (which, of course, works best with competent and well-motivated employees).

TABLE 15–1   Advantages of a bureaucracy

---

1. Machinelike efficiency
2. Personally given orders become unnecessary
3. Repetition of orders is unnecessary
4. Control of people from a distance
5. Punishment becomes legitimate
6. Equitable division of resources
7. Promotion of democracy in the workplace

Control of people from a distance. Top management can control people from a distance when those individuals are governed by a rational set of rules and regulations. When first-line supervisors are given a thorough grounding in machine safety, including rules in writing, frequent on-the-spot checks should not be necessary. At the other extreme, when management has not established a clear set of rules, there is need for extensive visitation to remote areas of the organization. An effective set of rules allows people to be managed properly without constant supervision.

Punishment becomes legitimate. In some instances, reprimands or punishments are necessary in a complex organization. Since most people resent punishment, they tend to question its legitimacy. A college policy may state that any individual who fails to attain a C average will not graduate. A person with a 1.8 average cannot cry "unjust punishment" when he or she does not graduate. A supervisor has every right to dismiss a forklift truck operator who drives his or her truck while drunk. The rules make such punishment legitimate.

Equitable division of resources. In a bureaucracy, the job each manager is supposed to perform is well defined. Each manager would prefer that he or she have substantial resources to carry out his or her mission. Most managers, if given a choice, would prefer that another staff member be added to the department. A bureaucracy usually prevents people overallocating resources for their own purposes. Managers at the top of the hierarchy try to divide up resources in an equitable fashion. Unfortunately, this advantage of a bureaucracy is sometimes subverted through the practice of **empire building**—adding people to your organizational unit more to acquire power than to serve the good of the firm.

Promotion of democracy in the workplace. In its ideal form, a bureaucracy fosters democracy in the workplace. Weber developed his bureaucratic model to help overcome the arbitrary treatment of employees.[4] In a bureaucracy personal favoritism is supposed to be minimized. Furthermore, the bureaucratic form of organization has had a significant democratizing effect in advancing certain minority interests and in implementing certain democratic principles. These principles include representation, democratic decision making, and equality.

The heavy reliance on group decision making and committees found in a bureaucracy also contributes to the democratic process. Each committee member, for example, has the opportunity to express his or her opinion on the issue under consideration. Although this contributes to the slowness in decision making characteristic of a bureaucracy, it does allow the democratic process to take place.

PROBLEMS CREATED BY A BUREAUCRACY

Despite these potential advantages of the bureaucratic form of organization, bureaucracies are better known for their disadvantages. Bureaucracies are currently under attack because they are frequently perceived as cumbersome and inefficient. The problems sometimes created by a bureaucracy are described following and summarized in Table 15–2.

Delays in decision making. Bureaucracies move painfully slowly on complex decisions. Recognition of this problem has led many large organizations to eliminate one or two layers of management in order to hasten decision mak-

---

Table 15–2   Disadvantages of a bureaucracy

1. Delays in decision making
2. Confusion and inefficiency
3. High frustration and low job satisfaction
4. Inversion of means and ends
5. Insensitivity to individual problems
6. Rigidity in behavior
7. Adverse changes in personality
8. Avoiding responsibility
9. Weakening of the connection between hard work and rewards

---

ing. The delay occurs because so many people have to concur before a final decision is made on important issues. In some bureaucracies, minor as well as major decisions are made slowly, as illustrated by this incident.

> A credit representative sent the vice president of finance a two-page memo outlining what steps he thought should be taken to make sure the company was an "equal opportunity lender." According to the representative's analysis, a disproportionate number of minority business owners were being denied credit by the company. Three months later, the credit rep received a memo back from the vice president. The memo began, "Sorry that your memo got chewed up in our corporate machinery. Nevertheless, your suggestions are being carefully reviewed by the appropriate levels of management. Your manager will discuss your proposal with you in the near future."

Confusion and inefficiency. When bureaucracies become large, they often breed confusion and inefficiency. Large firms are needed to carry out large-scale tasks. Nevertheless, there is a growing recognition that a small organization, or small subunit within a larger organization, is more efficient than a large, complex organization. It is common practice for large firms to subcontract some tasks to smaller firms because the smaller firms can perform the work more inexpensively. Also, many large firms are discovering that increasing their size decreases their effectiveness. The accompanying box describes the problem of bigness in the advertising business.

WHY MANY CLIENTS ARE LEAVING MEGA-AGENCIES

In recent years, many large advertising agencies have merged with each other creating mega-agencies with unprecedented total billings. One example was the merger of three major agencies to form the Omnicom Group. Another was the acquisition of Ted Bates Worldwide by the British firm of Saatchi & Saatchi, to create an ad group with annual billings of $7.5 billion.

The judgments of the clients of these huge agencies is that bigger is not necessarily better. A large number of important clients have quit the two supergroups mentioned above. One such advertiser took away $32 million in accounts from Omnicom and $96 million from Saatchi & Saatchi/Ted Bates. The chairman of the advertiser observed that the mergers may help the shareholders and managements of the agencies, but service to the client may not have been improved.

At the time of the mergers, the supergroups boasted that their worldwide scope would help clients reach international markets. However, some clients believe that the increased size of the agencies will create as many drawbacks as benefits. One concern is that creativity will be stifled in such large organizations. Another problem is that different ad agencies in the same group represent competitive companies. Morale can also suffer because of the layoffs that are needed to eliminate redundant jobs resulting from a merger. Another concern is that such a powerful ad agency will change the usual relationship in which the agency is subservient to the client.

As a result of the concerns about the size of the mega-agencies, a number of smaller ad agencies have picked up clients who are shopping for an agency of more traditional size.

Source: Facts derived from Stephen Koepp, "The Not-So-Jolly Advertising Giants," *Time,* Nov. 17, 1986.

High frustration and low job satisfaction.   Untold numbers of people find life in a bureaucracy frustrating and dissatisfying. Among the sources of frustration and dissatisfaction are "red tape," loss of individuality, and inability to make an impact on the organization.

Research evidence has been collected providing additional support to the belief that working in a bureaucracy creates some job dissatisfaction. The subjects were seventy-eight staff employees drawn from six large manufacturing organizations in the Midwest. They represented the areas of accounting, personnel, engineering, architecture, and market research. Among the information collected were measures of the style of organization (bureaucratic, collaborative, coordinative) and job satisfaction. A major finding was that job satisfaction decreased as the bureaucratic properties of the organization increased. According to the authors of the study, "This can be explained by the lack of individual responsibility and control characterizing bureaucratic structures."[5]

Inversion of means and ends.   A major problem associated with bureaucracy is the **inversion of means and ends,** a situation in which the methods for attaining a goal become more important than the goal itself. The inversion typically occurs when rigid adherence to rules or following procedures becomes an end in itself. Under these circumstances, the people involved become more concerned about following or carrying out procedures than accomplishing organizational objectives. Understanding the nature of a means-end inversion will help you develop insight into the potential pitfalls of a bureaucracy. Cost control sometimes results in an inversion of means and ends, as observed in the following case history:

> Top management in one company decided to exert tight controls over the use of photocopying in an effort to save money and therefore increase profits. In order to stay in the good graces of top management, many middle managers went out of their way to minimize their use of photocopying machines. Soon there was an increase in the number of mistakes made in handling customer requests because employees were quite often not sent copies of important information. Also, it was observed that many secretaries were being asked to print several originals of documents on word processors—a much more costly procedure than photocopying. Following the rules of limiting photocopies was the means by which the end of improved profits was supposed to take place. But rigidly following these rules was actually interfering with achieving the objectives of the organization.

Another variation of a means-end inversion occurs when tools become more important than the problems they were intended to solve. Equipping managers with personal computers sometimes results in a peculiar inversion of means and ends. The purpose of managers using personal computers is to improve productivity. However, some managers have become so enamored of the computers that they neglect dealing with their people. As a result, their true productivity as a manager declines.

Insensitivity to individual problems. Since rules in a bureaucracy are applied uniformly, individual circumstances are sometimes ignored. The person whose situation deserves an exception to the rule does not receive a waiver, particularly from lower-level organization officials. Here is an example.

> A woman attempted to purchase two stereo speakers with her consumer credit card. Because of the size of the purchase, a check was made of her available line of credit. The sales associate reported back to the woman, "I'm sorry, our records show that you are not allowed to charge any more merchandise until you pay the amount you have past due." The woman protested that a serious error had been made by the computer. Somehow a charge of $556 was entered for a purchase she had never made. She had already spent one hour on the phone trying to resolve this mistake. The associate said that she knew nothing about the phone conversation; therefore, the woman could not use her credit card to purchase the stereo equipment. Only by demanding to see the store manager did the woman resolve her problem. The store manager checked with the central credit department to finally iron out the problem.

Rigidity in behavior. Literal compliance with rules and regulations results in a rigidity in interpreting policy and carrying out procedures. The sales associate would not listen to the customer's explanation, or even bother to check. Robert Merton offers an explanation of why some bureaucrats are so rigid. The clients the bureaucrat serves become disenchanted because the impersonal treatment given by the bureaucrat doesn't take into account individual problems. Faced with this dissatisfaction, the bureaucrat relies increasingly on rules, routines, and impersonality as defense mechanisms.[6]

Adverse changes in personality. Besides being rigid, the person who works for a long time in a bureaucracy may show **bureaupathic behavior,** a strong need to control others based on insecurity. The need to control leads to an increasing number of rules and a decreased tolerance for deviation from them.

Bureaupathic behavior becomes more pronounced when managers have administrative responsibility over specialists whose work they do not understand. The performance of these specialists directly influences the performance of the manager, intensifying the problem of insecurity. The bureaupathic personality responds to this insecurity by issuing more rules, regulations, and procedures. As the result, organizational effectiveness may not improve, but the manager feels more in control.

As the superior exerts more and more control, conflict between the manager and the employee increases. An unfortunate amount of modeling may also take place. As the employee is controlled from above, he or she becomes more formal in relating to subordinates. Attempts at formalizing the organization eventually reach pathological proportions.[7]

Avoiding responsibility.   A bureaucracy is designed to pinpoint responsibility, yet in practice many people use bureaucratic rules to avoid responsibility.[8] Faced with a decision that he or she does not want to make, the buck-passing official will say, "That's not my job," or "That decision lies outside my sphere of influence," or "I'm afraid you will have to speak to my boss about that problem."

Closely related to avoiding responsibility is the avoidance of innovation so frequently found in a bureaucracy. Rather than risk trying a new procedure, the bureaucratic boss may say, "What you are suggesting violates tradition. Around here we don't do things that way." This was the response a marketing-oriented banker received from his boss when he suggested that the bank hold a "money sale." (It consisted of an advertising campaign offering loan rates lower than the competition.) The young banker whose suggestion was denied became doubly irritated when three months later a competitive bank held a successful money sale.

Weakening of the Connection Between Hard Work and Rewards

Based on extensive interviews with managers, Robert Jackall has written scathing indictments of bureaucracy. Men and women of the corporation, he finds, no longer regard success as necessarily connected to ability, talent, and dedicated effort. Instead, they are convinced that promotion is based on office politics, slick talk, strong connections, and luck. To get ahead, the bureaucrat must concentrate on impressing others, making contacts, and avoiding blame.[9] Furthermore, bureaucracy creates a confusion about moral values in this manner:

> In the bureaucratic world, one's success, one's sign of election, no longer depends on one's own efforts and on an inscrutable God but on the capriciousness of one's superiors and the market; and one achieves economic salvation to the extent that one pleases and submits to one's employer and meets the exigencies of an impersonal market.[10]

ORGANIZATIONAL COPING STRATEGIES

Bureaucracies often create problems for their members and outsiders. Yet it is unreasonable to conclude that bureaucracy does not serve a useful purpose. A more constructive approach to overcoming the problems of a bureaucracy is to make the bureaucracy more adaptable to the demands of a given situation. Five approaches toward this end are (1) use bureaucracy for recurring tasks, (2) use flexible organizational units within the bureaucracy, (3) use flat structures, (4) decentralize decision making, and (5) focus more on people than structures.

Use Bureaucracy for Recurring Tasks

The bureaucratic form of organization is the best structure for organizations dealing with a stable, predictable, relatively homogeneous environment. One such environment would be the processing of social security payments by the federal government. Bureaucracy is noted for its efficiency in handling recurring problems. Rather than create a new policy or rule for each situation, the manager applies a previously prepared rule or policy, and the problem is solved.

Use Flexible Organizational Units

Although a bureaucracy is geared to dealing with a large-scale, repetitive operation, it must also deal with some small-scale, unique problems. Thus if a bureaucracy is to be totally effective, parts of the organization must be more loosely structured. For example, temporary task forces and project teams may be embedded within the larger organization structure. According to the concept of **contingency organization design,** you choose the structure best suited to deal with the problem at hand.

The appropriate organizational structure depends to a large extent on the production technology and the external environment. When the environment and technology are stable and predictable, the traditional pyramidal organization appears to work best. Thus, if you are a production supervisor in a mass production assembly operation, accept the fact that a bureaucracy is best suited to accomplishing the task at hand.

In contrast, where the product is customized and the environment is unpredictable, a loose, nonhierarchical structure appears more appropriate. Should you be assigned to an intelligence operation within the Central Intelligence Agency, your mission would probably be best accomplished by a project or task force organization structure. The ombudsman described in Chapter 6 is another valid example of how a bureaucracy can be made more responsive to the problems of its members.

The skunk works organizational unit described in Chapter 4 is another example of the value of creating small, semi-autonomous units within the larger organization. You may recall that these small units offer two important advantages—they encourage innovation, and they can accomplish results quickly.

Use Flat Structures

A logical alternative to the multilevel bureaucracy is to use flat organization structures, as diagrammed in Figure 15–2. Eliminating several layers of management serves two important ends. First, there is a substantial cost

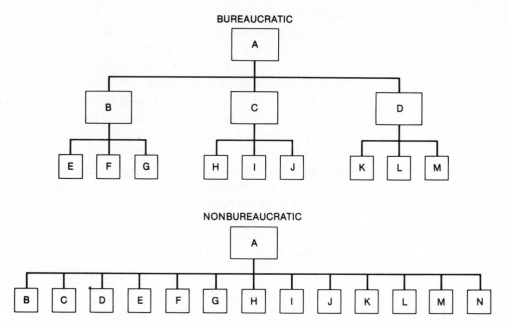

FIGURE 15–2 The Contrast Between a Bureaucratic (Tall) and a Nonbureaucratic (Flat) Organization Structure

Note: This figure represents the contrast between two organizational subunits. A comparison between two total organizations would depict several more layers of management.

savings in running an organization with fewer managers. Second, decisions can be made more quickly because fewer people pass judgment on a given decision. Major corporations that have flattened their organization structure in recent years include Saks Fifth Avenue, Unisys, Digital Equipment Corp., and Chase Manhattan Bank. Small businesses have traditionally used flat structures because they "run lean."

Consultant Tom Peters reports that many firms today have moved toward an organization structure in which the ratio of managers to nonmanagers is 1 to 100 at the bottom of the firm, and 1 to 20 at the top. The traditional number of employees supervised by one manager is about 1 to 15 at the bottom at 1 to 5 at the top of the organization.[11] Peter Drucker predicts that the flattening trend will continue. He estimates that business corporations after the year 2000 will have fewer levels than today. Also, they will have two thirds less managers.[12]

The flattening of organization structures does not mean that most middle managers will be terminated or that fewer business graduates will be hired. Instead of working as middle managers, many of these people will contribute directly to the enterprise through sales, product development, research, and manufacturing. Also, many people who would have worked as middle managers will now work as first-level supervisors. One reason is that the position of first-level manager has grown in stature and responsibility in recent years. Many supervisors now perform some of the work performed by middle managers in the past.

Decentralize Decision Making

Bureaucracies can also be made more efficient by granting more decision-making authority to lower-level managers. In a highly bureaucratic firm, managers at the top of the hierarchy (the executives) make most of the important decisions. Delegating decision-making authority to lower levels offers the same advantage as flat structures. Decisions can be made more quickly because lower-ranking managers do not need so many approvals from higher-ranking managers.

A decentralized organization is more palatable to workers at lower levels because their manager has reasonable decision-making authority. A store manager describes her reaction to the company's shift to decentralized decision making:

> My job is more fun now. If I have an idea for a special promotion, I can get it approved by speaking to only my boss. In the past she needed three levels of approval. Once I had an idea for a Halloween promotion that I suggested in August. By the time I received approval, it was time to get ready for Thanksgiving.

Focus More on People Than Structure

Bureaucracies are sometimes more effective when managers are not so preoccupied with the organization structure. The underlying principle here is that the capabilities of the people are far more important than the specific organization design. A recent analysis suggests that the most successful companies do not meet today's challenges by searching for the ideal structure. Instead, they focus more on developing the abilities, behavior, and performance of individual managers.[13]

Focusing on people rather than structure is relevant here because executives in a bureaucracy put so much effort into making changes in the organization structure. Bureaucracies are characterized by frequent changes in the organization structure, such as regrouping divisions and changing reporting relationships. Included in these shifts, however, are some nonbureaucratic structures, such as projects reporting to top management.

INDIVIDUAL COPING STRATEGIES

Individuals, too, play an important role in coping with the problems sometimes created by a bureaucracy. The most general strategy is for you as a person embedded within a large bureaucracy to understand why the problem exists. For example, many people complain bitterly about the amount of "red tape" in government without recognizing why the problem came into being. Recognition, in turn, often leads to tolerance. A serious study of red tape offers an explanation of its origins in big government: "There are watchdogs who watch watchdogs watching watchdogs. . . . Much of the often-satirized clumsiness, slowness, and complexity of government procedures is merely the consequence of all these precautions."[14]

Here we will offer a number of tactical (and perhaps political) approaches to coping with problems often created by a bureaucracy. The reader is cautioned to select that strategy or strategies that best fits his or her personality and circumstance.

Be persistent. A slow-moving bureaucracy is difficult to rush. If you want your legitimate demand met, repeated requests may be necessary. If you are an outsider to the bureaucratic system, even more persistence and patience may be required. The persistence becomes doubly necessary when you are shunted back and forth among organizational officials:

> After exercising a buy option on a leased car, a man inquired about the return of his security deposit. The local credit manager said corporate headquarters was responsible for returning the money; corporate headquarters said the regional office was responsible; and the regional office said the local dealer was responsible. Three months and eleven phone calls later, the local dealer mailed the distraught customer his check.

The competent person trick. However disorganized and ineffective a large bureaucracy may appear, there is usually a cadre of people at the lower levels who process the work. It is these people who keep track of the important transactions of the firm and who can furnish the information you might need to get your job accomplished. Once you discover one of these competent individuals, write down his or her name and telephone extension.

Exchange favors. Reciprocity is another method commonly used by people who successfully cut their way through red tape. Usually this technique is a follow-up step to having identified a competent person. After he or she provides you the information you need to get your job accomplished, you reciprocate at some later date.

Do not put everything in writing. In a bureaucracy, once something goes into writing, it becomes a permanent record and could be subject to misinterpretation by any one of several people who receive the original or a copy. The person who did you a favor that required bending of a policy is therefore liable for reprimand.

Explain your problem to the right person. A curious aspect about most bureaucratic organizations is that many of the people who listen to your complaints are not empowered to do anything about them. Even if these *organizational buffers* are sympathetic to your problem, the best they can do is represent your point of view to a higher-ranking official. Taking your story to the right person eliminates the frustration of having to repeat your complaint several times.

Explain how your proposition fits into the system.   If your demand or proposition can be tucked under an existing regulation or policy, it has a reasonable chance of being approved. If new policy is necessary in order to accept your proposition, its chances for acceptance are lowered. A case in point was the situation of a plant superintendent who wanted the plant repainted during a period of limited expenditures for refurbishing. He was able to acquire funds for repainting by tying the request into a proposal for reducing energy costs. The white paint he requested would pay for itself in the decreased amount of illumination required in the plant because of the painting.

Explain the problems created by a particular regulation.   One logical approach to overcoming red tape is to confront the responsible official with the problems created by an unreasonable rule or regulation. The responsible official may be lacking a firsthand report of the way in which a particular directive is creating a dysfunction. One national field service manager was faced with the problem of high turnover among field engineers. Basically the job of field engineer consisted of repairing broken equipment under tight time constraints. An informal survey by the manager revealed that the field engineers were quitting because they were looking for promotion to managerial positions. The national service manager then requested that the "college graduate only" regulation be removed from the hiring standards.

The manager reasoned that field engineers who graduated from technical institutes would be less concerned about promotion to managerial positions. They would therefore remain longer in field engineering assignments. Confronted with the negative implications of the regulation about hiring only college graduates, the president said to the national service manager:

> It looks like we goofed on that one. You're the national service manager. Make up your own qualification list for field engineers. But don't overcompensate in the process by giving anybody who likes to tinker with mechanical equipment a job as a field engineer in our company.

Summary of Key Points

- In its technical meaning, bureaucracy refers to a form of organization in which the division of effort, rank, and rules and regulations are carefully defined. Ultimate control of the organization rests at the top of the organization. At its best, a bureaucracy is a rational, systematic, and precise form of organization.

- A bureaucracy is designed for maximum efficiency. Among its characteristics are (1) a division of labor based on functional specialization, (2) a well-defined hierarchy of authority, (3) a system of rules covering the rights and duties of employees, (4) procedures for dealing with work situations, (5) impersonality in handling people, (6) promotion and selection based on technical competence.

- A bureaucracy offers many potential advantages: (1) machinelike efficiency, (2) personally given orders become unnecessary, (3) repetition of orders is unnecessary, (4) control of people from a distance, (5) punishment becomes legitimate, (6) equitable division of resources, and (7) promotion of democracy in the workplace.

- A bureaucracy also has some potential disadvantages: (1) delays in decision making, (2) confusion and inefficiency, (3) high frustration and low job satisfaction, (4) inversion of means and ends, (5) insensitivity to individual problems, (6) rigidity in behavior, (7) adverse changes in personality, (8) avoiding responsibility, and (9) weakening of the connection between hard work and rewards.

- Five organizational strategies for coping with problems created by bureaucracy are (1) use bureaucracy for recurring tasks, (2) use flexible organizational units, (3) use flat structures, (4) decentralize decision making, and (5) focus more on people than structures.

- You can better cope with a bureaucracy if you understand why certain forms of red tape exist. In addition, be persistent, use the competent person trick, exchange favors, do not put everything in writing, explain your problem to the right person, explain how your proposition fits into the system, explain the problems created by a particular regulation.

Questions and Activities

1. What connotation does the term "bureaucrat" have for most people?
2. Is your local Pizza Hut a bureaucracy? Use the characteristics of a bureaucracy described in this chapter to help you develop your answer.
3. Why are so many people quite content to work in a bureaucracy?
4. Many small business owners contend that they dislike bureaucracy. Nevertheless, these same people prefer large bureaucratic firms as customers. How do you reconcile these two points of view?
5. A small service firm in New York City, called "The Red Tape Cutters," specializes in running errands for people. What appears to be the logic behind the name of this firm?
6. Bureaucracies are characterized by an abundance of meetings. What factors do you think contribute to this preference for so many meetings?
7. How might the decentralization of decision making contribute to the development of managers?
8. It has been observed that once an organization prospers and then stabilizes in growth, it inevitably becomes a bureaucracy. Why might this be true?
9. How do the individual coping strategies relate to organizational politics?
10. Ask an employee of a large bureaucracy, such as the U.S. Postal Service or Citibank, his or her perception of the advantages and disadvantages of a bureaucracy. Be prepared to discuss your findings in class.

A HUMAN RELATIONS CASE PROBLEM
The Remaking of Bart (Bay Area Rapid Transit)

BART's new management team says that the transit agency is overburdened with bureaucracy. Management has found that many employees avoid making decisions, and some are rewarded just for showing up at work. John Haley, deputy general manager, says that the agency is so crippled by feuding between employees and layers of authority that basic tasks, such as cleaning a station, are left undone.

Employees spend more time either avoiding a decision or trying to defer it to another official than it would take to do the job, said Haley. As a result, BART suffers from stagnation.

"I don't think it is unreasonable that part of the problem is to get people to treat one another in a civil fashion and to understand the other person's point of view," Haley comments.

He sees the only solution as a complete restructuring of the agency, as well as the instillation of new work habits in employees. Managers would be sent to weekend retreats to discuss their jobs, goals, and gripes. As Haley sees it, the problem is not lazy employees but a burdensome structure that stifles the workers and makes it easier to do nothing than to take action.

Haley blames the problem on a vague management structure used for ten years by the former general manager. The structure encouraged employees to buck decisions to managers at higher levels. Haley believes that employees are not accustomed to making decisions. In the past they had no stake or ownership in what was going on, or they had only a minimal stake in making sure that something was done properly.

As a result of these problems, the correct number of railcars sometimes does not go out for the morning commute. Also, after a minor accident, no one wants to assume responsibility for ordering a routine drug test.

Haley said that with the reorganization, employees will be rewarded for good job performance, taking risks, and making decisions. But first, they will need to be taught new skills.

"We are in the business of providing transportation. Yet some employees get so hung up with planning for the sake of planning or budgeting for the sake of budgeting that they don't relate to what's happening," concludes Haley.

1. Evaluate Haley's plan for overcoming problems created by the BART bureaucracy.
2. What additional suggestions can you offer for overcoming the problems facing BART?
3. What evidence can you find of an inversion of means and ends taking place in the agency?

Source: As reported in Harre W. Demoro, "BART Says It Must Make Itself Over," *San Francisco Chronicle,* Aug. 15, 1990, p. A6.

A HUMAN RELATIONS CASE PROBLEM
The Intractable Savings Bank

Carla Mendez, the owner of budget printing center, began to earn a profit two years after setting up shop. She then took the initiative to establish a Keogh Plan (a retirement plan for the self-employed). Carla's plan was established at a local savings bank. The Keogh Plan she chose allowed the investor to make deposits of any size, and at any time during the year.

Each month Carla would make deposits into her plan of anywhere from $50 to $275. Once her taxes were filed, Carla would know precisely how much she could pay into her plan, since a Keogh Plan owner can contribute up to 15 percent of net profits to the plan annually. Each time a Keogh Plan owner makes a deposit into his or her account, the contributor is assigned a new account number. Over the first five years of the plan, Carla made fifty-one deposits and received fifty-one account numbers.

Carla then relocated to new headquarters a few blocks away from her original location. She filed all the necessary address changes, including notifying the savings bank. Mysteriously, the bank continued to send most—but not all—of its correspondence to Carla's old address. Carla filed another address change with the bank, but the problem persisted. Irritated, Carla called the savings bank and was given this explanation of what happened:

"According to our regulations, each account requires a separate change of address. We send out correspondence based on individual account numbers. So far you have only notified us of an address change for one account number. If you want all your mail going to your new address, you will have to file fifty-one change of address notices—one for each account. I'm sorry, but these are our regulations."

1. In what way is the bank behaving bureaucratically?
2. How could one defend the bank's position?
3. How should Carla handle this situation?
4. If you were Carla, would you file fifty-one change of address notices?

A HUMAN RELATIONS EXERCISE
Do You Have A Bureaucratic Orientation?

A person with a bureaucratic orientation is one who fits comfortably into the role of working in a bureaucracy. Unless the world were populated with people who adjust readily to working for a bureaucracy, organizations such as AT&T or the Ford Motor Co. could not function. Other people—those with a low bureaucratic orientation—experience feelings of discomfort working for a bureaucracy. The bureaucratic orientation scale presented next gives you a chance to acquire tentative (not scientifically proved) information about your position on this important aspect of work life.

Directions: Answer each question "mostly agree" or "mostly disagree." Assume that you are trying to learn something about yourself. Do not assume that your answer will be shown to a prospective employer.

		MOSTLY AGREE	MOSTLY DISAGREE
1.	I value stability in my job.	_____	_____
2.	I like a predictable organization.	_____	_____
3.	The best job for me would be one in which the future is uncertain.	_____	_____
4.	The military would be a nice place to work.	_____	_____
5.	Rules, policies, and procedures tend to frustrate me.	_____	_____
6.	I would enjoy working for a company that employed 85,000 people worldwide.	_____	_____
7.	Being self-employed would involve more risk than I'm willing to take.	_____	_____
8.	Before accepting a job, I would like to see an exact job description.	_____	_____
9.	I would prefer a job as a freelance house painter to one as a clerk for the Department of Motor Vehicles.	_____	_____
10.	Seniority should be as important as performance in determining pay increases and promotion.	_____	_____
11.	It would give me a feeling of pride to work for the largest and most successful company in its field.	_____	_____
12.	Given a choice, I would prefer to make $70,000 per year as a vice president in a small company to $80,000 as a staff specialist in a large company.	_____	_____

	MOSTLY AGREE	MOSTLY DISAGREE
13. I would regard wearing an employee badge with a number on it as a degrading experience.	_____	_____
14. Parking spaces in a company lot should be assigned on the basis of job level.	_____	_____
15. I would generally prefer working as a specialist to wearing many hats.	_____	_____
16. Before accepting a job (given a choice), I would want to make sure that the company had a good program of employee benefits.	_____	_____
17. A company will probably not be successful unless it establishes a clear set of rules and regulations.	_____	_____
18. Regular working hours and vacations are more important to me than finding thrills on the job.	_____	_____
19. You should respect people according to their rank.	_____	_____
20 Rules are meant to be broken.	_____	_____

Scoring and interpretation. Give yourself a plus one for each question that you answered in the bureaucratic direction:

1. Mostly agree	8. Mostly agree	15. Mostly disagree
2. Mostly agree	9. Mostly disagree	16. Mostly agree
3. Mostly disagree	10. Mostly agree	17. Mostly agree
4. Mostly agree	11. Mostly agree	18. Mostly agree
5. Mostly disagree	12. Mostly disagree	19. Mostly agree
6. Mostly agree	13. Mostly disagree	20. Mostly disagree
7. Mostly agree	14. Mostly agree	

Although the bureaucratic orientation scale is currently a self-examination and research tool, a very high score (15 or over) would suggest that you would enjoy working in a bureaucracy. A very low score (5 or lower) would suggest that you would be frustrated by working in a bureaucracy, especially a large one.

Notes

1. Richard W. Weiss, "Weber on Bureaucracy: Management Consultant or Political Theorist?" *Academy of Management Review,* April 1983, p. 243.

2. Elliott Jaques, "In Praise of Hierarchy," *Harvard Business Review,* January–February 1990, p. 127.

3. Max Weber, *Essays in Sociology,* quoted in Gary Dessler, *Organization and Management* (Englewood Cliffs, NJ: Prentice Hall, 1976), p. 31.

4. Michael J. Wriston, "In Defense of Bureaucracy," *Public Administration Review,* March–April 1980, p. 179.

5. Nicholas Dimarco and Steven Norton, "Life Style, Organization Structure, Congruity, and Job Satisfaction," *Personnel Psychology,* Winter 1974, pp. 581–91.

6. Robert K. Merton, "Bureaucratic Structure and Personality," *Social Forces,* vol. 18, 1940.

7. Christopher W. Allinson, *Bureaucratic Personality and Organization Structure* (Brookfield, VT: Gower, 1984).

8. B. J. Hodge and William P. Anthony, *Organization Theory: An Environmental Approach* (Boston: Allyn & Bacon, 1979), p. 435.

9. Robert Jackall, *Moral Mazes: The World of Corporate Managers* (New York: Oxford University Press, 1988).

10. Robert Jackall, "Moral Mazes: Bureaucracy and Managerial Work," *Harvard Business Review,* September–October 1983, p. 130.

11. The Tom Peters Group, *A World Turned Upside Down* (Palo Alto, CA: Excel, 1986), p. 16.

12. Peter F. Drucker, "The Coming of the New Organization," *Harvard Business Review,* January–February 1988, p. 45.

13. Christopher A. Bartlett and Sumantra Ghoshal, "Matrix Management: Not a Structure, a Frame of Mind," *Harvard Business Review,* July–August 1990, p. 145.

14. Herbert Kaufman, *Red Tape: Its Origins, Uses, and Abuses* (Washington, DC: The Brookings Institution, 1977).

Suggested Reading

FAZIO, ROBERT A. "Beyond Bureaucracy: Riding the New Wave in HR." *Personnel,* February 1988, pp. 28–35.

FISCH, FRANK, and SIRIANNI, CARMEN, eds. *Critical Studies in Organization and Bureaucracy.* Philadelphia: Temple University Press, 1984.

GREENBERG, ERIC ROLFE. "The 1989 AMA Survey on Downsizing." *Personnel,* October 1989, pp. 38–44.

HUMMEL, RALPH P. *The Bureaucratic Experience,* 3rd ed. New York: St. Martin's Press, 1987.

MINTZBERG, HENRY. *Mintzberg on Management: Inside Our Strange World of Organizations* (New York: Free Press, 1989).

NELSON, GARY L. "Restructure for Excellence: The Secret in Downsizing." *Management Review,* February 1990, pp. 44–47.

PITURRO, MARLENE C. "Decentralization— Rebuilding the Corporation." *Management Review,* August 1988, pp. 31–34.

TRACEY, WILLIAM R. "Deft Delegation: Multiplying Your Effectiveness." *Personnel,* February 1988, pp. 36–42.

16

Organizational Culture and Change

LEARNING OBJECTIVES

After reading and studying this chapter and doing the exercises, you should be able to

1. Describe the meaning and key dimensions of organizational culture.
2. Describe how organizational cultures are formed.
3. Specify the consequences and implications of organizational culture.
4. Explain the attributes and limitations of Japanese human resources management.
5. Describe the key elements of managing resistance to change.
6. Describe how organization development attempts to bring about changes in the organizational culture.

S o far our study of organizations has focused on the nature of effective organizations and dealing with a bureaucracy. In this chapter we explore two related major topics, organizational culture (or character), and bringing about constructive change. Both organizational culture and change have a direct bearing on organizational effectiveness. Healthy organizations have positive cultures, and methods of bringing about change are used to increase organizational effectiveness.

ORGANIZATIONAL CULTURE

Many top executives perceive organizational culture as the force behind success. When the chairman and chief executive of Corning was reorganizing the company, he said that he was aiming for a complete change in the corporate culture. He aimed for "a leaner, stronger company that seeks the ideas of workers as well as managers and gives women and minorities a more prominent role."[1]

Because culture has become so important, it has been defined in many ways, as shown in Figure 16–1. Despite these variations in meaning, the definition of culture presented in relation to work motivation encompasses most meanings of the term: **Organizational** (or **corporate**) **culture** is a system of shared values and beliefs that actively influence the behavior of organizational members. Our description of culture centers around its dimensions, formation, and consequences.

1. Unspoken rules and assumptions that determine how the organization operates and what it is like.
2. Norms by which the organization operates.
3. The character of an organization.
4. The soul of an organization.
5. The sum total of an organization's beliefs, values, philosophies, traditions, and sacred cows.
6. A subtle and complex set of unwritten rules and matter-of-fact prejudices; a value system.
7. The customary or traditional ways of thinking and doing things, which are shared to a greater or lesser extent by all members of the organization and which new members must learn and at least partially accept in order to be accepted in the service of the firm.

FIGURE 16–1 Representative Definitions of Organizational Culture

Source: The first six definitions reflect current thinking about organizational culture. The seventh definition is from Elliott Jaques, *The Changing Culture of a Factory* (London: Tavistock Institute, 1951), p. 251.

Dimensions of Organizational Culture

Pinpointing the dimensions of culture is important because it helps explain the nature of the subtle forces that influence every employee's actions. For instance, the dimension of risk taking will encourage employees to try new procedures without undue concern that they will be punished for failed ideas. Many of these dimensions are interrelated. To illustrate, a firm with a steep hierarchy is also likely to have many rites and rituals, such as formal management meetings.

Values. Values are the foundation of any organizational or corporate culture. The organization's philosophy is expressed through values, and values guide behavior on a day-to-day basis. Representative values include concern for employee welfare, a belief that the customer is always right, a commitment to quality, and an enduring desire to please stockholders. A manager whose firm's strongest value was to please stockholders would be willing to lay off employees in order to increase short-range profits.

Heroes and heroines. Corporate heroes and heroines are the people who introduce innovations, who "make waves," inspire others, and have a vision of the future of the firm. Terrence Deal and Allan Kennedy draw a contrast between heroes and heroines and the managers who are more disciplined and take care of the status quo.[2] Among the terms used to identify heroes and heroines are "crown princes and princesses," "comers," and "fast trackers." In some firms these people are given special opportunities for good assignments and special training. At AT&T Communications, for example, heroes and heroines make up the Manager Succession Group.

Rites and rituals. Part of an organization's culture is its traditions, its rites and rituals. Few organizations think they have rites and rituals, yet an astute observer can always identify them. Examples include regular staff meetings, retirement banquets (even for fired executives), and receptions for visiting executives. More details about organizational rites are presented in Figure 16–2. Do you see most of these rites as serving a useful purpose?

Cultural networks. Cultural networks function as grapevines for telling stories that communicate organizational norms. The networks are indispensable for maintaining a culture, because cultural values, beliefs, and practices, are unwritten. A story that circulates throughout Domino's Pizza concerns how pizza dough was flown into a branch location that was running short. The message is that customer satisfaction is so important the company will spend huge sums of money to avert dissatisfaction, even for one night. (Note that stories told through the cultural networks can be real or imagined. The Domino's story is true.)

Type of rites	Examples
Rites of passage	Induction and basic training in army
Rites of degradation	Firing and replacing top executive
Rites of enhancement	Mary Kay seminars (for sales reps of beauty products)
Rites of renewal	Organizational development activities (see later in this chapter)
Rites of conflict reduction	Collective bargaining
Rites of integration	Office holiday party

Figure 16–2 Organizational Rites

Source: Adapted with permission from Harrison M. Trice and Janice M. Beyer, "Studying Organizational Cultures Through Rules and Ceremonials," *The Academy of Management Review,* October 1984, p. 657.

Relative diversity. The existence of an organizational culture assumes some degree of homogeneity. Nevertheless, organizations differ on how much deviation from conformity they tolerate. Many firms are highly homogeneous: Executives talk in a similar manner and even look alike; people from similar educational backgrounds and fields of specialty are promoted into key jobs. Many conglomerates, for example, promote only managers with financial backgrounds into key positions. Here is a representative example of a cultural value against diversity:

> After moving into several floors of a New York City office building, the chief executive officer (CEO) had an assistant make regular tours of all offices. There had been a corporate "decorating" plan dictating the number and style of wall decorations, placement as well as style of furniture, and a clear rule that nothing was to be left out on horizontal surfaces at the end of the work day. Violators spotted by the presidential assistant received sharply worded reprimands from the president.[3]

Resource allocation and rewards. How money and other resources are allocated has a critical influence on culture. The investment of resources sends a message to people about what is valued in the firm. Assume the head of a government agency contends that client service must be improved. If new budget allocations are made to support programs for improved service, employees will believe that client service is important. Conversely, if no new resources are allocated, employees will believe that talk about improved client services is only rhetoric.

The status system of the organization is also shaped by decisions about resource allocation. Increasing an organizational unit's budget and providing it with new office space increases the unit's status. Conversely, receiving a substantial budget cut results in a loss in status. Being moved to a lesser office has a similar effect.

Steepness of the hierarchy. The culture of some organizations is very hierarchical (bureaucratic). Such a culture is maintained by heavy emphasis on formal, written memos; going through channels; and the discouragement of informal contacts. Bypassing a layer of management is taboo, and few people have contact with the CEO except for immediate subordinates. Another cultural feature of a steep hierarchy is that senior managers rarely visit the work sites. In a flatter organization, top managers regularly visit the offices, factories, and stores (operations).

Degree of stability. A fast-paced, dynamic organization has a different culture and climate from a slow-paced, stable one. Top management sends out signals, by its own energetic or lethargic stance, about how much it welcomes innovation. "Change-oriented organizations have a distinctive tempo; everything moves faster and more deliberately, in contrast to the slow-paced beat to which stability-oriented organizations march.[4]

Administrative practices. A final dimension of culture to be considered here are the various administrative practices of key functional groups, such as finance, accounting, or production. One example is how much emphasis the firm has traditionally placed on reaching financial targets. For instance, if the firm values ever-increasing yearly profits, it may be difficult to invest heavily in modernization of equipment and facilities. Administrative practices that emphasize financial performance may also discourage managers from investing too much time and money in the development of personnel. This situation is similar to a basketball coach not giving lesser players much playing time in order to maximize winning margins.

The dimensions described here can lead to an understanding of the culture of a given organization. Simultaneously, they hint at how organizational cultures are formed.

The Formation of Organizational Cultures

An organization's culture typically has its origins in the values, administrative practices, and personality of the founding executives. In many practices, a charismatic founder shapes the culture of the organization. A prime example is Thomas Watson of IBM, who originated the values of going to great lengths to please customers, and insisted that employees observe rules carefully. Culture responds to and mirrors the conscious and unconscious choices, behavior patterns, and prejudices of top management. Furthermore, top managers are not the victims, but the architects of the organizational climate.[5]

Another major way in which cultures are established is through **socialization,** how employees come to understand the values, norms, and customs essential for adapting to the organization.[6] Socialization is therefore a method of indoctrinating employees into the organization in such a way that they perpetuate the culture. If new employees were not socialized, the culture would lose its distinctiveness. Socialization continues throughout an employee's stay with the firm, for there are constant subtle reminders of which behaviors and values are appropriate.

The socialization process is carried out formally and informally. Larger firms are more likely to have a formal socialization process that includes training and orientation programs. A well-known investment firm, for example, sends its new financial consultants to a six-week training program in New York City. Aside from intensive training to prepare for a broker's license, the recruits are familiarized with the beliefs and values of the firm. Trainees are given tips on dress codes, professional appearance and behavior, and ethical client behavior. Directors of the program are encouraged to help weed out those men and women who show resistance to these norms.

Informal socialization take such forms as listening to more experienced workers, and observing what others are doing and saying. New employees are often not consciously aware that they are being socialized. Yet they gradually incorporate key aspects of the culture into their behavior and speech. One example is the new employees hired by a U.S. Navy support group. Several months after joining, the employees will pepper their speech with the question, "How does this support the fleet?" The value they are expressing is that everything one does in this organization should ultimately help the sailors at sea.

Stephen P. Robbins notes that a formal socialization process is more controllable; there is a higher probability that the culture will be perpetuated in the desired way. The informal socialization process is dependent upon whom the new employee uses as a socializing agent.[7] Some employees subscribe more to the culture than do others.

After the corporate culture is formed, it resists change. Nevertheless, under unusual circumstances cultures do change. The Apple Computer experience described in the accompanying box is one such unusual experience.

CULTURAL SHIFT AT APPLE COMPUTER INC.

Apple Computer Inc.'s headquarters is normally a hotbed of giddy enthusiasm and evangelical zeal. Much of the company's past success has been attributed to its free-spirited, risk-taking, and sometimes hokey enthusiasm, which the upbeat Apple culture has shown through its marketing campaigns, product development, and customer relations. Now many employees are worried that Apple is losing its prized corporate culture.

Disillusioned employees are wondering whether the belt-tightening and increased emphasis on discipline will so seriously hurt the quirky culture that it cannot be revived. "The culture is changing, and I'm not sure it is altogether for the better," says a six-year employee.

Apple executives acknowledge that attempting to impose more structure on the company is risky. What the company needs to acquire, says the human resources director, is more financial discipline and personal accounta-bility. The challenge is to add the discipline with-out losing the company's essence—passion, openness, and value of the individual.

Over the years, the company's devotion to changing the world with computers turned into a heady atmosphere. Annual meetings took the form of rock concerts with pulsating music, glitzy product introductions, and syrupy market-ing slogans. At company headquarters, employ-ees are treated to a fitness center, Friday afternoon beer busts, and parties with celebrity entertainers. Even low-level employees could seek support for their ideas without ever having received official direction from their boss.

In the past, rank-and-file employees were given special treatment, such as massages to re-lieve stress. Now recently hired top executives

are receiving huge perks. Disillusionment spread throughout the ranks when two facts were dis-closed. A new chief financial officer received a signing bonus of $1.5 million, and other execu-tives received severance packages of up to $2.1 million.

"It's not clear that everyone feels that we're working for the same organization," says one em-ployee. Says another, "There is more of a division than there ever was before between management and the rank and file." Many employees resented lower-level cutbacks in the workforce when the company showed a 6 percent sales growth in a re-cent quarter.

Source: As reported in Evelyn Richards, "Apple May Be Los-ing Its Cultural Core," *Washington Post* syndicated story, Feb. 26, 1990.

Consequences and Implications of Organizational Culture

Organizational culture has received much attention because it has a pervasive impact on organizational effectiveness. The major consequences and implications of organization culture are outlined in Figure 16–3 and summarized following.

Productivity and Morale

A major justification for studying, or trying to change, an organiza-tion's culture is that it influences the level of productivity and morale.[8] A culture that emphasizes productivity encourages workers to be productive, and a culture that values the dignity of human beings tends to foster high morale and job satisfaction. Conversely, a culture that encourages medio-cre performance leads to low productivity, and a culture that has no real commitment to the welfare of employees is beset with problems of low morale and low job satisfaction.

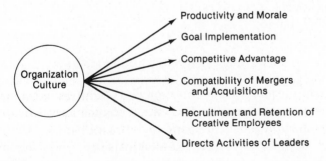

FIGURE 16–3 Consequences and Implications of Organizational Culture

Implementation of Organizational Goals

Many firms have found that they can devise new strategies that make sense from a marketing or financial viewpoint. Yet often they cannot implement those strategies because they require changes in values and beliefs that differ from the culture. One company could not implement the goal of selling to a less sophisticated market because the salespeople unconsciously looked down upon these new potential customers.[9]

Competitive Advantage

An example of a valuable culture is one that contains the eight characteristics of a successful organization cited by Peters and Waterman (see Chapter 14). A rare culture is one that is statistically infrequent, such as a firm in which employees volunteer to take a pay cut when business is poor. A unique or special culture is important, because it prevents other firms from becoming directly competitive. One of the many reasons such a culture may be difficult to imitate is that it has developed over a long period of time.[10]

Compatibility in mergers and acquisitions

Approximately 60 percent of corporate mergers and acquisitions lead to poor results—the performance of the combined partners often decreases. The major reason for these failed mergers is incompatibility between the cultures of the merged firms.[11] Correspondingly, a reliable predictor of success when contemplating a merger of two or more firms is the compatibility of their respective cultures. Great American Bank found this to be true, based on their experience with sixteen acquisitions. Specifically, Great American found that their most effective mergers took place between companies with values, ethical standards, and ways of conducting business that meshed with its own.[12]

Recruitment and Retention of Creative Employees

Creative employees prefer a corporate culture that encourages risk taking and latitude in how assignments are carried out. When a culture conducive to creativity is lacking, it may be difficult to recruit and retain creative employees. Do you recall the comments about "quirky culture" that used to be characteristics of Apple Computer Inc.?

Directing Leaders' Activities

Yet another important consequence of culture is that it directs the activities of organizational leaders. Much of a leader's time is spent working with the subtle forces that shape the attitudes and values of organization members. Schein states that leadership is the ability to manage culture.

However, this is a complex and confusing role, because culture determines such things as how the internal system of authority and work is organized.[13]

JAPANESE-STYLE MANAGEMENT AND ORGANIZATION CULTURE

The culture characteristics of large, successful Japanese firms have been of interest to other countries in recent years. The interest in the Japanese style of human resources management (and its corresponding culture) is attributed to the high levels of productivity and quality achieved by many Japanese firms. Here we describe the Japanese style of human resources management, along with an evaluation of its strengths and weaknesses.

The Japanese-Style Human Resources Management

The essence of Japanese management, and its corresponding organization culture, is a focus on human resources development. The focus on human resources is expressed in three interrelated strategies, and six techniques, as diagrammed in Figure 16–4. A major reason for this emphasis on human resources development is that Japan is limited in natural resources, such as oil, coal, and land.

Focus and general strategies. If a firm truly focuses on the development of its human resources, the other components of the model shown in Figure 16–4 fall into place. The human resources focus leads to three general strategies.

Develop an internal labor market. A policy in large Japanese companies is that when a male employee is hired after graduation from high school or college, an effort should be made to retain him for his entire working career. In contrast, the female workforce is temporary. Using women part-time workers and subcontractors helps Japanese firms adjust to changing business conditions while at the same time claiming to have a full-employment policy. Another method Japanese firms use to minimize job hopping is to underpay workers at early stages of their careers, relative to what they contribute. Later in their careers they are somewhat overpaid: The wages of high-seniority employees may exceed the pay of new employees by 200 to 400 percent. Highly paid senior workers are rarely hired by other firms.

Articulate a unique company philosophy. Many chief executives of large Japanese firms have written manuals and books expressing their philosophy of work and management. The firm is often depicted as a family with a unique character. *Wa* (harmony) is the norm of family life most frequently articulated, to the point that some observers believe that *wa* is the distinguishing characteristic of Japanese firms.

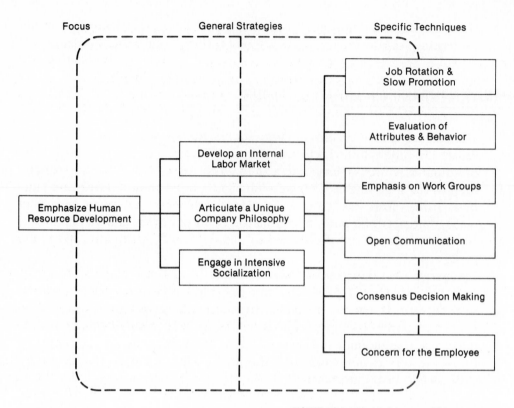

FIGURE 16-4 A Model of Japanese Management

Source: Adapted from Nina Hatvany and Vladimir Pucik, "An Integrated Management System: Lessons from the Japanese Experience," *Academy of Management Review,* July 1981, p. 470.

The commitment of the corporate family to the employee is expressed in policies of avoiding layoffs and providing ample employee benefits. Without this reasonable employment security, it would be almost impossible to foster the spirit of cooperation and teamwork known as *wa.*

Engage in intensive socialization.   Japanese personnel policies are geared toward developing a cohesive workforce. A major reason for bringing recent graduates into the firm is that they can be readily assimilated into the firm's unique environment—they can be more readily socialized the way the company prefers. To be hired, the young person must display moderate views and a harmonious personality. Job competence is obviously important. Nevertheless, applicants may be eliminated during the selection process if they arouse suspicion that they cannot get along with people, possess radical views, or come from an unfavorable home environment. After a while each employee is expected to assume the identity of a "company person." The employee's occupational specialty or professional identification is much less important. The socialization process begins during orientation, as illustrated at a Japanese bank.

Mitsubishi Trust and Banking Co. hands its new employees a brief list of "do's and don'ts" to get them started on the right foot. It warns them to respond with a quick "yes" when a superior calls them, and to stand up immediately to receive instructions; never to scratch their legs or arms in front of customers or superiors; never to smoke while talking with a superior; and never to criticize the company or its management.[14]

Techniques

Job rotation and slow promotion. Under a strategy of lifetime employment, employees must learn to accept relatively slow promotion unless an organization is expanding dramatically. Since unplanned job vacancies occur rarely, job rotation plays a major role in career development. Carefully planned lateral transfers also add substantial flexibility to job reward and recognition.

Flexibility in promotion is also enhanced by a dual promotion ladder. Promotion in status is based on past performance appraisals and seniority within the firm. Promotion in position depends on past appraisals and vacancies in the level above. A person can be given a status promotion and receive a salary increase, along with more respect.

Evaluation of attributes and behavior. In the Japanese organizational culture, employees are not made to feel that productivity is the main factor in evaluating performance. Japanese managers reason that such outputs may be beyond the control of the worker. Instead, the evaluation criteria include performance measures and desirable personality traits and behaviors, such as creativity, loyalty, and cooperation. It is also reasoned that the right traits and behaviors will ultimately contribute to productivity.

Although work-group harmony is valued, employees are appraised in comparison to each other. A somewhat counteracting force is that group performance is used as a criterion of individual performance. Peer pressure is therefore exerted on the individual to contribute to group performance. It might help your performance appraisal if somebody performs more poorly than yourself, but you still need that employee's help to achieve decent group performance.

Emphasis on work groups. Harmonious work groups are critical to the success of a Japanese firm, as they are to firms almost anywhere. Japanese companies create policies that foster strong work groups. Quality circles are a prime example of this emphasis. Typically, tasks are assigned to groups rather than to individuals. This, along with job rotation and feedback on group performance, encourages group cohesion.

Open communication. Extensive face-to-face communication takes place in Japanese companies. It is encouraged by the emphasis on team spirit in work groups and the friendships that employees develop during their long stay with the firm. Open communication is also built into the physical

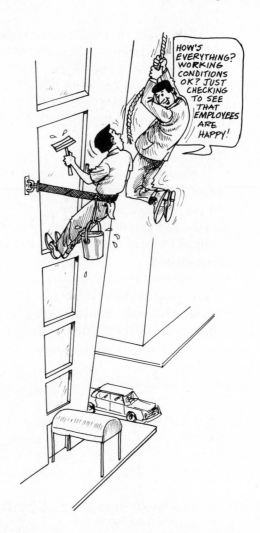

setup of the Japanese firm. Work spaces are open and crowded with employees at different levels in the hierarchy. Workers at all levels are aware of what others are doing, and even executives rarely have private offices.

A well-publicized feature of the open communication in Japanese firms is "management by wandering around." Japanese executives regularly circulate among and converse with employees on the shop floor and in the production yard. Middle managers are also expected to interact with employees and help out with the manufacturing process.[15]

Consensus decision making.   In Japanese firms, subordinates participate in all decisions that they will be responsible for implementing. The extent of participation varies somewhat, as it does in American firms. Many firms appear to use consensus decision making, in which everybody involved in a decision places a personal stamp of approval *(hanko)* on the decision. In other firms, management consults with employees before making a final decision, but personal approvals are not necessarily sought.

An important point is that ratification of the decision does not indicate unanimous approval, but it does imply a willingness to implement the decision. Thus, whether a specific Japanese firm uses a participative or consultative decision-making style, the result is a decision that subordinates stand willing to implement. Managers in Japanese firms spend many hours after 5:00 P.M. interacting with co-workers in order to build consensus.

Concern for the employee. The Japanese firm expresses concern for the employee in a number of formal and informal ways. Formal expressions of concern include the sponsoring of various cultural, athletic, and other recreational activities, resulting in a busy schedule of company social affairs. Among the formal benefits are family allowances, employee housing (dormitories), and company scholarships for employees' children. One informal expression of concern for employees is the great deal of time spent talking to them about everyday matters. Another expression of concern is an attempt to build a good relationship with each subordinate.

Evaluation of Japanese Management and Organizational Culture

The Japanese style of management and organizational culture has achieved an enviable track record. Japanese firms have met with considerable success in worldwide competition, and Japanese-owned firms in the United States have generally been quite successful. Nevertheless, many myths surround the success of Japanese human resources management practices. Here we attempt a balanced evaluation of the strengths and weaknesses of Japanese-style management and organizational culture.[16]

1. *The Japanese system has been able to produce high-quality products.* Many Japanese products are world leaders in quality, and Japanese companies are recognized as producing higher-quality automobiles and consumer electronic products than American companies have. However, when automobile safety is considered part of quality, Japanese cars do not fare better than those produced by other countries.

2. *Although the Japanese organizational culture reflects concern for some workers, many others are treated harshly.* Japanese companies, both in Japan and overseas, tend to exclude all but Japanese males from good job opportunities. Yet an increasing number of women are being promoted to management jobs. Middle managers in Japanese firms often work sixty to eighty hours per week for relatively low pay. A recent grave concern is that many Japanese managers and professionals are victims of *karoshi,* or death from overwork. A recent Health Ministry report called *karoshi* the second leading cause of death (after cancer) among Japanese workers.[17]

3. *Japanese productivity per worker does not exceed that of Americans.* American productivity per worker still exceeds that of Japanese

workers, yet Japanese workers have made impressive gains in recent years. Over the last decade, Korean workers showed higher productivity increases than either Japanese or Americans. The Japanese organizational culture has therefore not catapulted its workers into the highest productivity levels.

4.   *Japanese workers are neither more satisfied nor more committed than American workers.* A study compared Japanese, Korean, and American workers in diverse organizations. The conclusion reached was that Japanese and Korean employees are actually less committed to their organization than are U.S. employees. Another studied compared five Japanese electronic companies with the Western Electric Co. The quit rate for the Japanese companies was higher than for Western Electric.

5.   *The vast majority of Japanese workers are not offered lifetime employment.* Less than 30 percent of Japanese workers are guaranteed lifetime employment, and these are employees of large corporations. Layoffs of large numbers of employees have become more frequent in Japan, such as Nippon Steel eliminating 19,000 jobs.

6.   *Japanese workers receive better orientation and training than do their American counterparts.* Part of the Japanese organizational culture and management style is to invest heavily in orientation and training. For example, new hires typically spend about three months in orientation, vs. three days for American workers.

7.   *Japanese companies make more effective use of human resources management techniques, such as quality circles, consensus decision making, and cooperative union relationships.* The Japanese culture more readily adapts itself to democratic processes, such as quality circles and consensus decision making. The adversarial approach to union-management relations so characteristic *previously* in the United States is uncommon in Japan. Faced with increasing international competition, the United States is now moving closer to the Japanese model of labor relations.

Richard M. Hodgetts and Fred Luthans note that the Japanese business successes can in general be attributed to (1) better ability to apply technology, (2) greater commitment to orientation and training, and (3) better use of modern human resources techniques, such as consensus decision making.[18]

MANAGING RESISTANCE TO CHANGE

The necessity for changing the organizational culture, or some less comprehensive aspect of a firm, is almost inevitable. Frequently the major reason for change is because of a lack of fit between the external environment and the internal organizational activity. The aim should then be for the organization to readapt and reestablish a good fit between itself and the environment.[19] For example, an organization that restricts career opportunities for minority group members is out of sync with the environment.

When significant change is brought into the organization, employees react in various ways (as would be predicted from the model of human behavior described in Chapter 2). Some employees perceive major change so negatively that they experience job stress. At the other extreme, some employees are predisposed to react positively to change. They welcome the excitement and challenge of a major disruption.

A more typical reaction to change than shock or joy is direct or indirect resistance. Direct resistance may take the form of outright refusal to do something, such as the employee who says, "Sorry, I refuse to work a four-day week, ten hours per day. I'd rather quit." Indirect resistance takes the form of passive-aggressive behavior (being hostile by not taking appropriate action). An example would be the disgruntled employee who does not report a quality defect that he or she knows will create major problems for the company.

Why Workers Often Resist Change

When people resist change, it is usually because they think the particular change will do them more harm than good. Expectancy theory (refer back to Chapter 3) has been used as a general model to predict whether people will resist or welcome change. People formulate subjective hunches about the effects of a particular change. If their subjective probability is high that the change will be beneficial, they are positively inclined toward the change. Conversely, if they calculate that the odds of the change helping them are not in their favor, they resist change.[20]

Six more specific factors will be reviewed here that seem to account for most of the reasons employees sometimes resist (or even obstruct) change: financial reasons, fear of the unknown, disruptions in personal relationships, personal inconveniences, difficulty in breaking a habit, and negative experiences with change.

Financial reasons. Money enters into the decision-making process of most workers. If the organization introduces a change that employees think will provide them more money, they will be positively disposed toward that change. If employees think that a work-related change will cost them money, they will most probably resist that change. For example, sales representatives often resist new compensation plans because they question whether it will be to their economic advantage.

Fear of the unknown. An exception to the idea that people accept change that they think is potentially beneficial relates to fear of the unknown. People sometimes resist change simply because the outcome of the change is not entirely predictable. The situation of a supervisor in Buffalo, New York, who developed sinusitis, illustrates this principle:

A physician told the supervisor that the only permanent cure would be to live in a warm, dry climate. The supervisor succeeded in obtaining a transfer to a distribution center the company operated in Phoenix, Arizona. At the point of making final arrangements, the supervisor declined the transfer. His explanation to both the company and his wife was, "I guess I'll suffer along with a pain in the head a little longer. At least I know what I'm dealing with here in Buffalo. Who really knows what's going to happen to us in Phoenix?"

Disruptions in personal relationships.   A classic discussion about overcoming resistance to change contends that employees rarely resist technical changes. What they do resist is changes in personal relationships associated with technical changes. One sales company came close to going out of business because it overlooked the importance of changes in personal relationships.

Management decided to hire its own commission sales representatives to replace the manufacturer's sales representatives it had been using for ten years. Shortly after making these changes, the business suffered a 40 percent decrease in sales. The old customers resented losing long-established contacts with the manufacturer's representatives.

Instead of continuing to order from the same company, thus dealing with new people, they continued their association with the manufacturer's reps. The difference was that the reps now represented another company. Most of the customers had formed allegiances to the manufacturer's reps, not the company. Differences in product were not a factor, because the company sold novelty items of very low technology.[21]

Personal inconveniences.   Most changes encountered by employees result in personal inconvenience of some kind. Relocation of an office, even within the same city, is a prime example. Because of the move some employees will have to get up earlier and return home later; others will be forced to change their bank; and virtually everybody will face the problems of clearing out files, packing, and unpacking. Inevitably some important items will be temporarily misplaced.

Difficulty in breaking a habit.   Closely related to some of the problems involved in relocation is the problem of breaking an established habit. Each major habit is usually associated with a series of minor habits that people also resist breaking. If a new layer of management is introduced into a firm, many employees will have to learn new habits of bringing information to new managers. Simultaneously they will have to break old habits of going directly with problems to certain other managers.

Employee habits retard change, but most employees eventually do acquire new habits that are important to their work. Many employees first forced to work with computers were worried that "an entire day's work can be wiped out with one press of the wrong button." After a while this resistance was overcome to a large extent because the one-button disaster is relatively rare. (Or has it happened to you?)

Negative experiences with change. A person who had bad experiences with change in the past will resist change in the future. The relevant previous experiences can trace back into childhood. One pertinent example has to do with the prospects of moving. Adult attitudes toward relocation vary dramatically. Among the many contributing factors (including how much family inconvenience is anticipated) is how well relocation has worked out for the person in the past.

Reducing Employee Resistance to Change

Since changes are inevitable and many employees resist change, a manager often faces the task of reducing or overcoming such resistance. A general strategy for introducing change effectively is to take into account the reasons why people will probably resist the particular change. A change strategy can then be formulated. Seven tactics are described next for reducing or overcoming resistance to change that take into account most of the reasons for resistance described in the previous section.[22]

Understand the process of change. The famous psychologist Kurt Lewin presented a three-step analysis of the change process. First, unfreeze the status quo. Second, move to the desired change. Third, refreeze the new level, which becomes the new status quo.[23] The balance of the techniques described here incorporate this basic model of the change process. In brief, it works this way:

1. *Unfreezing* involves reducing or eliminating resistance to change. As long as employees are dragging their heels about a change, it will never be implemented effectively. A recent analysis of the change process notes that to accept change, first we must deal with and resolve our feelings about letting go of the old. Only after people have dealt successfully with endings are they ready to make transitions.[24]

2. *Moving to a new level or changing* usually involves considerable two-way communication, including group discussion. According to Lewin, "Rather than a one-way flow of commands or recommendations, the person implementing the change should make suggestions, and the changes should be encouraged to contribute and participate."

3. *Refreezing the status quo* involves such factors as pointing out the successes of the change and looking for ways to reward the people involved in implementing the change.

Allow for participation. The best documented way of overcoming resistance to change is to allow people to participate in the changes that will affect them. An application of this concept is allowing workers to set their own rules in order to increase compliance. The tactic is based on the principle that people who have a voice in setting rules of behavior are less likely to violate them.

Several years ago Borden Inc. asked a group of employees to devise a smoking policy for the company's headquarters. The group—comprised of smokers and nonsmokers, executives and office assistants, oldtimers and newcomers—set rules that were more restrictive than the smokers wanted. Yet the new rules stopped short of the total ban that many nonsmokers were pushing. Few loud grumblings or rule violations ensued.[25]

Avoid change overload.   Too much change in too short a period of time leads to stress for many people. It is therefore often helpful to avoid overloading employees with too many sweeping changes over a short time period. This suggestion would appear to run counter to the sentiment sometimes expressed as, "Let's make all our layoffs at once. This way we won't have people sitting around wondering who is next." In this case, however, the stress from ambiguity is greater than the stress from the change of having co-workers laid off. Therefore, the sentiment is probably correct, and so is the suggestion.

Allow for discussion and negotiation.   Resistance to change can be reduced by discussing and negotiating the more sensitive aspects of change. The two-way communication incorporated into discussion helps reduce some of the concern employees might have about pending work changes. Discussion often leads to negotiation, which further involves employees in the change process. One firm that ended the practice of providing certain employees company cars negotiated the issues of mileage allowance on personal cars and a new cost-of-living adjustment. At $0.30 per mile and a $3,000 per year adjustment, most complaints about eliminating company cars subsided.

Point out the financial benefits.   Since so many employees are concerned about the financial consequences of work changes, it is helpful to discuss these matters openly. (The example above is germane here too.) If employees will earn more money as a result of the change, this fact can be used as a selling point. An unwritten rule seems to exist in work organizations that a change toward a more hazardous (or more inconvenient) assignment carries with it a boost in pay. For example, U.S. and Canadian citizens who relocate to the Middle East are compensated far beyond the differences in cost of living between the two areas.

Avoid social upheavals.   One way to reduce resistance to change is to minimize changes in personal relationships stemming from the change. Some types of change, such as geographic relocation, inevitably result in social changes unless an entire organization is relocated. Under those extreme circumstances, there are still major changes in social contacts outside of work.

It is a difficult task for a manager to control most social changes when a major modification takes place, such as the formation of work teams instead of departmental structures. Nevertheless, sometimes employees can be asked to nominate individuals with whom they would like to work. Where feasible, teams could be formed of people who wanted to work together, thus minimizing social upheavals. Two precautions are in order. One, employees may nominate people with whom they socialize too much, with lowered productivity as the result. Two, some employees might not be nominated by anybody!

Place adaptable people in key spots. An important strategy for the effective introduction of change is to place the right people into jobs most directly associated with the change. The "right people" in this instance are those with a reputation for being adaptable and flexible. When a new machine is introduced into the workplace, there are usually grumbles to the effect that the new machine is inferior. If an adaptable, flexible, and optimistic person is the key operator of the new machine, this person will help bring about acceptance.

We have examined managerial strategies for the successful introduction of change (including overcoming its resistance). Our attention turns next to formal programs of bringing about change in organizations.

ORGANIZATION DEVELOPMENT AS A METHOD OF CREATING CHANGE

When it is necessary to bring about long-term, significant changes in the organization, a formal method of creating change—organization development—is often used. **Organization development (OD)** is any strategy, method, or technique for making organizations more effective by bringing about constructive, planned change. In its pure form, organization development attempts to change the culture of the firm. Quite often, however, organization development specialists are engaged in lesser changes, such as improving the design of jobs.

At its best, organization development is considered a method of corporate transformation, aimed at revitalizing the organization.[26] Another key point is that organization development is value driven. Organization development represents an effort to expand humanization in the workplace by supporting the values of openness, power sharing, and trust.[27] Here we describe a standard method of organization development, and then comment on one of its potential dangers.

Survey Feedback

The **survey feedback** is an organization development method that involves taking a survey of organizational problems and feeding this information back to management and survey participants. It is a well-structured, well-organized method that has a long history of good performance. In essence, the survey feedback involves (1) administering a survey of organizational problems through questionnaires and interviews; (2) reporting these results back to the organization; (3) developing action plans to overcome the problems uncovered; and (4) following up.

Administering the survey.   A survey designed by a specialist in attitude measurement is administered to a total organization, an organizational unit, or a representative sample of either. Both multiple-choice and write-in questions are found in the questionnaire, as illustrated in Figure 16–5. The most effective surveys ask questions that both apply to any organization and relate to specific concerns of the company being surveyed. Pressing topics are usually revealed by conversations with managers and human resources specialists.

An employee attitude survey (another name for the survey feedback method) typically asks the following types of questions:

Objective questions

	STRONGLY DISAGREE	DISAGREE	NEUTRAL	AGREE	STRONGLY AGREE
1. We have a major communications problem here.	_____	_____	_____	_____	_____
2. Our management makes all the decisions.	_____	_____	_____	_____	_____
3. Most people are proud to work for our company.	_____	_____	_____	_____	_____
4. Our employees are treated with dignity and respect.	_____	_____	_____	_____	_____

Sample write-in question:

In your opinion, what are the three biggest problems facing our company? Write your answer in the space provided below. Use the back of this page if necessary.

_____

_____

_____

_____

_____

_____

FIGURE 16-5 Sample Questions For an Attitude Survey

Goals. Do you have clear and reasonable goals? Does your department have clear and reasonable goals? Does your organization have clear and reasonable goals?

Managerial leadership. Are your managers and supervisors supportive and friendly? Do they encourage you and help you with work problems?

Co-worker relationships. Are your co-workers friendly? Do they listen to your problems and help you attain job standards?

Job satisfaction. Are you happy with your job, your salary, your opportunities for advancement, and your boss?

Organizational culture. Is your company interested in your welfare? Does the company try to improve working conditions?

Role conflict. Do you have enough authority to carry out your job? Do you have a clear statement of what is expected of you on the job? Do you report to two or more bosses?[28]

Feedback sessions. After an analysis of the survey results has been conducted, the information is fed back to survey participants. Feedback at this point typically takes the form of small group discussions held between members of a unit and an organization development specialist.

Develop action plans. A major difference between organization development and merely "conducting a survey" is contained in this step. Participants are asked for recommendations about how some of the problems uncovered in the survey should be resolved. A final report of the survey is not released until the action plans developed by people at several levels in the organization have been incorporated. At the University of Michigan Survey Research Center, the following rule has been formulated:

> No report containing recommendations based solely on their own analysis of data will be given to the client. Instead, they present data in preliminary form and involve members of the client organization in interpreting the data and deciding on specific courses of action.[29]

A dominant theme uncovered in one organization development survey was that employees were unsure of the future of their company. Many people wrote in comments such as these: "Rumors have it that our plant will be closed within six months. That's no way to live when you have a daughter ready for college." The action plan developed by middle management was straightforward and workable. They suggested an open meeting with top management to discuss the future of the company at that location. Top management complied. In the meeting it was explained that the rumors had a grain of truth, but were essentially incorrect. The company would not close the plant, but all expansion would take place in states with lower tax and utility rates.

Follow-up. Without continuous feedback and correction, organization development fails, or at best is a short-lived, interesting experience. Several months after the survey is conducted, a check should be made to determine if the action plans developed in the earlier stages are being implemented. In one company an action plan was developed to realign the wage scale of first-line supervision. A three-month checkup revealed that nothing had been done. Prodding by the organization development consultant and a representative from first-line supervision helped management begin some long-needed changes.

Potential Problems with Organization Development

Organization development programs have frequently been evaluated by researchers. In recent years, many of these studies have been characterized by careful attention to the requirements of scientific research.[30] Frequently evaluations of organization development programs show good results in terms of such objective criteria as turnover, profits, quantity, and quality. However, many organization development programs show neutral or negative results (conditions actually worsen).

One potential problem with organization development is that its specialists are sometimes too grandiose and zealous. They may impose their values and techniques on an organization that is not quite ready for a massive transformation. Pacific Bell experienced the problem just cited, and dropped the organization development program after two years of turmoil.

Employees complained about the strange jargon used by the organization development consultants, the confusing concepts, and threats they would lose their jobs if they did not conform. The training, with its enforced value system, was perceived as a Japanese-style "corporate religion." A major problem cited was forcing change at a time when Pacific Bell was trying to establish a more participative, less authoritarian culture. Attendance at the organization development sessions was mandatory. "Every quarter, everyone had to go, no matter what," said a Pacific Bell manager. The company later shifted to transformation on a division-by-division basis instead of companywide.[31]

Summary of Key Points

- Organizational culture is a system of shared values and beliefs that actively influence the behavior of organizational members. The various dimensions of organizational culture include values, heroes and heroines, rites and rituals, cultural networks, relative diversity of members, resource allocation and rewards, steepness of the hierarchy, degree of stability, and administrative practices.

- An organization's culture typically has its origins in the values, administrative practices, and personalities of the founding executives. Cultures are also formed and perpetuated through socialization, the process of understanding the values, norms, and customs essential for adapting to the organization.

- The major consequences and implications of organizational culture are (1) productivity and morale, (2) goal implementation, (3) competitive advantage for the firm, (4) compatibility of mergers and acquisitions, (5) recruitment and retention of creative employees, and (6) directing the activities of leaders.

- The essence of Japanese management, and its corresponding organization culture, is a focus on human resource development. Three general strategies are used to achieve this focus: Develop an internal labor market; articulate a unique company philosophy; and engage in intensive socialization of employees. Six related techniques stem from the focus and general strategies: (1) job rotation and slow promotion, (2) evaluation of attributes and behavior, (3) emphasis on work groups, (4) open communication, (5) consensus decision making, and (6) concern for the employee.

- The Japanese style of management has both strengths and weaknesses. For example, the Japanese system has been able to produce high-quality products, but Japanese middle managers work excessively long hours. The Japanese business successes can in general be attributed to better ability to apply technology, greater commitment to orientation and training, and better use of modern human resources techniques.

- Although the general topic of this chapter is organizational change, change must first be understood as it affects individuals. Among the responses to change are enthusiasm, aggressive behavior, and resistance. The general reason people resist change is that they think it will do them more harm than good. Specific reasons for resistance include (1) financial concerns, (2) fear of the unknown, (3) disruptions in personal relationships, (4) personal inconveniences, (5) difficulty in breaking a habit, and (6) negative experiences with change.

- Strategies for reducing employee resistance to change include (1) understand the basic process of change (unfreezing, changing, and refreezing), (2) allow for participation, (3) avoid change overload, (4) allow for discussion and negotiation, (5) point out the financial benefits, (6) avoid social upheavals, and (7) place adaptable people in key spots.

- Organization development (OD) is a general strategy for making organizations more effective by bringing about some kind of constructive, planned change. In its pure form, organization development attempts to transform the culture of the firm in the direction of openness, trust, and participation.

- Survey feedback is a well-structured form of organization development. Its key components are (1) take a survey of organizational problems through questionnaires and interviews, (2) report these results back to the organization, (3) develop action plans to overcome the problems, and (4) follow up to see if the action plans are implemented.

Questions and Activities

1. What similarity do you perceive between the meanings of "culture" and "organizational culture"?
2. Consultant and author Tom Peters contends that his rumpled clothing made him a poor fit at his former employer, the consulting firm of McKinsey and Co. What does Peters' statement tell you about the culture at McKinsey?
3. Visualize a Pizza Hut restaurant (or visit one soon). What conclusions about its culture can you make?
4. How might the organizational culture of a school influence the behavior of its students?
5. Assume that an American works for a Japanese subsidiary in the United States. What steps should the American employee take to increase his or her chances for promotion?
6. Many Japanese middle managers (called "corporate warriors") work approximately eighty hours per week. What aspect of the Japanese organizational culture encourages such behavior?
7. Why might it be true that older workers tend to be more resistant to change than younger workers? If you think that younger workers are more resistant to change, why might that be true?
8. How might management be able to overcome resistance to change in a hurry?
9. Why would an organization want to bother transforming its culture?
10. In what way might student ratings of instructors be used as a form of organization development?

A HUMAN RELATIONS CASE PROBLEM
The Electronic Mail Resistors

Deborah Winslow, chief administrator at Tuscon Group Health, was proud of her accomplishment. After 13 months of negotiation with other executives, including the board of directors, her health maintenance organization (HMO) converted to an electronic mail system. She realized that no other HMO in Arizona had made such a complete move to decrease paperwork in favor of electronic mail. Winslow thought that Tuscon Group Health employees were wasting too much time sending printed memos to each other. Now with one hour of training any employee could learn to communicate to other employees via electronic mail. Winslow was looking toward an annual cost savings of $30,000.

Four months after the start-up, Dr. Aaron Goldfarb, Winslow's boss, asked her how well the new electronic mail system was performing. Cupping her chin in her right hand, Winslow replied, "I have to give you a two-sided answer. From a technological standpoint, we have bought a beautiful piece of office automation. We have not had one serious malfunction with the system. It is also very user-friendly. Nobody has said that he or she can't learn how to operate electronic mail."

"What's the other standpoint?" asked Goldfarb.

"We have bombed out from a human use standpoint," Winslow replied. "Despite the electronic mail system, our employees are still dropping by each other's offices and cubicles to chat. Any time they have an important message they bypass electronic mail. Let me be candid. We are using the new system to pass along trivial messages to each other. So far electronic mail has not become a real time saver. It hasn't even improved communications in the office. My feelings are that HMO employees think that electronic mail is too impersonal. They prefer the human touch."

"I'm no expert on office communications," said Goldfarb. "However, that's a pretty expensive toy you've installed. If you can't get our employees to use it in a meaningful way, I'd say remove the system."

1. What might be the reasons why HMO employees are not making more extensive use of electronic mail?

2. What tactics and strategies do you recommend to Winslow if she wants to keep her system?

3. What do you think of the effectiveness of Goldfarb's approach to handling this problem?

A HUMAN RELATIONS CASE PROBLEM
"Get Me a New Culture"

Sunny Chai, human resource specialist at the Security Oceanic Trust Company, was working with a team of outside consultants to diagnose problems the company might be facing. As Chai pored over the results of the survey, he thought: "The data are as clear as any I've seen in any survey. The reason why our bank is not performing as well as management would like is that our culture doesn't fit the times. Loads of our employees see each other as being too conservative, too unwilling to take risks.

"It's too bad they don't see themselves as part of the problem. If they did, maybe we could move faster as a company and increase our profits."

Two weeks later, Chai, along with two members of the outside consulting firm, presented their findings to top management. Chai and the consultants went into detail about how the culture of "not making waves" and "protecting your hide at all costs" was slowing the progress of Security Oceanic.

After hearing the complete presentation, the president said: "I'm convinced what you say is right. I've noticed some of those problems myself. I agree that things have got to change. Sunny, I would like you and the two consultants to give us a new culture within forty-five days."

1. How should Chai respond to the president's request?
2. How realistic is the president's request?

A HUMAN RELATIONS EXERCISE
Describing the Organizational Culture

The class will form teams of four or five people who will attempt to measure and describe the culture of the organization in which you are taking this course (college, school, institute, company, and so forth). Before venturing out on the task, the group will agree on what questions should be asked of organization members in order to measure culture. Clues can be obtained from the section called "Dimensions of Organizational Culture." A sample question to ask people would be, "What are some of the most important values held by people around here?"

After the teams have completed their investigation, discuss the results and draw a composite picture of the culture of the organization in which you are taking this course.

Notes _____

1. Phil Ebersole, "Corning: Company Is a Lot More than Glass," *Rochester Democrat and Chronicle,* July 30, 1989, p. 1F.
2. Dimensions 1 through 4 are from Terrence Deal and Allan Kennedy, *Corporate Cultures: The Rites and Rituals of Corporate Life* (Reading, MA: Addison-Wesley, 1982), pp. 13–14; dimensions 5 through 9 are from Leonard R. Sayles and Robert V. L. Wright, "The Use of Culture in Strategic Management," *Issues & Observations,* November 1985, pp. 1–9.
3. Sayles and Wright, "The Use of Culture," p. 2.
4. Sayles and Wright, "The Use of Culture," p. 2.
5. Sayles and Wright, "The Use of Culture," p. 2.
6. Sayles and Wright, "The Use of Culture," p. 8.
7. Stephen P. Robbins, *Organizational Behavior: Concepts, Controversies, and Applications,* 4th ed. (Englewood Cliffs, NJ: Prentice Hall), 1989, pp. 465–77.
8. Guy S. Saffold III, "Culture Traits, Strength, and Organizational Performance: Moving Beyond 'Strong' Culture," *Academy of Management Review,* October 1988, pp. 546—-58.
9. Edgar H. Schein, "Are You Corporate Cultured?" *Personnel Journal,* November 1986, p. 84.
10. Jay B. Barney, "Organizational Culture: Can It Be a Source of Sustained Competitive Advantage?" *Academy of Management Review,* July 1986, p. 662.
11. Richard J. Petronio, "Why Mergers Fail: The Clash of Cultures," *The Surcon Report,* Special Issue, 1989, p. 5.
12. James F. Kelley, Jr., "Talk Eased Merger Stress for Great American Employees," *Personnel Journal,* October 1989, pp. 77–85.
13. Schein, "Are You Corporate Cultured?" p. 96.
14. Margaret Shapiro, "Japanese People Country's Greatest Resource," *The Washington Post* syndicated story, May 21, 1989.
15. James S. Bowman, "The Rising Sun in America (Part Two)," *Personnel Administrator,* October 1986, p. 83.
16. Richard M. Hodgetts and Fred Luthans, "Japanese HR Management Practices: Separating Fact from Fiction," *Personnel,* April 1989, pp. 42–45; Andrew Weiss, "Simple Truths of Japanese Manufacturing," *Harvard Business Review,* July–August 1984, pp. 119–25.
17. Gail Rosenblum, "Thousands in Japan Dying Suddenly of Overwork, Stress," Gannett News Service story, Aug. 11, 1990.
18. Hodgetts and Luthans, "Japanese HR Management," p. 45.
19. Paul Dainty and Andrew Kakabadse, "Organizational Change: A Strategy for Successful Implementation," *Journal of Business and Psychology,* Summer 1990, p. 464.
20. Joseph Tiffin and Ernest J. McCormick, *Industrial Psychology,* 5th ed. (Englewood Cliffs, NJ: Prentice Hall, 1965), p. 425.
21. Howard Klein, *Stop! You're Killing the Business* (New York: Mason & Lipscomb, 1974).

22. Stan Kossen, *The Human Side of Organizations,* 3rd ed. (New York: Harper & Row, 1983), pp. 292–97; R. Wayne Mondy, Robert E. Holmes, and Edwin B. Flippo, *Management: Concepts and Practices,* 2nd ed. (Boston: Allyn & Bacon, 1983), pp. 430–33.

23. Kurt Lewin, *Field Theory and Social Science* (New York: Harper & Row, 1964), chapters 9 and 10.

24. Harry Woodward and Steve Bucholz, *Aftershock: Helping People Through Corporate Change* (New York: Wiley, 1987).

25. Claudia H. Deutsch, "Workers Comply When They Set Their Own Rules," *The New York Times* syndicated story, July 20, 1990.

26. Ralph H. Kilmann, Teresa Joyce Covin, and associates, *Corporate Transformations: Revitalizing Organizations for a Competitive World* (San Francisco: Jossey-Bass, 1988).

27. Robert T. Golembiewski, *Organization Development: Ideas and Issues* (New Brunswick, NJ: Transaction Books, Rutgers University, 1989).

28. Robert J. Sahl, "Company-specific Attitude Surveys," *Personnel Journal,* May 1990, pp. 46–51; Gene Milbourn and Richard Cuba, "OD Techniques and the Bottom Line," *Personnel,* May–June 1981, p. 39.

29. George F. Wieland and Robert A. Ulrich, *Organizations: Behavior, Design, and Change* (Homewood, IL: Irwin, 1976), p. 504.

30. John M. Nicholas and Marsha Katz, "Research Methods and Reporting Practices in Organization Development: A Review and Some Guidelines," *Academy of Management Review,* October 1985, p. 37.

31. Barbara Block, "Creating a Culture All Employees Can Accept," *Management Review,* July 1989, p. 45.

Suggested Reading

GINSBERG, ARI, and BUCHHOLTZ, ANN, "Converting to For-Profit Status: Corporate Responsiveness to Radical Change." *Academy of Management Journal,* September 1990, pp. 445–77.

GREINER, LARRY, and SCHEIN, VIRGINIA. *Power and Organization Development: Mobilizing Power to Implement Change.* Reading, MA: Addison-Wesley, 1988.

NEUMAN, GEORGE A., EDWARDS, JACK E., and RAJU, NAMBURY S. "Organizational Development Interventions: A Meta-Analysis of Their Effects on Satisfaction and Other Attitudes." *Personnel Psychology,* Autumn 1989, pp. 461–90.

QUINN, ROBERT E., and CAMERON, KIM S., eds. *Paradox and Transformation: Toward a Theory of Change in Organization and Management.* Cambridge, MA: Ballinger, 1988.

SCHULTHEISS, EMILY E. *Optimizing the Organization: How to Link People and Technology.* Cambridge, MA: Ballinger, 1989.

SMITH, PETER B., and PETERSON, MARK F. *Leadership, Organizations, and Culture.* Newbury Park, CA: Sage, 1988.

WALTON, RICHARD E. *Innovating to Compete: Lessons for Diffusing and Managing Change in the Workplace.* San Francisco: Jossey-Bass, 1987.

WILKINS, ALAN L., and BRISTOW, NIGEL J. "For Successful Organization Culture, Honor Your Past." *The Academy of Management Executive,* August 1987, pp. 221–28.

YOUNG, JOSEPH A., and SMITH, BARBARA. "Organizational Change and the HR Professional." *Personnel,* October 1988, pp. 44– 48.

17

Developing
Your Career

LEARNING OBJECTIVES

After reading and studying this chapter and doing the exercises, you should be able to

1. Recognize your responsibility for developing your own career.
2. Understand how people find career fields for themselves.
3. Establish career goals and a tentative career path for yourself.
4. Describe at least five strategies and tactics for advancing your career by taking control of your own behavior.
5. Describe at least five strategies and tactics for advancing your career by exerting control over your environment.
6. Explain how career switching fits into career development.
7. Appreciate the importance of integrating the demands of career and personal life.

P rofessional and managerial job opportunities have been greatly affected by the baby boomers (those Americans and Canadians born between 1946 and 1964). As the majority of these people have reached middle age, they are competing for a shrinking number of professional and managerial jobs. People younger than the baby boomers must therefore invest time in careful career planning in order to find rewarding and satisfying positions. For some, this planning will be aimed at moving up the organization. Others will learn to derive equal satisfaction primarily from growing within their jobs.

Employers today are assisting employees in planning and developing their careers. **Career development** is a planned approach to achieving growth and satisfaction in work experiences. Today there is a growing recognition that career development benefits employers and employees alike. Despite this current awareness of the value of career development, you must still assume the major responsibility for developing your career. One fundamental reason is that you might change employers, voluntarily or involuntarily. Another is that you and your employer might have a different perception of what constitutes a satisfying and rewarding career.

This chapter emphasizes information about career development from the perspective of the individual taking the initiative to plan his or her career. The other perspective would be that of the organization providing career development programs for the individual. Much of the information in this chapter is organized according to the logical flow of events a person generally experiences in developing a career:

Finding a field → establishing career goals and a career path →
selecting relevant career advancement strategies and tactics →
switching careers if the need arises

Another aspect of career development, conducting a job campaign, is described in Appendix B. Use this information to supplement job-finding assistance provided by your school.

FINDING A SUITABLE FIELD

Finding a field that holds the promise of bringing you personal satisfaction and material rewards is a critical early step in developing your career. We say "early" because it is difficult to establish a zero point in career development. As soon as you even begin to think about making an occupational choice, you have begun to develop your career. Despite the importance of choosing a career, the process is usually done unsystematically. Few people are even aware that this major life choice can be done systematically. Among the more frequent ways in which people find a field—or occupation within that field—to pursue are these:

1. *Influence of parent, relative, or friend.* "My aunt owned a restaurant, so I became interested in restaurant management at an early age."

2. *Reading and study.* "While in high school I read about investments, so I decided to become a stock analyst."

3. *Natural opportunity.* "I was born into the business. Who would give up a chance to be a vice president by the time he was 25? Our family has always been in the retail business."

4. *Forced opportunity.* "I had never heard about electronics until I joined the army. They told me I had aptitude for the field. I enjoyed working as an electronics technician. After the army I applied for a job with IBM as a field service engineer. It has worked out well."

5. *Discovery though counseling and or testing.* "I took a computer-based guidance program after I entered business school. The program indicated that I had interests similar to those of an industrial sales representative. Not knowing what else to do, I decided to become a sales rep for machine tools."

6. *Matching yourself with a compatible person.* A novel way of finding a field and occupation within that field is first to locate a person with whom you have similar interests. You then choose that person's field of work for yourself, using this reasoning: "I seem to like what that person likes in most things. All things being equal, I would probably like the kind of work he or she does."

The Use of Occupational Information

In addition to the methods just listed, it is important to seek valid information about career fields so you can find a good fit between yourself and existing opportunities. Most libraries and bookstores are well supplied with this type of information.

Reference books about career information. The most comprehensive source document of occupational information is the *Occupational Outlook Handbook,* published every two years by the U.S. Department of Labor. Each occupation listed is described in terms of (1) nature of the work, (2) places of employment, (3) training, (4) other qualifications for advancement, and (5) employment outlook. Using the *Handbook,* one can find answers to such questions as, "What do city planners do and how much do they earn?" A similar source is the *Encyclopedia of Careers and Vocational Guidance.*

Computer-assisted career guidance. Several career guidance-information systems have been developed for access by computer. The information contained in these systems is designed to help users plan their careers. Guidance-information systems go beyond printed information, because you can interact with the software. For instance, when you are keyed in on a specific occupation, you can ask: "What is the promotion outlook? "What effect will technology have?"

A widely used career-guidance information system is DISCOVER.[1] It is intended for use by post-secondary students and by people seeking a new career direction. DISCOVER has two approaches. The information-only approach allows quick access to information files in the system. For example, direct access is permitted to detailed information about 458 occupations included in the DISCOVER files.

The more comprehensive approach to DISCOVER is Guidance Information, containing nine major modules. It is designed to support users for the complex process of making career and educational decisions. The modules are (1) beginning the career journey, (2) learning about the world of work, (3) learning about yourself, (4) finding occupations, (5) learning about occupations, (6) making educational choices, (7) planning next steps, (8) planning your career, and (9) making transitions. DISCOVER is comprehensive and complex, but so is the process of finding and developing your career.

Career information in newspapers and magazines. The topic of careers is of such interest today that it is regularly covered in newspaper and magazine articles. The business section of most newspapers regularly runs both career columns and feature stories about people in different occupations. These articles are usually based on current industry surveys, recent government statistics, and interviews with people who are firsthand sources of information.

Speaking to people. By speaking directly to informed people yourself, you can generate firsthand information about occupations. Many people have identified a field to pursue precisely in this manner. Seek out a person gainfully employed in any field or occupation in which you might be interested. Most people welcome the opportunity to talk about themselves and the type of work they do. If you do not know anyone engaged in the career field that interests you, do some digging. A few inquiries will usually lead to a person you can contact. It is preferable to interview that person in his or her actual work setting to obtain a sense of the working conditions people face in that field.

Speaking to people at different stages and levels of responsibility can be illuminating. If you ask a neophyte teller about the banking field, you will receive a very different answer from that of a 40-year-old vice president of commercial loans.

CAREER ORIENTATIONS OF TODAY'S WORKERS

According to popular belief, everyone wants to get ahead and climb the organizational ladder. C. Brooklyn Derr contends that this widely held assumption has never been true, and is even less true in today's world of changing career values. Yet many managers still manage employees as if they had the same career goal—vertical growth. As a result, people are mismanaged, and productivity and morale suffer. It is helpful for both the individual and the organization to recognize that people have different career orientations. Understanding your orientation will help you establish meaningful career goals. Derr's research points to these five orientations:[2]

Getting ahead—pursuing the traditional definition of career success involving vertical mobility in the organization. Many employees perceive themselves to be failures if they are not promoted at least once every five years.

Getting secure—seeking job security and an identity with the firm more than advancement or challenge. The security seeker typically is a low risk taker because taking risks is often associated with low job security. If you do not take big risks, you lower the probability of failing.

Getting free—wanting autonomy and independence, and the opportunity to choose one's own methods of solving problems. Many professional workers, such as accountants, computer scientists, and engineers, have this orientation. William J. Kuchta adds further that for many professionals, success does not consist of occupying the executive suite. For these people, management positions are an interlude during which they grow, only later to return to their true interests in a specialized field.[3] Similarly, many workers today are more interested in improving their technical and professional skills than in being promoted into administrative work.

Getting high—valuing excitement, challenge, and the content of the work. The orientation of getting high in a career is characteristic of those with a strong need for thrill seeking (refer back to Chapter 3).

Getting balanced—giving equal priority to one's career, family, friends, leisure, and self-development. People with a strong "getting balanced" orientation value total life satisfaction as much as job satisfaction. Rarely do they become workaholics or career dropouts. Instead, they seek a healthy balance between work and personal life.[4]

ESTABLISHING CAREER GOALS AND A CAREER PATH

Career planning, in the form of goal setting and establishing a career path, ideally precedes finding a job. This sequence, however, is not rigid. In practice, most people do not engage in serious career planning until they have some job experience in their field. Thus they establish career goals sometime after conducting a successful job campaign.

Establishing Career Goals

A person's chances for achieving career success and personal satisfaction increase if he or she establishes career goals. The opposite of goal setting is referred to as *winging it*. A fortunate few "wingers" work their way into rewarding jobs and careers.

Most of your career goals should be realistic in terms of your capabilities and job opportunities. As you achieve each goal, you can continue to raise your sights. Nevertheless, it is good for your mental outlook to entertain some fantasies about extraordinary accomplishments for yourself. Typically, a fantasy goal is far beyond attainment at your present stage in life, but could someday become a realistic goal.

Career goals become the basis for a **career path,** a series of positions in one or more organizations leading to a long-range goal. A career path laid out in one firm should be integrated with the present and future demands of the organization. For instance, if a company is decreasing the number of staff positions and increasing the number of line positions, a career path should consider this circumstance.

It is also desirable for a career path to integrate personal plans with work plans. Some lifestyles, for example, are incompatible with some career paths. It would be difficult to develop a stable community life if one aspired to occupying a field position with the Central Intelligence Agency.

Contingency plans should also be incorporated into a well-designed career path. For instance: "If I don't become an agency supervisor by age 35, I will seek employment in the private sector," or, "If I do not get promoted within two years, I will enroll in a business school program."

A sample career path is shown in Figure 17-1. Each rung on the ladder represents a position the person would have to attain to reach his or her long-range goal.

CAREER ADVANCEMENT STRATEGIES AND TACTICS

The strategies and tactics of organizational politics described in Chapter 11 can be interpreted as ways of advancing your career because they help you acquire more power. Described here are specific career advancement tactics, divided into two groups. The methods in the first group relate to taking control of your own behavior, while those in the second relate to controlling the external environment. Indiscriminate use of any of these approaches may backfire. For example, if you overdo the tactic of "find the right employer," you may never find an employer suited to your needs.

Advancement Through Taking Control of Yourself

The unifying theme to the strategies, tactics, and attitudes described in this section is that you attempt to control your own behavior.

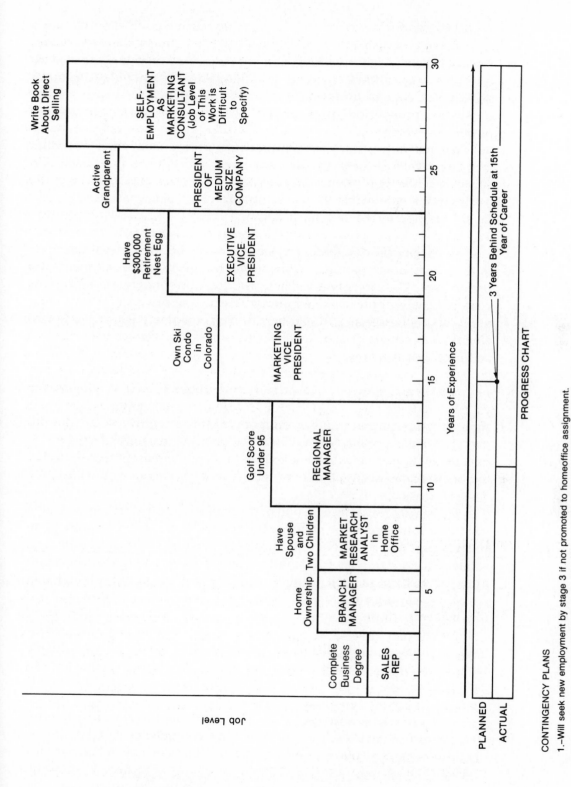

FIGURE 17-1 Sample Career Path for a Marketing Professional

CONTINGENCY PLANS

1.–Will seek new employment by stage 3 if not promoted to homeoffice assignment.

2.–If not promoted to marketing vice-president by stage 5, will purchase established retail business.

3.–If develop stress disorder, such as cardiac disease, at any point, will seek employment as inside sales representative in well-managed (non-hectic) company.

473

Develop a code of professional ethics.   A valuable starting point in developing a career is to establish a personal ethical code. An ethical code determines what behavior is right or wrong, good or bad, based on values. The values may stem from cultural upbringing, religious teachings, and professional standards. A code of professional ethics helps a person deal with such issues as accepting bribes, backstabbing a co-worker, or sexually harassing a powerless person.

When confronted with an ethical conflict, a recommended procedure is to talk to management. In some situations, for example, the worker perceives that the boss wants the business at all costs. Consequently, the worker takes action that is uncomfortable or illegal when management would have preferred an ethical option.[5]

Make an accurate self-appraisal.   An important part of career development is to have an accurate picture of your strengths, areas for improvement, and preferences. The career development inventory presented at the end of this chapter is an example of a self-appraisal instrument that an individual completes without assistance from others. Self-appraisal will be more accurate when it is supplemented by feedback from superiors, co-workers, friends, and career counselors.

Stick with what you do best.   The primary path to career success is to identify your best talents and build a career around them. Becoming wealthy and achieving recognition is a by-product of making effective use of your talents. The late columnist Sydney J. Harris claims that the only advice he ever gave to young people who came to him for career counseling consisted of ten one-syllable words: "Find out what you do best and stick with it."[6]

Display good job performance.   Good performance is the bedrock upon which you build your career. Job competence and talent are still the number one success ingredients in all but the most heavily political firms. All other talk about success strategies is fanciful without first assuming that the ambitious person turns in good job performance. Before anybody is promoted in virtually every organization, the prospective new boss asks, "How well did this person perform for you?"

An effective strategy for getting your good performance recognized is to make yourself more valuable to your boss. Ways of being more valuable include keeping your skills current, knowing your job responsibilities, and having a positive attitude.[7]

Create a good first and lasting impression.   The impression you create can influence your career because people often judge competence based on immediately observable behavior. One communications consultant believes that it takes about seven seconds for others to size up a person. In these instances they are responding to your facial expressions, voice tone, ges-

tures, stance, and energy.[8] Your manner of dress also contributes to a first impression.

Three controllable ways of creating a good first and lasting impression on others is through handshake, eye contact, and remembering names. The handshake should be firm, dry, and brief. Looking someone straight in the eye sends the message that you are confident and sincere. Remembering names is particularly important because so few people do it well. Upon hearing the name for the first time, repeat it to yourself, then make some association to that name.[9] Should you meet Wendy Katz for the first time, visualize her with cats who are eating Wendy's hamburgers.

Document your accomplishments. Keeping an accurate record of what you have accomplished in your career can be valuable when you are being considered for promotion. An astute person can point specifically to what he or she has accomplished in each position. Here are two examples from different types of jobs:

1. As ski-shop store manager, increased sales to hearing-impaired skiers by 338 percent in one year by hiring an interpreter to work in our shop on Saturday mornings.
2. As manufacturing technician, saved my company $36,000 in one year by switching from steel to nylon ball bearings in our line of bicycles and baby carriages.

Manage luck.   Good fortune weighs heavily in most successful careers. Without one or two good breaks along the way (such as your supervisor quitting suddenly, and a replacement being needed immediately) it is difficult to advance rapidly. The effective strategist to some extent manages luck by being prepared for the big break. (Luck has been defined as preparation meeting opportunity.) The person who has completed school and has an updated résumé on file is well positioned to be chosen for the supervisory position just mentioned.

Exerting Control Over the External Environment

In this section we emphasize strategies and tactics requiring you to exert some control over the outside environment. If you do not fully control it, at least you can try to juggle it to your advantage.

Identify growth fields and growth companies.   A sound strategy for career advancement is to seek jobs in growth situations. Generally this means seeking growth industries, but it can also mean seeking growth firms or areas of the country with plentiful job opportunities. Information about growth opportunities may be found in government reports (such as the *Occupational Outlook Handbook*), books on the topic, and newspapers. Local banks and the chamber of commerce can be a valid source of information about growth firms in your area. A summary of good job opportunities for the next decade is shown in Table 17-1.

Find the right employer for you.   Ideally, you should work for an organization in which there is a good fit between your style and its culture. For example, if you are adventuresome and aggressive, you would most likely prosper in a firm that welcomes employees with these characteristics. Although finding a fit between your personality and the personality of the organization may sound difficult to achieve, it may prove vital to your career advancement.

Information about a potential employer can be found through such means as reading annual reports (if it is a business corporation) and asking the opinion of a broker, customer, or supplier. Best of all, seek the opinion of several current or past employees. Choosing the wrong organization can be hazardous to your career. An organization that is "wrong" for you can be "right" for another person, and vice versa. You may not be able to tolerate an organization that expects its higher-level employees to work a fifty-five-hour week under intense pressure. Another person might thrive in such an atmosphere.

Achieve broad experience.   A widely accepted strategy for advancing in responsibility is to strengthen your credentials by broadening your experience. Broadening can come about by performing a variety of jobs, or a series of special assignments in one firm. Another approach is to perform

TABLE 17–1 Good job opportunities for the next decade

Professional and technical jobs

Business specialists

Accountant and auditor; advertising specialist; bank officer; customer service representative; human resources specialist; financial services sales representative; telemarketing specialist; retail store buyer; purchasing agent or buyer (industrial company); logistics (distribution and transportation) specialist.

Computer specialists

Operator; programmer; service and repair technician; systems analyst; computer-aided manufacturing technician.

Engineering

Civil engineer; electronic and electrical engineer or technician; mechanical engineer; industrial engineer; manufacturing technician; laser engineer or technician; hazardous waste technician.

Administrative and support services

Administrative assistant; medical secretary; legal secretary; paralegal assistant (fastest growing occupation in United States); office automation equipment operator.

Health care provider

Dental assistant; dental hygienist; registered nurse; licensed practical nurse; nurse's aide; physician's assistant; CAT scan or MRI technician; physical therapist.

Managerial jobs

Sales and customer service

Telemarketing supervisor; brand manager; customer service supervisor; international sales coordinator.

Finance

Security investments manager; general accounting; bank manager; chief internal auditor.

Personnel and human resources

Management training director; personnel and human resources manager; labor relations director; employee training and development manager.

Manufacturing

Plant manager; quality assurance manager; materials handling manager; purchasing manager.

Computers and information systems

Service and repair manager; management information systems director; computer operations supervisor.

Public service

City manager; urban planning manager.

Sources: Based on information in John Stodden, "Ten Best Careers for the '90s," *Business Week Careers How to Get a Job Guide* (1988 edition); "The Fastest-Growing Professions," *HR Focus* (in *Personnel,* April 1990, p. 7); "A Futurist Looks at Management Skills in Greatest Demand," *Personal Report for the Executive,* July 15, 1989, pp. 1–2.

essentially the same job in different organizations. Job hopping (moving from firm to firm) is widely practiced by top managers working for large companies. Rosabeth Moss Kanter explains that many executives are forced to switch firms because of the many corporate takeovers. In the process, however, they become more valuable.[10]

Because many employers value a stable employment record, and seniority is often rewarded, the ideal approach is to advance within one organization. Unfortunately, many employers cannot reciprocate by offering long-term job security to employees.

Find a sponsor.   A swift route to career progress is to find somebody at a high place in the organization who is impressed with your capabilities. Such a person can even be a blood relative or one by marriage. One reason why task force and committee assignments are so helpful to career progress is that they provide you with the opportunity to be seen by a variety of key people in your organization. Many an individual who has performed well in an activity such as fundraising for the United Way has found a bigger job in the process. In general, any tactic that brings favorable attention to yourself can help you find a sponsor.

Find a mentor.   A **mentor** is a boss who takes a subordinate under his or her wing and teaches and coaches that person. An emotional tie exists between the protégé (or apprentice) and the mentor. A relationship with a sponsor involves much less teaching, coaching, and forming of emotional ties. Effective mentors are said to perform these functions for their protégés: providing resources, supplying information, showing an interest in the apprentice's work, being a role model, setting high standards, building the apprentice's confidence, coaching him or her, and protecting the apprentice when the latter makes poor decisions.[11]

Mentoring is typically an informal relationship. Several organizations, however, have formalized mentoring by assigning a senior manager a group of junior managers to mentor. Among these organizations are Johnson & Johnson, Merrill Lynch, and the Internal Revenue Service. Sometimes the junior manager is given a choice of mentors. The purpose of these mentor programs is to develop managers.[12]

One criticism of the mentor system is that if your mentor (or sponsor) leaves, or falls out of power, your career is set back. Another criticism of mentoring is that women have a more difficult time finding mentors. One problem is that women may have fewer interactions than men with powerful people in the workplace. Also, male managers often find it more natural to develop mentorships with males.[13]

Rely on networking.   Establishing a network of contacts is valuable for finding a job and for advancing one's career. The value of networking is so widely accepted that formal networking groups have emerged. In many cities, for example, nightclubs hold an occasional "networking night" in which businesspeople exchange information and business cards, and develop contacts. Another example of formalized networking is a national organization called "Xerox-X," consisting entirely of former Xerox Corp. employees. Members of Xerox-X share information on job opportunities, business services, and investment opportunities, and can develop sales leads.

The current trend in networking is for men and women to become part of the same network. The "good old boy" and "good old girl" systems are being replaced by the "good old friend" system. For example, the networking clubs mentioned earlier attract both men and women. These networks are also helping women overcome the problems of attracting mentors. The accompanying box describes a specific method that women are using to make valuable business contacts.

WOMEN ARE CLUBBING THEIR WAY TO SUCCESS

For an increasing number of working women, the latest career decision involves which golf club to use. Women have found that playing golf is a way to mingle with influential people and boost their careers. Consequently, women are flooding the golf courses. Of the 6 million women playing golf in the United States and Canada, 47 percent have professional, managerial, and administrative jobs. In addition to exercise and fresh air, golf gives businesswomen:

— something to talk to other businesspeople about. Because so many people in power are interested in golf, bringing up golf can facilitate rapport. "You suddenly pick up a bond you would not otherwise," said Kathy Graper, an airline account executive who has played golf for twelve years.

— something to do with businessmen.

"After the meetings, all the men packed up and went to the golf course," said Candice Caldwell, an account executive with a credit card company. "Because I didn't golf, I was cut off from the mainstream of the meeting." Caldwell has now learned golf as a self-defensive maneuver.

— a way to keep someone's attention while trying to make the big sale. Golf courses are quiet, and have no telephones or fax machines on the greens. You can slip in some talk about your company and your products between swings—or maybe at the "19th hole" refreshment place. "Golf is a soft sell. Once you have played golf with someone, you're in the door," said Graper.

Source: As reported in Mindy Fetterman, "Women Are Finding Golf, Business Mix Well," Gannett News Service story, Aug. 19, 1990.

Learn to manage career plateaus. A **career plateau** is the point where it becomes evident that further job advancement is permanently or temporarily blocked. The vast majority of the workforce reaches a career plateau at least once or twice.[14] Some people reach an early plateau and stay there until retirement. The worldwide economy has settled into a period of stability or gradual expansion. It follows logically that many more people than in the past will encounter plateaus (no vertical growth and no slippage) in their careers. The best antidote to a plateau is to control your impatience and make constructive use of the time. Specifically, you might consider these strategies:

1. Learn to appreciate growth within your job. Develop new skills on your present job that will help you when you finally do receive a promotion in the future.
2. Since the demands on your time tend not to be excessive during a career plateau, invest some of that time in self-development, including reading in your field, attending workshops and seminars, and increasing your formal education.

Work comfortably with cultural diversity.   The workforce in the United States and Canada has become more culturally diverse. The fastest growing segments of the workforce are women and people of color. Succeeding in a diverse environment requires more than avoiding discriminatory behavior. Instead, success is facilitated by working comfortably with people of different sexes, races, religions, ethnicity, values, sexual orientations, and physical capabilities.

The vast majority of readers are already accustomed to working and/or studying with culturally diverse people. Nevertheless, many people in the workforce still have difficulty relating comfortably to people of different cultural backgrounds. To help employees overcome this hurdle, some companies conduct **diversity awareness programs.**[15] These programs provide an opportunity for employees to develop the skills necessary to deal effectively with each other and customers in a diverse environment. For example, a group of co-workers might listen to a Vietnamese woman explain how she feels excluded from the in-group composed of whites and African-Americans in her department. (Refer back to Chapter 13.)

CAREER SWITCHING

Career switching (making a relatively complete change from one career to another) is becoming more common. People switch careers for such reasons as boredom, relief from job stress, being laid off and unable to find a job in their present field, or being forced into early retirement.[16] Switching careers effectively requires long-range planning. Sometimes an avocation can be converted into an occupation, assuming that a high-level of skill has been developed. For example, a brand manager in a food company who played competitive tennis switched careers to become a tennis pro in a Caribbean island.

In order to switch careers effectively, you should follow the suggestions offered for finding a field or a first career. To avoid making what might turn out to be a costly and time-consuming error, you should:

1. narrow your interests to a few specific areas and job titles,
2. try part-time or evening work in your desired area,
3. get into an apprenticeship program (this usually requires completion of some specialized education),
4. do volunteer work in your field of interest,
5. take a course or two in the potential new field,
6. determine if you should return to college full-time or part-time.[17]

CAREER DEVELOPMENT PROGRAMS IN ORGANIZATIONS

Although individuals have the primary responsibility for managing their careers, company-sponsored career development programs make an important contribution. Above all, they help to integrate the career goals of individuals with the requirements of the organization. Career development programs take many forms but include such basic features as developing a career path, performance appraisal counseling, exploration of job opportunities within the company, and career counseling. The career development program at Corning is exemplary. Its essential features are outlined in Figure 17–2. Observe that the organization, the individual worker, and the supervisor play key roles.[18]

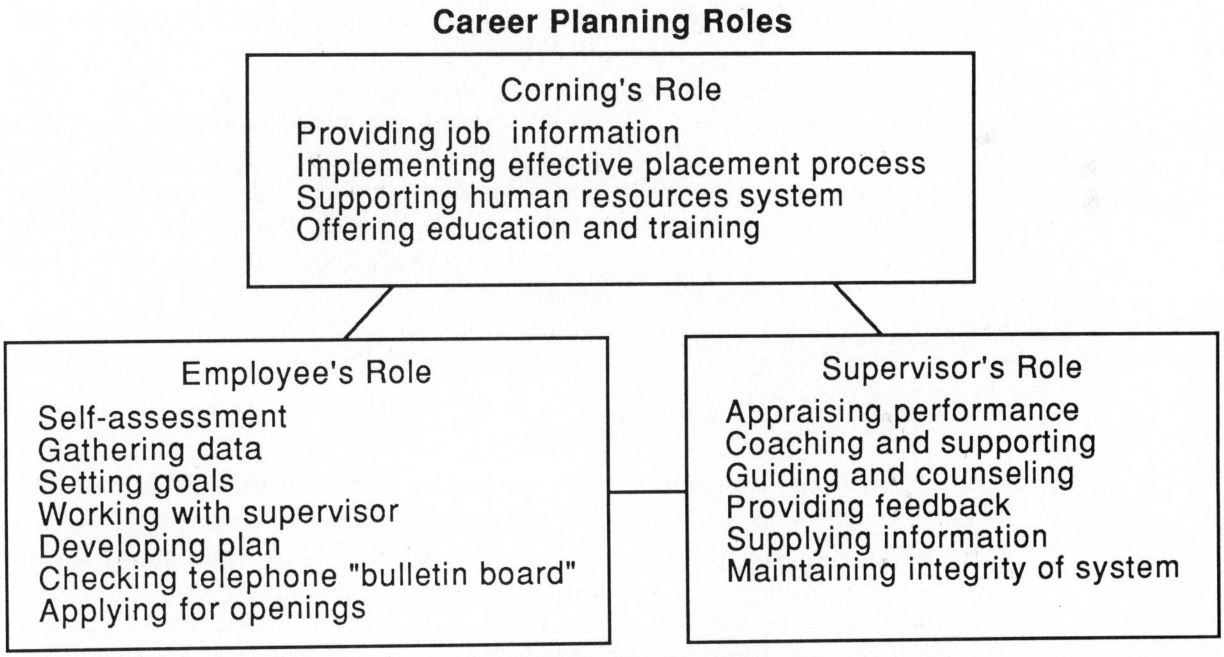

Career Planning Roles

Corning's Role

Providing job information
Implementing effective placement process
Supporting human resources system
Offering education and training

Employee's Role

Self-assessment
Gathering data
Setting goals
Working with supervisor
Developing plan
Checking telephone "bulletin board"
Applying for openings

Supervisor's Role

Appraising performance
Coaching and supporting
Guiding and counseling
Providing feedback
Supplying information
Maintaining integrity of system

FIGURE 17–2 The Career Development Program at Corning

Source: Zandy B. Leibowitz, Barbara H. Feldman, and Sherry H. Mosley, "Career Development Works Overtime at Corning Inc.," *Personnel,* April 1990, p. 44. Reprinted with permission.

As part of a career development program, the individual may receive career counseling. It is also possible to work privately with a career counselor. The vast majority of people manage their careers with no outside professional help. But what is common practice is not always best. Using a career counselor may be a sound investment in time and money, but not every counselee is helped.[19] Two key advantages of career counseling are that (1) it might provide you new insights into yourself, and (2) you may become aware of more alternatives. Next is a sampling of a counseling session that provided the counselee new insights and new alternatives:

Counselor:	You say that there is almost nothing else in life an engineering technician can do but work as an engineering technician.
Engineering technician:	Darn right. That's my problem. As I explained last week, I'm tired of sitting at a desk or in front of a computer solving detailed problems. I need some space, some freedom.
Counselor:	Okay, so you've burnt out a little on solving technical problems. So have lots of people. Do you think if you put your technical problem-solving skills to work just part of the time you would be happy?
Engineering technician:	You mean I should work just part-time? I can't afford it. I've got too many expenses.
Counselor:	(*Laughs good naturedly.*) What I'm talking about is putting your analytical skills to work in a job that also gives you some freedom and space. My impression is that companies that sell high-technology products are always looking to convert technical people into sales reps or sales engineers.
Engineering technician:	Why didn't I think of that? I bet I could make it as a sales rep for our firm. I know the product. I think I would just have to brush up on my speaking skills.
Counselor:	It sounds as if you're excited about this idea. What are you going to do about it?
Engineering technician:	I'm going to try to get an interview with the sales manager, real soon.

INTEGRATING THE DEMANDS OF CAREER AND PERSONAL LIFE

To achieve a successful life it is necessary to balance the demands of work and personal life. Achieving this balance has become a major challenge facing today's workforce. Career researcher Douglas T. Hall says that work/

family balance has become *the* hot career issue of the 1990s.[20] The challenge is particularly intense for employees who are part of two-wage-earner families—a group that includes close to 60 percent of the workforce in the United States and Canada. Consequently, employee caregivers often find themselves needing time away from work. They may need time to take care of a child's illness, school appointments, medical appointments for an elderly family member, or any of a number of family crises.[21]

Here we describe a few of the steps individuals can take, including assistance from the organization, to better balance the demands of career and personal life.[22]

Discuss work commitments with partner or prospective partner. Substantial conflict over work vs. family demands can be prevented if each partner has an accurate perception of the prospective mate's work schedule and work values. For example, some people are prepared to work sixty hours per week to achieve their career objectives, while others prefer to avoid working over forty hours. Partners who cannot agree or compromise on how much time is suitable to invest in a career may not be compatible.

Plan ahead for family events. Advance personal planning can minimize conflict between work and important family events. This would involve marking on one's office calendar, at the beginning of each year, important family dates, such as birthdays. In this way an attempt could be made to minimize business travel and late meetings on those dates. Similarly, the family could be advised of times when work demands would be at their peak.

Divide household chores equitably. Many women who work outside the home rightfully complain that they are responsible for too much of the housework. In the extreme, they function as both career people and full-time homemakers. Under this arrangement, conflict at home is highly probable, making it more difficult to concentrate on work. The recommended solution is for the working couple to divide household tasks in some equitable manner. Equity could mean that tasks are divided according to preference or the amount of effort required. Each couple should negotiate for themselves what constitutes an equitable division of household tasks.

Choose a "parent track." In a highly controversial article, Felice Schwartz identified two groups of corporate women. *Career-primary women* put career first and are willing to make sacrifices in their personal lives, such as forgoing child rearing. *Career-and-family women* are willing to sacrifice some career growth and compensation for freedom from excessive working hours. The latter group would be placed on a "mommy track."[23] Many men have placed themselves on a "daddy track" in order to invest more time in childrearing, and others would like to. A survey of 1,000 workers revealed that 74 percent of men said that they would choose a daddy track. Such a career track was defined as having flexible jobs that offer slower career advancement but more time for family life.[24]

In short, another way of integrating the demands of work and family life is to place oneself on a track that would most likely allow sufficient time to do a good job of parenting. Some career accomplishment would be sacrificed in order to be a better caregiver.

Rely on organizational support systems.   Employers are providing an increasing number of programs and services that support workers attempting to balance the demands of work and family life. Among these programs are child care, elder care (day care for elderly people who cannot care for themselves entirely), and parental leave. A sympathetic and patient supervisor is a major part of the support system.

Modified work schedules, as described in Chapter 4, make a major contribution to balancing work and family demands. An authority on work and family challenge issues advocates job sharing and work-at-home programs to integrate work and family demands.[25] New research has shown, however, that telecommuting is not always an ideal solution. Despite the allure of telecommuting to parents of young children, it is very difficult to concentrate on work and care for preschoolers simultaneously.[26]

Summary of Key Points

- Careful planning is required in order to find rewarding and satisfying career opportunities. You must accept the major responsibility for developing your career, despite whatever help is offered by your employer. Career development is a planned approach to achieving growth and satisfaction in work experiences.

- Finding a field is a critical early step in developing your career. Systematic methods of selecting a field include making use of valid occupational information (both written and computerized), and talking to jobholders in fields of potential interest to you.

- People have different career orientations, including a desire to get ahead, find exciting work, find security, and have freedom to pursue work of high interest. Consequently, not all workers plan their career toward achieving managerial positions.

- An important part of career development is to establish career goals and map out a career path. A career path is a series of positions in one or more organizations leading to a long-range goal. In laying out a career path, personal plans can be integrated with career plans. Contingency plans should also be incorporated into a well-designed career path.

- Career advancement strategies and tactics geared toward taking control of yourself include (1) develop a code of professional ethics, (2) make an accurate self-appraisal, (3) stick with what you do best,

(4) display good job performance, (5) create a good first and lasting impression, (6) document your accomplishments, and (7) manage luck.

- Career advancement strategies and tactics geared toward exerting control over the external environment include (1) identify growth fields and growth companies, (2) find the right employer for you, (3) achieve broad experience, (4) find a sponsor, (5) find a mentor, (6) rely on networking, (7) learn to manage career plateaus, and (8) work comfortably with cultural diversity.

- Company-sponsored career development programs make an important contribution to integrating the career goals of individuals with organizational requirements. Career development programs include such features as developing a career path, performance appraisal counseling, exploration of job opportunities, and career counseling. The latter may help you acquire useful insights about yourself and an awareness of a wide range of career alternatives.

- To achieve a successful life it is necessary to balance the demands of work and personal life. Achieving this balance has become a major challenge facing today's workforce. To work toward this balance, individuals might (1) discuss work commitments with a partner or prospective partner, (2) plan ahead for family events, (3) divide household chores equitably, (4) choose a parent track, and (5) rely on organizational support systems such as child care and modified work schedules.

Questions and Activities

1. How might the organization benefit from individuals doing a good job of career development?

2. What steps have you already taken to develop your career?

3. Is "getting ahead" the only suitable career orientation for a highly motivated person? Explain your reasoning.

4. How do lateral transfers (job assignments at the same level) fit into a career path?

5. How does one know if a particular business practice is unethical?

6. Aside from job hunting, how does making a good first impression help a person on the job?

7. Which of the career advancement strategies and tactics described in this chapter would you describe as being very political? Why?

8. How candid would you be in revealing your career path to an employer, especially if you planned to leave the organization in a few years?

9. What do you see as the advantages and disadvantages of telling an employer that you wish to be placed on a parent track?

10. Ask two successful people to describe the career advancement tactics they used to achieve success. Be prepared to discuss your answers in class.

A HUMAN RELATIONS CASE PROBLEM
The Golden Career Path

Terry Lee, a 21-year-old student majoring in business, submitted the following career path as part of the requirements for a course entitled "Human Relations in the Workplace."

Work: First, I will work two years as a first-line supervisor at a manufacturing company. Then I will take a one- or two-year tour of duty as an assistant plant manager. After that I will work for one or two years as a plant manager. Next, I would take on an international assignment to help prepare me for an executive position. After that I will have reached my medium-range goal of becoming an operations manager.

After three years as an operations manager, I will become a division head. I will then take on an assignment as the president of a small company for three years. My first presidency will be followed up by the presidency of a medium-sized company. Next, I will shift to the presidency of a major business corporation. I will stay there until I am approximately 50 years old, when I will buy my own spacecraft company or some other high-technology company.

My contingency plan concerns the presidency of a major corporation. If that does not materialize, I will buy my own firm sooner. While working for smaller companies, I will receive part of my compensation in stocks. As these investments pay off, I will have accumulated enough money to make a down payment on a company. I will pay off any loans with profits from the company I buy.

Personal plans: I intend to remain single until age 35. At that time I will marry the right professional woman. We will have four children of our own or adopt four from a Rumanian orphanage. We will own a house in the country where I am employed, plus a vacation villa in the Caribbean or France. I will stay in shape by doing exercise at my desk and weight lifting three times per week.

1. What criticisms do you have about Terry Lee's career path?
2. What positive comments do you have about his career path?
3. What career advancement strategies and tactics should Lee use to increase his chances of reaching his goals?
4. Should Lee's instructor offer him encouragement?

A HUMAN RELATIONS CASE PROBLEM
The Faltering Mentor

Alana Wong entered her company as a management trainee. One year later she was given a permanent assignment in the purchasing department as an assistant buyer. Al Bolton, the vice president of purchasing, took a strong interest in Wong's career. He regarded her as intelligent and ambitious. After a while, Wong became Bolton's protégé, and most people in the purchasing department thought Wong was headed for a purchasing manager's position early in her career.

After several months of association, the working relationship between Bolton and Wong became closer. With the approval of his boss, Bolton gave Wong a series of special assignments. When Bolton gave a presentation to other executives, he brought along Wong, who was asked to assist in the presentation.

Scarlett Overmeyer, Wong's boss, invited her to lunch one day. She said to Alana, "The news I have for you isn't very pleasant. But it's something you should know. Al Bolton has fallen out of power. He's made several really bad purchasing decisions that have cost the company close to $1,000,000. If I were you I would drop him as a mentor right away. If he goes, you are likely to go, too."

"Are you sure, Scarlett?" asked Alana.

"Absolutely," replied Scarlett. "Two independent sources have told me the same story."

1. What should Wong do next?
2. How might Wong discuss this topic with Bolton?
3. Has Overmeyer overstepped her bounds?

A HUMAN RELATIONS EXERCISE
The Career Development Inventory

Career development activities inevitably include answering some penetrating questions about yourself. Following are 12 representative questions to be found on career development inventories. You may need several hours to do a competent job answering these questions. After individuals have answered these questions by themselves, it may be profitable to hold a class discussion about the relevance of the specific questions. A strongly recommended procedure is for you to date your completed inventory and put it away for safekeeping. Examine your answers in several years to see (1) how well you are doing in advancing your career, and (2) how much you have changed.

Keep the following information in mind in answering this inventory: William Mihal conducted an experiment in which he documented the fact that people are generous in their self-evaluation when they answer career development inventories.[27] So you might want to discuss some of your answers with somebody else who knows you well.

1. How would you describe yourself as a person?

2. What are you best at doing? Worst?

3. What are your two biggest strengths or assets?

4. What are the two traits, characteristics, or behaviors of yours that need the most improvement?

5. What are your two biggest accomplishments?

6. Write your obituary as you would like it to appear upon your death.

7. What would be the ideal job for you?

8. Why aren't you more rich and famous?

9. What career advice can you give yourself?

10. Describe the two peak experiences in your life.

11. What are your five most important values? (The things in life most important to you.)

12. What goals in life are you trying to achieve?

Notes

1. DISCOVER for Colleges and Adults, The American College Testing Program.

2. William J. Kutcha, "Options in Career Paths," *Personnel Journal,* December 1988, p. 28.

3. C. Brooklyn Derr, *Managing the New Careerists: The Diverse Career Success Orientation of Today's Workers* (San Francisco: Jossey-Bass, 1986).

4. "Ethics: Can You Keep Your Values and Your Job?" *Personal Report for the Executive,* March 1, 1990, p. 1.

5. Sydney J. Harris, "Career Advice: Stick with What You Do Best," syndicated column, Sept. 16, 1982.

6. Greg Livadas, "Make Yourself More Valuable to Your Boss," careers supplement, *Rochester Democrat and Chronicle/Times Union,* June 22, 1990, pp. 1, 5.

7. Roger Ailes, "The First Seven Seconds," *Success,* November 1988, p. 18.

8. "Make an Impression: Improve Your Greeting," *Working Smart,* Sept. 15, 1990, p. 7.

9. Rosabeth Moss Kanter, "From Climbing to Hopping: The Contingent Job and the Post-Entrepreneurial Career," *Management Review,* April 1989, pp. 22–27.

10. Gene W. Dalton and Paul H. Thompson, *Novations: Strategies for Career Management* (Glenview, IL: Scott, Foresman, 1986).

11. Michael G. Zey, "A Mentor for All Reasons," *Personnel Journal,* January 1988, pp. 46–51.

12. Raymond A. Noe, "Women and Mentoring: A Review and Research Agenda," *Academy of Management Review,* January 1988, pp. 67–71.

13. James F. Kelly, Jr., "Coping with the Career Plateau," *Personnel Administrator,* October 1985, p. 65.

14. Susanne Elshult and James Little, "The Case for Valuing Diversity," *HRMagazine,* June 1990, p. 51.

15. O.C. Brenner and Marc G. Singer, "Career Repotters: To Know Them Could Be to Keep Them," *Personnel,* November 1988, p. 58.

16. Linda Kline and Lloyd L. Feinstein, "Creative Thinking for Switching Careers," *Success!,* March 1983, p. A2.

17. Zandy B. Leibowitz, Barbara H. Feldman, and Sherry H. Mosley, "Career Development Works Overtime at Corning Inc.," *Personnel,* April 1990, pp. 38–46.

18. Vernon C. Zunker, *Career Counseling: Applied Concepts of Life Planning,* 2nd ed. (Monterey, CA: Brooks/Cole, 1986).

19. Douglas T. Hall, "Moving Beyond the 'Mommy Track': An Organization Change Approach," *Personnel*, December 1989, p. 23.

20. Renee Magid, *The Work and Family Challenge* (Management Briefing) (New York: American Management Assoication, 1990), p. 31.

21. Douglas T. Hall and Judith Richter, "Balancing Work Life and Home Life: What Can Organizations Do to Help?" *The Academy of Management Executive,* August 1988, p. 213; Magid, *The Work and Family Challenge;* Hall, "Moving Beyond the 'Mommy Track,'" pp. 23–29.

22. Felice Schwartz, "Management Women and the New Facts of Life," *Harvard Business Review,* January–February 1989, p. 70.

23. Cited in "Men Are Choosing the 'Daddy Track' Over the Fast Track," *The Los Angeles Times* syndicated story, Oct. 28, 1989.

24. Magid, *The Work and Family Challenge,* pp. 41–45.

25. Andrew J. DuBrin and Janet C. Barnard, "Comparison of the Job Satisfaction and Productivity of Telecommuting versus In-house Employees," *Psychological Reports*, 1991, pp. 1223–34.

26. William L. Mihal, "An Assessment of the Accuracy of Self-Assessment for Career Decision Making," paper presented at the Academy of Management meeting, August 1983.

Suggested Reading

Adler, Nancy, and Izraeli, Dafna (eds.). *Women in Management Worldwide.* Armonk, NY: Sharp, 1988.

ARTHUR, MICHAEL B., HALL, DOUGLAS T., and LAWRENCE, BARBARA S., (eds.). *Handbook of Career Theory.* New York: Cambridge University Press, 1989.

BREIDENBACH, MONICA E. *Career Development: Taking Charge of Your Career.* Englewood Cliffs, NJ: Prentice Hall, 1989.

CAMERON, RANDOLPH W. *The Minority Executive's Handbook.* New York: Warner, 1989.

COMO, JAY. *Surviving on the Job,* 2nd ed. Mission Hills, CA: Glencoe, 1990.

GAERTNER, KAREN N. "Managers' Careers and Organizational Change." *Academy of Management Executive,* November 1988, pp. 311–18.

GALLIN, AMIRA, and BENOLIEL, BARBARA. "Does the Way You Dress Affect Your Performance Rating?" *Personnel,* August 1990, pp. 49–52.

GREENHAUS, JEFFERY H. *Career Management.* New York: Dryden, 1987.

KLUBNIK, JOAN. "Putting Together a Career Development Program." *Management Solutions,* January 1988, pp. 31–36.

MARMER, CHARLENE SOLOMON. "Careers Under Glass." *Personnel Journal,* April 1990, pp. 96–105.

18

Improving Your Work Habits and Time Management

LEARNING OBJECTIVES

After reading and studying this chapter and doing the exercises, you should be able to

1. Become more productive.

2. Develop insight into how you can decrease any personal tendencies toward procrastination.

3. Identify attitudes and values that contribute to effective work habits and time management.

4. Identify skills and techniques that contribute to effective work habits and time management.

5. Prepare an action plan for improving your work habits and time management.

B y improving your work habits and time management, you can improve your productivity on the job and enhance your personal life. As time management expert Alec Mackenzie observes, "The value of time management is not control of time per se, but the ways you can use time to improve your life."[1] Good work habits and proper management of time improve productivity because they result in more being accomplished in the same amount of time. Improved work habits and time management improve personal life for two main reasons. First, you have more time available for personal life. Second, since your work is under control you can concentrate better on—and therefore derive more enjoyment from—personal life.

Good work habits and time management practices are also important for defensive reasons. People are much more likely to be fired from the job or flunk out of school because of poor work habits rather than because of poor aptitude or insufficient basic skills.

We have organized information about developing better work habits and time management practices into three categories. One is overcoming procrastination, a problem that plagues almost everybody to some extent. The second is developing the attitudes and values that allow you to become more efficient and effective. The third category is developing the proper skills and techniques that lead to personal productivity.

DEALING WITH PROCRASTINATION

Procrastination is the delaying of action for no good reason. It is the major time waster for most people. Unproductive people are the biggest procrastinators, but even highly productive people have some problems with procrastination. If these people did not procrastinate, they would be even more productive. The enormity of the problem makes it worthwhile to examine the most probable underlying causes of procrastination and the tactics for minimizing procrastination. Only a charlatan would propose that procrastination can be *eliminated*. Before reading ahead, see Figure 18–1 to obtain further insight into the signs of procrastination.

Why People Procrastinate

Procrastination has many roots. One major cause is a fear of failure, including a negative evaluation of one's work.[2] For example, if you delay preparing a report for your boss, that person cannot criticize its quality. The fear of bad news is another contributor to procrastination. If you think the monitor on your personal computer is burning out, delaying a trip to the repair shop will postpone the diagnosis: "You're right. Your monitor is on its way out. We can replace it for $375."

When you have no valid excuse for not getting things accomplished, you are probably procrastinating. The signs of procrastination can also be much more subtle. You might be procrastinating if one or more of the following symptoms apply to you:

- You overorganize a project by such rituals as sharpening every pencil, meticulously straightening out your desk, and discarding bent paper clips.
- You keep waiting for the "right time" to do something, such as getting started on an important report.
- You underestimate the time needed to do a project, and say to yourself, "This won't take much time, so I can do it next week."
- You trivialize a task by saying it's not worth doing.

FIGURE 18-1 How Do You Know When You are Procrastinating?

Source: Based on information in "Procrastination Can Get in Your Way," *Research Institute Personal Report for the Executive,* Dec. 24, 1985, pp. 3–4.

Fear of success is another cause of procrastination. People who fear success share the conviction that success will bring with it some disastrous effect, such as isolation or abandonment.[3] Or some may simply prefer to avoid the responsibility that success will bring. And a quick way to avoid success is to procrastinate over something important, such as completing a key assignment.

A deep-rooted reason for procrastination is **self-destructive behavior,** a conscious or unconscious attempt to bring down personal failure. For instance, a person might be recommended for an almost ideal job opportunity. Yet the person delays sending along a résumé for so long that the potential employer loses interest. Self-destructive behavior and fear of success are closely related: The person who fears success may often engage in self-destructive behavior.

Procrastination may also stem from a desire to avoid uncomfortable, overwhelming, or tedious tasks. A person who itemizes tax deductions might delay preparing his or her tax return for all these reasons.

People frequently put off tasks that do not appear to offer a meaningful reward. Suppose you decided that your computer files need a thorough updating, including deleting inactive files. Even if you know it should be done, the accomplishment of updated files might not be a particularly meaningful reward.

Finally, people often procrastinate as a way of rebelling at being controlled. Procrastination, used this way, is a means of defying unwanted authority.[4] Rather than submit to authority, the person might say silently, "Nobody is going to tell me when I should get a report done. I'll do it when I'm good and ready."

Ways of Reducing Procrastination

A general method of coping with procrastination is to raise your level of awareness about the problem. When you are not accomplishing enough to meet your work or personal goals, ask yourself if the problem could be that you are procrastinating over some important tasks. Then try to overcome that incident of inaction. In addition, consider using one or more of the six strategies described next, and summarized in Table 18–1.

Calculate the cost of procrastination.   Alan Lakein believes that you can reduce the extent of your procrastination by calculating its cost. One example is that you might lose out on obtaining a high-paying job you really want by not having your résumé and cover letter ready on time. Your cost of procrastination would include the difference in salary between the job you do find and the one you really wanted. Another cost would be the loss of potential job satisfaction.

Apply behavior modification to yourself.   You can implement this strategy by reinforcing yourself with a pleasant reward soon after you accomplish an arduous task instead of procrastinating. You might, for example, go swimming with a friend after completing a research paper on time. A second part of the strategy is to penalize yourself with something you abhor immediately after you procrastinate.[5] How about cleaning out a barn floor as a punishment for mailing out bills late?

Counterattack the problem task.   Forcing yourself to do something overwhelming, frightening, or uncomfortable helps to prove that the task was not as bad as initially perceived.[6] Assume that you have accepted a new position, but have not yet resigned from your present one because resigning seems so uncomfortable. Set up a specific time to call your manager to schedule an appointment. Force yourself, further, to show up for the resignation appointment. After you break the ice with the statement, "I have something important to tell you," the task will be much easier.

TABLE 18–1   Ways of reducing procrastination

---

1. Calculate the cost of procrastination.
2. Apply behavior modification to yourself.
3. Counterattack the problem task.
4. Cut the task down into manageable chunks.
5. Focus on starting rather than finishing.
6. Make a public commitment.

Cut the task down into manageable chunks.   To reduce procrastination, cut down a project that seems overwhelming into smaller projects that seem less formidable. If your job calls for your inspecting twenty locations within thirty days, begin by making dates to inspect the two closest to home. It also helps ease the pain by planning the job before executing it. In this situation you would plan an itinerary before starting the inspections. The planning would probably be less painful than actually getting started making all the arrangements.

Focus on starting rather than finishing.   The thought of meeting a distant deadline is anxiety-provoking for procrastinators because they envision having to do the whole job at once.[7] If this might be part of your problem, think in terms of starting rather than finishing tasks. Similar to cutting the task down into manageable chunks, the project facing you will appear less formidable. Starting becomes even easier when you begin with a very easy task, such as taking out a new manila folder.

Make a public commitment.   Here you try to make it imperative that you get something done on time by making a commitment to one or more other people. You might simply announce to co-workers that you are going to get something accomplished by a certain date. If you fail to meet this date you are likely to feel the pangs of embarrassment. One manager used this technique to help him get performance appraisals (an arduous task) done on time. He would announce in a department meeting, "Your performance reports will be done by September 30. If I'm late with even one of them I want you to write a complaint letter to the president."

PRODUCTIVE ATTITUDES AND VALUES

Developing good work habits and time-management practices is often a matter of developing the right attitudes toward your work and toward time. If, for example, you think that your job is important and that time is a precious resource, you will be on your way toward developing good work habits. In this section we summarize a group of attitudes, values, and beliefs that can help a person make good use of time and develop productive work habits. These attitudes and values are summarized in Table 18–2.

Establish goals and develop a strong work ethic.   As described in Chapter 3, setting goals can directly improve performance. One reason goal setting helps in this way is that being committed to a goal propels you toward good use of time. Imagine how efficient most employees would be if they were told, "Here are five days' worth of work facing you. If you get it finished in less than five days, you can have all that saved time to yourself." One negative side effect, however, is that the employees might sacrifice quality for speed.

TABLE 18-2   Productive attitudes and values for work habits and time management

---

1. Establish goals and develop a strong work ethic.
2. Value your time.
3. Value good attendance and punctuality.
4. Learn to say no.
5. Strive for both quantity and quality.
6. Ask, "What is the best use of my time right now?"
7. Avoid perfectionism.
8. Avoid workaholism.
9. Avoid being a computer goof-off.
10. Try to discover mental blocks.

Closely related to establishing goals is developing a strong **work ethic**—a firm belief in the dignity and value of work. Developing a strong work ethic may lead to even higher productivity than goal setting alone. For example, one might set the goal of earning a high income. It would lead to some good work habits, but not necessarily a high commitment to quality. A person with a strong work ethic believes in quality, is highly motivated, and minimizes time-wasting activities.

Value your time.   People who place a high value on their time are propelled into making good use of time. If a person believes that his or her time is valuable, it will be difficult to engage that person in idle conversation during working hours. Valuing your time can also apply to personal life. Two economists have estimated that the yield from clipping grocery coupons is an average of $7 per hour.[8] Would a busy professional person therefore be better off clipping coupons or engaging in self-development for the same amount of time?

Value good attendance and punctuality.   Good attendance and punctuality are essential for developing a good reputation. Conversely, poor attendance and tardiness are the leading reason for disciplinary action against employees. Attendance and punctuality are also important because you cannot accomplish much if you are away from the work area. The same principle applies for telecommuters—you must also value starting work on time in order to be productive. Another caveat is that being late for or absent from meetings communicates the message to most people that you do not regard the meeting as important.

Learn to say no.   You cannot take care of your own priorities unless you learn tactfully to decline requests from other people that interfere with your work. Your boss, of course, is more difficult to turn down than a co-worker. If your boss interrupts your work with an added assignment, point out how the new task will conflict with higher-priority ones and suggest alternatives.[9] When your boss recognizes that you are motivated to get your major tasks accomplished, and not to avoid work, you may be able to avoid getting saddled with less important tasks.

A word of caution: Do not turn down your supervisor too often. Much discretion and tact is needed in using this approach to work efficiency.

Strive for both quantity and quality.   You will recall that productivity takes into account both quantity and quality. Most employers want a great deal of work accomplished, but they also need high-quality work. Thus a commitment to both quality and quantity leads to effective work habits. As a first principle, work as rapidly as you can just before the point at which you are committing an unacceptable number of errors. Striving for perfection is not worth the price, but achieving high-quality goods and services is highly valued in most firms today.

Ask, "What is the best use of my time right now?"   A key mental set for improving your efficiency and effectiveness is to ask this important question. It helps you justify your every action. Lakein notes that a particularly good time to ask this question (which he originated) is when you have been interrupted by a visitor or phone call. When it is over, he advises to check whether you should go back to what you were doing or on to something new.[10]

Avoid perfectionism.   Thoroughness is a virtue in most jobs until it reaches the point of diminishing returns. If every typographical error were removed from a newspaper, the price of the paper would have to be increased to an unrealistic level. Even worse, the paper would usually be late. Striving for excellence is certainly worthwhile, but striving for perfectionism is often self-defeating. Two work-habit consultants advise us:

1. Don't run all over town looking for a particular report folder when second-best will do.
2. Don't have letters rewordprocessed to be picture perfect; the recipients will just file them or throw them away.
3. Realize that *below average to a perfectionist often is perfectly acceptable to others.*[11]

Avoid workaholism.   A valid attitude to maintain is that overwork can be counterproductive, leading to negative stress and burnout. Proper physical rest contributes to mental alertness. **Workaholics,** people who are obsessed with work, often approach their jobs in a mechanical, unimaginative manner. True workaholics have such an excessive need to work that it hampers the well-being of themselves and those around them.[12] A person who works excessively out of financial necessity or love of work—and is highly productive—should therefore not be labeled a workaholic.

Constant attention to work or study is often inefficient. It is a normal human requirement to take enough rest breaks to allow oneself to approach work or study with a fresh perspective. Each person has to establish for himself or herself the right balance between work and leisure, within the bounds of freedom granted by the situation. A middle manager painted this picture of working conditions at his company:

> Sure, I believe in leading a balanced life. But at my company you can't if you want to climb the ladder. Management expects us to work about sixty hours per week. You dare not be caught entering the building after 8 A.M. or leaving before 6:30 P.M.

Avoid being a computer goof-off. We are all aware of the productivity improvements possible through computers. An unproductive use of computers, however, is to tinker with them to the exclusion of more important work. Many people have become intrigued with computers to the point of diversion. They become almost addicted to creating new reports, using exquisite graphics, and even playing computer games on company time. Some managers become so involved with computers that they neglect leadership responsibilities, thus lowering their productivity. In short, avoid becoming a computer goof-off.

Try to discover mental blocks. Some forms of poor work habits and time-management practices have deep psychological roots. If you can figure out what your problem is, you might be able to overcome problems like forgetting to do important assignments. One potential block is fear of success, described previously. It would take a shrewd bit of self-analysis to determine if you feared success. A recommended approach would be to supplement self-analysis by discussing the topic with a trusted friend and/or professional counselor.

Unresolved personal problems can also block personal efficiency and effectiveness. This is especially true because effective time utilization requires good concentration. When you are preoccupied with a personal problem, it is difficult to give your full attention to the task at hand. The solution is to do something constructive about whatever problem is sapping your ability to concentrate. Sometimes a relatively minor problem, such as being out of checks in your checkbook, can impair your work concentration. At other times, a major problem, such as a broken romance, interferes with good work habits. In either situation, your concentration will suffer until you take appropriate action.

PRODUCTIVE SKILLS AND TECHNIQUES

In addition to minimizing procrastination and developing attitudes, values, and beliefs, you also need the right skills and techniques to become efficient and effective. Most books, articles, and workshops dealing with the topic of work habits and time management cover similar ground. Following we summarize most of the skills and techniques mentioned in these sources, along with a few original ones. The same skills and techniques are listed in Table 18–3. The goal of this information is to help you work "smarter rather than harder."

Prepare a list and set priorities.   At the heart of every time-management system is list making. Almost every successful person in any field composes a list of important and less important tasks that need to be done. Some executives and professional people delegate their list making and errand running to a subordinate.

Before you can compose a useful list, you need to set aside a few minutes a day to sort out the tasks at hand. Such activity is the most basic aspect of planning. As a person's career advances, his or her list becomes longer. Many people find it helpful to set up "to do" lists for both work and personal life. The list a small-business owner brought to a time-management workshop is presented in Figure 18–2.

When "to do" lists are placed on index cards or small pieces of paper, they become readily lost or misplaced. One solution is to affix the index

---

TABLE 18–3   Skills and techniques for effective work habits and time management

1. Prepare a list and set priorities.
2. Use a time log and minimize time wasters.
3. Build flexibility into your system.
4. Concentrate on important tasks.
5. Concentrate on one task at a time.
6. Work at a steady pace.
7. Schedule similar tasks together.
8. Set a time limit for certain tasks.
9. Keep an orderly work area (within reason).
10. Stay in control of paperwork.
11. Make use of bits of time.
12. Remember where you put things.
13. Stand instead of sit for certain tasks.

From the Desk of Hank Evans

JOB

Find new grill for '78 Corvette
Do estimate on '86 Toyota
Find Vacation replacements for Tony and Jim
Call accountants to work on books
Pay utility bill
Have broken phone fixed
Call insurance company about payment for Caddy job
Estimate doll-up price for Buick Electra
Have outside sign fixed

HOME

Order pizza for tonight
Birthday present for Margot
Heels replaced on two pairs of shoes
Doctor's appointment for Knee cartilage
Buy grass fertilizer
New pair of jeans
Keg of beer for Saturday's party

HANK'S COLLISION SERVICE
Atlanta, Georgia   **FIGURE 18-2** A Sample "To Do" List

card or slip of paper inside a pocket appointment calendar. More widely recommended is to put these lists in a combined daily planner and calendar, such as the one illustrated in Figure 18–3. Such calendars also serve as a convenient place to log expenses and to make comments on the status of projects.

Not everything on a "to do" list is of equal importance; therefore priorities should be attached to each item on the list. A typical system is to use A to signify critical or essential items, B to signify important items, and C for the least important ones. Although an item might be regarded as a C (for example, refilling the paper clip jar), it still has a contribution to make to your management of time and well-being. Many people report that they obtain a sense of satisfaction from crossing off an item on their list, however trivial. Second, if you are at all conscientious, small, undone items will come back to interfere with your concentration. As you try to enjoy your evening, that unfilled paper clip jar will be lurking in the back of your mind.

Use a time log and minimize time wasters. An advanced tool for managing time efficiently is to prepare a time log of how you are currently investing time. For five full workdays, write down everything you do, including such activities as answering mail and taking rest breaks.[13] An activity calendar (see Figure 18–3) is ideally suited to preparing a time log. One of the most important outputs of a time log is the uncovering of time leaks. A **time leak** is anything you are doing or not doing that allows time to get away from you.

A major time leak for many workers is **schmoozing**— informal socializing on the job, including small talk and conversations with friends. Schmoozing is useful in relieving tension and increasing job satisfaction,

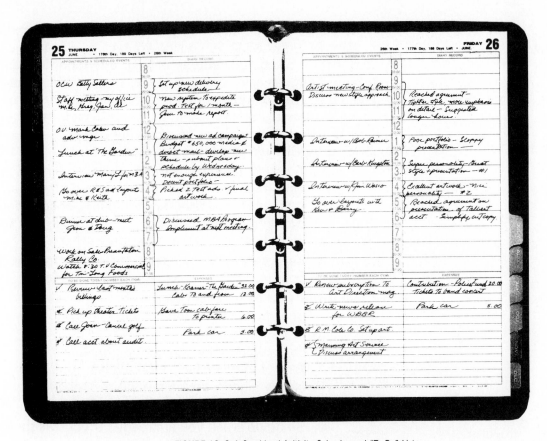

FIGURE 18-3 A Combined Acitivity Calendar and "To Do" List

Source: Reprinted with permission from Desk-Day Timer Inc., Allentown, PA 18001.

but too much of this activity is a major loss of productive time. Investigations conducted by Mackenzie revealed the following top time wasters:

1. Telephone interruptions
2. Crisis management, shifting priorities
3. Lack of objectives, priorities, and planning
4. Drop-in visitors (see Figure 18–4)
5. Ineffective delegation (assigning tasks to subordinates)
6. Attempting too much
7. Meetings
8. Personal disorganization, cluttered desk
9. Inability to say "no"
10. Lack of self-discipline.[14]

Build Flexibility into your system. A common misperception is that an effective time manager has every working minute carefully budgeted. In reality, a good time-management system allows some room for flexibility in taking

What should you do when your co-workers want to socialize, but you want to work? Must you resign yourself to a forty-five-minute illustrated lecture on the adventures of your co-worker's grandchild when you have a difficult sales presentation to prepare? Or should you risk offending the proud grandfather by throwing him bodily out of your office? Fortunately there is some middle ground. Consider this list of suggestions for politely but firmly protecting your privacy—and your sanity—published by GF Business Equipment Inc.

1. A direct statement is most effective. Simply say, "I'm sorry, but I'm busy and can't be disturbed." If you are concerned that others will take this personally or consider you antisocial, compensate by going out of your way to be friendly with these people at other times.

2. Keep your responses brief and let your tone of voice convey your reluctance to engage in conversation.

3. Avoid eye contact with unwelcome visitors. It's harder for people to sustain conversation with people who won't look at them.

4. If you were about to make a phone call when someone enters, do not replace the receiver. Keeping it in your hand clearly signals your intention to proceed momentarily.

5. Do not sit down if you want to keep the visit brief.

6. Stand up when you are ready for your visitor to leave. This is an unmistakable signal.

7. If you occupy a work space with relatively low partitions (five feet or less), place or attach articles such as plants, in/out trays, lamps, clocks, or vases on the partition surface or edge to prevent others from leaning into your space.

8. If possible, use task lighting to focus on your work. This emphasizes your absorption in your task and creates a bond between you and your work that others will hesitate to break.

FIGURE 18–4 Protecting Your Privacy

Source: GF Business Equipment, 229 E. Dennick Ave., Youngstown, OH 44501.

care of unplanned activities. Only events under your control can be planned.[15] It is therefore important to build some time into your work schedule to handle unplanned activities, such as emergency meetings, traffic jams, and interruptions by higher-ranking people. Reviewing your time log is an effective way of determining if you are too tightly scheduled.

Concentrate on important tasks. To become more productive, you have to concentrate on tasks in which superior performance could have a large payoff. Concentration on these tasks facilitates achieving peak performance.

Charles A. Garfield observes that an important behavior of peak performers is their goal orientation: "They do not waste time on activities that are not tied to reaching their goals."[16] No matter how quickly Hank Evans takes care of making sure that his utilities bills are paid on time, this effort will not make his collision shop a success. However, if he gets the work out on time and the quality is high, the reputation of his shop will spread.

In following the A-B-C system, you should devote ample time to the essential tasks. You should not pay more attention than absolutely necessary to the C (least important) items. Many people respond to this principle of time management by saying, "I don't think concentrating on important tasks applies to me. My job is so filled with routine that I have no chance to work on the big breakthrough ideas." True, most jobs are filled with routine requirements. The antidote is to spend some time, perhaps even one hour a week, concentrating on tasks of potentially major significance.

Concentrate on one task at a time.   Productive people have a well-developed capacity to concentrate on the problem or person facing them. The best results from concentration are achieved when you are so absorbed in your work that you are aware of virtually nothing else at the moment. Concentration is also useful because it reduces absentmindedness. If you concentrate intensely on what you are doing, the chances diminish that you will forget what you intended to do.

Researchers have discovered that conscious effort and self-discipline can strengthen concentration skills. "There are two types of concentration: passive and active," explains Auke Tellegen. "The former is used when you are drawn into something riveting, such as a good novel. The latter demands self-constraint." The best way to sharpen your concentration skills is to set aside fifteen minutes a day and focus on something repetitive, such as your breathing or a small word. The same approach is used in meditation to relieve stress.[17]

Work at a steady pace.   In most jobs, working at a steady clip pays dividends in efficiency. The spurt worker creates many problems for management. Some employees take pride in working rapidly, even when the result is a high error rate. An important advantage of the steady-pace approach is that you accomplish much more than someone who puts out extra effort just once in a while. The completely steady worker would accomplish just as much the day before a holiday as on a given Monday. That extra hour or so of productivity adds up substantially by the end of the year. Despite the advantages of maintaining a steady pace, some peaks and valleys in your work may be inevitable. The seasonal demands placed on public accountants is a prime example.

A by-product of working at a steady pace is that it allows you to leave work at a regular time because you have evened out many of the peak loads. Being caught up enables you to better handle surges in workload. The philosophy of steady pacing also keeps you from leaving early (either physically or mentally), thus keeping you current with work.

Schedule similar tasks together.   An efficient method of accomplishing small tasks is to group them together and perform them in one block of time. To illustrate, you might make most of your telephone calls in relation to your job from 11:00 to 11:30 each workday morning. Or you might reserve the last hour of each workday for correspondence and filing. It is also helpful to group your visits to people away from your work area. In this way you minimize the amount of time you are away from your own work area. Time spent "traveling" on company premises is usually not very productive. (And remember to minimize schmoozing).

By scheduling similar tasks together you develop the necessary pace and mental set to go through chores in short order. In contrast, when you jump from one type of task to another, your efficiency may suffer.

Set a time limit for certain tasks.   As a person becomes experienced with certain projects, he or she is able to make accurate estimates of how long a new project will take to complete. Thus Hank Evans might say, "I think we can fix this wreck in ten working days." A good work habit to develop is to estimate how long a job should take, then proceed with strong determination to get the job completed within the estimated period of time.

A variation of this technique is to decide that some low-priority and medium-priority items are only worth so much of your time. Invest that much time in the project, but no more. A new employee might say, for example, "Learning about the company policies and philosophy is of medium importance. Therefore, I'll study the company manuals one hour per week. But that's it. It's more important that I learn my new job well."

Keep an orderly work area (within reason).   A controversy in time management is whether or not a clean, well-organized work area reflects an uncluttered, organized mind. Some people contend, "What difference does the appearance of my desk make? What counts is whether I know where things are." Some time-management specialists contend that an orderly desk is not linked directly to productivity.[18]

A partial resolution of the controversy is to recognize that a tidy work area is more important for some types of work than others. Executives tend to prefer a well-organized desk, whereas artists, writers, scientists, and professors tend to prefer a cluttered desk. If you work in a bureaucracy, an orderly desk is impressive. A disorderly desk gives you a negative image.

An orderly work area has two striking advantages. For one, it helps you concentrate on one piece of paper at a time—an important habit for accomplishing things. Second, it decreases drastically the amount of time you devote to searching for notes, forms, and other work-related material. Despite these two impressive arguments for an organized, tidy desk, some highly successful people have disastrous looking desks.

Stay in control of paperwork.   Although it is fashionable to decry the necessity of having to do paperwork in responsible jobs, the effective career person does not neglect paperwork. Paperwork includes reacting to correspondence, computer printouts, memos, and to advertisements sent through the mail. Unless paperwork is handled efficiently, a person's job may get out of control. Once a job is out of control it leads to lowered productivity and stress. Ideally, a small amount of time should be invested in paperwork every day to prevent the task from getting out of hand. Paperwork also includes *electronic work*, such as electronic mail and voice mail.

Most systems of managing paperwork are similar to making up a list of tasks and setting priorities. You sort out the papers facing you and assign them priorities. Dru Scott recommends that every day you sort all your papers into three priority piles:

I. Centrals and essentials
II. Secondary matters
III. Marginal matters[19]

The ideal is to get rid of as many papers on the spot as you can. This means throwing away as many of the marginal matters as possible so you won't have to handle them again. The secondary matters should be put in a special place for later action. (An example of a secondary matter might be a request for you to participate in a company survey.) A decision must be reached about each piece of paper with a priority of I (centrals and essentials):

1. What action should be taken?
2. Who should take it?
3. What should the timetable be?

One example would be a memo from your boss asking for your opinion on reorganizing the department. Your answers to the above might be: (1) I should write a report and request to discuss it with my boss; (2) I'm the one who has to take action; and (3) This is a top priority item. I'll get it done within three working days.

Make use of bits of time.   A truly efficient person makes good use of miscellaneous bits of time, both on and off the job. While waiting in line at a bank or post office, you might update your "to do" list; while waiting for an elevator you might be able to read a 100-word report; and if you have finished your day's work ten minutes before quitting time, you can use that time to clean out a drawer in your desk. By the end of the year your productivity will have increased much more than if you had squandered these bits of time.

Remember where you put things.   How much time have you wasted lately in looking for items such as an important file, your keys, or a copy of your computer password? If you can remember where you put items of this nature, you can save a lot of wasted time and motion. Turla and Hawkins offer two practical suggestions for remembering where you put things:[20]

1. *Have a parking place for everything.* This would include putting your keys and pocket calculator back in the same place after each use.
2. *Make visual associations.* In order to have something register in your mind at the moment you are doing it, make up a visual association about that act. Thus if a woman named Alison parks her car in section A-6 of a giant parking lot, she might say to herself, "I parked at A-6 and it makes sense. 'A' stands for Alison, and '6' stands for the number of letters in my first name."

Stand up for certain tasks.   According to Merrill E. Douglass, standing rather than sitting is one of the most overlooked secrets for getting more done during working hours. People tend to take longer to accomplish things when they sit down. If forced to stand, they will answer you more quickly rather than become engaged in a long conversation. Because of this fact, many managers schedule stand-up meetings when an agenda is not too long or complicated. Also, some companies have experimented successfully with stand-up conference tables.[21]

Standing is perceived by most people as more formal than sitting. Because people tend to respect time more in formal than informal settings, they make better use of standing time. Also, they waste less time than when slouched in chairs. A physical reason for people getting things done more quickly while standing is that they find it less comfortable than sitting. To avoid discomfort, they get to the point quickly.

Do you think that stand-up meetings have pushed comfort and courtesy too far in the quest for high productivity?

GETTING STARTED IMPROVING YOUR WORK HABITS AND TIME MANAGEMENT

Assume you were able to implement every suggestion in this chapter and you also followed carefully the decision-making steps outlined in Chapter 7. You would now be on the road toward being one of the most productive and well-organized people in your field. The flaw in this logic is that no one is equipped to implement, immediately, every suggestion. One limiting factor is that you might not be able to identify or do much about the underlying problems blocking your productivity.

The recommended way to begin improving your work habits is to start small. Select one or two strategies that seem focused on a major work-habit or time-management problem facing you. Try the strategy. Monitor your progress and move on to another strategy.

A helpful starting point for almost anyone seeking to improve work habits is to sort out the tasks facing you and make a prioritized list. An equally valid approach would be to do the human relations exercise at the conclusion of this chapter. It helps you identify areas where you might be deficient. Act first on those areas where you have a problem. For example, if you are courageous enough to admit that your biggest problem is a tendency to procrastinate, you would act first by attempting to decrease your procrastination.

How personal characteristics influence ability to improve one's work habits. Some people will find it easier than others to improve their productivity. Above all, one needs the right talent and motivation to make much improvement feasible. Another factor is that certain personality characteristics are related to work habits and time management. At the top of the list is **compulsiveness,** a tendency to pay careful attention to detail and to be meticulous. A compulsive person takes naturally to being well-organized and neat. If you are less concerned about detail and meticulousness by nature, it will be more difficult for you to develop exceptional work habits. People who are spontaneous and emotional also tend to be naturally inclined toward casual work habits.

A note of caution: Compulsiveness can sometimes be detrimental to productivity. Compulsive people may have a difficult time concentrating on important tasks. They often get hung up on details and fail to see the "big picture." The truly productive person finds an optimum balance between concern for detail and being able to look at the "big picture."

Decisiveness is another personality factor that exerts an important influence on time management. When faced with a small problem, a decisive person makes up his or her mind in several seconds. When faced with a major decision, the same person moves quickly through the decision-making steps, and then implements the chosen alternative. Indecision and agonizing over past decisions consumes time, thus lowering productivity.

Summary of Key Points

- By improving your work habits and time management, you can improve your job productivity and enhance your personal life. Also, improving in these areas can help prevent one from flunking out of school or being fired.
- Procrastination is a major problem for many people. The major causes of procrastination are fear of failure, fear of bad news, self-destructive behavior, and the desire to avoid uncomfortable, overwhelming, or tedious tasks.

- Awareness of the procrastination problem may lead to its control. Six other methods for reducing procrastination are (1) calculate the cost of procrastination, (2) apply behavior modification to yourself, (3) counterattack the problem task, (4) cut the task down into manageable chunks, (5) focus on starting rather than finishing, and (6) make a public commitment about performing the task.

- Developing good work habits and time-management practices is often a matter of developing the right attitudes toward your work and toward time. Ten such attitudes, values, and beliefs are as follows:

  1. Establish goals and develop a strong work ethic.
  2. Value your time.
  3. Value good attendance and punctuality.
  4. Learn to say no.
  5. Strive for both quantity and quality.
  6. Ask, "What is the best use of my time right now?"
  7. Avoid perfectionism.
  8. Avoid workaholism.
  9. Avoid being a computer goof-off.
  10. Try to discover mental blocks.

- Thirteen skills and techniques to help you worker smarter rather than harder (and therefore be more productive) are:

  1. Prepare a list and set priorities.
  2. Use a time log and minimize timewasters.
  3. Build flexibility into your system.
  4. Concentrate on important tasks.
  5. Concentrate on one task at a time.
  6. Work at a steady pace.
  7. Schedule similar tasks together.
  8. Set a time limit for certain tasks.
  9. Keep an orderly work area (within reason).
  10. Stay in control of paperwork.
  11. Make use of bits of time.
  12. Remember where you put things.
  13. Stand instead of sit for certain tasks.

- The best way to begin improving your work habits and management of time is to start small. Select one or two attitudes, beliefs, strategies, or methods that appear particularly relevant to your circumstances and give them a try. Monitor your progress, and then move on to another tactic. In trying to improve, be aware that if you are not somewhat compulsive, it will require extra effort to become neat and well-organized. Being decisive also facilitates good time management.

Questions and Activities

1. A critic of this chapter said, "If you took all this advice too seriously, you would become obsessed. You would never have any time to relax. It would be work, work, work." What is your response to this critic?

2. What does a person's speech and appearance tell you about his or her work habits and time management?

3. What can you learn about a person's work habits and time management from the appearance of his or her automobile?

4. What is your reaction to the contention that people who are tightly organized are usually not very creative?

5. What applicability do the methods and techniques described in this chapter have for school work?

6. One time-management practice was deliberately omitted from this chapter. Called "double up on time," it deals with such behaviors as sorting through mail while conducting a phone conversation. Why do you think it was omitted?

7. How can a telephone answering machine or voice mail be used to improve task scheduling?

8. What do companies do that encourages workaholism among their employees?

9. What is it about being busy that makes it difficult to practice good work habits and time management?

10. How does the slogan "Just do it" (popularized in Nike commercials and T-shirts) relate to the material in this chapter?

A HUMAN RELATIONS CASE PROBLEM
How To Cure Pilomania

Jeffrey J. Meyer says that you are suffering from *pilomania,* the piling up of papers on the desk, if your desk is buried under piles of papers. It doesn't matter if the papers are in neat orderly piles, in stackable trays, or totally disorganized.

Many people suspect that out of sight is out of mind, and therefore hesitate to put things away for fear of misplacing them. Ultimately you are working less efficiently because your desk area is being improperly used. Meyer claims that if you eliminate the clutter you will save at least thirty minutes a day because you will be able to find all the unfinished work hidden in the piles.

To cure pilomania, begin by making a two-hour appointment with yourself. Use that time to go through every piece of paper on your desk. Keep papers calling for work yet to be done or an action not yet taken. Throw out the rest. Next, go through your keeper file and create a *master list*—an inventory of all your unfinished work and ongoing projects.

For each paper on your list, ask: Is there any work that needs to be done, such as a phone call to make, an electronic message to send, a letter to write? Record the action to be taken on the master list. After you have made your entry, either throw out the paper or place it in a properly labeled file.

The master list is modeled after the directory on a computer, which lists all the files located within its memory. With the master list you have a directory of your unfinished work stored in hard copy. Meyer proposes that you use your master list all day long. It should be the first thing you look at when you start work, and the last thing you look at before leaving.

Part of the master list system is to develop an efficient filing system. Place all papers that deal with a customer, client, or project in a manila folder. Label your files by hand according to whatever categories fit best, such as by project or customer.

New items are added to the master list as the day progresses, and old items are crossed off when they are done. To get the biggest productivity gain from your master list, follow these additional suggestions:

— Use a lined legal- or letter-size pad. Avoid small pieces of paper because you will end up with piles of lists.

— Write on every line, but do not number the items.

— When you have filled up a page, continue on the next one. After half the items on a page are completed, transfer the unfinished items to the next page.

— Date your lists so you know how long some unfinished items have been there.

— Keep your master list on top of your desk where it can be readily located. Do not put it inside a file folder.

— Each evening before going home, scan your list and ask yourself, "What is the most important thing I must do tomorrow?"

1. How effective do you think this system would be for most office workers?

2. What other suggestions for improved work habits and time management does the master list replace?

3. What problems might the master list method create?

Source: Jeffrey J. Meyer, *If You Haven't Got the Time to Do It Right, When Will You Find the Time to Do It Over?* (New York: Simon & Schuster, 1990); "Curing Pilomania," *The Pryor Report,* July 1990, p. 4.

A HUMAN RELATIONS CASE PROBLEM
The Overwhelmed Administrative Assistant

Mary Converse looked into the storeroom mirror and thought to herself, "You're looking bad, kid. Somehow you've got to get your life straightened out. You're on a treadmill, and you don't know how to get off. But it's a bad time to be thinking about myself right now. It's time to meet with my boss, Beatrice. I wonder what she wants?"

Beatrice Reynolds began the meeting with Converse in her usual open manner: "Mary, I'm concerned about you. For a long time you were one of the best administrative assistants in our firm. You received compliments from me and the other department heads who had contact with your department. Now you're hardly making it. You've become so irritable, so lacking in enthusiasm. And a lot of your work contains glaring errors and is also late. The reason I'm bringing the subject up again is that things have gotten worse. What's your problem?"

"I wish it were only one problem, Beatrice. I feel like the world is caving in on me. I work here about forty hours a week. I'm trying to upgrade myself in life. As you know, I'm taking two courses in a business program. If I can keep up the pace, I'll have my degree by next spring. But it's getting to be a grind."

"How are things at home, Mary?"

"Much worse than they are here. My husband works too, and he's getting fed up with never seeing me when he comes home. It seems that when he's home, I'm either working late at the office, in class, or studying at the library. Thursday is the one weekday night I'm home for sure. And that's Tony's bowling night.

"Our son Steve isn't too happy either," Converse continued. "He's only 5 but the other day he asked me if Daddy and I were getting divorced. Steve doesn't see us together much. When he does see us, he can feel the tension between us."

"So, you're under pressure at the office and at home," said Reynolds.

"Add school to that list. I'm having a devil of a time getting through my business statistics course. If I flunk, my chances of getting a degree are set back considerably."

"Do the best you can, Mary. I'm sympathetic, but I need better performance from you."

As Converse left Reynolds' office, she said: "Thanks for being candid with me. My problem is that my boss, my husband, my child, and my professors all want better performance from me. I wish I knew how to give it."

1. What suggestions can you offer Converse for working her way out of her problems?
2. Why is this case included in a chapter about improving your work habits and time management?
3. What stress symptoms is Converse experiencing?
4. How well do you think Reynolds handled the interview?

A HUMAN RELATIONS EXERCISE
Improving Your Work Habits and Time Management

Casually reading this chapter will rarely lead to improvements in personal productivity. You need to back up these ideas with a specific action plan for improvement, as described in the section entitled "Getting Started Improving Your Work Habits and Time Management." A useful mechanical aid toward achieving this end is to scan the checklist presented next. It covers the strategies, techniques, and tactics described in this chapter. Select the six areas on this checklist in which you need the most help. For each item you select, write a one- or two-sentence action plan. Suppose you checked "Work at a steady pace." Your action plan might take this form: "I'm going to use self-discipline to make sure that I treat every day as if it were a Monday. In other words, I will try to keep a steady flow of high-energy work going most of the time. I'll especially try to avoid the slow process of working myself back up to speed after vacations and long weekends."

THE WORK HABIT AND TIME MANAGEMENT CHECKLIST

PROCRASTINATION
1. Calculate the cost of procrastination.   _____
2. Apply behavior modification to yourself.   _____
3. Counterattack the problem task.   _____
4. Cut the task down into manageable chunks.   _____
5. Focus on starting rather than finishing.   _____
6. Make a public commitment.   _____

ATTITUDES AND VALUES
1. Establish goals and develop a strong work ethic.   _____
2. Value your time.   _____
3. Value good attendance and punctuality.   _____

4. Learn to say no. _____
5. Strive for both quantity and quality. _____
6. Ask, "What is the best use of my time right now?" _____
7. Avoid perfectionism. _____
8. Avoid workaholism. _____
9. Avoid being a computer goof-off. _____
10. Try to discover mental blocks. _____

SKILLS AND TECHNIQUES

1. Prepare a list and set priorities. _____
2. Use a time log and minimize time wasters. _____
3. Build flexibility into your system. _____
4. Concentrate on important tasks. _____
5. Concentrate on one task at a time. _____
6. Work at a steady pace. _____
7. Schedule similar tasks together. _____
8. Set a time limit for certain tasks. _____
9. Keep an orderly work area (within reason). _____
10. Stay in control of paperwork. _____
11. Make use of bits of time. _____
12. Remember where you put things. _____
13. Stand instead of sit for certain tasks. _____

Notes

1. Alec Mackenzie, *The Time Trap* (New York: AMACOM, 1990), p. 14.

2. Jane Burka and Lenora Yuen, *Procrastination: Why You Do It, What to Do About It* (Reading, MA: Addison-Wesley, 1984).

3. Bryce Nelson, "Do You Fear Success?" *The New York Times* syndicated story, Feb. 16, 1983.

4. Theodore Kurtz, "Ten Reasons Why People Procrastinate," *Supervisory Management,* April 1990, pp. 1–2.

5. Alan Lakein, *How to Gain Control of Your Time and Your Life* (New York: Wyden, 1973), pp. 141–51.

6. "Don't Procrastinate," *Practical Supervision,* January 1989, p. 3.

7. Neil Fiore, "How to Get Procrastinators Up to Speed," *Working Woman,* March 1989, p. 32.

8. John Charles Pool and Ross M. Laroe, "Is Coupon Clipping Worth the Hassle?" *Rochester Democrat and Chronicle,* June 27, 1988, p. 9D.

9. Edwin C. Bliss, "Give Yourself the Luxury of Time," *Mainliner,* December 1976, p. 56.

10. Lakein, *How to Gain Control,* p. 99.

11. Peter A. Turla and Kathleen L. Hawkins, "The Flaws of Perfectionism," *Success!,* December 1983, p. 23.

12. Ruth Haas, "Workaholics: Good News—Bad News," *Human Resources Forum,* July 1990, p. 1.

13. "Time Management: Beyond the Crutches," *Executive Strategies,* April 3, 1990, pp. 6–7.

14. Sarah Stiansek, "Making Time," *Success!,* April 1990, p. 18; Mackenzie, *The Time Trap,* p. 55.

15. Merrill Douglass, "The Oats Formula: How to Better Plan Your Time," *Supervisory Management,* February 1990, p. 11.

16. "Peak Performance—It Can Be Learned and Taught," *Management Solutions,* June 1986, p. 26.

17. "Increase Your Powers of Concentration," *Research Institute Personal Report for the Executive,* Jan. 7, 1986, p. 7.

18. See, for example, Dru Scott, *How to Put More Time in Your Life* (New York: New American Library, 1980), p. 172.

19. Scott, *How to Put More Time in Your Life,* p. 175.

20. Peter A. Turla and Kathleen L. Hawkins, "Remembering to Remember," *Success!,* May 1983, p. 60.

21. Merril E. Douglass, "Standing Saves Time," *Executive Forum,* July 1989, p. 4.

Suggested Reading

DOUGLASS, MERRILL. "Timely Tips: Sorting Mail Reduces Paperwork." *Executive Forum,* August 1989, p. 4.

FRAM, EUGENE H., and AXELROD, JOEL. "The Distressed Shopper." *American Demographics,* October 1990, pp. 44–45.

JAMES, TAD, and WOODSMALL, WYATT. *Time Line Therapy and the Basis of Personality.* Cupertino, CA: Meta Publications, 1990.

MAYER, JEFFREY J. *If You Haven't Got the Time to Do It Right, When Will You Find the Time to Do It Over?* New York: Simon & Schuster, 1990.

SEIWERT, LOTHAR J. *Time Is Money: Save It.* Homewood, IL: Dow Jones Irwin, 1989.

STIASEN, SARAH. "Making Time: How Tracking the Hours Yields Hidden Benefits." *Success!,* April 1990, p. 18.

WINSTON, STEPHANIE. *The Organized Executive.* New York: Norton, 1986.

Research in Human Relations and Organizational Behavior

LEARNING OBJECTIVES

The purpose of this appendix is to help the reader understand how the scientific method and research contribute to knowledge about human relations and organizational behavior. Four topics are chosen to achieve this purpose

1. The contribution of theory and research.
2. Methods of data collection.
3. Research methods.
4. Sources of error in research about human behavior.

THE CONTRIBUTION OF THEORY AND RESEARCH

Many people with job experience who are taking their first course in human relations or organizational behavior comment, "Skip the theory and research. Let's get to practical applications. I'm taking this course so I can improve my effectiveness on the job." Although this text takes a job-oriented approach, it has not entirely skipped theory and research. Sound research, followed by sound theory, leads to generalizations that will help you function more effectively on the job.

A case in point is the accumulated wisdom about goal setting described in Chapter 3. Behavioral scientists have demonstrated through research that setting realistic goals leads to improved performance. Practicing managers can now use such knowledge as a guide to action. Thoman H. Jerdee explains how theory and research contribute to knowledge about human behavior on the job:

> Theory is simply the orderly summarization of verified knowledge about phenomena and their interrelationships. As such, it is the well-spring of human progress in mastering the environment. Prescriptions for action must be derived from theory, and different people may reasonably derive varying prescriptions from the same theory, depending on their values and priorities. Here, perhaps, is where the real gap between theoretician and practitioner develops, rather than in regard to theory itself.[1]

Despite these comments, the establishment of theory sometimes precedes data collection. A human relations specialist, for example, might develop a theory through "armchair reasoning" and then test the theory by collecting data. An important purpose of the theories presented in this book is to help you understand human behavior in organizations. If we merely describe what happens—without providing explanation—human relations is entirely unscientific.

METHODS OF DATA COLLECTION

The four most frequently used methods of collecting data in human relations and organizational behavior are questionnaires, interviews, direct observation of behavior, and unobtrusive measures.

Questionnaires

Questionnaires have appeared at various places in this text, and you have probably filled out dozens of research questionnaires. Before preparing a final questionnaire, a scientist collects relevant facts and generates hypotheses (educated guesses) about important issues to explore. The questionnaires are carefully designed to measure relevant issues about the topic under survey. Review the Bureaucratic Orientation questionnaire presented in Chapter 15 for a sampling of how a questionnaire touches upon relevant issues. Questionnaire construction is a complex art, despite the deceptively straightforward appearance of one that is well designed.

Interviews

The researcher about human behavior on the job relies heavily upon the interview as a method of data collection. Even when a questionnaire is the primary method of data collection, it is probable that interviews were used to obtain ideas for survey questions. Interviews are also helpful in uncovering explanations about phenomena and furnishing leads for further inquiry. For instance, a researcher conducting interviews about productivity uncovered the fact that workers "goofing off" was a major source of low productivity. Written questions would probably have missed this issue. Fill-in questions on written surveys, such as "Is there anything else you would like to add?," may also be useful in providing explanations and diagnostic information.

Another advantage of interviews is that a skilled interviewer can probe for additional information. One disadvantage of the interview method is that skilled interviewers are required. Another disadvantage is that the interviewer has to be trusted in order to obtain accurate results.

Interviews can be classified into *structured* and *unstructured*. The structured interview asks standard questions of all respondents. Highly structured interviews take on the tone of a written questionnaire, particularly when they ask two-response-category questions, such as "Are you satisfied with your pay?"

Unstructured interviews encourage the free flow of conversation and appear less scientific than structured interviews. The unstructured interview is used to gather general impressions about the job, the firm, or the employee. During the unstructured interview, the interviewer shifts to whatever questions seems suited to uncovering important information. By contrast, the structured interview follows a more rigid pattern.

Systematic Observation

Much information about human behavior on the job is collected by observers placing themselves in the work environment. Systematic observations are then made about the phenomena under study. One concern about this method is that the people being observed may turn in atypical performances when they know they are being observed.

A variation of systematic observation is *participant observation*. The observer becomes a member of the group about which he or she is collecting data. For instance, to study the job stress experienced by some VDT operators, a researcher might work in a word-processing department.

Unobtrusive Measures

One problem with the method of data collection mentioned so far is that the researcher interacts with the person providing the data. To get around this problem, some researchers collect information without the awareness of the people being studied. One example would be observations about the job satisfaction of sales associates in a store made by visiting the store as a customer. If people do not know what a participant observer is doing, that person is using unobtrusive measures.

RESEARCH METHODS

The methods of data collection just described are the basic tools for conducting research about human behavior in organizations (and in business). These methods of data collection are applied to different methods or strategies for conducting an investigation. Research methods can be classified as follows: case study, correlational study, and experiment (including laboratory and field experiments).

Case Study

Cases have been presented throughout this text. Although they are a popular teaching method, cases are often looked upon critically as a method of conducting research. Case information is usually collected by an observer recording impressions in his or her mind or in a notepad. People have a natural tendency to attend to information specifically related to their own interests or needs. The following incident illustrates the problem of filtered perceptions:

> One researcher prepared a case report showing examples of how the initiative of word processing technicians was hampered by an authoritarian supervisor. Another researcher prepared a report in the same department emphasizing how much the technicians enjoyed not having to make decisions themselves.

Both researchers were correct within the limits of their selective perception. Both sets of events probably took place, but each researcher saw only a partial view of reality. Despite this subjective element in the case method, cases provide a wealth of information that can be used to explain what is happening in a given situation.

Correlational Study

A widely used research method is to correlate scores on one measure (an independent variable) with scores on some outside criterion (a dependent variable). Often the dependent variable represents "hard data" (objective information), such as salary, number of units shipped, or number of patents issued. The independent variable is typically measured by a questionnaire. An example of this type of study would be correlating a measure of leadership style with group productivity.

A major limitation of correlational studies is that they can be misinterpreted as revealing the cause of something. All that can be safely concluded from a correlational study is that the two variables measured vary in a similar fashion. In the example above, a particular leadership style might not be the true cause of group productivity. The true cause might be that one style of leader encourages more goal setting than does another.

Experiment

An experiment is the most rigorous research method. The essence of conducting an experiment is to make sure that only the variable under study is influencing the results. This procedure is referred to as *controlling* for the influence of independent variables. The two most frequently used experiments in organizational behavior and human relations are the laboratory experiment and field experiment.

Laboratory experiment. A major characteristic of the laboratory experiment is that the conditions are supposedly under the experimenter's control. A group of people might be brought into a room to study the effects of stress on problem-solving ability. The stressor the experimenter introduces is an occasional blast from a siren. In a field setting, assuming the experiment were permitted, the experimenter might be unaware of what other stressors the employees were facing. A major concern about laboratory experiments is that their results might not be generalizable to the outside world.

Field experiment. Field experiments are an attempt to apply the experimental methods to real-life situations. Variables can be controlled more readily in the laboratory than in the field, but information obtained in the field is often more relevant. The experiment about flexible working hours described in Chapter 1 illustrates a field experiment. Here we provide more details about the nature of the experimental method.

Suppose an experimenter were interested in studying the influence of assertiveness training (AT) on the career progress of women. One experimental method to investigate this matter would be to measure how AT influences the salary growth and rate of promotion of women. A conventional research design to study this problem is shown in Figure A–1.

Procedures and steps	Experimental group	Control group I	Control group II
Assign women randomly to groups	Yes	Yes	Yes
Record current salary	Yes	Yes	Yes
Record current job level	Yes	Yes	Yes
Administer AT program	Yes	No	No
Conduct group discussions about careers	No	No	Yes
Allow time to pass without interacting with participants	Yes	Yes	Yes
Record salary level at one- and two-year periods	Yes	Yes	Yes
Record job level at one- and two-year periods	Yes	Yes	Yes

FIGURE A-1 A Research Design Based on the Experimental Method

The experimenter would make statistical comparisons of the salary progress and job-level progress of the experimental and control groups. If the women who underwent AT scored higher in salary and job level, it would be concluded tentatively that AT helped career progress more than did (1) no such training or (2) group discussions about career progress. Using the second control group helps to rule out the possibility that talking about improving one's career is as effective as AT.

Sources of Error in Research on Human Behavior in Organizations

Research in human relations and organizational behavior has many more problems than does research in most physical and biological sciences. Here we mention ten of the most common sources of error when conducting research on human behavior in organizations.

1. *Inaccurate information.* For example, people sometimes respond to questionnaires insincerely, and productivity figures used as dependent variables may be misleading and unreliable.

2. *Limited generalizability of results.* Research is often conducted in healthy organizational climates characterized by trust between top managers and employees. When the same techniques are applied in less trustful environments, the results might not be as good.

3. *Apathy, indifference, and anxiety of participants.* People participating in research studies may not care about the study or may be fearful of telling the truth. Consequently, the results of the study are inaccurate, leading to the experimental error listed above.

4. *The social desirability factor.* Participants often say things in response to research questions that they think will make them look

good (be socially desirable). For instance, virtually all managers contend that they consult with employees before making a decision. And few people blame themselves for productivity problems.

5. *Invalid measures of experimental variables.* Many questionnaires are not a true measure of what they intend to measure, thus limiting the possibility of achieving useful results. For example, a questionnaire about leadership style might really be measuring how much the respondent enjoys working with people.

6. *Influence of the measuring instrument on the outcome (reactivity of methods).* A measurement is *reactive* when an attempt to measure something alters the state of the person being measured. For instance, if a person begins to experience stress symptoms while completing a questionnaire about job stress, the questionnaire is reactive. Asking people about job satisfaction may bring to mind issues of dissatisfaction.

7. *Extraneous influences on the dependent variable.* Sometimes an outside factor enters the experiment during the course of the study. The outside factor then changes the results. For example, a study might be conducted about the influence of flexible working hours on productivity. During the experiment, a new manager is appointed who is so effective that productivity increases because of her leadership approach. Leadership style thus becomes the extraneous influence on the outcome of this study, and the possible influence of flexible working hours is difficult to measure.

8. *Nonrandom selection.* When people are assigned to experimental and control groups on any basis other than random selection, the results could be biased. An illustrative source of bias is that volunteers for a given program or experiment are sometimes psychologically different from nonvolunteers. For example, they might be more adventuresome and self-confident, thus tending to do well in a given training program or respond well to any treatment.

9. *Loss of subjects.* In field research, particularly, some participants may drop out of the experiment before it is completed. Randomness is thus not ensured. In the AT and career development program mentioned earlier, it is conceivable that some of the subjects who responded well to AT may have become so assertive that they left the firm for better opportunities elsewhere.

10. *The influence of moderator variables.* In most research about human behavior in organizations, certain factors are present which influence the results for some groups but not for others. These factors are referred to as **moderator variables**, factors that specify the condition under which an independent variable influences a dependent variable. One factor mentioned in the text was the moderating influence of employee preference on the effectiveness of job enrichment. A study might show that job enrichment had no impact on job satisfaction. As-

sume that the criterion groups were categorized into those who wanted job enrichment versus those who did not want job enrichment. The outcome of the experiment would then be quite good—for the criterion group that wanted job enrichment.

Note

1. Thomas H. Jerdee, book review in *Personnel Psychology,* Winter 1976, p. 655.

Suggested Reading

ANASTASI, ANNE. *Psychological Testing,* 6th ed. New York: Macmillan, 1988.

DANSEREAU, FRED, ALUTTO, JOSEPH A., and YAMMARINO, FRANCIS J. *Theory Testing in Organizational Behavior: The Variant Approach.* Englewood Cliffs, NJ: Prentice Hall, 1984.

GIBSON, JAMES L., IVANCEVICH, JOHN M., and DONNELLY, JAMES H., JR. *Organizations: Behavior, Structure, Processes,* 7th ed. Homewood, IL: Irwin, 1991, Appendix A.

LAWLER, EDWARD E. III, and associates. *Doing Research That Is Useful for Theory and Practice.* San Francisco: Jossey-Bass, 1985.

LOCKE, EDWIN A. *Generalizing from Laboratory to Field Settings.* Lexington, MA: Lexington Books, 1986.

SZILAGYI, ANDREW D., and WALLACE, MARC J., JR. *Organizational Behavior and Performance,* 5th ed. Glenview, IL: Scott, Foresman/Little, Brown Higher Education, 1990, pp. A1–A14.

Conducting
a Job Campaign

LEARNING OBJECTIVES

The purpose of this appendix is to help the reader conduct a job campaign.
Three topics are chosen to achieve this purpose

1. Job-hunting tactics
2. The job resume and cover letter.
3. Handling yourself in a job interview.

Most people have to conduct a job campaign upon graduation, and perhaps at various times in their career. The process usually takes about six months. The three major aspects of the job campaign are job-hunting tactics, preparing a résumé, and performing well in an interview.

JOB-HUNTING TACTICS

We recommend using the tactics shown in Table B–1 as a checklist to ensure that you have not neglected something important. The list should be supplemented with suggestions from placement offices and from an entire book about the topic, such as *What Color is your Parachute?*

Identify Your Objectives

An effective job search begins with a clear perception of what kind of job or jobs you want. Your chances for finding employment increase considerably if a large number of positions will satisfy your job objective.

Identify Your Potential Contribution

A man responded by phone to a want ad with this initial comment: "Hello, this is Tom Crawford. I've just got to have a job. I've been laid off and I have a family to support. I need something right away." Poor Tom probably did need the job, but the company he was calling was more interested in *receiving* than in *giving* help. If Tom had used the following approach he might have increased his chances for being granted an interview (and getting hired): "Hello, this is Tom Crawford. I see you need somebody to help ship packages. I know how to ship packages in a fast and economical way. When could I talk to you about it in person?"

TABLE B–1   Key job-hunting tactics

---

1. Identify your objectives.
2. Identify your potential contribution.
3. Use multiple approaches and tactics.
4. Use networking.
5. Persist.
6. Take rejection in stride.
7. Avoid common mistakes.

Use Multiple Approaches and Tactics

No one job-hunting approach or tactic works best in most situations. The job seeker is therefore advised to use several of the tactics described in this section, and to explore several sources of job leads. Among the possible approaches are school placement offices, employment agencies, government employment services, classified ads in local and national newspapers, ads in trade magazines, employment booths at trade associations and conventions, inquiries through friends and relatives, and cold canvassing. You might also have your résumé entered into a computerized database. Subscribers to the system across the country would then have access to your résumé.

Another standard approach is to place a situation wanted ad in local and national newspapers. The following ad helped one graduate find a job: "Productivity-minded problem solver wants in on your management training program. Try me. I'll give you a big return on your investment. Write Box 7943 this newspaper."

Use Networking

Networking is particularly helpful because it taps you into the "insider system" or internal job market. The internal job market is the large array of jobs that have not been advertised, and that are usually filled by word of mouth or through friends and acquaintances of employees. The best way to reach these jobs is by getting someone to recommend you for one. When looking for a job, it is important to tell every potential contact of your job search. The more influential the person, the better. Be specific about the type of job you are seeking. A variation of this approach is to ask people how a person with qualifications such as yours might find a job. This approach does not put people on the spot as much as asking directly for a job lead.

To use networking effectively, it may be necessary to create contacts aside from those you already have. Potential sources of contacts include almost anybody you know, as summarized in Table B–2.

Another way of reaching the internal job market is to write dozens of letters to potential employers. A surprisingly large number of people find jobs by contacting employers directly. Prepare a prospective employer list, including the names of executives to contact in each firm. The people who receive these letters become part of your network.

Persist

Finding a job is a tedious and time-consuming activity for many people. Persistence is vital in turning up good leads, and may help you find a job even after you have had some rejections.

TABLE B-2   Potential sources of contacts for a network

Friends
Parents and other family members
Faculty and staff
Former or present employer (assuming you hold a temporary job)
Graduates of your school
Athletic teams
Community groups, churches, temples, and mosques
Trade and professional associations
Student professional associations
Career fairs
People met in airports and on airplanes

Source: Many of the items on this list are from Karen O. Dowd, "The Art of Making Contacts," *The Honda How to Get a Job Guide,* published by *Business Week's Guide to Careers,* 1985, p. 24.

Take Rejection in Stride

Finding a new job is fraught with rejection. It is not uncommon for a recent graduate or an experienced career person to send out 150 letters of inquiry to find one job. When your job search is confined to places that are trying to fill a position that matches your specialty, you still may have to be interviewed many times in order to find one job. Often you will be rejected even when it appears to you that your qualifications match perfectly those required for the job opening. The employment interviewer may have interviewed another applicant that he or she thinks is even better qualified than you.

Avoid Common Mistakes

Be aware of mistakes to avoid in searching for a job. Several of these mistakes cover the points mentioned above. Robert B. Nelson suggests that the job seeker avoid the following:

- Not knowing what type of work you want to do.
- Not taking the initiative to generate job leads.
- Going to too few prospects.
- Not viewing the job from the employer's perspective. (Employers are more interested in knowing what you can do for them, rather than vice versa.)
- Asking too directly for a job. (It is preferable to discuss job opportunities in an "informational interview.")
- Not making contact with the people with whom you would be working.

- Approaching prospects in an impersonal way. (Never address a letter "To Whom It May Concern." Instead, write to a specific person whose name can be found through a directory or phone call.)
- Overlooking your selling points. (For example, you might have exceptional computer skills or communication skills.)
- Not making follow-up contacts after you have generated a lead.
- Having a poor résumé.[1]

THE JOB RÉSUMÉ AND COVER LETTER

Your résumé must attract enough attention to invite you for an interview. Effective résumés are straightforward, factual presentations of a person's experiences and accomplishments. They are neither overdetailed nor too sketchy. Considerable debate and subjective opinion exists about the desirable length for a résumé. Certainly less than one page would seem superficial, while a three-page or longer résumé may irritate an impatient employment specialist. Two pages is therefore recommended.

To attract attention, some job seekers print résumés on tinted paper, in a menu-like folder, or on an unusual size of paper. If done in a way to attract positive attention to yourself, the nonconventional résumé formats have merit. The menu-like folder has worked well for a number of job seekers, but do not (as one joker did) label your job objective "the appetizer," your work experience, "the entree," and your education, "the dessert." Unconventional résumés work best for jobs requiring artistic creativity, such as advertising copywriter. Avoid using a video for a résumé unless you have acting experience.

Three Types of Résumés

The three most commonly used formats are the chronological, functional, and target. Consider using one of these types, or a blend of them, based upon what information about yourself you are trying to highlight. Whichever format you choose, you must include essential information.

The chronological résumé presents your work experience, education, and interests, along with your accomplishments in reverse chronological order. A chronological résumé resembles the traditional résumé, with the addition of accomplishments and skills. Some people say the chronological résumé is too bland. However, it contains precisely the information that most employers demand, and it is easy to prepare. A sample chronological résumé is presented in Figure B–1.

The functional résumé organizes your skills and accomplishments into the functions or tasks that support the job you are seeking. A section of the functional résumé might read:

Jack Paradise
210 Alabaster Road
Dallas, Texas 75243
(312) 381-8902

JOB TARGET: Industrial sales position, handling large,
                             complex machinery. Willing to work largely
                             on commission basis.

MAJOR BUSINESS ACCOMPLISHMENT:

                             In one year sold at a profit $250,000 worth
                             of excess machine inventory. Received letter
                             of commendation from company president.

WORK HISTORY:

    1991–present   Industrial account representative,
                             Bainbridge Corporation, Dallas. Sell line of
                             tool and die equipment to companies in
                             Southwest. Duties include servicing estab-
                             lished accounts and canvassing for new ones.

    1988–1991   Inside sales representative, Bainbridge Cor-
                             poration. Answered customer inquiries.
                             Filled orders for replacement parts. Trained
                             for outside sales position.

    1984–1988   Tool and die maker apprentice, Texas Metals
                             Inc., Dallas. Assisted senior tool and die
                             makers during four-year training program.
                             Worked on milling machines, jigs, punch
                             presses, numeric control devices, CAD/CAM.

FORMAL EDUCATION:

    1986–1988   Madagascar College, Dallas, Texas. Associate
                             Degree in Business Administration; graduat-
                             ed with 3.16 grade point average. Courses in
                             marketing, sales techniques, consumer be-
                             havior, accounting, and statistics. President
                             of American Marketing Association, student
                             chapter.

    1982–1986   Big Horn High, Dallas. Honors student; aca-
                             demic major with vocational elective. Played
                             varsity football and basketball. Earned part
                             of living by selling magazine subscriptions.

CAPABILITIES AND SKILLS:

                             Competent sales representative. Able to size
                             up customer's manufacturing problem and
                             make recommendation for appropriate ma-

chinery. Precise in preparing call reports and expense accounts.

PERSONAL INTERESTS AND HOBBIES:

Personal computer enthusiast (write programs for own computer), scuba diving, recreational golf player, read trade and business magazines, dance competitively.

FIGURE B–1 A General-purpose Résumé

Supervision: Organized the work activities of ten employees as a restaurant manager, resulting in two years of high profits and customer satisfaction.

Trained and supervised five data-entry technicians to produce a smooth-running data-entry operation.

The functional résumé is useful because it highlights the things you have accomplished and the skills you have developed. An ordinary work accomplishment might seem more impressive following this format. For instance, the tasks listed under "supervision" may appear more impressive than listing the jobs of "assistant restaurant manager" and "data-entry supervisor." One problem with the functional résumé is that it omits the factual information many employers demand.

The targeted résumé focuses on a specific job target, or position, and presents only information that supports the target. Using a targeted résumé, an applicant for a sales position would list only sales positions. Under education, the applicant would focus on sales-related courses, such as communication skills and marketing. A targeted résumé is helpful in dramatizing your suitability for the position you are seeking. Yet this type of résumé omits other relevant information about you. Also, a new résumé must be prepared for each target position.

Common Mistakes in Résumés

Despite the abundance of useful information available about résumé preparation, many job seekers continue to prepare résumés that virtually disqualify them from further consideration. Do your best to avoid most of these errors by editing your own résumé and asking at least two other people to do the same:

- Lacking a skill section. Today's employers emphasize skills.
- Too lengthy, containing much useless information.
- Disorganized, including the same type of information presented under different headings.

- Poorly typed or word processed, including narrow margins and writing in the margins.

- Skimpy or insufficient information—only dates, titles, and incomplete addresses.

- Excessive information including inconsequential information (such as facts about a company you worked for).

- No listing of accomplishments or skills.

- Misspellings, typographical errors, poor grammar, and the frequent use of the word "I."

- Overly elaborate résumé, such as fancy typesetting or plastic binder.

- So much emphasis on nontraditional réumé that basic facts are missing (for example, work experience and addresses of schools attended). Since the company official cannot verify facts or assess qualifications, he or she places résumé in circular file.

- Inflating facts about yourself that prove to be untrue when references are checked. This type of résumé error usually leads to immediate disqualification. If the error is discovered after the candidate is hired, he or she is liable for dismissal.

The Cover Letter

A résumé should almost always be accompanied by a cover letter explaining who you are and why you are applying for this particular job. The cover letter serves to customize your approach to a particular employer, while the résumé is a more general approach. Even a targeted résumé is sent to more than one employer. Most job applicants use the conventional (and somewhat ineffective) approach of writing a letter attempting to impress the prospective employer with their background. A sounder approach is to capture the reader's attention with a punchy statement of what you might be able to do for them. Later in the letter you might present a one-paragraph summary of your education and the highlights of your job and educational experience. Here are two examples of opening lines geared to two different types of jobs:

1. Person seeking employment in credit department of garment maker: "Everybody has debt-collection problems these days. Let me help you gather in some of the past-due cash that you have a right to."

2. Person looking for position as administrative assistant in hospital where vacancy may or may not exist: "Is your hospital drowning in paperwork? Let me jump in with both feet and clear up some of the confusion. Then you can go back to taking care of sick people."
   If the above approach is too brash for you, just mention your interest in the position.

HANDLING YOURSELF IN A JOB INTERVIEW

Job hunters typically look upon the employment interview as a game in which they must outguess the interviewer. A sounder approach is to present a positive but accurate picture of yourself. The suggestions presented next should help you appear to be a sincere and responsible job seeker.

1. *Rehearse being interviewed.* Being a good interviewee requires practice. Some of this practice may be acquired while going through interviews. In addition, you can rehearse simulated job interviews with friends. Practice answering the questions in Figure B–2. Videotaping these interviews is valuable because it provides feedback on how well you handled yourself.

2. *Prepare in advance.* Be familiar with pertinent details about your background, including your social security number and names and addresses of references. It is also important to know some important facts about your prospective employer. Annual reports, brochures about the company, and newspaper and magazine articles can be helpful. Also, speak to current and past employees of the prospective employer.

A useful way of preparing for job interviews is to rehearse answers to the kinds of questions you will most likely be asked by the interviewer. The following questions are of the same basic type and content encountered in most employment interviews. Rehearse answers to them prior to going out on job interviews.

1. What are your career goals?
2. What do you expect to be doing five years from now?
3. What are your present income requirements?
4. How much money do you expect to be earning ten years from now?
5. What are your strengths (or good points)?
6. What are your weaknesses (or areas for improvement)?
7. Why did you prepare for the career you did?
8. How would you describe yourself?
9. How would other people describe you?
10. Why should we hire you instead of other candidates for the same job?
11. If hired, how long would you be working for us?
12. How well do you work under pressure?
13. What makes you think you will be successful in business?
14. What do you know about our firm?

FIGURE B–2 Questions Frequently Asked of Job Candidates

3. *Dress appropriately.* So much emphasis is placed on dressing well for job interviews that some people overdress. Instead of looking businesslike, they appear to be dressed for a wedding. The safest tactic is to wear moderately conservative business attire when applying for most positions.

4. *Ask a few good questions.* The best questions to ask the interviewer are sincere ones that reflect an interest in the nature of the work itself. Following are several questions that will usually meet with good reception in an employment interview. Ask them during a period of silence or when you are asked if you have any questions.

 a. If hired, what would I actually be doing?

 b. What kind of advancement opportunities are there in your firm for outstanding performers?

 c. Whom would I be working with aside from people in my own department?

 d. What is the company's attitude toward people who make constructive suggestions?

 e. What kind of person would you ideally like to hire for this position?

 f. What would I have to do to be considered an outstanding performer in your firm?

 g. Is there anything else I've said so far that requires elaboration?

5. *Be ready to discuss your strengths and weaknesses.* Most employment interviewers will ask you about your strengths and weaknesses. Being unable to describe personal strengths would suggest a lack of self-confidence. Being unable to identify areas for improvement would suggest a lack of insight or defensiveness. A mildly evasive approach is to emphasize weaknesses that could be interpreted as strengths. A case in point: "People say I'm too much of a perfectionist about pleasing the customer."

6. *Show how you can help the employer.* Explain to a prospective employer what you think you can do to help the company. This gains more for you than telling the prospective employer of your good qualities and characteristics.

7. *Allow the interviewer to talk.* Although a skilled interviewer lets the interviewee do most of the talking, there may be times when the interviewer wants to communicate something to you. In addition, make a few encouraging comments to the interviewer, such as "That's very informative."

Note

1. Robert B. Nelson, "10 Common Mistakes Job Hunters Make," *Business Week's Guide to Careers,* November 1986, pp.91–93.

GLOSSARY

Abrasive personality A self-centered individual who is isolated from others, perfectionistic, contemptuous, and prone to attack.

Achievement need The desire to set and accomplish goals for their own sake.

Action plan A description of the steps that need to be taken to achieve an objective or bring performance back to an acceptable standard.

Affiliation need A desire to seek out close relationships with others and to be a loyal employee or friend.

Aggressive personality A person who physically or verbally attacks other people frequently.

Anger A feeling of extreme hostility, indignation, or exasperation.

Anxiety Generalized feelings of fear and apprehension that usually result from a perceived threat. Feelings of uneasiness and tension usually accompany anxiety.

Appeals procedure A formal method of resolving conflict by bringing the issue to a higher level of authority.

Artificial intelligence (AI) The capability of a computer to perform functions usually considered part of human intelligence, such as learning, reasoning, and listening.

Assertive Forthright with demands, expressing the specifics of what the person wants done and the feelings surrounding the demands.

Assertiveness training (AT) A self-improvement program that teaches people to express their feelings and act with an appropriate degree of openness and candor.

Attitude A predisposition to respond in a particular way.

Autocratic leader A person in charge who attempts to retain most of the authority granted to the group.

Behavior modification An attempt to change behavior by manipulating rewards and punishments.

Behavior shaping The rewarding of any response in the right direction and then rewarding only the closest approximation.

Brainstorming A conference technique of solving specific problems, amassing information, and stimulating creative thinking.

Brainwriting Arriving at multiple solutions to problems by working alone and jotting the solutions down yourself.

Bureaucracy A form of organization in which division of effort, rank, rules, and regulations are carefully defined.

Bureaupathic behavior A strong need to control others based on insecurity.

Burnout A state of emotional, mental, and physical exhaustion in response to prolonged job stress.

Career development A planned approach to achieving growth and satisfaction in work experiences.

Career development program A planned approach to helping employees enhance their careers while at the same time integrating individual and organizational goals.

Career path A series of positions in one or more organizations leading to a long-range goal.

Career plateau The point in a career where it becomes evident that further job advancement is permanently or temporarily blocked.

Career switching Making a relatively complete change from one career to another.

Charisma Personal charm and magnetism that is used to lead others.

Coaching A method of helping employees grow and improve their job competence by providing suggestions and encouragement.

Coalition A specific arrangement of parties working together to combine their power.

Coercive power The ability to punish for noncompliance.

Cognitive resource theory A theory of leadership emphasizing that intelligent and competent leaders make more effective plans, decisions, and strategies than do leaders with less intelligence or competence.

Cognitive viewpoint (or model) An explanation of human behavior that emphasizes the internal mental processes that take place whenever a person is subject to an external force.

Command group A clustering of workers consisting of a manager and his or her subordinates.

Committee A group of people brought together to help solve a problem.

Communication The sending, receiving, and understanding of messages.

Communication climate The degree to which an organization permits or promotes a free and open exchange of ideas and information among its members.

Comparable worth The doctrine that people who perform similar jobs with different titles, but of comparable value to the firm, should receive equal pay.

Compressed work week A full-time work schedule that allows forty hours to be accomplished in less than five days.

Compromise Settlement of differences by mutual concession.

Compulsiveness A tendency to pay careful attention to detail and to be meticulous.

Computer-aided monitoring Using a computer to help keep track of employee output and activity.

Computer stress A strong negative reaction to being forced to spend many more hours working at a computer than one expected or desires.

Conflict A situation in which two or more goals, values, or events are incompatible or mutually exclusive.

Consensus leader A person in charge who encourages group discussion about an issue and then makes a decision that reflects the general agreement (consensus) of group members.

Consensus A state of general agreement or harmony with a reasonable amount of disagreement still present.

Consultative leader A person in charge who solicits opinions from the group before making a decision, yet does not feel obliged to accept the group's thinking.

Contingency organization design Choosing the best organization structure to deal with the problem at hand.

Contingency theory of leadership An explanation of leadership that specifies the conditions under which a particular leadership style will be effective.

Contingency viewpoint The idea that the best solution to a given problem depends upon certain key factors in the situation.

Control group A comparison group that is similar to the experimental group except that it is not exposed to the variable being studied.

Corporate culture *See* **Organizational culture.**

Corrective discipline Any type of discipline that emphasizes improving employee behavior.

Counseling A formal discussion method for helping another individual overcome a problem or improve his or her potential.

Cultural awareness training A formal method of helping people develop a sensitivity to local and national customs, and to their importance in effective interpersonal relations.

Creative problem solving The ability to overcome obstacles by approaching them in novel ways.

Creative worker Someone who approaches problems in a new or unique way.

Creativity The ability to develop good ideas that can be put into management.

Customer orientation The delivery of goods and services is focused on customer needs and concerns.

Decision making The process of choosing among the alternatives that exist to solve the problem.

Decision-making leave A paid one-day suspension to help an employee think through a disciplinary problem.

Decision-making software Any computer program that helps the decision maker work through the problem-solving and decision-making steps.

Defensive communication The tendency to receive messages in such a way that one's self-esteem is protected.

Democratic leader A person in charge who turns over final authority to the group.

Denial The suppression of information we find uncomfortable.

Developmental need A specific area in which a person needs improvement.

Disparate treatment A form of job discrimination in which members of a protected group receive unequal treatment or are evaluated under different standards.

Diversity awareness program A training exercise that provides an opportunity for employees to develop the skills necessary to deal effectively with each other and customers in a diverse environment.

Early executive mortality A tendency for recently retired executives to die much sooner than expected.

Ego state As defined in transactional analysis, the three parts of the human personality (parent, adult, child).

80-20 principle The generalization that 80 percent of the results or problems are usually caused by 20 percent of the activities.

Empathy In communication, imagining yourself in the receiver's role, and assuming the viewpoints and emotions of that individual.

Empire building Adding people to your organizational unit more to acquire power than to serve the good of the firm.

Employee assistance program (EAP) A formal organizational unit designed to help employees deal with personal problems adversely affecting job performance.

Empowerment The process by which a manager shares power with subordinates, thereby enhancing their feelings of self-efficacy.

Enriched job (job enrichment) One that allows the worker to perform more interesting and responsible tasks.

Entrepreneur A person who converts an innovative idea into a business.

Environmental determinism The doctrine of behaviorism stating that our past history of reinforcement determines, or causes, our current behavior.

Eustress A positive force that is the equivalent of finding excitement and challenge.

Eureka factor The sudden illuminating flash of judgment that guides many executives.

Expectancy In expectancy theory, the probability assigned by the individual that effort will lead to performing the task correctly.

Expectancy theory (ET) An explanation of work motivation based on the premise that how much effort people expend depends upon how much they expect to receive in return.

Expert power The ability to control others through knowledge relevant to the job.

External locus of control The belief that external forces control one's life.

Extinction In behavior modification, decreasing the frequency of undesirable behavior by removing the consequences of such behavior.

Fear Worry and anxiety about a punishment that might be forthcoming.

Feeling-level communication A form of sending and receiving messages that emphasizes the feelings, emotions, and attitudes that are exchanged when people communicate.

Fight-or-flight response The body's physiological and chemical battle against the stressor in which the person tries to cope with the adversity head-on, or tries to flee the scene.

Flextime A method of organizing hours of work so that employees have flexibility in choosing their own hours.

Fogging Responding to manipulative criticism as if you were a fog bank.

Formal communication pathways The official, sanctioned route over which messages are supposed to travel in the organization.

Formal group A work unit deliberately formed by the organization to accomplish specific tasks and achieve objectives.

Frame of reference The fact that people perceive words and concepts differently because their vantage points and perspectives differ.

Free-rein leader A person in charge who turns over virtually all the authority to the group.

Frustration A blocking of need or motive satisfaction.

Gainsharing A group incentive program that enables employees to share in the financial benefits of any improvements in productivity to which they contribute.

g (general) factor A factor in intelligence that contributes to the ability to perform well in many tasks.

Goal What a person wants to accomplish.

Gossip Idle talk or tidbit of information about people that are passed along informal communication channels.

Grapevine The major informal communication channel in an organization.

Grievance procedure A formal mechanism for filing employee complaints.

Group Two or more people who interact with each other, are aware of each other, are working toward some common purpose, and perceive themselves to be a group.

Group cohesiveness The attractiveness of the group to its members, which leads to a feeling of unity and "togetherness."

Group norms The unwritten set of expectations for group members.

Groupthink A deterioration of mental efficiency, reality testing, and moral judgment in the interest of group solidarity. Also, an extreme form of group consensus.

Hawthorne effect The tendency for people to behave differently when they receive attention because they respond to the expectations of the situation.

Hearing officer A staff specialist who is employed by the firm to arbitrate disputes between employees and management.

Hostile takeover A corporate takeover in which one firm takes over another against its will.

Hot-stove rule A guideline for administering discipline, recommending that it include a warning, be immediate, consistent, impersonal, and appropriate.

Human relations The art and practice of using systematic knowledge about human behavior to achieve organizational and/or personal objectives.

Humble decision making Admitting when choosing among alternative solutions to a problem that all the relevant facts cannot be gathered and processed.

Image exchanging A method of conflict resolution in which the two antagonists make it clear that they understand each other's point of view.

Individual contributor Employees who accomplish work primarily by themselves rather than through others.

Industrial humanism The philosophy that emotional factors are a more important contributor to productivity than physical and logical factors.

Informal communication pathway An unofficial network of communications used to supplement a formal pathway or channel.

Informal group A group that arises out of individual needs and the attraction of workers to one another.

Information overload The state of receiving more information than one can handle. As a result, the person becomes overwhelmed and does a poor job of processing information.

Insight A depth of understanding that requires considerable intuition and common sense.

Instrumentality In expectancy theory, the probability assigned by the individual that performance will lead to certain outcomes or rewards.

Integration A situation that occurs when the subparts of the organization fit together and therefore are not in severe conflict or working at cross purposes.

Intelligence Problem-solving ability.

Interactive video A computer-assisted video system in which the trainee interacts with the training material.

Intermittent reward A reward that is given for good performance, occassionally but not always.

Internal locus of control A belief that fate is pretty much under one's control.

Interorganizational group A formal group composed of members of organizations with common concerns who meet regularly.

Interpersonal skill training The teaching of skills in dealing with others so the skills can be put into practice.

Intrapreneur A company employee who engages in entrepreneurial thinking and behavior for the good of the firm.

Intrinsic motivation theory The idea that the work itself is rewarding.

Inversion of means and ends A situation in which the methods for attaining a goal become more important than the goal itself. An example would be a computer programmer who cares more about writing interesting programs than solving company problems.

Jelly bean motivation The heaping of undeserved rewards upon another person.

Job burnout A state of emotional, mental, and physical exhaustion in response to prolonged job stress.

Job discrimination An unfavorable action brought against a person because of a characteristic of that person unrelated to job performance.

Job satisfaction The amount of pleasure or contentment associated with a job.

Job sharing A modified work schedule in which two people share the same job, both usually working half-time.

Job stress The body's response to any job-related factor that threatens to disturb the person's equilibrium.

Law of effect Behavior that leads to a positive consequence for the individual tends to be repeated, while behavior that leads to a negative consequence tends not to be repeated.

Leader-match concept The idea that leadership effectiveness depends on matching leaders to situations where they can exercise the most control.

Leadership The process of influencing employees to attain organizational goals, excluding illegal and immoral methods of persuasion.

Leadership Grid A framework for simultaneously examining the concern for production and people dimensions of leadership, thus classifying a leader's role.

Leadership style The typical pattern of behavior engaged in by the leader when dealing with employees.

Leading by example A simple way of influencing group members in which the leader acts as a positive model.

Lean organization An organization in which there is a minimum of nonessential functions and employees.

Legitimate power Power granted by the organization.

Life script In transactional analysis, a plan or drama acted out during a person's life.

Limited tolerance for ambiguity A tendency to be readily frustrated when situations and tasks are poorly defined.

Line authority The right to make decisions dealing with the primary purposes of the firm.

Lose-lose conflict situation After conflict is resolved, nobody wins.

Machiavellian tendencies A desire to manipulate other people.

Management Working with and through other people to accomplish organizational goals.

Management by objectives A system of goal setting and review in which employee evaluation is linked to how well objectives were attained.

Management by wandering around The managerial process of visiting worksites and informally chatting with people about their work, as a means of collecting input and boosting morale.

Manager Person who accomplishes work through others and has the authority to use resources, such as money, to get things done.

Maslow's need hierarchy A theory of motivation emphasizing that people strive to fulfill needs, arranged in a hierarchy of importance—physiological, safety, belongingness, esteem, and self-actualization. People strive for satisfaction of needs at one level only after satisfaction has been achieved at the previous level.

Mentor A boss who takes a subordinate under his or her wing and teaches and coaches that person.

Mirroring Subtly imitating someone.

Moderator variable A factor that specifies the condition under which an independent variable influences a dependent variable.

Modified work schedule Any formal departure from the traditional hours of work, excluding shift work and staggered work hours.

Morale A mixture of feelings, attitudes, and sentiments that contribute to a general feeling of satisfaction.

Motivation An internal state that leads to effort expended toward objectives. Also, an activity performed by managers or any other person to get others to accomplish work.

Motivational state Any active interests and needs of a person at a given time.

Motive A socially learned force that requires satisfaction, such as the desire to accumulate power.

Need An internal striving or urge to do something.

Negative affectivity A tendency to experience aversive emotional states.

Negative lifestyle factor Any behavior that predisposes one to stress, such as poor eating habits, exercise habits, and heavy ingestion of caffeine, alcohol, and other drugs.

Negative reinforcement Rewarding people by taking away an uncomfortable consequence of their behavior. It is the withdrawal or termination of a disliked consequence.

Negotiating (bargaining) Conferring with another person in order to resolve a problem.

Networking Seeking out friends and acquaintances and building systematically on these relationships to create a still wider set of contacts to gain employment or advance one's career.

Nominal group technique A group problem-solving technique that calls people together in a structured meeting with limited interactions.

Noncognitive viewpoint An explanation of human behavior emphasizing that behavior is determined by the rewards and punishments an individual receives from the environment.

Nonprogrammed decision A decision for which a new solution is required because alternative solutions have not been prescribed in advance.

Nonverbal communication (NVC) The transmission of messages through means other than words.

Ombudsman A neutral person designated by the firm to help resolve employee conflicts.

Open-door policy A policy in which any employee can bring a gripe to higher management's attention without checking with his or her immediate manager.

Organic organization An organization with the ability to adapt to necessary changes.

Organization development (OD) Any strategy, method, or technique for making organizations more effective by bringing about constructive, planned change.

Organizational behavior (OB) The study of individual and group behavior in organizations.

Organizational culture A system of shared values and beliefs that actively influence the behavior of organizational members; the organizational norms.

Organizational effectiveness The extent to which an organization is productive and satisfies the demands of its interested parties.

Organizational politics Gaining advantage through any means other than merit or luck.

Outplacement Company-sponsored programs to minimize the personal and organizational trauma associated with job loss.

PACT model A framework stating that a well person has perspective, autonomy, connectedness, and tone.

Participative leader One who shares decision-making authority with the group.

Perception The process of interpreting events in the external world.

Perceptual block A traditional, or rigid, way of looking at something.

Performance appraisal A formal system of evaluating employee performance and conveying this evaluation to the employee.

Performance-reward-satisfaction model An explanation of job satisfaction stating that if you perform well and receive an equitable reward, your satisfaction will increase.

Personality The persistent and enduring behavior patterns of the individual that are expressed in a wide variety of situations.

Personality clash An antagonistic relationship between two people based on differences in personal attributes, preferences, interests, values, and styles.

Personality quirk A persistent peculiarity of behavior that annoys or irritates other people.

Personal power The ability to control others derived from characteristics and qualities of the controller.

Politics Any methods used to acquire and retain power.

Positive discipline An approach to improving substandard performance and behavior that emphasizes coaching, individual responsibility, and a mature problem-solving method.

Positive mental attitude A conviction that you will succeed.

Positive reinforcement Increasing the probability that behavior will be repeated by rewarding people for making the desired response.

Power The ability to control anything of value.

Power need (or motive) The desire to control other people and resources.

Practical intelligence The belief that intelligence is composed of several aspects, such as creativity, in addition to academic intelligence.

Problem solving A method for closing the gap between the actual situation and the desired situation.

Procrastination The delaying of action for no good reason.

Productivity The ratio of output to input, taking quality of work into account.

Programmed decision A decision in which the alternative solutions are determined by rules, procedures, or policies.

Progressive discipline Administering punishments in increasing order of severity until the person being disciplined improves or is terminated.

Punishment The introduction of an unpleasant stimulus as a consequence of the person having done something wrong.

Quality Conforming to requirements.

Quality circle (QC) A small group of employees from the same department who voluntarily and regularly meet in order to identify, analyze, and solve problems related to work groups.

Quality of work life (QWL) The extent to which workers are able to satisfy important needs through their job and other experiences with the organization.

Realistic goal A goal that is challenging but not set so high that frustration is the inevitable result.

Referent power The ability to control others stemming from one's personal charactersitics.

Reinforcement model *See* **Noncognitive viewpoint.**

Relaxation response A bodily reaction in which the person experiences a slower perspiration rate and heart rate, lowered blood pressure, and lowered metabolism.

Reward power The ability to control by giving employees rewards for compliance.

Role A set of behaviors or attitudes appropriate to a particular position, regardless of who occupies that position.

Role ambiguity A condition in which the job holder receives confusing or poorly defined expectations.

Role conflict Having to choose between competing demands or expectations.

Role confusion Being uncertain what role you are occupying.

Role overload A burdensome workload.

Role underload Having too little work to perform.

Rumor A message transmitted through an organization, although not based on any official word.

Sanction The use of threats of punishment or actual punishment to get somebody to act in a particular way.

s (special) factors Specific components of intelligence that contribute to problem-solving ability.

Schmoozing Socializing on the job.

Self-concept What you think of yourself or who you think you are.

Self-defeating behavior A pattern of doing something to oneself that interferes with goal attainment and happiness.

Self-destructive behavior A conscious or unconscious attempt to bring about personal failure.

Self-determination theory The idea that people are motivated when they experience a sense of choice in initiating and regulating their actions.

Sense of identity For an organization, an awareness of what it is and what it is trying to accomplish.

Sexual harassment Any unwanted advance toward another individual, including spoken comments, touching, or demands for sexual favors.

Skunk works A secret place in an organization to conceive new products.

Socialization How employees come to understand the values, norms, and customs essential for adapting to the organization.

Specialist or **individual contributor** An employee who gets things accomplished primarily working alone rather than through others.

Staff authority The right to make decisions and carry out tasks dealing with the secondary purposes of the firm, such as the authority of a safety and health specialist in a manufacturing firm.

Strain The adverse effects of stress on an individual's mind, body, and actions.

Stress *See* **Job stress.**

Stressor A force bringing about stress.

Subordinate power Any type of power organizational members can exert upward in the organization.

Substance abuse The overuse of any substance that enters the bloodstream.

Summary discipline The immediate discharge of an employee for having committed a major offense.

Superordinate goals Common ends that might be pursued by two or more groups, yet cannot be achieved through the independent efforts of each group separately.

Supervision First-level management, or the art and practice of achieving results through people.

Survey feedback A method of organization development that involves taking a survey of organizational problems and feeding back this information to management and survey participants.

Synergy A combination of things with an output greater than the sum of the parts.

Task force A group of employees assigned to carry out a specialized activity, often with a time deadline.

Team building A systematic method of improving the interpersonal and task aspects of regular work groups.

Telecommuting An arrangement in which employees perform their regular work duties from home or at another location.

Theory X Douglas McGregor's famous statement of the traditional management view that considers people as usually lazy and needing to be prodded by external rewards. A rigid and task-oriented approach to management.

Theory Y Douglas McGregor's famous statement of an alternative to traditional management thinking. It emphasizes that people seek to fulfill higher-level needs on the job and that management must be flexible and human-relations-oriented.

Time leak Anything you are doing or not doing that allows time to get away from you.

Traditional mental set A conventional way of looking at things and placing them in familiar categories.

Transcendental meditation (TM) A process of establishing a physiological state of deep rest.

Transformational leader A person in charge who helps organizations and people make positive changes in the way they do things.

Two-factor theory (of work motivation) Herzberg's theory contending that there are two different sets of job elements. One set of elements can satisfy and motivate people (motivators). The other set can only prevent dissatisfaction (dissatisfiers or hygiene factors).

Transactional analysis (TA) A technique for improving interpersonal relationships that focuses on the exchanges between people.

Transformational leader A person in charge who helps organizations and people make positive changes in the way they do things.

Type A behavior Behavior that is demanding, impatient, overstriving, and hostile, therefore leading to distress.

Type T personality An individual who is driven to a life of constant stimulation and risk taking.

Value A strongly held belief that guides action.

Valence In expectancy theory, the value, worth, or attractiveness of an outcome.

VDT stress An adverse physical and psychological reaction to prolonged work at a video display terminal (VDT).

Wa A Japanese word for harmony, unity, kinship, or love. It is said to lead to cooperative manager-employee relationships.

Wellness A focus on good health rather than simply the absence of disorder.

Wellness programs Formal programs to help employees stay well and avoid illness.

Whistle blowing The disclosure of organizational wrongdoing to parties who can take action.

Win-win conflict resolution An approach to resolving conflict in which both sides gain something of value after the conflict has been resolved.

Workaholic Person who is obsessed with work to the point that it hampers his or her well-being and those around him or her.

Work ethic A firm belief in the value and dignity of work.

Work flow The routing of work from one person or department to another.

Work motivation Effort expended toward organizational objectives.

Wrongful discharge The firing of an employee for arbitrary or unfair reasons.

Zone of indifference The area of behavior in which an employee is prepared to accept direction or influence. Orders that lie within the zone of indifference are seen as lawful and within the employee's value system.

NAME INDEX

SUBJECT INDEX